Individual Health Insurance Planning:
Medical, Disability Income, and Long-Term Care

Huebner School Series *Walt Woerheide, Editor*

Financial Planning: Process and Environment
Don A. Taylor and C. Bruce Worsham (eds.)

Fundamentals of Insurance Planning
Burton T. Beam, Jr., and Eric A. Wiening

Individual Health Insurance Planning: Medical, Disability Income, and Long-Term Care
Thomas P. O'Hare and Burton T. Beam, Jr.

Fundamentals of Income Taxation
James F. Ivers III (ed.)

McGill's Life Insurance
Edward E. Graves (ed.)

McGill's Legal Aspects of Life Insurance
Edward E. Graves and Burke A. Christensen (eds.)

Group Benefits: Basic Concepts and Alternatives
Burton T. Beam, Jr.

Planning for Retirement Needs
David A. Littell and Kenn Beam Tacchino

Fundamentals of Investments for Financial Planning
Walt J. Woerheide and David M. Cordell

Fundamentals of Estate Planning
Constance J. Fontaine

Estate Planning Applications
Ted Kurlowicz

Planning for Business Owners and Professionals
Ted Kurlowicz, James F. Ivers III, and John J. McFadden

Financial Planning Applications
Thomas P. Langdon and William J. Ruckstuhl

Advanced Topics in Group Benefits
Burton T. Beam, Jr., and Thomas P. O'Hare (eds.)

Executive Compensation
John J. McFadden

Health and Long-Term Care Financing for Seniors
Burton T. Beam, Jr., and Thomas P. O'Hare

Financial Decisions for Retirement
David A. Littell and Kenn Beam Tacchino

Huebner School Series

Individual Health Insurance Planning:
Medical, Disability Income, and Long-Term Care

Thomas P. O'Hare
Burton T. Beam, Jr.

The American College Press/*Bryn Mawr, Pennsylvania*

270 South Bryn Mawr Avenue
Bryn Mawr, PA 19010
(888) AMERCOL (263-7265)
www.theamericancollege.edu

Library of Congress Control Number 2007938739
ISBN 1932819568

Printed in the United States of America

To my wife Christine

TPO'H

To L.H. for all her hard work

BTB

Contents

Preface

Over the past several years, we have been responsible for a course in The American College's professional designation programs on the subject of individual health insurance. For this course, we used separate books on the three forms of health insurance—medical expense insurance, disability income insurance, and long-term care insurance. Because of the many commonalities of these forms of health insurance, the use of separate books sometimes resulted in overlap and repetition. In addition, the three books were not always consistent in how they approached various topics.

As a result, we made a decision to develop a single book that focused on all forms of individual health insurance. This enabled us to focus on the commonality that exists across all forms of health insurance, and this is the basis for the first six chapters of the book. After that, we explore the unique characteristic of each form of health insurance.

The highlights of our changes from the three older books include the following:

- increased emphasis on planning for financing health care expenses, including alternatives to private health insurance products
- updating of statistics, the legislative environment, and product developments where needed
- broader coverage of the tax treatment of premiums and benefits
- expanded coverage of claims
- expanded coverage of Medicare supplement policies and their latest variations
- expanded coverage of Medicare Advantage plans and the Medicare prescription drug program
- expanded coverage of high-deductible health plans and health savings accounts.
- more in-depth coverage of disability income products

As with any new book, there are many people who have contributed to our endeavor.

We would like to thank our students, whose questions and comments have resulted in many of the refinements in the book. We would also like to thank other readers of the previous books, including instructors, who have offered us suggestions. In addition, we appreciate the time that numerous people have taken to answer specific questions that we asked.

There are also a few people that we want to acknowledge by name for their contribution to this book. The book is better because of all of them:

- Ed Auble and Sara Taylor, Broker Resource Center
- Tom Musco, United States Department of Health and Human Services
- Nancy Morith, NP Morith, Inc., and an adjunct professor at The American College
- Ed Graves and Rich Dulisse, our faculty colleagues at The American College
- Virgina Webb and Mary Anne Adler, The American College Library
- Evelyn Rice, our production assistant who puts up with our constant demands
- Wendy de Pinho, our always excellent editor

We as authors, however, have the ultimate responsibility for providing you with the best book possible, and we have tried to do that. It would be foolish to believe that any book is perfect. Please take some time to give us your constructive comments on how we can improve future editions.

Thomas P. O'Hare
Burton T. Beam, Jr.

About the Authors

Thomas P. O'Hare, STB, MBA, HIA, is an adjunct professor of insurance at The American College. He received his BA and STB degrees from the University of St. Mary of the Lake, Mundelein, Illinois, and his MBA from Loyola University of Chicago. Prior to joining The American College, Mr. O'Hare served in leadership positions with the Health Insurance Association of America (HIAA) in both Chicago and Washington, D.C. Most recently as vice president of membership and special programs and director of insurance education, he led the revision and update of HIAA's education curriculum, including the establishment of the Managed Healthcare Professional (MHP) designation program and the creation of the course material to support it. He previously worked for the American Hospital Association in Chicago, where he was a hospital payment/reimbursement specialist with responsibilities for membership consulting on regulatory compliance. Mr. O'Hare is author of *Individual Medical Expense Insurance* and coauthor of *Meeting the Financial Need of Long-Term Care* and *Health and Long-Term Care Financing for Seniors.* He is also a member of the National Association of Health Underwriters.

Burton T. Beam, Jr., CLU, ChFC, CPCU, CASL, is associate professor of insurance at The American College. Mr. Beam did his undergraduate work at the University of Oregon and holds graduate degrees from that institution and the University of Pennsylvania. Prior to joining The American College, Mr. Beam was on the faculties of the University of Florida and the University of Connecticut. He has written extensively in the areas of group and health insurance and has had articles published in several professional journals. He is the author of *Group Benefits: Basic Concepts and Alternatives.* He is also coauthor of *Meeting the Financial Need of Long-Term Care, Health and Long-Term Care Financing for Seniors*, and *Employee Benefits,* a textbook used at many colleges and universities. Mr. Beam is an assistant editor of the *Journal of Financial Service Professionals.* He is a member of the National Association of Health Underwriters, the CPCU Society, and the Society of Financial Service Professionals.

Individual Health Insurance Planning:
Medical, Disability Income, and Long-Term Care

1

Introduction

Learning Objectives

An understanding of the material in this chapter should enable you to

1-1. Explain why a person should have health insurance.

1-2. Define individual health insurance and its three component forms.

1-3. Explain how other health insurance programs affect the need for individual health insurance.

1-4. Describe the fundamental importance of health insurance planning and the role of the health insurance agent.

1-5. Describe the developments in the current environment that are making the need for individual health insurance and the role of the health insurance agent increasingly important.

1-6. Summarize the development of each form of health insurance from earlier decades to the present.

Chapter Outline

Health insurance protects financial security as a person anticipates and moves through life's various stages. At each stage in life, a responsible person endeavors to maintain a reasonable level of financial security. Financial security affects both the quality of that person's life and that of his or her spouse and children as well. Financial security remains a requirement throughout life, although its purpose and means may change significantly. At varying times in a person's life, it may support education and career building, marriage and family obligations (including child rearing), wealth accumulation, and ultimately retirement and estate planning. For most people, earned income provides the means of financial security. Saving and investing income over time also provides financial security by creating assets that become increasingly important, especially in retirement.

Adequate health insurance helps to build and maintain financial security by shielding a person from financial setbacks that could compromise that security should ill health or injury occur at any stage in life. Few individuals can afford to be without health insurance. According to a study published in 2005, adverse health-related events account for over 45 percent of personal and family bankruptcies.[1] When filing for bankruptcy, these debtors, who are typically under age 45 with some college education, cited one or more of the following circumstances:

- illness or injury
- uncovered medical bills
- lost work-related income
- mortgaged home to pay medical bills

Example: Roger is a 31-year-old engineer and had a good job with a small construction company. His wife, Linda, was able to be a stay-at-home mom for their two young children. Like many young couples, Roger and Linda had only limited savings and large mortgage payments for a home they had recently purchased.

While installing Christmas lights on their house, Roger fell off a ladder and broke his back. He had adequate insurance for most of his medical expenses. However, he was unable to work for 9 months, and his disability benefits from his employer continued for only 2 months. During the remaining 7 months, he and his wife exhausted their savings, fell behind on their mortgage loan payments, and took cash advances to the full limit of their credit cards. Linda was unable to return to work because she needed to care for Roger.

When Roger returned to work, his condition was such that he was only able to work part-time. Linda also got a job, but little income was left after child-care expenses. As a result, Roger and Linda were unable to recover financially. After the bank started foreclosure proceedings on their house, they decided to file for bankruptcy.

The need to file for bankruptcy would have been significantly minimized or eliminated if Roger had had an individual disability income policy.

An insured person enjoys peace of mind to the degree that health insurance forestalls the financial effects of such occurrences and thereby preserves financial security. Whether the reader is a financial services professional, such as a health insurance agent or financial planner, or a consumer, this book has the same underlying goals:

- understanding individual health insurance products, the coverage they offer, and the benefits they provide
- understanding health insurance planning that is essential to the security of an overall financial plan

INDIVIDUAL HEALTH INSURANCE BROADLY DEFINED

individual health insurance

A broad definition of *individual health insurance* is a personally purchased contract of insurance that provides benefits in the event of an insured's illness or injury. This book, as its title suggests, presents individual health insurance in three forms: medical expense, disability income, and long-term care. Each form provides distinct health-related benefits:

medical expense insurance

disability income insurance

long-term care insurance

- *Medical expense insurance* pays for or provides access to services of medical professionals, facilities, and institutions required for the treatment of illness or injury, or the maintenance of well being.
- *Disability income insurance* partially replaces the income of persons unable to work because of injury or illness.
- *Long-term care insurance* pays for custodial and skilled-nursing care over an extended period at home, in an adult day care center, in an assisted living facility, or in a nursing home.

As subsequent chapters explain, many features and components constitute the benefits within each form of health insurance. In addition, a single policy, often called a hybrid policy, may encompass two or even three forms of health insurance.

PLAN OF THIS BOOK

The rest of this chapter sets the stage for the discussion in subsequent chapters by (1) describing the relation of individual health insurance to other available health insurance programs, (2) identifying the need for health insurance planning and the role of the health insurance agent, (3) reviewing the changing environment that encourages an increased reliance on individual health insurance, and (4) reviewing the development of health insurance to better understand today's policies.

All forms of health insurance have several common aspects, which are discussed in chapters 2 through 6. Chapter 2 focuses on the process of purchasing individual health insurance and takes into account the sources of coverage and the consumer's decision-making process leading to the purchase. Chapter 3 addresses the nature and importance of the contract that is at the heart of any health insurance policy. Chapters 4 and 5 explore underwriting and claims processing, two common functions essential to the successful operation of health insurance programs. Chapter 6 covers regulation and tax treatment that affect the extent of coverage, benefits, costs, availability, and marketing.

Chapters 7 through 11 are devoted to medical expense insurance. Chapter 7 introduces medical expense insurance and the considerations that affect the decision to purchase an individual medical insurance policy. Chapter 8 explains the principal policies of medical expense insurance that provide substantial benefits for the major portion of a person's health care expenses and constitute the insured's fundamental program of medical expense protection. Chapter 9 focuses on the recent development of consumer-directed medical expense plans aimed at promoting the cost effective use of medical services and describes how tax-preferred savings accounts work in conjunction with high-deductible insurance plans.

However, even a principal policy or program of medical expense insurance typically does not pay all of a person's medical expenses. For example, although most Americans are eligible for Medicare at age 65, that program does not fully cover a beneficiary's medical expenses. Chapter 10 addresses ways in which many retirees obtain coverage to fill some of these gaps and obtain benefits for otherwise uncovered services.

Some persons may want other types of supplemental medical insurance policies in the event of a critical illness, for example. When a person travels, he or she might need an international travel medical expense policy. Still other persons want dental insurance. Chapter 11 presents the wide variety of interim, supplemental, and ancillary medical expense policies that are available to meet these and other needs.

Chapters 12 through 15 cover disability income insurance, the second form of health insurance that this book presents. Chapter 12 introduces this form of health insurance by reviewing some of the features unique to the product and consumers' pattern of benefit purchases. Chapter 13 explains how a person selects an appropriate level of disability income benefits that will provide needed income in the event of a disability while avoiding excess benefit levels that could create obstacles to a return to work.

Chapter 14 reviews the unique policy provisions of disability income insurance, including contractual provisions and optional benefits that differentiate it from other forms of coverage. Chapter 15 concludes the discussion of disability income insurance by explaining its uses for the protection of a person's business interests.

Chapters 16 through 20 focus on financing long-term care costs that are left uncovered by medical expense insurance and Medicare. Chapter 16 looks at the reasons why there is a growing need for long-term care and describes the variety of settings in which such care might be received. Most individuals have noninsurance resources to meet some of their long-term care needs. These may include assets, income, and family support. Chapter 17 addresses these personal resources and other programs for which they may be eligible.

In most cases, despite the personal resources that may be available, an individual or couple will likely need long-term care insurance. Chapter 18 traces the development of this relatively new form of health insurance and chapter 19 describes its characteristics. Chapter 20 concludes the book with a review of consumer attitudes about long-term care insurance and the decisions consumers have to make when purchasing it.

INDIVIDUAL HEALTH INSURANCE AND OTHER HEALTH INSURANCE PROGRAMS

Individuals may have health insurance protection from a variety of sources, and this often introduces complexity into the decision to purchase an individual health insurance policy. Many persons have coverage under government programs. These programs are often thought of as the first building block of economic security. The second building block is provided through employee benefit plans. For some individuals, these sources provide adequate protection. However, for many other individuals, these building blocks are inadequate and an additional building block is necessary: the purchase of individual health insurance.

Although this book emphasizes individual health insurance planning, proper planning cannot take place without an understanding of what an individual already has in the form of government and employer-provided protection. Individual health insurance is typically purchased because benefits under these other programs are either nonexistent or insufficient. These other programs also influence the reasons for some of the provisions in and the underwriting of individual policies. In addition, employee benefit programs are often coordinated with government programs.

The following very brief discussion looks at government programs and employer-provided benefits. Where appropriate later in the book, they are discussed in somewhat more detail. No attempt, however, is made to analyze the programs in depth. That is the purpose of other books.

Government Programs

Government programs encompassing health insurance fall into two broad categories: public assistance, often referred to as welfare, and social insurance.

Public Assistance

Medicaid

The major government public assistance program for health insurance is Medicaid. Approximately one-sixth of Americans have coverage under this program, which provides medical expense coverage and, in most states, long-term care coverage. Eligibility is limited to various classes of individuals who have low incomes and limited assets. Each state has its own *Medicaid* program that is established under federal guidelines; the federal government finances a major portion of each state's program as well.

Individuals who are eligible for Medicaid include the aged, the disabled, and families with dependent children. In many cases, these persons are not employed and do not have the resources to purchase individual health insurance. However, many states also provide benefits for the medically needy. These are persons whose income exceeds the level normally required for benefits but who have significant medical expenses that they are unable to pay. This is how many seniors are able to qualify for long-term care benefits. However, with proper planning, some of these persons can avoid having to rely on Medicaid.

Example 1: Tom and Marie are retired and have modest income and assets. They realize that they will be unable to afford the cost of long-term care if it is needed for more than a few months. They are willing to let Medicaid pick up the tab if the need arises.

Example 2: Dave and Jackie are also retired and have modest income and assets. They worked hard for the assets they have and want to leave them to their children. They also do not want to rely on public assistance or their children if it can be avoided. Ten years ago, they purchased long-term care insurance policies. They did not have the income to purchase policies with the benefit amounts or durations they would have preferred, but they feel they have adequate protection as long as any stay in a nursing home is not more than 2 years.

Chapters 7 and 17 discuss Medicaid in more detail.

Social Insurance Programs

social insurance programs

Social insurance programs are run or regulated by the government and designed to solve social problems that affect a large portion of society. Eligibility for benefits is not based on need. Rather, benefits are prescribed by law and offered to eligible persons as a matter of right.

There are four important programs that provide health-related benefits. All states have worker's compensation programs that provide medical expense and disability income coverage for persons who have suffered work-related accidents or illnesses. In addition, five states (California, Hawaii, New Jersey, New York, and Rhode Island) and Puerto Rico require that employers provide short-term disability income coverage to their employees. These so-called temporary disability programs provide benefits up to a statutory maximum. Employees may be required to pay part of the cost of coverage. All of these programs are discussed in more detail in subsequent chapters.

The two major programs that provide health-related benefits are federal programs—Social Security and Medicare.

Social Security

Social Security. Almost all employed persons are covered by *Social Security*. It provides retirement income to almost all elderly Americans and survivor benefits to many children and spouses of deceased workers. It also provides disability income to disabled workers, generally after 6 months of disability. However, benefit levels are inadequate for higher-paid individuals, and the criteria for benefits are more stringent than for private disability income programs. Unless an employer provides adequate supplemental benefits, many individuals need individual disability income policies.

Example: Sarah is a self-employed consultant. She is in good health and has a high-deductible medical expense policy and a health savings account to which she makes the maximum allowable contribution. She nets over $100,000 per year and realizes that her potential disability benefit from Social Security is no more that $2,000 per month. Therefore, Sarah recently purchased an individual disability income policy so that her income will be $65,000 per year if she is disabled.

Medicare

Medicare. Most Americans aged 65 or older and certain younger disabled workers are eligible for medical expense benefits under *Medicare*. Under the original Medicare program, benefits are less adequate than what most people had prior to Medicare eligibility, and supplemental coverage is often needed. Some individuals are fortunate enough to have this as a retiree benefit from their employers. Other individuals may elect a Medicare Advantage plan through a private insurer or purchase a Medicare supplement (medigap) policy. Chapter 10 covers Medicare Advantage plans and Medicare supplement policies.

In addition, Medicare beneficiaries must decide whether they need to purchase prescription drug coverage. The federal government heavily subsidizes this coverage as long as it meets certain standards, but the actual coverage is purchased from private insurers.

Example: Joe's employer does not provide any medical expense coverage for retirees, so Joe worked until age 65 when he became eligible for Medicare. He soon became aware of Medicare's limitations and decided to find some type of supplemental coverage. He discovered that many insurers sold Medicare supplement policies. He also looked at the only Medicare Advantage plan in his area. Although it was a less expensive than a Medicare supplement policy, it was structured as an HMO—a feature that was not particularly appealing to him because he often traveled outside its service area. Therefore, Joe purchased a Medicare supplement policy.

Joe also realized that Medicare did not provide nursing home coverage except in very limited circumstances and only for a very short duration. Fortunately, he had the resources to purchase a long-term care policy and wonders why he had not done so at an earlier age when the annual premium would have been much less.

Employer-Provided Benefits

The major source of health insurance benefits for many Americans is through an employer. In many cases, employers pay a portion of the cost of the coverage through what are commonly referred to as group insurance or employee benefit plans. Employers may also have voluntary benefit plans under which employees who elect coverage pay its full cost.

Group Insurance Plans

Although many small employers provide few if any health-related group insurance benefits, the majority of Americans are employed by organizations that offer medical expense coverage and pay a portion of its cost. Coverage is generally comprehensive and often better than what can be obtained in the individual marketplace. It is also less expensive to employees as long as the employer makes a significant contribution towards the cost of a plan. Employer contributions for an employee's coverage are often very substantial, with an employee either paying nothing or a small monthly premium. However, employers often pay a much smaller portion of the cost of dependent coverage. This may lead to an employee finding less costly protection for his or her family in the individual marketplace.

Example: Gary is self-employed. Maryanne, his wife, has group coverage for which her employer pays all but a small monthly premium. However, the employer makes only a small contribution for coverage of dependents and spouses. By looking in the individual marketplace, Gary was able to find a policy that was less expensive than if Maryanne added him to her group insurance plan.

Many employers provide some type of short-term disability income protection to their employees. A smaller number of employers provide long-term disability income protection, particularly for lower-income employees whom the employer deems to have adequate protection from Social Security. Even when coverage is provided to higher-income employees, the benefit level may be low enough to encourage them to purchase an individual policy.

Example: Harriet's employer has a very generous disability income plan that provides benefits of up to 66 2/3 percent of predisability income when coordinated with Social Security. However, for underwriting reasons, the employer's insurance carrier insists on a maximum month benefit of $5,000. Harriett is a vice president of the firm and earns $18,000 per month. She purchased an individual policy that will pay an additional $4,000 per month if she is disabled.

Voluntary Benefits

voluntary benefits

Many employers make one or more *voluntary benefits* available to their employees. Under such plans, employees can obtain coverage as long as they are willing to pay the full cost of that coverage. Advantages of voluntary benefits include the ease of payroll deductions and possibly liberalized underwriting and favorable premiums. However, liberalized underwriting may also result in premiums that are higher than what a healthy person might find in the individual marketplace.

Example 1: Jack's employer recently made several voluntary benefits available to its employees. These include critical illness insurance, long-term disability income insurance, and long-term care insurance. During the initial enrollment period, there is minimal underwriting. Although Jack considers himself in good health, he has diabetes that is controlled through diet and exercise. Jack realizes that this disease will make it difficult for him to find coverage in the individual marketplace. Therefore, he is looking closely at the benefits available through these voluntary plans.

Example 2: Karen works for the same employer as Jack. She has been considering long-term care insurance, and the offering of this new voluntary benefit has increased this interest. However, she was able to find coverage in the individual marketplace at a somewhat lower cost and with features she considered more attractive.

One final comment about voluntary benefit plans: They generally are portable in the sense that an individual can continue coverage after leaving employment by paying the premium directly to the insurance company.

HEALTH INSURANCE PLANNING AND THE HEALTH INSURANCE AGENT

As with any other program that has financial security as its goal, such as life insurance or investing, health insurance requires planning. Indeed, health insurance planning can be understood as securing the foundation that life insurance and investment planning can build upon. Financial planners who do not sell insurance routinely refer their clients to health insurance agents to make sure that the health insurance component of an overall financial plan is secure. Insurance agents who have a good relationship with financial planners may find this leads to additional clients.

Even though most people are serious about planning when it comes to financial security and their future, they can easily fail to anticipate the full effects of ill health in terms of medical bills, lost income, and incapacity. The fundamental role of the health insurance agent and/or financial planner is to assist clients to choose the health insurance policies and benefit levels that provide both present and future financial security for themselves and their families. The health insurance agent or planner must evaluate a client's needs before making any recommendations for health insurance coverage and benefits, and must understand the implications of those recommendations as well.

During this process, the agent or planner should gather complete and accurate information about the client's finances, including the client's priority goals and objectives as well as the health benefit programs for which the client is enrolled or eligible. A client's age or stage in life also affects health insurance needs. As clients age and take on greater responsibilities, they are more likely to call upon health insurance benefits. The agent or planner should counsel clients to purchase insurance protection well in advance of any need and preferably at a younger age when coverage is more affordable and available.

INDIVIDUAL HEALTH INSURANCE IN A CHANGING ENVIRONMENT

Several developments are changing the current environment and are making the need for individual health insurance planning and the role of the health insurance agent more important than ever. Among these developments are declining employer funding of benefits, longer post-retirement life expectancy, potential Medicare reductions, and increased personal responsibility.

Declining Employer Funding of Benefits

Continuing a current trend, employers are likely to reduce funding for or even eliminate health benefits for active workers and retirees.

Medical expense insurance provides the most striking examples of this development. Although most employers offer medical benefits, active and retired workers are experiencing various combinations of rising premiums, greater out-of-pocket expenses, and more stringent eligibility requirements. Significantly, the percentage of employers offering health benefits has fallen from 66 percent to 60 percent over a recent 5-year period. Only a third of firms with 200 or more workers offer benefits to assist retirees with medical expenses unpaid by Medicare, which is half the percentage of firms that offered these benefits 20 years ago.[2]

Less than half the employers in private industry offer short-term disability income insurance (39 percent). Even fewer (31 percent) offer long-term disability income insurance.[3] Generally, these levels have shown no increase since the mid-1990s, except with regard to short-term disability coverage among companies with less than 100 workers, where they declined substantially.[4]

Although an increasing number of employers are sponsoring long-term care insurance plans, only 12 percent of full time employees have access to these plans—a level that changed little in the past few years.[5] More importantly, when employers offer long-term care insurance, they usually do so on a voluntary basis with employees paying the entire premium.

To control costs, employers are turning increasingly to voluntary benefit plans, not only for long-term care insurance, where such plans are dominant, but also for medical expense and disability income insurance. However, voluntary benefit plans often have drawbacks that may encourage employees to seek coverage in the individual health insurance market outside the workplace.

The employer typically selects benefits and maximum benefit levels for voluntary benefits, even though the employee pays the entire premium. For example, long-term care policies may lack the automatic benefit increase for inflation that is available in the individual marketplace. In addition, disability income policies may have lower maximum monthly benefits. Because enrollment is self selected, voluntary plan premium rates are likely to be higher than in plans where the employer pays most or all of the premium. Consequently, employees have an incentive to turn to the individual insurance market where they may find preferred rates and benefits that suit their needs better. The increasing number of self-employed persons and owners/employees of newly established companies are also likely look to this market as the primary source of their health insurance.

Longer Post-Retirement Life Expectancy

The latest available data from the National Center for Health Statistics reports that the average additional life expectancy at age 65 is 20 years for women and 17.1 years for men. In just over 50 years, the average life expectancy at age 65 increased 5 years for women and just over 4 years for men.[6] In general, the challenge of a longer life expectancy is to maintain financial security throughout these additional years, which for half the persons reaching age 65 will be longer—in some cases, much longer— than these average statistics indicate. For the purpose of this book, the individual health insurance component of a financial plan must also anticipate the potential effects of increased longevity on health-related expenses.

Potential Medicare Reductions

Medicare, the primary payer of medical expenses for older Americans, requires beneficiary cost-sharing features that involve premiums, deductibles, and copayments for covered services. As chapter 10 indicates, these cost-sharing features are significant. As a result, most Medicare beneficiaries have some form of insurance to supplement Medicare benefits.[7] Because employer funding of retiree benefits continues to decrease, the number of beneficiaries seeking Medicare supplement benefits through individual insurance policies should increase as beneficiaries place greater reliance on them.

Moreover, Medicare beneficiaries must recognize the extent to which their medical and other health-related expenses are left uncovered by Medicare. A recent study reports that a married couple who reaches age 65 in 2006 with an average additional life expectancy (82 for a man and 85 for a woman) could need as much as $295,000 to cover premiums for health insurance coverage and out-of-pocket expenses during retirement.[8]

The study also notes that for several reasons, these projections can easily underestimate the financial resources needed. First, the half of the Medicare beneficiary population that lives beyond the average remaining life expectancy will need to dedicate greater resources to health care. A couple living to age 95, for example, will need over 80 percent more than the amounts needed by a couple with an average life expectancy. Second, with limited exceptions, Medicare excludes coverage for assistance with activities of daily living (custodial care) when beneficiaries are long-term care recipients. These projections do not consider the cost of long-term care. Third, a looming financial crisis in Medicare program is likely to cause beneficiaries to incur substantial additional cost sharing in the future.

By 2010, Medicare is expected to spend more to cover program services than it will receive in income. Public policy changes must address the Medicare budget shortfall because Congress is just as likely to reduce Medicare benefits as to raise taxes to maintain them. Regardless of the outcome, Medicare beneficiaries will have greater responsibility for the cost of their medical care. Of course, to the extent that financial and insurance planning are done in advance of age 65, persons will have more time to anticipate and to save for retirement health care expenses.[9]

Increased Personal Responsibility

Taken together, declining employer funding of benefits, longer post-retirement life expectancy, and potential Medicare reductions increase personal responsibility for health-related expenses. In turn, this responsibility encourages people to use individual health insurance to protect themselves and their families against the potential of these expenses to erode financial security, especially, but not only, in retirement years. These factors also increase the importance of the health insurance agent and financial planner as an advisor to clients on the policies and benefits that best fit their needs.

The advent of consumer-directed health plans in recent years greatly expands the potential for increased personal responsibility in the selection and use of medical expense insurance. Such plans are referred to as "health plans," although they are actually only for medical expenses. While employers may sponsor consumer-directed health plans for their employees, individuals and families with or without an employment relationship may also establish these plans. Consumer-directed health plans commonly feature a high-deductible medical expense insurance arrangement and an annual deposit of funds to a tax-preferred savings account. One objective of these plans is to give insureds a strong incentive to buy medical services using the accumulated amounts in the plan savings account with the same prudence and economy they would use when purchasing services with their own money. Consumers must be well informed if these plans are to contain costs successfully. Consequently, properly implemented consumer-directed health plans provide access to and education on the effective use of comparative price and quality data for the purchase of medical services along with wellness information.

In turn, because insureds under these plans now have an increased level of personal responsibility, health insurance agents and financial planners must educate themselves in order to advise their clients on choosing and effectively using consumer-directed medical expense policies and their associated support tools. Chapter 9 discusses consumer-directed health plans in detail.

THE DEVELOPMENT OF HEALTH INSURANCE

Health insurance policies that are currently available developed and evolved over the years in response to many forces, including legislation and regulations, economic and social conditions, the financial stability of insurance companies, and competition and other demands of the market. Because these forces are ongoing, current products will continue to evolve and new products will develop.

A brief review of the development of today's health insurance products can promote a health insurance agent's or advisor's understanding of these products and how they can protect a client's financial security. Although health insurance can trace its history over hundreds of years, our review begins more recently with the early years of the 20th century. By then, state government investigations had led to regulations governing company operations and policy provisions. Although these regulations originally governed life insurance, they would also affect the newly developing forms of health insurance. An association of state insurance commissioners developed the model Standard Provision Law, later succeeded by the Uniform Individual Accident and Sickness Policy Provision Law. All states eventually enacted some form of this law or similar legislation that afforded consumers greater uniformity and fairness in the provisions of health insurance policies they purchased.

From that era through subsequent decades, we can recognize the development of the current forms of health insurance: medical expense, disability income, and long-term care.

Medical Expense Insurance

Medical expense insurance rose from virtual nonexistence at the beginning of the 1930s to become a primary payment structure for the nation's medical care. Without this form of health insurance in the private sector, the United States may have had little choice other than to establish a totally government-funded system for financing medical care.

The 1930s-The Initial Decade

Rampant unemployment during the Great Depression years of the 1930s significantly affected the development of medical expense insurance. The swelling ranks of the unemployed forced workers and their families to consider the repercussions that job loss would have on their physical well-being. Twentieth-century medicine was advancing more rapidly, but with progress came higher costs. For the first time, the ability to pay for medical services began to rank among the necessities.

At the same time, skyrocketing unemployment and severe economic conditions caused health care provider income to decline significantly, as many persons experienced difficulty in paying for their medical care.[10] Hospitals exhausted their charitable resources.

The modern era of medical expense insurance resulted from the response to these economic and social conditions by three types of organizations: Blue Cross and Blue Shield plans, health maintenance organizations (HMOs), and insurance companies.

Blue Cross and Blue Shield Plans. The forerunner of Blue Cross plans is generally considered to be the prepaid arrangement for 21 days of hospital service established in 1929 at Baylor University Hospital for the Dallas school teachers. Throughout the 1930s, many Blue Cross plans developed around the country, with strong backing from local hospitals. Physicians soon followed the hospitals' approach and established medical society-sponsored Blue Shield plans offering physician and surgeon benefits.

A number of common features distinguished the maturing Blue Cross and Blue Shield plans. Prominent among them were the following characteristics:

- establishment as not-for-profit (and tax-exempt) hospital and/or medical prepayment plans
- favorable service and reimbursement agreements with most health care providers in the community
- a single average enrollee premium rate, known as community rating
- first-dollar benefits with no out-of-pocket costs, known as service benefits
- provider claims filed directly with the plan

- governance heavily influenced by health care providers who agreed to accept lower reimbursement if the plan operated at a loss

Initial benefit designs provided a limited duration of coverage, such as 21, 30, 60, or 90 days for hospital services, and a schedule of physician and surgeon fees with a total maximum payment per period.

Special state legislation exempted them from many organizational, financial, and other regulatory requirements imposed on insurance companies. Because they were regarded as quasi-public entities, Blue Cross and Blue Shield plans were often required to provide guaranteed issue and community rating of individual coverage as well as community service and health promotion programs. The advantages these plans enjoyed, including the strong support of health care providers and organized labor, promoted their rapid and continued growth over ensuing decades.

Health Maintenance Organizations (HMOs). At the same time, prepaid group practice plans, later known as health maintenance organizations (HMOs), also began to emerge. What is usually considered to be the first HMO, the Ross-Loos Clinic, was founded in Los Angeles in 1929. Other HMOs, such as Kaiser Permanente, began in the 1930s.

These organizations shared a number of characteristics with Blue Cross and Blue Shield plans and enjoyed many of the same financial and business advantages. Early HMOs were established as not-for-profit enterprises and used community rating. Doctors and hospitals provided benefits to HMO enrollees under service and reimbursement contracts.

HMOs were also innovative. The actual provision of care was coupled with prepaid service benefits. Medical services were comprehensive and went beyond inpatient hospital and surgical care with an emphasis on preventive medicine. Unlike Blue Cross and Blue Shield plans that sought to contract with as many health care providers as possible, HMOs entered into contracts with or hired a limited number of these providers; the number of doctors and hospitals was based on the service needs of the enrolled population. Although their market penetration remained low until the last few decades, HMOs eventually became prominent and many of their initially innovative features permeate today's medical expense plans.

Insurance Companies. Seeing the success of Blue Cross plans, insurance companies entered the market for hospital insurance in the 1930s and later added coverage for surgical and physicians' expenses. The initial patterns of medical expense insurance benefits, which prevailed into the

1950s, were largely confined to hospital care and physicians' services—principally surgery in the hospital.

The 1940s and 1950s—Development and Refinements

By 1940, over 9 percent of the population had some type of medical expense insurance.[11] The 1940s witnessed significant growth related to World War II, the rising strength of unions, and the growth of labor union health and welfare funds. The period through the end of the 1940s onward might be characterized as the refining process for the formative developments.

During the 1950s, previous regulatory and legal developments that promoted its growth deeply ingrained medical insurance within the institutional fabric of American life. Taken together, these developments permitted collective bargaining for health benefits and allowed employer tax deductions for the cost of health insurance.

In the early 1950s, health insurance companies, which had been only modestly successful in competing with Blue Cross and Blue Shield plans, introduced policies with an innovative benefit structure, known as major medical insurance.[12] These policies provided more comprehensive, more all-inclusive coverages for inpatient and outpatient treatment, physicians' office visits, and required diagnostic testing and therapies.[13] In many cases, insurers wrapped a program of major medical coverage (known as supplementary major medical) around the more limited basic plan of inpatient benefits provided by Blue Cross and Blue Shield plans.

Major medical insurance policies implemented a contractually imposed deductible and coinsurance benefits, which required the covered person to share in the payment for medical care services. An insured must pay a deductible, which is a specified dollar amount such as $200, for covered services before major medical benefits begin. In the case of a wraparound or supplementary major medical policy, that deductible (known as a corridor deductible) occurs after the basic plan pays its benefits. Coinsurance is the percentage of covered expenses paid as a benefit once the deductible is satisfied.

Major medical expense insurance gained rapid public acceptance.[14] As the 1950s gave way to a new decade, over two-thirds of Americans had some form of medical expense coverage.[15]

The 1960s—Government Involvement

While medical expense insurance policies underwent little change during the 1960s, there was one major development in the middle of the decade. For the first time, the federal government became a major player in providing medical expense coverage by creating national health insurance programs for the elderly and poor. These two programs are Medicare and Medicaid.

Medicare effectively eliminated the private insurance market as a principal source of medical expense benefits for the 65-and-over population. At the same time, however, this population constituted an expanded market for more affordable individual and group supplemental and ancillary benefit programs, which filled the gaps in Medicare coverage and extended benefits for senior citizens into new areas.

Significantly, Medicare and Medicaid reimbursed only the cost of the care of its beneficiaries and recipients. As a result, health care providers, especially hospitals, usually recovered the cost for the care of patients who did not pay their bills by increasing their charges to the insured and self-pay patients, a practice known as *cost shifting.* Because their reimbursement contracts precluded this practice, many Blue Cross and Blue Shield plans enjoyed a competitive advantage over insurance companies.

cost shifting

Nevertheless, private insurers enjoyed a period of unprecedented growth as the number of persons covered by medical expense insurance plans grew rapidly during the decade and insurance companies began offering more comprehensive coverage with higher limits. Maximum benefits under major medical policies ranged from $50,000 to several million dollars.[16]

The 1970s—The First Reactions to Spiraling Costs

In 1950, expenditures for health care equaled 4.1 percent of the nation's gross domestic product (GDP); they increased to 5.1 percent in 1960 and 7.0 percent in 1970.[17] The infusion of revenues from new government and expanding private-sector benefit plans, an aging population, higher service utilization, technology advances, and cost shifting were having a dramatic effect on health care cost increases. Employers and individuals sought to control their spiraling premiums that reflected these cost increases.

Insurers and employers implemented modified benefit plan designs with increased cost sharing through higher deductibles, coinsurance, and copayments. New plan designs also featured coordination of benefits when more than one benefits plan applied, coverage of lower-cost service alternatives, and utilization controls. Individual medical expense policies incorporated these plan design changes, and had greater levels of cost sharing and somewhat lower benefits compared to group plans in an attempt to maintain a more affordable premium for persons who had to pay the entire amount themselves.

The 1980s and 1990s—Accelerated Costs and Accelerated Change

Attempts to rein in the cost of medical care in the 1970s had little overall effect. By 1980, health care expenditures reached 8.8 percent of the GDP.

This figure climbed to 12.0 percent by 1990, and estimates are that it topped 16 percent in 2005.[18]

The federal government moved aggressively to control its costs under Medicare by paying hospitals prospectively determined per case rates and using fee schedules based on the relative values of procedures to pay doctors. With federal government approval, many states implemented alternative payment programs to contain their Medicaid costs.

Many of the key changes in private sector plans that occurred in these decades can be summarized under the headings of managed care, specialty benefit and service organizations, legislation, and consolidations among insurers. These changes affected individual medical expense policies as well as group health plans.

Managed Care. The most significant change over the last two decades has been the dramatic shift from traditional major medical expense plans to managed care plans. A medical expense insurance plan is considered "managed" when its structure incorporates contracts with a network of health care facilities and professionals to provide medical care to an enrolled population. Enrollees usually must use the network to obtain full benefits, or perhaps any benefits, under the plan. The contracts with health care providers contain agreements and payment incentives to promote appropriate utilization of medical care and contain costs.

The most fully developed and integrated managed care structure is the health maintenance organization (HMO). However, in the 1980s, a new type of managed care structure developed—the preferred provider organization (PPO). Under PPO plans, participants may receive care from any provider, but they are encouraged through financial incentives (higher benefits) to use the network of providers that contract with the plan. Since their institution, PPOs have far outpaced HMOs in the numbers of persons enrolled. In fact, most individual major medical policies are structured as PPO products.

Many organizations, including Blue Cross and Blue Shield plans, insurance companies, and other managed care entities, offer a wide portfolio of managed care products including HMO and PPO plans. Chapter 8 discusses managed care.

Specialty Benefit Organizations. A specialty benefit organization provides services in one or more of the following areas: behavioral health care, chronic condition and disease management, rehabilitation after catastrophic injury, and transplant surgeries. Historically, insurers and other health plan sponsors used the programs these organizations offer, known as carve outs, to achieve cost savings and/or better outcomes. These organ–izations often operate as managed care plans in their specialty care areas.

Legislation. Continued cost escalation, the nagging problem of the uninsured, and the dominance of managed care evoked conflicting legislative reactions from states and the federal government. These efforts sought to make coverage more available, yet at the same time mandated benefits that made insurance more costly.

After early opposition, the insurance industry backed properly structured state high-risk pools for the medically uninsurable, as well as tax-supported assistance and increases in public programs like Medicaid—especially for children. The most sweeping of these proposals was the Health Insurance Portability and Accountability Act of 1996 (HIPAA) that established federal regulatory standards for private health insurance products sold in both the group and individual markets.

HIPAA provides a measure of health insurance portability for people who change or lose their jobs. Insurers and employers sponsoring self-funded plans now must credit prior coverage toward preexisting-condition requirements when an employee (new or current) changes health plans. Persons losing their group medical benefits are assured of the availability of individual medical insurance at some premium. HIPAA also gradually increased the deduction for health insurance premiums of the self-employed to 100 percent.

Consolidations among Medical Expense Insurers. After five decades of continuous growth, the market for medical expense insurance peaked with the over-65 population covered by Medicare and more than 77 percent of the under-65 population covered by private insurance.[19] The remaining population consisted of Medicaid participants and the uninsured, who were outside the private insurance market mostly for economic reasons.

Industry growth in premium revenue was due almost exclusively to increases in the cost of medical care. Insurers competed for an increased share of a fairly defined total market of insureds based on price and service. As in any mature industry, this competition led to consolidation. Consolidation began within the ranks of traditional insurance companies, Blue Cross and Blue Shield plans, and HMOs. More significant, however, were subsequent rounds of consolidation that often dissolved the boundaries between these traditional organizational structures. In the process, many Blue Cross and Blue Shield plans and HMOs abandoned their tax-exempt and non-profit status as well as their community rating practices. As a result, they became taxed and regulated like health insurance companies, many of which also converted from not-for-profit mutual insurers to stock companies.

The New Century Begins—Development of Consumer-Directed Health Plans

The early years of the new century witnessed the return of significant inflation in medical expense insurance premiums. The annual increases in these costs in some years are reminiscent of the double-digit increases of an earlier era. Two factors are often cited as eroding the early cost-containment potential of managed care: consumer and provider rejection of rigorous cost-containment features and the absence of plan members' financial stake in restraining medical costs due to continued low copayments for many services. This erosion focused attention on the potential of newly developing consumer-directed (also referred to as consumer-driven or consumer-choice) health plans to contain benefit costs.

Consumer-directed health plans promise to restore personal financial incentives as a restraint on spending for medical services while maintaining broad benefits and freedom of choice. A consumer-directed health plan commonly features a high-deductible insurance arrangement and an annual deposit or crediting of funds to an account used for the payment of health care expenses unreimbursed by the insurance arrangement. Unused funds at year end remain in the account to accumulate and the account may grow through subsequent deposits and investment. Legislatively enacted tax law changes authorized the creation of qualified health savings accounts (HSAs) and high-deductible health plans (HDHPs) on a tax-preferred basis. These plans may be established either with or without an employment relationship. Chapter 9 reviews the requirements for participation in qualified HSAs and HDHPs, as well as other types of tax-preferred medical expense plans.

Although there is significant initial interest in consumer-directed health plans, their growth depends on continued broad appeal and acceptance by employers and consumers. Consumer access to and effective use of comparative price, treatment, and quality of care data along with wellness promotion information is essential to the success of these plans.

Disability Income Insurance

By the second decade of the 20th century, insurance companies began to offer today's general form of disability income insurance policies. At this time, disability income insurance became available routinely as a separate policy apart from other forms of insurance, such as life insurance. Benefits, although not always at the same level, were extended to disability from illness as well as disability from accidents. Some of these new policies were *guaranteed renewable*, meaning that the insurance company could not make any unilateral changes in a policy's provisions and the insured had the right to continue coverage through timely payment of premiums. The insurance company retained the right to revise rates periodically for broad classes of insureds, however. Many newer policies were also *noncancelable*, meaning that in addition to continuing coverage without change, insurance companies would establish premium rates in advance that would remain effective for the life of the policy.

Disability income insurance grew significantly throughout the 1920s. This growth marked the first phase of many cycles in the industry that began with expansion, competition, new companies entering the market, and product liberalizations. Product liberalizations included loosening contract language and underwriting rules accompanied by increased benefits limits and reduced pricing, all of which lead to narrowed profit margins. The second phase of the cycle involved an economic downturn that produced significant insurance company claim losses followed by product design restrictions, sales contraction, significant premium increases, and a consolidation of companies in the disability income market. Although these cycles shared common features, especially as they relate to industry growth, there was usually a unique economic event or set of events that precipitated the downturn.

The 1930s to the 1950s

In the 1930s, with the deepening Depression, insurance companies learned for the first time, how, after a period of strong growth, a worsening economy affects disability income insurance claims. With large numbers of workers unemployed, both the number of claims and average length of claims increased. This caused insurance companies to limit the issuance of new policies and avoid liberal provisions in the policies that they did issue. After the Depression years and through the 1950s, disability income insurance began to grow again. However, there was very little enthusiasm or incentive for companies to make significant changes or liberalizations in product language or underwriting rules. The typical individual disability income contract called for up to $200 per month of disability benefits, had a definition of disability that was strictly determined by the applicant's ability to work in "any occupation," and had a maximum period for which benefits were to be paid that was rarely more than 2 or 3 years.

Nevertheless, in the early 1950s, disability income policies increasingly exhibited some liberalizations:

- a benefit period that could be fully restored after a disability. Previously, when the total number of days on disability equaled the benefit period, even though separate disabilities occurred, the policy terminated.
- extension of the longer benefit periods that previously applied only to disabilities from accidents to disabilities from sicknesses
- increased availability of both noncancelable and guaranteed-renewable contracts
- extension of the maximum contract age to 65 without a reduction on the amount of the benefit payments or change in premium under noncancelable policies
- continuation of the policy in force after age 65 as long as an insured remained actively at work with the insurer retaining the option to increase premium for persons who continued their policy beyond that point

The 1960s to the 1980s

Disability income insurance continued to progress and prospered into the 1960s. However, that decade witnessed significant changes that affected the industry: consolidated sources of disability insurance coverage; substantial benefit increases; and government-sponsored programs that reduced the market for disability income insurance.

Consolidated Sources of Disability Insurance Coverage. The sources of disability income insurance became concentrated among a few specialty insurers that successfully used brokers rather than their own agents to distribute their products. These insurers discovered that despite their initial concerns about antiselection and poor persistency, the disability income brokerage business came primarily from well-established and professional life insurance agents. These agents needed a reliable source of disability income policies and were not seeking only to minimize premium and maximize commissions.

Substantial Benefit Increases. Following several years of profitable experience, insurance companies relaxed their issue-limit maximums. They also targeted the professional and self-employed business market as a source of large-premium and persistent and quality business. By the early 1970s, issue limits of $3,000 and $3,500 per month became commonplace and the maximum period for which benefits were payable under disability income contracts was extended significantly for sickness coverage from 10 years to age 65. Traditional underwriters of disability income insurance failed to recognize the effect that these increased issue-limit maximums could and would have on their claim experience.

Government-Sponsored Disability Income Programs. A major event that affected the business in the 1960s was the entry of the federal government into the disability income business. In 1960, Congress expanded the 1956 legislation that provided disability benefits under the Social Security program. The amended disability rules authorized payment of benefits to workers of any age and to their dependents after a waiting period of 5 full calendar months from the onset of a worker's disability. Over the course of many previous years, a few states had developed their own temporary disability programs (identified earlier) to cover disabilities that were not covered under the workers' compensation program.

Because the amount of disability insurance covered by insurers is directly related to the applicant's earned income, and because both federal and state programs offered a greater proportion of income protection to lower-income individuals, the lower-income markets made up of middle-income and blue-collar workers began to disappear. By the mid-1970s, the Social Security program coupled with state temporary disability programs effectively eliminated the markets on which many individual disability income insurers had built their businesses. Nevertheless, because of the government programs, many lower-and middle-income insureds who had bought or maintained disability income policies were now overinsured and had a significant incentive to make and continue a disability claim.

In addition, a negative feature promoting disability claims was embedded in the formula for calculating disability income under the Social Security program. In some instances, the benefits actually paid exceeded a recipient's net and gross income. Benefit increases tended to run much higher than the rate of inflation. Congress largely alleviated this problem with legislated changes to the benefit formula in the late 1970s and 1980.

When the recession of the mid-1970s occurred, it was clear that the significant changes in the 1960s, had set the stage for the most severe economic losses that the disability income insurance industry had suffered in its previous 40 years. Overinsurance resulting from government programs, overliberalizations by the industry, and erosion of traditional work-ethic patterns all aggravated the normal adverse pressures that the disability business undergoes during a recession.

The 1980s to the Present

By the early 1980s, the industry had begun to rebuild its confidence in underwriting, product language, and rate structure. With a favorable economic environment through 1986, the disability industry began a new business cycle as it experienced substantial growth. This period was characterized by even further liberalizations in contract language, increased issue limits, more relaxed underwriting, and increased competition as companies expanded their portfolios and their emphasis on disability income products.

However, very substantial changes in markets and products had resulted. Because the lower-income, blue-collar markets had been abandoned to the federal government, new premium volume was even more concentrated in the professional, white-collar markets. High professional incomes demanded higher benefit limits, and some companies raised their limits during this period to $15,000 or even $25,000 per month.

The continued attractiveness of the professional market resulted in both insurers and agents concentrating in this area, particularly on the physician profession. Many insurance companies grew so rapidly in the physician market that one-third or more of their entire premium came from this source. However, with a change in physician motivation and stability, morbidity would increase, and this large concentration of premium would significantly affect earnings. That is what emerged in the 1990s.

Even though physicians were highly motivated and stable in their profession, they had experienced enormous changes that affected their motivation negatively and caused their morbidity to deteriorate. Among those changes were increased government regulation and the threat of malpractice suits. In addition, government programs such as Medicare and Medicaid, as well as the dominance of managed care plans in the private sector, affected the way physicians treated patients and the fees they could charge. The result was that some physicians elected early retirement based on medical impairments that in the past would not have been enough to cause total disability.

Not surprisingly, by the mid-1990s, companies introduced numerous product, rate, commission, and underwriting restrictions. Among those that affected professional classes (physicians in particular) were the following:

- Some companies ceased writing noncancelable disability contracts and reverted to guaranteed renewable policies that allowed rate increases when claims experience deteriorated.
- Rates were increased for all occupation classes, but the rate changes for physicians were especially substantial.
- Own-occupation definitions of disability became more restrictive, lifetime benefits were removed, and cost-of-living benefits were curtailed.
- Most companies added restrictive language to their contracts for mental and nervous disorders, an impairment area that had seen large claim experience increases since the late 1980s.

- Underwriting issue limits were curtailed, again especially for physicians and other professionals. Limits that had grown to $25,000 per month were reduced to maximums of $10,000 or $15,000.
- Commission levels were substantially reduced during the same period, with the most substantial reductions occurring in physician and other professional classes.

Companies had directed their market emphasis away from the professional areas and were following the age-old insurance principle of spreading their business risk among other occupations. As the effects of the restructuring took hold in the latter half of the 1990s, claim experience and profit margins improved. In 1999 and beyond, sales of both noncancelable and guaranteed-renewable policies increased over the previous years.

At the same time, some companies exited the disability market. The considerable restructuring and consolidation within the industry reduced by half the number of disability income insurers that were doing business in the early 1980s. By the time the new century began, the three largest individual disability insurers had all merged to form one company.

Long-Term Care Insurance

As we have seen, it is common for insurance coverages to develop over time. However, the evolution of long-term care products has been dramatic with respect to the magnitude of the changes and the speed with which these changes have occurred.

Early Policies

The long-term care policies in existence in the early 1980s were primarily designed to provide care during the recovery period following an acute illness. They seldom met the needs of persons who required long-term care for chronic conditions. Until the 1980s, the following provisions were characteristic of many of these policies that were called nursing home policies because no benefits were available in other settings.

- short benefit periods
- modest daily benefits
- a prerequisite for benefits in a skilled-nursing facility, often a prior hospitalization of 3 to 5 days
- a prerequisite of a higher level of out-of-hospital care before benefits could be received for a lower level of care. For example, custodial care might be covered, but only if a person received 3 to 5 days of skilled-nursing care in a nursing home.

- exclusion of benefits for preexisting conditions
- exclusion of benefits for care needed as a result of Alzheimer's disease or other organic brain diseases
- no benefits for home health care
- no inflation protection to meet higher long-term care costs in the future
- lack of guaranteed renewability provisions

In addition, the sale of early long-term care policies was often accompanied by improper sales practices. Consumers were led to believe that policies were much more comprehensive than they actually were. In effect, policyowners felt that they were purchasing "nursing home" insurance that would cover them any time nursing home care was needed. Only when such care was needed did these policyowners realize how limited their coverage was.

Finally, for many years, no favorable tax treatment was given to long-term care insurance. Premiums for coverage were not deductible, and employer-paid premiums under group plans resulted in taxation to employees.

Evolution of Coverage

Criticism of early long-term care policies created pressure for change. Consumer groups argued for more government regulation. The federal government conducted studies and held hearings, with the results painting a less than flattering picture of long-term care policies. Change itself, however, resulted primarily from the actions of insurance companies themselves and from state regulators of insurance. However, the threat of federal regulation was always present. Negative publicity about early long-term care policies (and also Medicare supplement policies) dampened the public's acceptance of long-term care insurance. This led many insurance companies to modify their policies and companies entering the business to offer more comprehensive policies. At the same time, the National Association of Insurance Commissioners (NAIC) took an active interest in long-term care insurance. This culminated in the adoption of the Long-Term Care Insurance Model Act in 1987. In 1988, the Long-Term Care Insurance Model Regulation was issued to enable the states to implement the model act. The act and the regulations have been amended almost every year since. Sometimes these amendments changed previous act provisions; at other times, new issues were addressed.

All states now regulate long-term care insurance. Most states have adopted the model act, which chapter 18 discusses in more detail. However, the version in force in a given state is often not the latest NAIC version. The remaining states have adopted legislation different from the model act, although it may be similar to that recommended by the NAIC.

Considerable changes have also taken place at the federal level with passage of the Health Insurance Portability and Accountability Act in 1996. HIPAA provides favorable tax treatment to long-term care insurance contracts that meet certain standards. Such a contract is referred to as a *tax-qualified policy*. Chapter 18 also discusses the requirements for these policies.

Most insurance companies' long-term care policies have gone through many revisions. Although coverage is still not always complete, there is little comparison between the early policies and most of what is marketed today; policies have become more comprehensive over the last few years. For a while, premiums also tended to drop as competition intensified and as more credible statistics about long-term care claims became available. Currently, premiums for new business are increasing and a few companies have raised premiums for existing policies. Enhancements to policies, such as a lifetime benefit period and an automatic benefit increase, also require an additional premium increase.

Most companies that write individual policies now issue only the tax-qualified contracts prescribed by HIPAA. Some companies issue both tax-qualified policies and non-tax-qualified policies. Although purchasers of non-tax-qualified policies do not receive the new tax advantages, these policies usually include provisions that make it easier to qualify for benefits.

Effect of Changes on Existing Policyowners. As policies have evolved, insurance companies have been faced with how to treat existing policyowners. Until recently, many policy upgrades were also accompanied by reduced future premiums for the entire policy. At one extreme, companies did not let existing policyowners know of these changes. If a policyowner found out, he or she might have been allowed to exchange an old policy for the newer form. However, the premium may or may not have been based on the original age of issue. If the conversion was based on the attained-age rates (the rates at the policyowner's current age), a higher premium might have resulted. In some cases, the policyowner could get the new policy only if current underwriting rules were satisfied. Finally, for some insurers, policy provisions of the new policy, such as preexisting-conditions provisions, were again applicable.

At the other extreme, many insurance companies took a more consumer-oriented approach. Policyowners with no claims history were automatically given the enhanced coverage at issue-age rates (the original-age cost) and without any policy restrictions.

Current enhancements to long-term care products usually result in increased premiums. Again, insurance company practices vary. Some companies allow the policyowner to add the enhanced benefits by paying the new premium based on the policyowner's original age of issue. Other companies require evidence of insurability and use attained-age rates.

Where We Are Now

Since the early 1980s, long-term care insurance has evolved from being virtually nonexistent to being an important form of insurance that provides protection to over 6 million persons with annual premiums of about $9 billion. Of this total, individual policies cover approximately 4.5 million lives with almost $8 billion in premium, while about 1.8 million lives covered by group plans generate over $ 1 billion in premium.[20] About 45 insurers offer long-term care products. However, a relatively small number of companies account for the vast majority of the coverage; for example, 10 companies accounted for 86 percent of the new individual premium written in 2006. The group market is even more concentrated, with the top five writers accounting for 97 percent of the new premium in the same year.[21] The major providers of employee benefits now also make group products available.

Long-term care insurance can best be described as having grown from infancy to somewhere between the childhood and teenage years. Coverage will undoubtedly continue to evolve to meet consumer demands and expectations, and the largely untapped market for coverage will continue to grow as the American population ages.

CHAPTER REVIEW

Key Terms

individual health insurance
medical expense insurance
disability income insurance
long-term care insurance
Medicaid
social insurance program
Social Security
Medicare
voluntary benefits
cost shifting
guaranteed renewable
noncancelable

Review Questions

Review questions are based on the learning objectives in this chapter. Thus, a [1-3] at the end of a question means that the question is based on learning objective 1-3. If there are multiple objectives, they are all listed.

1. a. How does health insurance protect a person's financial security? [1-1]
   b. What relevant circumstances do persons filing health-related bankruptcies often cite? [1-1]

2. What are the three forms of health insurance? [1-2]

3. a. What are the building blocks of health insurance coverage that lead to economic security? [1-3]
   b. How does individual health insurance planning relate to these building blocks? [1-3]

4. What types of government programs provide health insurance protection? [1-3]

5. Under what circumstances would persons eligible for benefits under Social Security, Medicare, and/or employer group programs also wish to purchase individual policies of health insurance? [1-3]

6. a. What is the fundamental role of the health insurance agent in health insurance planning? [1-4]
   b. Why do clients need this agent service? [1-4]
   c. What actions should the agent take as part of the health insurance planning process? [1-4]

7. How does each of the following developments make planning for individual health insurance and the agent's role increasingly important?
   a. declining employer funding of benefits [1-5]
   b. longer post-retirement life expectancy [1-5]
   c. potential Medicare reductions [1-5]
   d. increased personal responsibility [1-5]

8. What efforts did insurers implement to contain their medical expense premium increases in the each of the following periods?
   a. the 1970s [1-6]
   b. the 1980s and 1990s [1-6]
   c. the year 2000 to the present [1-6]

9. From the 1930s to the present, what insurer practices and economic factors are associated with the disability income business cycles of (i) growth and (ii) retrenchment? [1-6]

10. What unique effects did government-provided disability income benefits have on the disability income market and the insurance companies that served it? [1-6]

11. a. What were some of the drawbacks to early long-term care insurance policies? [1-6]
    b. What actions led to changes in these policies? [1-6]

12. How can existing policyowners obtain enhancements to long-term care insurance policies? [1-6]

NOTES

1. "MarketWatch: Illness and Injury as Contributors to Bankruptcy" by Himmelstein, Warren, Thorne, and Woolhandler, *Health Affairs,* February 2, 2005, http://content.healthaffairs.org/cgi/content/full/hlthaff.25.63/DC1.
2. *Employer Health Benefits: 2007 Annual Summary of Findings*, The Kaiser Family Foundations and Health Research and Educational Trust, 2007, pp. 31, 174.
3. *Employee Benefits in Private Industry, Summary 2007*, U.S. Department of Labor, Bureau of Labor Statistics.
4. Ibid; *Employee Benefits in Small Private Establishments, 1994, Bulletin 2475*, U.S. Department of Labor, Bureau of Labor Statistics, Table 1 and *Employee Benefits in Medium and Large Private Establishments, 1995, Bulletin 2496*, U.S. Department of Labor, Bureau of Labor Statistics, Table 1.
5. *Employee Benefits in Private Industry, Summary 2007*, U.S. Department of Labor, Bureau of Labor Statistics, and Employee Benefits in Private Industry, 2002–2003, U.S. Department of Labor, Bureau of Labor Statistics, Table 6, p. 10.
6. *Health, United States 2006*, With Chartbook on Trends in the Health of Americans, National Center for Health Statistics, Hyattsville, Maryland: 2006, Table 27.
7. *Savings Needed to Fund Health Insurance and Health Care Expenses in Retirement*, Employee Benefits Research Institute (EBRI), Issue Brief, No. 295, July 2006, p. 10.
8. Ibid. pp. 1, 13.
9. *Can America Afford Tomorrow's Retirees: Results from the EBRI-ERF Retirement Security Projection Model*, No. 263, November 2003, p. 4.
10. J. F. Follmann, Jr., *Medical Care and Health Insurance*. Homewood, IL: Richard D. Irwin, Inc., 1963, p. 108.
11. Ibid., p. 107.
12. Ibid., p. 133.
13. Ibid., p. 116.
14. Ibid. p. 133.
15. U.S. Department of Health, Education and Welfare, Social Security Administration, Division of Program Research, 1960.
16. *Source Book of Health Insurance Data.* Washington, DC: The Health Insurance Association of America, 1999–2000, p. 2.
17. The gross domestic product (GDP) is a measure of the output of goods and services of the United States calculated by the Commerce Department. Health expenditures as a percentage of GDP is based on *Health, United States, 2002*, National Center for Health Statistics, and "National Health Expenditures Projections," Table 1, Centers for Medicare & Medicaid Services, Office of the Actuary.
18. Ibid., and National Health Expenditures Projections: 2005–2015, Table 1, Centers for Medicare & Medicaid Services, Office of the Actuary.
19. Employee Benefits Research Institute tabulations of data from the March 1987–2002, Current Population Surveys, Table 26.1, Health Insurance Coverage of the Nonelderly, and Table 36.1, Health Insurance Coverage of Elderly Americans.
20. *Individual LTC Insurance, Annual Review 2006*, LIMRA International, Inc., 2007, pp. 2 and 3, and *Group LTC Insurance, Annual Review 2006,* LIMRA International, Inc., 2007, p. 2.
21. Ibid.

2

Purchasing Individual Health Insurance

Learning Objectives

An understanding of the material in this chapter should enable you to

2-1. Describe the factors that make a health insurance risk insurable and the unintended consequences that insurers must guard against.

2-2. Identify the entities that provide health insurance and describe how they may differ organizationally and with respect to the products they offer.

2-3. Describe the agency and direct response distribution systems and how they differ.

2-4. Explain why persons may turn to the individual market for their health insurance.

2-5. Identify the criteria that consumers should use when evaluating insurers and their agents.

Chapter Outline

Purchasing individual health insurance is a process that relies on a number of fundamental components. Among these components are the insurability of health-related expenses, sources for individual health insurance, and the market for individual health insurance.

INSURABILITY OF HEALTH-RELATED EXPENSES

Medical bills, income lost to disability, and the cost of assistance with activities of daily living due to infirmities must constitute insurable risks if they are to be covered by a health insurance policy. *Risk* can be defined simply as the possibility of undesired and unintended loss. It is at the heart of all insurance. The potential loss associated with high health-related expenses presents an insurable risk because persons who incur these expenses face a potentially severe and even catastrophic financial setback. Most Americans deal with health-related risks through the purchase of one or more forms of health insurance. Despite the important value that it provides, health insurance, like any other kind of insurance, creates unintended consequences that insurers must guard against.

risk

An Insurable Risk

Insurance usually involves both a transfer and a combination of risk. The transfer is made to the insurer who is willing to combine the risk of many individuals, all of whom wish to be protected from a loss that only some of them will actually incur. In exchange for this protection, individuals pay the insurer a specified amount, called a premium, which forms a pool of funds that the insurer draws on to pay for the large expenses or losses of those who incur them.

Not all risks are insurable. In order to be insurable, the potential loss incurred through health -related expenses must be:

- significant
- unexpected
- calculable

These requirements are far from absolute. For example, while many medical expenses are unpredictable and large, such as hospitalization for emergency surgery, others are routine and relatively inexpensive, such as annual physicals and routine tests. Although the expense of such routine services is frequently a benefit under a medical expense policy, people need insurance for the nonroutine and catastrophic expenses. Routine expenses are not insured so much as they are pre-funded; in any case, they account for a small part of the overall premium cost.

Significant

To be insurable, expenses must be significant enough in total to be the principal component in the premium rate. Health-related expenses can meet this criterion. For example, medical expenses associated with a hospital stay for a serious condition, the loss of a year's earned income from an inability to work, or an extended period of long-term care can easily produce an expense or loss of tens or even hundreds of thousands of dollars, an amount that most Americans would consider significant. As the previous chapter indicates, health-related expenses are a leading cause of personal and family bankruptcies. The significance of these expenses is reflected in the maximum benefit limits of some policies, which in some cases can run into many millions of dollars. If a potential expense is of no great consequence, then the insurer's cost to provide a benefit for it could outstrip the amount of the expense itself.

Unexpected

As stated earlier, the definition of risk means that the loss is undesired and unintended. The loss also must be unexpected and uncommon. If the loss is so common as to be expected, it is considered uninsurable. To be insurable, large health-related expenses must be chance or random occurrences for the persons affected.

Calculable

A third and broad prerequisite of health-related expenses as insurable risks is that they be reasonably calculable. The insurable event, though unexpected, must permit a clear and definitive measurement of the value of the loss associated with the occurrence. The actual occurrence of an event to one person is difficult to predict, so the insurer must generate a reasonable projection of future loss through the law of large numbers and experience over time.

The Law of Large Numbers (The Law of Averages). When an insurer combines the risk of individuals seeking protection, their number must be large enough to allow the insurer to predict the incidence of losses and the associated expenses. This way a proper premium can be charged to all insureds so that those who do not incur a loss generate sufficient funds to pay for those who do. Premiums also must be equitable so that those who pose a greater risk pay a commensurably higher premium than those with a lower potential for loss. Thus, for example, the premium charged older persons and less healthy persons is typically higher than the amounts charged to younger and healthier persons.

Experience Over Time. The incidence of hospitalizations, disabilities, and long-term care can be determined within a specific period, usually a period of years, and in relation to their associated losses or costs. Thus, insurance can cover the risk of health-related expenses where losses or costs may be reasonably predicted or where judgment based upon experience permits a calculated estimate of their aggregated cost.

Unintended Consequences

The presence of insurance generates unintended consequences that could drive up the cost of insurance, even to the point of making it unaffordable. Among them are the potential for adverse selection, moral hazards, and attitudinal hazards. Insurers guard against these unintended consequences by using underwriting requirements. Underwriting assesses an individual's health status, occupation, hobbies, and other pertinent information that may result in preexisting-conditions limitations, exclusions of benefits, waiting periods before benefits become effective, higher premiums, or even a refusal to offer coverage. Chapter 4 discusses the underwriting requirements of individual health insurance in detail.

Adverse Selection

adverse selection

Adverse selection is the natural tendency of individuals who are vulnerable to specific losses to purchase insurance to cover those particular losses. For example, a person who has a history of illness would be very interested in obtaining medical expense insurance.

Moral Hazard

moral hazard

Moral hazard is the perverse human tendency that increases the frequency and severity of a loss because insurance is in force. Patients and health care providers may commit unethical acts to fraudulently profit by insurance; examples include filing false claims or providing unnecessary services to maximize reimbursement. Because insurers can pay claims only by collecting premiums from other insureds, moral hazards raise everyone's premiums.

Attitudinal Hazard

attitudinal hazard

Attitudinal hazard consists of carelessness or indifference as to whether a loss occurs or the size of the loss if it does occur. It differs from moral hazards that generally involve dishonesty. In relation to health insurance, an attitudinal hazard can take many forms. Some persons may undertake or continue unhealthy or self-abusive lifestyles because of the knowledge that the loss of income from or treatment for any resulting health problems will be underwritten. For these persons, tobacco use, poor dental hygiene, and alcohol abuse are examples of attitudinal hazards. For others, this hazard may result in the unnecessary use of health care services simply because the insurer is footing the bill.

SOURCES FOR INDIVIDUAL HEALTH INSURANCE

Bringing an insurance product to market has two fundamental requirements, an entity to accept the risk of the financial loss, known as the insurer, and a distribution system that brings insurance products to consumers who purchase them. Insurers may use a distribution system that relies on an agency system, direct marketing, and/or some combination of the two.

Insurers

An insuring entity accepts the risk of health-related losses from an identified population, known as insureds, and combines or pools the potential losses in return for a premium paid by all the insureds that is also pooled. The pool of premiums pays the losses of the insureds who incur them, funds reserves, covers operational expenses, and provides net income or profits to maintain and build the insuring entity's business.

There are various types of insuring entities established under law in the field of health insurance. They include insurance companies, Blue Cross and Blue Shield plans, and managed care organizations, such as health maintenance organizations (HMOs). All of these insuring entities may offer their health insurance products as group and/or individual insurance. Our focus is on individual health insurance.

Insurance companies are the insuring entities for medical expense, disability income, and long-term-care insurance. Blue Cross and Blue Shield plans and managed care organizations for the most part limit their products to medical expense insurance, although in some cases they offer other forms of health insurance through separately incorporated subsidiary or holding companies.

Insurance Companies

Insurance companies, including those that provide health insurance, are typically classified by their form of legal organization either as stock companies or as mutual companies. A stock insurance company is a corporation organized as a profit-seeking venture owned by stockholders. A mutual insurance company is owned by its policyowners. It has no stockholders and is organized primarily to provide insurance for its policyowners, rather than to seek a profit. Stock companies are more numerous than mutual insurance companies in the provision of health insurance. The number of mutual insurance companies is declining as they reorganize as stock companies in a process known as demutualization. Demutualization allows an insurance company to raise capital more easily by issuing stock and debt instruments and earn profits. As a mutual company, the capital these organizations might need for expansion, acquisition, and other purposes would be limited to profits and borrowings.

Blue Cross and Blue Shield Plans

Historically, Blue Cross plans and Blue Shield plans were founded in specific geographic regions as separate organizations to provide hospital and physician/surgeon benefits, respectively. Although they initially operated independently in these regions, most plans merged over the course of many years into single local Blue Cross and Blue Shield plans. With further consolidation, these local organizations became regional and even national in their operations, while maintaining local plan identification and management. Thus, the more than 130 separate Blue Cross plans and Blue Shield plans of an earlier era are now fewer than 40 companies.

Blue Cross and Blue Shield plans must be members of the national Blue Cross and Blue Shield Association, which sets membership standards for local plans. While maintaining close ties to health care providers, plan boards must be independent. Each plan must participate in a national program that offers portability of coverage and benefit availability for insureds outside the plan's service area.

Although Blue Cross and Blue Shield plans and insurance companies were once quite different, they evolved over the years and now probably have more similarities than differences. Many plans continue to exist under special enabling legislation, which may give them advantages, such as favorable state taxation, but also limits their underwriting and rating flexibility. Many Blue Cross and Blue Shield plans also continue their founding structure as not-for-profit organizations, making them similar to mutual insurance companies. Profits are not disturbed to shareholders or policyowners, but some of the plans have accumulated a substantial surplus despite their nonprofit status. However, several Blue Cross and Blue Shield plans converted to the traditional forms of stock or mutual insurance companies. Others established holding companies and/or subsidiary organizations that are structured to operate as traditional insurance companies.

Managed Care Organizations

Managed care organizations are identified typically as HMOs or preferred-provider organizations (PPOs).

HMOs. As mentioned in the previous chapter, the most fully developed and integrated managed care structure is the HMO. Most state laws require an HMO to be organized as a corporation rather than as a partnership or other legal entity. Although early HMOs were not-for-profit organizations, for-profit organizations now dominate the field with the majority of enrollees. Today, HMOs may be sponsored or owned by insurance companies, Blue Cross and Blue Shield plans, consumer groups, physicians, hospitals, labor unions, or private investors.

PPOs. In the 1980s, the competition between the more cost-restrictive HMOs and the maximum flexibility but greater cost of traditional major medical plans offered by insurance companies provided the opportunity for PPOs to develop. PPOs, in effect, offered a middle ground between HMOs and traditional health insurance; unlike HMOs, insureds could receive some benefits for care received from any provider. However, full benefits are available only when the PPO's network of hospitals and doctors provide care. Initially, PPOs were separate organizations, although their sponsorship and ownership became as diverse and entrepreneurial in nature as that of HMOs. As a result, over time, the term PPO, like the term HMO, identified not just an organization, but also a type of managed care plan offered by the spectrum of insuring entities for medical expense benefits. Today, many types of medical expense insuring organizations typically provide PPO plans, as well as HMO plans, sometimes incorporated as subsidiary companies, regardless of the parent organizations' own corporate structure.

Distribution Systems

In general, insurers use two distribution systems to bring insurance products to the consumer: the agency system and direct response.

Agency System

The complex and intangible nature of insurance and its significance to the insured can make personal contact through an intermediary very valuable in the sale of most insurance, including health insurance.

The applicant for individual health insurance usually makes contact with insurers through agents or brokers. These representatives may also be financial planners if they are directly involved in helping their clients protect their security through the purchase of insurance. Generally, all these representatives are compensated by commissions, which are a part of the insurance premiums paid to the agent or broker in the first and frequently subsequent years when coverage is in effect.

An insurance agent is often referred to as a producer because he or she produces business for the insurance company or companies that he or she represents. Legally, any agent represents a principal; an insurance agent's principal is an insuring organization. These organizations appoint agents to solicit prospects for insurance, to negotiate with these prospects, and, in some cases, to put contracts of insurance into effect. The agent's powers are defined by his or her agency contract with the insurer.

Brokers legally represent their clients rather than the insurer and can offer significant advice and counsel to their clients. A broker is an independent contractor. Although the broker assists the applicant for insurance by finding coverage, the broker is usually paid by the insurer. The broker's duties are similar to those of agent, just described, except that the brokers' legal duties pertain more directly to the applicant or policyowner whom he or she represents.

Policyowners sometimes do not differentiate between an insurance broker and an agent. The insurance agent is acting under specific and delegated authority from the insurer and is sometimes authorized to bind coverage within specific limits. The broker, on the other hand, has no such authority. Many insurance agents are licensed so that they can operate as either an agent or a broker.

An exclusive agent, also known as a captive agent, represents only one insurance company, while an independent agent usually represents several insurance companies or groups of companies. When agents work in the same office, the office is known as an agency. From a legal standpoint, agents are also classified as a general agent or a limited agent.

General agents typically represent property/casualty insurers with the authority to issue a binder to a client that commits the insurer to make insurance effective immediately and prior to the actual issuance of the policy. However, with regard to health insurance, agents are usually limited agents with more restrictive powers. Generally, these agents are authorized to solicit, receive, and forward applications for the contracts their companies write. The insurer issues the contract in conformance with its underwriting policies only after receiving the written, signed application and, often, a medical examination report. As the following chapter explains, health insurance coverage may be effective immediately if the applicant at the time of completion of the application and submission of the required premium payment is eligible for insurance under the insurer's normal underwriting standards. However, a limited agent may not commit the insurer to covering the applicant immediately.

Direct Response

Under a direct-response distribution system, the insurer deals directly with the applicant through salaried employees of the insurer. (Such persons are often required to have an agent's license, however.) For example, health insurers commonly use direct mail, television, or Internet advertising for certain types of medical insurance such as critical illness, specified disease, hospital indemnity, or long-term care. All communication occurs directly between the company and the prospect. The insurance contract is written and serviced by mail or telephone.

Mixed Distribution Systems

Mixed distribution systems that utilize both the agency system and direct response forms of insurance distribution are also common. For example, some insurance agents and brokers market insurance through the Internet. Other insurance companies market through agents and also market directly to consumers through the Internet or through mail.

THE MARKET FOR INDIVIDUAL HEALTH INSURANCE

This section discusses the market for individual health insurance from the standpoint of who are the purchasers of individual health insurance policies.

In the process, these purchasers are also selecting a health insurer and very likely a health insurance agent or broker. They should be confident in these selections by making careful evaluations.

Who Purchases Individual Health Insurance

The purchasers of individual health insurance are found in five general situations:

- persons with access to group insurance programs at their place of employment

- persons with access to insurance through association plans
- persons without access to group health insurance from an employer or association plan
- businesses in certain circumstances
- seniors with Medicare

Persons with Access to Group Insurance

Most persons under age 65 obtain much of their health insurance through group benefit programs at their place of employment. For example, 9 out of 10 people in this age category obtain their medical expense insurance in this way. There are good reasons that support their decision to do so.

In many cases, employers pay a significant portion of the premium. Again, taking an example from medical expense insurance, a recent survey reports that on average employees pay only 16 percent of the premium for single coverage and 28 percent for family coverage.[1] Underwriting requirements for an employer group rarely, if ever, cause a rejection of coverage of individual employees and covered dependents based on personal health status. However, such coverage must be accepted when the employer first offers it, usually upon hiring or during an annual election period. In addition, there are economies associated with the administration of an insured group that are absent when health insurance is purchased on an individual basis.

Nevertheless, persons with access to group insurance may have good reasons to seek health insurance in the individual market. This occurs primarily because an employer does not offer the coverage they want or they can obtain it less expensively on an individual basis.

Example 1: Parnell, age 26 and just out of graduate school, joins a small start-up Internet security firm that offers a competitive salary and stock options should the company ever go public. However, the group health benefits that the company sponsors are all voluntary with no employer premium contribution. He contacts Jackson, his family's insurance agent of many years, to determine what alternatives may be available in the individual health insurance market. Because he is younger than the average age of his coworkers and is in excellent health, he is able, with Jackson's help, to purchase a policy that matches the employer's voluntary medical benefit at a lower premium. For the same age and health reasons, Jackson encourages

Parnell to purchase an individual disability income policy at a lower premium. This policy will replace two-thirds of his income after a 90-day waiting period after a disability begins. Although he purchases the disability policy, Jason declines the recommendation to purchase a long-term care policy that Jackson also makes.

Example 2: In a continuation of the previous example, Parnell's company has some success and after 5 years now makes some health insurance premium contributions. Parnell is now married. His wife, Chloe, a landscape architect who works from home, is covered under Parnell's policy. Parnell has some decisions to make.

The company now covers 90 percent of employees' medical premium, but pays 25 percent toward dependent coverage. Parnell enrolls in the company's medical plan because of its low cost. However, Chloe now obtains her own individual medical expense policy in the private market. Jackson persuades her to select a high-deductible health (medical) plan that at her age and health status produces a significant savings compared to the out-of-pocket payment for the dependent premium required by Parnell's employer. Jackson arranges for Chloe to open a health savings account (HSA) to which she makes tax-preferred contributions for the payment of her deductible and other out-of-pocket medical expenses. As they are planning a family, Jackson makes sure that maternity coverage is included in the policy and points out that when they have a child, he will convert Chloe's coverage to a high-deductible family policy that allows increased contributions to the HSA.

The company also provides 60-day short-term disability coverage at no cost to employees. Long-term disability remains a voluntary benefit, however. Parnell welcomes the short-term disability coverage, but maintains his individual disability income policy.

Persons with Access to Insurance through Association Plans

association plans

Many professionals, business persons, or other persons with common interests join together as members of organizations called associations to advance their common goals. Among the services that these associations frequently offer their members are one or more forms of health insurance, known as *association plans*. These plans, which are marketed under the association's name through an arrangement with an insurance company, may have lower policy premiums than comparable coverage available elsewhere in the individual market. For an insurance company, an association's members constitute an easily contacted and potentially preferred population; they are more likely to purchase coverage because of the association's endorsement and their risk factors often suggest better-than-average claim experience.

The list of associations that sponsor such plans is seemingly endless; it includes the Society of Financial Services Professionals, The American Medical Association, and AARP, to name just a few. As a result, association plans are a significant source of health insurance for persons seeking individual coverage, including retirees. Association plans may also provide policies for employer groups.

Example:

Dr. Florence, having completed all her medical education and residency requirements, proudly hangs out her shingle for the first time as a family practice specialist. One of the challenges in beginning her practice is to find a source for health insurance. In her start-up practice, she relies entirely on part-time staff, for whom she provides no benefits (at least for now). Thus, she needs coverage only for herself. Her residency mentor reminded Dr. Florence that The American Medical Association (AMA), which she had joined in her medical school days, offers health insurance along with other insurance products.

After a brief review of the AMA's Web site, Dr. Florence discovers a high-deductible medical expense insurance policy that is affordable and allows her to contribute to a health savings account on tax-preferred basis. She also finds a disability policy that meets her needs and uses a favorable "own occupation" definition of disability for 5 years. She applies for and obtains both policies. At her age, Dr. Florence declines long-term care insurance that is also available through the association, but makes a note to discuss that form of health insurance with her parents.

A few years later, her practice has grown quite a bit and she has established a full-time staff complement that now includes clerical support, nurses, a physician's assistant, and a family practice specialist as a partner. Once again, she turns to her association, which also offers health insurance on an employer group basis.

Persons without Access to Group Health Insurance from an Employer or Association Plan

Obviously, persons without access to group health insurance or an association plan would likely turn to the individual market to find coverage for themselves and their families. Persons in this category could be employed or perhaps have no employment relationship at all.

Employed persons could be self-employed (such as business owners, professionals, or farmers) or work for an employer, especially a small employer that provides or sponsors no health insurance.

In some cases, however, employers may pay part or all of the premiums for individual health insurance policies of employed persons. For example, a small business may be ineligible for group coverage, or may find such coverage too costly and elect to purchase individually underwritten policies of medical insurance for employees. In another case, an employer may pay the premiums for individual policies of disability income insurance or long-term care insurance for executives or senior managers.

Persons who have no employment relationship are usually in one of the following situations:

- termination of employment for such reasons as quitting voluntarily, being fired or laid off, becoming disabled, or taking early retirement
- termination of spouse or child coverage, even when employee coverages continue because of divorce, separation, or a child surpassing dependent age
- not being in the labor market. Some people have the resources to forgo employment. Others are unable to find or hold jobs.
- international travel

Example: Jason retired at age 55. He continued his employer's group medical expense coverage for himself and his wife, Eulalia, by electing COBRA coverage for 18 months, the maximum period allowed in his situation. Subsequently, when their COBRA coverage terminated, Estelle, their insurance agent, was able to obtain coverage for Jason and his wife in the underwritten individual market because they continue to enjoy good health. By accepting an underwritten policy, they avoided the need to obtain coverage at above standard rates through the state's high-risk pool that guarantees access to individual medical expense coverage under federal law. To obtain a more attractive premium at their ages, Jason purchased a high-deductible health (medical) plan and opened an HSA to pay for the deductible and other medical out-of-pockets, if necessary. Jason is hoping to minimize their use of the HSA in order to allow the funds to grow year to year as a potential investment vehicle after age 65 with accumulated tax-preferred annual contributions and accrued income.

Jason would have included his twin daughters under his new coverage, but according to the terms of the policy, they are ineligible to be covered as dependents because they are 23 years old and have just graduated from college. Jason purchases a temporary medical expense policy for each daughter at a very favorable premium. Jason plans to pay their premiums for 6 months or so—a period within which he expects they will find employment in their chosen field as well as group health benefits.

Estelle also suggests that Jason and Eulalia, given their relatively young ages and good health, should seriously consider purchasing long-term care insurance. Estelle points out that if they wait, they will find a substantially increased premium and possible difficulty in obtaining coverage should their health deteriorate. After considering their families' longevity and health history, they decide to purchase the long-term care policy that covers them both.

Jason also decides to become a self-employed consultant. Because his expertise is in great demand, he earns a good income while working 20 hours a week. With documentation of his annual income and long-term engagements under contract, Jason applied for a disability income policy that together with Social Security disability income would replace approximately two thirds of this income in the event of a disability. Estelle secured this coverage for Jason until age 65, when he plans to discontinue his consulting practice.

With newly found additional income and available time, Jason and Eulalia intend to travel extensively. Estelle quickly points out that his new policy has some limitations on benefits for foreign travel and he should purchase an international travel medical policy to supplement their benefits as needed, especially for emergency air evacuation back to the United States if necessary.

Businesses in Certain Circumstances

In some circumstances, businesses, especially small, closely held firms, may be the purchasers of individual health insurance policies. Such situations occur most frequently with medical expense policies and disability income policies for owners, partners, or senior executives, who are the beneficiaries. A business may also purchase various types of disability policies that help the enterprise to continue if an owner, partner, senior executive, or other key person is disabled.

Seniors with Medicare

Another segment of the population that often obtains individual health insurance coverage consists of persons eligible for Medicare. As chapter 10 explains, Medicare has limitations that include no out-of-country coverage and higher copayments than major medical policies. As a result, more than 60 percent of persons over age 65 have elected some type of coverage to supplement Medicare. More than a third of these persons obtain that coverage through individual Medicare supplement policies.[2]

Although Medicare together with a Medicare supplement policy can provide adequate coverage and benefits for medical care, other health-related areas are unaddressed. For example, Medicare provides very limited benefits for long-term care and no benefits for dental and vision care.

Example: Giselle retired after a career as a personnel director for a company in the upper Midwest. At age 65, she is now eligible for Medicare and her employer does not provide medical expense coverage for retirees. As a result, she decided to purchase a Medicare supplement (medigap) policy. She thought this would be appropriate for her because she will be spending up to 2 months of the year with her daughter and two sisters who live in a sunshine state. In addition, because she plans to take at least two 3-week international trips a year, she will need the foreign travel emergency benefit that her medigap policy offers. Generally, Medicare pays nothing for emergency medical care outside the United States. Giselle is pleased that she can continue her long-term care policy that she purchased 10 years ago as a voluntary benefit program through her company. However, her dental and vision plans were not similarly portable. Giselle is able to purchase these useful forms of coverage through her personnel managers' professional association.

Selecting Insurers and Agents

Insuring organizations and their representatives are integral to the market for individual health insurance. Anyone seeking individual health insurance must select an insurer and more than likely an agent or broker from whom to purchase the coverage. Consumer evaluation of insurers and agents is an important part of the process of purchasing individual health insurance.

Selecting an Insurer

In addition to comparing and evaluating the provisions of health insurance policies, it is important for a consumer to ensure that he or she is purchasing a policy from a reputable company at an appropriate price. In many cases, the consumer will rely on the advice of an insurance agent or financial planner who specializes in health insurance and is perhaps in a better position to make this evaluation. The evaluation should focus on three basic considerations: financial strength, reputation, and cost.

Financial Strength. Probably the single most important criterion in evaluating an insurer is financial strength. Because an insurer's basic function is to pay claims, care must be taken to select only those insurers that are most likely to have the financial strength to do so if and when the need arises. In light of past insolvencies and near insolvencies among insurers, this claims-paying ability cannot simply be taken for granted.

Detailed financial information can be obtained from the annual reports that insurance companies must file with state insurance departments. These reports are public information. Although an evaluation of this information is beyond most individuals' ability, it has been performed by several rating organizations that publish the financial history, ratings, and analyses of individual insurers. These organizations include A.M. Best Company, Fitch Ratings, Moody's Investors Service, Standard & Poor's, and Weiss Ratings. A few words of caution are in order with respect to reliance on ratings assigned by these organizations, however. First, criteria and methodology differ among the rating organizations, so an insurer may receive different ratings from different organizations. Second, a rating of A, which many people associate with excellence, may not be particularly good. For example, Best's has two ratings higher than A, and Standard & Poor's has five ratings higher than A. Third, some rating agencies seem to be more generous in their ratings than others. Fourth, not all insurers are assigned ratings by all of the rating organizations. In light of all of these differences, it is wise to choose insurers that have very high ratings from at least two or three of the rating organizations.

These ratings may be available from public libraries, the Internet, insurer brochures, or state insurance departments. A link to state insurance department Web sites appears at the NAIC Web site.

Reputation. With hundreds of companies writing one or more forms of individual health insurance, there is no reason to purchase coverage from any insurer that has other than a good reputation. Reputation arises from many factors. For example, are current customers satisfied with the insurer? What is the insurer's track record for fair and prompt claims settlement? How are insureds treated when the insurer introduces new or improved policies? What commitment and experience does the insurer have with health insurance products? Does the insurer have a reputation it wants to protect and thus may be willing to "do the right thing"?

A good insurance agent or financial planner, through experience and interaction with colleagues, should have a feel for an insurer's reputation within the insurance industry. Another source of information is the records about consumer complaints that state insurance departments receive. There are also consumer publications that periodically evaluate insurers based on costs, claims handling, consumer satisfaction, and other factors.

However, reputation is of little value if an insurer does not have adequate financial strength. Unfortunately, a few insurers that were once highly regarded have become insolvent.

Cost. It is important to look at the variations in cost among insurers for similar policies. Consumers or their insurance agents or brokers working on their behalf should compare premiums by insurer for policies with the same or similar benefits and major policy provisions. There can be and are substantial premium variations among insurers for the same or similar policies.

However, cost comparisons must be used with care for several reasons. First, it is important that they are for comparable policies; policies are often not identical. Even though benefits may be similar, different policy provisions may apply. For example, do policies have the same waiting periods before benefits begin or the same provisions for preexisting conditions? Is the payment of premiums waived during an illness or disability? Or do preferred premium rates apply?

Second, what is the financial strength of each of these insurers? Low premiums may be an indication that an insurer has inadequate reserves or is trying to increase revenue in the short run because of a poor financial position.

Third, are the levels of service from the insurers the same? For example, an insurer with a low premium may have the reputation of being very strict in its claims-paying practices.

Last, but not least, is the topic of premium increases. What is an insurer's history of premium increases? What is the likelihood of future premium increases? Insurers with premiums that are among the lowest might be new to the business and have little experience in pricing specific forms of health insurance policies, or they might be using a low premium as a method for increasing market share. In either case, they may increase premiums in the future and make policies unaffordable for some insureds. It is worth asking an insurer about past rate increases; some states also provide this information. Some insurers with low premiums have a reputation for frequent price increases, while other insurers with somewhat higher premiums have infrequent or no increases because of more realistic pricing assumptions.

All of this is not to say that price differentials are not important. However, they must be analyzed with care.

Selecting an Agent

Because most individual health insurance is written through the agency system, the choice of a competent and reliable insurance agent or broker is often an important decision for the insurance buyer. Because of the complex nature of various risks, insurance coverages, and rates, the insurance agent or broker should be selected with the same care and discrimination used to choose other professional advisors.

If an exclusive agent who represents one insurer only is chosen, this selection also determines the insurer with which business is conducted. If an independent agent is chosen, the insurance buyer often leaves the selection of the insurer up to the agent, or at least relies heavily on the agent's recommendations. Good companies and good agents usually work together.

A person may use a single agent rather than several for all of his or her health insurance needs. Such an agent can more easily understand and satisfy a person's health insurance needs. A single agent can more easily gather and maintain the comprehensive information needed to analyze a client's overall insurance requirements and recommend an integrated program of health insurance protection. Nevertheless, because of the specialized nature of some products, an agent may sell only a specific form of health insurance. Thus, for example, it is not unusual for someone to deal with separate agents for disability income insurance and for long-term care insurance.

Choosing an agent or broker is an important step toward a sound program of health insurance essential for a client's financial security. Some of the criteria that might be used to evaluate insurance agents and brokers include knowledge and ability, integrity and character, and representation.

Knowledge and Ability. The agent or broker must learn about the client's insurance needs and help the client understand the value of the services rendered. The agent must have the background and experience necessary to identify and analyze what the client needs and recommend the appropriate policies and benefit levels.

Agents who are fully committed to the insurance business are more likely to do a successful job for their clients by developing their professional skills and keeping abreast of rapidly changing knowledge requirements. One method to evaluate the agent or broker's knowledge and ability in the area of health insurance is to ask questions about their professional designations such as "Are you a CLU, LUTCF, RHU, or REBC?' In addition, a financial planner may have a CFP or ChFC designation. If not, ask if the agent has or is working toward these or other educational objectives on a regular basis. Also, ask if they are members of professional organizations such as NAIFA (National Association of Insurance and Financial Advisers) or NAHU (National Association of Health Underwriters). Such organizations are dedicated to maintaining and enhancing their members' ability to meet client needs through education, professional development, and ethical conduct.

Integrity and Character. Because insurance is purchased to reduce uncertainty; clients must have confidence in their agent or broker when discussing their financial needs and goals. They must trust the recommendations they are receiving. Thus, agents or brokers must have integrity and character to earn a client's confidence and trust, as would a doctor, a lawyer, or an accountant.

Essentially, integrity and character come from professional behavior that adheres to a code of ethics—a statement of values that promotes appropriate conduct and avoids inappropriate activities. In general, this means that agents and brokers must seek the best interest of their clients in all their dealings with them. Specific ethical actions include:

- promotion and sale of valuable products that clients need
- truthful and complete presentation of products and their features
- avoidance of unnecessary replacement of existing policies
- maintenance of confidentiality of client information
- maintenance of up-to-date product knowledge

Conformance to the laws and regulations that chapter 6 presents pertains largely to ethical behavior. However, an agent or broker's adherence to a code of ethics should go well beyond obeying laws and regulations; it should encompass complete forthrightness and honesty in all business relationships and activities, particularly those dealing with clients.

At the outset of a relationship, a client may have difficulty determining the integrity and character of an agent or broker. Nevertheless, a client should inquire if the agent has pledged adherence to a code of ethics that guides his or her business conduct. Ask for a copy. The professional designations mentioned previously require the professionals who receive them to subscribe to a code of ethics. Similarly, the professional organizations also mentioned impose a code of ethics on their members. Indeed, the companies that agents and brokers represent should also have a code of ethical conduct to which they subscribe. Many insurers belong to the Insurance Marketplace Standards Association (IMSA), which is the market conduct and compliance standards-setting organization serving the life insurance marketplace. Finally, a client may contact the state insurance department to inquire about complaints or investigations of agents, brokers, or insurers, especially those that pertain to unethical behavior.

Representation. Good agents and brokers must represent or have contacts with one or many insurers that can provide the required protection and services for the policyowner. Ideally, all necessary health insurance coverages should be available through the agent at a reasonable cost. The agent or the insurers that he or she represents should be capable of writing many different kinds of insurance, including newer coverages and benefit options designed to meet an individual's particular needs.

Insurance agencies and brokerage firms vary from a single-person agency to organizations that have large staffs and offer a wide range of specializations. These organizations differ in the services they offer, their methods of doing business, and the types and kinds of insurance they handle. Frequently, specialists in a large agency may limit their activities to health insurance. Even within the area of health insurance, specialists may exist for medical expense, disability income, and long-term care insurance. Thus, when selecting the agent or broker, the insurance consumer should consider whether the particular agent and agency office have the needed experience and service capabilities.

CHAPTER REVIEW

Key Terms

risk
adverse selection
moral hazard
attitudinal hazard
association plans

Review Questions

Review questions are based on the learning objectives in this chapter. Thus, a [2-3] at the end of a question means that the question is based on learning objective 2-3. If there are multiple objectives, they are all listed.

1. What factors allow a risk to be insurable and why are they relevant? [2-1]
2. What are the unintended consequences that insurers must guard against? [2-1]
3. a. What are the insuring entities that provide health insurance? [2-2]
   b. What organizational characteristics may differentiate them? [2-2]
   c. What forms of health insurance does each typically offer? [2-2]
4. What differentiates each of the following representatives in the agency system of insurance distribution?
   a. agent and broker [2-3]
   b. exclusive agent and independent agent [2-3]
   c. general agent and limited agent [2-3]
5. In what ways does a direct response distribution system differ from an agency system? [2-3]
6. a. Why would a person with access to group insurance turn to the individual market to obtain health insurance? [2-4]
   b. What conditions, relative to the purchase of individual health insurance, are associated with persons who have no employment relationship? [2-4]

c. Why would persons eligible for Medicare purchase individual health insurance? [2-4]

7. a. What criteria should consumers use when selecting a health insurer? [2-5]
   b. What questions might a consumer ask agents to determine their knowledge and ability? [2-5]

8. a. What are specific ethical actions that a client should expect from an agent? [2-5]
   b. What information can a client obtain to aid in evaluating an agent's integrity and character? [2-5]

NOTES

1. *Employer Health Benefits: 2007 Annual Survey,* The Kaiser Family Foundation and Health Research and Education Trust, p. 66.
2. *Health Insurance Coverage of the Elderly,* EBRI, 2006, p. 1.

3

The Insurance Contract

Learning Objectives

An understanding of the material in this chapter should enable you to

3-1. Describe the unique nature of an insurance contract, and explain the importance of its terms to the policyowner and the insurance company.

3-2. Describe offer and acceptance as the core element of a binding contract created in the proposal process with the submission of a properly completed application.

3-3. Explain the importance of true and complete information in an insurance application.

3-4. Summarize the other elements essential to a legally binding contract.

3-5. Describe the special characteristics of insurance contracts that also affect health insurance policies.

3-6. Describe the key and miscellaneous provisions of an insurance contract.

3-7. Summarize the goal and requirements of the Uniform Electronic Transactions Act and its effect on insurance transactions.

Chapter Outline

Health insurance, like all forms of insurance, is a contract. Agents and brokers use written contracts of insurance, called insurance policies, as products of great value that give their clients peace of mind as they protect them against significant losses. An insurance policy is of great value because of the important obligations undertaken by the parties to the contract—the client who becomes the policyowner and the insurer. Agents and brokers must understand the products that they are selling. This understanding extends to the characteristics of contracts generally as well as the distinctive features of contracts of insurance. This chapter reviews many of these often legal characteristics and features.

The chapter begins with an overview of the unique nature of an insurance contract. The discussion continues with a review of the essential elements of a legally valid contract; a detailed analysis of offer and acceptance, and a discussion of legal purpose, consideration, and competent parties. The chapter then turns to the characteristics that typify an insurance contract and continues with a description of the provisions that serve as the framework for the typical insurance contract. The chapter concludes with a review of the conduct and enforceability of electronic insurance transactions within the structure of state and federal legislation. Throughout, the chapter relates the discussion to individual health insurance.

THE NATURE OF AN INSURANCE CONTRACT

contract

Insurance is fundamentally a contract. A *contract* may be defined as a binding or legally enforceable agreement between two or more parties for the provision of goods or services through an exchange of value.

The purchase of insurance is unlike most purchases of goods and services that provide immediate satisfaction or enjoyment. Insurance is a promise of financial protection in the event of a covered loss that may be unlikely to occur. With the agent's help, however, the buyer understands that insurance provides relief from anxiety and freedom from worry about the possibility of an extraordinary financial loss or need, even if the covered event does not occur. If the event does occur, the value of the insurance benefit is likely to exceed what has been paid in premiums.

In an individual insurance contract, the agreement is in writing and is called a policy. The parties to the contract are the insurance company and insurance applicant, who becomes the policyowner when the contract is formed. The contract's beneficiaries may be the policyowner and/or other persons allowed by company practices and state laws, such as certain dependents. The provision of services under a health insurance contract is the insurer's promise to assume or undertake financial responsibility for losses or expenses related to illness, injury, or other incapacity. This responsibility may include payment for medical expenses, lost income due to disability, or the cost of long-term care.

The insurance company must use the policy's provisions as a basis for making and carrying out its promises. The policy provisions permit, as well as require the insurance company to satisfy obligations when they come due for specific policyowners. The potential for future claims must be determined and well defined if the insurer is to establish and maintain the financial capacity, administrative functions, and other services that support the promises contained in the policy. If the insurer cannot rely on the policy provisions to identify its responsibilities as well as noncovered events for which it is not responsible, it cannot reliably conduct its business.

Hence, the insurance policy is important because it is both the tangible expression of the promises made by an insurer and the document upon which the policyowner must rely as evidence of those promises. Through its many provisions, the policy spells out all the terms and conditions of the agreement and defines the rights and obligations of the parties involved. Both parties—the policyowner and the insurance company—have every reason to insist that policy provisions be legally binding and enforceable. To accomplish that mutual objective, the insurance policy must conform to the legal requirements, features, and provisions of a contract—the subject of this chapter.

OFFER AND ACCEPTANCE

In order to be legally binding, a contract must include several essential elements. The core element of a binding agreement is offer and acceptance. The discussion of the proposal process that results in an offer and acceptance of an insurance contract leads directly to the closely related areas of the insurance application and the effects of untrue and incomplete information.

The Proposal Process

A legally binding contract requires an offer by one party and acceptance by the other. The first step in forming a contract occurs when one party extends an offer to another party. An offer is deemed complete when no further action by the party making it is required in order for the other party to accept it. However, as we will see, the date an insurance policy is issued may differ from the effective date of coverage.

Although an insurer actively solicits business through a wide range of activities that include advertising and direct solicitations by agents, the insurance offer-and-acceptance process itself is usually initiated by the prospective insured via a written application for coverage. If the prospective insured's completed application includes the required initial premium, the applicant's offer is considered complete. However, submission of the application without the initial premium only presents the insurer with an invitation to make an offer.

Thus, there are two initial offer-and-acceptance scenarios in the insurance proposal process: submission of an application with required premium and submission of an application only.

Submission of an Application with Required Premium

Insurers typically require the submission of the required premium when a person applies for a medical expense, disability income, or long-term care insurance policy. In this scenario, the offer is considered complete; no further action by the applicant is required in order for the insurer to accept it. Acceptance by the insurer is held by most courts to occur if the applicant at the time of the offer satisfies the insurer's normal underwriting standards, even before the insurer's review of the application and the conduct of a medical examination, if required. This means a contract can be formed and coverage can become effective as early as the date of the application and premium payment. In many cases, however, the applicant may select another date so that coverage is effective with the termination of an existing policy, for example, or some other relevant event. In such a situation, the contract is usually subject to the condition that the applicant satisfy the insurer's normal underwriting standards on the date the coverage is to become effective, not the date of the application and premium submission.

Most often, the policy is issued as applied for because the applicant does in fact meet the company's underwriting standards. However, if the insurer declines the offer as proposed (usually because of the applicant's failure to meet underwriting standards), there is no acceptance, no binding agreement, and no contract. Alternatively, the insurer may make a counterproposal by modifying either the policy provisions, usually the benefits, as embodied in the application and/or the premium amount. This counterproposal now becomes an offer to the applicant. If the applicant agrees to the new terms, offer and acceptance has occurred and a contract is formed. Otherwise, there is no contract and the insurer must return the premium paid.

Submission of the Application Only

In some cases, applicants may find a health insurer that accepts an application without payment of the required premium. Should this situation occur, the submission of the application alone is not considered an offer, but rather an invitation for the insurer to make an offer. Again, the insurer has three options after evaluating the applicant's eligibility for coverage: make the offer of insurance as applied for, refuse to make an offer of insurance, or make an offer of insurance on terms other than those applied for.

Obviously, if the insurer makes an offer that provides the requested coverage, it is assumed the applicant will accept. Acceptance is confirmed when the applicant receives the policy and pays the premium. Typically, before accepting the premium, the applicant is asked to sign a statement declaring that his or her insurability has not changed since the completion of the application. Then, the contract is formed and the coverage becomes effective.

On the other hand, the insurer may decline to make an offer on the existing terms (again, usually for underwriting reasons) or may make an offer on alternative terms. If the prospective insured accepts the offer on the alternative terms by receiving the policy and paying the premium, offer and acceptance are achieved, the contract is established, and coverage becomes effective.

Example: Herbert and Hubert, who are business partners, both decided to purchase disability income insurance.

When Herbert completed the application, he gave the agent a check for 2-month's premium and received a conditional receipt (explained later). Hubert, however, submitted the application only, preferring instead to pay the premium when the policy was actually issued.

On their way home together, they were involved in a serious automobile accident that required both of them to undergo several months of rehabilitation and convalescence before they were able to return to work. Within 10 days after the accident, the insurer had reviewed Herbert and Hubert's applications and determined that they both met the insurer's underwriting requirements at the time of application. The insurer is obligated to pay disability income benefits to Herbert commencing at the conclusion of the 60-day elimination period for his current disability as required by the policy. The insurer has no such obligation to Hubert, who is similarly disabled, because no contract was completed due to the nonpayment of premium.

Elements of an Application

As we have seen, submission of an application for insurance is an important part of the offer-and-acceptance process that forms a binding contract. Completing an application, prepaying the premium—even the receipt given to the applicant by the agent are important functions in that process and must be done with integrity and in proper form if they are to support a binding contract.

The Completed Application

The application furnishes essential information that is critical to appropriate rating and underwriting. An insurer may base recision (the act of revoking a policy by an insurer once it is issued) of the contract on the application if the information it contains is inaccurate or incomplete. To ensure an accurate record of the applicant's information, an insurer must include an exact copy of the application as part of the subsequently issued policy. The questions must be phrased so as to preclude (as nearly as possible) any misunderstanding by the applicant. Courts usually construe ambiguity or lack of clarity in the questions against the insurance company.

If an answer on the application is ambiguous or incomplete to the extent that it merits further inquiry, the insurer must obtain clarification at the time of underwriting and before policy issue. Failure to do so at this time may prevent the insurer from rescinding the policy once it is issued, even if the insurer later learns that the ambiguous answer contained false information.

The insurer can reasonably expect applicants to know when they last consulted a physician or whether they have a specific disease. Other questions that the applicant may not be able to answer on a precise, factual basis are phrased to permit an answer that is accurate to the best of the applicant's knowledge.

The application contains a statement above the applicant's signature indicating that the information provided by the applicant is true to the best of his or her knowledge and belief. The agent who solicits the application witnesses the applicant's signature. The agent's signature on the application serves two purposes: to verify that the applicant signed the application in the presence of the soliciting agent and to fulfill the regulatory requirement of some states that the application identify the soliciting agent.

If any answer on the application must be changed or corrected after the application is submitted to the insurer, the applicant must almost always give written concurrence even if the change is only a minor administrative one. Any change made without the applicant's written consent may invalidate the insurer's right to revoke the policy if material misrepresentation on the application is discovered later because the policy did not contain a complete and identical copy of the original application.

Initial Premium Payment

As stated earlier, an initial premium payment usually accompanies the submission of the completed application. Money paid by the applicant when the application is completed, known as a prepayment or advanced payment, is advantageous to both the applicant and the insurer. An applicant is more likely to confirm acceptance of the insurance policy when it is delivered if it has already been paid for. The advantage to the applicant also may depend on the insurer's commitment to encouraging prepayment, which is set forth in the receipt the agent gives the applicant. In addition, note that the insurer has the use of the money earlier than it would have otherwise.

modal premium

Insurers normally require the initial premium amount to be a *modal premium,* which is the premium amount at the interval allowed by the insurer and elected by the applicant, such as annually, semiannually, quarterly or monthly. For example, if the applicant elects to pay premiums on an annual basis, an annual premium must accompany the application. A frequent exception to this general rule occurs if the applicant wishes to pay premiums monthly. In that case, many insurers require that that the premiums for the first 2 months accompany the application.

Receipt

The terms and conditions in the receipt given for any payment made with the application may affect or confirm the date coverage becomes effective, which, as stated previously, may be different from the date of the application or the date the insurance policy is issued. Generally, receipts for health insurance are classified as conditional receipts or temporary insurance agreements.

conditional receipt

Conditional Receipts. A *conditional receipt* can be classified further as an "insurability type" or "approval type."

- The type of conditional receipt that health insurers typically use is the insurability receipt, which makes coverage effective either on the date of payment (provided the applicant was acceptable on that date for the coverage applied for) or the date when the application's information requirements are completed, if later. This type of receipt may also allow the applicant to select a specific effective date of coverage, but usually not more than 90 days from the application completion and prepayment date. Any change of insurability after the date selected would not be used in determining whether the policy would be issued. This is why it is a good idea to pay the initial premium with the submission of the application; prepayment protects the applicant against change in insurability during the period between the date coverage is to be effective and the subsequent date of policy issue. However, if the applicant is ultimately deemed unacceptable to the insurer, the insurer may reject or decline the applicant and coverage never takes effect.
- The rarely used approval-type receipt provides less protection for the applicant. Coverage begins only upon approval of the application by the company's underwriting department.

temporary insurance agreement (TIA)

Temporary Insurance Agreements. In response to court decisions and laws in several states, insurers have developed a receipt with a *temporary insurance agreement (TIA)*. Such an agreement typically provides interim coverage between the initial premium payment and application completion date and the date the insurer notifies the applicant of the underwriting decision. The insurer reserves the right to reject the application, but does agree to provide coverage until underwriting is completed, regardless of the applicant's ultimate insurability. The insurance provisions and benefits are often the same as those in the policy applied for, but may be more restrictive in some policies.

A TIA also affords some protections to the insurer. The TIA does not impair the insurer's ability to apply underwriting standards to the application and to reject it if the proposed insured does not qualify. Indeed, no payment is accepted and no interim coverage is provided if responses on the application indicate that the proposed insured may be an unacceptable risk. Incorrect or misleading statements in the application void the agreement. Benefits for preexisting conditions are excluded, as is duplicate payment for the same medical services under the TIA and the subsequently issued policy. Under temporary coverage, benefits are limited to a specific period, such as one year after a claim begins.

Generally, interim coverage runs until actual policy issue or rejection of the application. Upon rejection, the insurer notifies the applicant and returns the payment advanced, regardless of whether a claim has been filed or benefits paid under the TIA.

The Effects of Untrue and Incomplete Applicant Information

A contract's validity is based on the presentation of information that materially affects the offer-and-acceptance decisions made by both parties. In establishing a contractual relationship, both the insurer and the applicant have an ethical obligation to be honest in their presentation of information to each other. The contract is one of utmost good faith; both parties to the agreement must stand on an equal footing in that regard. Chapter 6, which explains the regulation of insurance companies, focuses on insurer obligations.

At the time of application, a major focus is also on the applicant's ethical obligations. He or she must disclose to the insurer all relevant material or important facts that are his or her exclusive knowledge. Because the insurer has a right to properly underwrite, price, and issue the policy with the full knowledge of the potential for loss being undertaken, the insurer must depend upon the applicant's statements as being truthful and complete.

The agent also has an ethical responsibility to the insurer. To the extent it is within his or her power to do so, the agent must ensure that the applicant's information is true and complete and record all applicant-provided information relevant to the issuance of the policy. The person to be insured is usually physically present to the agent during the application process, so many material facts essential for an appraisal of potential loss are within the agent's range of observation.

Untrue and incomplete information provided at the time of application may cause the insurer to deny a subsequent claim and/or render the insurance contract voidable. The terms void and voidable are sometimes used

void contract

interchangeably, but this usage is not correct. A *void contract* is an agreement that is entirely without legal effect, and neither party may enforce it. The law institutes certain requirements for a contract's validity; in the absence of these requirements, the contract is void. For example, a contract having an illegal objective, such as illegal gambling, may not be enforced legally by either party.

voidable contract

A *voidable contract* may be affirmed or rejected at the option of one of the parties but is binding on the other. For example, if the policyowner has failed to comply with a condition of the contract, the insurer may elect to fulfill its part of the agreement or may choose to rescind the contract. There are many potential circumstances that can give the insurer the technical right to treat a contract as voidable, but in the interests of equity and good public relations, the insurer often decides not to. Only seldom does the policyowner have the right to treat a contract as voidable—perhaps when the insurer or its agent has grossly misrepresented the contract benefits.

The effects of untrue and incomplete information when the contract is established are considered under the headings of misrepresentation and concealment. Misrepresentation and concealment can make insurance contracts voidable, but not void. Intentionally erroneous and incomplete information provided subsequent to the issuance of the policy, such as the filing of false claims, is not a basis for making the contract voidable, although it may be a basis for other actions, including nonrenewal.

Misrepresentation

misrepresentation

Prospective insureds are required to make statements in the form of responses to questions on the application for insurance. These statements are often called representations. A *misrepresentation,* then, is a false statement that, under insurance contract law as interpreted by the courts, must be made knowingly. Also, a misrepresentation may be considered knowingly made even when a person is unaware or unsure of the facts, but reasonably could be expected to determine what they are. Thus, a person may feel quite confident that a "no" response to the question, "Have you had a complete physical exam within the past 2 years?" is correct. However, that statement could be a misrepresentation if the answer should have been "yes" because the person could have confirmed the actual date of the exam as 18 months ago by reviewing personal files, but failed to do so.

If a misrepresentation is material, the insurance policy can become voidable. A misrepresentation on an insurance application is material if , the insurance company would have declined coverage or provided coverage under different terms had the facts been known. Which misrepresentations reach the threshold of "material" must be evaluated in a given situation, by the courts if necessary. For example, a response of "no" by a person applying for health insurance to the question, "Have you seen a health care provider in the last 5 years?" might be considered a material misrepresentation if, in fact, the applicant "forgot" a cancerous cyst removal that occurred 2 years earlier. However, it would not be considered such if the event was a routine wart removal that happened 4 years ago.

Example 1: Madison, only recently retired from her school teaching career, went to a neurologist about occasional but unusual memory lapses that her daughter had pointed out. The doctor, whom her daughter recommended, confirmed that she was in the very early stages of dementia. Because this was the first time she visited this particular doctor and had done so without a physician referral, her regular doctors received no report of Madison's evaluation.

With strong encouragement from her family, she agreed to obtain a comprehensive long-term care insurance policy. In completing the insurance application, she made a false statement by responding "no" to the question, "Have you ever been diagnosed with any form of senile dementia, including Alzheimer's disease?" In addition, she intentionally omitted the name of the neurologist whom she visited recently from her list of all current and previous health care providers requested in the application. The insurer issued Madison the long-term care insurance policy she requested.

Although initially she experienced only occasional episodes of forgetfulness and confusion, her condition deteriorated rapidly. After 18 months, her family persuaded her to file a claim under her long-term care policy for home care assistance and supervision.

Upon investigation of the claim, the insurer discovered the true situation regarding the onset of Madison's condition. The insurer informed her that it was denying the claim, rescinding the long-term care policy, and refunding her premiums. The insurer explained that Madison's responses to questions on the application made the policy voidable. Her knowingly untrue statement regarding senile dementia was a material misrepresentation, and she also intentionally omitted the name of her doctor. The insurer explained further that if the facts were known, it would not have issued the policy under the company's underwriting requirements.

Example 2: Kildare, a surgical specialist, applies for disability income insurance. In the process, the agent informs the doctor that the insurer offers a maximum monthly benefit in the event of disability that is limited to 60 percent of current income. Kildare is still relatively early in his career and expects to have significantly greater income in the years ahead, much more that the guaranteed insurability options (explained in a later chapter) the insurer would provide. He is concerned that his family's lifestyle will suffer if he must call on a disability benefit in the future that is based on his current income. As a result, he justifies the submission of fictitious income statements and tax forms in support of a disability benefit that far exceeds his current income. The insurer unknowingly accepts the fictitious information as true and issues the policy at the benefit level requested.

A year later, tragedy strikes when Kildare, during the completion of a weekend home improvement project, severely injures his hand on a table saw. The injury prevents him from practicing his specialty, at least for the foreseeable future. When processing Kildare's ensuing claim, the insurer discovers his true income level and his misrepresentation on the application. The insurer informs Kildarc that his submission of the fictitious income information that enabled him to obtain coverage at the level provided was a material misrepresentation. If his true income were known, the coverage would have been issued under different terms. The company denies the claim, rescinds the contract, and returns the premium.

Concealment

concealment

Neither party can practice concealment. *Concealment* is a failure by one party to a contract to disclose affirmatively to the other all of the important facts that are the exclusive knowledge of the first party. Misrepresentation and concealment are not identical. The applicant misrepresents if an untrue statement is made knowingly; he or she conceals if silence is maintained when there is an obligation to make or provide a statement. Concealment, almost by definition, must also be intentional because it is done knowingly. Ordinarily, to avoid concealment, the applicant needs only to answer the insurer's inquiries fully and in good faith. As with misrepresentation, if the insurer would have declined the application or issued the policy under different terms if it had possessed all the facts, the concealment is material and the policy becomes voidable.

An exception to the ordinary rule may occur when important facts bearing on the application for insurance are so unusual that they would not normally be questioned or readily discovered by the insurer. In that case, the obligation of affirmative disclosure by the applicant is present, whether or not a specific inquiry has been made.

Example:

Whitaker is a self-employed creator of computer games. Although the market success of his many games has made him very wealthy, he does not enjoy a tranquil life. He has a long-running dispute with his former business partner, Rodney, over the ownership of proprietary software essential to Whitaker's current products and the key to his success. Of late, the dispute has grown especially acrimonious after Rodney lost his last legal battle to obtain major royalty payments or alternatively to prevent Whitaker from using the software. Fearing for his physical safety, Whitaker, is considering obtaining a restraining order against Rodney after he made several threats.

Whitaker, who previously gave little thought to the subject, is also seeking health insurance in the event Rodney makes good on his threats. Whitaker visits an agent and provides truthful and complete answers to all the health insurance application questions. The agent remarks that she very rarely has a client complete simultaneously applications for medical expense, disability income, and long-term care insurance. Whitaker responds that he just thought it was time.

Whitaker has made no misrepresentations on the applications in the form of untrue or incomplete statements. Nevertheless, he is practicing concealment: he is silent about the physical threats he is under and has an obligation to disclose this situation, which is unknown to the insurer and unlikely to be the subject of specific inquiry. The concealment is material because Rodney's threats against Whitaker would almost certainly influence significantly the insurer's decision on providing coverage and/or the extent of its liability under the health insurance policies.

OTHER ESSENTIAL LEGAL ELEMENTS

In addition to offer and acceptance, other essential elements of a legally binding contract include legal purpose, consideration, and competent parties.

Legal Purpose

A legally binding contract must have a legal purpose or object. The courts do not enforce an insurance contract if it has an illegal purpose or is contrary to public policy.

Consideration

consideration

A valid contract requires *consideration* to be exchanged by both parties to the agreement—a right or something of value given up, or an obligation assumed. In insurance, the applicant typically makes a premium payment and meets other conditions of the contract. While payment of the initial premium is required before the contract becomes effective, continued payment of premiums is required to maintain the policy in force and to avoid a lapse in coverage. The insurer's consideration is its promise to pay for specified losses or to provide other services to the policyowner as stated in the policy.

Competent Parties

The final element of a binding agreement is that the parties must be competent. Individuals must be legally and mentally capable of entering into a contract, and insurers must have the organizational and legal capacity to enter into a contract.

The most common individual requirement arises in conjunction with applicants' attainment of legal majority age. Legal majority age gives an applicant the legal capacity to enter into contracts on themselves or on others in whom they have an insurable interest. Even though they may fully understand the contract's terms and willingly accept them, applicants under the age of legal majority are considered minors except for the purchase of basic necessities, such as food, clothing, and shelter. They may repudiate any other purchases up to the time they reach legal adulthood; in the case of insurance, they may demand a full return of all premiums paid. Recognizing the importance of insurance to minors, some states have made an exception for life, health, and auto insurance contracts by establishing special age limits of 14 or 16 beyond which minors are considered to have the legal capacity to insure themselves. These insurance contracts are binding.

Others who have reached the age of majority nevertheless may remain incapable of understanding any agreement and its terms. Examples would include individuals with significant and permanent mental handicaps as well as those incapacitated (even temporarily at the time of application) due to alcohol and/or substance abuse.

Organizations, including insurers, must be competent to contract by meeting state charter and license requirements. Nevertheless, even when such legal capacity is deficient, many courts hold the insuring organization or its executives responsible for the contracts to avoid penalizing good-faith purchasers of coverage.

SPECIAL CHARACTERISTICS OF INSURANCE CONTRACTS

In addition to the essential requirements of a legally binding contract, there are a number of special features that affect insurance policies, including health insurance policies. These characteristics include the following:

- unilateral structure
- conditional nature
- aleatory recovery
- indemnity payment
- insurable interest
- contract of adhesion

Unilateral Structure

unilateral contract

A contract is unilateral if only one of the parties makes a legally enforceable promise; it is bilateral if both parties have a legal obligation to perform. Insurance is typically a *unilateral contract* because only the insurer has made legally enforceable promises. In the case of medical expense insurance, for example, if the insurer fails to provide benefits for a covered medical expense, the insurer may be held liable for breach of contract. The insured, however, makes no such promise after the contract comes into force.

Of course, he or she must pay the premiums when due or the insurer is released from the contract, but the insurer cannot sue the policyowner to enforce continued payment of premiums.

Conditional Nature

conditional contract

One party's obligation to perform may be conditioned upon the performance of the second party. A clause in an insurance contract requiring such a performance is usually referred to as a condition. One party's failure to perform under such a *conditional contract* relieves the other party of any obligation under the contract. As explained later in the section on key insurance contract provisions, a condition may precede or be subsequent to the time at which a promise becomes binding on the promisor.

Aleatory Recovery

aleatory contract

Insurance is called an *aleatory contract* because one of the parties may recover a great deal more actual dollar value than the other, depending upon the occurrence of some possible future event. For example, under a disability income insurance contract, the insured could become disabled in an accident and begin receiving disability income benefits amounting to hundreds of thousands of dollars over the course of the disability after paying only a few months' premiums. On the other hand, the insured may pay premiums for many years with little or no corresponding benefit because of continuing good health.

Indemnity Payment

indemnity contract

A health insurance contract is often an *indemnity contract*. A contract of indemnity is a common law[1] concept, modified by state statute, that means an insured is entitled to payment under a policy only to the extent of financial loss or legal liability. In other words, the insured should remain in the same financial position that existed prior to a loss and should not be allowed to profit from the loss. Contracts of indemnity are tied to actual expenses incurred, such as for medical care and long-term care. An insured is indemnified only up to the policy limits and is subject to policy provisions, such as deductibles and percentage participation amounts.

Example: Sydney purchases an individual major medical expense policy with a $5 million lifetime maximum. The policy limits hospital room-and-board benefits to the cost of semiprivate accommodations. Sydney is subsequently hospitalized and incurs $25,000 in hospital bills, $1,200 of which is for the extra cost of a private room upgrade that she requests without medical necessity. The policy reimburses her based on an allowed hospital expense amount of $23,800, minus policy deductibles and the insured's percentage participation amount. Therefore, Sydney has been indemnified within policy limits and provisions.

---

valued policy

Some health insurance contracts, such as disability income policies, some long-term care policies, and some medical expense policies, are valued policies rather than policies of indemnity. A *valued policy* pays a precise dollar amount per day, per week, or per month without a direct relation to an expense incurred or a loss sustained. However, through underwriting, insurers try to eliminate payments in excess of losses by making sure that there is a reasonable relationship between the applicant's income and/or potential medical or long-term care expenses and the benefit (indemnity) amount. Nevertheless, in certain circumstances, persons may receive policy benefits that exceed the loss incurred. For example, a person owning a disability income policy with a benefit established at a high income may elect subsequently to pursue an opportunity in a new field, but at a substantially lower income, at least initially. Should this person become disabled at the outset of the new career, he or she may receive a disability benefit that exceeds income and is, in that sense, overindemnified.

Insurable Interest

insurable interest

All insurance contracts should contain an element of insurable interest. An *insurable interest* is a right or relationship with regard to the subject matter of the insurance contract such that the policyowner would suffer financial loss from damage, loss, or destruction to the subject matter.

The purposes of requiring an insurable interest in insurance contracts are to prevent gambling, to decrease moral hazard, and to help measure actual loss. Without an insurable interest, a contract is gambling or a wager because the risk assumed by the parties is created by the agreement itself and would not exist in the absence of the agreement. The absence of an insurable risk also could be an undesirable incentive for some persons to cause losses or injuries on purpose. In an insurance contract, the insurable interest means that the risk insured against exists regardless of the contract. When an insurable interest exists, no profit results because policyowners merely receive repayment for the loss they have suffered.

The continuance of life and good health serves as the basis for many examples of insurable health-related interests. Injury, sickness, disability, and other incapacities may result in financial losses to the persons insured or to their families. The right of persons to insure themselves, as well as the right of close family members to insure certain blood relatives and spouses (and possibly domestic partners), is based on this insurable interest. Insurable interests for health insurance are also based upon actual losses (either increased expenses or reduced income potential) resulting from other relationships to the insured, such as those of creditors, business partners, or employers. The business uses of disability insurance presented in chapter 15 provide examples of these types of insurable interests.

Contract of Adhesion

contract of adhesion

An insurance contract is said to be a *contract of adhesion* in that it is ordinarily prepared in all its details by the insurer; the policyowner has no part in drawing up its clauses or determining its wording. In applying for insurance, the applicant's actions are limited to: (1) acceptance of the policy as prepared by the insurer (adherence to it); (2) refusal to purchase the insurance; or (3) purchase of another insurer's policy that may use different policy wording. Although insurance contracts are sometimes modified to meet individual needs, the contract with its amendments is still prepared by the insurance company. By contrast, a bargaining contract is one in which both parties contribute to the terms and conditions.

For the most part, then, the parties to an insurance contract do not have equal bargaining power. The insurer is judged to be the party of superior strength and knowledge, with the applicant having limited resources and expertise. As a result, three significant contract-related actions flow from the imbalance inherent in a contract of adhesion:

- the benefit of the doubt to the policyowner in the event of dispute
- the need for the policyowner to read and understand the policy
- the rise of extracontractual considerations that may modify the policy terms

Benefit of Doubt to the Policyowner

Because the insurer has the advantage of drawing up the agreement and is expected to clearly represent the intent of the parties, it is generally held that where the terms of the policy are ambiguous, obscure, or susceptible to more than one interpretation, the construction most favorable to the policyowner must prevail. The rule is based on the assumption that the insurer has a duty to make its meaning clear; when the insurer's language is unclear, the benefit of the doubt goes to the policyowner. This applies only when a court decides that the contract is unclear, not every time the policyowner misinterprets or does not understand a provision. However, this principle may afford the policyowner an advantage that offsets his or her lack of participation in drawing up the contract.

Need for the Policyowner to Read and Understand the Contract

Where there is no ambiguity, the contract is to be enforced in accordance with its terms. If the contract is clear and understandable, its meaning may not be distorted by interpretations. Consideration must be given to the generally understood meaning of the terms used and to the entire context to determine the nature and extent of coverage. A corollary to the strict compliance rule is that the law binds persons to the terms of a written contract that they sign or accept, regardless of whether they have taken the trouble to acquaint themselves with all of its terms and conditions.

Many insurance contracts are complicated and difficult to understand. It is probably safe to state that, regardless of the clarity or obscurity of the terminology, most people do not read their policies; they simply assume that the policy meets their needs. When a loss occurs, however, it is no defense to claim ignorance of the policy's terms because of failure to read the agreement. Neglecting to read the contract does not change or extend the policyowner's rights as stated in the written policy. An agent's or broker's advice to their clients should be: "To avoid problems (and uncertainties), know what is in your insurance policy by reading it, having it explained to you, or both."

Extracontractual Considerations

The insurance policy contains the written expression of the agreement between the parties and should provide the only reference for rights and obligations. Thus, the contract is ordinarily not subject to modification by considerations external to the written terms. For example, a policyowner may not usually contradict the written contract by claiming that the agent told him or her that the policy covered a specific type of loss. The policy's language is nevertheless not binding in clear cases of mutual mistake of fact or where there is a mistake on one side and fraud inducing it on the other. In such cases, the injured party has a legal right to ask that the contract be reformed to the true agreement. An example of a clear mistake of fact might be a contract that insured the wrong dependent based on incorrect oral information from an applicant.

However, certain factors external to the written contract terms may have a bearing on the contractual relationship. Two of these factors are the insurer's advertisements for its products and the actions of the agent.

Advertisements. Advertisements are a prime inducement to the insured to enter into a contract of insurance. Therefore, they must reflect accurately the benefits a policy provides. An insurer's advertisements are such an important factor in the offer process that the NAIC has a model regulation to control health insurance advertisements. The regulation, adopted by many states, aims to ensure that advertising accurately describes the advantages and disadvantages of the insurance product without either exaggerating the benefits or minimizing the limitations.

Some courts have held that if an advertisement suggests that the policy provides more than it in fact does, the advertisement is construed to contain a promise that the insurance company must honor. Consequently, to ensure that the insurer does not have to provide benefits beyond the policy's terms and conditions, it is crucial for policy advertisements to accurately portray benefits and limitations and promise no more than the policy can deliver.

Actions of the Agent. Although it is unwise for policyowners to assume that courts will be lenient in excusing them from a contract's written terms, special situations sometimes occur when policyowners have reasonably relied upon an insurance agent's advice. Even though the application and the policy itself contain warnings about the limitations on the agent's authority, state rulings may extend the policy terms to representations made by the agent who induced the applicant to purchase the contract. In addition, many states impute to the insurer any knowledge and information the applicant has given to the agent—even information that the agent has failed to reveal to the insurer—regardless of any language to the contrary in the application. Consequently, it is vital that agents properly understand the products they are selling, have adequate training in the special nature of health insurance, accurately represent the policies, and include in the applications all pertinent information given to them by the applicants.

KEY INSURANCE CONTRACT PROVISIONS

Insurers take considerable care to set forth in policy language, called provisions, exactly what coverage they intend to provide. The legal characteristics of the insurance contract make the drafting of provisions exceedingly complex and intricate. Health insurance contract provisions can vary widely due to differing practices of insurance companies and the determinations of state legislation and regulation. The NAIC's model laws and regulations have resulted in some uniformity in those states adopting the models. Despite the variations in formats that insurers use, certain key provisions are common. Typical insurance contract provisions can be grouped into the following categories, depending on the purposes they serve:

- declarations
- insuring and consideration clause
- right of examination
- policy continuation and premium change
- definitions
- dependent eligibility
- benefit provisions
- exclusions
- conditions
- waiver of premium
- riders
- execution clause

Declarations

declaration

Every insurance contract has a set of declarations, although they are not always labeled as such. A *declaration* is a factual statement identifying the specific person, property, or activity being insured and the parties to the insurance transaction; it also provides descriptive information about the insurance being purchased. Declarations are usually grouped together in the initial section of the policy.

Insuring and Consideration Clause

insuring and consideration clause

In general terms, the *insuring and consideration clause* is the insurer's promise to pay benefits. This contract provision, which is at the core of any insurance policy, expresses the promise to pay, and summarizes the scope and limits of coverage. This provision also expresses the applicant's consideration, which includes the application and payment of the premium. For example,

> "We will pay benefits for a loss as set forth in this policy. This policy is issued in exchange for and on the basis of your application and payment of the first premium."

Right of Examination

free-look period

States commonly require a provision for a *free-look period* under which the applicant has the right to examine the policy for a specific period after it has been issued. In most states, the period is 30 days, but a few states have 10-day periods for some medical expense policies. During this time, the policy is effective and binding. If the applicant—now the policyowner—is dissatisfied during this period, he or she may nullify the otherwise valid contract. In this case, the contract is considered to have never been issued and the insurer is required to refund any premium amounts paid.

Notice of the right to examine the policy and to return it must appear on the front page of the policy. It might read as follows:

> "If you are not satisfied with this policy, you may return it within 10 days of receipt. Mail or deliver the policy to the agent who sold it to you, to our home office, or to the agency office through which it was delivered. We will then refund any premium paid. The policy will then be deemed never to have been issued."

Policy Continuation and Premium Change

One of the more important provisions in an insurance policy relates to both the policyowner's right to continue the coverage in force and the premium that must be paid for the continuation. Policy continuation and premium change provisions in health insurance policies generally fall into four categories:

- guaranteed renewable
- noncancelable
- conditionally renewable
- nonrenewable

Most health insurance policies are guaranteed renewable. Some policies that provide broader renewal rights to the policyowner are noncancelable. Other polices that are conditionally renewable provide the lowest level of renewability of the three categories. In addition, some health insurance polices are simply nonrenewable.

However, HIPAA severely limits an insurer's ability to nonrenew major medical, HMO, and similar comprehensive policies of individual medical expense insurance. With certain exceptions, these types of medical expense policies are renewable solely at the policyowner's option with insurers retaining the right to set an appropriate premium. Because age is not an exception for these policies, a medical expense policy subject to HIPAA must be renewable up to and even after age 65 in the unlikely event that the policyowner, now a Medicare beneficiary, wishes to pay premiums to continue it. Consequently, any limitations on renewal discussed below apply only to the HIPAA-"excepted" benefits noted in chapter 6, such as the benefits contained in policies covering disability income, long-term care, and limited medical expense benefits.

Guaranteed Renewable

A guaranteed renewable policy provision gives the policyowner the right to renew the coverage at each policy anniversary date. In addition, the policy may not be canceled by the insurer during the period of coverage. However, in a guaranteed renewable policy, the insurer does not guarantee future rates for the coverage. Instead, the insurer retains the right to raise rates for broad classifications of insureds (such as by age or occupation), but not just for one individual with poor claim experience.

Medical expense, long-term care, and many disability income policies are typically guaranteed renewable. However, the term as it is commonly used may not be as broad as it first seems. Most disability income policies and some limited benefit forms of medical expense policies are guaranteed renewable only to a stated age, such as 65. In addition, some states also have adopted NAIC language that allows disability income policies to be labeled as "guaranteed renewable" if at a minimum they are renewable until age 50 or for at least 5 years if issued to a person aged 44 or older.

Noncancelable

A noncancelable policy provision is sometimes called noncancelable and guaranteed renewable or simply "Non-can." Such a provision gives the policyowner both guaranteed renewal rights and a premium rate guarantee. Thus, the policyowner has the right to renew the coverage at each policy anniversary date; the policy may not be terminated by the insurer during the period of coverage and no changes to any provisions can be made unilaterally while the policy is in force. In addition, in a truly noncancelable policy, future rates for coverage are guaranteed (though not necessarily level) in the contract itself.

Because of their rate guarantee aspects, noncancelable provisions are an unlikely occurrence in medical expense and long-term care policies. The uncertainties associated with medical and health care cost inflation and utilization make such guarantees in these types of policies impractical, if not impossible. Consequently, noncancelable provisions occur only in some disability income policies and perhaps some limited benefit types of medical expense policies.

The renewal terms of noncancelable polices, as in the case of guaranteed renewable policies, may not be as broad as they first seem. Like guaranteed renewable policies, noncancelable policies may be renewable only to some stated age, such as 65. In addition, the states that have adopted the NAIC language mentioned above for minimum age requirements of guaranteed renewable disability income policies also apply these same age minimums to policies labeled as noncancelable.

Conditionally Renewable

conditionally renewable

The *conditionally renewable* provision in some policies allows the insurer to refuse to renew the policy for specifically listed conditions. These policies may also be labeled as nonrenewable for stated reasons only. In health insurance policies, thc insurcr may reserve the right not to renew the policies held by an entire group of insureds classified by age, policy form, date of issue, or geographic area. (However, if age is the only condition, the policy still often qualifies as guaranteed renewable.) The conditions listed may not single out for cancellation a specific policyowner's coverage, based on claims experience, for example. The insurer may also adjust the premium and change the benefits by class.

Although this type of renewability provision rarely appears in today's health insurance policies, some medical expense, disability income, and early long-term care policies may be conditionally renewable. While a conditionally renewable provision is the lowest level of renewability compared to the two types of continuation provisions just discussed, it provides more protection than policies that are nonrenewable.

Nonrenewable

Some policies are purchased to provide insurance protection for a specifically defined period and are nonrenewable upon the expiration of the coverage period. Health insurance policies with nonrenewable provisions include term disability income insurance for unique employment situations and interim medical expense insurance that provides term, international travel, and student coverage.

nonrenewable

A *nonrenewable* provision gives the insurer the unilateral right to refuse to renew a policy at the end of any period for which premiums have been paid. This type of policy affords the insured the least security in terms of continuation of coverage. Even if the insurer agrees to continue coverage by issuing another policy of the same type, it has the right to alter the policy's provisions. These alterations could eliminate coverage for certain types of losses or injuries to certain parts of the body, or limit the extent of coverage for certain occurrences.

Definitions

Because an insurance policy is a contract of adhesion, the insurer must define exactly what it wishes to cover or not cover. Otherwise, words and phrases that are not specifically defined in the contract are interpreted by the courts and regulatory officials according to the following general principles:

- Everyday language is given its ordinary or normal meaning.
- Technical terms are assigned their technical definitions.
- Terms that have an established legal meaning are given that meaning.
- Where appropriate, meanings of words take into account local, cultural, and trade usage considerations.

As mentioned earlier, contractual ambiguities are likely to be construed against the insurer. The definitions section of the policy functions to make the insurer's intentions precise.

Health insurance is designed to provide benefits for "loss" sustained under specific conditions and circumstances. Certain words must be given a very specific and precise meaning so that the policy clearly states the nature of such losses and the conditions and circumstances for coverage. Health insurance policies usually have many terms in common, such as physician, licensed health care practitioner, and preexisting conditions. However, not every insurer defines these terms in precisely the same way. Insurers may also define differently terms that are unique to each form of health insurance. Such common and unique terms include the following:

- in medical expense insurance—average semiprivate room rate, hospital, medical emergency, prevailing charge
- in disability income insurance—accident, any occupation, disability, injury, loss of income, own occupation
- in long-term care—adult day care center, assisted-living facility, hands-on assistance, loss of functional capacity, stand-by assistance, substantial supervision

Dependent Eligibility

Every policy defines who is eligible—the person or persons covered by the policy and eligible for benefits. At a minimum, eligibility includes the insured person, who is most often also the policyowner. In medical expense policies and long-term care policies, eligible persons may also include close family members, frequently called dependents. Subsequent chapters explain dependent eligibility under each form of health insurance policy.

Benefit Provisions

The benefit provisions section is the essence of any insurance contract. Development of these provisions is generally a cooperative effort of the insurer's actuarial, legal, claim, underwriting, and marketing areas. The benefits provided by a policy must be clearly spelled out in a manner that affords the policyowner easy reference and understanding. A summary of these provisions is customarily presented on a separate schedule of benefits; this schedule includes the policy number and date of issue, the insured's name, types and amounts of benefits, the initial annual premium, maximum benefit periods, waiting periods, and other variables.

The benefit provisions set forth the insurer's promises. Each benefit is explained in detail, indicating what is to be paid, conditions that establish the insurer's liability to make payment, conditions under which payment is to be made, the nature and extent of benefits payable, and the applicable benefit limitations.

Benefit provisions must be drafted with the utmost care. They must be clear and precise, but at the same time broad enough to cover virtually any claim situation that could conceivably arise.

Exclusions

exclusions

Every insurance policy has *exclusions,* sometimes referred to as exclusions and limitations, which are items that the insurer does not intend to cover. The following are typical exclusions in health insurance policies:

- certain uninsurable perils, such as loss due to war
- conditions that pose a major increase in costs not contemplated in the basic premium, such as expenses of long-term custodial care under a basic medical expense policy
- losses that are designed to be covered by other types of policies, such as workers' compensation or Medicare coverages
- coverage of losses that would pose a potential moral hazard, such as coverage for intentionally self-inflicted injuries
- benefits that are not desired by most policyowners, such as hair transplants

A practical result of exclusions, if not a reason for their use by insurers, is to hold down the premium cost of coverage for policyowners. Although good reasons exist for exclusions, they do restrict coverage. Consequently, it is very important that the insurer's limits on its liability appear in a prominent place in the policy and be expressed in clear and understandable terms.

Conditions

The insuring agreement is not an absolute promise by the company with "no strings attached." Instead, the promise is a qualified one, enforceable only if the policyowner fulfills a number of *conditions* that are spelled out in the policy. Those conditions may be grouped together in a section of the policy labeled "Conditions," or they may be scattered throughout the policy and its endorsements or riders (discussed in the following section). Most policy conditions must be fulfilled by the policyowner before the insurer may be held liable for a loss.

Conditions are usually regarded as either precedent (before) or subsequent (after) the time at which a promise becomes binding on the insurer. An illustration of a common condition precedent, which must take place before a promise becomes binding, is the requirement in many insurance contracts that an insurer must have proper notice and proof of loss before the claim is payable. Note that the policyowner does not have to file a claim, but the insurer is not obligated to pay unless the policyowner does so in the proper manner. An example of a condition subsequent is an insured's obligation to cooperate with the insurer. For example, a disability income policy and a long-term care policy typically permit the insurer to have its own physician examine the insured to confirm the disability or incapacity. If the insured fails to comply with this condition, that failure subsequently relieves the insurer of its earlier obligation to pay.

Waiver of Premium

waiver of premium

Waiver of premium is a provision in a health insurance policy that maintains the policy in force and allows benefits to continue without the payment of premium when the insured is seriously ill. Although this provision is found in many health insurance policies and has the same objective, its application in each type of policy varies. Specific waivers of premium as they apply to medical expense, disability income, and long-term care policies are discussed later in the book.

Riders

rider

Health insurance policies frequently contain a rider. A *rider* (also known as an *endorsement* or *amendment*) to an insurance contract is a provision added to the policy, sometimes for an extra premium charge, by which the scope of its coverage is clarified, restricted, or enlarged.

There are three types of riders:

- *language riders.* Language riders amend or add policy language so that, for example, the policy conforms to state requirements. The language rider may amend a 30-day notice of nonrenewal to conform to a 60-day notice requirement or limit the insurer's right to void the policy for only specified reasons.
- *benefit riders.* Benefit riders are supplementary agreements that provide optional benefits not contained in the basic policy; these benefits require a separate additional premium. Examples that might be offered by rider are maternity benefits for attachment to medical expense policies and accidental death and dismemberment benefits for attachment to disability income policies. Benefit riders may be attached to the policy when it is issued or they may be added later. When added, they immediately become part of the contract of insurance.
- *exclusion riders.* Exclusion riders restrict the scope of coverage by excluding a specifically named medical condition or certain activities or avocations. Insurers may require this form of rider as a precondition for issuing a policy; this is one type of counteroffer. If the applicant signs the rider and accepts the policy as offered, this creates a binding contract. A copy of the signed rider remains attached to the policy. Refusal to accept the exclusion rider constitutes a rejection of the counteroffer.

As a general principle, whenever a rider's wording conflicts with terms of the policy to which it is attached, the rider takes precedence. The assumption underlying this principle is that an alteration of the basic agreement between the policyowner and insurer more accurately reflects the true intent of the parties than does the basic agreement itself.

Execution Clause

Just as the applicant must sign the application, the insurer must, through an authorized executive officer, sign the insurance policy. This execution clause signifies that the insurer has entered into the contract and is bound by its terms. In today's policy issue systems, the signature is a facsimile printed on the policy.

OTHER PROVISIONS

The previous section discussed standard or key contract provisions that are common and similarly defined in all forms of health insurance policies. Other common provisions, such as grace periods and reinstatement, are covered in chapter 6. However, some other provisions are unique to or defined uniquely under each form of health insurance. Among these provisions, which later chapters discuss, are:

- in medical expense insurance—extension of coverage, out-of-pocket limit, restoration of benefits, separate service maximum
- in disability income insurance—elimination period, presumptive disability, nonoccupational clause, qualification period, relation of earnings, restoration of benefits
- in long-term care insurance—elimination period, nonforfeiture, pool of money, shared benefit, restoration of benefits

ELECTRONIC COMMERCE

Electronic commerce is the conduct of business using computers as well as computer-related interface devices that are linked by telephone, cable lines, or satellite communication. Electronic commerce also involves the establishment and transmission of contracts, including insurance contracts and other transactions that relate to them. The Internet is the most common vehicle for these kinds of transactions, in which digitized information is communicated from one person or entity to another and stored without the use of paper. Almost all states have enacted the Uniform Electronic Transactions Act (UETA) developed by the National Conference of Commissioners on Uniform State Laws to support the use of electronic commerce, including insurance transactions. In the few states that have not yet adopted UETA, federal statute provisions govern electronic insurance transactions.

Uniform Electronic Transactions Act

The goal of UETA is to make sure that electronic transactions in the marketplace are as enforceable as transactions memorialized on paper and with manual signatures, but without changing any of the substantive rules of law that apply.[2] It does not prohibit paper records and manual signatures, nor does it require the use of electronic transactions or reliance upon electronic records and signatures. Thus, parties to binding electronic transactions must agree to conduct their transactions electronically.[3] Generally, this agreement involves a separate statement that has consent to conduct transactions electronically as its primary purpose. That agreement could be achieved when a person simply clicks "I accept," "I agree," or "OK" at the place indicated on a computer screen. Such consent may not be imbedded as a provision in a standard contract form unless that provision is conspicuously displayed and separately agreed to.

Basic rules of law, like the law of contracts, continue to apply. In other words, an electronic record of a transaction is the equivalent of a paper record, and an electronic signature should be given the same legal effect as a manual signature. UETA's main objectives are as follows:

- A record or signature may not be denied legal effect or enforceability solely because it is in electronic form.
- A contract may not be denied legal effect or enforceability solely because an electronic record was used in its formation.
- An electronic record satisfies any law that requires a record in writing.
- Any signature requirement in the law is met if there is an electronic signature.

An electronic signature is defined as an electronic sound, symbol, or process attached to or associated with a record and executed or adopted by a person with the intent to sign the record.[4] While the law facilitates the use of a digital signature, which is a method of encryption, and other security procedures, nothing in UETA requires the use of a specific digital signature or security procedure. The identifier is technologically neutral. Persons can use the most up-to-date digital signature technology or less sophisticated security procedures, such as passwords, personal identification numbers (PINs), or even a typed name.

Other provisions determine when information is legally sent and received in electronic form. To be properly sent, electronic information must be properly addressed or directed to the recipient using the recipient's designated system. When the record enters the system that the recipient has designated and to which the recipient has access (and in a form capable of being processed by that system), the record is received whether or not the recipient ever retrieves the record.

Another important aspect of UETA is that it clearly validates contracts formed by electronic agents. An electronic agent is a computer program that is implemented by its principals to do business in electronic form. A person may form a contract by using an electronic agent and the person or entity that provides the program is bound by the contract that its agent makes.

Insurance Transactions

As the electronic provision of insurance products and services to consumers increases, some legal and compliance issues for insurers, agents, brokers, and other persons and entities have arisen. The NAIC has developed a model bulletin on electronic signatures and records used by states to address these areas under UETA requirements or federal statute.[5]

Under UETA Requirements

The state exercises jurisdiction over electronic media (such as Web sites) that solicit, sell, or negotiate insurance products or services. Electronic media are generally subject to the same rules governing insurance in other media. Thus, the requirements for advertising, document format, record keeping, and document delivery remain the same regardless of medium.

Advertising. If the content or changes to the content of a Web site are of the type that would require approval as a print advertisement, then the Web display change requires approval as well. However, changes in the appearance of a Web site, with no changes in substantive content, would not generally require approval or separate record keeping.

Document Format. Specific format requirements originally established for printed documents are satisfied for electronically transmitted or displayed records by using characteristics that are designed to meet the same regulatory objective. For example, a requirement to use a specific color or font can be met in an electronic format by having the same emphasis or distinguishing proportions for the print characters relative to the rest of the document.

Record Keeping. Electronic record keeping is generally subject to the same timelines and other standards as record keeping in other media. Thus compliance with the state's record keeping requirements is observed if a regulated entity can reassemble the original information upon request. For example, in cases where there is no paper document, a regulated entity (person, company, or organization) is in compliance if it can produce the information or data that accurately represents the electronic record of communication with the policyowner.

Document Delivery. For purposes of document delivery and other communications required or permitted by state law and regulations, delivery and communication by electronic or other verifiable means is not precluded where agreed to by the parties involved. The burden is on the regulated persons or entities to meet all existing requirements for delivery regardless of the method by which the policy or other record(s) is actually delivered to the recipient.

Any policy, other record, or communication delivered to an individual must be maintained in accordance with applicable retention schedules, and the regulated entity must provide, on demand, an easily readable electronic or paper copy of the policy or document to the regulator or other party entitled to the information. If a law or regulation requires a record, notice, or document to be attached to or enclosed with other records, documents, or notices, the law or regulation can be satisfied in the electronic environment as long as it is clear that the attached or enclosed record, document, or notice is logically associated with or linked to the same electronic record as the principal record, document, or notice.

Under Federal Statute

The federal Electronic Signatures in Global and National Commerce Act (E-SIGN) contains its own specific procedures or requirements for the use or acceptance of electronic records or electronic signatures to establish the legal effect, validity, or enforceability of contracts or other records. However, E-SIGN provisions, which are similar to UETA provisions, are preempted when a state passes UETA. The statute was enacted in 2000 over concerns that several years might elapse before all states passed UETA. Therefore, Congress introduced broad legislation that would give nationwide validity to electronic records and signatures. E-SIGN is now largely superfluous because state passage of UETA is almost universal. Even in the absence of UETA, E-SIGN would not apply to certain state law notice requirements, such as written notice requirements for the cancellation or termination of life and health insurance benefits.

CHAPTER REVIEW

Key Terms

contract
modal premium
conditional receipt
temporary insurance agreement (TIA)
void contract
voidable contract
misrepresentation
concealment
consideration
unilateral contract
conditional contract
aleatory contract
indemnity contract
valued policy
insurable interest

contract of adhesion
declaration
insuring and consideration clause
free-look period
conditionally renewable
nonrenewable
exclusions
waiver of premium
rider

Review Questions

Review questions are based on the learning objectives in this chapter. Thus, a [3-3] at the end of a question means that the question is based on learning objective 3-3. If there are multiple objectives, they are all listed.

1. a What is unique about an insurance contract? [3-1]
   b. Why are the terms of the policy important to both the insurer and the policyowner? [3-1]

2. a. What are two initial offer-and-acceptance scenarios in the insurance contract process? [3-2]
   b. What is the effect of the payment of the initial premium on acceptance of the applicant's offer to contract, and what implications does it have for the applicant? [3-2]

3 a. Why must the questions on an insurance application be clear and unambiguous? [3-2]
   b. Why is it important that responses be accurate and complete? [3-2]
   c. Why does the agent sign the application? [3-2]
   d. Why is including a premium payment along with the application advantageous to both the insurer and the applicant? [3-2]

4. a. On what dates may coverage become effective under the two types of conditional receipts provided upon completion of a health insurance application and payment of the required initial premium? [3-2]
   b. What unique advantage does a receipt with a temporary insurance agreement provide to an applicant? [3-2]

5. What effects may untrue and incomplete information have on an insurance contract? [3-3]

6. a. What makes a misrepresentation or concealment material? [3-3]
   b. What effect may a material misrepresentation or material concealment on an insurance application have on a subsequently issued policy? [3-3]

7. a. In addition to offer and acceptance, what are other essential elements of a legally binding contract? [3-4]
   b. Briefly explain their significance. [3-4]

8. Why do insurance contracts require an insurable interest? [3-5]

9. What are the three significant contract-related consequences that result from the imbalance inherent in a contract of adhesion? [3-5]

10. What part may advertisements and agent statements play in modifying the written contract terms? [3-5]

11. What is the purpose of each of the following contract provisions or sections?

    a. right of examination [3-6]
    b. definitions [3-6]
    c. dependent eligibility [3-6]
    d. benefit provisions [3-6]
    e. conditions (precedent and subsequent) [3-6]
    f. execution clause [3-6]

12. a. What are the three methods of policy continuation that usually apply to health insurance policies? [3-6]
    b. Why are some health insurance policies nonrenewable? [3-6]
    c. What is the effect of HIPAA on nonrenewal? [3-6]

13. a. What is the purpose of each of the three types of riders used with medical insurance policies? [3-6]
    b. What assumption is made in the event of conflict between a rider's terms and the terms of the policy to which it is attached? [3-6]

14. a. What are the main objectives of the Uniform Electronic Transactions Act (UETA)? [3-7]
    b. How do UETA's requirements affect electronic insurance transactions with regard to advertising, document format, record keeping, and document delivery? [3-7]

NOTES

1. Common law is defined as the body of law developed in England primarily from judicial decisions based on custom and precedent, unwritten in statute or code, and constituting the basis of the English legal system and of the system in all of the United States, except Louisiana.
2. This material was adapted from the Web site of the National Conference of Commissioners on Uniform State Laws, at www.nccusl.com under *Uniform Electronic Transactions Act, Summary*, 2003.
3. UETA excludes transactions subject to the following states laws: the Uniform Commercial Code (UCC), except for the sections on sales and leases; the Uniform Computer Information Transactions Act (UCITA); laws governing estates and trusts; and other specific laws that a state wants to exempt from the rules applied in UETA.

   The UCC is a well-established body of state laws governing commercial transactions. The UCITA is a recent model law on comprehensive computer information licensing, also developed by the National Conference of Commissioners on Uniform States Laws. Although UCITA has been enacted in only a few states, it is being considered by many more.

4. Other examples of electronic signatures include: a digitized image of a handwritten signature that is attached to an electronic document; a secret code or personal identification number (PIN) to identify the sender to the recipient; a code that the sender of a message uses to identify himself or herself; and a unique biometrics-based identifier, such as a fingerprint or a retinal scan.
5. This material was adapted from *Model Bulletin: Regulatory Issues Associated with the Provision of Insurance Electronically,* National Association of Insurance Commissioners, December 5, 2000.

4

Underwriting

Learning Objectives

An understanding of the material in this chapter should enable you to

4-1. Describe the underwriting process in general and its key role in providing insurance.

4-2. Describe the relationship between the agent and home office underwriter that a successful underwriting process requires.

4-3. Explain the significance of the classification categories used by health insurance underwriters and how they apply to the specific forms of health insurance.

4-4. Describe the insurance application process and its importance.

4-5. Identify the additional sources of information that a health insurance underwriter relies on and describe the extent to which the underwriter may use them.

4-6. Describe alternative final underwriting actions and reunderwriting and how they apply to the specific forms of health insurance.

Chapter Outline

underwriting

Underwriting is an essential function in all forms of insurance. It is the process of evaluating an insurance applicant, making decisions about the applicant's acceptability for insurance coverage, and determining the appropriate basis on which to provide coverage and charge a premium. The applicant for individual health insurance must generally provide evidence of insurability. This means that he or she must meet the standards that the insurance company has determined are necessary before it will issue a policy. Company and product underwriting standards vary—widely so in some cases. Although it may deny coverage altogether, an insurer may also use this process to issue a policy with restricted coverage and benefits and/or charge a higher premium. Thus, underwriting has important implications for the availability and cost of health insurance coverage.

The discussion opens with an overview of underwriting. The remaining sections examine the steps in underwriting individual health insurance that include classification categories, sources of information, underwriting actions, and renewal underwriting. Although many underwriting features are common to all forms of health insurance, there are specific features that are more relevant and even unique to one form or another. Consequently, the discussion points out both the similarities and differences in underwriting features as they relate to medical expense, disability income, and long-term care insurance.

OVERVIEW

A brief explanation of the key role of underwriting and the essential relationship between the agent and home office underwriter affords an overview of the underwriting function.

Key Role of Underwriting

An understanding of why an insurer rejects some applicants or restricts their coverage or benefits makes it clear that underwriting is one of an insurer's major functions. Underwriting enables an insurance company to provide its services to insureds—including the payment of claims—and to make a profit. Without underwriting, the company would be vulnerable to financial loss caused by adverse selection. Adverse selection means that those who are likely to have claims are also those who are most likely to seek insurance. It is the underwriter's responsibility to minimize adverse selection so that the insurance company can obtain the "average" group of insureds assumed in the rate structure.

Underwriting relates directly to the premiums paid by those covered by an individual policy. If the premium does not reflect the assumed average potential for health claims, then the insurance is a bargain for some and an overcharge for others, setting the stage for adverse selection. Those with likely medical expenses try to obtain insurance in much larger numbers than those who are less likely to have such expenses. Premiums rise as a result and individuals who are less likely to incur claims become more likely to drop coverage. Moreover, many other potential applicants who previously found health insurance difficult to afford might now find its cost completely prohibitive.

It would seem that the best way to avoid adverse selection would be to accept only the best applicants for insurance. However, if underwriting is too restrictive, agents may direct their clients to other companies, making it difficult for an underwriter to meet the insurer's profit objectives. As a result, underwriting must balance adverse selection with selecting only the best applicants. It results in the selection of most applicants for insurance, but it also involves rejecting some applicants or accepting them with conditions attached. In some cases, traditional underwriting that would lead to rejection of a health insurance applicant is modified by state or federal laws.

Although underwriting plays a key role in a company's ability to conduct the business of insurance, underwriting practices are far from uniform; they vary significantly by company and form of coverage. Underwriting can be

persistency

sophisticated and is often based on a solid body of experience, but it is not an exact science; scrutiny and judgment are required. Among other reasons, an insurer determines the stringency in underwriting a specific policy based on such factors as company philosophy, the aggressiveness of its marketing, policy premium levels, the level and stability of claims, and *persistency*—the length of time an insured maintains a policy in force. Consequently, clients, as well as their agents, should be aware that if one company denies an applicant coverage or offers less favorable terms, one or more other companies may accept that applicant or offer coverage at more favorable terms.

The Agent and the Home Office Underwriter

Underwriting is accomplished by the insurer's home office (or regional office) underwriter and the field underwriter—the agent. Their roles are complementary and mutually supportive. Timely and effective communication between them is essential for a successful underwriting process. The insurer's underwriting department determines the underwriting rules to be carried out by its agents and its company personnel. Agents receive instruction on what types of applications are unacceptable and what kinds of business the company particularly desires.

Well-qualified agents choose clients who meet the insurer's underwriting rules. In the application process, insurers regularly stress to agents their responsibility to obtain a complete and accurate application, especially with respect to the applicant's medical condition. The agent must also communicate all known or even suspected relevant facts about the applicant. Insurers encourage agents to identify special circumstances or any other issues, as well as to clarify questionable situations. Extra efforts in these areas bolster the home office underwriter's confidence in the agent and facilitate the approval of current and future applications. Thus, completeness and candor assist both the agent and the applicant to avoid a subsequent declination of a claim or rescission of a policy for misrepresentation. Moreover, underwriters are often able to monitor the quality of an agent's business based on data that insurers gather by agent, including claims and persistency. If there are problems, the company may underwrite more closely the applications the agent submits or, in serious cases, terminate its relationship with the agent.

In turn, the underwriter should process the agent's applications in as timely a manner as possible with prompt communication about the pending and final status of applications. As explained later, this does not mean that underwriting is completed quickly; it often takes some period of time to conclude the process. When an underwriter declines an application, the agent needs as much background information regarding that decision as the underwriter can legally divulge in order to communicate sensitively and effectively with the applicant. Helping the agent to deal effectively with a client is an essential aspect of maintaining good field force morale.

As we will see, the home office underwriter, however, is not totally dependent on the agent as the sole source of applicant information. Without diminishing the importance of the agent's role as the field underwriter, the home office underwriter may access information from the applicant directly through a variety of sources, such as a follow-up telephone interview, a face-to-face assessment, or a review of medical records. The use of these sources of direct applicant information varies significantly among insurance companies and by insurance product.

CLASSIFICATION CATEGORIES

An underwriter must first identify the categories into which applicants may be classified. These categories, which determine the premium to be charged, are also used by the underwriter to evaluate an applicant's acceptability for insurance. Thus, they are established by an insurance company's actuaries with input from underwriters. However, there are federal and state laws that prohibit classification based on certain factors, such as race, ethnic origin, and religion.

Applicants for health insurance are classified typically according to some or all of the following categories:

- number of insureds
- age
- gender
- geographic area
- tobacco use versus nonuse
- occupation
- income
- duplicate coverage
- lifestyle factors
- medical condition
- underwriting classes

Some classification categories are factual, so entries and responses can be assigned easily, quickly, and accurately. Such categories include the number of insureds applying for coverage, age, gender, geographic area, and duplicate coverage. Nevertheless, despite the evident objectivity, the underwriter is likely to verify applicant information in these categories by using sources in addition to the application, which are discussed subsequently. Other categories such as medical condition, tobacco use, other lifestyle factors, insurable income for disability income coverage, and underwriting class require not only verification, but also scrutiny and judgment about the appropriateness of the applicant's assignment.

The underwriter views all categories—those that are factual and those requiring analysis—not in isolation, but in relation to one another; they all affect the decision on the applicant's insurability and the conditions under which coverage and benefits may be offered. Thus, for example, a benefit level that an insurer might approve for an applicant at a younger age may differ if the applicant were older. A company's excessive claims experience in a certain geographic area may prompt a more extensive underwriting process than normally required or serve to limit benefit maximums in that area.

Number of Insureds

The number of insureds is a category that for the most part is pertinent to medical expense policies. Such policies may cover the applicant as well as the applicant's immediate family, usually a spouse and possibly dependent children under a certain age. The number of insureds covered under a single policy determines the premium and the underwriter must obtain sufficient information to determine the acceptability for coverage of each person applying for insurance.

For purposes of setting rates and charging premiums, insurance companies vary in the ways they aggregate insureds when more than one person is covered under the same policy. Whatever structure is selected takes into account gender and the inclusion of a spouse and the number of children to be covered under the policy.

Example: An insurer offers a PPO plan in suburban Chicago with a $1,000 per person annual deductible. The plan is very comprehensive and includes prescription drug coverage. The monthly cost for this coverage for an applicant aged 45–49 is as follows:

Category	Monthly Premium
Single male	$258
Single female	274
Applicant and spouse	533
Applicant and 1 child	347
Applicant and 2 or more children	466

Applicant, spouse, and 1 child	622
Applicant, spouse, and 2 or more children	741

Note that these premiums would be more than 20 percent lower if the deductible were raised to $2,000.

Although most long-term care policies that are issued cover only the applicant, many companies will insure a spouse under the same policy. Disability income policies, however, cover only the applicant, although some variations are discussed in a later chapter under the business uses of disability income insurance.

Age

Age is such a definitive predictor of health claims that it also forms an explicit basis for establishing product premium rates for all forms of health insurance. This is true for at least two reasons. First, the older an applicant is, the more likely he or she is to have claims. Second, the younger the applicant is, the longer the insurer is likely to collect premiums before the more significant claims payments associated with older ages are required. Usually, this means that a younger person is more likely to obtain coverage as applied for and at a more favorable premium than an older person.

In disability income insurance, however, the age factor can be more complex than it is in medical or long-term care insurance. While it is true that the chance of a disability, especially from illness, increases with age, there can be other, somewhat offsetting considerations. Younger persons are judged to have less *stability*, defined as permanence in personal, family, employment, and community relationships, than older persons. Underwriters associate lower stability with poorer claims experience. Older persons also have a shorter period of potential benefits because many disability income policies terminate by age 65, and they are often more likely to return to work sooner after a disability than a younger person. For underwriting disability coverage, age is a less important predictor of disability claims than occupation and income.

stability

Age-Rating Methods

The two common age-rating methods are attained age and issue age. A level (no-age) rate in which the same premium is charged for all age classes is not generally found in health insurance (except as required by law for medical expense policies in some states), but it is sometimes used in accident and travel policies. Insurers also impose limits on the ages at which they will offer health insurance coverage.

attained-age rates

Attained-Age Rates. Using *attained-age rates*, the insurer charges insureds the same premium at the same age for the same coverage without regard to when the insureds initially purchased a policy or how long they have maintained it. Premium increases, when they occur, apply as the insured ages, with the insured being charged the same premium the company charges all insureds at that increased age. The premium levels and their increases may be established in 5- or 10-year-range age bands or for each year of age.

Example 1: Jane purchased a major medical policy from her agent last year when she was 47.

The monthly premiums at that time for selected age categories were:

Age	Monthly Premium
45–49	$278
50–54	$347
55–59	$366
60–64	$384

This year, the company's premiums have increased and are:

Age	Monthly Premium
45–49	$305
50–54	$381
55–59	$402
60–64	$422

Jane will pay $305 to renew her policy, which is the monthly premium that a new applicant of age 48 also would pay.

Example 2: Using the premium rates listed in Example 1, if Jane had been 49 when she purchased her policy initially, the premium would still have been $278 per month. However, at renewal this year, her monthly premium would increase to $381, the premium now being charged to persons in the 50 to 54 age bracket.

Attained-age rates are more typical in medical expense insurance because they generally produce lower—and therefore more attractive—initial rates than the issue-age method. However, declining persistency as rates increase with age is a drawback of the attained-age method.

issue-age rates

Issue-Age Rates. *Issue-age rates*, also known as at-entry rates, charge the same premium to all insureds who initially purchase the same policy at the same age. In turn, future premium increases for these insureds also reflect their experience aggregated by their age when they initially purchased their policies.

Example: Bob purchased a long-term care insurance policy last year at age 56.

The annual premiums for a policy from his insurer for persons at selected age are:

Age	Monthly Premium
55	$1,668
56	$1,740
57	$1,812
58	$1,884
59	$1,996
60	$2,040

His insurer has never increased premiums, even though it could do so by class. When Bob renews his policy at age 57, his annual premium will remain at $1,740. However, a new applicant with the same insurer this year at age 57 would pay $1,812.

This method maintains persistency. Despite higher premiums at first, year-to-year rate increases are more restrained than under attained-age rates. Disability income and long-term care insurance policies most frequently use issue-age rates.

Age Limits. Although variations exist among insurance companies with respect to the age limits for which they will issue health insurance policies, these limits usually fall into similar patterns.

Medical expense insurance has a broad span of ages for policy issue, with coverage offered usually to persons ranging from birth up to age 65 and possibly longer. Under a family policy, unmarried children are eligible for coverage as dependents to a specified age, such as 19 or older if a full time student. Comprehensive medical expense polices are generally not offered to persons aged 65 and older, as these persons are normally eligible for

Medicare. Supplemental medical expense polices of various kinds are available at these older ages, however.

Very little disability income coverage is written below age 20 or in the 60 to 70 age range. Persons below age 20 lack sufficient stability and the age 60 and older market contains special risks and hazards for the insurers because it is a population with a much higher percentage of sickness-related disabilities. However, this may change as more older persons remain in the job market. The average age of the population is increasing, many Americans remain in the workplace longer, and the availability of the full Social Security retirement benefit now goes beyond age 65.

Variations also exist among insurance companies with respect to the age at which long-term care policies are available. At a minimum, a person between the ages of 40 and 75 is eligible for coverage from almost all insurance companies. Most companies also have an upper age in the range of 84 to 89, beyond which coverage is not issued. Restrictive policy provisions and very high premiums often accompany coverage written at age 85 or older when available.

Gender

Separate gender-based rates are quite common in the individual market for medical expense and disability income insurance. Prior to middle age, women tend to incur greater medical expenses than men. As middle age approaches, theses differences narrow. At older ages, men have poorer claims experience than women. For disability income insurance, premium rates have typically been higher for women than for men because of more frequent claims and poorer persistency, particularly in younger ages. However, antidiscrimination laws have encouraged the creation of unisex rates in some states that place both men and women in the same class for premium purposes for one or more forms of health insurance. As a rule, unisex rates are typical in long-term care insurance despite expected differences by gender in the use of long-term care services.

Geographic Area

The price and utilization of health care services vary significantly by state and region. In addition, urban areas are more expensive than rural areas. These differences are due to many factors, including the cost of living, availability of health care facilities and services, physician practice patterns, individual attitudes, and socioeconomic status. Although geographic area is not a major factor in disability income insurance, it directly affects the cost of most medical expense and long-term care policies.

For medical expense insurance, areas with similar medical expense and/or utilization levels are grouped into rate categories to reflect these differences. Depending on the type of medical expenses insurance, these rate categories may be broad enough to include several states or narrow enough to reflect differences by zip code groupings.

Example: Roger is a consulting engineer who lives in Pocatello, Idaho. He moves to San Francisco to better serve a major client with whom he obtains a significant 5-year contract. After the move, the premium for his comprehensive medical expense policy increases by 28 percent.

Benefits for facility and at-home care under long-term care policies are usually based on the cost of care or the anticipated cost of care where the applicant lives or expects to retire.

Tobacco Use versus Nonuse

The use of tobacco, including smoking cigarettes, cigars, or pipes, as well as chewing, poses a health hazard that is significant for all forms of health insurance. Therefore, some insurers have separate rates for tobacco users and nontobacco users to reflect the anticipated differences in claims and to encourage good health habits. For some insurers, this price differential may be 40 percent or more in some policies. Other insurers that do not have separate rates will often consider tobacco use when reaching a final underwriting decision on the applicant's acceptability for coverage.

Occupation

At the very least in all forms of health insurance, occupation serves as a proxy for such socioeconomic indicators as education, income, and lifestyle, which underwriters relate directly to an applicant's likelihood to file claims and persistency. For the most part, however, the relevance of an applicant's occupation to the underwriter depends on the form of health insurance for which the person is applying.

Medical Expense Insurance

For medical expense insurance, the underwriter is interested in occupations that have higher than average potential for illness or injury and attendant claim costs—costs that must be reflected in an insurer's rates.

Dangerous occupations, such as movie stunt persons or workers on oil derricks, or those with excessive claim experience usually are not insurable under individual medical expense policies.

Occupation is gaining importance as an underwriting factor because of the increase in self-employed individuals, who constitute a primary market for individual medical expense insurance. These individuals usually are not subject to workers' compensation laws, and the nature of their occupations may exhibit a wide spectrum of potential for medical expenses.

Finally, identifying occupation permits the insurer to inquire about the existence or availability of employment-based coverage that may signal either possible adverse selection or a duplicate coverage situation (discussed latcr).

Disability Income Insurance

Occupation plays a critical role in underwriting disability income insurance. Applicants with higher classifications receive a more favorable premium because they are judged to be less at risk for a disability and more likely to have shorter disabilities than persons classified in a lower occupation category. Experienced and conscientious agents can assist the underwriter greatly by accurately assigning the applicant to the proper occupation class.

Traditional Classes. Historically, occupations were classified only on the degree of their physical requirements and skill levels. Applicants with light physical requirements and mostly mental skills received a higher occupation classification than persons with more hazardous occupations and lower skill levels. Thus, a clerical worker received a higher occupation classification than a construction worker. Some occupations, however, remain uninsurable for individual disability income insurance because of the nature of the physical risk, such as jockeys. Others were deemed uninsurable because of instability, such as actors and bartenders.

More Refined Classes. Today, the trend in underwriting individual disability income insurance is to go beyond job hazard as insurers refine their methods of classifying occupations. Insurers are increasingly aware that an individual's level of responsibility in his or her occupation, stability in that occupation, income, age, and the desire to go to work are measures of occupation class that are just as important as the occupation's level of physical hazard.

The length of time an individual has been in his or her present employment is an important element in measuring stability. The longer an employee works in the same occupation, the more dependable the employee, the more favorable his or her work ethic, and the lower the expected morbidity. Thus, employees of longer tenure often receive a higher classification than those employed at a firm for a shorter time.

Business owners (including the self-employed) and managers, both in skilled trades and in professions, have a greater personal stake in the performance of their businesses than do their employees. Typically, they will push themselves to continue working despite physical problems, whereas employees, even though they are in the same work environment, are more likely to claim a disability when faced with similar problems. When disabled, business owners and managers are also more likely to return to work sooner than are employees. Thus, business owners and managers, because of their higher level of motivation, may be assigned a higher occupation class than employees. On the other hand, clerical employees may be in a lower occupation class than their managers with whom they may work directly because as a group they generate less favorable morbidity.

Insurers typically have four to eight classifications into which an applicant is initially classified by occupation. The insurer's claims experience is the primary criteria for assigning each occupation to the classification.

Example: One insurer has seven occupational classifications:

- Class 7 includes persons in certain occupations that have demonstrated the most favorable claims experience because of stability of employment and income, training, and experience. Examples that fall in this class include pharmacists and CPAs.
- Class 6 contains certain medical and managerial professionals that have had the most favorable claims experience. These include dentists and attorneys.
- Class 5 consists of other professionals whose claims experience has been less favorable than the two higher classes. These include psychologists and advertising account executives.
- Class 4 includes semi-professional occupations with office duties and some types of sales duties. These include opticians and executive secretaries.

- Class 3 consists of occupations that require more physical activities or have had less favorable experience than class 4. These include violin makers and locksmiths.
- Class 2 includes occupations for which light manual or skilled work is involved, but no unusual hazards exist. These include hairdressers and harbor masters.
- Class 1 includes blue-collar occupations requiring heavy manual duties or where there are accidental or environmental hazards. These include heavy equipment operators and drill press operators.

Several occupations may fall into more than one class. For example, most physicians are in class 6. However certain physicians are in class 5. These include anesthesiologists, obstetricians, and surgeons. Economists may fall into classes 4, 5, or 6 depending on the type of academic degree they hold. And veterinarians who treat small animals are in class 6, but those who treat bigger animals are in class 4.

There are also occupations for which the insurer will not write coverage. Some of these include actors, military personnel, and chimney sweeps.

As stated previously, the higher the classification, the lower the premium. In addition, persons in higher classifications are often able to have more favorable provisions in their policies, such as more liberal definitions of disability, shorter elimination periods, and longer benefit periods. However, the underwriting in each classification may lead to a person being moved to either a higher or lower classification, depending on a combination of such factors as ownership interest, age, income, and years in their current business.

Example: Lucia, an architectural engineer, is president and founder of a successful firm that builds and manages commercial properties. When she applies for disability income insurance, her agent assigns her initially to the insurer's highest occupation class by emphasizing her ownership interest as well as her executive and management level responsibilities. Additional information obtained in the underwriting process reveals, however, that Lucia is a hands-on manager and frequently visits her hard hat construction job sites, often in unfinished areas well above ground level.

Underwriters consulting on the application suggest that Lucia's on-the-job site activities would justify a reduction of two levels. However, the lead underwriter decides to reduce Lucia's occupation class by only one level below the top class because of her education, ownership interest, and high motivation level. The underwriter also notes the declining extent of her job site visits coincident with company growth and her increased delegation of responsibility. The offer of coverage notes that the insurer will reevaluate the occupation class reduction in 2 years.

Working at Home. Disability insurers have been reluctant to insure individuals working at home because the determination of when a person working at home is disabled is more difficult. In some cases, insurers will provide no coverage and in other situations they may limit the amount of benefits. Nevertheless, as the frequency of at-home work situations, including telecommuting, increases, this market grows.

As a result, insurers are becoming more likely to provide disability income coverage for at-home workers, but the underwriting is more intense and the benefits are less liberal. Underwriters review all of the following factors when reaching a decision on offering coverage to those who work at home:

- nature of the work
- duration of at-home employment
- part-time versus full-time workload
- income level and income stability
- relationship to a business located elsewhere

Long-Term Care Insurance

Generally, occupation is not an issue in underwriting long-term care insurance, although an underwriter might be interested in knowing much of the same information relating to occupational hazards and motivation that were discussed under medical expense and disability income insurance. However, the degree of interest is substantially less. The average applicant for individual long-term care coverage is age 60 or over. Consequently, the focus of the underwriter's attention is less on the potential for acute care expense and more on the likelihood of cognitive and physical impairments that would require dependency on other persons to conduct activities of daily living.

Income

Income is also a consideration in underwriting health insurance. Similar to occupation, its degree of importance differs depending on the form of coverage being applied for.

Medical Expense Insurance

While the applicant's income may be more significant in other forms of health insurance, it remains a concern in underwriting medical expense insurance. For example, an insurer would be concerned about issuing a hospital indemnity policy with a daily benefit that could quickly exceed the insured's income and potential hospital expenses. Often coverage is geared to the average semiprivate room rate in the applicant's geographic area to ensure adequate coverage. In addition, an underwriter might be concerned about fraudulent claims and a policy remaining in force if the premium represents a disproportionate share of an applicant's personal or family income.

Disability Income Insurance

For disability income insurance, as its name suggests, income is of primary importance; it is the insurable interest. Consequently, a major focus of disability underwriting is insurable income and how much of that income to insure. Only earned income is insurable and to avoid overinsurance, the amount to be insured is limited to a percentage of such income. The precise meaning of income and the percentages insurers will insure is covered in chapters 12 and 13.

Long-Term Care Insurance

For long-term care insurance, the concern about income relates to the personal value such coverage may have to the applicant and the applicant's ability to purchase coverage and to maintain it over the years, even in the event of premium increases. Chapter 17 discusses the importance of these aspects of income to long-term care insurance.

Duplicate Coverage

Duplicate coverage is an important factor that must be taken into account when underwriting all forms of individual health insurance; it can easily create an overinsurance situation in which an insured can profit from claims and therefore have an incentive to file them. Consequently, an insurer needs information about similar forms of insurance that a person requesting coverage may presently have in force or that he or she has applied for.

Medical Expense Insurance

In individual medical expense insurance, duplicate coverage is a special concern. There is usually no coordination between two individual (non–group) policies covering the same person that would limit total benefits paid by both policies to no more than the insured's incurred expenses. Often such coordination does not exist between an individual medical expense policy and an employer's medical benefit plan. As result, two major medical policies covering the same person might easily result in insurance payments in excess of the insured's incurred medical expenses. In general, companies decline to issue comprehensive self-only or family policies to applicants if duplicate coverage remains in effect through any group or other individual insurance source without the applicant's stated intention to terminate that coverage. If subsequent information confirms that the previous group or individual policy continues, the insurer retains the right to rescind its policy within the contestable period (2 years in most states).

Disability Income Insurance

The underwriter of disability income policies must also identify duplicate coverage as the discussion on income indicates. This effort is an important part of the disability income underwriting process and frequently involves additional investigation and questions of the applicant. The agent and underwriter must be knowledgeable about the array of programs that may provide income or other payments to the applicant in the event of a disability. Such programs include: Social Security disability income; workers' compensation; salary continuation; employer group disability; and even debt payment protection plans.

If other disability income sources would continue to exist after policy issue and if the agent had not done so already, the underwriter would reduce the benefits requested to take these sources into account. The total of all disability-related income amounts available to the applicant must be subtracted from the otherwise maximum amount allowed as a replacement ratio to determine how much room there is for the additional disability coverage being applied for. If the difference between the benefits under the coverage(s) being maintained and the company's determination of the insurable income amount leaves little or no room for additional coverage, the underwriter would have no choice but to decline the application.

Long-Term Care Insurance

As chapter 18 explains, the NAIC model legislation requires the insurer to obtain information about any long-term care insurance currently in force or in force during the prior 12 months. In addition, the applicant must state whether the new policy is intended to replace an existing policy. Even without the NAIC requirements, many underwriters would still want information about duplicate coverage because overinsurance provides an incentive for the insured to profit from the use of long-term care benefits.

Lifestyle Factors

Lifestyle factors are personal or living environment characteristics of an applicant's life that may have underwriting significance. Although they may be subjective in some cases, these factors can affect the premium an insured pays because of their potential to affect the frequency and severity of claims. Among these factors are marital status, living arrangements and activities, habits, moral hazard, and avocation.

Marital Status

Marital status can be an indicator of personal stability, which an underwriter views as an indicator of claims potential and persistency for any form of health insurance. Although it rarely generates premium rate differences for medical expense and disability income insurance, marital status frequently affects the premiums charged for long-term care insurance.

Some long-term care insurers grant a spousal discount, which may be 10 percent, to any applicant who lives with his or her spouse. Other insurers give a spousal discount, which may be 20 to 30 percent or more, only if they insure both spouses. Insurers offer spousal discounts because experience has shown that long-term care claims from married persons are less frequent and of shorter duration than claims from single or widowed persons. This favorable claim experience results because many married couples take care of each other for as long as possible before long-term care services are needed.

Insurers may also apply these discounts to siblings who live together and/or to unmarried couples who have committed relationships.

Living Arrangements and Activities

An underwriter of long-term care insurance may want to know if an applicant owns and lives in his or her own home. Such persons are less likely to move to a long-term care facility than persons who rent an apartment. The same is true of single or widowed persons who have support from family and friends. Evidence also indicates that a person who works, drives, has hobbies, or participates in social, recreational, and volunteer activities is less likely to need long-term care than a person who leads a much less active lifestyle.

Habits

Habits—or, more properly, bad habits or vices—also concern underwriters of all health insurance policies. Drug addiction usually results in refusal to issue coverage, but there are degrees of alcohol abuse. An underwriter would likely decline coverage for a person who has a serious problem with alcohol. In less severe circumstances, the underwriter may take action ranging from standard issue to an extra premium rating.

Moral Hazard

Moral hazard is the dishonest tendency that may increase the frequency and/or severity of a loss because insurance, including any form of individual health insurance, is present. Persons who present moral hazards are those who might be dishonest in their dealings with the insurer. The underwriter must approach the subject with an objective viewpoint, considering the type of job a person has and other lifestyle factors. Warning signs of moral hazard are unethical or questionable business practices, bankruptcies, criminal records, actual or attempted overinsurance, and excessive claims experience.

Avocation

An avocation is a hobby or other personal activity pursued for enjoyment rather than financial gain. If most of the population participates in an activity of similar hazard, such as driving an automobile, the cost of the extra hazard would be covered by the regular premium structure. However, if only a small percentage of the population actually participates, the underwriter must determine the increased exposure to danger. Some insurers require completion of a special questionnaire when there is evidence that an applicant engages in a specific hazardous avocation, such as scuba diving, hang gliding, mountain climbing, or motorcycle racing. From this questionnaire, an underwriter can determine whether the exposure to danger is minimal and can be safely ignored or whether the exposure is excessive.

Where permitted by law, the underwriter may decline coverage, although the usual remedy is an exclusion rider eliminating coverage for injury resulting from certain types of activities. In some cases, an extra premium may be used. Avocation is more of a concern in underwriting medical expense and disability income insurance than it is in long-term care insurance. Nevertheless, as the average age of those applying for long-term care insurance continues to decline and an increasing proportion of claims arise from insureds under age 65, some insurers are now asking about hazardous avocations.

Medical Condition

Medical condition is the most important single factor in underwriting individual medical expense, disability income, and long-term care insurance; it determines largely the basis on which insurance is offered or refused and, when coverage is offered, the premium to be charged. Underwriters evaluate the probable influence of an applicant's medical condition on future claims specific to the form of health insurance being applied for. Underwriters classify applicants according to the extent that their medical condition differs from that of unimpaired applicants.

For medical expense insurance, this evaluation considers the likelihood a medical condition involving acute illness would require future medical treatment, hospitalization, or a prolonged period of recovery.

For disability income insurance, medical condition is especially significant if it relates directly to the major causes of disability claims. Among such causes would be musculoskeletal deficiencies leading to back problems, knee problems, and arthritis, as well as psychiatric problems. For long-term care insurance, these same problems could develop into physical and cognitive impairments requiring dependency on others for the basic activities of daily living.

It is important to point out that while all underwriting requires a great deal of skill and judgment, long-term care insurance is a relatively new type of insurance, and many potential claims from existing policies have yet to occur. Therefore, the underwriter must use a greater degree of subjectivity and conservatism than is necessary for other types of health insurance for which decades of claim experience is available. As a result, significant variations exist, particularly among the underwriting standards of long-term care insurers with respect to the evaluation of medical condition.

The underwriter evaluates medical condition by reviewing the applicant's medical history, current physical status, and family information.

Medical History

Underwriters review histories of previous conditions to determine the

- possibility of recurrence
- effect on the applicant's general health
- complications that may develop at a later date
- normal progression of any impairment
- interaction of disease progression on future illnesses from an unrelated cause

Some prior diseases have a tendency to recur. An applicant with a history of digestive disorders is more likely to require hospitalization for those conditions in the future than someone who has never had them. Many previous acute disorders can be disregarded, however, if recovery has been prompt and complete and without evidence of any residual impairment. Examples include bone fractures and appendectomies.

Current Physical Status

In addition to medical history, current physical status also needs to be assessed. To do this, the underwriter evaluates

- evidence of current medical care and expense
- current medical conditions that need, or will shortly need, treatment
- physical conditions, such as high cholesterol level, that increase the likelihood of future illness

Sometimes a condition, such as diabetes, has current and future implications for health; it is likely to require ongoing care and may lead to disability and loss of independence. Similarly, excess weight and elevated blood pressure are considered indicators of future cardiovascular impairment with implications for the likely use of medical, disability income, and long-term care coverage.

Family Information

The importance of family information in health insurance underwriting is limited. In medical expense coverage, as previously stated, if the application requests coverage for eligible family members, the underwriter must have medical history and current physical status information on each family member. Some insurers also may require a statement verifying that coverage has been requested for eligible family members.

If family members are not part of the medical expense coverage being applied for, insurers may question the reasons for their omission because they may affect the risk of insuring the applicant. Thus, insurers may directly or implicitly seek to ascertain if family members have been diagnosed or are being tested or treated for a contagious disease, including acquired immunodeficiency syndrome (AIDS) or AIDS-related complex (ARC). However, the omission from proposed coverage may be accounted for by such reasons as other insurance or military service of a son or daughter.

morbidity

Insurers only rarely include questions on family history for underwriting medical expense insurance policies. Historically, *morbidity* (the incidence of sickness and disability) statistics have not shown family medical history to be important except in limited instances. Also, regulators and public policy makers may perceive the gathering of a family's medical history as an initial incursion into genetic information. However, family medical history is routinely the subject of life insurance applications. Diabetes or hemophilia, for example, may prompt additional tests or adverse action. To the extent that certain medical policies, such as critical illness and specified disease insurance, emulate life insurance by providing sizable lump-sum benefits, family history may be subject to underwriter inquiry.

Nevertheless, there is a noticeable increase in requests for family history information on some insurer's applications for long-term care insurance. Inquiries may ask about: the status of parents, if living or deceased; if deceased, at what age they died; and their history of dementia, stroke, vascular disease, and diabetes.

Underwriting Classes

Each insurer has one or more underwriting classes for health insurance. Some insurers have a single underwriting class; applicants are accepted at the company's standard rate structure, denied coverage, or subjected to additional underwriting evaluation to offer coverage on a basis other than applied for. Other insurers establish two or more classes, each with a different premium. In such cases, as explained later, the agent as the field underwriter often assigns the underwriting class (at least initially) when an application is submitted. In the underwriting process, the insurer may deny coverage at the initially assigned class, but offer such coverage at the higher premium requirement of another available class. Even with several underwriting classes, there are still applicants who will be unacceptable to the insurer.

When more than one underwriting class is available, the applicant's medical condition largely determines into which class he or she will fall. Other factors such as tobacco use and lifestyle can also affect the class assigned. For example, applicants in excellent health with no medical impairments who are tobacco nonusers may be insured in a preferred class with rates that are 85 percent of the insurer's standard rates. An underwriting class with a standard rate may apply to applicants of average health who may have minimal medical impairments. In addition, there may be one or more substandard underwriting classes for applicants who remain insurable but whose health is somewhat impaired by varying degrees of moderate medical conditions. Rates in substandard classes may range from 25 percent higher to as much as 125 to 200 percent of the standard rate. The extent of coverage and benefits selection in substandard classes are often restricted.

SOURCES OF INFORMATION

The underwriter must select those applicants who are within the insurer's range of acceptability, as determined by the insurer's underwriting objectives for types of policies issued and claims experience anticipated. In the process of classifying applicants to determine insurability, the underwriter relies on many sources of available information. These sources fall into the following categories:

- the application
- telephone interviews
- attending physician's statements
- inspection reports
- personal evaluations
- MIB Group, Inc.

Although these categories are typical, an underwriter may use other forms of communication, such as a requiring that the applicant complete a supplemental information request, to determine insurability. The extent to which the underwriter uses any source of information beyond that contained on a properly completed application varies within companies by form of health insurance and geographic area, the extent of the potential loss, and company experience. Thus, for example, a dental policy with a maximum $1,000 annual benefit requires a much different (lower) level of underwriting information than a disability income policy with a 60 percent replacement ratio for a person with annual net income of $200,000. An application for a catastrophic major medical policy with a $20,000 deductible by a 30-year-old might require a review of only the most significant health history. On the other hand, an application from a 50-year-old for a comprehensive major medical policy with a $250 deductible and a $2,000 out-of-pocket limit with a $100,000 accidental death rider would require more detailed inquiry and scrutiny.

The spectrum of information sources accessed also depends on a company's satisfaction with the responses to routine questions contained in the application. Indeed, based on their experience with certain products and in certain areas of the country, for some products a company may rely exclusively on the information contained in the application.

Nevertheless, in addition to the application and the agent's statement that accompanies it, the telephone interview and attending physician's statements remain routine information sources for underwriters. Other sources, such as inspection reports, personal evaluations, and the use of MIB, Inc., are enlisted selectively to resolve questions that arise from the application and routine information sources. To a large extent, these information sources are common to all forms of health insurance. However, the discussion points out unique product-specific information sources, as well as the relevance of common information sources to specific forms of health insurance.

The Application

The application is a legal document because it becomes a part of the contract of insurance when issued; the application must be approved by the various state jurisdictions before it can be used. The application is also the basis for the underwriter's decision to provide the requested coverage, to modify it, to try to obtain more information, or to reject the application entirely. When completed properly, the application represents a bridge between the field agent and the home office underwriter and between the applicant and the company. When incomplete or inaccurate, it results in the underwriting process ceasing or being delayed before coverage is approved.

After the policy is issued, the application may become the basis for action by the claims department. For example, claims for illness or disability shortly after the policy becomes effective could prompt a review of the statements on the application. If an insurer determines before the end of the contestable period that there was a false statement or incomplete disclosure of material information on the application, the insurer may reject a claim and rescind the contract. Therefore, the application requires careful drafting to elicit truthful and complete answers from the applicant and to ensure that the agent's recording of all information is accurate.

The agent is a vital link in the application completion and submission process. Thus, the agent's care in completing the application, skill and training in developing correct information, and reputation in the home office (based upon prior reliability) all come together in determining the confidence the home office places in the information on a particular application.

The format of the application and the depth and direction of its questions vary by insurer and by its specific product use. If the application is to be used with only one form of health insurance, then the questions elicit only the information pertinent to underwriting that form of coverage. However, if the application allows the applicant to select other types of insurance such as life and/or supplemental accident insurance, then the questions meet the underwriting information needs of these other types of insurance as well. The application and the application process are discussed under the headings of qualifying the applicant and information sought in the following areas:

- personal information
- other insurance
- coverage and benefit selection
- mode of premium payment
- acknowledgements and authorizations
- financial and occupational information
- medical and other health-related information
- agent's statement (certifying completeness of the information)

These areas may not constitute separately titled sections in an application, but they represent the information content of an application which may be spread throughout its various sections.

Qualifying an Applicant

The application is fundamentally a form, but it is more significantly the beginning of the underwriting process. Professional health insurance agents are not simply order takers who accept an application, no matter how complete and truthful, from anyone wishing to purchase insurance. Rather, they are field underwriters who take applications only from candidates who are within the broad range of acceptability established by the insurance companies that they represent. Agents, therefore, must qualify the applicants to whom they are selling insurance. To accept applications from persons who are clearly outside the insurance company's range of acceptability is unfair to the applicant who will be denied coverage and an unnecessary expense to the insurance company that is being asked to evaluate an application for no purpose.

Insurance companies assist agents to qualify candidates by providing them with an underwriting guide for each health insurance product that the agent is authorized to sell. These guides list medical conditions for which the insurer requests the agent not to submit an application as well as conditions that are generally acceptable to the insurer, frequently with the applicable rating class within which they may be acceptable. Medications associated with unacceptable and acceptable conditions are similarly listed. The underwriting guide also often states that multiple medical conditions may affect the applicant's acceptability or the rating class in which the applicant might be placed. In such cases, the guide typically suggests that the agent contact the insurance company's underwriting department before submitting an application.

For all forms of health insurance, then, if the agent becomes aware when taking the application (either by observation, or through prior knowledge of the client) that the applicant is outside the company's range of acceptability, the agent should decline to complete or submit the application. In addition, disability income insurance through the use of preliminary applications and long-term care insurance through the use of prequalification questions and personal worksheets build prerequisites directly into the application process.

Preliminary Applications. An agent completing a disability income insurance application may choose instead to complete and submit a preliminary or trial application. The underwriter may examine this form briefly to determine whether there is a possibility of acceptance for coverage, thereby deferring the expense of completing all underwriting requirements until the possibility of an offer of coverage is confirmed. Usually, a trial application is used with health-impaired applicants or with persons in hazardous occupations or avocations. In these situations, the agent accepts no premium payment and provides no receipt.

Prequalification Questions and Personal Worksheets. Prospects wishing to complete an application for long-term care insurance are qualified using prequalification questions and personal worksheets.

When placed into the application itself, prequalification questions, sometimes known as preapplication screens, are usually close to the beginning of the form. Most applications contain a series of between four and 10 questions designed to prequalify applicants for coverage. If an applicant answers "yes" to any of these questions, the applicant is not eligible for coverage from that insurer. In these cases, the agent and, indeed, the applicant are often advised not to submit an application. At a minimum, most insurers will ask questions like the following. (The list will be much longer for insurers that have stringent underwriting standards.)

- Do you currently reside in, or has a health professional advised you to enter, a nursing home or any type of assisted living facility?

- Are you currently receiving home care services or attending adult day care?
- Do you currently require the assistance or supervision of another person with activities such as bathing, dressing, eating, getting in or out of a bed or chair, using the toilet, or maintaining continence?
- Do you use any medical devices, aids, or treatments such as a motorized scooter, wheelchair, walker, multi-prong cane, hospital bed, dialysis, oxygen, or stair lift?
- Have you ever been diagnosed or treated for Alzheimer's disease, dementia, senility, any type of organic brain disorder, or Parkinson's disease?
- Have you ever been diagnosed with or tested positive for acquired immunodeficiency syndrome (AIDS), AIDS-related complex (ARC), or human immunodeficiency virus (HIV)?
- Because of mental retardation, do you currently require or receive human help or supervision with activities such as living independently, preparing meals, taking medications, using transportation, shopping, walking, or making decisions about money?

By state law, an applicant (with the agent's assistance) must complete a personal worksheet which asks questions about the applicant's income and assets to help the applicant and company determine if the applicant should purchase coverage. If the applicant fails to meet the insurer's guidelines, because, for example, the premium is greater than 7 percent of income and assets are less than $30,000, the agent may decline to accept the application for long-term care insurance.

Personal Information

Personal information inquiries serve primarily to identify the applicant and provide basic information such as age, gender, birth date, address, phone number, Social Security number, and marital status. If not asked for elsewhere, the applicant may also be asked to record height and weight, and possibly changes to those measurements over time. Applications for a medical expense policy require similar personal information on a spouse and any dependents to be covered under the policy. An application for long-term care insurance also asks whether a spouse or domestic partner or other household member has coverage or is applying for coverage with the same insurance company as the applicant. If so, that person is identified as well.

Other Insurance

For the reasons cited previously, applications for all forms of health insurance inquire about the existence of other forms of health insurance, whether group or individual, that may exist or are being applied for. Insurers also inquire about the applicant's intent to maintain or terminate existing coverage and if coverage being applied for is intended to replace other coverage. There are several reasons for these inquiries.

First, insurers want applicants to be properly insured, but not overinsured because overinsurance may encourage claims. Insurers typically do not issue coverage if duplicate coverage is in force, unless the applicant indicates that the other coverage will terminate. Indeed, if duplicate coverage continues after the policy being applied for takes effect, some companies will rescind the policy or reduce benefits.

Second, if the new coverage is substituting for existing coverage, they also do not wish to have an applicant prematurely cancel coverage before the coverage applied for becomes effective.

Third, insurers wish to determine if another insurer (1) denied the applicant any form of coverage; (2) offered coverage on a basis other than what was applied for; or (3) terminated coverage (for fraud or nonpayment of premiums, for example).

In the case of medical expense insurance, HIPAA and state laws may require that prior coverage for qualified individuals results in a guaranteed issue of coverage and/or offsets in whole or in part a preexisting-conditions exclusion period.

As might be expected, disability income insurance has the most extensive inquiries on existing and pending insurance, in particular with respect to other forms of disability income coverage and what percent of an applicant's income the other coverage already represents.

Coverage and Benefit Selection

The coverage and benefit components of an application are unique to each form of health insurance. The following listings display the illustrative health insurance coverage and benefit areas by product from which applicants may select available options. Subsequent chapters explain many of these terms. Each form of health insurance also may include options for other types of insurance, such as life and supplemental accident coverage.

Individual Medical Expense

- annual deductible amounts
- copayments, coinsurance, and percentage participation levels
- annual out-of pocket maximums (for selected services and for all covered services)

- lifetime maximum
- optional medical coverage riders (for example, maternity care, prescription drugs)

Disability Income

- term of coverage (5 years, age 65, lifetime)
- elimination period (30-day, 90-day, 180-day)
- benefit amount (from $100 to $5,000 per month in $100 units)

Long-Term Care

- facility-only coverage (nursing home, assisted living facility, adult day care) or comprehensive coverage (home care as well as all levels of facility coverage)
- benefit amount (daily, weekly, or monthly amount at minimum and maximum levels, often with a separate choice of home care benefit level when coverage is comprehensive)
- benefit period (3 years, 5 years, 7 years, or lifetime)
- elimination period (20/30/60/90 days)
- nonforfeiture option
- return of premiums
- joint benefit options (if spouse or partner have policy with the same company)

Of the three forms of health insurance, long-term care presents an applicant with the most extensive array of coverage and benefit choices. Because of the complexity of these choices, some insurance companies suggest alternative combinations of choices using packaged plan options, while maintaining the applicant's ability to further customize a plan.

Mode of Premium Payment

mode of premium payment

Mode of premium payment is the frequency of premium payment selected by the applicant from the several options that an insurer may offer. Generally, for all forms of heath insurance, an applicant may select a mode of payment that is annual, semiannual, quarterly, or monthly, with annual payment representing the lowest total premium amount for a 12-month period. Regardless of the mode, premiums are typically paid as long as a policy is in force. However, long-term care insurance policies often allow accelerated premium payments (described in chapter 19).

Modal factors are used to determine the payment amount when premiums are paid more than once a year. For example, one insurer's modal factor (identical to that of many other insurers) for semiannual payments is 0.52. This means that semiannual payments of $520 are required if the policyowner elects this mode of payment rather than a single annual premium of $1,000. The result is that the policyowner pays an additional premium of $40 to postpone payment of $500 for 6 months—an effective interest rate of 16.7 percent.[1] The modal rates for quarterly and monthly payments are 0.27 and 0.09, respectively. These result in quarterly payments of $270 and monthly payments of $90. In either case, the policyowner is paying $80 per year to make premium payments less than annually.

As a result, a policyowner should realize the high cost of paying premiums more than once a year. If resources are available, a single annual payment is financially prudent unless the policyowner is earning a significant return on his or her investments.

When selecting the mode of payment, the applicant also designates the method of payment, which usually includes direct billing (when the mode of payment is quarterly, semiannually, or annually) or automatic bank draft withdrawal (when the mode of payment is monthly or quarterly). Usually an initial premium may be paid by credit card.

Acknowledgements and Authorizations

Although the agent usually asks the questions and fills in the answers on the application, the applicant must sign the form. The applicant's signature is required in one or more areas that may be described as acknowledgments and authorizations. The applicant's signature follows a list of acknowledgements typically signifying agreement that

- responses provided in the application are complete and true and are the basis on which insurance is to be issued
- the terms of the contract, conditions under which coverage is to be issued, and policy limits (including preexisting-conditions limitations) are understood and accepted
- if specified, similar coverage currently in force must be terminated under penalty of recision
- the insurance being applied for is in force only upon issuance by the company, receipt and acceptance by the applicant, and payment of the first premium

Authorizations require the applicant's signature as well. Authorizations permit the underwriter to obtain required information from outside sources to the extent required by responses in the application. Specifically, the applicant authorizes a blanket release of information from health care providers, other insurance companies, and other organizations that have relevant personal and medical information. The applicant is notified of and agrees to a follow-up telephone interview, a face-to-face assessment, possible physical examination, investigative report, and the use of the MIB information exchange services. These authorizations usually have an effective time limit, such as 24 or 30 months from the date the application is signed. An authorization to debit the premiums from the applicant's account is also required.

Financial and Occupation Information

Applications for all forms of heath insurance are likely to request financial and occupation information. In the case of medical expense insurance, that request is minimal. As previously explained, an application for long-term care insurance asks for extensive financial information using a personal worksheet. The worksheet, which can be part of the application itself, helps to understand whether or not the applicant has sufficient income and assets to make the purchase of long-term care insurance an appropriate choice.

Disability income insurance, however, has the most extensive application sections on financial and occupation information, typically requiring responses to detailed questions in the following categories:

- employment and occupation
- business ownership interest
- nature and extent of occupational duties and responsibilities
- additional employment and occupations, if any
- full-time versus part-time occupation status
- length of time continuously at work and any interruptions due to sickness or injury
- income and net worth
- personal or business bankruptcy filings

Medical and Other Health-Related Information

Applications for medical expense, disability income, and long-term care insurance ask remarkably similar questions about an applicant's medical history and current physical status, including medications taken. They all inquire about diagnoses, disorders, treatments, recommendations for treatment, and advice sought for a list of medical conditions covering every bodily system (usually with gender specificity) as well as psychiatric and substance abuse conditions. The look-back period for these conditions may range from the last 2, 5, 7, or 10 years to any time in the applicants life. The relevant period for a specific condition varies by company, the form of insurance, and, most importantly, the nature of the condition itself. Any positive response requires additional information on treatment, dates of care, and contact information for health professionals or institutions that provided or are providing care.

In this area, the application may ask for several other types of information with health-related implications. The following are typical of these inquiries, which largely relate to lifestyle:

- Select from the levels indicated in the following list the level that best represents your use of tobacco, alcohol, and recreational drugs.
- From the following list, identify the recreational activities, sports, and hobbies in which you are involved.
- What is your height and weight? Has there been a change? If so, by how much?

Not surprisingly, disability income and long-term care insurance applications have specific questions on income from any source received or denied because of a disability or injury. Disability income application questions may also extend to driving and criminal records.

To reveal a higher-than-average need for long-term care in the future, long-term care applications contain specific questions on:

- memory loss or forgetfulness
- use of medical equipment such as a cane, brace, crutches, or a wheelchair
- assistance required for ordinary daily activities, such as shopping, managing finances, meal preparation, transportation, laundry, or taking medications
- use of a nursing home, adult day care center, assisted living facility, any other senior care facility, home care services, or hospital in the past 2 years

Agent's Statement

Most insurers devote space on their applications for the agent to supply additional information and to witness the applicant's completion and signing of the form. The questions in the agent's statement may include the following:

- Did you personally interview the applicant and witness his or her signature?
- Do you certify that all information presented by the applicant has been truly, accurately, and completely recorded?

- Do you certify that to the best of your knowledge there is no other medical information about the applicant than that provided in the application?
- Did you review the applicant's current health insurance coverage and determine that the proposed insurance is appropriate for the applicant's needs?

State regulations may require the agent to list any other health insurance policies he or she has sold to the applicant within the last 5 years, whether or not the policies are in force.

Applications for long-term care insurance would likely ask the following specific questions of the agent who is in a position to make a face-to-face assessment:

- Did you observe any physical or mental impairment with respect to memory, walking, or speaking? If so, explain.
- Did you observe any tremor? If so, explain.

Companies also encourage agents to identify and record any other information that could have underwriting significance. Extra efforts in these areas bolster the home office underwriter's confidence in the agent and facilitate the approval of current and future applications.

Telephone Interviews

After a health insurance application is received in the home office, the proposed insured is often contacted for a telephone interview, also know as a personal health interview, which typically takes 30 minutes or less. Although some companies may contract with specialized agencies to conduct telephone interviews as their authorized agents, most companies use their own personnel, who are likely to be registered nurses or other persons with qualifications as health care professionals.

For all forms of health insurance, telephone interviews provide an independent verification of responses on the application and a chance to obtain additional information, especially on the applicant's medical conditions and medications. Also, they afford an opportunity to clarify information both reported on the application and/or obtained subsequently from other sources, such as medical record information through an attending physician's statement. Increasingly, the telephone interview is integrated with the application; the application solicits a defined but general level of information, leaving required, specific inquiries to the telephone interview. When this is the case, the interview will last longer than usual.

Telephone interviews are very commonly conducted when underwriting disability income and long-term care insurance because of their unique underwriting requirements in addition to medical condition and medication information. Indeed, the application form for these coverages may explicitly advise the applicants of the likelihood of a telephone interview and, when requesting contact information, inquire about the best time to call.

For disability income insurance, telephone interviews are a reliable method of obtaining the detailed income and occupation information that may be absent from the completed application, but required to make the proper underwriting decision. These interviews focus on accurate explanations of income and occupation. They review length of employment, specific duties, job risks, and any other special circumstances. The interviewer may also inquire about a variety of additional information concerning employment stability and avocation.

In underwriting long-term care insurance, especially for applicants in certain age categories, telephone interviews are also used to detect the presence and extent of early cognitive loss. With a few basic questions, a properly trained interviewer can evaluate an applicant's memory, ability to understand questions, and sense of time and place. The interviewer also inquires about the applicant's ability to function independently in everyday tasks like bathing and dressing.

Attending Physician's Statements

The application, or any other source of underwriting information, may disclose a serious or questionable medical condition. In that case, underwriters of every form of health insurance routinely request an attending physician's statement covering the applicant's medical condition over the past 3 or 5 years or longer. The term *attending physician's statement (APS)* as used here may be actual medical records from the applicant's primary care physician, other physicians (for example, specialists), and/or hospitals that have treated the applicant for conditions bearing on underwriting. Alternatively, an APS may be a written explanation or statement from these health care providers regarding the history or significance of a specific condition. The statement may also ask the physician or other provider to supply information about dates of treatment, length of treatment, tests ordered, medications prescribed, and the degree of recovery or control achieved over medical conditions. Health care providers charge for and insurers routinely pay for an APS.

attending physician's statement (APS)

Attending physician's statements are the best source of information for an accurate description of an applicant's medical condition; they provide insight into the nature and severity of a medical condition and may reveal to the underwriter conditions undisclosed on the application. At the same time, these statements may allow the underwriter to determine that the applicant meets the insurance company's underwriting guidelines because a health condition that otherwise would cause coverage to be declined is stable and presents no insurability problem.

Although underwriters of all three forms of health insurance routinely request an APS, the broader use of multiple or substandard underwriting classes heightens the need for this type of information in underwriting disability income and long-term care insurance policies.

Inspection Reports

inspection report

An *inspection report* is completed by an independent agency that specializes in insurance investigations. These reports are valuable not just for gathering factual data but also for identifying a prospect's poor habits or risk of moral hazard through such sources as employers, neighbors, or associates. The report, which usually is written, covers such pertinent factors as occupation, financial status, and health history. Credit reports and driving records may also be obtained.

Although used infrequently for medical expense and long-term care insurance, inspection reports can be an important source of underwriting information when needed. These reports are more commonly used, however, when underwriting a disability income policy, especially to verify income and occupation information. Nevertheless, because companies have found that properly trained telephone specialists can elicit a large amount of good quality underwriting information, inspection reports for disability income insurance are now largely limited to applications for high benefit amounts.

Personal Evaluations

In a personal evaluation, a representative of the insurer obtains medical and related information directly from the insurance applicant through an in-person appraisal. These evaluations, which may be summarized as either medical examinations or face-to-face assessments, are conducted by qualified professionals and usually involve various types of tests. Like other sources of information, although they may be used by most insurers, personal evaluations are conducted selectively based usually on applicant circumstances that warrant the additional information, such as specified medical condition(s), age, or benefit levels above certain amounts. Personal evaluations may be conducted in place of or as supplements to other information sources.

Medical Examinations

A medical examination is an in-person physical evaluation that is performed by a physician or paramedical personnel to determine or verify the applicant's medical condition. Regardless of who conducts the examination, various tests are typically required and commonly include blood tests, urinalysis, drug screening, and X-rays. Vital capacity (lung) tests and electrocardiograms may be required as well. The examination takes less than an hour and usually is conducted in a doctor's office if performed by a physician or in the applicant's home or office if performed by paramedical personnel. Medical examinations in health insurance are conducted most frequently for disability income insurance.

Insurers often prefer paramedical personnel to do the examination rather than physicians because of the speed and ease with which they are arranged and conducted as well as the considerable volume of medical information they provide to the home-office underwriter at a modest cost. Paramedical personnel also tend to give more detailed information without making judgments as to its importance. Thus, examinations are conducted by paramedical personnel in the majority of instances in which medical examinations are required, except for those cases that require the specific skills of a physician. For example, in some instances, uncertain or unfavorable results of the paramedical examination or the need for a greater level of clinical detail on a medical condition may prompt a request for an assessment by a physician. An applicant is more likely to discuss previous medical history with a physician than with an agent or a paramedical professional.

Face-to-Face Assessments

Face-to-face assessment is a term that usually describes an evaluation of applicants for long-term care insurance. This type of assessment conducted by paramedical personnel, usually in the applicant's home, focuses on the applicant's cognitive and functional abilities. Memory tests are administered and the ability to independently perform routine tasks such as bathing, dressing, preparing meals, and paying bills is noted. In some ways, this assessment is similar to a medical examination described above, although no blood test or urine analysis is required. However, the status of medical conditions and required medications are reviewed and simple screenings such as measurement of blood pressure, weight, and height may be conducted.

Face-to-face assessments not only serve to identify applicants who are unacceptable because they are likely to suffer cognitive or functional loss, but also may allow coverage to be offered to some applicants who have experienced a stroke, multiple medical conditions, or joint replacement. These applicants remain insurable if their functional loss is limited and stable.

MIB Group, Inc.

For many health insurance companies, MIB Group, Inc., (often referred to as MIB) is an important resource when underwriting medical, disability income, and long-term care insurance. *MIB* is a not-for-profit association of over 500 U. S. and Canadian insurance companies that serves as a repository of information on persons who apply for life and health insurance and file certain claims. MIB's purpose, much like that of a credit bureau for lenders, is the protection of insurers, and ultimately their policyowners, from losses by facilitating the detection and deterrence of fraud by those who may omit or try to conceal facts essential to proper insurance underwriting.

MIB

MIB's databases consist of information submitted by its member companies on persons who complete insurance applications or file certain claims. These persons sign authorizations that allow insurers to contribute their information to MIB's databases and to obtain reports on them using any information already on record with MIB. A report from a search of an MIB database is only one step that an insurer might use in the underwriting process. The insurer who receives an MIB search report compares the results with information already received on the application and from other sources. If the report is not consistent, the insurer must seek further information about the applicant. An insurance company may not make an adverse decision on an application based solely on an MIB report; the company must verify the information with the applicant or another information source.

MIB is largest insurer-sponsored organization that serves as a medical-related data resource for the insurance industry. However, there are other independent organizations that now provide similar services as part of a broader portfolio that may include risk management and investigation services to the legal, clinical, and business communities, including the insurance industry. MIB, as well as these independent companies, must comply with federal legislation dealing with credit reporting and privacy. Insurers must also comply with federal privacy legislation as well as state privacy requirements based on the NAIC Insurance Information and Privacy Protection Model Act.

MIB maintains three databases, all of which are helpful to underwriters of medical expense, disability income, and long-term care insurance: Underwriting Services, Disability Income Record Service (DIRS), and Health Claims Index (HCI).

Underwriting Services

The underwriting services database maintains a coded list of more than 200 medical conditions and/or test results that are of underwriting significance. Conditions commonly reported include height and weight, blood pressure, EKG readings, and X-ray results. Submitted information does not indicate what action a reporting member company took, nor does it indicate the type or amount of insurance applied for or issued. The MIB Underwriting Services database provides three basic reporting services: Checking Service, Follow-Up Service, and Insurance Activity Index.

- Checking Service allows members to compare the applicant-supplied information against information in the MIB database.
- Follow-Up Service provides a company with any future information about an individual reported to MIB during the 2-year contestable period. This service alerts companies to nondisclosure of conditions that if known at the time of the original application would have caused the insurer to rate the original application differently or to decline it.
- The Insurance Activity Index alerts the company to applicants who might be applying for life, health, disability income, critical illness, and/or long-term care policies with multiple companies and informs the insurer of the purpose of earlier searches.

DIRS

DIRS is a shared database that helps avoid overinsurance by individuals applying for disability income policies. Reports from the database provide information on the amount of both applied-for and in-force insurance and identify the company or companies that submitted the information. DIRS subscribers may contact one another when an application for disability income insurance has been made. Disability insurers typically use DIRS and the underwriting services database simultaneously when processing an application for disability income insurance in order to obtain medical underwriting and overinsurance information.

HCI

HCI is a shared disability income claims database that alerts claims professionals to the filing of multiple claims. It also provides a 2-year follow-up to all new claims reported, and thus helps to detect overinsurance, speculation, fraud, and abuse at the time of claim.

FINAL UNDERWRITING ACTION

Underwriting information is collected until the underwriter determines that there is enough information to make a final decision. This process may require anywhere from several days to several weeks to complete because the underwriter may have to obtain and review information from one or more of the sources just discussed in addition to the information provided on a properly completed application. For example, physicians may not view the completion of an attending physician's statement for an applicant as a high-priority item. As a result, a wait of 30 days or more to receive an underwriting decision is not unusual and is not necessarily an indicator that coverage will be declined. In the meantime, however, the insurer should acknowledge receipt of the application to the applicant and the agent and explain, at least generally, the requirements remaining before coverage is issued.

The final underwriting decision may be standard issue (issue exactly as applied for), modified issue (issue on an other-than-applied-for basis), or declined. In the event coverage is declined, well-informed agents are able to assist clients who are difficult to insure.

There are also situations in which a decision is suspended. The suspension may simply be a postponement of the decision when an applicant currently has a medical condition from which he or she is expected to recover or at least achieve a status that is stable, controllable, and insurable. In that case, the insurer will identify a time period after which the applicant may reapply for coverage. In other cases, a suspension occurs because insufficient or incomplete information is received. After a period of time, such files are closed.

Standard Issue

standard issue

For all forms of health insurance, *standard issue*, the approval of the insurance coverage as applied for, is the usual underwriting decision. Over 62 percent of persons submitting completed applications for comprehensive medical expense policies are offered standard issue coverage.[2] Between 55 to 70 percent of applications for disability income insurance are approved as standard issue.[3] Over 80 percent of applicants for long-term care insurance receive offers of coverage, most at standard or preferred rates.[4]

Modified Issue

modified issue

Modified issue or modified underwriting approval is perhaps the most difficult aspect of health insurance underwriting. It means that the insurer is offering coverage on a basis other than what was applied for because the applicant does not satisfy the underwriting criteria for standard issue coverage. The modification may be an extra premium, a change in benefits, an exclusion rider, or some combination of these approaches. Approximately 23 percent of applicants for medical expense insurance who receive an offer of coverage receive that offer on a modified issue basis.[5] The level of modified issue offers is comparable for disability income insurance applicants.[6] The level of applications for long-term care insurance approved as modified issue is less than 10 percent.[7]

The goal of modified issue underwriting is to achieve the same loss ratio on this type of business overall that the company experiences on its standard issue business. As a result, some applicants, largely those with prior medical histories or conditions, will require underwriting modification to the coverage they applied for (mostly through increased premium), based on the anticipated aggregate experience of all applicants (not the individual applicant) with similar impairments.

Extra Premiums

Some conditions, such as nervous disorders, are too broad in scope and too difficult to define to be covered adequately by excluding them using a rider, as a subsequent section explains. Many other conditions, such as obesity, hypertension, or diabetes, have too many complications that would have to be excluded. For such conditions, an exclusion rider would be either too broad to protect the insured or too narrow to protect the insurer. One answer to this dilemma is to give the policyowner full protection through use of the extra-premium approach. Payment of an additional premium that grants the insured full coverage usually is more acceptable to the applicant than an exclusion. Consequently, insurers generally prefer to use extra premiums rather than exclusion riders for modifying coverage. Over the years, with increasing underwriting sophistication of all forms of health insurance, the use of additional premiums, has become the typical method for modified issue coverage.

If an insurer offers more than one underwriting class and the applicant's condition is only mild, the extra premium may be obtained by simply reclassifying the applicant to a class with a higher premium. Likewise, in disability income insurance, the issue of concern to the underwriter can be resolved by placing the applicant in a lower occupation class.

Conditions that are insurable but nevertheless of concern to an underwriter usually have more than a mild degree of severity. Consequently, the underwriter, regardless of the number of rating classes an insurer may have, typically places applicants with these more significant conditions in a special rating or substandard class in which the extra premium is expressed as a percentage above the standard premium. The substandard class premium usually ranges from 25 to no more than 100 percent above the standard premium, although some insurers may allow even higher rates.

Example 1: Gilbert has high cholesterol and an enlarged, but nontumorous, prostate. Both conditions are being managed with prescription medications when he applies for medical expense insurance. Gilbert receives an offer of coverage at a premium that is 25 percent above the standard rate. Because his policy covers prescription drugs, the insurer also limits Gilbert to a policy with no less than a $2,000 deductible.

Example 2: Camrod has a bad driving record. When he applies for disability income insurance, he receives an offer with a premium that is 20 percent higher than the standard premium.

Example 3: Gordon has hypertension (abnormally high blood pressure) that is controlled through medication. When he applies for long-term care insurance, he receives an offer of coverage that places him in an underwriting class with a premium that is 15 percent above the standard rate.

Change of Benefits

Another method of modification is to change the benefits to something other than what the applicant requested. Change-of-benefit modifications are often used when some question exists about the applicant's overall acceptability for standard coverage. Sometimes, benefit modifications occur in conjunction with extra premiums or exclusion riders. Such modifications may entail a larger deductible on a major medical expense policy, a longer waiting period for benefits under a disability income policy, or facility-only coverage rather than a comprehensive coverage in a long-term care policy. Alternatively, the long-term care insurer might insist on a longer elimination period, lower daily benefit, or reduced maximum benefit. Such changes may be coupled with a higher premium.

Example 1: Holly goes skydiving frequently as a member of an active club. When she applied for disability income insurance, the company offered coverage with a full exclusion for any loss resulting from skydiving. Because she has been pursuing her avocation safely over as number of years and was recognized as quite skilled, Guy Wisely, her agent, suggests that she apply to another insurer, where she finds that she can obtain coverage without the exclusion for an additional premium of 30 percent and an elimination period of 180 days applicable to disabilitics arising from her avocation instead of the 60-day waiting period applicable to all other disabilities covered by the policy.

Example 2: After an operation for a serious melanoma 5 years ago, Bruno finds that he is rejected for long-term care insurance because the company to which he applied requires a 7-year period without recurrence before it considers insuring persons with such conditions. However, his agent, Gloria Cleverly, directs him to another insurer which considers someone in Bruno's situation as insurable, but impaired. The company places Bruno in an impaired risk class with a premium that is 25 percent above the standard premium and benefits limited to facility-only care.

Exclusion Riders

exclusion rider

Exclusion riders (also called waivers) are a traditional means of issuing coverage to persons who would otherwise have to be declined. Today, however, an exclusion rider is the least used method of modified issue coverage for all forms of health insurance. As the following examples indicate, such a rider may require a full or only a limited-period exclusion. The full exclusion eliminates the payment of any claim resulting from a particular medical problem (such as a back disorder) or an unusually hazardous occupation or avocation (such as automobile racing). The rider may be worded to exclude coverage for only a specific disorder, or it may exclude an entire system or bodily area. The actual wording is determined by the nature and severity of the applicant's medical history or impairment as well as by the insurer's underwriting philosophy. Although exclusion riders generally eliminate all coverage for the condition named in the rider, some insurers use a limited-period exclusion that may be long or short depending on the condition. A limited period exclusion may be used in conjunction with an extra premium and/or a change in benefits.

Example 1: Clarice noted her chronic neck problem on her application for medical expense insurance. After reviewing her medical record, the insurance company's offer of coverage contained the following statement:

> "This contract excludes coverage for any expense incurred or care required due to or resulting from a condition of the cervical spine."

Clarice has an offer of coverage with a full exclusion rider.

Example 2: Rocco has a history of kidney stones that pass without the need for surgery. When he reports this problem on his application for disability income insurance, he receives an offer of coverage with the following statement:

> "This contract excludes coverage for any loss due to kidney stones for the first 180 days of a disability with benefits thereafter limited to 2 years."

Rocco has received an offer of coverage with both a limited-period exclusion and a benefit modification.

Example 3: Rush has a chronic peptic ulcer. When he applies for disability income coverage, he receives an offer of coverage that excludes "any loss from a disease or disorder of the stomach or digestive system." Ginger Smartly, his agent, tells Rush that the company has applied an exclusion rider for an entire bodily system. She suggests he apply for coverage to another company she represents known for its less restrictive exclusion riders. Rush subsequently receives a limited exclusion rider from that company that narrows the exclusion to losses resulting from ulcers.

Declination of Issue

The most drastic and fortunately the rarest underwriting action is to decline any coverage. This decision is required only for serious medical or other reasons that cause the applicant to exceed a particular company's parameters for acceptance. For comprehensive medical expense policies, approximately 18 percent of applicants are denied coverage. Most of these rejections (more than two-thirds) are for medical reasons. Non-medical reasons may include lifestyle factors discussed previously.[8] For disability income insurance, rejection rates between 6 and 10 percent of applicants are common.[9] Again, most of these are for medical reasons; only a small percentage is for occupation or income related problems. The comparable number for long-term care insurance applicants is in the 13 to 20 percent range.[10]

When coverage is denied, the insurance company should promptly communicate that decision to the applicant and agent with at least a general explanation. If the specific reason for the decision is based on medical information obtained from sources other than directly from the applicant, the insurer may identify the source but without describing the specific reason for the decision. In this case, the insurer also should explain how the applicant may arrange to discuss the medical information directly with his or her physician.

Many insurer companies allow an applicant to request an appeal when coverage is denied. Coverage may be available from another insurer with less restrictive underwriting standards, although the premium might be higher.

Assisting Difficult-to-Insure Clients

Inevitably, an agent will have clients whose applications for health insurance are declined, typically for medical reasons. In the event of such an outcome, a well-informed agent can remain of service to his or her client by being aware of and suggesting potential alternatives.

As just mentioned, a possibility of appeal may exist which can be successful if there is a misunderstanding of the applicant's true situation or there is some combination of modified issue features that had not yet been considered. As also pointed out, insurer underwriting standards vary widely and an agent's up-to-date knowledge of these differences can encourage the client to apply for coverage to one or more other insurers. Indeed, some health insurers specialize in offering various forms of coverage to higher-risk persons.

If a person is uninsurable, the agent may suggest other alternatives. For example, over 30 states have high-risk pools that provide medical expense coverage, usually at above standard premium rates. Persons who are uninsurable for a disability income policy should be aware of government programs such as Social Security and state disability benefits, as well as workers' compensation benefits. Someone who is uninsurable for long-term care coverage should be informed of Medicare's limited benefits for long-term care services, as well the benefits that Medicaid and the Veterans Administration offer to eligible persons who need long-term care.

REUNDERWRITING

There are situations in which persons who have health insurance may be subject to reunderwriting.

A person who has received health insurance coverage on a modified issue basis may request reconsideration if there is an improvement in his or her circumstances, including medical conditions and lifestyle circumstances (cessation of tobacco use or dangerous hobbies), that warranted the original decision. In some instances, the underwriter may offer to reconsider the modified issue underwriting decision after a certain period of time has elapsed. If the original decision was based on a medical condition, reconsideration is normally subject to medical evidence that there has been no recurrence or worsening of the condition. Reconsideration may result in an exclusion rider being removed, thereby allowing full coverage, sometimes for an extra premium charge.

Reunderwriting often takes place if the insured wishes to make changes in a policy, usually by adding coverage and/or enhancing benefits. A person with a medical expense policy may wish to add maternity coverage, while someone with disability income insurance may request an increased benefit level due to significantly increased earned income.

As long-term care insurance, the most recent form of health insurance, continues to mature and improve product features, there are frequent requests for policy changes. For example, an insured might want to add adult day care or assisted living care or increase the overall maximum policy benefit to newly accepted levels. These actions require submitting an application for increased coverage that will be underwritten in a manner similar to the original application. A new policy is issued if the insured meets the insurer's current underwriting standards. Typically, the new premium blends the rate applicable to the coverage that is new at the insured's current age with the rate applicable to the previously existing coverage when originally purchased. A reduction in policy benefits will usually not require additional underwriting. However, some insurers may not allow certain benefit reductions, such as dropping an inflation rider.

Finally, reunderwriting may be required to reinstate a lapsed policy or reissue an interim medical expense policy.

CHAPTER REVIEW

Key Terms

underwriting
persistency
stability
attained-age rates
issue-age rates
morbidity
mode of premium payment
attending physician's statement (APS)
inspection report
MIB
standard issue
modified issue
exclusion rider

Review Questions

Review questions are based on the learning objectives in this chapter. Thus, a [4-3] at the end of a question means that the question is based on learning objective 4-3. If there are multiple objectives, they are all listed.

1. a. Why is insurance underwriting important? [4-1]
   b. Why must underwriting strike a balance between adverse selection and choosing only the best applicants? [4-1]
   c. Why do underwriting practices differ? [4-1]

2. a. Why are the roles of the agent and the home office underwriter mutually supportive and complementary? [4-2]
   b. Why is the home office underwriter not totally dependent on the agent for applicant information? [4-2]

3 Describe how each of the following classification categories is relevant to an applicant's insurability or premium rate for at least one form of health insurance (medical expense, disability income, or long-term care):

   a. number of insureds [4-3]
   b. gender [4-3]
   c. geographic area [4-3]
   d. tobacco use [4-3]
   e. duplicate coverage [4-3]
   f. lifestyle factors [4-3]

4. a. Why is age such an important factor in underwriting health insurance? [4-3]
   b. Why is age a more complex factor in underwriting disability income insurance than in other forms of health insurance? [4-3]

5. a. Why is occupation a more significant factor in underwriting disability income insurance than in other forms of health insurance? [4-3]
   b. How does today's trend toward more refined occupation classes in underwriting disability income insurance differ from traditional classes? [4- 3]
   c. What factors do insurers consider when underwriting disability income insurance for persons who work at home? [4-3]

6. When underwriting disability income insurance, what do insurers consider insurable income? [4-3]

7. a. Why is medical condition the most important factor in determining if an applicant should be offered health insurance? [4-3]
   b. What specific aspects of medical conditions do underwriters evaluate under medical history and current physical status? [4-3]
   c. How is the availability of more than one underwriting class relevant to the medical condition of a health insurance applicant? [4-3]

8. a. How does an agent qualify an applicant for (i) disability income insurance and (ii) long-term care insurance before completing an insurance application? [4-4]
   b. What information does a health insurance application normally request? [4-4]
   c. Apply each area of information to at least one specific form of health insurance (medical expense, disability income, or long-term care). [4-4]

9. What determines the extent to which additional sources of underwriting information are used? [4-5]

10. Identify how information from each of the following sources contributes to the underwriting decision for at least one form of health insurance (medical expense, disability income, or long-term care):

    a. telephone interviews [4-5]
    b. attending physician's statements [4-5]
    c. inspection reports [4-5]
    d. personal evaluations [4-5]
    e. MIB Group, Inc. [4-5]

11. a. Compare modified underwriting actions using exclusion riders, extra premiums, and change in benefits. [4-6]
    b. What are the advantages and disadvantages of an exclusion rider? [4-6]

c. What alternatives may an agent suggest to a difficult-to-insure health insurance client? [4-6]

12. Under what circumstances may reunderwriting of health insurance policies occur? [4-6]

NOTES

1. To determine the annual percentage rate, assume that the insured has initially paid $520 of the $1,000 premium in advance and is financing the other $480 for 6 months. Therefore, $40 of the second semiannual payment represents the interest for this loan.
2. *Individual Health Insurance: A Comprehensive Survey of Affordability, Access, and Benefits,* America's Health Insurance Plans, August 2005. pp 9–11.
3. Charles E. Soule, *Disability Income Insurance: The Unique Risk.* Bryn Mawr, Pa: The American College Press, 2002, pp. 183, 188.
4. Nancy P. Morith, Richard A. Dulisse, Kirk Okumura, Glenn E. Stevick, and C. Bruce Worsham, *Essentials of Long-Term Care Insurance.* Bryn Mawr, Pa: The American College Press, 2008, p. 7-23.
5. *Individual Health Insurance,* pp. 9–11.
6. Soule, *Disability Income Insurance,* pp. 183, 188.
7. Morith, et al, *Essentials of Long-Term Care Insurance,* p. 7-23.
8. *Individual Health Insurance,* pp. 9–11.
9. Soule, *Disability Income Insurance,* pp. 183, 188.
10. Morith, et al, *Essentials of Long-Term Care Insurance,* p. 7-23.

5

Claims Payment

Learning Objectives

An understanding of the material in this chapter should enable you to

5-1. Identify what constitutes a loss under each form of health insurance.

5-2. Describe settlement practices that are deemed unfair.

5-3. Explain how agents may help clients meet their claims payment expectations.

5-4. Summarize the steps in the claims payment process that are common to health insurance policies.

5-5. Explain how medical expense claims are paid on a service basis and an indemnity basis.

5-6. Describe the claims payment features specific to disability income policies.

5-7. Identify the claims payment features specific to long-term care policies.

Chapter Outline

claims payment

Like underwriting, claims payment is essential to all forms of insurance. *Claims payment* is the process whereby an insurer determines its obligations under a policy for a claimant's covered losses and provides benefits for such occurrences in accordance with the policy's terms. In medical expense insurance, the covered loss is typically medical expenses incurred or services received due to injury, illness, or maintenance of health. In disability income insurance, income forgone because of an illness- or injury-related inability to earn a living constitutes the covered loss. In long-term care insurance, the covered loss relates to a cognitive or physical impairment that results in an inability to care for oneself and dependency on others.

From the claimant's viewpoint, claims payment is the purpose for which the insurance was purchased. At the very least, the claimant rightfully expects this process to be easily accessible, accurate, fair, complete, and prompt. The service and performance that an insurer demonstrates in the claims payment process are the true measures of the insurance contract's value to the policyowner.

At the same time, an insurer's claims payment practices represent a major source of possible mistreatment of claimants. Most states now have enacted laws patterned after the NAIC's model laws and regulations pertaining to unfair claim settlement practices. Some of the practices that are regarded as unfair are the following:

- failing to investigate claims promptly
- failing to communicate with or acknowledge communications from claimants on a timely basis
- failing to provide a reasonable explanation as to why a claim was denied
- failing to maintain procedures for handling complaints about claims
- misrepresenting pertinent policy provisions that affect claims
- failing to try to settle a claim once the insurer's liability becomes clear
- attempting to settle a claim for far less than a reasonable person would expect based on the insurer's advertising material

The agent, who is essential to the underwriting process, also has a key role in the success of the claims payment process. Health insurance claims usually occur when insured persons are unprepared: they are dealing with an illness, accident, disability, or loss of independence. They are also unlikely to be fully aware of the details of their policy's provisions, especially those relating to claims payment. By serving as an advisor to insureds at this time with respect to both coverage and claims provisions, the agent provides an important client service function. The agent can explain a policy's claims process as well as assist with claims filing and reporting on claims payment status. Insurers encourage this important agent role by providing the agent with claims payment resource information, including forms to assist an insured who is filing a claim. Understanding claims payment, consequently, equips the agent to be a better client advocate.

Example: Anita is a career agent with significant experience in long-term care insurance. When her clients receive their policies, she counsels them to call her if they believe they need to file a claim. She reinforces this recommendation by relating the story of a wife who called her long after her husband had been receiving covered home care services only to find out that some of her claims were being denied; the caregivers in many cases were uncertified as the policy required.

When clients call as she requests, Anita carefully reviews all the claims payment requirements of their policies. In this way, she assists her clients to avoid claims pitfalls and to maximize the payment of appropriate benefits. Among the topics she covers are: timely filing of claims; the types of care services covered; the extent and limitations of benefits for covered services; documentation required; and the advantages of the using a care coordinator as allowed or required under the policy. She emphasizes that claims filed under a plan of care developed by a care coordinator who has certified the need for care are more likely to be accepted by the insurer and processed problem free.

In general, as the following discussion indicates, the payment of health insurance claims under medical expense, disability income, and long-term care policies share many common features. These common features result from the NAIC's Uniform Individual Accident and Sickness Policy Provision Law (UPPL), which all states have adopted in some form. Chapter 6 discusses the UPPL in more detail. The discussion in this chapter also notes claims payment features that are specific to each of these forms of health insurance.

COMMON FEATURES

Each policy spells out the steps that the claimant must follow, as well as his or her responsibilities following a loss. In certain cases, the claimant will be both the policyowner and the insured. In other cases, such as under a medical expense policy that covers family members, the claimant will be the policyowner who files claims for a child or other insured family members. The claimant's failure to follow any necessary procedures may jeopardize the receipt of benefit payments and the ability to bring legal actions against the insurance company if disputes arise. However, at times, especially with disability income and long-term care coverage, the claimant may be incapacitated and the necessary duties of complying with claims provisions will fall to the claimant's legal representative.

The steps in the claims payment process, including those applicable to health insurance policies, fall into four general categories: (1) the claimant furnishes a notice of loss to the insurer, (2) the policyowner files a proof of loss with the insurer, (3) the insurer examines the claim, and (4) the insurer makes or denies the claim payment, sometimes after negotiating the amount to be paid. These steps are logically distinct and may extend over the course of weeks or even months in the case of disability income and long-term care insurance claims. Alternatively, two or more of these steps may occur at the same time. For example, in the case of medical expense insurance, these steps often occur in rapid succession and nearly simultaneously thanks to electronic data transmission technology.

Notification

The claimant must first notify the insurer that a claim is being made. Notification to the insurer must be provided as spelled out in the policy. Often, the time frame is specified as "immediately," "promptly," or "as soon as reasonably possible" after a loss occurs or a covered service is received. Some policies may require notice within a specific time frame, such as within 30 or 180 days after the occurrence of a loss. In most cases, the policies contain the insurer's contact information. Many insurers prefer written notification of a claim rather than notice by phone or through the Internet. Some insurers initially do little other than send the claim forms to the claimant with instructions to have them completed and returned to the insurer. The insurer must supply claim forms within 15 days after the insured gives notice of claim. However, many insurers are proactive and work with the claimant to ensure that all necessary paperwork is properly completed. In practice, an insurer rarely penalizes a claimant for failure to give timely notice, if the insurer suffers no detriment as a result.

Proof of Loss

In the second step of the process, the insurer requires that it receive a proof of loss. For most medical expense policies, as explained later, a health care provider often accomplishes this step directly with the insurer. Disability income and long-term care policies as well as some medical policies state that no claim will be paid unless a proof-of-loss form is filed within a specified time, which may range from 90 days to one year after the start of covered services or the commencement of a disability claim, unless the claimant is legally unable to comply. As in the case of notification, companies sometimes do not adhere strictly to the required time period and may accept claims filed beyond the period specified in the policy.

The proof of loss under health insurance policies usually is submitted using claim forms supplied by the insurer to determine its payment responsibility. These forms consist of a claimant's statement as to the dates and nature of the loss incurred and/or treatment received. Statements on the form or attached to the form from a physician or other licensed health care provider must document that the claimant meets the conditions to qualify for benefits. For disability income and long-term care claims, providers must specify how long the claimant's condition is expected to continue. The claim form also contains an authorization from the claimant or other covered person which permits any medical provider to release records or information concerning the claimant's medical history and current condition. Information gained from such a release is often essential to the claim because it demonstrates proof of loss. In the case of disability income insurance, this authorization extends to employer release of information indicating the dates and reasons that a claimant's active employment ceased. The insurer also reserves the right, at its own expense, to have the claimant examined by a physician of its own choice as may be reasonably necessary to verify a claim.

Periodically, during an extended claim-paying period, the insurer may also require verification that the claimant continues to satisfy the criteria to receive benefits. Continued verification is more likely under disability income and long-term care policies due to their extended periods of benefits than under a medical expense policy.

Examination

Claims examination, the third step, determines whether a loss occurred and, if so, whether the policy covers it. Some of the questions that may have to be resolved include the following:

- What is the effective date of coverage?
- When did the loss occur and was the coverage in effect on that date?

- Is the loss covered, and if so, what benefits, exceptions, and exclusions, if any, apply?
- What conditions affecting the claim must occur or be satisfied?
- Is there evidence of misrepresentation?

contestable period

With specific reference to this last point, misrepresentation calls into question the validity or legitimacy of claims with respect to the truth of their content and possibly to the truth of statements made previously on the application for insurance. As chapter 3 explains with examples, if there is material misrepresentation on an application, insurers have the right to deny claims and rescind (with a return of premium) or deny the claim and offer to reform a contract. Insurers generally maintain this right for a period of time, known as the *contestable period.* The contestable period is usually 2 years after a policy is issued, but some states allow 3 years. Thus, any claims filed within the contestable period are subject to a special level of investigation to determine if the information provided on those claims also provides evidence of misrepresentation on the application. Most misrepresentations pertain to health conditions prior to the date of the application, but may also extend to misrepresentation of income in applications for disability income coverage.

Payment

Finally, the amount to be paid must be determined in one of three ways: (1) payment of the claim in full, (2) payment of a different amount than the claimant might initially expect, or (3) denial of the claim. Numerous policy provisions may be applicable. These include provisions that

- deal with other insurance covering the same loss;
- provide for a deductible, coinsurance amount, or waiting period;
- and/or impose a specific limit on the insurer's responsibility for certain types of claims or the total of all claims.

Payment may be a single action or decision, as it is when a medical expense claim is paid for a one-time treatment of a minor illness in a physician's office. For all forms of health insurance, however, payment is more frequently complex; multiple payment decisions must be made because claims for each loss or event usually have several related components. Moreover, these more complex claims often involve component claims that occur over a period of time. A medical expense claim may involve a hospital stay as well as follow-up physician office visits, or therapy extending over weeks or months. In the event of a disability or the need for long-term care, the period is likely to be many months or years. In addition, multiple losses and events may occur over the period that a health insurance policy remains in force. Consequently, the payment of claims also requires management of claims; a specific claim or component of a claim must be paid within the context of a policy's applicable benefit provisions for covered losses or events as well as its maximum lifetime benefits.

Health insurance benefits can generally be assigned to providers of care as is common in the case of medical expense and long-term care insurance. Benefits may be assigned to another party if such an assignment is permissible under state law and the insurance contract.

facility-of-payment provision

If an insured person is physically, mentally, or otherwise incapable of giving a valid release for any payment received, a *facility-of-payment provision* allows payments to be made to a legal representative, frequently referred to as a guardian.

Example: Marcia is senior software engineer at a small information management company whose employment benefit program does not contain long-term disability coverage. Marcia, wishing to better protect her six-figure-income lifestyle, obtains an individual disability income policy with a 90-day waiting period. Within a year after the policy issued, she is diagnosed with multiple sclerosis, a permanent and degenerative disease of the central nervous system. Although periods of remission allow Marcia to remain on the job for several months after her diagnosis, the rapid progression of the disease, which severely affects her sensory and motor functions, soon prevents her from performing the duties of her job.

Marcia notifies her insurer of her disability in a timely manner and receives claims forms which she completes and submits along with attending physician's statements describing her disability. Because Marcia's claim falls within the 2-year contestable period, her insurer thoroughly investigates her claim and the information previously provided on her insurance application together with all relevant medical record data over the last several years. The insurer also accesses MIB's Disability Income Record Service and Health Claims Index to make sure no unusual policy application or claim activity has occurred since the policy was issued.

The insurer confirms Marcia's disability status and finds no evidence of any misrepresentation or concealment with respect to the diagnosis or treatment of her current condition prior to her application for insurance. Her claim is approved. Because she is totally disabled, the insurer begins to pay Marcia the full monthly disability benefit upon the expiration of the 90-day waiting period.

SPECIFIC FEATURES

Claims payment features are also specific to the form of health insurance. The following section highlights some of the unique features of medical expense, disability income, and long-term care insurance. Subsequent chapters that cover regulations and benefits of each health insurance product provide further explanations of these and other claims payment provisions.

Medical Expense Insurance

indemnity basis

The previous discussion on the presentation of proof of loss requiring the filing of claims forms is largely relevant to medical expense policies (as well as other types of policies) that provide benefits on an *indemnity basis*. Such policies often reimburse a claimant for the incurred expense of medical services received and therefore require documentation concerning the occurrence, nature, and extent of each claim.

service basis

capitation

In today's market, however, managed care plans—in particular PPOs as well as HMOs and the plans of other organizations like Blue Cross and Blue Shield plans—dominate the comprehensive medical expense insurance market. These plans provide benefits on a *service basis* because they have contractual agreements with health care providers and networks of health care providers for the delivery of medical care to covered persons and generally do not require these insureds to file claim forms. Rather, the providers of services perform any necessary paperwork and are then reimbursed directly without any need for an assignment of benefits from the claimant. Some network providers have arrangements that pay them on a per-member-per-month basis to render any service to an insured (referred to as a plan member or enrollee) who uses that provider for care. This practice is called *capitation*. The providers file patient encounter forms with the insurers that are like claim forms but produce no payment for a specific service.

When physicians and other licensed health professionals or institutions present a claim to the insurer whose plan provides benefits on a service basis, the insurer must determine one or more of the following:

- the care provider's status as a network participant
- the primary or specialty care nature of the service if rendered by a network participant
- the applicability of medical management requirements, including authorizations for service, utilization or care quality parameters, and care management
- the pricing of the claim, including determination of the payment amount, the amount paid to the provider, and the claimant's cost sharing

Depending upon the plan's stringency, the provider's reimbursement may be denied altogether or be far less than the amount charged if the claimant receives services from a nonnetwork provider or if a specialist is seen without a required referral. In turn, the payment made to the provider determines whether the enrollee must pay a modest copayment, a more substantial amount under an indemnity benefit as described above, or the total amount if a claim is denied.

Example: Alex has a medical expense policy that requires him to receive care from physicians who participate in a preferred provider network. After an office visit to Dr. Lexa, who participates in the network, Alex pays a $10 copayment and the doctor files a claim for Alex's office visit directly with the insurer in whose network she participates. The doctor subsequently receives payment of $70 which together with Alex's copayment represents the negotiated rate for Alex's service.

Alex's brother, Axel, also visits Dr. Lexa and receives the same level of service. However, Dr. Lexa does not participate in the network utilized by Axel's insurer. In addition, Dr. Lexa does not accept assignment of insurance benefits and requires Axel to pay her standard $90 fee for an office visit at the time of service. As a courtesy, Dr. Lexa does file the claim with Axel's insurer who subsequently makes the claim payment directly to Axel, subject to applicable deductible and personal participation amounts required under the policy.

Disability Income Insurance

Claims payment features specific to disability income insurance are summarized under the headings of the complexity of the claims examiner's responsibility, the definition of disability, and rehabilitation.

Claim Examiner Responsibility for Claims

Similar to the importance of the underwriter's determining what investigation is necessary when first evaluating the insurance application, the disability claim examiner must determine the legitimacy and severity of the disability early in the claim process. Although contract language and definitions help to resolve many potential problems, each individual claimant has a set of complex circumstances and motivations. As a result, determination of a legitimate disability is not always clear and frequently has many subjective qualities. An insured's decision to file or extend a disability claim can be effected by such subjective factors as a:

- business downturn
- desire to "retire" early
- lack of financial incentive to promptly return to work

Proper investigation and analysis of available information are critical to the proper handling of the claim. Naturally, the depth and detail of the investigation depend on the claim's circumstances—particularly the projected length of disability, the severity of the disability, and the subjectivity of the impairment. All of these variables must necessarily be weighed against other variables, such as the claimant's occupation and age. In addition to obtaining the types of routine claim form information discussed previously, the claim examiner may utilize other information sources that include the following:

- Disability claim examiners frequently develop important and reliable information on a disability by dealing directly with the claimant over the telephone.
- Inspection reports (similar to those discussed in the previous chapter on underwriting) may be used when there is a question of the degree of disability, verification of occupation information, income

questions, or possible overinsurance. These reports may take the form of an investigation and even surveillance, if there is suspicion of misrepresentation or fraud.

- A CPA or other financial consultant available to claim examiners may review certain claims involving large amounts, residual benefits, business insurance, or complex financial situations.
- Independent medical examinations (IMEs) are reserved for those instances where a disability is of potentially long-term duration and where the degree of recovery is in question. Calling in an IME at the insurer's expense is an important method of obtaining third-party input concerning the disability's severity.
- In recent years, many companies have used functional clinical evaluations (FCEs) to determine more accurately the extent or degree of disability. The criteria used in these evaluations are much like the standards for the ability to perform activities of daily living used in long-term care insurance.
- MIB's Disability Income Records System (DIRS) alert insurers to problems of overinsurance, particularly during the contestable period.
- Although only a small percentage of claims result in a personal visit and contact from a claim department representative, face-to-face verification of the circumstances surrounding the claim is necessary in some situations.

Disability Definition

The general concept of the payment of claims under a disability income policy is clear—replacement of a portion of an insured person's income when that person becomes totally disabled. However, the term disability may be defined and understood in many ways. Insurers strive to define disability as precisely as possible. Nevertheless, its application to a specific person's situation for the payment of only legitimate claims requires skill and good judgment. Claims payment denials based on the definition of disability are a frequent cause of litigation involving disability income policies.

The two major definition categories are total disability, in which the full disability benefit is paid, and less than total disability, in which only a portion of the full benefit is paid. The various definitions of disability are discussed in chapter 12.

Rehabilitation

By paying claims, all forms of health insurance to a greater or lesser degree have rehabilitation as one of their purposes. Medical expense insurance pays benefits to restore and maintain a person's health. Although less frequently the case in long-term care insurance, the claims paid may allow a person to become independent once again. However, rehabilitation is most visibly associated with the claims payment function under disability income insurance. Rehabilitation provisions in a policy or in benefit administrative practices can effectively encourage a claimant to return to work as soon as reasonably possible, thereby eliminating or reducing claims payments. Some companies have introduced strong rehabilitative policy language in response to claims problems. These may include contractual provisions that

- require that a claimant be receiving appropriate medical care for his or her impairment.
- include mandatory rehabilitation to maintain benefits, if the claimant is a candidate for return to work or rehabilitation.

disability management program

Rehabilitation, as implemented by disability income insurers, encompasses a comprehensive set of procedures and functions usually known as a *disability management program.* A disability management program includes:

- early intervention in a disability case by coordinating the handling of specific claims and the entire claims record for the disability
- coordinated use of various professionals (physicians, nurse case managers, psychiatric nurses, rehabilitation specialists, and accountants) to determine the right approach for a specific case
- assisting claimants with the process of filing for disability benefits under Social Security when the circumstances warrant it

---

Example: In a continuation of the earlier disability income insurance example, Marcia's insurer implements a disability management program that, along with her medical treatment, encourages her to perform a portion of her duties by working from home during periods of remission. Marcia is pleased with this arrangement for a number of reasons including the fact that her reduced salary is supplemented by a partial disability benefit payment allowed in this situation under her policy. As result, she suffers little in the way of lost net income. Although this arrangement works well over the next couple of years, it is only temporary; Marcia's periods of remission become fewer and shorter. As a result, she returns to total disability status and again receives the full monthly disability benefit.

Long-Term Care

When insureds file a claim under a long-term care policy, the policy provisions spell out the procedures that must be followed. These procedures generally follow the claims payment features common to health insurance policies as discussed previously. Nevertheless, there are claims payment features specific to long-term care policies. In many cases, the insured will be incapacitated and the necessary duties of complying with claim provisions will fall to the insured's legal representative. In such situations, the assignment of benefits to providers of care reduces a family's involvement in handling financial matters directly. However, benefits cannot be paid, assigned, or pledged as collateral for a loan.

Other claims payment features specific to long-term care policies can be summarized under the headings of the payment basis, use of a care coordinator, and the effect of federal legislation. Chapter 19, which explains the benefit provisions of long-term care insurance policies, describes these features in greater detail.

Payment Basis

A long-term care insurance policy may pay benefits on a per diem basis or a reimbursement basis.

per diem basis

Under policy that uses a *per diem basis*, benefits are paid at the policy's daily, weekly, or monthly benefit level regardless of the actual cost of care. In this case, a policy with a daily benefit of $200 will pay $200 even if actual charges for care for the day are only $150. Indeed, some of these policies, known as disability-based policies, pay benefits even if no expenses are incurred as long as the claimant meets the criteria for a covered cognitive or physical impairment.

reimbursement basis

The majority of newer policies, however, pay benefits on a *reimbursement basis*. These policies reimburse the claimant for actual expenses up to the specified policy limit. Thus a policy with daily benefit amount of $200 will pay only $150 if that was the claimant's actual charge for a day's care covered by the policy.

Care Coordinator

When the claimant notifies the insurer that a claim is being made, the insurer may provide the services of a care coordinator, also known as a care manager, at no additional charge to the policyowner. Care coordinators occupy a pivotal position in the determination of benefits in some long-term care insurance policies, although their use varies by both company and policy. Some policies require the use of a care coordinator. In others it is optional, and in still others it is not available, particularly in older policies.

care coordinator

A *care coordinator* is a health professional whose responsibilities include screening claimants, determining eligibility for services, conducting provider referrals, monitoring outcomes, and counseling families. The coordinator also develops a plan of care based on a comprehensive assessment of the claimant's physical and cognitive needs, social situation, health condition, and other factors. The physician, the claimant, and the claimant's family participate in its development. The plan not only addresses care needs, it also identifies associated issues that may affect family stability and require the use of community services as well. Much of the planning revolves around the use of home care versus community care services and which services best match the needs of all parties involved. In some policies, the use of a care coordinator may waive the elimination period for certain services. Typically, insurers contract with care coordination firms to provide the service to their policyowners.

Federal Legislation

Federal legislation, known as HIPAA (discussed in the following chapter), grants tax-preferred status to long-term care policies that contain specific provisions (discussed in chapter 18). As a result, more than nine out of ten policies now sold comply with these provisions, which affect claims payment in a number of ways. Benefits may be paid only if the insured is certified as meeting the definition of chronically ill required by the law. In addition, the chronic illness must be expected to last at least 90 days, with recertification no less than every 12 months. The initial and any subsequent certifications must be made by a physician or other licensed health care practitioner.

CHAPTER REVIEW

Key Terms

claims payment	capitation
contestable period	disability management program
facility-of-payment provision	per diem basis
indemnity basis	reimbursement basis
service basis	care coordinator

Review Questions

Review questions are based on the learning objectives in this chapter. Thus, a [5-3] at the end of a question means that the question is based on learning objective 5-3. If there are multiple objectives, they are all listed.

1. What constitutes a covered loss under each form of health insurance? [5-1]
2. a. What claims practices are identified as unfair? [5-2]
   b. What do claimants expect from the claims payment process and how can health insurance agents help them meet their expectations? [5-3]
3. What time frames may be associated with a notification of loss? [5-4]
4. a. How is proof of loss typically submitted under a health insurance policy? [5-4]
   b. What kinds of statements and authorizations are required? [5-4]
   c. Why may continued verification be required? [5-4]
5. What questions are typically resolved in determining whether a loss occurred and whether the policy covers it? [5-4]
6. a. What policy provisions are applicable when determining the amount of a claim payment? [5-4]
   b. Why does claims payment often require multiple claim decision for the same event? [5-4]
7. Under what circumstances can benefits be assigned? [5-4]
8. How does the process for paying medical expense claims differ depending on whether benefits are paid on a service basis or an indemnity basis? [5-5]
9. a. What factors make the disability claims examiner's responsibilities complex? [5-6]
   b. What information sources may the disability claims examiner utilize? [5-6]
10. Why is it important for a policy to precisely define the term disability? [5-6]
11. a. What contractual provisions pertaining to rehabilitation have some companies introduced in response to disability claims problems? [5-6]
    b. What disability management procedures and functions might a company implement? [5-6]
12. Describe the elements that a care plan developed by a care coordinator may include. [5-7]

6

Regulation and Tax Treatment

Learning Objectives

An understanding of the material in this chapter should enable you to

6-1. Identify the purposes and sources of health insurance regulation.

6-2. Describe the types of state regulations that affect individual health insurance policies.

6-3. Describe the federal laws affecting individual medical expense policies.

6-4. Summarize the income-tax treatment of health insurance policies.

Chapter Outline

An understanding of health insurance requires a basic knowledge of insurance regulation. The business of insurance is generally considered to serve the public interest. Consequently, the goal of insurance regulation is to protect the public against insurer insolvency and unfair treatment by insurers. Health insurance, then, is arguably the most heavily regulated type of insurance; it protects almost irreplaceable personal values that are directly related to health and well being, earning a living, and the conduct of life's basic activities. Additional reasons for regulation of health insurance include past abuses by some insurers and agents when dealing with vulnerable consumers, in particular those who are older and more susceptible to less-than-ethical sales practices.

For the most part, the regulation of health insurance is conducted by the states. However, a number of federal laws and regulations are also applicable. In the area of tax treatment, a specific form of regulation, both the federal tax laws as reflected in the Internal Revenue Service Code and many state tax laws strongly encourage the public to purchase health insurance. All these regulations are the subjects of this chapter.

Both state and federal regulation may come from three sources:

- legislatures
- regulators
- courts

Legislation is the foundation of insurance law because state legislatures and Congress pass laws that pertain to insurance. Actual enforcement of the laws is given to regulatory bodies that often have considerable leeway to interpret these laws and do so by issuing regulations that must be followed. At the state level, this regulatory body is usually the state insurance department, although other agencies may be involved. For example, managed care organizations, such as HMOs, that provide medical expense insurance also may be regulated by the state health department. At the federal level, it may be one of several agencies, such as the Department of Labor, the Internal Revenue Service, or the Centers for Medicare & Medicaid Services.

The courts regulate insurance in two primary ways. First, they may declare laws unconstitutional or overrule regulations as being beyond the scope of the regulatory agency. Second, they may be called on to resolve disputes between insurers and their insureds.

This chapter consists of two related parts: a discussion on the regulation of health insurance policies and a summary of the tax treatment of those policies. The discussion on regulation looks at both state and federal regulations, which may overlap. In some cases, both types of regulation may apply and insurers must design policies that meet both sets of regulations. In other cases, federal regulation may preempt state law. In still other cases, federal regulation applies only if there is either no state regulation or no regulation that meets specified standards. In the case of health insurance, tax laws are quite favorable and strongly support the purchase of health insurance. The second part of the chapter describes these laws as they affect the premiums paid for and benefits received from health insurance policies. The chapter provides mainly a regulatory overview; subsequent chapters present greater detail on regulations as they affect the specific types of health insurance policies.

STATE REGULATION

NAIC (National Association of Insurance Commissioners)

State regulation of health insurance falls into several categories. While the categories are the same in all states, the type and extent of regulation varies among the states and significant variations often exist. However, the *NAIC (National Association of Insurance Commissioners)* is a voluntary association of all insurance commissioners whose goal is the promotion of uniformity in legislation and administrative rules affecting insurance. It has developed many model laws and regulations which states and insurance commissioners may or may not adopt. Numerous states have adopted many of them, although sometimes with modifications.

The prominent categories of state regulation that apply broadly to policies of medical expense, disability income, and long-term care insurance are:

- licensing
- financial standards
- policy forms
- market conduct
- premium rates
- renewability
- policyowner complaints

In addition, this section also discusses two categories of regulations that are unique to medical expense insurance: 1) mandated benefits and 2) access and affordability.

Licensing

Every state requires the licensing of insurance companies that sell insurance in the state. The primary objective of insurer licensing is to evaluate whether the company can provide the coverage it promises to its insureds. When licensing an insurer, the states look at the insurer's financial strength as well as its management and business practices. For example, a new company owned or managed by persons who had been convicted of defrauding clients in past business ventures would most likely be denied a license.

Although most agents and applicants for insurance have little reason to suspect it, a very small number of organizations have been known to sell insurance without a license. It is always wise to make sure that one is dealing with a licensed insurer. If there is any doubt, call the state insurance department.

Licensed insurance agents are responsible for ascertaining that the companies for which they are selling are approved by the department of insurance in that state.

Example: In the state of Florida, any agent who sells coverage from an unauthorized entity faces the risk of regulatory penalties, liability for unpaid claims, and imprisonment on a felony charge. An *unauthorized entity* is an insurance company (or other organization, either real or fictitious) that has not gained approval to place insurance business from a department of insurance in the jurisdiction where it or its agent wants to sell insurance.

unauthorized entity

Financial Standards

In addition to its financial strength at the time a company is licensed, a state is concerned with the insurer's ongoing financial viability. To guarantee this financial strength, there are regulations regarding investment practices and the maintenance of reserves for claims and other contingencies.

Even when regulation is very good, some insurers encounter financial difficulties and are unable to meet their obligations to insureds. In such situations, state insurance departments will step in and attempt to rehabilitate the insurer and possibly liquidate it. In some cases, another insurer may take over a block of business and coverage will continue, although premiums might be increased. In other cases, the insurance coverage will cease. However, existing claims are almost always paid by state *guaranty funds*. These funds are established by state law for paying the claims of insolvent insurers and are typically financed by assessments of other insurers that are licensed in the state.

guaranty funds

Chapter 2 describes an approach that prospective insureds may use when assessing the financial strength of an insurer and identifies the independent organizations that evaluate insurers.

Policy Forms

policy form

A *policy form* is a standardized contract that an insurer offers to its policyowners. Most states require an insurer to file these forms, along with any attached applications and riders, with the insurance commissioner's office. Policies must follow prescribed formats and define specified terms. For example, a state may dictate the order in which provisions are presented in a policy and the size of type that must be used. Gone are the days when exclusions were printed in such small type that even people with excellent eyesight would have trouble reading them. Also, exclusions must be conspicuously labeled as such, and there must also be separate and clearly identified paragraphs describing preexisting conditions and policy limitations.

States also have standards for defining many of the terms used in health insurance policies. Examples include hospital, accident, sickness, disability, occupation, preexisting condition, physician, nurse, mental and nervous disorder, convalescent nursing care, and home health care.

Uniform Individual Accident and Sickness Policy Provision Law (UPPL)

Laws also require that certain provisions be contained in policy forms and prohibit the use of other provisions. The *Uniform Individual Accident and Sickness Policy Provision Law (UPPL)* can be considered the primary model law governing health insurance policy forms. The UPPL or its equivalent has been adopted by all states and applies to medical expense, disability income, and long-term care insurance. Although the following discussion focuses on UPPL provisions, other policy provisions mentioned later in this chapter also fall into the broad category of regulation of policy forms.

Note that to a great extent, the UPPL's provisions are reflected throughout the chapter 3 discussion of contracts, particularly in the sections on special characteristics of insurance contracts and key insurance contract provisions. Chapter 5 also presents UPPL provisions relating to the common features of claims payment.

In addition to UPPL's required provisions, other provisions may be optional on the part of the insurer, but if they are used they must adhere to specified standards.

Prominent among the required provisions are the following:

entire contract provision

- *entire contract provision.* This provision states that only those items actually included in the policy, including any riders or attachments, are part of the contract of insurance. A change in the policy is not valid until approved by an executive officer of the insurance company and an appropriate endorsement is attached to the policy. An agent does not have authority to change the policy or waive any of its provisions.

This provision is advantageous to both the insured and the insurer because it limits the contract's terms to the contents of the written policy. Representations made in the application also bind the insured when a copy of the application is made part of the policy—which it usually is.

- *time limit on certain defenses and the incontestable clause.* The time limit provision restricts an insurer's right to rescind or void a policy because of nonfraudulent misstatements to 3 years (2 years in most states). However, if the misstatements were fraudulent, meaning that they were intended to deceive the insurer and would have caused the insurer to take a materially different action if the truth had been known, the time limit provision does not apply. The intent to defraud is difficult to prove.

incontestable clause

The *incontestable clause* is a frequently used alternative to the time limit provision. This clause not only limits an insurer's right to contest the policy (contestable period) to 3 years (2 years in most states), but it also makes the policy fully incontestable after that time with respect to any misstatement made by the insured on the application.

grace period

- *grace period.* This provision gives an insured a specific number of days beyond the due date to pay each premium. During this grace period, the premium can be paid and the policy maintained in force. States usually require a 31-day grace period for most policies.

reinstatement provision

- *reinstatement provision.* If a premium is not paid before the end of the grace period, coverage ceases. This provision sets forth the procedures for allowing the insured to apply for reinstatement of the policy and affording the insurer the opportunity to reevaluate the risk.

If an insurer (or the insurer's agent) accepts a premium without requiring an application for reinstatement, the policy is automatically reinstated upon receipt of the premium. If the insurer does require an application and issues a conditional receipt for money paid with such an application, it has 45 days to decide whether or not to accept the risk again. If it fails to notify the insured within 45 days that the application has been declined, the policy is reinstated automatically at the conclusion of such period.

Upon the date of reinstatement of a medical expense policy, the policy initially covers only accidental injuries. Coverage for losses due to sickness is restored 10 days after reinstatement. The 10-day delay for coverage of sickness is designed to avoid claims for illnesses in existence at the time of reinstatement.

- *claims provisions.* The following provisions deal with the filing and payment of claims:

  - *notice of claim.* Written notice must be given to the insurer within 20 days of loss or as soon as is reasonably possible. (As mentioned in chapter 5, most health insurance policies are more liberal.)
  - *claims form.* The insurer must supply forms within 15 days after the insured gives notice of claim.
  - *proof of loss.* Depending on the type of health insurance policy, the insured usually has anywhere from 90 days to one year to file a formal proof of loss with the insurer.
  - *time of payment of claims.* Claims must be paid promptly.
  - *payment of claims.* Benefits must be paid to the insured, to a policy beneficiary, or (with the insured's permission) to the person or institution rendering services.
- *physical examinations and autopsy.* This provision gives an insurer the right to have the insured examined at its own expense while a claim is pending. The examination provides the insurer with an independent opinion as to the extent of loss or impairment. In the case of death, the provision also permits an insurer to have an autopsy performed where it is not forbidden by law, but insurers rarely request an autopsy in the case of health insurance claims.
- *legal action.* Under this provision, the policy states that the insured must wait at least 60 days after submitting proof of loss before starting legal action against the insurer. Furthermore, it prohibits the insured from bringing legal action more than 3 years after proof is required.

  This provision protects the insurer against untimely lawsuits begun before it has a reasonable opportunity to investigate the claim. The provision also allows the insurer to consider claims closed 3 years after the final action. The 3-year limit is usually shorter than the statutory limit on contract actions in general, which in some states is 5 or 6 years.

Some of the optional provisions that an insurer may include in various types of health insurance policies include the following:

- *misstatement of age.* If the insured's age has been misstated, all benefits payable under the policy are typically paid at a level that the premium paid would have purchased at the correct age. In some health expense insurance policies, there may be a provision that allows the payment of an additional amount to reflect the premium at the correct age if the insured understated the age but remains eligible for coverage. If the covered person is ineligible for coverage at the correct age, then the misapplied coverage is rescinded and any applicable premium refunded.

- *insurance with other insurers.* Insurers sometimes attempt to lessen the possibility of claimants profiting from insurance by including "other insurance" provisions. Such provisions allow an insurer in the presence of valid coverages with other insurers to limit its payment responsibility to a proportionate amount of the insured's allowable benefits under its policy. Other valid coverage may include group and individual coverage. Without such a stipulation, other valid coverage is not considered duplicate insurance.
- *conformity with state statutes.* This provision specifies that any policy provision which, on its effective date, is in conflict with the statutes of the state in which the insured resides is made to conform to the minimum requirements of such statutes.

Market Conduct

All states have standards aimed at the market conduct of insurers. These standards relate to many aspects of health insurance marketing and operations, including advertisements, claims settlement practices, unfair discrimination, conduct of agents, replacement of insurance, and privacy protection.

Advertising

The purpose of advertising standards is to provide the insurance-buying public with an accurate, clear, and truthful presentation and a specific description of insurance products in both the advertising media and material issued and/or used by agents and insurers. That purpose is achieved through standards that prevent unfair, deceptive, and misleading advertising. Because advertising can occur after a policy sale, the definition extends to material that accompanies a policy when it is delivered and material used in the solicitation of renewals and reinstatements.

The standards specify required information as well as the methods of its disclosure in form and content. Required information must be conspicuous with a prominent arrangement of text and captions. Advertisements must fairly and accurately describe benefits and premium payable. The standards also specifically prohibit deceptive and exaggerated words and phrases, enumerate the conditions under which examples and illustrations may be given, and establish acceptability criteria for testimonials and statistics relating to the insurer or policy used in advertising. The manner in which an insurer identifies itself to the public is delineated. The insurer cannot advertise beyond the geographic area in which it is licensed unless the area of licensure is disclosed. No advertisements may make disparaging comparisons of other insurers, their products, or their methods.

The most extensive requirements are applied to advertising that constitutes an invitation to contract because it directly solicits the purchase of insurance; they go well beyond fair and accurate descriptions and avoidance of misleading statements. An advertisement that is an invitation to contract must disclose:

- exceptions, reductions, and limitations affecting the basic provisions of the policy
- the amount of any deductible, copayments, and coinsurance percentage
- the extent to which any loss is not covered if the cause of the loss is traceable to a condition existing prior to the policy's effective date
- provisions relating to renewability, cancelability, and termination

Each insurer is required to maintain a complete file of all its advertising materials. This file is subject to inspection by the insurance department. A few states also require the filing of certain advertisements with the department.

Claims Settlement Practices

An insurer's practices in paying claims represent a major source of insured and claimant dissatisfaction and can be an area of abuse because of unfamiliarity with the insurance contract's technical details. Therefore, states have imposed regulations aimed at eliminating unfair claim settlement practices. Chapter 5 presents a list of the actions that are regarded as unfair claim practices.

Some states go further and spell out limits in terms of a specific number of days in which the insurer must acknowledge a claim, furnish claim forms, answer a claimant's correspondence, and pay or deny a claim. If an investigation is necessary, the insurer must notify the claimant within a given time and must periodically inform the insured of the reason for any continuing delay. In an increasing number of states, the insurer must pay the claimant interest on amounts that are due but were not paid within a certain number of days.

Unfair Discrimination

Most states prohibit "unfair discrimination" between individuals of the same class and essentially the same hazard. Such regulations limit the insurer's ability to decline coverage and to underwrite and rate individuals applying for or seeking to renew their health insurance. Specific regulations deal with several topics, including gender and marital status, blindness, physical or mental impairment, and AIDS. The following are common regulations:

- *regulation to eliminate unfair gender discrimination.* This regulation prohibits insurers from denying availability of coverage or restricting any term, condition, or type of coverage on the basis of gender or marital status. In most states, the purpose of this regulation is to enforce a standard of equal access, not to impose uniformity in premium rates. Therefore, insurers are allowed to use gender-distinct rates for individual insurance products, except in the few circumstances when a state requires unisex rates.
- *regulation on the basis of blindness or partial blindness.* This regulation prohibits actions by an insurer based solely on an applicant's blindness or partial blindness. The actions prohibited include: refusing to insure or refusing to continue to insure; limiting the amount or kind of coverage available; and charging a different rate for the same coverage.
- *unfair discrimination in life and health insurance on the basis of physical or mental impairment.* This regulation applies to unfair discrimination among individuals in the same class on the basis of physical or mental impairment with respect to (1) issuance and renewal of coverage, (2) the amount, extent, or kind of coverage, and (3) rates. However, different treatment of applicants and insureds is allowed if that different treatment is based on sound actuarial principles or it is related to actual or anticipated experience. While such treatment could be called discrimination, it is not "unfair" discrimination under the regulation.
- *guidelines outlining minimum standards for insurance application questions and underwriting relating to AIDS.* Many states have guidelines that outline minimum standards for insurance application questions relating to acquired immunodeficiency syndrome (AIDS) and the underwriting of persons with AIDS. An insurer must refrain from asking questions designed to elicit information about an individual's sexual orientation or preference. Information about sexual orientation cannot be used in the underwriting process and is not to influence the decision on whether an individual is considered insurable. Insurers are permitted to ask questions of a strictly medical nature, such as whether an individual had been diagnosed or treated for the human immunodeficiency virus (HIV) or AIDS.

Conduct of Agents

States also have laws that prohibit fraudulent and unethical acts of agents and brokers. The regulations exact fines and, more importantly, suspend or revoke licenses as penalties for violations. Examples of such unfair practices include:

twisting

- *twisting.* This is a special form of misrepresentation in which an agent may induce the policyowner to cancel disadvantageously the contract of another insurer in order to take out a new contract.

misappropriation

- *misappropriation.* This occurs when an agent unlawfully keeps funds belonging to others.
- *commingling of funds.* This is prevented in some states by requiring a separate bank account for the agent's premium funds.
- *misleading advertising.* This is restrained by many regulators by requiring full and fair information in advertisements by insurers and agents.

rebating

Most states also prohibit *rebating*, which is the return of any part of the premium to the policyowner by the insurer or agent as a price-cutting sales inducement.

Policy Replacement

Application forms must include questions as to whether the policy is intended to replace any other health insurance in force. If so, the applicant must be given a notice warning that preexisting conditions possibly covered by the old policy may not be covered by the new one. The notice advises the insured to consult the previous insurer or its agent before terminating the old coverage. The insured is also cautioned to be certain that the questions on the application are answered truthfully and completely, because any misrepresentation in the application may result in recision of the policy.

Privacy Protection

Most states have privacy protection regulations. Although not targeted directly at health insurance, these regulations are relevant because of the personal information gathered in the health insurance contract and claims processes. Federal regulations mentioned in the following section do address directly the privacy and security of health information. State privacy protection regulations often include the following features:

- *restrictions* designed to minimize intrusiveness—in particular, pretext interviews (interviews in which the investigator's purpose is not disclosed).
- *a mechanism* to enable people to find out what information is being or has been collected about them. Before gathering information, the insurer must notify the individual that personal information may be gathered from, and disclosed to, other parties and that he or she has a right to obtain access to the information and to make corrections to it. On request, the individual may obtain a more detailed description of the types of information to be sought, the parties from whom it is to be sought, and the method of investigation to be used.
- *prescribed procedures* for granting the individual access to the information, permitting corrections, or including explanatory information.
- *safeguards* to limit disclosure of information. These safeguards include prescribed authorization forms, specific time limits for the use of authorizations (usually 30 months in the case of an authorization obtained for underwriting purposes and the duration of the claim when the authorization is used for claim investigation), and rules severely restricting further dissemination of information without the insured's specific consent.
- *notification* of adverse underwriting decisions. Insurers are required to notify individuals of the reasons for an adverse underwriting decision and of the procedures for obtaining more detailed information about the decision.

Premium Rates

Health insurance is difficult to price. Despite regulations, benefit provisions are not totally standardized, although benefits do fall into certain patterns. Actuaries base premiums largely on the average loss experience for similar benefits in the past. At the same time, they must anticipate future changes in the cost and utilization of covered services. In projecting future costs, actuaries evaluate inflationary trends observable in the most recent periods.

Each insurer develops its own rates, and most states require insurers to file these rates with the insurance department. States typically stipulate that health insurance policies maintain a certain minimum loss ratio, which may be defined generally as the aggregate percentage of the overall premiums received returned to insureds in the form of benefits paid. For example, a loss ratio that a state may impose as a minimum for individual medical expense policies may be 60 percent. States require a statement describing the anticipated loss ratio for the policy form in question and may also require an actuarial memorandum showing how the rates were developed. Commissioners reject policy form submissions if they conclude that the benefits provided are unreasonable in relation to the premium.

Each year insurers are required to file loss ratio information with the insurance department for each policy form being used. The loss ratio shows the premium-dollar percentage used to pay claim benefits and gives commissioners the opportunity to check the experience. If they find that the loss ratio on a given policy form is unreasonably low, they may question the insurer for clarification. In addition, a growing number of states now have complex and detailed requirements for rate analysis and for maintaining and reporting claim experience.

It is sometimes necessary for insurers to revise their rate tables when they find themselves paying out more in claims than they anticipated. This situation has arisen, especially in medical expense coverages, as a result of escalating hospitals' and physicians' charges and increased utilization of services. In filing for a rate increase, insurers are usually required to report their claims and premiums for the past few years on the policy form and give evidence that adverse experience is likely to continue.

Renewability

Health insurance policies usually are written for a period of one year, and the policy determines whether the policyowner has the right to continue coverage for an additional period. In most cases, as chapter 2 states, coverage is guaranteed renewable. This means that the policyowner must be given the right to renew the policy. However, the insurer is allowed to change the premium rate at time of renewal and may do so especially a result of claims experience. The increased rates must apply to all policyowners in a given class of business and cannot be applied selectively to a certain person or groups of persons within the established class.

Policyowner Complaints

Dealing with policyowner complaints is an important function of the state insurance departments. Even with the best intentions and efforts, no insurance company can avoid some policyowner dissatisfaction. This is inherent in the technical nature of the insurance contract. Furthermore, considerable time often elapses after the original sale of the policy before a claim occurs. The claimant's understanding of the policy provisions may have become blurred. In the case of health insurance, the somewhat more subjective nature of the risk increases the possibility of misunderstanding. Consequently, most insurance departments report more complaints arising from health insurance than from most other lines of insurance.

The first step an insurance department takes in processing a complaint is to ask the insurer to state the reasons for its position. The insurer's reply usually satisfies the department that the insurer's position is correct. On the other hand, the department sometimes learns of some fact unknown to the insurer, or it has some other basis for asking the insurer to reconsider its position. Most often, differences of opinion between the department and the insurer are resolved. However, in relatively rare instances where the issue has broad implications, the department may require the insurer to attend a hearing on the matter. If a violation of the law is found to have occurred, the department can impose penalties.

In recent years, most states have enacted laws or regulations that provide for an independent, external review of certain types of benefit decisions, particularly those involving the denial of benefits because a treatment was not medically necessary or because it was experimental.

Mandated Benefits

mandated benefits

Mandated benefits generally apply only to medical expense insurance policies. Every state has passed laws that are known collectively as *mandated benefits* because they require that these policies contain coverage requirements for certain populations, providers, alternative care settings, specific conditions, diagnostic tests and exams, treatments, and services and products. These mandates have proliferated over the last four decades from fewer than 100 in the 1960s to over 1,000 today. Initially most mandates applied only to group insurance. However, states now often require individual medical expense policies to contain many of these mandates.

For consumers, mandated benefits present issues of affordability and equity. State-mandated benefit laws are estimated to increase health insurance premiums from 4 to 13 percent. To the extent these increases make medical insurance less affordable, the number of individuals without medical insurance is increased.

Mandated benefits challenge an insurer's ability to remain price competitive and profitable. The extent of the challenge from any specific mandated benefit or set of benefits varies significantly by company due to the unique mix of products, insured populations, market share, and claims expense experience that is specific to each company's book of business. Many of these benefits can easily lead to very expensive claims that can create significant losses for affected companies. Just as each insurer carefully includes in each contract the provisions required by the state in which it is to be sold, each insurer also thoroughly evaluates the continued viability of its medical expense products in each market.

The range of enacted mandates is quite extensive and may be categorized according to the object of the benefits they require:

Populations

Historically, the most common populations singled out for mandated benefits are newborn and handicapped children. Family policies ordinarily set an age limit (such as 19 or 23) at which dependent children's coverage stops. In states that have adopted the handicapped children provision, this age limit does not apply to any dependent child who is mentally or physically unable to earn her or his own living.

Example: In the state of Illinois, individual medical expense policies must cover persons in the following groups:

- adopted children
- handicapped children (after attaining the age limit when coverage would normally cease)
- newborns

Provider Recognition

Many states have passed statutes requiring that insurers recognize the services of specified providers as long as they are acting within the scope of their licenses and the service is covered by the policy. Frequently identified providers include chiropractors, dentists, naturopaths, optometrists, and psychologists. Insurers do not necessarily have to spell out in their policies all of the types of providers whose services are covered. Policy definitions of such terms as "duly licensed physician" or "duly qualified physician" indicate that the insurer recognizes every type of provider licensed by the state to treat injuries and illnesses covered by the policy. These requirements, however, do not preclude benefit limitations for specific services.

Alternative Care Settings

To encourage methods of treatment that are less costly than hospital confinement, some states require that medical expense policies provide coverage for an ambulatory surgical facility or "surgicenter"—that is, a facility apart from a inpatient hospital setting where outpatient surgery is performed. A growing number of states also require individual policies to cover medical care and therapies when provided at home.

Conditions

Many state legislatures have passed statutes requiring coverage for specified conditions. In some cases, the identified condition must be covered just like any other illness, although in others these statutes permit more limited coverage. Some of the more common specific condition mandates include alcoholism, chemical dependency, congenital defects, Lyme disease, mental illness, and temporomandibular joint (TMJ) syndrome.

Example: The state of Illinois requires that individual medical expense policies must provide benefits for the following conditions:

- alcoholism
- osteoporosis

Diagnostic Tests and Exams

Increased interest in preventive health care services has stimulated mandates for certain diagnostic tests. Among the more common examples are colon cancer exam, mammography, osteoporosis screening, prostate exam, ovarian cancer screening, and pelvic exam.

Example: The state of Illinois requires that individual medical expense policies must provide benefits for the following tests and exams:

- colorectal cancer screening
- mammograms
- prenatal HIV testing

Treatments

Perhaps the largest category of benefit mandates is specific treatments. They often include acupuncture, autologous bone marrow treatments, cosmetic surgery, dental services for disabled insureds, experimental drugs, human organ transplants, immunizations, investigational therapies for cancer, mastectomy hospital stay, mental health or substance abuse hospital stay, occupational therapy, and physical therapy.

Example: The state of Illinois requires that individual medical expense policies must provide benefits for the following treatments:

- breast implant removal
- dental adjunctive services (anesthesia and other services for inpatient/surgical dental care)
- post surgical care and reconstruction following mastectomy
- pregnancy complications
- multiple sclerosis preventive physical therapy
- organ transplants (However, there are guidelines under which experimental and investigational transplants can be denied.)

Services and Products

In addition to treatments, a number of health-related services and products are also the subject of mandates. Examples include diabetes self-management training and equipment as well as marriage and pastoral counseling.

Example: The state of Illinois requires that individual medical expense policies that cover prescription drugs must provide benefits for the following services and products:

- contraceptives
- prescription inhalants (and refill limits do not apply)

mandated option laws

The more recent rise of *mandated option laws*, which allow insurers to offer mandated benefits for purchase at the consumer's option, permits policies to be issued without mandates. Optional benefits are often difficult to price appropriately because they may also be expensive and are likely to be purchased by individuals who are more likely to use them than the general insured population, thereby creating adverse selection. While that approach has the advantage of keeping basic coverage more affordable, it may further aggravate a company's loss situation.

Example 1: The state of Virginia requires that individual medical expense policies offer and make available the following benefits:

- periodic review of a child's physical and emotional status
- bone marrow transplants
- treatment of morbid obesity

Example 2: The state of Illinois requires that individual medical expense policies offer benefits (which may be limited to $10,000 annually) for participation in approved cancer research trials.

Access and Affordability

Most states have used their regulatory authority to improve access and affordability in the individual medical expense insurance market, primarily (though not exclusively) for people with previous health problems. More than a dozen states require guaranteed issue of one or more products to all applicants. Approximately 20 states have passed legislation limiting variations in premium rates or the use of such factors as health status, claims experience, age, or gender in determining rates for individuals. More than 20 states also limit the use of preexisting-conditions exclusions. However, some states allow insurers to issue a rider that excludes coverage for identified conditions (such as heart problems) for the duration of the policy.

In addition to direct individual product regulation, more than 30 states have high-risk health insurance plans that offer comprehensive medical expense benefits to uninsurable individuals. Chapter 7 discusses specific government initiatives to improve access to and affordability of medical expense coverage that include state high-risk health insurance plans.

FEDERAL REGULATION

Federal regulations also affect individual health insurance. However, the effect of federal regulations varies greatly in intensity depending on whether the policy is one of medical expense, disability income, or long-term care insurance. Medical expense insurance policies, which have the greatest degree of federal regulation, are governed by the Health Insurance Portability and Accountability Act (HIPAA), the Women's Health and Cancer Rights Act, and Medicare supplement legislation.

Individual disability income policies are virtually devoid of direct regulation at the federal level. Of course this form of insurance is affected greatly by the expansion of Social Security disability, which created serious problems for disability insurers. Social Security disability, along with programs of temporary income replacement initiated by certain states (as chapter 1 describes), have restricted the market for privately insured disability income products in many cases and created overinsurance problems as well.

HIPAA brings about significant changes in long-term care insurance by granting federal tax-favored status to policies that meet the standards specified in the law. The remainder of this section, however, is dedicated to a general discussion of federal regulations affecting policies of individual medical expense insurance.

HIPAA

HIPAA

In 1996, Congress enacted the Health Insurance Portability and Accountability Act, usually referred to as *HIPAA*. Despite the name *Health* in its title, the act applies only to medical expense insurance and medical information. The primary purpose of the act addresses the problem of employees losing their medical expense coverage after they changed or terminated employment. In addition, the law provides for federal tax law changes (discussed in the following section on taxation) and privacy and security of medical information.

HIPAA affects individual medical expense insurance with respect to both availability of coverage and privacy and security of medical information. In both instances, state laws apply to the extent that they contain provisions that are more favorable to consumers.

Availability

Unless a state has a federally qualified mechanism for insuring the unhealthy, an insurer offering policies of comprehensive medical coverage in the individual market must guarantee issue and renew coverage to an eligible individual and may not impose any preexisting-conditions exclusion with respect to such coverage. Generally, as just mentioned, eligible individuals are persons who have changed or terminated employment. HIPAA requires insurers to offer at least two different policy forms to eligible individuals as long as both forms are made generally available and actively marketed to both HIPAA eligible and other individuals. However, there is no federal regulation of the premiums that can be charged.

In many states, the guaranteed issue requirements do not affect insurers directly. Over 20 states have opted to use their risk pools for the medically uninsurable (referred to in chapters 2 and 4) as an alternative mechanism to guarantee coverage in the individual market under HIPAA. In the remaining states, unless there is a single insurer of last resort or some other alternative in place, all insurers providing individual coverage remain subject to the guaranteed issue requirements in this market. It should be pointed out that the HIPAA guaranteed issue and renewal rules do not apply to disability income or long-term care insurance policies or to limited or supplemental medical insurance policies.

Privacy of Medical Information

In general, insurance companies that sell medical expense policies and/or long-term care policies are covered entities under HIPAA's privacy provisions. However, a company that sells disability income insurance only or life insurance only is not subject to the HIPAA privacy provisions. Nevertheless, it is common for some companies that sell medical expense policies or long-term care policies to sell disability income or life insurance, as well. These companies may elect to be treated as hybrid entities. A hybrid entity must identify which of its products are subject to HIPAA privacy provisions and establish firewalls to guard against unauthorized use or disclosure of HIPAA-protected information with regard to these products. HIPAA provisions then apply to these products only. If such a multi-line company declines hybrid status, HIPAA's provisions apply to all the company's products.

protected health information (PHI)

Insurance companies that are covered entities must conform to HIPAA's privacy standards. These standards (known as the privacy rules) protect individually identifiable health (medical) information, called *protected health information (PHI),* that is used or disclosed by a covered entity in any form or media, whether electronic, paper, or oral. Agents as business associates of insurers are also specifically subject to these requirements because they perform functions that include the use and disclosure of PHI. Accordingly, agents are prohibited from using or disclosing PHI in any manner that would violate the privacy standards if done by the insurer itself.

A covered entity or its business associate may not use or disclose PHI, except either: (1) as the privacy standards permit or require, or (2) as the individual subject of the information (or the person's personal representative) authorizes. Authorization is defined as written permission from individuals to use and disclose their PHI.

Nevertheless, an extensive range of activities allow, but do not require, authorizations. In general, a covered entity or business associate may use or disclose PHI without written authorization for treatment, payment, or health care operations and other situations permitted by the privacy rule. Health care operations constitute a broad spectrum of administrative services that support or otherwise relate to the delivery of health care services and include many insurance functions, such as underwriting, rating, and reinsurance.

Women's Health and Cancer Rights Act

With a few exceptions, federal law does not mandate benefits that an individual medical expense insurance policy must include. One of these exceptions is the provisions of the Women's Health and Cancer Rights Act. Any policy that provides medical and surgical benefits for mastectomy must also provide coverage for the following:

- reconstruction of the breast on which the mastectomy was performed
- surgery and reconstruction of the other breast to maintain a symmetrical appearance
- prostheses and physical complications of all stages of mastectomy, including lymphedemas

Prior to the act's taking effect, such services or items were often not covered because of exclusions, particularly exclusions that applied to cosmetic surgery. Benefits can be subject to deductibles and coinsurance provisions as long as they are consistent with those provided for other procedures under the plan or policy.

Medicare Supplement Legislation

Medicare supplement insurance in the individual marketplace became directly subject to federal regulation in 1990, when Congress directed the National Association of Insurance Commissioners to develop a group of standard Medicare supplement policies and mandated several of the requirements for the sale of such policies. This was the first time the federal government had intervened this broadly into a regulatory area normally left to the states. The specific features of these regulated policies are discussed in chapter 10.

FEDERAL TAX TREATMENT

Taxation is a type of regulation. The final two sections of the chapter focus on federal and state income tax laws as they affect individual medical expense, disability income, and long-term care insurance. Federal tax laws as embodied in the Internal Revenue Code are largely favorable to health insurance; to a great extent, premiums paid for individual health insurance and/or benefits received under these policies have a tax-favored status. In effect, federal tax laws generally reflect broad public support for health insurance. That support increases the value of health insurance policies and encourages their purchase. As a result, for many persons, these policies are financially more attractive and more affordable than they would be in the absence of their tax-favored status. In some cases, however, tax-favored status is contingent on an insurance policy containing specific provisions.

The tax laws vary by form of health insurance, and each form is discussed separately.

Medical Expense Insurance

Medical expense insurance premiums may be deductible in determining a person's taxable income, while medical expense benefits received by an insured are generally not counted as taxable income.

Federal legislation now extends tax-preferred status to health savings accounts established in conjunction with certain kinds of medical expense policies, known as high-deductible health plans. Nevertheless, all high-deductible medical expense policies are tax preferred with respect to premiums and benefits as described below, whether or not they meet the rules governing their use with tax-preferred accounts. Chapter 9 discusses the rules governing tax-qualified savings accounts and the health plans with which those accounts are linked.

Deductibility of Premiums

The scope of policies classified as medical expense policies whose premium can qualify for a deduction is quite broad. Such policies may be comprehensive, as in the case of major medical, PPO, or HMO coverage, or more limited in their coverage. Coverage may be supplementary as in the case of specified disease, critical illness, and Medicare supplement policies. Still other policies may cover only dental, vision, hearing, or prescription drug expenses. Medical expense policies may provide benefits on a service basis and/or pay benefits on the basis of incurred expenses. Others pay benefits as per diem amounts or as a lump sum. Even comprehensive policies may have low or high self-responsible amounts by way of deductibles, copayments, and other out-of-pocket expenses. These policies are discussed in detail in later chapters.

Although the premiums paid to purchase all these medical expense policies are potentially deductible, everyone is not able to deduct the premium from taxable income in the same way or to the same extent. How medical expense insurance is purchased or obtained largely determines how premiums are able to be deducted. The following discussion looks at the general tax rules. However, more favorable rules apply to persons who are self-employed. In addition, the tax treatment may be somewhat different if individual medical expense policies are purchased by employers as benefits they provide to employees.

General Tax Rules. The Internal Revenue Code allows an individual to deduct medical expenses paid for the medical care of the taxpayer, the taxpayer's spouse, and the taxpayer's dependents under certain circumstances. First, the taxpayer must itemize deductions. Second, the deduction is only for expenses that are not reimbursed by insurance or some other source. Third, the deduction is limited to expenses that exceed 7.5 percent of the taxpayer's adjusted gross income.

Finally, the deduction is allowed only for medical expenses as defined by the Internal Revenue Service. These expenses include amounts paid for the diagnosis, cure, treatment, or prevention of disease or for the purpose of affecting any structure or function of the body. This definition is broad enough to include dental care. The definition also generally includes premiums for medical and dental insurance. However, medical expense premiums for policies that pay a stated periodic payment to a person while hospitalized, regardless of benefits from other sources, are considered premiums for disability income insurance and are not deductible. One final point should be mentioned. Expenses for long-term care are classified as medical expenses. Premiums for long-term care insurance, as explained in a following section of the chapter, are also classified as medical expenses up to specified amounts.

Example: Clara and Bill, who are each aged 62, file a joint federal income tax return and have an adjusted gross income of $60,000 from investments and retirement plans. Since their retirements, they have purchased an individual major medical policy that has an annual premium of $8,000 for the current tax year. In addition, they have $3,000 in unreimbursed medical expenses. As long as they itemize their deductions, they can deduct medical expenses that exceed 7.5 percent of $60,000, or $4,500. Therefore, $6,500 of their total medical expenses of $11,000 is deductible.

Detailed information about deductible medical expenses can be found in IRS Publication 502 on the IRS Web site: www.irs.gov.

Purchases by Self-Employed Persons. The IRS Code gives even more favorable tax treatment to the self-employed. They are able to deduct the total amount of their premiums for medical expense insurance in determining adjusted gross income even if they do not itemize deductions. The only restriction is that the deduction for these premiums cannot exceed earned income from self-employment. Other medical expenses can also be deducted, but only if expenses are itemized and then to the extent they exceed the 7.5 percent limitation.

Example: After her divorce 2 years ago, Lily decided to quit her corporate job and work from home so she could spend more time with her young daughter. She became a freelance editor and makes $35,000 in self-employment income. Her ex-husband's medical insurance policy covers her daughter. For herself, Lily carries a high-deductible policy that has an annual premium of $3,000. During the last year she has incurred $1,000 in medical expenses that have not been covered by her policy because of the deductible. Lily can fully deduct her health insurance premium because it is less than her self-employment income. The additional medical expenses are deductible only to the extent they exceed 7.5 percent of Lily's adjusted gross income. Unless she has significant adjustments to her self-employment income when she determines her adjusted gross income, this is unlikely to occur.

There is a significant disparity in the treatment of the deduction of individual medical insurance premium paid between the self-employed and most others persons in the workforce who may pay all or part of their premiums for individual health insurance or for an employer-provided health plan. This disparity has fueled ongoing debate in Congress about ways to allow all personally paid premiums for medical expense insurance to be deductible from taxable income in much the same way as they are for self-employed persons. Proposals to achieve that objective are usually labeled as granting an "above the line" deduction, meaning that the premium or health plan payments create a dollar-for-dollar reduction in taxable income. This type of deduction would eliminate the need to include the premiums with other itemized medical expenses subject to the 7.5 percent limitation.

Employer-Paid Premiums. It is common for employers to have benefit plans that provide medical expense insurance to employees and possibly retirees. Although such coverage is typically through a group insurance policy or a self-funded benefit plan, employers sometimes purchase individual insurance policies. If the employer is a C corporation, which is the form of a corporation that most people work for, these premiums are deductible to the business and do not represent taxable income to the employees or retirees. Any employee contributions for employer-provided coverage are treated for income tax purposes the same as individually purchased insurance and subject to the general tax rules previously described. Note that if an employer merely reimburses an employee for coverage that the employee purchased, this represents taxable income to the employee.

The situation is different if the employer is a sole proprietor, partnership, or S corporation. Any premiums paid on behalf of a proprietor, a partner, or a person who owns more than 2 percent of the stock of an S corporation are deductible at the business level, but they are included in the person's gross income. Such payments by the business are considered a distribution of profits to the employee(s)/owner(s) and are taxable. A sole proprietor is allowed the self-employment deduction previously described, even if the policy is purchased in the name of the sole proprietorship. Partners and more-than-2-percent owners of an S corporation may also claim the self-employment deduction, but only if the policy is in the name of the business.

There are other types of business organizations than those previously mentioned. These include the limited liability company (LLC)—a common and popular business form for professionals, such as doctors, lawyers, and accountants. LLCs have many attributes of corporations, particularly with respect to the liability of their members (as the owners are called). The organization is given a choice of being taxed as a corporation or partnership. In almost all cases, it elects partnership treatment, and the members are treated as described in the previous paragraph with respect to medical expense coverage.

Tax-Free Receipt of Benefits

Benefits received from a medical expense policy purchased by an individual are generally not taxable to the individual even if they exceed any medical expenses incurred. The only exception is that any reimbursements for expenses deducted in a prior year must be included in income. For example, such a situation might occur if a taxpayer paid a medical bill in December and deducted the expense in calculating income taxes for the year in which the bill was paid. If the taxpayer received any insurance benefit payments for this expense in the following year, they would need to be included in income for that year.

There is one difference if benefits are received from an employer-provided medical expense plan, whether or not the plan is funded with individually purchased policies. In such cases, benefits are taxable to the extent they exceed any expenses actually incurred. However, plan design almost always prevents this situation from occurring.

Disability Income Insurance

The tax treatment of disability income insurance is different than that of medical expense insurance, primarily due to the inability of individuals to deduct individual policy premiums. But as with medical expense insurance, the tax implications may vary if a policy is purchased by an employer.

Individually Purchased Policies

The Internal Revenue Code does not allow a deduction for disability insurance premiums paid by an individual. Thus, even a self-employed person may not deduct individual disability income premiums to determine his or her adjusted gross income. In addition, self-employed and other persons who personally purchase individual disability income insurance may not include such premium payments with their otherwise allowable medical expense insurance premiums and medical expenses to determine deductibility of amounts in excess of the 7.5 percent of adjusted gross income, as discussed previously.

Benefits received from individually purchased policies are received income tax free.

Example: Joe works for an employer that does not have long-term disability income coverage for its employees. As a result, Joe purchased an individual disability income policy that has an annual premium of $2,000. The premium is not deductible. However, any benefits Joe receives will be tax free.

Treatment of Employer-Provided Policies

Just as with medical expense insurance, an employer may purchase individual policies to fund a disability income plan for employees. In the usual situation, premiums paid by the employer are tax deductible to the employer and result in no taxable income to employees. Any benefits attributable to employer premiums, however, are considered income to an employee who receives such benefits. Nevertheless, as the result of a 2004 IRS Revenue Ruling, an employer can design a disability income plan so that an employee can receive tax-free benefits financed with employer contributions. This requires the employee to elect to have the employer-paid premium reported as taxable income. Such an election applies separately to each employee and must be made prior to the beginning of a plan year. Few plans have incorporated such a plan-design provision, however. It creates administrative burdens for the employer, and most employees prefer to minimize their income-tax burden on a current basis. If an employer makes such an option available, an employee should discuss its implications with a tax advisor before making an election.

If an employee contributes to the cost of employer-provided disability income coverage (either individual or group policies), such contributions are treated as premiums for individually purchased coverage, and premiums and benefits are subject to the rules described for individually purchased coverage. This means that a portion of the benefits are received income-tax free. For example, if an employee pays 40 percent of the cost of his or her coverage, 40 percent of the benefits are received tax free, and 60 percent of the benefits must be included in income for tax purposes.

As with medical expense insurance, disability income insurance premiums paid by a business for a sole proprietor, a partner, a more-than-2-percent owner of an S corporation, or most members of LLCs are deductible by the business but must be reported as income for such a person. In effect, these persons are treated for tax purposes as having individually purchased coverage and benefits are tax free. Note that the deduction for the self-employed that is available for medical expense premiums is not available for disability income premiums.

In addition to purchasing policies to provide disability income to employees, businesses often use individual disability insurance policies for a variety of other reasons. These include business overhead insurance, key person insurance, and the funding of disability buy-sell agreements. These techniques are described in chapter 15 along with the potential tax consequences associated with each.

Long-Term Care Insurance

The enactment of HIPAA in 1996 made the tax treatment of long-term care insurance more favorable. To a great extent (although with limitations), long-term care insurance now has the same tax-preferred status as medical expense insurance. Favorable tax treatment is given, however, only if long-term care insurance policies meet prescribed standards. Policies that meet these standards are designated as qualified long-term care insurance contracts. However, the more commonly used terminology is *tax-qualified contracts* or simply *qualified contracts*. As a result, the nature of most long-term care insurance coverage has changed. In many cases, the imposition of federal standards resulted in broader coverage for consumers. However, Congress seemed to have been concerned with the revenue loss associated with this tax legislation. As a result, policies that were modified to comply with the federal standards sometimes actually provide more limited access to benefits than had been previously required in several states. Chapter 18 discusses in detail HIPAA requirements for long-term care policies as qualified contracts.

Although HIPAA brings about changes in long-term care insurance primarily through changes in the federal income tax code, states still have the authority to regulate long-term care insurance contracts. They have no obligation to bring state rules and regulations into conformity with these tax changes. However, all states allow tax-qualified contracts so that consumers can obtain the favorable federal tax benefits. Estimates are that at least 95 percent of contracts sold are tax qualified.

Federal taxation of qualified long-term care insurance policies is discussed here under the headings of deductibility of premium and tax-free receipt of benefits. The tax treatment of policies that are not tax qualified is also briefly mentioned.

Deductibility of Premiums

General Tax Rules. The general tax rules that apply to the deductibility of long-term care insurance premiums for tax-qualified policies are essentially identical to those for medical expense insurance premiums. However, there is one major exception in that only a portion of the premiums are deductible for individually purchased coverage. These limits, which are based on a covered individual's age and subject to annual cost-of-living adjustments, are shown for 2008 in table 6-1.

TABLE 6-1
Long-Term Care Deductible Limits

Age	Annual Deductible Limit per Covered Individual
40 or younger	$ 310
41–50	580
51–60	1,150
61–70	3,080
Older than 70	3,850

The deductible amount is added to any other medical expenses and deductible to the extent it exceeds 7.5 percent of adjusted gross income.

Example: Winnie, aged 59, has a tax-qualified long-term care insurance policy that has an annual premium of $4,000. Based on table 6-1, she can include $1,150 of this amount as a medical expense when she prepares her income tax return. To the extent her total medical expenses exceed 7.5 percent of her adjusted gross income, she will be allowed a deduction as long as she itemizes her deduction.

Purchases by Self-Employed Persons. Self-employed persons are able to deduct premiums for long-term care insurance even if they do not itemize deductions. However, the deduction is limited to the amounts shown in table 6-1. In addition, the total deduction for medical expense insurance premiums and long-term care insurance premiums cannot exceed earned income from self-employment.

Employer-Paid Premiums. Very few employers have employee benefit plans under which they pay any portion of the premiums for the long-term care insurance premiums of employees. If they do make such contributions, the employer's share of the premium is fully deductible to the employer and does not represent taxable income to the employees. Employee contributions are treated as individually purchased coverage and deductible to the extent previously described under general tax rules.

If an employer is a sole proprietor, partnership, S corporation, or LLC, the tax treatment parallels that described earlier for medical expense coverage.

Tax-Free Receipt of Benefits

Like medical expense insurance benefits, benefits received under a tax-qualified long-term care contract are generally received tax free. This is always the case if the policy is written on a reimbursement basis so that it only pays benefits for expenses actually incurred. However, some policies are written on a per diem basis and pay a fixed daily benefit regardless of actual expenses incurred. Under such contracts, benefits are excludible from income in amounts up to $270 per day in 2008. (This figure is indexed annually.) Amounts in excess of $270 are also excludible to the extent that they represent actual costs for long-term care services.

Non-Tax-Qualified Policies

There is a small percentage of long-term care insurance polices that do not meet the requirements for tax-qualified policies. Premiums for such policies are not deductible. Furthermore, there is uncertainty over the tax status of benefits received from such policies. There is no specific provision in the Internal Revenue Code that allows for tax-free receipt of benefits. There are arguments that such a provision is unnecessary because the policies qualify as accident and sickness insurance, but not all tax experts agree with this position. To make matters worse, the IRS has so far not issued a ruling on this matter, and IRS employees' stated opinions have been inconsistent.

STATE TAX TREATMENT

Almost all states levy a state income tax. In many cases, they follow the federal income tax rules previously described. However, in other states, the rules are much different, particularly with respect to deductibility of insurance premiums. Some states have a tax that is a percentage of income with no deductions allowed. At the other extreme, some states are more generous than the federal government. For example, they may allow a full deduction for long-term care insurance premiums or allow deductions for medical expenses that exceed a smaller percentage of adjusted gross income than 7.5 percent.

The states are much like the federal government in that benefits from individually purchased health insurance policies are generally received income tax free.

It is beyond the scope of this book to detail the tax laws of every state. However, financial planners and insurance agents should familiarize themselves with the laws of the states within which they do business.

CHAPTER REVIEW

Key Terms

(NAIC) National Association of Insurance Commissioners
unauthorized entity
guaranty funds
policy form
Uniform Individual Accident and Sickness Policy Provision Law (UPPL)
entire contract provision
incontestable clause
grace period
reinstatement provision
twisting
misappropriation
rebating
mandated benefits
mandated option laws
HIPAA
protected health information (PHI)

Review Questions

Review questions are based on the learning objectives in this chapter. Thus, a [6-3] at the end of a question means that the question is based on learning objective 6-3. If there are multiple objectives, they are all listed.

1. Why is health insurance regulated? [6-1]
2. What are three sources of health insurance regulation? [6-1]
3. What is the primary purpose for licensing insurers? [6-2]
4. What are the types of state regulations that apply to policy forms? [6-2]
5. What is the purpose of advertising standards for health insurance policies? [6-2]
6. What types of regulations are aimed at prohibiting unfair discrimination in health insurance? [6-2]
7. What types of regulations apply to the replacement of health insurance policies? [6-2]
8. What types of regulations apply to each of the following?
   a. premium rates [6-2]
   b. renewability [6-2]
   c. policyowner complaints [6-2]
9. What types of mandates may apply to medical expense policies? [6-2]
10. How have states used regulatory authority to promote access to and affordability of medical expense insurance? [6-2]
11. How does each of the following federal laws affect individual medical expense insurance?
    a. HIPAA [6-3]
    b. Women's Health and Cancer Rights Act [6-3]
12. What are the general tax rules for the deductibility of medical expense premiums for federal income tax purposes? [6-4]
13. How do the federal tax rules for the deductibility of medical expense premiums differ under the following circumstances?
    a. The policy is purchased by a self-employed person. [6-4]
    b. The policy is purchased with employer-paid premiums. [6-4]
14. When are benefits from individual medical expense policies considered income for federal income tax purposes? [6-4]

15. What is the federal tax treatment of premiums paid for and benefits received from individual disability income policies when they are purchased in the following circumstances?
    a. by an individual [6-4]
    b. in employment-related situations [6-4]

16. In what ways does the federal tax treatment of HIPAA-qualified policies of long-term care insurance differ from that of medical expense policies with respect to?
    a. deductibility of premiums [6-4]
    b. taxation of benefits [6-4]

17. How might state income tax laws differ from federal rules with respect to health insurance premiums? [6-4]

7

Introduction to Medical Expense Coverage

Learning Objectives

An understanding of the material in this chapter should enable you to

7-1. Explain why people need protection against medical expenses.

7-2. Describe the programs of medical expense protection sponsored by federal and state governments and the populations they protect.

7-3. Explain how COBRA allows employment-related coverage to continue.

7-4. Describe the effect of a conversion provision on medical expense coverage.

7-5. Explain how HIPAA allows persons to obtain medical expense coverage when they change, lose, or terminate their jobs.

7-6. Summarize the types of individual medical expense insurance and their purposes.

Chapter Outline

This is the first of five chapters on policies of individual medical expense insurance. The discussion of this form of health insurance begins in this chapter by exploring broadly how persons may obtain protection against the expenses of medical care other than through active employment.

Although most persons obtain this protection through an employer-sponsored plan, many persons may not be covered in this way. An employer may not offer a medical benefit program, or the coverage may be insufficient. Even if an employer does offer an adequate plan, some employees may be ineligible or may decline participation for many reasons, including the cost of single or family coverage. Others may have changed or left employment or otherwise have no direct connection to a workforce where such plans are available. Many of these persons and others successfully turn to the individual medical expense insurance market to obtain coverage for themselves and their families. This market, nevertheless, may be an unlikely source of coverage for those whose economic situation does not allow them to pay the required premiums or whose health status prevents insurers from offering them coverage, even if they could otherwise afford the premiums. These persons must turn to government programs or private programs operating under government regulations.

In summary, individuals who either prefer to or must obtain medical expense coverage without reliance on active employment status must select an available program that best suits their and their families' economic and health-related circumstances. Beyond the coverage obtained through active employment, the sources of coverage—the subjects of this chapter—can be summarized as government programs, a continuation of coverage as a result of prior employment, and individual medical expense insurance.

Health insurance agents and financial advisors should understand broadly all sources of coverage so they know the place the policies they sell occupy in the spectrum of payment programs for medical care services. In doing so, they can assist their clients to make better coverage decisions.

A review of protection against the expenses of medical care and the extent of its availability precedes the discussion of the sources of coverage.

THE NEED FOR PROTECTION AGAINST MEDICAL EXPENSES AND ITS AVAILABILITY

Most people do not need to be convinced about the need for protection against the cost of medical care: More than 211 million Americans under age 65 have such protection through employment-based coverage, individually purchased policies, or government programs. Virtually all of the approximately 40 million persons aged 65 and over have coverage under Medicare. Thus, the value of medical expense coverage is almost universally appreciated by Americans, so much so that many policymakers and government leaders increasingly refer to having such coverage as a "right." Not surprisingly, expansions of government programs and regulation of private insurance programs aim to improve the availability of coverage and the number of persons covered.

The Need

The need for protection against medical expenses arises from the potential for unexpected and/or serious illnesses or injuries and the extraordinary cost of the medical services that a person experiencing them incurs.

While most persons appreciate the protection that medical expense coverage offers, they often fail to understand the magnitude of the expenses—expenses that they would probably be unable to pay in the absence of such coverage. Major advances in medicine have occurred for both inpatient and ambulatory care and include new diagnostic technologies, new forms of surgeries and treatments, and drug therapies. As a result, the price of medical services has increased and continues to increase dramatically; it is well above the average of all others items that consumers buy. For example, the price of hospital services has increased at more than double the average increase of all items in the consumer price index over the last 10 years.[1] Such amounts become even more prohibitive when they go beyond routine episodes of care to include major surgeries or continuing treatment for chronic and catastrophic or dread diseases, such as cancer, a stroke, or a paralyzing accident. These expenses can easily rise to tens of thousands, if not hundreds of thousands of dollars or more. As medical advances and their associated expenses continue, a person's or family's ability to pay for them in the event of a serious health problem or accident has become an extraordinary expense best managed through coverage under some type of program for the payment medical expenses.

Availability

For more than three decades before the establishment of any major government programs of medical expense coverage, private sector programs of medical expense insurance and medical benefit plans grew and flourished where virtually none existed previously. The success of these programs established them as the primary vehicle of financial access to needed medical care. Medical expense insurance became arguably the most important type of insurance protection and the type of protection that causes the most anxiety if it is lost or unaffordable. It is also the line of insurance for which the greatest dollar outlay is made. Understandably, then, the continuing public policy debate over the last decades has focused on the cost, availability, and benefits of medical expense insurance for those who have coverage, but in particular for those who do not—the uninsured and uninsurable.

Although private programs continued their success, there remained populations to which private coverage appeared unavailable, unaffordable, or both. Thus, not surprisingly, Medicare and Medicaid were established under federal legislation to provide coverage for the elderly, low-income children and families, and the disabled. State high-risk pools, now established by over 30 states, offer coverage to the medically uninsurable. Persons leaving or changing jobs were also viewed as potentially vulnerable for loss of medical expense insurance if they were unable to replace their coverage because of previous acute or chronic heath conditions. COBRA and HIPAA, programs of federal legislation discussed later in the chapter, allow such persons to continue their coverage or obtain coverage when terminating, leaving, or changing jobs. Many states have additional programs that expand coverage beyond the populations and limits required by these federal statutes.

Coverage Alternatives

The resulting interplay of coverage available through medical expense insurance, insurance required by regulation, and government programs frequently provides many persons and their families with alternatives. For example, many persons coming off employer coverage are eligible for coverage under COBRA, but for various reasons may wish to consider other options. Making a selection when alternatives present themselves depends on a number of factors such as person's age, medical condition, financial resources, family status, and the cost of coverage.

Example: Hector and many of his coworkers are losing their jobs in a major cutback. They do not expect to find comparable employment anytime soon. Although he is eligible to continue his medical expense coverage under COBRA, Hector finds that in his circumstances, the family premium is un–affordable—$950 per month for himself, his wife Harriet, and daughter, Henrietta.

When Hector discusses the matter with his terminating coworkers, he finds that a number of the younger workers, including some with families, are declining COBRA; they can obtain individual medical expense insurance at a rate much lower than the COBRA premium due to their age and good health. Other workers are at or near age 65 and soon will be Medicare eligible. Still others in their late 50s find that, because of their age, the premium for individual medical expense insurance exceeds the COBRA premium, which is based on the average age of their employer's generally younger workforce. They decide to continue coverage under COBRA, which, fortunately, they can afford for the time being.

Hector is in a quandary. His own younger age and good health would allow him to purchase an affordable, yet comprehensive, medical expense policy for himself in the private market. However, both his wife and daughter have medical conditions that would exclude them from such coverage. Despite its cost, COBRA appears to be the only option that will allow Hector to obtain coverage for his family without medical underwriting.

A coworker introduces Hector to Sam Sage, an insurance agent. Sam informs Hector of alternatives he may have and helps him evaluate them. COBRA allows dependents to be covered even when a worker personally declines such coverage. Their state also has a high-risk pool for persons with uninsurable health conditions as well as state health insurance program for children in families with moderate income (SCHIP). For Harriet, the state high-risk pool premium at 200 percent of the standard rate is comparable to the COBRA premium, but provides somewhat less comprehensive coverage. Henrietta is eligible for SCHIP because Hector's family income is within the state's income eligibility requirement—300 percent of the federal poverty level.

Hector makes his decisions. For himself, he purchases an individual medical high-deductible medical expense policy from Sam for about $100 per month. He continues Harriet's coverage under COBRA for $350 per month and enrolls Henrietta in SCHIP with no premium required. The total amount that Hector pays is less than half the COBRA premium required for his entire family.

As the example illustrates, making an informed decision requires knowledge of the coverage alternatives that may be available.

Consumers as well as agents and others who advise them can obtain information on the availability of coverage in the private market, both employment-based and individually purchased, as well as government-sponsored programs of medical coverage by visiting http://www.nahu.org/consumer/healthcare/index.cfm. This Web site, sponsored by The National Association of Health Underwriters (NAHU), contains an interactive state-by-state coverage options database. The site also identifies sources of assistance and contacts to obtain coverage.

The Foundation for Health Care Coverage at its Web site www.coverageforall.org provides a similar state-by-state database as well as an interactive function to help determine an individual's eligibility for specific plans.

State insurance departments typically are an information resource on health insurance coverage that is available in the private market and through government-sponsored programs.

The following two sections on government programs and continuation of coverage as a result of prior employment explain these sources of coverage and what they provide. This chapter's final section presents individual medical expense insurance as a major source for coverage of medical care expenses in the private sector for those persons who are outside of the realm of active employment or government program eligibility.

GOVERNMENT PROGRAMS

Both the federal government and state governments are deeply involved in providing protection against medical care expenses through Medicare, Medicaid, veterans' benefits, the State Children's Health Insurance Program, and state high-risk health insurance plans. All of these programs were established because public policymakers and government leaders believe that in general the populations served by the programs are unable or unlikely to obtain medical expense insurance in the private market.

Medicare

First established by federal legislation in 1965, Medicare is a medical expense insurance program for people aged 65 or older, people under age 65 with disabilities, and people with end-stage renal disease (permanent kidney failure requiring dialysis or a transplant). Medicare provides coverage to over 40 million Americans, known as beneficiaries. Because of continuing increases in the aged population (for which this program is primarily designed) as well as longer life expectancies, Medicare enrollment continues to climb.

Almost all Medicare beneficiaries become eligible for benefits when they reach age 65, as long as they are entitled to monthly retirement benefits from Social Security or the Railroad Retirement Board (although they may not be actually receiving them, as in the case of persons who must wait past age 65 to receive those benefits). Thus, Medicare is an entitlement program with eligibility unrelated to income or health status. Although many Medicare eligible persons could, in the absence of the program, find insurance under a private medical expense insurance policy, for many others the situation is likely to be different. Persons with no earned income from employment often cannot afford the premiums, and those with deteriorating health would likely be uninsurable even if the cost of the premiums was affordable.

Nevertheless, with Medicare as its principal coverage, this population is eligible for coverage under Medicare supplement policies in the private market. They are also eligible in many cases for comprehensive coverage through federally approved alternative plans to original Medicare, known as Medicare Advantage plans. Chapter 10 explains Medicare, policies that supplement Medicare, and Medicare Advantage plans.

Medicaid

Medicaid is a federal/state program that is the largest source of payments for the medical care of eligible individuals and families with low incomes and assets. Medicaid has nearly 55 million beneficiaries, with annual expenditures consisting of state funds and matching federal funds in excess of $300 billion.

Within broad federal requirements, each state (1) establishes its own eligibility standards, (2) determines the type, amount, duration, and scope of services, (3) sets the rate of payment for services, and (4) administers its own program. Medicaid policies for eligibility, services, and payment are complex and vary considerably. Thus, a person who is eligible for Medicaid in one state might be ineligible in another state. Likewise, the services provided by one state may differ considerably in amount, duration, or scope from services covered in a neighboring state.

At the same time, ongoing legislative and regulatory changes continue to increase a state's ability to obtain federal matching funds for an array of services and eligibility alternatives that go beyond federally mandated requirements. Generally, these changes broaden the low-income populations that can qualify for Medicaid. The best place to begin the search for detailed information on Medicaid is at the federal government's Web site, www.cms.hhs.gov/medicaid. This site contains consumer information on Medicaid with access to specific state Medicaid program information. In addition, some local governments (cities and counties) provide health care programs for residents that a state's Medicaid program may not provide.

In general, to qualify for Medicaid, a person must satisfy low income and resource criteria that each state determines within federal guidelines. However, poverty alone is not sufficient; a person must also be in an eligible category. Medicaid covers three main groups of low-income Americans: the elderly (persons aged 65 and over), the disabled (including the blind), and parents and children. Fifty-three percent of Medicaid beneficiaries are children, with an additional 24 percent being parents, mostly women, in families with children. About 11 percent are elderly and 12 percent are disabled. [2]

The array of Medicaid benefits are summarized under the headings of medical benefits, medical benefit variations, and long-term care benefits.

Medical Benefits

For most recipients, Medicaid benefits encompass acute medical care services provided by a broad spectrum of health care professionals and institutions and may include services such as dental and vision care. With few exceptions, Medicaid's payment to care providers for services is payment in full, and the recipient has no further payment responsibility. States may impose nominal deductibles, coinsurance, or copayments on some Medicaid recipients for certain services, however. Most states administer their Medicaid benefits through plans conducted to some degree by private sector managed care organizations.

Medical Benefit Variations

Medical benefit variations include assistance with Medicare premiums and cost sharing and coverage of three optional populations

Assistances with Medicare Premiums. States are also required to offer assistance by way of payment for Medicare premiums and cost sharing (but not any other Medicaid benefits) to categories of low-resource and low-income Medicare beneficiaries. This assistance is identified as the Medicare Savings Program.

Medicaid pays Medicare Part A premiums, if any, and Part B premiums and cost shares for those eligible in the lowest income category, but limits such assistance to payment of the Medicare Part B premium for other persons who may qualify. In addition, qualified persons can receive federal assistance with premiums for prescription drug coverage and other drug cost-sharing amounts as low-income beneficiaries if they enroll in the Medicare prescription drug program (explained in chapter 10).

Of course, Medicaid recipients who are generally entitled to Medicaid benefits and are also Medicare eligible, known as dual eligibles, are entitled to the same assistance as well.

Three Optional Populations. Three federal eligibility categories give states the option to extend limited Medicaid coverage to three populations of uninsured or potentially uninsured low-income individuals, including childless individuals under 65 who are not disabled. These populations are: (1) newly unemployed workers and others entitled to COBRA continuation coverage, (2) individuals infected with tuberculosis, and (3) women diagnosed with breast or cervical cancer.

Persons qualifying in the first category who pass an income and resource test receive a premium subsidy, but no other Medicaid benefits. Persons who qualify in the second category by passing an income and resource test receive Medicaid benefits only for the treatment of tuberculosis.

The eligibility of persons qualifying in the third category, however, is not determined using an income or resource test. Instead, women are qualified if they (1) are not already covered as a mandatorily eligible Medicaid beneficiary, (2) are under age 65, (3) have been screened at the early detection program funded by the Centers for Disease Control and Prevention and need treatment for breast or cervical cancer, and (4) do not have private health insurance or other health care coverage. Qualified women are entitled to Medicaid's medical benefits package. Most states have elected to implement this option.

Long-Term Care Benefits

As chapter 17 explains, the Medicaid program is also the largest payer of long-term care services in institutional settings and will continue to be so in the years ahead. Moreover, in the upcoming decades, Medicaid is projected to be second only to Medicare in payment for home health services. Not surprisingly, then, the proportion of the population needing long-term care that relies on Medicaid is greater than the proportion of the population that relies on Medicaid for payment of medical expenses. Chapter 17 includes a more complete discussion of Medicaid eligibility requirements.

Veterans' Benefits

Another potential government source of medical expense coverage is the health care program of the Department of Veterans Affairs, often referred to as the VA. Eligibility and benefits can change from year to year because they depend on congressional appropriations. Current information on veterans' health care programs is available at the Web site of the Department of Veterans Affairs, www.va.gov.

Eligibility

In general, veterans are eligible for enrollment in the VA program in a priority order based on the extent of their service-related injuries and/or their financial resources. Currently, about 6 million veterans are enrolled in the program.

Some of these veterans must rely entirely on their veterans' benefits for their medical care because of their uninsurability and unemployability. Nevertheless, anyone who is eligible for veterans' benefits, even if they have other medical coverage, may seek care from the VA program. Such care may provide a special type and quality of service for their personal health needs, especially if that care is for a service-connected medical condition. In addition, there is little or no out-of-pocket expense for most categories of eligible veterans. For these persons, care in a VA facility could be less expensive than paying the self-responsible amounts of their medical benefit plans for services received outside the VA system.

However, the VA is authorized to recover reasonable charges from private medical expense plans for medical care for non-service-connected medical conditions. Although the VA cannot bill Medicare for medical services provided to veterans, it can bill for services that are covered by a Medicare supplement policy but not covered by Medicare.

Benefits

Benefits are comprehensive; they include a broad array of inpatient and outpatient services which may be received from VA facilities or other providers under contract to the VA. All services are not available at all VA locations, however. The VA also provides long-term care services, which chapter 17 discusses.

State Children's Health Insurance Program

State Children's Health Insurance Program (SCHIP)

As one of its provisions, The Balanced Budget Act of 1997 authorized states to implement a new child health program, known as the *State Children's Health Insurance Program (SCHIP)*. States that implement SCHIP receive federal matching funds to initiate or expand health insurance coverage to uninsured children 18 years old or younger with low family incomes who are ineligible for Medicaid. All 50 states, as well as the District of Columbia, have implemented this program. In addition to state appropriations, a state's sources of matching funding may include foundation grants, county and other local funds, and private donations as well. Within the limits of the federal requirements, states determine eligibility and may impose cost sharing on recipients through enrollment fees, premiums, deductibles, and copayments.

States have the option of implementing SCHIP through an expansion of Medicaid, designing or building a separate (from Medicaid) child health program, or using both approaches. Because of its greater flexibility in determining the benefits provided and the specific age and income groups served, over 40 states use a separate child health program, either on a stand-alone basis or in addition to an expanded Medicaid program. However, the separate program option requires adherence to one of several benefit package benchmarks or approval from the Secretary of HHS for an acceptable alternative.

Nevertheless, the Secretary has authorized the use of program funds in innovative ways, including premium assistance to buy into employer-sponsored insurance coverage and even the extension of coverage to parents in the hope that inclusion of families will increase the enrollment of their children. Currently hundreds of thousands of parents and/or pregnant women are enrolled in SCHIP together with several million children.

Some facets of the program's implementation may provide incentives to drop existing private-sector coverage in favor of SCHIP. Such a substitution of a public program for a private-sector program is known as "crowd-out." The income eligibility threshold for SCHIP significantly exceeds the Medicaid level in all states, and states continue to increase it. Some states go beyond 200 percent of the federal poverty level and frequently dispense with asset tests. Coverage often has a lower premium and more comprehensive benefits compared to private coverage. Employers, too, may also have an incentive to discontinue dependent coverage or reduce their premium contributions if SCHIP coverage is available for their low-wage workers. States attempt to control "crowd-out" through (1) a waiting period after the loss of health insurance, (2) program benefit designs comparable to those available in the private sector, and (3) inquiries of applicants and their employers about existing or available coverage.

SCHIP is controversial due to its scope and its funding. Some congressional leaders seek significant expansion of the program to include parents as well as children at family income levels that are much higher than those currently authorized, with annual funding at multiples of previously budgeted amounts. Other leaders observe that a significant number of eligible children have not enrolled in SCHIP as it is. They argue that any future legislation should aim to achieve the program's original objective by increasing SCHIP's funding levels moderately and improving outreach to eligible but unenrolled children.

State High-Risk Health Insurance Plans

State high-risk health insurance plans were initiated under state legislation over the last three decades, beginning with Connecticut and Minnesota. The main feature of these plans is a mechanism to broadly share the risk of above-standard financial losses for the benefit payments of comprehensive medical insurance offered to individuals whose preexisting health conditions denied them standard coverage in the private market. This mechanism, operated as a not-for-profit association, is known as a *high-risk pool*. More than 30 states now have a health insurance high-risk pool or a similar program that provides coverage for uninsurable persons. Pools in a few of these states may not be fully operational, and some may limit access. About half the states have opted to use their high-risk pools to guarantee coverage in the individual market required by HIPAA for people who leave their employer or other source of group coverage.

high-risk pool

On an annual basis, the total number of enrollees for all states exceeds 190,000, with each state's participation level ranging from a few hundred (Florida) to approximately 31,000 (Minnesota). Risk pool insurance typically costs more than standard coverage in the private market but by law maintains a cap on premiums. Most state premium limits range from 125 to 150 percent of average for a comparable plan in the private market, although some states may allow up to 200 percent of average. Total claims from operational programs are approaching $1.5 billion annually.[3]

Each pool loses money because it is not feasible to pool a group of individuals with known major health problems and expect their premiums to cover the entire cost. Consequently, each pool requires a subsidy of over 40 percent on average that states generate from various sources. The sources for funding the subsidy may include the following:

- an assessment of all insurers, including HMOs and other health plans
- shared funding of the subsidy whereby the assessment of insurers is offset by a state tax credit

- an appropriation from state general tax revenue
- a designated revenue source, such as a tobacco tax, or a hospital or health care provider surcharge

Risk pools are not created expressly to serve the indigent or poor who cannot afford health insurance; they are designed to serve people who are unable to purchase health insurance because it is simply unavailable or because they are uninsurable. Thus, these pools largely serve uninsurable persons who would otherwise be in the same market as that served by standard insurance products: small business owners, employees of small businesses that do not offer insurance, the self-employed, and other individuals. Nevertheless, some state risk pools do have a subsidy for lower-income, medically uninsurable people.

An appointed board of directors governs the programs with day-to-day administration by a private third party, typically with supervision by the state's insurance department.

Example: Nadine, a self-employed interior designer, is a single mother with a 6-year old son. She moved to another state to be near her elderly parents so she can provide them some assistance with their daily living activities. In making the move, she gave up coverage under her local HMO where she has had an individual policy covering herself and her son for several years. Because of several health conditions, she is unable to obtain medically underwritten coverage in the individual market in her parents' state. COBRA and HIPAA coverage requirements do not apply to her situation. However, she turns to her new state's high-risk insurance pool that allows her to obtain coverage at 150 percent of standard premium. She purchases a separate medically underwritten policy for her son at a low premium in the private insurance market because of his age and robust health.

Under the Trade Adjustment Assistance Act of 2002, the federal government for the first time provided seed grants to encourage states that currently do not have qualified high-risk pools to establish them. In addition to allocating up to $1 million for each new state program, the act also provides operational grants in similar amounts to offset up to 50 percent of the losses of established qualified high-risk pools. However, these pools must cap premiums as a percent of the standard rate (150 percent), offer at least two plan options, and ensure a mechanism for continued funding after the last year for which a grant is provided. The State High Risk Pool Funding Extension Act of 2006 extended the program through 2010. The extension legislation implements some changes in the operational grant requirements, including a required allocation of funds based on a state's uninsured population and number of pool enrollees, a conditional relaxation of the previous premium cap (200 percent), and bonus grants to encourage benefit improvements.

CONTINUATION OF COVERAGE AS A RESULT OF PRIOR EMPLOYMENT

Approximately 90 percent of the persons under age 65 who have medical expense insurance obtain it as an employee benefit. Although the extent of their contributions continues to decline, employers pay a major portion of the cost of their employees' coverage.

Even though employer-provided benefits vary widely, enrolling in an employer-sponsored plan is generally the first choice for any eligible employee and his or her dependents because coverage at all employee group-size levels is generally more comprehensive and a better value than other forms of coverage. Consequently, the ability to continue that valuable coverage when an employee's status as part of the active workforce changes represents a desirable option. In the absence of any provision for continuation or conversion, employer-provided coverage on an employee and dependents generally ceases on the date employment terminates or the end of the last period for which the employee has made any required contribution.

However, insurance coverage often is available past these dates because of federal legislation or employer practices. The most notable coverage continuation requirements under federal legislation are COBRA, conversion, and group-to-individual coverage portability under HIPAA. COBRA involves a continuation of prior employer-provided coverage. The other options allow a person to obtain individual coverage without evidence of insurability. To properly advise clients, it is important for an agent, broker, or financial planner to understand these options.

Continuation of Coverage under COBRA

COBRA

A federal law known as *COBRA*[4] (because it was part of the Consolidated Omnibus Budget Reconciliation Act of 1985) requires that group health plans allow employees and certain family members to extend their current health insurance coverage at group rates for up to 36 months following a "qualifying event" that results in the loss of coverage for a "qualified beneficiary." In many cases, the continuation of employer-provided coverage is the most cost-effective method for employees under age 65 to obtain medical expense coverage. However, the duration of the coverage is limited.

The term *group health plan* as used in the act is broad enough to include medical expense plans, dental plans, vision care plans, and prescription drug plans, regardless of whether benefits are self-insured or provided through other entities, such as insurance companies, HMOs, or PPOs. Long-term care and disability income coverages are not included in the definition of a group health plan and are not subject to COBRA.

COBRA also applies to voluntary (employee-pay-all) group health plans as long as an employee would not be able to receive the coverage at the same cost if the employment relationship ended. COBRA does not apply if the voluntary plan has a portability provision whereby an employee can continue the coverage on an individual basis at no increase in cost.

Certain church-related plans and plans of the federal government are exempt from COBRA, but the act applies to all other employers who had the equivalent of 20 or more full-time employees on a typical business day during the preceding calendar year.

Qualified Beneficiaries

qualified beneficiary

Since the passage of COBRA, a *qualified beneficiary* has been defined as any employee, or the spouse or dependent child of the employee, who on the day before a qualifying event was covered under the employee's group health plan. The Health Insurance Portability and Accountability Act (HIPAA) expanded the definition to include any child who is born to or placed for adoption with the employee during the period of COBRA coverage. This change gives the child automatic eligibility for COBRA coverage.

Each qualified beneficiary has his or her own COBRA election rights.

Qualifying Events

qualifying event

Under COBRA, each of the following is a *qualifying event* if it results in the loss of medical expense coverage by a qualified beneficiary:

- death of the covered employee
- termination of the employee for any reason except gross misconduct. This includes quitting, retiring, or being fired for anything other than gross misconduct.
- reduction of the employee's hours so that the employee or dependent is ineligible for coverage

- divorce or legal separation of the employee and his or her spouse
- for spouses and children, the employee's eligibility for Medicare
- a child's ceasing to be an eligible dependent under the plan

The act specifies that a qualified beneficiary is entitled to elect continued coverage without providing evidence of insurability. The beneficiary must be allowed to continue coverage identical to that available to employees and dependents to whom a qualifying event has not occurred. Coverage for persons electing COBRA continuation can be changed when changes are made to the plan covering similarly situated active employees and their dependents. In addition, a qualified beneficiary who moves out of an area served by a region-specific plan must be given the right to change coverage if the employer is able to provide coverage under another of its existing plans.

Example 1: Herb and his wife Susan are covered by his employer's medical expense plan, under which 200 employees are insured. Herb expects to retire next year when he and Susan will be aged 64 and 62, respectively. They will both then be eligible for COBRA coverage for a maximum of 18 months. If they elect COBRA, Herb's coverage will cease upon his entitlement to Medicare at age 65. Susan's coverage will continue for the full 18 months, at which time she will need to find another source for her medical expense protection until she turns age 65.

Example 2: Michael, aged 42, was unexpectedly laid off because of a restructuring by his employer. He does not expect to have difficulty finding new employment, but realizes it may take a few months. Bccause of his diabetes, for which he takes medication, he realizes that it may be difficult to find coverage on his own. Therefore, he decides to elect COBRA coverage.

Length of Coverage

Each qualified beneficiary must be allowed to continue coverage from the qualifying event until the earliest of the following:

- 18 months for employees and dependents when the employee's employment has terminated or coverage has been terminated because of a reduction in hours. This period is extended to 29 months for a qualified beneficiary if the Social Security Administration determines that the beneficiary was or became totally disabled at any time during the first 60 days of COBRA coverage.

- 36 months for all other qualifying events
- the date the plan terminates for all employees
- the date the coverage ceases because of a failure to make a timely payment of premium for the qualified beneficiary's coverage
- the date the qualified beneficiary subsequently becomes entitled to Medicare or becomes covered (as either an employee or dependent) under another group health plan, provided the group health plan does not contain an exclusion or limitation with respect to any preexisting condition. If the new plan does not cover a preexisting condition, the COBRA coverage can be continued until the earlier of (1) the remainder of the 18- or 36-month period or (2) the time when the preexisting-conditions provision no longer applies.

If a second qualifying event (such as the death or divorce of a terminated employee) occurs during the period of continued coverage, the maximum period of continuation is 36 months as long as the event would have resulted in a loss of coverage if it had been the first qualifying event.

Example: Fritz elected COBRA continuation coverage for himself and his wife Edna when he retired at age 61. At his death 15 months later, a second qualifying event occurred for Edna. The normal period of COBRA continuation resulting from the death of an employee is 36 months. However, because Edna has already had COBRA coverage for 15 months, the second qualifying event extends her coverage period for an additional 21 months.

At the termination of continued coverage, a qualified beneficiary must be offered the right to convert to an individual insurance policy if a conversion privilege is generally available to employees under the employer's plan. Conversion is discussed later.

Notification of COBRA Rights

Notification of the right to continue coverage must be made at two times by the administrator of an employer plan. First, when a plan becomes subject to COBRA or when a person becomes covered under a plan subject to

COBRA, notification must be given to an employee as well as to his or her spouse, generally within 90 days. A single letter to the employee and spouse satisfies this requirement as long as they reside at the same location. Second, when a qualifying event occurs, the employer must notify the plan administrator, who then must notify all qualified beneficiaries within 14 days. In general, the employer has 30 days to notify the plan administrator. However, an employer may not know of a qualifying event if it involves divorce, legal separation, or a child ceasing to be eligible for coverage. In these circumstances, the employee or family member must notify the employer within 60 days of the event, or the right to elect COBRA coverage is lost. The time period for the employer to notify the plan administrator begins when the employer is informed of the qualifying event, as long as this occurs within the 60-day period.

Recent changes to COBRA rules also require plan administrators to provide notification to qualified beneficiaries in two other circumstances. First, if a plan beneficiary receives a notice of a qualifying event and the qualified beneficiary is ineligible for COBRA coverage, the plan administrators must explain why the qualified beneficiary is not entitled to coverage. Second, if COBRA coverage is terminated before the end of the maximum duration, the plan administrator must explain when and why the coverage is being terminated and inform the qualified beneficiary of any available rights to other coverage.

COBRA Elections

The continuation of coverage is not automatic; a qualified beneficiary must elect it. The election period starts on the date of the qualifying event and may end not earlier than 60 days after actual notice of the event to the qualified beneficiary by the plan administrator. Once coverage is elected, it is effective retroactively to the date coverage would otherwise have ceased, and the beneficiary has 45 days to pay the premium for the period of coverage prior to the election.

COBRA Premiums

Under COBRA, the cost of the continued coverage may be passed on to the qualified beneficiary, but the cost cannot exceed 102 percent of the cost to the plan for the period of coverage for a similarly situated active employee to whom a qualifying event has not occurred. The extra 2 percent is supposed to cover the employer's extra administrative costs. (The one exception to this rule occurs for months 19 through 29 if an employee is disabled, in which case the premium can then be as high as 150 percent.) Qualified beneficiaries must have the option of paying the premium in monthly installments. In addition, there must be a grace period of at least 30 days for each installment.

It is important to point out that an employer can charge less than 102 percent for COBRA continuation and may even pay the full premium for a period of time as part of a severance or early-retirement package.

Example: Clark, aged 50, was laid off. Prior to retirement, he paid $100 per month toward his medical expense coverage, and his employer paid the remaining $400 of the $500 total premium. The employer can charge him a monthly COBRA premium of up to $510 (102 percent of $500). However, as part of a severance package, his employer has agreed to charge him a monthly COBRA premium of $100 for the first 6 months of any COBRA election, or the same amount of his contribution while employed. After 6 months, the monthly premium will be the full $510.

COBRA has resulted in significant extra costs for employers. Precise statistics are difficult to obtain, but one insurer indicates that coverage is elected by approximately 20 percent of those persons who are entitled to a COBRA continuation. The length of coverage averages almost 1 year for persons eligible for an 18-month extension and almost 2 years for persons eligible for a 36-month extension. Although significant variations exist among employers, claim costs of persons with COBRA coverage generally run about 150 percent of claim costs for active employees and dependents. Moreover, administrative costs are estimated to be about $20 per month for each person with COBRA coverage.

Is COBRA Coverage Worth the Cost?

Premiums under employer-provided plans tend to be the same for all employees, regardless of age. Therefore, continuation of coverage under COBRA is often the most cost-effective way for an older former employee to obtain medical expense coverage for as long as it lasts. However, circumstances vary, and the other alternatives that are mentioned in this and later chapters need to be explored as well. Younger employees may have little difficulty finding less expensive coverage in the individual marketplace, particularly if they are healthy.

Example 1: Harry, who is single, decided to retire at age 62. His employer currently pays an insurance premium of $400 per month for each actively working single employee. The employer has set the monthly COBRA premium at 102 percent of this amount, or $408. The least expensive comparable coverage Harry can find in the individual marketplace has a monthly premium of $500. Therefore, COBRA continuation is less expensive than an individual policy. However, Harry will need to find alternative coverage in 18 months when COBRA coverage is no longer available.

Example 2: After receiving an inheritance from his grandmother, Larry, aged 30, decided to quit his job and spend a year studying for an MBA. When shopping around, he found that he could buy an individual policy at about half the cost of the premium for COBRA coverage.

One final point worth mentioning involves comparing COBRA coverage with coverage available in the individual marketplace. In many cases, employer-provided coverage includes more comprehensive benefits than individually purchased coverage. As a result, any comparison of the two should look at benefits as well as cost. In addition, persons who are in good health and who are willing to assume higher deductibles and copayments can often find individual coverage that is less expensive than COBRA continuation.

State COBRA Laws

Some states have continuation laws for insured medical expense plans that require coverage to be made available in situations not covered by COBRA. These laws are often referred to as state COBRA laws or mini-COBRA laws. One example is coverage for employees of firms with fewer than 20 employees; another is coverage for periods longer than those required by COBRA.

These state laws do not apply to self-funded plans. Such plans, which insure about one-half of the country's workers and their families, are exempt from state legislation of this type because of ERISA, another federal law.

Conversion

conversion provision

Except when termination results from the failure to pay any required premiums, medical expense contracts often contain (and may be required to contain) a *conversion provision*. With such a provision, most covered persons whose group coverage terminates are allowed to purchase individual medical expense coverage without evidence of insurability and without any limitation of benefits for preexisting conditions. Covered persons have a specified number of days (typically 31) from the date of the group coverage's termination to exercise this conversion privilege; coverage is then effective retroactively to the date of termination.

This conversion privilege is typically given to any employee who has been insured under the group contract (or under any group contract it replaced) for at least 3 months, and it permits the employee to convert his or her own coverage as well as any dependent coverage. In addition, a spouse or child whose dependent coverage ceases for any other reason may also be eligible for conversion (for example, a spouse who divorces or separates, and children who reach age 19).

State laws and insurance company practices vary with respect to the conversion provision and COBRA. In some cases, conversion is contingent upon an individual electing COBRA coverage and maintaining it for the maximum election period. At that time, a conversion policy is available. In other cases, a person who is eligible for both the conversion privilege and the right to continue the group insurance coverage under COBRA has two choices when eligibility for coverage terminates. He or she can either elect to convert under the policy's provisions or elect to continue the group coverage under COBRA. If the latter choice is made, the COBRA rules specify that the person must again be eligible to convert to an individual policy within the usual conversion period (31 days) after the maximum continuation-of-coverage period ceases. In either situation, policy provisions may also make the conversion privilege available to persons whose coverage terminates prior to the end of the maximum continuation period. If the conversion option is elected, there are no COBRA rights if the conversion policy terminates.

The provider of the medical expense coverage has the right to refuse the issue of a conversion policy to anyone (1) who is covered by Medicare or (2) whose benefits under the converted policy, together with similar benefits from other sources, would result in overinsurance according to the insurance company's standards. These similar benefits may be found in other coverages that the individual has (either group or individual coverage) or for which the individual is eligible under any group arrangement.

The word "conversion" is often a misnomer. In actuality, a person whose coverage terminates is only given the right to purchase a contract on an individual basis at individual rates. Most Blue Cross and Blue Shield plans and some HMO plans offer a conversion policy that is similar or identical to the terminated group coverage. However, many insurance companies offer a conversion policy (or a choice of policies) that contains a lower level of benefits than existed under the group coverage.

Some plans offer a conversion policy that is written by another entity. For example, an HMO might enter into a contractual arrangement with an insurance company. In some cases, the HMO and insurance company are commonly owned or have a parent-subsidiary relationship.

Self-funded medical expense plans, which are exempt from state laws mandating a conversion policy, may still provide such a benefit. Rather than providing coverage directly to the terminated employee, an agreement is usually made with an insurance company to make a policy available.

Historically, the persons who elect to convert coverage have been relatively unhealthy, and the premiums for this coverage often reflect this fact. Persons in good health can often find less expensive coverage in the individual marketplace. Persons in poor health may also find better and less expensive coverage by purchasing an individual policy under provisions of HIPAA. As a result, conversion is seldom used. However, it is an available option to explore and occasionally may be the best option.

Group to Individual Portability under HIPAA

A major purpose of HIPAA, introduced in the previous chapter, is to maintain medical expense coverage for workers and their families when they change, lose, or terminate their jobs. As long as they had prior employer-provided medical expense coverage, they are guaranteed access to and renewability of coverage provided in the individual market (There are also HIPAA rules that guarantee access to the coverage of a new employer, but these rules are beyond the scope of this book.) The name of the act (the Health Insurance Portability and Accountability Act) is somewhat misleading because workers and their families do not keep the same insurance program and are likely to have different benefits under the subsequent program. *Portability* means that preexisting-conditions limitations for medical insurance purposes are defined under the act and once satisfied may not serve to deny, limit, or delay a qualified person's coverage or the renewal of that coverage as required by the act. State laws apply to the extent that they contain provisions that are more favorable to consumers.

portability

It is important to point out several things that HIPAA is not. First, it is not applicable if a person changes from one individually purchased medical expense policy to another. Second, HIPAA does not guarantee that insurance protection will be available at a price everyone can afford; it only guarantees access to available coverage. Because of adverse selection, individual policies available under HIPAA often have a high cost. Finally, HIPAA coverage is not necessarily the only available medical expense coverage. Too often it is viewed as the only alternative to someone with medical problems.

Example: Jack and his wife Charlotte, both aged 62, selected COBRA coverage when Jack retired 18 months ago. Now they must obtain individual coverage until they are eligible for Medicare. They have heard that they can obtain guaranteed coverage under HIPAA without any preexisting-conditions exclusions. However, in exploring the situation they have found that the HIPAA coverage is significantly more expensive than identical coverage that is individually underwritten. Even though they have minor medical problems, individually underwritten coverage is available to them at a price lower than HIPAA coverage.

General Provisions

HIPAA individual market provisions apply to major medical, HMO, and similar types of principal medical insurance benefit programs (described later in the chapter). These provisions establish requirements for the guaranteed issue and renewal of individual medical expense coverages for eligible individuals. To a great extent, health insurers are only indirectly affected; more than 40 states satisfy the HIPAA individual insurance requirements by implementing a federally qualified alternative mechanism. About half of these states have opted to use their high-risk pools (discussed earlier) for the medically uninsurable as the alternative mechanism to guarantee coverage in the individual market under HIPAA. Modifications to some of these programs qualified them as an alternative mechanism under the federal requirements. The alternative mechanism in other states may be the use of the state's existing guaranteed issue and renewal mandates in the individual market or reliance on a single insurer of last resort.

In several states and the District of Columbia, which have no alternative mechanism, insurers providing individual coverage in these markets are subject to HIPAA's federal fallback standards (discussed later) for guaranteed issue and renewal. However, these standards do not apply to insurers offering coverage only in conjunction with group medical expense plans, including one-life group and group conversion policies. In addition, there are special rules for association plans.

Note that the HIPAA rules do not apply to many types of medical expense plans or apply only under certain circumstances. These include:

- coverage for accidents, including accidental death and dismemberment
- disability income insurance
- limited vision or dental benefits, long-term care insurance, nursing home insurance, home health care insurance, and insurance for community-based care if these benefits are offered separately rather than as an integral part of a medical expense plan
- coverage for a specific disease or illness or for hospital or other fixed indemnity insurance if the benefits (1) are provided under a separate policy, certificate, or contract of insurance and (2) are not coordinated with other coverage under a medical expense plan
- Medicare supplement insurance or other similar supplemental coverage if the policy is offered as a separate insurance policy rather than as a continuation of coverage under a plan that also covers active employees

Guaranteed-Issue Requirements

To be eligible for guaranteed issue of medical expense coverage under HIPAA, a person must have

- 18 months of "creditable qualifying coverage," the most recent of which was under an employer, government, or church group health plan
- no gaps in coverage of 63 or more full days within or after the 18 months of creditable coverage
- exhausted any other coverage, if eligible under COBRA or similar state programs
- no eligibility for another group medical expense plan, Medicare, or Medicaid
- no other medical expense coverage
- no cancellation of prior coverage for fraud or nonpayment of premium

creditable qualifying coverage

Creditable qualifying coverage is prior coverage under a medical expense plan or policy. HIPAA does not require that individuals without prior coverage be insured, nor does it provide guaranteed issue for individuals moving from one individual medical insurance policy to another. Furthermore, it leaves to the states the decision regarding limitations to be imposed on premiums charged for individual health insurance coverage required by HIPAA.

In the absence of a federally qualified state mechanism, a carrier offering coverage in the individual market is subject to the federal fallback standards mentioned previously. Under these standards, a carrier may not refuse coverage or enrollment to an eligible individual under at least two of its medical expense policies and may not impose any preexisting-conditions exclusions with respect to such coverage. There are standard exceptions to this requirement for insurers that have insufficient financial capacity or whose provider network (in the case of managed care plans) does not encompass the location where an eligible individual lives, resides, or works.

Although individual insurers may elect to offer coverage to eligible individuals under all of their current policy forms, HIPAA allows insurers two other elections, which may be more appealing. Under these elections, insurers may limit the policy forms available to eligible individuals to either (1) their two most popular policies, as measured by the largest and second-largest premium volume; or (2) two representative individual medical expense insurance policies typically offered by the insurer in the state. These two representative policy forms must include a lower and higher level of coverage, each of which is substantially similar to other levels of coverage offered by the insurer in the state as determined by specified actuarial value tests. Blocks of business closed under applicable state laws may be excluded from calculating premium volume. Policies under these two elections must be made generally available and actively marketed to both HIPAA-eligible and other individuals. Whatever election an insurer makes must remain effective for not less than 2 years and must apply uniformly to all HIPAA-eligible individuals in the state.

Guaranteed Renewability Requirements

HIPAA requires health insurers offering individual medical insurance coverage to renew such coverage at the individual's option. Exceptions to these requirements include: (1) nonpayment or untimely payment of premiums, (2) fraud, (3) termination of coverage in the market in accordance with applicable state law, (4) the individual no longer living, residing, or working in the plan's service area, and (5) discontinuance of membership in a bona fide association.

The guaranteed renewal provisions also apply to individuals with existing individual coverage, regardless of whether or not they were originally offered coverage as "eligible individuals" under the HIPAA provisions. In addition, similar to group plan requirements, all insurers in the individual market must provide certifications of prior creditable coverage automatically to beneficiaries when their individual coverage ceases and forward the same information upon request to new plans in which the beneficiaries may enroll. These certificates of individual coverage help persons to reduce or eliminate preexisting-conditions limits or delays in benefits when obtaining coverage under a group plan.

Eligibility for Medicare is not a basis for an insurer to decline to renew or terminate an individual's medical expense insurance coverage in the individual market. If permitted by state law, however, policies that are sold to individuals before they attain Medicare eligibility may contain provisions that exclude payment under the policy to the extent that Medicare provides benefits. Many persons terminate principal policies of medical expense insurance at age 65 and may purchase Medicare supplement policies.

Association Plans under HIPAA

As chapter 2 states, association plans are a significant source of health insurance for persons seeking individual coverage. In general, HIPAA requires medical expense insurance policies offered through associations to be issued and renewed on a guaranteed basis. The full extent of these requirements applies if the organization meets HIPAA's definition of a bona fide association—one that has a nature and purpose other than the provision of insurance. Insurers may decline to renew individual insurance through an association plan if the insured individual leaves the association. However, HIPAA does require insurers to renew an association master contract or, if the insurer withdraws the plan from the market, offer the association all other products that it sells in that market.

INDIVIDUAL MEDICAL EXPENSE INSURANCE

Individual medical expense insurance encompasses a significant array of programs that play a crucial role in the payment of personal medical care expenses. Recently available statistics indicate that almost 18 million Americans, or approximately 7 percent of the population under age 65, are covered by policies of individual medical expense insurance as the principal source of their health care cost protection. These statistics represent an increasing trend; approximately 16 million persons were similarly insured in 2000.[5] Typically, these insureds do not qualify for either employer-provided coverage or a government-sponsored program. Many circumstances account for the need for individual medical expense insurance. These include:

- lack of employer-provided coverage for some employees (usually those who work for small employers)
- termination of employment for such reasons as voluntarily quitting, being fired or laid off, becoming disabled, or retiring early
- termination of spouse or child coverage, even when employee coverages continue, because of divorce, separation, or a child surpassing dependent age
- self-employment status of businessowners, professionals, and farmers
- not being in the labor market; some people have the resources to forego employment, while others are unable to find or hold jobs
- gaps in existing coverage, despite its comprehensiveness
- international travel

Of the circumstances listed above, self-employed persons and employed persons who do not have employer-provided coverage available to them constitute the key markets for individual medical insurance of persons under age 65. This segment of the market may be expected to grow because of the rise in self-employed professionals, the increased start-up of small entrepreneurial enterprises that often provide no medical insurance plans, and the frequency of international travel in a global economy.

Even when a person has a comprehensive program of medical expense coverage, it will not likely cover every medical or health-related expenses that may arise from an illness or incapacity. Individual supplemental medical expense insurance has a broad appeal to those who already have adequate principal coverage Millions of people of all ages seek to enhance their protection through a wide variety of individual programs of supplemental medical insurance that provide cash benefits when the insured is sick or injured. The bulk of this market is persons aged 65 and over who are purchasing coverage to fill the gaps in original Medicare. Over 23 percent of individuals aged 65 and over have individual (nongroup) coverage to fill gaps in Medicare.[6]

Moreover, a person with a serious illness who is well protected by medical expense coverage may also need other forms of health insurance, such as disability income insurance to replace lost income and/or long-term care insurance if an illness requires a professional caregiver for personal or custodial care for an extensive recovery period. Nevertheless, financial advisors recommend that their clients maintain 3 to 6 months of income in reserve for unanticipated expenses even when they are well protected through policies covering all forms of health insurance.

Individual medical insurance generally falls into one of three categories: principal, supplemental, and ancillary coverage.

Principal Medical Expense Insurance

principal medical expense insurance

Principal medical expense insurance, as defined in this text, describes a plan that provides substantial benefits for the major portion of the expenses for needed health care services and generally constitutes the insured's fundamental program of medical expense protection. Covered services typically encompass a core of acute and nonacute hospital and physician services as well as directly related diagnostic and therapeutic services. Historically, principal coverage usually designated coverage for hospital confinements and surgeries. While that emphasis is still true for lower-premium programs, other principal coverages are typically more comprehensive. Chapter 8 explains principal policies of medical expense insurance.

Although most purchasers of a principal policy expect to maintain their coverage for an undetermined period of time, personal circumstances may require others to purchase medical expense insurance on an interim basis. Such a policy may provide temporary, international travel, or student medical expense insurance. It may also be principal medical expense insurance if it represents the insured's underlying or fundamental medical benefit program. Interim medical expense policies are discussed in chapter 11.

As chapter 8 also explains, major medical insurance is the foundation of most principal policies. These policies cover most types of medical expenses arising from hospital, other facility, and physician services, as well as diagnostic tests and therapies, regardless of setting. Coverages include a broad array of emergency, urgent, elective, and routine services. Benefits impose service-specific and overall plan limits and usually are subject to deductibles, copayments, and coinsurance benefit amounts with out-of pocket maximums. Over time, varying degrees of managed care features have accrued to these policies and modified their nature. The most significant of these is the provision under most policies requiring an insured to obtain medical services from a preferred provider network to obtain full benefits. More recently, certain major medical plans with high deductibles coupled with health savings account options create a basis for today's consumer-directed health plans. Chapter 9 covers consumer-directed health plans.

Supplemental Medical Expense Insurance

supplemental medical expense insurance

Supplemental medical expense insurance, which also falls into several categories, is intended to augment and may extend the benefits beyond those received under a principal policy by providing benefits for the direct, indirect, and/or personal expenses left uncovered as a result of illness or injury. Benefits are almost always paid without regard to any other type of medical insurance. Supplemental medical insurance encompasses Medicare supplement policies, which chapter 10 discusses. Supplemental policies also encompass accident only, hospital confinement indemnity, specified disease, and critical illness insurance. Chapter 11 describes these kinds of supplemental medical expense policies.

Medicare Supplement (Medigap)

These policies provide additional protection to people aged 65 and over who are covered by the original Medicare plan (Parts A and B). The additional protection appears in the form of payment of Medicare deductibles, coinsurance, and copayment amounts, with benefits typically extended beyond Medicare limits for covered and noncovered services.

Hospital Confinement Indemnity

These policies typically feature cash benefits in the event of hospitalization and surgery resulting from illness or injury. Coverage may extend to hospital outpatient services and physicians' office visits. Benefits frequently provide dollar payments per day of hospital confinement as well as a percentage of the plan's scheduled amounts for outpatient, physician, and surgical services. These programs typically have no out-of-pocket limits and contain overall plan and service maximums.

Accident Only

These policies provide coverage singly or in combination for death, dismemberment, disability, or hospital and medical care caused by an accident. Coverage may include most types of accidents or may be limited to specified types, such as automobile accidents. Benefits typically feature cash payments in the event of injury or death resulting from a covered accident within a specified period, usually 90 or 180 days, although the number of days varies by state. The hospital and medical care benefits payable under these policies are similar to those associated with hospital confinement indemnity policies.

Specified Disease

These policies assist in meeting the direct and indirect expenses incurred as a result of a covered condition, usually cancer. Current policies may extend coverage to 30 or more diseases, including cancer. Benefits usually include a lump-sum payment upon first diagnosis, with additional amounts paid upon receipt of identified services that may include therapies, transportation, and lodging for the patient and his or her family. Cash benefits for covered services may be determined via a schedule or based on actual charges up to a set maximum.

Critical Illness

These policies are similar to specified disease policies except that they emphasize the policyowner's selected maximum benefit amount (potentially more than $100,000), payable upon the first diagnosis of the covered illness or an event, such as heart bypass or major transplant surgery. Critical illness policies limit the number of covered conditions and the services for which a percentage of the maximum is payable. Optional coverage may provide a disability income benefit and/or an accidental death and dismemberment benefit.

Ancillary Medical Coverage

ancillary medical expense insurance

Ancillary medical expense insurance, as defined in this text, provides coverage and benefits for health care services that were historically considered incidental to medical care. Examples of ancillary coverages include dental, vision, hearing, and prescription drug services. Benefits for these services, even though they may be available through stand-alone coverages, are often incorporated into more comprehensive programs. Policies that provide this type of insurance are also commonly called limited-benefit policies. Chapter 11 also discusses ancillary medical expense insurance.

CHAPTER REVIEW

Key Terms

State Children's Health Insurance Program (SCHIP)
high-risk pool
COBRA
qualified beneficiary
qualifying event
conversion provision
portability
creditable qualifying coverage
principal medical expense insurance
supplemental medical expense insurance
ancillary medical expense insurance

Review Questions

Review questions are based on the learning objectives in this chapter. Thus, a [7-3] at the end of a question means that the question is based on learning objective 7-3. If there are multiple objectives, they are all listed.

1. Why are many persons not protected under an employer-sponsored program of medical expense coverage? [7-1]
2. Why do such individuals and their families need protection against medical expenses? [7-1]
3. a What are alternative sources for coverage of medical expenses to which a person may turn and how may they identify them? [7-2]
   b. On what basis may a person select from among available alternatives? [7-2]
4. a. Identify five government-sponsored programs of medical expense coverage. [7-3]
   b. What are the characteristics of the populations they serve? [7-3]
5. What types of group health plans are subject to COBRA? [7-4]
6. a. What individuals are considered qualified beneficiaries for purposes of COBRA? [7-4]
   b. What is a qualifying event for purposes of COBRA? [7-4]
   c. What COBRA rights are given to a qualified beneficiary who suffers a qualifying event? [7-4]
7. For what length of time must a qualified beneficiary be allowed to continue COBRA coverage? [7-4]
8. a. What must a qualified beneficiary do to start COBRA coverage? [7-4]
   b. When does coverage become effective? [7-4]
9. What is the maximum charge that can be made for continuation of health insurance coverage under the provisions of COBRA? [7-4]
10. Why may there be better alternatives than electing COBRA? [7-4]
11. a. What are typical characteristics of a conversion provision in a group medical expense plan? [7-5]
    b. How do practices vary with respect to the relation between such a provision and COBRA? [7-5]

12. a. To what types of individual health insurance plans or policies does HIPAA apply? [7-6]
    b. To what types of health insurance plans does it not apply, or apply only under certain circumstances? [7-6]

13. a. What criteria make a person eligible for guaranteed issue of individual medical expense coverage under HIPAA? [7-6]
    b. What are the ways that a HIPAA-eligible person may obtain this coverage? [7-6]

14. a. To which insurers and persons in the individual market do HIPAA's guaranteed renewability provisions apply? [7-6]
    b. What exceptions to these requirements are insurers allowed? [7-6]
    c. How does Medicare eligibility affect these renewal requirements? [7-6]

15. What circumstances account for the need for individual medical expense insurance? [7-7]

16. a. What are the types of supplemental medical expense insurance? [7-7]
    b. How might they appeal to those who have adequate principal coverage? [7-7]

NOTES

1. U.S. Department of Labor, Bureau of Labor Statistics, Consumer Price Index for All Urban Consumers, available at http://data.bls.gov/cgi-bin/dsrv, March 21, 2007, p. 3.
2. *Medicaid Enrollment and Spending by "Mandatory" and "Optional" Eligibility and Benefit Categories,* Kaiser Commission on Medicaid and the Uninsured, June 2005, p. 8.
3. *Comprehensive Health Insurance for High Risk Individuals*, 20th edition, 2006/2007, National Association of State Comprehensive Health Insurance Plans.
4. For a more complete discussion of COBRA provisions, see Burton T. Beam, Jr., and Thomas P. O'Hare (eds.), *Advanced Topics in Group Benefits*, 3rd edition. Bryn Mawr, Pa: The American College Press, 2008, and Burton T. Beam, Jr., *Group Benefits: Basic Concepts and Alternatives*, 11th edition, Bryn Mawr, Pa.: The American College Press, 2006.
5. Employee Benefits Research Institute (EBRI), *Sources of Health Insurance and Characteristics of the Uninsured; Analysis of the March 2007 Current Population Survey*, Health Insurance Coverage of the Nonelderly, Figure 1, p. 5.
6. EBRI, *Databook on Employee Benefits*, Chapter 36, Table 36.1, Health Insurance Coverage of Elderly Americans, updated October 2007.

8

Principal Medical Expense Policies

Learning Objectives

An understanding of the material in this chapter should enable you to

8-1. Describe the general nature of major medical insurance policies.

8-2. Identify the optional coverage and additional kinds of insurance that may be purchased with individual medical expense insurance.

8-3. Compare traditional high-deductible and catastrophic major medical policies.

8-4. Summarize the characteristics that make managed care plans effective.

8-5. Describe the managed care elements in major medical insurance, including the ways preferred provider organization (PPO) arrangements function.

8-6. Identify HMO characteristics and compare them with PPO arrangements and traditional major medical insurance without such arrangements.

Chapter Outline

For all the reasons cited in the previous chapter, many persons are likely to seek medical expense insurance in the individual market. Individual medical expense insurance offers coverage that may range narrowly or broadly across the spectrum of available health care services for treating illness or injury and maintaining health. The health care spectrum encompasses the services of virtually all recognized and licensed institutions and professional practitioners. Like covered services, benefits too can vary widely; they may provide protection for all or part of the expense of covered services or they can pay cash benefits without regard to actual expenses incurred. Truly, a kaleidoscope of coverages and benefits can be found among individual medical expense policies. In order to place that virtually endless variety of patterns in a logical framework, this book presents individual medical expense insurance in three main categories: principal, supplemental, and ancillary.

This chapter starts the discussion of principal medical expense policies that provide substantial benefits for the major portion of the expenses for needed health care services. These policies generally constitute the policyowner's or insured's[1] fundamental program of medical expense protection. Historically, principal policies usually were limited to hospital and physician services related to inpatient care and surgery and had fixed or scheduled benefit limits. Although products that seek to maintain low premiums still focus on inpatient care, most principal policies are more comprehensive. They include a broad array of additional services in hospital outpatient departments, ambulatory facilities (both surgical and nonsurgical), and doctors' offices, as well as routine physicians' services, diagnostic tests, and therapies regardless of setting. Coverage for other services, such as emergency transport and outpatient prescription drugs, is frequently included as well.

Insurance companies, Blue Cross and Blue Shield plans, and managed care organizations offer principal policies of medical expense insurance in the individual market. Over time, the traditional differences between these types of organizations have blurred because of mergers, acquisitions, the creation of subsidiaries, and product evolution. Today, many managed care organizations still specialize in selling products that are associated with their particular legal form of being a preferred-provider organization (PPO) or health maintenance organization (HMO). However, most insurers and Blue Cross and Blue Shield plans sell traditional health insurance products as well as managed care plans such as HMOs and PPOs.

Individuals and their advisors may identify the companies that are offering principal policies of medical expense coverage in a specific area by contacting the state department of insurance or searching the Internet.

Principal policies can take many forms. Until about 25 years ago, individual major medical insurance consisted almost totally of traditional indemnity, or fee-for-service, contracts. Under these policies, medical expenses were incurred and patients had considerable freedom in choosing providers of medical services. Claims were generally paid on the basis of charges billed by providers with few attempts to control costs. Beginning in the 1980s, and following what was occurring in the employer-provided market, insurers began to issue individual policies that contained elements of managed care. HMOs also became more likely to offer individual coverage.

Today, the typical policy purchased for individual medical insurance is a PPO plan, which represents more than eight out of ten policies sold. Well over half of these policies have deductibles in the range of $1,000 to $3,000 with over three-quarters of them having a lifetime benefit maximum between $5 million and $7.5 million.[2] Traditional major medical policies and HMO coverage are much less common.

This chapter begins with a description of the general nature of major medical policies, including optional and additional policy benefits that may be added. It then describes high-deductible and catastrophic major medical policies. The discussion then turns to the ways traditional policies have been modified by managed care provisions, often including the use of preferred-provider networks. Finally, HMOs are discussed.

MAJOR MEDICAL INSURANCE

Major medical policies are the foundation of most principal programs of individual medical expense insurance, including many managed care plans that are typically PPO plans. Even HMOs, especially those with a point-of-service (POS) option, incorporate major medical insurance features. In addition, many of the features and definitions included in major medical policies may also be found in the other forms of medical expense insurance (discussed in chapters 9 and 11).

major medical insurance

Individual *major medical insurance* pays for *covered health care services* through a *benefit structure* based on (1) the payment of a *deductible* by the insured, (2) a plan payment of a *percentage of allowable charges (co-insurance)* with an *out-of-pocket limit*, and (3) *benefit maximums*.

An explanation of the italicized terms in this definition forms the basis for understanding major medical insurance policies and indeed all types of medical expense policies, which share many of these same features.

Covered Health Care Services

Covered health care services may be limited to a core of services or may extend to a more comprehensive array.

All major medical programs provide at least a core of covered services for the treatment of illness and injury that focus largely, though not exclusively, on the inpatient setting. Programs that limit coverage to these core services are known as hospital/surgical major medical policies. The following is a typical list of core inpatient, outpatient, physicians', and other services.

Inpatient Services

Inpatient services fall into two categories: room-and-board services and other inpatient services.

Room and Board. Room-and-board services typically consist of

- hospital room, meals, and the services normally provided to inpatients, including routine nursing care in a semiprivate (two-bed) room for a standard level of care. The facility is usually a hospital but can be a nursing home or rehabilitative facility (for a short period of time) if skilled medical care is needed. If the facility has only private rooms, benefits do not exceed the most common semiprivate room rate in the area.
- higher levels of medically necessary hospital service requiring private rooms, intensive care, coronary care, or interim care units, possibly subject to day or dollar maximums.

Other Services. Other inpatient benefits include additional medically necessary services and supplies furnished by a hospital for inpatient care, such as

- operating room charges
- drugs
- surgical dressings
- laboratory and radiology services

Outpatient Services

Several types of services are covered on an outpatient basis to reduce the unnecessary use of more costly inpatient services. They usually include

- preoperative outpatient testing given in preparation for a scheduled inpatient admission (covered as part of the inpatient hospital stay,

provided that it would have been eligible as a covered service if received as an inpatient)
- surgery performed in a hospital outpatient department or a free-standing surgical center and related diagnostic services rendered within 72 hours prior to the surgery
- outpatient chemotherapy and radiation therapy treatments
- emergency accident and illness care if hospital admission occurs as a result of the accident or the illness within 72 hours of the emergency care; sometimes care is eligible as a covered service without a subsequent admission but with a greater out-of-pocket payment

Physicians' Services

The following physicians' services are typically covered:

- surgery performed by a physician, as well as any related diagnostic services received on the same day as the surgery
- anesthesia administered at the same time as a covered surgical procedure
- services provided by a physician who assists the operating surgeon in performing covered surgery
- inpatient visits in a hospital or skilled-nursing facility
- specialist consultations requested by the attending physician in a hospital or skilled-nursing facility
- reconstructive surgery (1) related to or following surgery for injury, trauma, infection, or disease, or (2) for the correction of a newborn child's birth abnormalities or congenital defects
- services that are associated with covered chemotherapy and radiation therapy
- services that are associated with covered emergency, accident, and illness care

Other Covered Services

Other covered services may include

- mammograms, Papanicolaou (Pap) smear tests, and associated office visits
- ambulance transportation in connection with a covered inpatient admission or covered emergency accident or illness
- initial prosthetic devices, special appliances, and surgical implants to replace all or part of an organ or tissue

Comprehensive Covered Services

Major medical policies that extend coverage beyond the core services for the treatment of illness and injury listed above are called *comprehensive*. They provide a broad scope of covered services for outpatient, routine, and preventive care. Included among these additional covered services are the following:

- physician services for the diagnosis and treatment of sickness or injury in or out of the hospital
- routine outpatient X-ray and laboratory tests for diagnosis and treatment of sickness or injury
- outpatient prescription drugs and medicines dispensed by a pharmacist. However, under some policies, prescription drug coverage is an optional benefit that requires an additional premium.
- blood or blood plasma
- oxygen and rental of equipment for its administration
- inpatient and outpatient private-duty nursing authorized by a physician up to an annual maximum, such as 30 days
- rental of a wheelchair, hospital bed, or other durable equipment
- outpatient occupational, physical, or speech therapy services on an ambulatory basis
- home health care
- outpatient and inpatient psychiatric care in licensed facilities other than acute-care hospitals
- treatment of alcoholism and substance abuse
- replacement of prosthetic devices
- hospice care
- routine preventive examinations and tests

Benefits for several of these additional covered services may be subject to separate maximums as listed in table 8-1 later in this chapter.

Benefit Structure

As indicated previously, the benefit structure for the specified covered services is based on (1) the payment of a deductible by the insured, (2) a plan payment of a percentage of allowable charges (coinsurance) with an out-of-pocket limit, and (3) benefit maximums.

Deductibles

deductible

Major medical benefits typically require a deductible. A *deductible* is the initial amount an insured must pay for covered services before the plan begins to pay its benefits. Insurers impose deductibles to avoid the cost of singly processing small initial claims and to give the insured a personal financial stake in obtaining less costly services, which would otherwise be subject only to a low patient out-of-pocket payment.

Thus, even though the services are covered, the insured must pay 100 percent of covered expenses up to the deductible amount. Charges for noncovered services and disallowed portions of charges for covered services do not count toward satisfying the deductible. A deductible may be applied (separately or in combination) per service, person, or family. Typically, the deductible is incurred only once per person per benefit period (almost always one calendar year) for the expenses of most covered services in aggregate. This type of deductible is often referred to as an *all causes* deductible. Although major medical policy deductibles may range from $250 to $10,000, the average deductible amount in recently purchased policies is approximately $2,000.[3] A deductible may also be applied to each separate injury or episode of illness. Such a *per cause* deductible, however, is not common.

If a policy covers a family, the traditional deductible applies separately to each covered person each year, and any family member who meets his or her own deductible may begin to receive benefits. Most policies waive any remaining deductible amounts for all family members after a certain number of family members (usually two or three) have satisfied their individual deductibles. If two or more covered persons are injured in the same accident, only one deductible is usually applicable to the expenses arising from the accident.

Some policies contain a deductible carryover provision so that expenses in the last 3 months of the year used to meet that year's deductible are also used to meet the following year's deductible. Separate deductibles often apply to specific services (as identified later in table 8-3) when other benefits are added to the policy.

Note, however, that the structure of the deductible is different in some respects if the policy has a high deductible and is used in conjunction with a health savings account. Chapter 9 addresses this structure.

Percentage of Allowable Charges (Coinsurance)

allowable charges

Allowable charges are the basis on which benefit payments are determined. Once a deductible is satisfied, the benefit payment is a specified percentage of the remaining allowable charge.

reasonable and customary (R&C) fees

Under traditional major medical policies, insurers determine allowable charges using *reasonable and customary (R&C) fees*. R&C fees (also known as usual, customary, and reasonable, or UCR) are defined as the lesser of the provider's fee, the fee most often charged by the providers for the same service, or the fee most often charged for comparable services in the area by providers with similar training and experience. Insurers may define "area" to mean a metropolitan area (or section thereof), a county, or a larger area if needed to find a representative sample of provider fees for a comparable service or supply. If the charges for covered services exceed allowable charges, the unallowed amount becomes the insured's responsibility.

More recently, under PPO arrangements, the allowable charge is the fee negotiated with participating providers. If insureds use a participating provider, they are not responsible for the payment of any charges above the negotiated fee. However, the negotiated fees are often the allowable amount or charges paid to nonparticipating providers. As a result, insureds in a PPO arrangement who receive services from nonparticipating providers are responsible for amounts charged above the negotiated levels. Some PPOs pay nonnetwork benefits using R&C levels, which are usually more generous.

coinsurance

The term *coinsurance* as used in this book refers to the percentage of allowable charges paid by a medical expense plan with the remaining percentage of such charges paid by the insured. Thus a policy with 80 percent coinsurance, sometimes referred to as an 80/20 policy, pays 80 percent of allowable charges for covered services, while the insured must pay the remaining 20 percent. The level or amount of the benefit paid by the insurance plan usually ranges from 50 percent to 90 percent, depending on the policy's terms, generally after the deductible has been satisfied. The coinsurance percentage is often the same for all covered medical services, but different percentages may be used for different services. Under PPO arrangements, the coinsurance percentage for services received from nonnetwork providers may be lower.

percentage participation

copayment

In some policies, the insured's percentage participation in paying allowable charges for covered services, such as 20 percent, is specified. As commonly used, a *percentage participation* refers to the percentage of covered medical expenses that is not paid by a medical expense policy and that the person receiving benefits must pay. Note that a percentage participation is sometimes referred to as a *copayment*, but this terminology usually implies a fixed dollar amount that the insured must pay for a covered service. A few insurers also refer to the percentage participation, rather than their portion of the benefit payment, as coinsurance.

Out-of-Pocket Limit

out-of-pocket limit

An *out-of-pocket limit* (also known as a *stop-loss limit*) is the maximum sum of all the percentage participation amounts paid by an insured after the receipt of benefits for covered services in a yearly benefit period. When this level is reached, the policy pays 100 percent of all subsequent allowable charges for the remainder of the calendar year. The average out-of-pocket limit across a spectrum of currently purchased policies ranges from $2,500 to approximately $5,000.[4] Under a family policy, the out-of-pocket limit is the total amount for all insureds covered under the policy. The family limit is usually set at two or three times the per person insured limit and can be satisfied by the accumulated expenses of one or more family members. The following expenses do not apply toward the out-of-pocket limit:

- disallowed charges for covered services (that is, above reasonable and customary or other limits)
- expenses incurred beyond separate covered service benefit maximums
- expenses for noncovered services
- benefit reductions or penalties for noncompliance with cost containment or other required policy provisions
- copayments (fixed dollar amounts for doctor's office visits and other outpatient services)

Under most policies, any deductibles paid are also not considered when determining the out-of-pocket limit. However, some policies do allow this amount to be considered.

Some insurers also explain the out-of-pocket limit as the level of allowable charges for covered services after which the policy's benefit increases to 100 percent of such charges. For example, a policy with a $2,000 out-of-pocket limit may state simply that after the insured pays the deductible, the coinsurance benefit is 80 percent of the next $10,000 of allowable charges for covered services; after that, the policy pays 100 percent of such charges up to the applicable benefit maximum.

Note that PPO arrangements encourage use of network providers by establishing separate annual out-of-pocket limits applicable to network and nonnetwork services.

Benefit Maximums

Major medical policies usually contain an aggregate maximum and separate covered service maximums that are designed to control plan cost, thereby maintaining affordability and stability in the product's premium price. Once again, note that under PPO arrangements, these maximums may be established separately for services received from providers that participate in the plan's network and services received from providers that do not.

aggregate maximum

Aggregate Maximum. An *aggregate maximum* (often called a lifetime maximum) is the overall amount of benefits payable under the policy for all covered services on behalf of each insured as long as the policy is in force. These maximum amounts vary by policy and may range from $1 million to $8 million; while some policies may be unlimited, the average maximum is

$5 million.[5] In the absence of any provision to the contrary, benefits paid reduce the aggregate maximum. However, policies often permit restoration of the aggregate maximum under certain conditions, such as the absence of claims for 2 consecutive calendar years. Some policies may impose a maximum per calendar year, such as $1 million, in addition to an aggregate (lifetime) maximum, such as $5 million.

separate service maximum

Separate Service Maximum. A *separate service maximum* (also called an internal limit) may apply to benefits for specific services, if covered, such as organ transplants, substance abuse and dependency, mental illness, home health care, skilled-nursing care, infertility treatments, and private-duty nursing. Illustrative separate service benefit maximums are presented in table 8-1. Note that the services shown may not be covered in all policies. These maximums may be imposed per lifetime, per year, or per service or episode of service, and they may be expressed as dollar amounts or units of service.

TABLE 8-1
Separate Service Benefit Maximums

Covered Services	Maximum*
Substance abuse and dependency, inpatient and outpatient	$1,000 per year
Organ transplants and high-dose chemotherapy	$100,000 per benefit treatment period
Home health care	1 visit per day up to 60 per year
Hospice	30 inpatient days and $3,000 lifetime
Mental illness, inpatient and outpatient services	Combined maximum $10,000 lifetime
Inpatient services	30 days per year
Outpatient services	20 visits per year and 1 visit per week with 50 percent coinsurance up to $25 per visit
Private-duty nursing	30 days per year
Routine preventive examinations and tests	$150 per year
Skilled-nursing facility care	60 days per year
Manipulative treatment, heat treatment, and ultrasound	$1,000 per year

*All benefits are subject to the overall aggregate (lifetime) maximum.

Although benefits remain subject to the overall aggregate (lifetime) maximums, charges that are incurred above the separate benefit maximums do not count toward the out-of-pocket limit. Applicable state law may inhibit an insurer's ability to implement these maximums.

Range of Available Benefits

Major medical policies offer a complete range of benefit provisions. Policies that have benefit provisions in the lower ranges of available aggregate maximums and coinsurance but have higher deductibles and out-of-pocket limits (and therefore higher out-of-pocket expenses for the insured) are considered lower-option plans. Policies that have higher lifetime maximums and coinsurance but have lower deductibles and out-of-pocket limits (and therefore lower out-of-pocket expenses for the insured) are considered higher-option plans. Thus, major medical expense insurance that provides either a comprehensive or core program of covered services may also provide either a high or a more limited level of plan benefits, based on the same structural elements.

Table 8-2 provides a representative list of benefit provisions and available options. Many of these alternatives are offered by the same insurance company and are frequently available in various combinations within the same policy form. Many individual major medical benefit provisions are quite similar to those available in the employer-sponsored insurance market.

TABLE 8-2
Major Medical Policies and the Range of Available Benefit Features

Benefit	Available Features
Aggregate (lifetime) maximum	$1 million to $8 million
Deductible per calendar year	Individuals: $250, $500, $1,000, $1,500, $2,500, $5,000, $7,500, $10,000 Family: 2 or 3 individual deductibles
Coinsurance percentage*	50; 80
Out-of-pocket limit per calendar year**	Individuals: $1,000, $1,500, $2,000, $2,500, $5,000, $7,000 Family: 2 or 3 times the individual level

*Policy pays 100 percent of allowable charges for covered services with deductibles of $5,000 or higher.

**The out-of-pocket limit must be $5,000 or higher if the 50 percent coinsurance option is selected.

Example: George is insured under a major medical policy with the following benefit features:

- $2 million aggregate (lifetime) maximum
- $500 individual annual deductible
- 80 percent coinsurance above the deductible
- $2,000 annual out-of-pocket limit

He incurs $60,000 in total medical expenses for the year, but $2,500 of these expenses is not allowable because this amount exceeds reasonable and customary charges.

If George has no other medical expenses during the yearly benefit period, the policy pays $55,000.

Incurred medical expenses	$60,000
minus disallowed charges	(2,500)
Allowable expenses	$57,500
minus deductible	(500)
Amount subject to coinsurance	$57,000
minus insured's 20% participation up to out-of-pocket limit	(2,000)
Benefit payment	$55,000

This payment also reduces the remaining aggregate maximum benefit by $55,000.

Note that the percentage participation normally would be calculated as 20 percent of the amount subject to coinsurance. However, this amount ($11,400) exceeds the policy's out-of-pocket limit ($2,000), so the latter is used. The effect of the out-of-pocket limit is that the benefit payment actually exceeds the policy's otherwise stated benefit of 80 percent of allowable expenses after the deductible.

George is responsible for $5,000 of the expenses that is not included in the benefit payment. These expenses consist of the nonallowable expenses ($2,500), the deductible ($500), and the out-of-pocket amount at the limit ($2,000), which the insurer may display in a benefit summary as follows.

	Benefit Payment	George's Payment
Disallowed charges	$ 0	$ 2,500
Deductible	$ 0	$ 500
Coinsurance applied to the next $10,000	$ 8,000	$ 2,000
Remaining allowable charges	$47,000	$ 0
Total	$55,000	$ 5,000

Exclusions

Major medical policies clearly state that only the services specifically identified in the policy are covered. Nevertheless, policies also typically list exclusions, with the following being among the more common:

- services furnished by or on behalf of government agencies, unless there is a requirement for the patient or the patient's medical expense plan to pay
- cosmetic surgery, unless (1) such surgery is to correct a condition resulting from illness, accidental injury, or a congenital defect of a newborn child covered under the policy since birth or (2) required by the Women's Health and Cancer Rights Act
- custodial or rest care services
- eye refraction (testing to determine the degree of vision acuity), or the purchase or fitting of eyeglasses or hearing aids (exclusion eliminated if coverage is provided as an additional benefit)
- expenses either paid or eligible for payment under Medicare or other federal, state, or local government medical expense programs
- unnecessary, ineffective, experimental, or investigational medical treatment
- expenses resulting from war, whether declared or undeclared
- expenses resulting from attempted suicide or self-inflicted injury
- any expense that the insured is not required to pay
- occupational injuries or diseases to the extent that benefits are provided by workers' compensation laws or similar legislation

As mentioned earlier, there are also exclusions for any benefits that are not purchased because they are optional. However, any exclusion for dental care typically does not apply to (1) treatment required because of injury to natural teeth and (2) hospital and surgical charges associated with hospital confinement for dental surgery.

preexisting condition

Most major medical policies also contain a provision that applies to *preexisting conditions.* A condition is treated as preexisting if several criteria are satisfied. First, the condition was not fully disclosed on the application. Second, it must have occurred within a specified period prior to the effective date of the policy. In addition, it is a condition (1) for which symptoms existed that would cause an ordinarily prudent person to seek diagnostic care or treatment, or (2) for which medical advice, treatment, or service was recommended by or received from a physician. Thus, a preexisting condition may exist without actual diagnosis or treatment having occurred prior to the policy's effective date. However, benefits for preexisting conditions usually become payable subsequent to a specific period after the policy's effective date, such as 12 months. A preexisting condition does not include known conditions revealed in the application or otherwise identified. An insurer may specifically exclude or limit coverage for such known health conditions as discussed in the subsequent section on riders. It may also decide to deny coverage or to issue the policy with an extra premium.

As chapter 7 explains, the preexisting-conditions exclusion may not apply or have full effect because of HIPAA provisions.

Optional Coverages

Major medical policies sometimes have optional coverages for which an extra premium is charged. If the optional coverage is not elected, benefits are excluded. These optional coverages might include outpatient prescription drugs (if not otherwise covered), dental services, and maternity services. Table 8-3 is an example of the separate benefit structures that often apply to these optional coverages.

Prescription Drugs

Outpatient prescription drug benefits, which are frequently provided under comprehensive major medical policies, may also be offered as an option. Deductibles, copayments, and coinsurance benefits may be separate from those applicable to the overall plan, possibly with no limit on out-of-pocket payments.

formulary

Whether it is covered under a comprehensive plan or added as an optional benefit, the prescription drug benefit is often administered as a separate program by a third party, often known as a pharmacy benefit manager, and uses a formulary. The *formulary* is a list of drug products that

TABLE 8-3
Separate Benefit Structures for Optional Coverages

Optional Coverages	Benefit Structures*
Prescription drugs	Deductible: $100 to $1,000, depending on medical plan deductible selected Copayment for retail pharmacy: $10 generic or $25 brand-name formulary, and $40 nonformulary for 30-day supply** Copayment for mail-order supply: $20 generic or $50 brand-name formulary and $80 nonformulary for 90-day supply**
Dental	Deductible: $50 per person per year with no family deductible Coinsurance: 50% to 80%, depending on the service Calendar maximum: $1,000 or $1,500
Maternity	Deductible: $1,000 Coinsurance: 80% after one or more years of coverage; 50% with less than one year of coverage

*Reasonable and customary limitations apply to all coinsurance levels; out-of-pocket amounts are not subject to any limits and do not contribute to the overall medical policy out-of-pocket limit.
**Coinsurance may also apply after deductible and copayment.

are preferred for dispensing to covered persons when appropriate and contains both generic and brand-name drugs. A generic drug product is one that is chemically equivalent to a brand-name drug whose patent has expired. A brand-name drug is manufactured and marketed under a trademark or name by a specific drug manufacturer.

Today, most drug coverage has a three-tier copayment structure. The lowest copayment is for generic drugs, with brand-name drugs on the formulary requiring a higher amount, and nonformulary drugs (if covered) requiring the highest copayment. Ordinarily, a generic drug is automatically substituted for a brand name if an equivalent is available, unless the doctor specifies otherwise on the prescription. The pharmacy plan usually limits a retail (walk-in) pharmacy prescription to a 30-day supply, although refills are covered. The plan's goal is to encourage the use of its lower-cost mail-order pharmacy, especially among insureds with chronic conditions and those who use maintenance drugs. Plans frequently suggest that when doctors first prescribe a drug that is to be taken for an extended or indefinite period, patients should request a 30-day prescription to be filled immediately at a network retail pharmacy. They should also request a second prescription for at least 90 days (with additional refills as appropriate) to be filled through the mail-order pharmacy. A financial incentive for the use of mail order is a lower copayment than would be the case if three 30-day supplies of the drug were obtained from the network retail pharmacy.

Prior approval is often needed before certain drugs will be dispensed. Those typically include high-cost drugs when there are often less expensive alternatives. However, these drugs are typically approved as long as a physician can justify their use.

Two techniques that are gaining wider use in prescription drug programs are a four-tier copayment structure and step therapy. With a four-tier copayment structure, there is a fourth tier for very expensive drugs. There is either a large copayment, which may be as high as $200 or $300 per prescription, or a high percentage participation, such as 25 or 50 percent. With step therapy, approval for higher-cost medications is contingent on an individual first trying lower-cost, often well-established drugs to see if they are effective.

Exclusions and Limitations. Prescription drug programs contain many exclusions and limitations. They often include the following:

- coverage for prescription drug products for any amount that exceeds the supply limits
- unit-dose packaging of prescription drug products
- drugs prescribed, dispensed, or intended for use while the covered person is in a hospital, skilled-nursing facility, or alternative facility
- experimental, investigational, or unproven services and medications; medications used for treatments and/or dosage regimens determined to be experimental
- drugs furnished or paid for by the government
- compounded drugs not containing at least one ingredient requiring a prescription order or refill
- over-the-counter drugs that do not require a prescription by federal or state law before being dispensed and any drug that is therapeutically equivalent to an over-the-counter drug
- injectable drugs except when (1) self-administered as defined by the plan and (2) injected subcutaneously or intramuscularly
- durable medical equipment, including prescribed and nonprescribed outpatient supplies, other than specifically covered diabetic supplies
- replacement of a lost, stolen, broken, or destroyed prescription order or refill

- certain types of drugs. Examples include:
  - vitamins, except prenatal vitamins, vitamins with fluoride, and B-12 injections
  - appetite suppressants and other weight-loss products
  - prescription smoking-cessation products
  - medications solely for cosmetic purposes
  - infertility drugs
  - contraceptive drugs
  - sexual dysfunction drugs

Dental Services

Coverage for preventive, basic, and major dental services is available, usually with a separate calendar-year deductible, varying coinsurance benefit levels depending on the services, and a separate calendar-year maximum. Dental benefit plan features are also explained in chapter 11 under ancillary benefits.

Maternity Services

A separate maternity option may be provided under individual medical expense policies (subject to state law) to cover the expenses of normal pregnancy, including prenatal and postpartum care, childbirth, and routine nursery care. Complications of pregnancy and treatment of sickness or injury of the newborn are covered whether or not there is an optional benefit for normal maternity care.

Additional Insurance

Some individual medical expense policies provide opportunities to purchase additional types of insurance, such as supplemental accident, term life, and accidental death and dismemberment (AD&D).

Supplemental Accident Insurance

Individual policies frequently offer supplemental accident insurance as a first-dollar accident benefit option. This type of insurance provides a maximum benefit (available from $300 to as high as $5,000) without copayments or deductibles for the charges of covered services incurred as a result of injuries received in an accident. Some policies require that initial treatment be received within 72 hours of an accident or injury and that claim expenses be filed with the insurer within 90 days of the event. Other policies allow initial expenses to be incurred within 6 months of the accident, with subsequent expenses incurred within 1 year of the accident.

Term Life Insurance and Accidental Death and Dismemberment (AD&D) Insurance

Term life insurance and accidental death and dismemberment (AD&D) insurance are sometimes offered in conjunction with a medical policy. Term life insurance is a form of life insurance in which the death proceeds are payable if the insured dies during a specified period. However, nothing is paid if the insured survives to the end of the period. A dependent term life option is frequently extended to a spouse, a child aged 14 days to 19 years, or an older child if he or she is a full-time student. Benefits available to dependents are substantially lower than those available to the insured policyowner, however.

Accidental death and dismemberment insurance is a policy or rider to a policy that designates a dollar benefit or *principal amount* payable at the insured's accidental death. The benefit under term life and AD&D insurance may be as high as $300,000. In the case of AD&D insurance, payment of all or part of the principal amount is also made in the event of the accidental loss of a hand, foot, and/or eye, or at a degree of complete and irreversible paralysis of the limbs.

High-Deductible Major Medical Insurance

high-deductible major medical insurance

As discussed earlier, individual major medical policies offer high-deductible options. Policies with deductibles of $1,000 and more constitute traditional *high-deductible major medical insurance*. Historically, these policies have been purchased alone. However, they are now the focus of attention as the high-deductible health plan (HDHP) component of consumer-directed medical expense plans when they satisfy certain criteria and are established in conjunction with a tax-preferred savings account. Consumer-directed health insurance medical expense plans are covered in chapter 9. Catastrophic policies constitute a variation of high-deductible major medical insurance.

Traditional High-Deductible Policies

Traditional high-deductible policies are major medical plans that have at least a $1,000 annual deductible per person, although as mentioned previously, deductible amounts may reach as high as $10,000. The assumption with these policies is that there is no other underlying insurance plan and the selected deductible level represents an insured's affordable out-of-pocket payment before benefits begin.

These policies are very popular. As stated previously, the average deductible for most medical expense policies that are purchased is $2,000. The majority of policies, then, are high-deductible policies. The reason for this popularity is most likely the lower premium compared to low-deductible/high-option programs. For example, depending on the geographic area and the specific benefit package, the premium for a 35-year-old male may decrease by more than 30 percent if he selects a $1,000 deductible instead of a $250 deductible. Indeed, with catastrophic-level deductibles discussed below, such as $20,000 or more, the premium reduction could exceed 80 percent.

Critics argue that high-deductible plans are attractive to those who are healthy and do not anticipate needing health care (sort of a reverse adverse selection), leaving less healthy persons in the remaining eligibility pool for non-high-deductible individual coverage. In addition, those with high-deductible coverage may tend to postpone routine expenses for diagnosis and treatment because they must be paid out of pocket. Such procrastination can sometimes worsen an insured's condition and thus drive expenses beyond the deductible. However, newer high-deductible policies may waive the deductible for certain types of preventive care.

Today, many high-deductible policies are designed to be used with health savings accounts. Chapter 9 discusses the requirements for such policies.

Catastrophic High-Deductible Policies

catastrophic high-deductible policies

There is a more limited market for *catastrophic high-deductible policies*, with individual and family deductibles ranging from $20,000 to $1 million per year and aggregate maximums up to several million dollars per person. Some policies permit the deductible to be satisfied over a 2- or 8-year period. In general, catastrophic plans operate as umbrella or excess major medical plans to fill gaps after an underlying principal plan reaches its maximum. However, an insured is not required to have an underlying plan to obtain this type of coverage. Some insureds also use catastrophic insurance as supplementary coverage when their HMO or PPO plans exclude or limit nonnetwork benefits.

Like most major medical insurance, catastrophic plans often contain internal limits on benefits for specific services, such as private-duty nursing and extended, home, and hospice care. Once a deductible is satisfied, benefits may continue for as long as 3 years without the insured having to satisfy a new deductible. Depending on the policy terms, the high-deductible amount may be satisfied by covered expenses paid out of pocket as well as those paid by an existing underlying plan, including Medicare. After the deductible has been met, catastrophic plans usually pay 100 percent of reasonable and customary charges for covered services but do not duplicate benefits paid by an underlying plan.

Example: Ian and Rhoda, both in their early 60s, are covered under a retiree medical plan of her former employer. The plan has a $250,000 lifetime maximum and numerous internal limits. Because a friend of theirs recently incurred medical expenses of about $500,000 as a result of a stroke, Ian and Rhoda have decided to purchase a catastrophic high-deductible policy. They have found one that has a $50,000 per person deductible and a $2 million lifetime limit. The premium for each of them is $300 per year.

MANAGED CARE

The growth of managed care plans over the last three decades has had a profound effect on medical expense insurance. While this growth has mostly influenced employer-sponsored medical plans, it has significantly affected individual medical expense insurance as well. Policies with varying elements of managed care are offered by many organizations and entities, including insurance companies, HMOs, Blue Cross and Blue Shield plans, physician groups, hospitals, labor unions, consumer groups, and private investors.

Managed Care Characteristics

Regardless of sponsorship, effective managed care plans have five distinguishing characteristics: controlled access to providers, risk sharing, utilization and quality management, preventive care, and high-quality care.

Controlled Access to Providers

It is difficult to control costs if plan members (the term commonly used for persons with managed care coverage, particularly from HMOs) have unrestricted access to physicians and hospitals. Through either direct employment of or contract with health care professionals, a managed care plan creates a participating provider network for the delivery of institutional, professional, and related health care services. Managed care plans channel their members to designated participating providers in order to obtain the benefits for covered services. Because a major portion of medical expenses results from referrals to specialists, managed care plans may use primary care physicians as gatekeepers to determine the necessity and appropriateness of specialty care. By limiting the number of providers and validating the need for services, managed care plans are better able to control costs through reduced utilization and favorable provider prices.

Risk Sharing

Managed care plans are most successful if providers share in the financial consequences of medical decisions. As part of their plan participation agreements, providers are given financial incentives and penalties to eliminate unnecessary utilization and expense through various types of payment mechanisms, such as capitation (payment per member per month without regard to services rendered) and other arrangements to encourage cost-effective care. For example, physicians who stay within budgeted diagnostic test and referral patterns may receive a bonus. Such arrangements intend to eliminate only unnecessary services, not medically appropriate care.

Utilization and Quality Management

Successful managed care plans perform utilization review at all levels and conduct quality assurance programs. This involves reviewing a patient's medical condition to determine the type of treatment necessary, monitoring ongoing care, and evaluating the appropriateness and success of treatment after it has been given.

Preventive Care

Managed care plans encourage preventive care through routine physicals, targeted age- and gender-specific diagnostic screenings, and immunizations as well as the attainment of healthy lifestyles.

High-Quality Care

A managed care plan is not well received by or selected by participants if it is known for inferior or inconvenient medical care. Managed care plans strive to select health care providers carefully throughout the plan's service area. In addition, they monitor quality on a continuing basis using practice parameters and guidelines for medical care processes and outcomes. The majority of the nation's managed care organizations voluntarily seek accreditation and performance rating by recognized external bodies, such as the National Committee for Quality Assurance (NCQA), URAC (formerly the Utilization Review Accreditation Commission), and the Joint Commission on Accreditation of Healthcare Organizations (JCAHO).

Managed Care Elements in Major Medical Expense Insurance

Managed care elements have permeated individual products to such an extent that it is difficult to find a major medical policy that does not incorporate these elements or offer them as an option. Managed care elements in current major medical insurance take the form of provisions for treatment authorization, designated outpatient surgeries, case and disease management, selected benefit management, centers of excellence, preventive care, and preferred-provider organization arrangements.

Treatment Authorization

Treatment authorization or certification requires that all nonemergency hospital admissions, including those for inpatient surgery, undergo a review process to determine their medical necessity. Authorization is frequently required for emergencies within 24 to 48 hours after admission to the hospital. A determination of the required length of the proposed hospital stay is also made, although a physician may request a reevaluation of the number of hospital days certified.

Failure to comply with the required certification process may result in a denial of benefits, but more often reduces benefits through an additional deductible and/or a reduction in the coinsurance payment. Outpatient surgeries and courses of treatment may also be subject to an authorization process.

Designated Outpatient Surgeries

Certain surgical procedures are designated for performance on an outpatient basis. If such surgery is performed on an inpatient basis, benefits are reduced. The outpatient requirement is waived if the physician provides satisfactory evidence that confinement is medically necessary or that appropriate outpatient facilities are unavailable in the insured's geographic area, usually defined as 50 miles. Selected examples of designated outpatient surgeries are

- carpal tunnel repair
- cataract removal
- dilation and curettage (D&C)
- certain endoscopic procedures

- certain excisions
- eye muscle surgery
- hernia repair
- hemorrhoidectomy
- tonsillectomy

Case and Disease Management

case management

Case management, usually called large or catastrophic case management, focuses on the provision of health care to disproportionately high-cost patients. These patients are identified when first hospitalized, as in the case of trauma, or prior to hospitalization, as in the case of high-risk pregnancy or end-stage renal disease. The goal is to coordinate the care to improve continuity, quality, and outcomes and lower expenses through cost-effective resource utilization.

disease management

A logical extension of case management is the related function of *disease management,* which is a continuous program of care conducted across a broad range of settings affecting the course of chronic illnesses, such as emphysema, asthma, diabetes, and heart disease. Disease management includes the use of care guidelines by physicians and self-care education of patients. Some companies offer participation in self-care programs involving proper diet and exercise to reduce the potential for illness, such as cholesterol control, and the need for more invasive treatment, as in the case of heart disease. The goal of disease management is to eliminate or reduce the frequency and severity of critical episodes associated with a chronic illness, thereby reducing costs as well.

Selected Benefit Management

In order to control costs, some insurers carve out selected services covered under the major medical plan. Benefits are then provided by a managed care plan that specializes in those services, such as prescription drugs, rehabilitation programs, and mental health and/or substance abuse programs. Managing services with these plans often allows for more generous benefits through coordinated care and cost controls that emphasize outpatient treatment. In addition, this approach to benefits management has been successful in encouraging people to begin prescribed treatment and to finish treatment once it has started.

Centers of Excellence

Specialized facilities may be placed under contract as designated centers for transplant surgeries, for example. Such specialized facilities are known as

centers of excellence

centers of excellence. If the facility is outside the insured's geographic area (more than 50 miles, for instance), travel (including emergency transport), lodging, and meal expenses incurred by the transplant patient and an accompanying family member would be covered, usually up to a specified limit (such as $10,000). While the same services may be received at a nondesignated facility, they may be subject to limitations, such as $100,000 per benefit treatment period.

Preventive Care

Major medical policies frequently highlight prevention benefits by providing each covered person with a routine physical exam and associated laboratory services. Additional regular examinations prompted by the insured's age and gender and by physician recommendation are often covered. Among these examinations are prostate exams, mammograms, Pap smears, and associated office visits. The prevention benefit often extends to childhood immunizations as well. Benefits for these services may be subject to the plan deductible and coinsurance or sometimes a flat dollar maximum benefit. Policies featuring participating provider network arrangements usually cover these same benefits subject only to a copayment if members use network providers.

Preferred-Provider Organization (PPO) Arrangements

preferred-provider organization (PPO)

Preferred-provider organization (PPO) arrangements represent the most extensive application of managed care elements to traditional major medical policies. As mentioned previously, more than eight out of ten individual polices of medical expense insurance sold contain such an arrangement. PPO arrangements can be defined in general as the features of health benefit plans that make available to insureds an identified network of participating providers to obtain cost-effective medical services. The network is considered risk based if provider compensation is adjusted for the utilization of plan services by members. A network in which providers may receive discounted payments but no adjustment for the utilization of services is a nonrisk-based network.

PPO arrangements involve well-structured negotiated agreements that establish a network of participating providers available to insureds for all or almost all covered services. The network includes primary care physicians, specialty physicians, and hospitals. Radiology, laboratory, and physical therapy services are also available through network providers.

These arrangements produce advantages for insurers, insureds, and providers; the savings from negotiated provider rates and utilization and quality management should allow the policy to compete effectively in the marketplace based on price and service.

Major medical plans with preferred-provider features can create powerful incentives to purchase this type of coverage and obtain care from network providers. Policies that offer preferred-provider features as an option sometimes encourage the insured to select them by doubling the aggregate (lifetime) maximum without additional premium. The major advantage of these arrangements to the insured is greater flexibility in the choice of providers than is allowed under a more restrictive HMO program. Services received from nonparticipating providers are still covered, albeit at a lower benefit. The insured may obtain primary and specialty physician or hospital care within the network without being locked into the same choices for future services. Although some referral requirements for specialists may exist under these arrangements, they are uncommon.

Under PPO network arrangements, providers typically bill the insurer directly, knowing the payment amount in advance with no disallowed charges—thereby also relieving the insured of the sometimes complicated claim-filing process. Providers anticipate increased patient volumes because the arrangement directs insureds to the providers by notifying insureds of the network participants and encouraging the use of these participants through a higher benefit. In addition, the network may be limited in size because the number of participating physicians is tailored to the size of the covered population. As a result, ensured patient volume levels may be incorporated into the provider reimbursement agreement.

Like major medical plans, covered services and benefit incentives are available in a broad array of alternatives. PPO arrangement alternatives are illustrated by the copay and standard models in table 8-4, whose features are frequently interchangeable.

Copay Model. There is a different benefit structure for network and nonnetwork services under the copay model PPO. As table 8-4 illustrates, the network benefits are provided using nominal copayments by the insured for many services. For radiology and pathology services, there is no copayment because the plan pays 100 percent of the expense. Routine/preventive care is usually covered only when received from a network provider. For the network services presented, there are no other payments by the insured for deductibles, coinsurance balances, or disallowed amounts. The nonnetwork benefits, on the other hand, follow a typical major medical plan structure and are less generous. Instead of a modest copayment, the insured must pay a deductible and a 30 percent payment in most cases. In many cases, the coinsurance benefit for nonnetwork providers may be determined as a percentage of the charges paid to network providers and therefore would likely be even less generous than traditional reasonable and customary charge levels would allow. For example, if an insured's incurred charge of $1,000 for nonnetwork services is fully allowable as a reasonable and customary benefit, the insured's payment at 30 percent would be $300. However, if the negotiated charge for the same services from a network provider is $800, then the nonnetwork benefit at 70 percent is $560, leaving the insured with a payment of $440.

TABLE 8-4
Payments by Insureds for Selected Covered Services under Alternative Formal PPO Arrangement Models

	Payment by Insureds under Copay Model		Payment by Insureds under Standard Model	
Covered Services	**Network[a]**	**Nonnetwork (after deductible and coinsurance)[b]**	**Network (after deductible and coinsurance)[c]**	**Nonnetwork (after deductible and coinsurance)[d]**
Inpatient hospital and surgical facility	$500 copay	30%	10%	40%
Physicians' visits (office or hospital)	$20 copay	30%	10%	40%
Radiology and pathology services	$0	30%	10%	40%
Routine preventive care	$20 copay	Not covered	10%	Not covered
Emergency room[e]	$50 copay	40%	10%	40%
Prescription drugs	$10 copay (generic) $25 copay (brand name, preferred) $40 copay (brand name, nonpreferred)	20% (generic) 30% (brand name, preferred) 40% (brand name, nonpreferred)	10% (generic) 20% (brand name, preferred) 30% (brand name, nonpreferred)	30% (generic) 40% (brand name, preferred) 50% (brand name, preferred)

a. Insured's payments for network services are not subject to any deductible or disallowances above maximum allowable amounts. However, these payments do not contribute to the satisfaction of the separate nonnetwork deductible or out-of-pocket limit.
b. The coinsurance benefit percentage paid to nonnetwork providers is based on the rates negotiated with network providers. Insured is responsible for any amount above those levels in addition to the out-of-pocket percentage payment indicated.
c. Insured's payments for network services are not subject to disallowances above maximum allowable amounts. Indicated payments apply to a separate network out-of-pocket limit.
d. Insured is also responsible for any amounts disallowed as exceeding reasonable and customary limits. Indicated payments apply to a separate nonnetwork out-of-pocket limit.
e. Paid as an inpatient hospital expense if insured is admitted.

Standard Model. Under the standard model PPO, the typical major medical benefit structure is used for both network and nonnetwork services. The incentive to use network providers is created by making the insured's payment (after deductible and coinsurance benefit) appreciably lower for services received from network providers compared to the payment applicable to services received from nonnetwork providers. Table 8-4 illustrates a much larger payment by insureds if they use nonnetwork services. As with the copay model, services such as routine/preventive care, are often covered only when rendered by network providers. Although the network provider services remain subject to the insured's payment of the deductible and coinsurance balance percentage, there are no disallowed charges because of the negotiated agreement on the price of services. However, some programs may eliminate the deductible for network services. This model also frequently establishes a separate deductible and out-of-pocket limit for both network and nonnetwork services to encourage the insured to continue to use network providers after the network deductible and out-of-pocket limit is satisfied and the policy benefit increases to 100 percent. Otherwise, after expenses exceed a single deductible and out-of-pocket limit, the insured would have a 100 percent benefit for nonnetwork services as well.

three-tier copayment or deductible structure

More recently, a few managed health care plans have implemented a *three-tier copayment or deductible structure* for network services. Under such a structure, members pay one of three copayment or deductible amounts for services, especially hospital services, depending on their selection of a network provider and the cost to the plan for using that provider.

Health Maintenance Organizations

The most fully developed and integrated managed care structure is the health maintenance organization.

health maintenance organization (HMO)

Health maintenance organizations (HMOs) are generally regarded as organized systems of health care that provide a comprehensive array of medical services on a prepaid basis to voluntarily enrolled persons living within a specified geographic region. HMOs act like traditional insurance companies and traditional Blue Cross and Blue Shield plans in that they finance health care. However, they also deliver medical services. HMOs can be either for-profit or not-for-profit organizations. HMOs may be sponsored or owned by insurance companies, Blue Cross and Blue Shield plans, consumer groups, physicians, hospitals, labor unions, or private investors.

Although HMOs have a limited presence in the individual medical expense insurance market, they also influence this market through their unique nature. Table 8-5 shows examples of HMO benefits and copayments.

TABLE 8-5
Selected HMO Covered Services and Member Copayment

Covered Services	Member Copayment
Hospital inpatient services (includes all room and board and other inpatient services as well as physician and specialist services)	$500 per admission
Outpatient services (includes physician and specialist visits and consultations as well as routine examinations, tests, and immunizations)	$20 per visit; waived for covered children up to age 3
Diagnostic testing and X rays	$0
Outpatient surgical procedures (includes facility charges for services, tests, drugs, and supplies)	$50
Urgent care services outside the service area	$20 per visit limited to a $500 maximum per year for continuing/follow-up care
Extended care in a skilled-nursing facility	$0 for up to 100 days per year following hospitalization
Home health and hospice service	$25 per day
Mental health services	
Inpatient	$500 per admission
Outpatient	$25 per individual visit after 3 visits; $45 per individual visit after 11 visits

Limited Presence in Individual Market

As managed care grew, HMOs also grew in the individual market, but not to the same extent as in the employer-sponsored market, where HMO coverage (including point-of-service plans) represents a third of the market.[6] Less than 6 percent of the individual market has HMO coverage. [7] Individual HMO coverage is not available in all states or even all areas of the states where it is available. Nevertheless, some organizations that provide HMO plans in the employer market frequently offer HMO coverage in the individual market. Important differences between the employer-sponsored and individual markets may cause this disparity in growth.

Employers who pay the majority of the cost for their medical plans have been a driving force in promoting HMOs because of their potential for cost containment. In addition, because HMOs traditionally serve the employer market, they would find the individual market unappealing for several reasons.

Individual insurance is uniquely regulated at the state level compared with employer-sponsored plans. This disparity is compounded when individual insurance, as in the case of HMOs, is directly tied to service delivery. Any attempt by an HMO to modify the premium or benefits would encounter government scrutiny not only of the premium, but also of the associated medical care delivery system. In turn, changes the HMO would need to make in the delivery system for sound management reasons, though achievable with relative ease in the employer market, could require approval of individual plan filings.

Also, the traditional HMO commitment to comprehensive benefits that limits enrollee cost sharing to copayments may place HMOs at a competitive disadvantage in the individual market. Individual non-HMO insurance products can present attractively priced premium options using a range of deductibles, coinsurance, and targeted benefit limits.

Indeed, a premium disparity with non-HMO products in the individual market can result in adverse selection against HMOs by those willing to pay a higher premium because of needed extensive medical care. HMOs may hesitate to adopt the vigilant underwriting and pricing standards and multiple product offerings necessary to support this market. The guaranteed issue and renewal requirements of HIPAA in the individual market provide HMOs with little encouragement to undertake or expand individual product offerings.

Unique Nature

HMOs are unique among managed care plans in several ways. First, HMOs provide for the delivery of medical services, which in some cases are performed by salaried physicians and other personnel employed by the HMO. Although this approach is in contrast to the usual fee-for-service delivery system of medical care, HMOs frequently contract with providers on a fee-for-service basis. Unlike PPOs and traditional major medical plans, HMOs often have unlimited lifetime benefit maximums.

Second, members are required to obtain their care from providers who are affiliated with the HMO. Because HMOs may operate in a geographic region no larger than a single metropolitan area, this requirement may result in limited coverage for members if treatment is received elsewhere. Most HMOs do have out-of-area coverage, but only for medical emergencies.

Third, HMOs emphasize coordinated care through the use of primary care physicians and specialists. Primary care physicians fulfill a gatekeeper function and historically have controlled access to specialists. The traditional HMO covers benefits provided by a specialist only if the primary care physician recommends the specialist, who may be a fellow employee in a group-practice plan or a physician who has a contract with the HMO. The member may have little or no choice regarding the specialist selected, which has been one of the more controversial aspects of HMOs and one that has discouraged larger enrollment. In response to consumer concerns, many HMOs now make the process of seeing a specialist easier. Referrals can often be made by nurses in physicians' offices or by HMO staff members, who members can contact by telephone. Some HMOs, referred to as direct-access or self-referral HMOs, allow members to see network specialists without going through a gatekeeper. However, the specialist may have to contact the HMO for authorization before proceeding with tests or treatment.

point-of-service (POS) option

The popularity of flexible preferred-provider arrangements has encouraged many HMOs to loosen strict exclusive-provider restrictions and specialist referral requirements to allow members to obtain covered services outside the network with additional out-of-pocket payments. This approach, known as a *point-of-service (POS) option*, would approximate the copay model for network and nonnetwork services in table 8-4.

DETERMINING THE APPROPRIATE POLICY

Determining which type of policy is best for a particular person involves a consideration of several factors:

- How comprehensive are benefits?
- To what degree is the person willing to accept limitations on the choice of providers?
- Are an adequate number of primary and specialty providers available?
- To what degree is the individual willing to have his or her medical care managed?
- How much is the person willing to spend on premiums?
- What is the cost of coverage? If all other factors are the same, premiums are lower with higher degrees of managed care.
- Has the person previously been covered by a managed care plan, and what has been his or her experience with managed care?
- How convenient is access to health care services?
- Can the person afford to pay the required deductibles and copayments in case of large medical expenses? High degrees of managed care are often accompanied by lower and fewer deductibles and copayments.
- How does the person feel about keeping receipts and filing claims?

Table 8-6 compares the major types of principal medical expense policies.

TABLE 8-6
Comparison of Health Insurance Plans

	Traditional Major Medical Insurance	PPOs	HMOs
Provider choice	Unlimited	Unlimited in network, but benefits are greater if network provider is used	Network of providers must be used; care from non-network providers covered only in emergencies
Required use of gatekeeper	None	None	Used for access to specialists
Out-of-pocket costs	Deductibles and percentage participation	Deductibles and percentage participation, which are lower if network providers are used; may have small copayment for network services	Small copayments for some services
Utilization review	Traditionally little, but several techniques are likely to be used now	More than traditional plans, but less than HMOs; network provider may be subject to some controls	Highest degree of review, including financial incentives and disincentives for providers
Preventive care	Little covered other than that required by law	Usually, more coverage than traditional major medical plan but less coverage than HMOs and POS plans	Covered
Responsibility for filing claims	Covered person	Plan provider for network services; the covered person for nonnetwork services	Plan providers

CHAPTER REVIEW

Key Terms

major medical insurance
deductible
allowable charges
reasonable and customary (R&C) fees
coinsurance
percentage participation
copayment
out-of-pocket limit
aggregate maximum
separate service maximum
formulary
preexisting condition
high-deductible major medical insurance
catastrophic high-deductible policies

case management
disease management
centers of excellence
preferred-provider organization (PPO)
three-tier copayment or deductible structure
health maintenance organization (HMO)
point-of-service (POS) option

Review Questions

Review questions are based on the learning objectives in this chapter. Thus, a [8-3] at the end of a question means that the question is based on learning objective 8-3. If there are multiple objectives, they are all listed.

1. a. How have principal policies of medical expense insurance evolved over recent decades? [8-1]
   b. What are the features of a typical principal policy of individual medical insurance? [8-1]
2. a. What are the core covered services under a major medical policy? [8-1]
   b. What additional services do comprehensive policies cover? [8-1]
3. What is the benefit structure for services covered under major medical policies based on? [8-1]
4. What is the difference between an aggregate maximum and a separate service maximum? [8-1]
5. a. What is a typical range of available benefits under major medical insurance? [8-1]
   b. What are the differences between higher- and lower-option plans? [8-1]
6. George maintains a major medical policy with the following plan features: (1) a $500 annual deductible; (2) an 80 percent coinsurance benefit and a 20 percent percentage participation; (3) a $2,000 out-of-pocket limit; and (4) an aggregate maximum of $2 million with an outpatient psychiatric maximum of $1,000 per year. In addition, George purchased the outpatient prescription drug rider that has a $100 deductible and a $10 copay per prescription.

   George has had a difficult year medically. A fall from a ladder generated total hospital charges of $5,000, all of which were allowable under his policy. His total bill for physician services was $1,000, of which $250 was disallowed as exceeding reasonable and customary limits. His continuing discomfort after discharge required an initial pain management prescription for 30 days that was refilled twice at a retail charge of $100 per prescription. The stress of his accident combined with job and personal challenges required counseling services, which equaled his plan's charge per visit and number of visit allowances.

What benefit payment should George expect to receive from his major medical plan? [8-1]

7. What exclusions are typical under a major medical policy? [8-2]
8. a. What are three optional coverages that may be provided under a major medical policy? [8-2]
   b. What types of benefit limitations may apply to them? [8-2]
   c. How do drug plans encourage the use of mail-order pharmacies? [8-2]
9. What additional kinds of insurance may be purchased in conjunction with a major medical policy? [8-2]
10. How do the benefit provisions of a catastrophic high-deductible major medical policy differ from those of a traditional high-deductible policy? [8-3]
11. Describe the characteristics of effective managed care plans. [8-4]
12. Briefly describe the managed care elements found in current major medical policies. [8-5]
13. a. What is the major advantage of PPO arrangements to insureds compared with more restrictive HMO programs? [8-5]
    b. What effect has the popularity of PPO arrangements had on HMOs? [8-5]
14. Under PPO arrangements, what are the key differences between the copay and standard models for network and nonnetwork services? [8-5]
15. a. In what ways are HMOs unique among managed care plans? [8-6]
    b. What types of member copayments do HMOs require? [8-6]

NOTES

1. The policyowner is the buyer of the insurance and is often the insured, although he or she may purchase coverage for another person only, such as a child. Under family policies, the policyowner is the insured along with other covered family members, such as a spouse and/or a child or children.
2. *Individual Health Insurance: A Comprehensive Survey of Affordability, Access, and Benefits*, America's Health Insurance Plans, August 2005, p.12.
3. Ibid., p.13.
4. Ibid., p. 16.
5. Ibid., p. 19.
6. The Kaiser Family Foundation and Health Research and Education Trust, *Employer Health Benefits*, 2007 Annual Survey, p. 62.
7. *Individual Health Insurance: A Comprehensive Survey of Affordability, Access, and Benefits*, p. 12.

9

Health Savings Accounts

Learning Objectives

An understanding of the material in this chapter should enable you to

9-1. Explain the nature of consumer-directed health care that incorporates tax-favored savings accounts.

9-2. Describe the characteristics of health savings accounts.

9-3. Explain the decisions consumers must make to establish and manage health savings accounts.

9-4. Explain how Archer MSAs are similar to health savings accounts and how they differ.

Chapter Outline

health savings account (HSA)

Most chapters in this book look at specific health insurance products and their role in planning for financial security. This chapter focuses primarily on a type of tax-favored savings account that is available to individuals as a means for paying medical expenses that are not reimbursed by an insurance policy. This account is the *health savings account,* commonly referred to as an *HSA*. The establishment and use of such accounts are subject to numerous rules and regulations, as is explained later.

The HSA is an example of consumer-directed health care, and the chapter begins with a discussion of this concept. The majority of the chapter is then devoted to HSAs—their characteristics and considerations in their establishment. The chapter concludes with a brief discussion of Archer medical savings accounts (Archer MSAs) and how they are similar to HSAs, as well as how they differ. Archer MSAs were the predecessors to HSAs, and a small number still exists.

CONSUMER-DIRECTED HEALTH CARE

A major issue facing the American economy is the spiraling cost of health care and the accompanying increase in insurance premiums. Even with numerous attempts to rein in these costs, expenditures for health care have risen from 12.2 percent of GDP in 1990 to almost 16 percent today. The Centers for Medicare & Medicaid Services project that this figure will rise to 20 percent by 2015. In addition, the number of persons without medical expense coverage continues to increase and is now estimated at about 47 million. For most of these persons, the lack of coverage is more an issue of affordability than availability.

consumer-directed health care

Over the past decade, there has been increasing interest in a concept that is referred to in this book as *consumer-directed health care.* This concept, also called consumer-driven health care or consumer choice, attempts to control costs by making the consumers of health care take a more active role in the purchase of such care. In the past, most Americans have had health insurance with generous benefits and relatively small deductibles and copayments. This has led to minimal concern on the part of consumers to seek out the most cost-effective sources of medical care.

Although there are several approaches to consumer-directed health care, the term is generally used to describe the use of high-deductible medical expense policies accompanied by tax-favored savings accounts that consumers can access to pay unreimbursed medical expenses. The rationale for this approach is that significant savings can occur for two reasons. First, the payment of small claims is largely eliminated as demonstrated by the fact that a major medical policy with a $2,500 deductible can often be purchased for about one-half the cost of a policy with a $250 deductible. Second, a policyowner has a direct incentive to avoid unnecessary care because any funds taken from the savings account are the policyowner's own money. In addition, these funds can be carried forward to future years if not used in the current year.

As with almost any approach to cost containment, consumer-directed health care has its critics. It is argued that individuals will minimize treatment for minor medical expenses and preventive care that would have been covered under a medical expense policy that paid benefits on a first-dollar basis or had a small deductible and copayments. Critics contend that this avoidance of medical care may lead to major medical expenses that could have been averted or minimized with earlier treatment. However, some types of consumer-directed plans pay benefits for many types of preventive care without regard to the deductible. Another criticism is that consumer-directed health care tends to favor the healthy who are less likely to access their savings accounts and people in high-income tax brackets who can afford to open such accounts and whose higher tax benefits make the tax savings from such accounts advantageous. A final criticism is that this type of approach does not adequately address the problem of the uninsured. This group has gone without coverage even though high-deductible policies have been available in the individual marketplace for many years.

The federal government has not shared these concerns. Under a pilot project that began in 1997, the Internal Revenue Code allowed the establishment of Archer MSAs for employees of small employers and the self-employed as long as these persons had medical expense coverage that contained certain features, including a high deductible. These accounts met with limited success and fewer than 100,000 were established. As a result, the federal government introduced the health savings account as part of the 2003 Medicare Prescription Drug, Improvement, and Modernization Act. HSAs have been allowed since 2004 and are available to a much wider range of individuals. In addition, the underlying policy deductibles can be lower and some of the rules governing such plans are more liberal. Consequently, HSAs have gained much wider acceptance than Archer MSAs, and there has been growth from year to year. By early 2007, there were 4.5 million people covered by the types of policies that would allow them to establish HSAs in conjunction with these policies.[1] Estimates are that slightly less than half these people actually opened such an account[2]; in other words, they elected to pay any unreimbursed medical expenses from other sources. The most common reason stated for the failure of eligible persons to have HSAs is that they did not have money to put in the account.[3] Other reasons include difficulty opening and managing the account, lack of sufficient tax benefits, and the complicated nature of such accounts.

Before continuing, several important points need to be mentioned. First, the remainder of this chapter is devoted primarily to the saving accounts used with consumer-directed health care in the individual marketplace—health savings accounts and Archer MSAs. These tax-favored savings accounts also can be established by persons other than those who purchase individual medical expense policies. They are available to persons who have employer-provided high-deductible medical expense coverage if their employer does not establish accounts for them and they otherwise meet the criteria discussed later. Even if the employer does establish such accounts, they are individual accounts in the name of each employee and belong to the employee upon termination of employment.

Second, employers may use alternative techniques to HSAs, such as health reimbursement arrangements (HRAs) and health flexible spending accounts (FSAs). Details about these approaches are covered in books on employee benefits.

Third, the nature of high-deductible policies in the individual marketplace is discussed in chapter 8. However, the criteria that such policies must satisfy for use with savings accounts are described in this chapter.

Finally, consumer-directed medical expense plans have continued to evolve. For example, the Tax Care and Health Relief Act of 2006 contained several provisions that affected HSAs. These provisions were heavily supported by Republicans who controlled Congress and who favored legislation that further encouraged their use. Democrats, who are now in control, tend to favor different approaches with respect to health care policy. As a result, the future of legislation with respect to HSAs can best be described as uncertain. To best meet the needs of their clients, financial services professionals must carefully follow legislative developments.

CHARACTERISTICS OF HEALTH SAVINGS ACCOUNTS

high-deductible health plan (HDHP)

An HSA is a personal savings account from which unreimbursed medical expenses, including deductibles, percentage participation, and copayments, can be paid. The HSA must be in the form of a tax-exempt trust or custodial account established in conjunction with what federal tax rules refer to as a *high-deductible health plan (HDHP)*. This plan may be an individual medical expense policy or employer-provided coverage as long as the plan satisfies the criteria mentioned later. An HSA is established with a qualified trustee or custodian in much the same way that an IRA is established. Any insurance company or bank (as well as certain other financial institutions) can be a trustee or custodian, as can any other person or entity already approved by the IRS as a trustee or custodian for IRAs.

HSAs are individual trusts, which prohibits a husband and wife from having a joint HSA. But as long as both are eligible, each may have a separate HSA.

Some insurers that sell HDHPs for use with HSAs also market the HSA accounts; other insurers leave it to the purchasers of an HDHP to establish their HSAs with other institutions.

This section of the chapter looks closely at HSAs with respect to several characteristics. These include eligibility, high-deductible health plan requirements, contributions, account growth and investment options, distributions, the effect of retirement, and estate tax treatment. A later section of the chapter dicusses some of the issues and procedures surrounding the establishment and maintenance of HSAs.

Eligibility

Anyone—employees, the self-employed, and the unemployed—can establish an HSA as long as the following rules for qualification are met:

- The individual must be covered by a high-deductible health plan. The HDHP, if offered by an employer, may be insured or self-insured.
- The individual is not eligible to be claimed as a dependent on another person's federal income tax return.
- With some exceptions, a person who is covered under an HDHP is denied eligibility for an HSA if he or she is covered under another health plan that does not meet the definition of a high-deductible plan but that provides any benefits that are covered under the HDHP. The exceptions include coverage for accident, disability, dental care, vision care, and long-term care insurance. Insurance for a specified disease or illness and insurance paying a fixed amount per period of hospitalization are also permitted.

An individual covered by Medicare (by attaining age 65 or becoming disabled) or receiving Veterans Administration benefits is considered as having another health plan and, therefore, may not establish an HSA. Such a person may continue an existing HSA but may not make additional contributions. Nevertheless, an individual who is (1) eligible for Medicare but not enrolled or (2) eligible to receive medical benefits through the Veterans Administration but not receiving them may contribute to an HSA.

An individual (whether employed or not) may establish his or her own HSA, and an employer can establish HSAs for its employees.

High-Deductible Health Plans

For purposes of HSA participation, a high-deductible health plan is defined as having the following deductibles and annual out-of-pocket limits for covered services. These figures are for 2008 and subject to annual inflation adjustments:

- In the case of self-only coverage, the deductible must be at least $1,100, and annual out-of-pocket expenses cannot exceed $5,600.
- In the case of family coverage, the deductible must be at least $2,200, and annual out-of-pocket expenses cannot exceed $11,200.

The out-of-pocket expenses include the deductible amount, copayments, and any required percentage participation. They do not include the premium for the coverage.

If high-deductible plans use preferred-provider networks, they can have higher out-of-pocket limits for services provided outside the network, and any deductibles for nonnetwork services are not taken into account when determining the out-of-pocket limits specified above.

One point should be emphasized about the deductible for family coverage. It is not a traditional family deductible as described in the chapter 7 discussion of major medical insurance. In that situation, there is an individual deductible that applies to each family member as well as a separate deductible for the family. The individual deductible is sometimes referred to as an embedded deductible, and policy benefits are paid for any family member once his or her deductible is satisfied, even if the family deductible has not been met.

In the case of a high-deductible policy used with an HSA, there will usually not be an individual deductible if the policy is written for a family. Rather, there will be a single deductible—referred to as a common deductible—that must be satisfied before any benefits are payable, even if all claims are for one family member. It is permissible, however, to use an embedded deductible, but only if the individual deductible is equal to at least the required minimum HSA family deductible. For example, a policy with an individual deductible of $2,500 and a family deductible of $5,000 would be acceptable.

The following incurred expenses do not count toward the plan's required deductible and out-of-pocket limit:

- payments for services not covered by the high-deductible health plan
- payments for services received from nonnetwork health care providers if the plan uses a preferred-provider network

- amounts above a plan's reasonable specific service or lifetime maximums
- amounts in excess of reasonable and customary fees
- penalties for failure to obtain a plan-required certification

Nevertheless, copayments count toward the out-of-pocket limit, even if the plan does not consider copayments as contributing toward the satisfaction of the deductible.

Generally, an HDHP established in conjunction with an HSA cannot provide benefits before the deductible is satisfied, but there is an exception for benefits for preventive care. An HDHP may provide benefits for preventive care before the insured satisfies the plan's required high deductible, but slightly more than half of persons with HSAs are covered by health plans with deductibles that apply to all health care services.[4] When preventive services are available, coverage may be on a first-dollar basis or subject to copayments. These services may include the following:

- annual physicals, immunizations, and screening services
- routine prenatal and well-child care
- tobacco cessation programs and obesity weight-loss programs
- employee assistance, disease management, or wellness programs
- treatment of a related condition that is incidental or ancillary to a preventive care service or screening, such as removal of polyps during a diagnostic colonoscopy
- drugs or medications taken by a person who has developed risk factors for a disease before the disease manifests itself or to prevent the reoccurrence of a disease from which the person has recovered. An example is the drug treatment of high cholesterol to prevent heart disease, or the treatment of recovered heart attack or stroke victims with medications to prevent a recurrence. Other prescription drugs that do not qualify under this exception remain subject to the plan's high deductible.

Preventive care generally does not include treatment of existing conditions.

Contributions

Contributions to an HSA may be made solely by individuals who have such accounts. They may also be made by employers that provide their employees with a high-deductible health plan.

Individual Contributions

Individuals often fund HSAs without employer contributions because they are not employers or because their employer makes no contribution to HSAs. Contributions must be in the form of cash, and they are deductible for federal income tax purposes even if the individual does not itemize deductions.

The maximum annual contribution to an HSA in 2008 is $2,900 if the account holder has self-only coverage and $5,800 if the account holder has family coverage. These amounts are subject to annual indexing for inflation. As a result of the Tax Relief and Health Care Act of 2006, the full maximum contribution is allowed even if it exceeds the deductible amount under the higher deductible health plan. Despite the maximum limits on HSA contributions, the majority of account holders who purchase high-deductible health policies in the individual marketplace make an annual contribution of less than $1,000.[5]

If both a husband and wife establish an HSA and have family coverage (that is, a single policy covering both of them), they can allocate the maximum contribution in any way they determine. If they have separate policies, each is subject to the limits that apply to self-only coverage.

Individuals aged 55 or older are also permitted an additional annual catch-up contribution of up to $900 in 2008. This amount will increase to $1,000 in 2009. If both a husband and wife are aged 55 or older, the catch-up contribution is available to each of them only if they have separate HSAs.

Annual contributions can be made in a lump sum or spread out over time. However, the contributions for a specific tax year cannot be made before the tax year begins or after the taxpayer's original filing date (without extensions) for that tax year. For most individuals, this is the earlier of April 15 of the following year or the date a return is filed. This is similar to the rules for IRA contributions.

Example: Jack and Eva, a married couple, retired last year when they each reached age 56. They purchased a family medical expense policy with a $5,000 deductible, and Jack established an HSA. The maximum contribution to the HSA for 2008 is $6,700, which consists of the regular $5,800 limit and an additional catch-up amount of $900 for Jack.

However, if they each established an HSA, they both would be eligible to make the $900 catch-up contribution to their own accounts. The $5,800 regular contribution could be allocated among the two accounts as they agree upon. The net effect is that the total HSA contributions would increase to $7,600.

These contributions can be made in one or more payments between January 1, 2007, and the date they file their 2008 tax return (but no later than April 15, 2009, if they obtain a filing extension).

If an individual quits participating in an HSA during a tax year, the actual HSA contribution that can be deducted for the tax year is limited to 1/12 of the annual amount, as described previously, times the number of months that an individual is eligible for HSA participation. Until 2007, the same rule applied if an individual began participating in an HSA after January of the tax-year—only a proportionate contribution could be made. The Tax Relief and Health Care Act changed the rule as long as an individual is still eligible to participate in an HSA during the last month of a tax-year. In such a situation, the individual is allowed to make the full annual tax-deductible contribution for the year. However, if he or she fails to remain eligible for an HSA for at least 12 months thereafter (other than because of death or disability), the contribution for the prior year that is attributable to months when the account holder did not have an HSA is includible in gross income and subject to a 10 percent penalty tax.

An excess contribution occurs to the extent that contributions to an HSA exceed the deductible limits or are made for an ineligible person. The account holder is subject to a 6 percent excise tax on excess contributions for each year these contributions are in an account. This excise tax can be avoided if the excess amount and any net income attributable to the excess amount are removed from the HSA prior to the last day prescribed by law, (including extensions) for filing the account holder's income tax return. The net income attributable to the excess contributions is included in the account holder's gross income for the tax year in which the distribution is made.

Example 1: Paul, aged 55, is eligible for an HSA and has a self-only high-deductible policy. In January 2008, he made a contribution of $2,000 to the HSA. On July 1, Paul decided to cease being a self-employed freelance editor and become an employee of a magazine. He cancelled his previous medical expense policy and enrolled in his new employer's, which did not qualify as a high-deductible health plan. As a result, Paul's allowable HSA contribution for the year is only 6/12 of $2,900, or $1,450. He is now in the position of having made an excess contribution for the year. As long as he withdraws the other $550 plus any earnings on this amount before filing his 2008 tax return, he will avoid any adverse tax consequences.

Example 2: Jane, aged 39, did just the opposite of Paul. She left her prior job with an employer and became a self-employed consultant. This occurred on November 1, 2008; she dropped her former HMO coverage through the employer and purchased a high-deductible medical expense policy for herself and her son. She also established an HSA. She is eligible to make the full 2008 contribution of $5,800 and took it as a deduction on her 2008 tax return. However, if she does not continue to be covered under a high-deductible health plan through 2009, a portion of this amount will have to be included as taxable income for 2009.

Roll-Over Contributions

An account balance from an Archer MSA can be rolled over to an HSA on a tax-free basis. Similarly, account balances from an existing HSA can be rolled over to a new HSA.

The Tax Relief and Health Care Act of 2006 also allows certain other types of tax-free rollovers in specific circumstances. For example, an account holder who establishes an HSA is allowed a one-time rollover of funds from an HRA or health FSA. The amount of the rollover, which is in addition to any regular contribution for the year, is limited to the lesser of the balance in such an account on (1) September 21, 2006, or (2) the date of the rollover. If the account holder does not remain eligible to participate in an HSA for at least one year after the rollover, the amount of the rollover is included in income for tax purposes and subject to a 10 percent penalty tax. Finally, an account holder may make a one-time-only rollover from an IRA. The amount of the rollover is limited to the tax-deductible HSA contribution for the year and reduces any regular contribution allowed.

Employer Contributions

Many persons with HDHPs have their coverage under an employer-provided plan, and their employer may make contributions to the HSAs of employees. Employer contributions belong to the employee and are nonforfeitable. The employer might make the maximum annual contribution as previously described. However, it is also possible that the employer contribution will contribute a lower amount. In this case, any remaining allowable contribution can be made by the employee.

An employer that makes contributions to HSAs is subject to a nondiscrimination rule that requires the employer to make comparable contributions for all employees who have HSAs. Failure to comply with this rule subjects the employer to an excise tax equal to 35 percent of the aggregate amount contributed to HSAs during the period when the comparability rule was not satisfied. However, full-time employees and part-time employees (those working fewer than 30 hours per week) are treated separately. The comparability rule generally requires that the employer contribute either the same dollar amount for each employee or the same percentage of each employee's deductible under the health plan. However, it is permissible for an employer to make larger contributions for nonhighly compensated employees than for highly compensated employees.

Account Growth

Unused amounts in an HSA accumulate on a tax-free basis and carry over to subsequent years without limit. The size of an HSA balance carried over from prior years has no effect on a current year's contribution.

Account balances in HSAs are rather modest overall, partially because of the newness of such accounts. In 2006, over 60 percent of HSAs had balances of over $1,000.[6]

As mentioned later, account growth could come from a wide variety of investment options.

Distributions

An individual can usually take distributions from an HSA at any time, but the trust or custodial document may put reasonable restrictions on both the frequency and minimum amount of distributions. Generally, accounts are set up so that they can be accessed with debit cards or checks written by the account holder as an alternative to actually filing for reimbursement. The amount of the distribution can be any part or all of the account balance. Subject to some exceptions, distributions of both contributions and earnings are excludible from an account holder's gross income if used to pay medical expenses of the account holder and the account holder's legal spouse and tax dependents as long as these expenses are not paid by other sources of insurance. There is no requirement that these family members be covered by a high-deductible health insurance plan. If both a husband and wife have HSAs, a reimbursement for any family member can come from either or both HSAs but together cannot exceed the amount of the unreimbursed expense.

For the most part, the eligible medical expenses are the same ones that would be deductible, ignoring the 7.5 percent of adjusted gross income limitation, if the account holder itemized his or her tax deductions. Tax-free withdrawals are permitted for the purchase of COBRA continuation coverage, or for the purchase of health coverage while an individual receives unemployment compensation. They are also permitted for the purchase of long-term care insurance up to the deductible limits shown in table 18-1 of chapter 18. However, tax-free withdrawals are not otherwise permitted for the purchase of health insurance by persons under age 65.

Example: Eric has had an HSA for the last 3 years and has accumulated $6,000 in the account during that time. Because his wife has medical expense coverage with her employer, Eric's high-deductible policy is for him only.

In February, Eric incurred his first medical expenses for the year when he severely sprained his wrist. He incurred $1,000 in medical expenses that were not covered under his policy because the $5,000 deductible had not been met. Eric can pay for these expenses with funds from his HSA.

In April, Eric had a routine eye examination that cost $120. This examination was not covered under his medical expense policy, but it qualifies as a medical expense for IRS purposes. Therefore, Eric can take a $120 tax-free distribution from his HSA.

In July, Eric's wife had a crown installed by her dentist. Her employer-provided health insurance paid only $600 of the dentist's. Eric can use his HSA to pay the remaining $400 because HSA funds can be used to pay unreimbursed medical expenses of an account holder's legal spouse. (Note that the IRS considers medical expenses to include charges for dental services.)

Even though contributions cannot be made after an individual reaches age 65 and becomes a Medicare beneficiary, tax-free distributions can still be used for any future qualified medical expenses, which include Medicare premiums, premiums for Medicare Advantage plans, and premiums for medical expense coverage under employer-sponsored plans. However, tax-free distributions cannot be used to pay premiums for Medicare supplement policies. (Medicare

Advantage Plans and Medicare supplement policies are discussed in chapter 10.)

It should be pointed out that from a financial planning standpoint, account holders may want to wait until after retirement or age 65 to take HSA distributions as long as they have the resources to pay for unreimbursed medical expenses prior to that time. This will allow their HSA balances to grow on a tax-favored basis for use in their older years when unreimbursed medical expenses may be higher and/or income may be lower.

Distributions are permitted for other reasons, but they are subject to income taxation and possibly to a 10 percent penalty tax. However, the penalty tax does not apply in the case of distributions after an individual's death, disability, or the attainment of age 65.

Example: Kirby has a balance of $7,000 in his HSA. At age 67, he rediscovered his childhood sweetheart and fell madly in love. She agreed to marry him, and he wants to give her a large diamond ring. Because she told Kirby that she would take care of him for life, he decided to cash in his HSA and apply the proceeds to the purchase of the ring. His tax accountant informed Kirby that this arrangement would not be a qualified medical expense. He can withdraw the funds without penalty because he is at least age 65, but the $7,000 must be included in his gross income for federal income tax purposes.

Effect of Retirement

Retirees can continue HSAs that were established prior to retirement, and the rules for contributions and distributions are as previously described.

Retirees who did not have an HSA prior to retirement can establish one at that time as long as all the rules are satisfied. Such an HSA may present an opportunity for a retiree to reduce income taxes. However, the requirement of having a high-deductible plan will probably negate this advantage if an individual has substantial medical expenses.

Example: Kathleen, a widow, retired at age 60 from her job as an attorney. Her medical expense coverage had been under an Archer MSA and a high-deductible health plan. Her current account balance is $9,360. She enjoys excellent health and is in a high income tax bracket. She likes the concept of consumer-directed health plans and has decided to establish an HSA and to roll over her Archer MSA balance into this account. In order to be eligible for the HSA, she purchased a major medical policy with an annual deductible of $2,500. She plans on making the maximum allowable contribution to the HSA until she is eligible for Medicare. She will then use her HSA balance to pay her Medicare premiums.

There are fees involved in establishing an HSA. These fees may affect any potential tax advantages if an HSA is established near the time of Medicare enrollment because of the short time horizon for making contributions.

Federal Estate Tax Treatment

Upon death, the remaining balance in an HSA is includible in the account holder's gross estate for estate tax purposes. If the account's beneficiary is a surviving spouse, the HSA belongs to the spouse and he or she can deduct the account balance in determining the account holder's taxable estate. The surviving spouse can then use the HSA for his or her medical expenses. If the beneficiary is someone other than the spouse, the HSA ceases to exist, and the beneficiary must include the fair market value of the account in his or her gross income for tax purposes. If no beneficiary is named or survives, the tax is payable by the estate or the estate's beneficiary.

ESTABLISHING AND MAINTAINING HEALTH SAVINGS ACCOUNTS

There are a number of issues that need to be evaluated by an individual who has the option to establish an HSA. Perhaps the most important question is whether such an account is appropriate. After a person decides to open such accounts, issues such as account fees, investment options for funds, and recordkeeping must be addressed.

Appropriateness

For some persons, an HSA is very appropriate and offers significant tax benefits and financial planning opportunities. For other persons, an HSA may not be an attractive financial commitment. An HSA's viability depends on individual circumstances such as income, tax rates, the funds available to fund such an account, when account balance will be withdrawn, earnings on account funds, and account fees. These issues are addressed in the examples below. Because HSA contributions are tax deductible, the tax savings must be estimated. The amounts used in the examples below are based on information provided by the Treasury Department on its Web site: www.treasury.gov. They are based on typical taxpayers at various income levels. Obviously, an analysis for any one individual depends on that person's specific tax situation.

Example 1: John and his wife, both aged 50, no longer have any dependent children. They are self-employed and have a joint income of $150,000. For the last few years, they have had an HSA-compatible policy with a $5,000 deductible, but have not established HSAs. They are in good health and have paid all unreimbursed medical expenses from current income. Their financial advisor has suggested that one or both of them should establish an HSA. They have decided to do so, and make an annual contribution of $5,000, which is an affordable financial commitment. This will result in an annual income tax savings of $1,300. The have also decided to continue paying any unreimbursed medical expenses from current income and to let the HSA funds accumulate until they retire at age 65. They plan on investing the funds in a mutual fund that they expect to grow at 9 percent per year. If this return is achieved, they will have a fund of about $150,000 when they retire. They will then withdraw the funds as needed on a tax-free basis to pay their Medicare premiums.

Example 2: Billie is a 35-year-old single mother with a young daughter. She earns $30,000 per year in her job as a hairdresser at a beauty salon that does not provide medical expense insurance. She has a medical expense policy with a $4,000 annual deductible for herself and her daughter. Her modest savings were largely depleted when she purchased a home 2 years ago, and Billie must watch her money carefully to meet her normal living expenses. She itemizes her income tax deductions. Because her medical expense premium already exceeds 7.5 percent of her adjusted gross income, any additional unreimbursed medical expenses are tax deductible. Both she and her daughter are healthy but still have about $1,000 of reimbursed medical expenses in a typical year. Billie could put this money into an HSA and receive an income tax deduction. However, she is already able to deduct the unreimbursed medical expenses, so there is no additional tax saving if she withdraws the funds to pay for medical expenses. In addition, there would be account fees with an HSA that would have the effect of reducing any tax savings. Therefore, Billie decides to just keep budgeting for $1,000 of annual medical expenses. She is concerned that a large medical expense might occur in any given year and wonders where she would get the funds to pay the deductible amount. Like many people in her financial situation, however, Billie does not feel she has the resources to put any money into an HSA for this purpose. She decided to rely on her meager emergency fund for whatever occurs, be it unreimbursed medical expenses totaling more than $1,000 or unexpected house or car repairs.

Example 3: For several years Craig, who earns $100,000 per year, has had medical expense coverage through an employer-provided plan for himself, his wife, and four children. All employee contributions have been paid with a salary reduction through a cafeteria plan. What few medical expenses Craig's family has incurred have been copayments for doctor's visits and prescription drugs. Craig's employer recently adopted a high-deductible health plan that has a $5,000 annual deductible for family coverage. This plan will save the employer money. Rather than putting some of this savings into employer-established HSAs, the employer has decided to reduce required employee contributions for coverage. In Craig's case, his contribution will decrease by $2,350 this year. Craig, his wife, and three of their children are very healthy and incur few doctor's bills, and what they do incur is usually in the form of preventive medicine that is reimbursed by the high-deductible health plan. However, his oldest son is diabetic and will have unreimbursed medical expenses that average about $3,000 per year. At a minimum, Craig feels that he should put this amount into an HSA because it will generate an annual income tax savings of $780. Craig's wife also reminds him that their dentist has indicated that all of their children will need orthodontic work over the next few years. This will cost several thousand dollars more than their dental insurance plan will pay. As a result, Craig and his wife decide to increase the HSA contribution to the maximum limit, which will result in further tax savings of about $700 per year.

Account Fees

One factor that varies widely among financial institutions that offer HSAs is the fees that they charge. If an individual uses an HSA that has been established by his or her employer, the employer may pay some of these fees. But no matter how an account is established, a potential account holder should look at the fees and their impact on the account balance. Unfortunately, this is not always easy to do. Although financial institutions often have information about their HSAs on Web sites or in print, the fee structure is often conspicuously absent or hard to locate. Unlike other types of financial products, such as IRAs, there are no requirements to provide potential account holders with a prospectus that details the fees. Therefore, it is often necessary to ask specific questions. As the next example demonstrates, these fees may have an effect on the decision to establish an HSA. Even if an HSA is an obvious choice, the account balance will be affected by the fee structure.

Fees fall into several categories. The fees that an HSA might have include one or more of the following:

- account setup fee. This is a one-time fee to establish the HSA. The authors of this book have found fees that range from $0 to $50, with $15 or $20 being common.
- annual fee. An HSA may have an annual fee that ranges up to $200, but amounts of $10 to $20 are most common.
- monthly maintenance fee. An HSA may have a monthly maintenance fee that ranges up to $10, but amounts like $2 to $3 seem most common. Although there may be both a monthly maintenance fee and an annual fee, this is very uncommon; there is usually one or the

other. In either case, the amount of the fee may be lower for higher account balances.

- transaction fee. An HSA may have a fee that is levied on each transaction. The fee may apply to contributions, but is most likely to be levied on withdrawals only. Fees may be as high as $5, but $.25 to $.50 are quite common. Sometimes a few transactions are allowed without a fee, but fees are levied on transactions in excess of this number.
- account closing fee. It is not unusual for an HSA to have an account closing fee that can range up to $25 or $30, although $10 is a more common amount.

Example: Amber is a self-employed editor who earns about $40,000 annually. She has a medical expense policy with a $3,000 deductible, the premium for which she deducts on Schedule C of her income tax return. Amber enjoys traveling and what money she has left is being saved for the down payment on a condo and a new car that she hopes to buy within the next 2 years. Amber is healthy and incurs about $500 in unreimbursed medical expenses annually. This typically includes two doctor's visits and quarterly refills of a prescription drug. To minimize her taxes, Amber decides to put the $500 into an HSA account and take a withdrawal each time she incurs an unreimbursed medical expense. This will lower her taxes by about $75. When she looks into establishing such an account with her local bank, she finds that they have an account set-up fee of $15. There is also a $2 monthly maintenance fee ($24 per year) and a $3 fee for each withdrawal ($18 for her six transactions). Therefore, she will incur expenses of $58 to save $75 the first year. When Amber finds out that her account balance will be too small to earn more than1 percent interest, she decides that an HSA is not worth the administrative hassle for such a minimal tax savings.

Investment Options

Financial institutions often offer several types of investment options for HSA funds. Account holders can invest HSA funds in essentially the same manner as IRA funds. Allowable investments include bank accounts, annuities, certificates of deposit, stocks, mutual funds, and bonds. Investments in life insurance policies or most types of collectibles are prohibited. In addition, an HSA trust or custodial agreement may limit the investment options available.

Although mutual funds and stocks may result in the best return over a number of years, they are probably unsuitable if an account holder has modest amounts in an HSA that will be used for medical expenses in the near future. Like many types of investments, they will fluctuate in value over time. Such investments may also be unavailable unless an account holder has an account balance of several thousand dollars. The example of John mentioned under the heading Appropriateness shows when such an investment makes sense.

In most cases, an individual will be using some type of bank account that allows easy access to the available funds. In this case, it is important to evaluate the return that these funds will earn, which is set by each bank. In some cases, nothing is paid unless the account exceeds a minimum balance, such as $1,000. Interest rates may also vary by the size of the account's average daily balance. In still other cases, a specified interest rate, which can change, is paid on any size balance. Even with these variations, there are significant differences paid among banks.

Recordkeeping

Custodians and trustees for HSAs report the amount of annual contributions to and distributions from each HSA to the IRS. Under IRS rules, it is the account holder's responsibility to determine whether distributions from HSAs are for eligible medical expenses. Therefore, individuals who establish such accounts should maintain records in case they are audited. They should also become familiar with the types of expenses that are deductible. Guidance can be found in IRS Publication 502, which is available on the IRS Web site: www.irs.gov.

ARCHER MEDICAL SAVINGS ACCOUNTS

Archer MSA

HSAs are designed to be successors to Archer MSAs. Like an HSA, an *Archer MSA* is a personal savings account from which medical expenses can be paid. In some respects, Archer MSAs are virtually identical to HSAs, but in several important circumstances, they are different.

No new Archer MSAs can be established after 2007 unless Congress extends a sunset provision. Those in existence at the end of 2007, however, can remain in effect, with future contributions still allowed for eligible participants. It is expected that most Archer MSAs will be converted to HSAs through tax-free rollovers.

How Archer MSAs Differ from HSAs

Archer MSAs differ from HSAs primarily with respect to eligibility, the nature of the high-deductible health plan used, contributions, and distributions.

Eligibility

Two types of individuals were eligible to establish and now to continue making contributions to Archer MSAs:

- a self-employed person (or spouse of a self-employed person) maintaining a self-only or family high-deductible health plan covering that individual
- an employee (or spouse of an employee) of a small employer who obtains self-only or family coverage through a high-deductible health plan sponsored by that employer. A small employer is defined as having an average of 50 or fewer employees on business days during either of the two preceding calendar years. After the initial qualification as a small employer is satisfied, an employer can continue to make contributions to employees' Archer MSAs until the first year following the year in which the employer has more than 200 employees. At that time, participating employees may take over contributions to their accounts, but no employer contributions can be made. Alternatively, the employer could convert the plan to an HSA.

Nature of High-Deductible Health Plan

An HDHP, for purposes of Archer MSA participation, is a plan that has the following deductibles and annual out-of-pocket limits. These amounts are for 2008 and subject to inflation adjustments.

- In the case of self-only coverage, the deductible must be at least \$1,950 and cannot exceed \$2,900. The maximum annual out-of-pocket expenses cannot exceed \$3,850.
- In the case of family coverage, the deductible must be at least \$3,850 and cannot exceed \$5,800. The maximum annual out-of-pocket expenses cannot exceed \$7,050.

The deductible must apply to all medical expenses covered by the plan, including preventive services.

Contributions

Either the account holder of an Archer MSA or the account holder's employer, but not both, may make a contribution to an Archer MSA. If the employer makes a contribution, even one below the allowable limit, the account holder may not make a contribution.

The amount of the annual tax-deductible contribution to an employee's account is limited to 65 percent of the policy deductible for the health coverage if the Archer MSA is for an individual. The figure is 75 percent if the account holder of an Archer MSA has family coverage. If each spouse has an Archer MSA and if one or both of the spouses has an HDHP with family coverage, the aggregate contribution is equal to 75 percent of the deductible for the family coverage with the lowest deductible. The contribution is split equally between the two persons unless they agree to a different division.

Distributions

The rules for distributions from Archer MSAs are less liberal than those for HSAs. Tax-free distributions cannot be made for medical expenses of an "ineligible individual" in any year that contributions are made to an Archer MSA. An ineligible individual is a person who incurs medical expenses when the individual is not covered by a high-deductible health plan.

Example: Derek has an Archer MSA. However, his wife is an ineligible individual because she is retired and covered by Medicare and therefore is not covered by a HDHP. As long as Derek or his employer contributes to the Archer MSA, he cannot take tax-free reimbursements for her unreimbursed medical expenses.

Note that when he retires and Archer MSA contributions are not made in a tax year, such a tax-free distribution would be allowed.

How Archer MSAs Are Similar to HSAs

Archer MSAs are essentially identical to HSAs with respect to account growth and estate tax treatment.

Effect of Retirement

Individuals who retire retain ownership of balances in their Archer MSAs. Distributions can be taken under the tax rules as previously described for HSAs, but no additional contributions can be made unless they continue to meet the eligibility requirements.

Retirees under age 65 may still wish to participate in a consumer-directed health plan. They may maintain their Archer MSAs, and they are eligible to establish HSAs. They can also roll over Archer MSA balances to such a newly established account on a tax-free basis.

CHAPTER REVIEW

Key Terms

health savings account (HSA)
consumer-directed health care
high-deductible health plan (HDHP)
Archer MSA

Review Questions

Review questions are based on the learning objectives in this chapter. Thus, a [9-3] at the end of a question means that the question is based on learning objective 9-3. If there are multiple objectives, they are all listed.

1. How can consumer-directed health care lead to cost savings with respect to health care? [9-1]
2. What are some of the criticisms that have been leveled at consumer-directed health care? [9-1]
3. What are the reasons why persons with high-deductible health plans often do not establish HSAs? [9-1]
4. Who is eligible to establish and maintain an HSA? [9-2]
5. What is the nature of a high-deductible health plan that a person must have before he or she can establish an HSA? [9-2]
6. a. What is the income tax treatment of HSA contributions? [9-2]
   b. What amounts can be contributed to HSAs? [9-2]
   c. What types of rollover contributions are allowed? [9-2]
7. a. When can distributions be taken from an HSA? [9-2]
   b. How are distributions taxed? [9-2]
8. How does retirement affect HSAs? [9-2]

9. What is the estate tax treatment of HSAs? [9-2]
10. What factors should be considered in determining the appropriateness of an HSA? [9-3]
11. What types of fees may be charged to HSA account holders? [9-3]
12. What types of investment options are available to HSA account holders? [9-3]
13. Why is recordkeeping particularly important with respect to HSA distributions? [9-3]
14. a. How do Archer MSAs differ from HSAs? [9-4]
    b. How are they similar? [9-4]

NOTES

1. "January 2007 Census Shows 4.5 Million People Covered By HSA/High-Deductible Health Plans," Center for Policy and Research, America's Health Insurance Plans, April 2007, p. 1.
2. Atlantic Information Services, Inc., *Inside Consumer-Directed Care,* Volume 4, Number 2 (January 27, 2006), p. 7.
3. Employee Benefit Research Institute, *The 2nd Annual EBRI/Commonwealth Fund Consumerism in Health Care Survey*, 2006, p. 21.
4. Ibid. p. 4.
5. Ibid. p. 18.
6. Ibid. p. 18.

10

Supplementing Medicare

Learning Objectives

An understanding of the material in this chapter should enable you to

10-1. Describe original Medicare with respect to eligibility and benefits.

10-2. Identify the gaps in original Medicare and the types of coverages available to fill these gaps.

10-3. Explain how individual Medicare supplement policies enhance the benefits available under Medicare.

10-4. Describe the Medicare Advantage program.

10-5. Describe the prescription drug coverage available under Medicare Part D.

Chapter Outline

Medicare is the principal source of medical expense insurance for many Americans aged 65 and older, as well as certain other persons. As explained later in this chapter, there are gaps in the Medicare program that are often filled by private policies of medical expense insurance. However, this coverage is often subject to guidelines established by both federal and state government regulations.

Although the purpose of this book is not to provide a detailed analysis of the Medicare program, some background is needed to explain why supplemental coverage is often necessary. Agents and brokers who sell these supplemental policies are also better able to serve their clients by being able to answer clients' questions about Medicare and to direct them to sources for more detailed information. Therefore, the chapter begins with a brief discussion of original Medicare and the gaps in the program.

The chapter continues by looking at the three most common ways these gaps in medical expense coverage are filled: Medicare supplement polices, Medicare Advantage plans, and Medicare prescription drug plans.

ORIGINAL MEDICARE

original Medicare

Original Medicare is the term used to describe Part A and Part B of Medicare, which is available to about 99 percent of all persons over age 65. This section looks at Medicare eligibility, benefits, gaps in benefits, and sources for additional information.

Eligibility

Part A, the hospital portion of Medicare, is available at no monthly cost to any person aged 65 or older as long as he or she is entitled to monthly retirement benefits under Social Security or the railroad retirement program.

Civilian employees of the federal government aged 65 or older are also eligible. It is not necessary for these workers actually to be receiving retirement benefits, but they must be fully insured for purposes of retirement benefits. The following persons are also eligible for Part A of Medicare at no monthly cost:

- persons aged 65 or older who are spouses (including certain divorced spouses) of fully insured workers aged 62 or older
- survivors aged 65 or older who are eligible for Social Security survivors benefits
- disabled persons at any age who have been eligible to receive Social Security benefits for 2 years because of their disability. This includes workers under age 65, disabled widows and widowers aged 50 or over, and children 18 or older who were disabled prior to age 22.
- workers who are either fully or currently insured under Social Security and their spouses and dependent children with end-stage renal (kidney) disease who require renal dialysis or kidney transplants. Coverage begins either the first day of the third month after dialysis begins or earlier for admission to a hospital for kidney-transplant surgery.

Most persons aged 65 or over who do not meet the previously discussed eligibility requirements may voluntarily enroll in Medicare. However, they must pay a monthly Part A premium and also enroll in Part B.

Any person eligible for Part A of Medicare is also eligible for Part B. A monthly premium must be paid for Part B, and is unrelated to age. The minimum premium ($96.40 in 2008) is adjusted annually and represents only about 25 percent of the cost of the benefits provided. The general revenues of the federal government finance the remaining cost of the program. As a result of the Medicare Prescription Drug, Improvement, and Modernization Act, the Part B premium will continue to equal 25 percent of Part B benefit costs, but only for beneficiaries with modified adjusted gross income of $82,000 or less for a single person and $164,000 for a couple (in 2008 and subject to indexing). Higher-income persons pay a larger premium that increases with income.

Persons who receive Social Security or railroad retirement benefits are automatically enrolled in Medicare if they are eligible. If they do not want Part B, they must reject it in writing. Other persons eligible for Medicare must apply for benefits. As a general rule, anyone who rejects Part B or who does not enroll when initially eligible may later apply for benefits during a general enrollment period that occurs between January 1 and March 31 of each year. The monthly premium is increased by 10 percent for each 12-month period during which the person was eligible but failed to enroll.

If a person continues to work after age 65, there are Medicare secondary rules that often make employer-provided medical expense coverage primary to Medicare. These persons (and any other Medicare-eligible persons still covered as active employees under their employers' plans) may not wish to elect Medicare because it largely constitutes duplicate coverage. When employer-provided coverage ends, these persons have a 7-month special enrollment period to elect Part B coverage, and the late enrollment penalty is waived.

Benefits

The original Medicare plan is Medicare's traditional pay-per-visit/service benefit arrangement. Medicare pays benefits when a beneficiary receives services from a hospital, doctor, or other health care provider.

Part A Benefits (Hospital Insurance)

Medicare hospital insurance, or Part A, helps pay for care in hospitals and certified skilled-nursing facilities, home health care, and hospice care under certain circumstances. After the patient pays a deductible ($1,024 in 2008) for the first admission in each benefit period, Medicare pays hospitalization benefits for approved inpatient care in a semiprivate hospital room at 100 percent for the first 60 days. The patient shares in the daily charges from the 61st to the 90th day of hospital confinement ($256 in 2008). The only coverage after 90 days in a benefit period is a 60-day lifetime reserve on which patients can draw. However, there is a large daily copayment ($512 in 2008).

Custodial care in a nursing home is not covered under Medicare, but care in a Medicare-approved skilled-nursing facility for a condition requiring at least a 3-day hospital stay within the previous 30 days is covered for up to 100 days. Daily copayments ($128 in 2008) are required from the 21st through the 100th day.

Medicare covers the cost of services performed in the patient's home by nurses, therapists, and health care providers other than physicians. In order to be covered, the services must be provided by Medicare-approved home health care agencies. If a person has only Part A, all home health care benefits are covered under Part A. However, if a person has both Parts A and B, the first 100 visits that commence within 14 days of a hospital stay of at least 3 days are covered under Part A. All other home health visits are covered under Part B.

Hospice benefits are also available under Part A. To qualify for hospice benefits, a beneficiary must be certified as terminally ill with a life expectancy of 6 months or less and elect such coverage in lieu of other benefits for the terminal condition. While benefits may be provided as an inpatient, if needed, they are primarily provided to patients in their own homes. In addition to physician services and the types of benefits described for home health care, hospice benefits also include drugs, bereavement counseling, and respite care when family members need a break from caring for the ill person. In order for benefits to be paid, the facility or agency providing benefits must participate in the Medicare program. Virtually all hospitals are participants, as are most other facilities or agencies that meet the requirements of Medicare.

Part B Benefits (Supplementary Medical Insurance)

Part B, called supplementary medical insurance, helps pay for a broad spectrum of expenses, mostly professional medical services, that are not covered under Part A. These expenses may be incurred for physician's services, inpatient and outpatient medical and surgical services, physical and speech therapy, diagnostic tests, and durable medical equipment. Beneficiaries may receive these services in any setting, including a doctor's office, clinic, nursing home, hospital, or at home. Essentially, Part B pays for 80 percent of Medicare-approved charges for various covered services after the patient has met a deductible for the calendar year ($135 in 2008). The Medicare beneficiary is responsible for the remaining 20 percent of approved charges and charges for noncovered services.

Most doctors and other suppliers of medical services accept an assignment of Medicare benefits and, therefore, are prohibited from charging a patient in excess of the approved charge schedule issued by the Centers for Medicare & Medicaid Services (CMS), which administers Medicare. They can, however, bill the patient for any portion of the approved charges that are not paid by Medicare because of the patient's annual deductible and/or percentage participation amount after coinsurance. They can also bill for any services that are not covered by Medicare.

Medical service providers who do not accept assignment may bill above the approved fee levels, although a limit is placed on the amount that nonparticipating doctors may charge. These balances must be borne by the Medicare beneficiary. However, the suppliers of ambulance services and durable medical equipment that do not accept assignment constitute an exception because they have no limits on what they can charge a Medicare beneficiary. In those cases, the beneficiary is responsible for all charges beyond the Medicare-approved amount.

Gaps in Benefits

As previously indicated, the original Medicare program has many limitations. These limitations create out-of-pocket costs for beneficiaries that fall into three categories: fully covered, partially covered, and uncovered services.

Benefit Gaps for Fully Covered Services

Benefit gaps for fully covered services include

- the Part A deductible for each hospital benefit period. A benefit period begins the day of initial confinement in a hospital or skilled-nursing facility and ends after subsequent hospital or skilled-nursing care has not been received for 60 consecutive days.
- any part A copayments after the first 60 days of hospitalization in a benefit period
- the Part B annual deductible
- the 20 percent participation share of charges for most covered services under Part B. It is important to note that Medicare does not have a maximum out-of-pocket limit.

Benefit Gaps for Partially Covered Services

Gaps in benefits for services that are only partially covered include

- home health care that does not meet the program's required conditions
- the first three pints of blood
- all costs for skilled-nursing facility care after day 100 in a benefit period
- all costs for hospital care after benefits are exhausted in a benefit period

Benefit Gaps for Services That Are Not Covered

Gaps due to services that are not covered (with a few exceptions) include

- outpatient prescription drugs
- routine vision care
- dental care
- hearing aids
- private duty nursing
- certain preventive services
- care while traveling or living outside the United States
- custodial/long-term care

Sources for Further Information

Readers may wish to obtain further information about Medicare or be able to direct their clients to sources for this information. The best source for this information is the official Medicare Web site: www.medicare.gov. This site contains numerous excellent booklets, brochures, and fact sheets. Unfortunately, they are not always that easy to find if a visitor is unfamiliar with the site. One recommended approach is to do a search for the "Medicare Publications Catalog." It lists all the documents that are available. With the name or the publication number, the reader can access the document. All publications are online and can also be ordered for delivery by mail. Many publications are in Spanish, braille, and/or large print. A small sample of the publications includes:

- Medicare and You
- Enrolling in Medicare
- Medicare Coverage of Durable Medical Equipment
- Medicare Hospice Benefits
- Medicare and Home Health Care
- Medicare and Your Mental Health Benefits
- Guide to Medicare's Preventive Services
- Medicare Coverage of Diabetes Supplies and Services
- Choosing a Medigap Policy
- Choosing a Medicare Health Plan
- Comparing Medicare Prescription Drug Coverage
- Your Medicare Rights and Protections

Each state also has a State Health Insurance Assistance Program (SHIP). These are state programs that get money from the federal government to give free health insurance counseling and assistance to people with Medicare. SHIP counselors can answer questions about Medicare on such topics as Medicare benefits, dealing with denials and appeals, Medicare rights and protections, sending complaints about care or treatment, and selecting the appropriate Medicare and prescription drug plan. A SHIP also should be able to offer guidance about enrolling in Medicaid, selecting a Medicare supplement policy, and buying long-term care insurance. Phone numbers for each state's SHIP can be found on the Medicare Web site.

FILLING THE GAPS

There are several ways to fill the gaps in Medicare, but no single way fills all the gaps. To meet long-term care needs, a person can purchase long-term care insurance, which is the subject of later chapters of this book. To obtain benefits for care when traveling outside the United States, a person can purchase an international travel medical policy. Such policies are described in chapter 11.

Precise statistics are difficult to obtain, but the majority of individuals have some type of coverage to supplement Medicare. About 30 percent of Medicare beneficiaries are still fortunate enough to have retiree benefits provided by their former employers, but this percentage is shrinking. Employer-provided coverage for retirees may take the form of either a Medicare carve-out or a Medicare supplement. With a Medicare carve-out, the employer-provided group benefits are reduced to the extent that benefits are payable under Medicare for the same expenses. As an alternative, some employers use a group Medicare supplement plan that provides benefits for certain expenses not covered by Medicare. Note that the term Medicare supplement in the group market is applied generically to any supplemental medical expense plan. These plans are not subject to the rules that apply to individual Medicare supplement policies as described in this chapter. The extent to which employer-provided coverage includes benefits for prescription drugs varies.

Another 30 to 40 percent have individually purchased Medicare supplement policies or are covered under Medicare Advantage plans, both of which are discussed in detail in this chapter. However, even with such coverage, a person may still need coverage for the cost of prescription drugs. This coverage can be obtained with Medicare prescription drug coverage, the final topic of the chapter.

MEDICARE SUPPLEMENT (MEDIGAP) POLICIES

Medicare supplement (medigap) insurance

Medicare supplement insurance in the individual marketplace is frequently referred to as *medigap insurance*. As the name implies, its objective is to fill some of the gaps left after Medicare benefits have been exhausted. When originally developed, Medicare supplement plans were as diverse as the companies that sold them. This led to confusion in the marketplace and to questionable sales practices and duplications of coverage. As a result, the federal government enacted legislation to address the structure and marketing of Medicare supplement plans.

In 1990, the Medicare supplement market became directly subject to federal regulation when Congress directed the National Association of Insurance Commissioners (NAIC) to develop a group of standardized Medicare supplement policies. Congress mandated several other features, including a 6-month open enrollment period, limited preexisting-conditions exclusions, prohibition of the sale of duplicate coverage, and increased loss ratios. Indeed, when describing the benefits of each of the Medicare supplement policies, insurance companies must use the same format, language, and definitions. They also are required to use a uniform chart and outline of coverage to summarize the benefits in each plan. These requirements are intended to make it easier for beneficiaries to compare policies and to choose among them based on service, reliability, and price.

Federal laws have also generated several restrictions on the markets to which Medicare supplement policies may be sold. Under these restrictions, known as antiduplication provisions, it is generally illegal for an insurance company to sell a Medicare supplement policy to

- a current Medicare supplement policyowner, unless that person states in writing that the first policy will be cancelled
- a Medicaid recipient
- an enrollee in a Medicare Advantage plan

A violation of these provisions is subject to criminal and/or civil penalties under federal law.

Basic Benefits

The NAIC originally adopted 10 standard Medicare supplement plans; all 10 required the inclusion of a core of specified basic benefits. States may approve, and insurers may offer, fewer than these 10 standard plans, but all states must permit the basic benefits to be sold alone (plan A). Most states permit the sale of all 10 plans, but a some limit the types sold, and a few states are not affected by the mandate because alternative standardized programs were already in place prior to the federal legislation. There are now two additional plans that contain consumer-directed health plan features. These two plans differ somewhat from the original 10 plans, which are discussed first.

Note that the following rules for standardized policies apply to the individual marketplace. Group Medicare supplements that employers offer to their retirees are not considered Medicare supplement policies and may differ. In addition, three states—Massachusetts, Minnesota, and Wisconsin—had Medicare supplement programs prior to the NAIC standards. These programs were allowed to continue, and the policies issued are somewhat different from those previously described. However, they are required to contain the basic benefits available in all other states.

The basic benefits that all 10 original plans must include consist of the following:

- hospitalization—the copayment or cost sharing of Part A benefits for the 61st through the 90th day of hospitalization and the 60-day lifetime reserve. In addition, coverage is extended for 365 additional days after Medicare benefits end.

- medical expenses—the Part B percentage participation for Medicare-approved charges for physicians' and medical services after a beneficiary has satisfied the Part B deductible
- blood—the payment for the first 3 pints of blood each year

Additional Benefits

The 10 original Medicare supplement plans that can be sold include, in addition to the basic benefits, an array of benefits for services that Medicare covers either in part or not at all. These benefits include paying

- the Part A copayment for the 21st through the 100th day of skilled-nursing facility care
- the hospital inpatient Part A deductible for each benefit period
- the Part B deductible
- charges for physicians' and medical services that exceed the Medicare-approved amount (either 80 or 100 percent of these charges)
- 80 percent of the charges for emergency care in a foreign country (with several limitations)
- an at-home provider to give assistance with activities of daily living (ADLs) while a beneficiary qualifies for Medicare home health care benefits. Coverage is limited to seven visits per week and a maximum benefit of $40 per visit and $1,600 per year.
- limited annual amounts for preventive care (annual shots, physicals, certain screening tests, and so forth)

The 10 plans are illustrated in table 10-1. The policies available in the individual marketplace must be identified by the letters A through J. Insurers can offer plans F and J as high-deductible policies with a deductible that is set annually by the federal government. The 2008 deductible is $1,900.

The most widely available Medicare supplement plans are A, C, D, and F. Plan A generally represents less than 5 percent of Medicare supplement sales, however. Plan F represents more than half, while plans C and D make up approximately a third of total sales. Plans K and L and Medicare SELECT policies (also described later), which are generally less available, represent no more than 10 percent of total Medicare supplement sales.

Plans H, I, and J were originally designed to pay 50 percent of outpatient prescription drug charges after a $250 deductible up to an annual $1,250 or $3,000 calendar limit. Beginning in 2006, insurance companies may no

TABLE 10-1
Medicare Supplement (Medigap) Policies

Benefits	A	B	C	D	E	F	G	H	I	J
Basic	X	X	X	X	X	X	X	X	X	X
Skilled-nursing facility (days 21–100)			X	X	X	X	X	X	X	X
Part A deductible		X	X	X	X	X	X	X	X	X
Part B deductible			X			X				X
Part B excess charges						100%	80%		100%	100%
Foreign travel emergency			X	X	X	X	X	X	X	X
At-home recovery				X			X		X	X
Preventive medical care					X					X
Prescription drugs								$1,250*	$1,250*	$3,000*

*Not available with newly sold policies; can be eliminated by an already insured person who enrolls in a Medicare prescription drug plan.

longer issue these policies to new insureds with a drug benefit included. Persons already insured under these policies have several options. They may continue to renew the policies with drug benefits included as long as the insured does not enroll in the Medicare prescription drug program (Part D). However, they will then probably be subject to the penalty for late enrollment if they later enroll in the program because the benefits under the Medicare supplement policy will likely not qualify as creditable coverage. If they enroll in the Medicare prescription drug program, they may keep in force their existing Medicare supplement policies but with the drug benefit eliminated and the premium adjusted accordingly. Alternatively, they can switch to another available Medicare supplement policy that has no drug benefit. Such a switch is allowed without evidence of insurability or a penalty for preexisting conditions as long as it occurs during the initial Part D enrollment period.

Other Plans

With two exceptions, insurance companies cannot offer policies that provide benefits that differ from those under Plans A through J. The first exception is that the companies can now offer two plans with consumer-directed features. Called plans K and L, these plans include the same basic hospital benefits as plans A through J and pay 100 percent of these amounts. In addition, these plans cover the following benefits:

- the Part A deductible
- the daily copayment for days 21 through 100 of skilled-nursing facility care
- the first three pints of blood
- the percentage participation for Part B services
- hospice and respite care cost sharing (not covered under Plans A through J)

Under Plan K, the insured must pay 50 percent of the amounts for these additional benefits except for Part B preventive services, which are covered at 100 percent. When the insured's out-of-pocket payments plus the Part B deductible equal $4,440 (in 2008 and subject to indexing), plan K will pay 100 percent of the self-responsible amounts (any required copayments and percentage participation for Medicare services other than prescription drugs) for the rest of the calendar year. However, provider charges that exceed Medicare-approved amounts (excess charges) do not count toward the annual out-of-pocket limit.

Plan L is identical to plan K except that the percentage the insured must pay is 25 percent rather than 50 percent. In addition, the out-of-pocket limit is $2,220 (in 2008).

Because of the more limited benefits and cost sharing, Plans K and L are significantly less expensive than Plans A through J.

Medicare SELECT policy

The second exception is for policies issued under the Medicare SELECT program, which has been in existence since 1994. A *Medicare SELECT policy* is one of the 12 standard Medicare supplement policies, but it can exclude or limit benefits (except in emergencies) for medical services if they are not received from network providers. Medicare SELECT policies are issued by insurance companies as PPO products and by some HMOs. As a general rule, the cost of a Medicare SELECT policy is 15 to 25 percent less than the cost of a comparable policy that does not use such preferred-provider networks. An insured who has a Medicare SELECT policy has the right to switch to a regular Medicare supplement policy the same company sells, as long as the new policy has equal or less coverage than the Medicare SELECT policy.

Eligibility

Persons aged 65 or older and anyone else eligible for Medicare may buy any available Medicare supplement policy, regardless of health status, at any time during the 6-month period after initial enrollment for Medicare Part B benefits. Insurance companies are allowed to exclude benefits for no more than 6 months because of preexisting conditions, but this period is reduced or eliminated by prior creditable coverage. Some policies, however, immediately provide benefits for preexisting conditions or have an exclusion period shorter than 6 months.

If a person initially elects a Medicare Advantage plan in lieu of original Medicare benefits, he or she will be eligible to purchase a Medicare supplement policy, without evidence of insurability, if he or she leaves the during the first 12 months of coverage and returns to original Medicare benefits. Similarly, a person who drops Medicare supplement coverage and elects a Medicare Advantage plan can regain Medicare supplement coverage if he or she decides to drop the plan during the first 12 months of coverage.

In addition, a person can obtain a Medicare supplement policy without evidence of insurability because of the termination of an employer-provided plan that supplements Medicare, or because a Medicare Advantage plan no longer provides coverage or the person loses eligibility by moving out of the plan's service area. Policies also have a free-look period and are guaranteed renewable.

MEDICARE ADVANTAGE PLANS

In 1985, Congress amended the Medicare program to allow a beneficiary to elect coverage under a health maintenance organization (HMO) as an alternative to original Medicare. In 1999, Part C of Medicare (originally called Medicare+Choice) went into effect. It expanded the choices available to most Medicare beneficiaries by allowing them to elect health care benefits through one of several alternatives to original Medicare, as long as the providers of these alternatives enter into contracts with the Centers for Medicare & Medicaid Services. However, beneficiaries must still pay Part B premiums. It is important to emphasize that these are private insurance plans. Although some plans market directly to Medicare beneficiaries, others use agents or brokers to sell their products.

These plans must provide all benefits available under Parts A and B of Medicare. They typically include broader benefits as part of the basic coverage at no additional cost or for an additional premium. These include coverage for the deductibles, copayments, and percentage participation of original Medicare. They may also include some benefits for vision, hearing, or dental care as well as some wellness benefits. As a result, beneficiaries have little or no reason to have a Medicare supplement policy. In fact, they are ineligible to purchase one. However, they still have a need for Medicare prescription drug coverage.

The initial reaction to Medicare+Choice was less than overwhelming. Few new providers of alternative coverage entered the marketplace, and the Medicare Advantage program had decreased after several years of growth.

Medicare Advantage

The situation, however, changed in 2005 as a result of provisions in the Medicare Prescription Drug, Improvement, and Modernization Act. The act changed the name of Medicare+Choice to *Medicare Advantage;* all materials for such plans must now use this terminology. The act makes numerous administrative changes to the program aimed at increasing participation. The method for calculating payment to participating plans has changed, and many plans now receive larger payments. This has already prompted some plans to increase benefits and/or lower premiums. And participation has begun to increase. Today, about one out of every seven Medicare beneficiaries is enrolled in a Medicare Advantage plan. About 85 percent of these enrollees are in HMO plans; the remainder are scattered among the other types of plans. The participation rate varies significantly among states, with some states having almost no participants and other states having participation rates over 20 percent. To some extent these statistics have been influenced by the fact that most Medicare Advantage plans are HMOs, and some parts of the country are either served by a single Medicare Advantage plan or have no such plans. In other parts of the country, there is a very competitive market.

Since 2006, PPOs have been able to offer regionally based Medicare Advantage plans that are broader than the typical service areas used for non–Medicare Advantage participants. The Secretary of Health and Human Services determines these regions. This gives PPOs a broader base from which to solicit members and should also increase competition. These regional plans must use a single deductible and out-of-pocket limit for Part A and Part B benefits.

Beneficiaries are generally able to enroll in a Medicare Advantage plan or switch plans (including reenrollment in Parts A and B) from November 15 to December 31.

Medicare Advantage plans are required to submit proposals to participate in the program. Such proposals are subject to negotiation, and the Secretary of Health and Human Services will determine whether a plan can participate in the program based on statutory criteria. This is similar to the procedure used to select the medical expense plans available to employees of the federal government under the Federal Employees Health Benefits Program.

Types of Plans

There are currently five types of Medicare Advantage plans. It is important to emphasize that if one of these options is selected, a beneficiary is still technically covered by Medicare. However, benefits are paid by the Medicare Advantage plan, not original Medicare. Any medical expenses not covered by the Medicare Advantage plan are the responsibility of the plan member.

- health maintenance organizations (HMOs). As with HMOs for persons who are not eligible for Medicare, beneficiaries typically must select a primary care physician from the plan's network. This physician must usually make referrals for specialty care. Some Medicare Advantage HMOs have a point-of-service option, under which a beneficiary can elect to go outside the plan's network, but the beneficiary will pay a portion of the cost of these services. HMOs, their nature, and their advantages and drawbacks, are discussed in chapter 8.
- preferred-provider organizations (PPOs). Medicare Advantage PPOs are essentially like the PPOs described in chapter 8. Beneficiaries can elect out-of-network care if they are willing to pay the additional cost for such care, which can be substantial.
- private fee-for-service (PFFS) plans. Beneficiaries can go to any provider who agrees to accept the payment rates determined by the plan, but they may be required to pay a portion of these rates in the form of cost sharing. If a provider does not accept the PFFS plan rates, the beneficiary is responsible for the entire balance above what the plan pays. PFFS plans are similar to traditional major medical plans, which are described in chapter 8. PFFS plans, not widely purchased until recently, are becoming increasingly common as more insurers are marketing such products.
- Medicare medical savings account (MMSA) plans. These are similar to HSAs (see chapter 9). A beneficiary has a high-deductible policy, with the size of the deductible varying from plan to plan. Medicare then puts an annual amount into a medical savings account that can be used for unreimbursed medical costs. MMSA plans are not yet widely purchased and are offered by only a small number of insurers in limited parts of the country.
- special needs plans (SNPs). SNPs are designed primarily to meet the needs of beneficiaries who are eligible for both Medicare and Medicaid (or who have certain chronic conditions) and who live in institutions such as nursing homes, or continue to live at home but need the level of care provided by such institutions. These plans help manage and coordinate the many services and providers needed by such beneficiaries. These plans are available only in limited geographic regions.

Is a Medicare Advantage Plan an Appropriate Option?

The selection of a Medicare Advantage plan is often a viable option that may provide broad coverage at a relatively modest cost, particularly if payments from Medicare remain at a level that such plans feel is sufficient. However, Medicare Advantage plans are not available in all parts of the country, and the number of plans in a given area may be very limited. In addition, most of the plans that currently exist are structured as HMOs. For a retiree who was covered by an HMO plan while working, the nature of the coverage will be familiar, and the HMO plan may even be with the same insurer that provided coverage previously. For other retirees, the inherent nature of such plans may be less than desirable. For example, HMOs control the selection of physicians that a member can use. The selection of a Medicare Advantage plan may require a retiree to stop seeing a long-time trusted physician and select a physician who participates in the HMO network. On the other hand, the retiree's physician may already be in the HMO network and no change will be necessary. HMOs also have limited coverage when a member receives medical care outside the plan's relatively small geographic service area. Retirees who plan to spend winter or summer months at another location may have limited coverage except in emergency situations unless they return home for treatment.

The decisions regarding HMO coverage are essentially the same for retirees as they are for actively working persons.

Other Medicare Alternatives

In addition to Medicare Advantage plans, there are three other types of health plans that are part of the Medicare program. Each is available only in limited parts of the country.

The first is referred to as a Medicare cost plan, which is a type of HMO. Unlike a Medicare Advantage HMO, which receives a set amount of money for each beneficiary, the plan is reimbursed for its reasonable cost by Medicare. The plan pays benefits only if a beneficiary uses a network provider. If services are received outside the plan's network, they are covered by original Medicare. Medicare costs plans predate Medicare+Choice plans and are no longer common. A person eligible for Medicare can enroll at any time as long as such a plan is accepting new members and may return to original Medicare at any time.

Medicare has also approved special projects in some parts of the country that are referred to as demonstration/pilot programs. The purpose of these programs is to test improvements in Medicare coverage, payment, and quality of care for specific groups of people. For example, one program is for persons who have been diagnosed with end-stage renal disease.

The final program is PACE (programs of all-inclusive care for the elderly). PACE combines medical, social, and long-term care services for frail elderly who live in and get care in the community. These are joint Medicare and Medicaid program in a few states that have chosen to offer them as an optional Medicaid benefit.

MEDICARE PRESCRIPTION DRUG COVERAGE

Along with numerous other changes to Medicare and the establishment of health savings accounts, the Medicare Prescription Drug, Improvement, and Modernization Act added a prescription drug program to Medicare—Medicare Part D.

Part D has been a subject of considerable controversy. Some members of Congress argue that it does not go far enough in meeting the needs of beneficiaries; other members of Congress contend that its cost will saddle the government with another major entitlement. Part D is also viewed by some as a boon to the pharmaceutical industry that will cost $400–$700 billion over the next 10 years. In addition, the rules for this program are very complex.

As with any new program of this magnitude, there will undoubtedly be situations that come to light during its infancy. As a result, changes no doubt will take place, and readers need to keep abreast of current developments. One source of such information is the Medicare Web site: www.medicare.gov.

Eligibility

Part D is a voluntary prescription drug benefit available to all Medicare beneficiaries enrolled in either Part A and/or Part B (original Medicare) or in any of the various Medicare Advantage plans. Each enrollee must pay a monthly premium. No one can be denied coverage because of income level or for health reasons. Hereafter, Part D benefits are referred to as *Medicare prescription drug plans*.

Medicare prescription drug plans

Types of Plans

Medicare prescription drug plans are private plans offered by insurance companies, managed care plans, and other organizations. These sponsors typically contract with pharmacy benefit managers to design plan formularies. The plans must meet certain standards and be approved by the Secretary of Health and Human Services. Like Medicare Advantage plans, Medicare prescription drug coverage may be marketed directly to Medicare beneficiaries or sold by agents or brokers.

There are two basic types of Medicare prescription drug plans. One type of plan is for persons enrolled in most Medicare Advantage plans. As long as the Medicare Advantage plan has such a prescription drug program, members can obtain their prescription drug coverage only through that program. The other type of plan, referred to as a *stand-alone plan,* is available to persons enrolled in original Medicare or in Medicare Advantage plans without prescription drug programs. The main differences between these two types of plans are in the process of enrollment and premium payment.

Standard Benefit Structure

The act provides for a standard prescription drug plan but also allows for alternative plans to be approved if certain requirements are met and the plans are at least as generous as the standard plan. Most plans that are now available provide broader coverage than the standard plan, as explained later.

The standard prescription drug program has an initial annual deductible of $275 in 2008. This amount and other dollar figures mentioned below will increase in later years if the expenditures for prescription drugs by Medicare beneficiaries increase.

After the deductible has been satisfied, the plan will pay 75 percent of the next $2,235 of prescription drug costs covered by the plan. Benefits then cease until a beneficiary's total drug costs (including the deductible) reach $5,726.25. This range where no benefits are paid is often referred to as the *coverage gap* or *doughnut hole*. Once the $5,726.25 amount is reached, the beneficiary will have had out-of-pocket costs of $4,050 (often referred to as *TROOP* or true out-of-pocket costs) in addition to the annual premium. For covered drug costs in excess of $5,726.25, the beneficiary will then pay for each prescription the greater of (1) 5 percent of the cost of the prescription or (2) a modest copay of $2.25 for a generic or $5.60 for a brand name drug. For all but inexpensive drugs, this means that the plan will pay 95 percent of the cost to fill a prescription.

coverage gap (doughnut hole)

It is important to point out that all of the above limits apply to drug costs covered by the plan. If a beneficiary purchases a drug that is not covered by the plan, the beneficiary must pay the full cost for the drug and cannot apply this amount toward the initial deductible or use it to satisfy the previously mentioned limits. In addition, certain other drug costs do not count toward the limits. These include the cost for drugs purchased outside the United States, the cost of drugs specifically excluded by Medicare, and any payments made by most other private or government drug programs. However, drug costs paid by family members and certain state assistance programs count toward these limits.

The following example shows that beneficiaries with $777 or less in annual prescription drug expenditures will receive no net benefit from the

Medicare prescription drug plan, assuming the prescription drug premium is $30 per month. Approximately half of Medicare beneficiaries fall into this category and will need to decide whether they should purchase coverage. The negative side of not signing up when initially eligible, as discussed later, is that there will be a financial penalty for enrollment at a later date when a beneficiary might have significantly higher drug costs.

Example: Bryan incurs $755 in covered drug costs during the year.

Payment by drug plan [.75 x ($755 – $275 deductible)]	$360
Minus premium ($30/month)	–360
Net benefit from plan	0
Percentage of drug cost paid by Bryan	100%

The next example shows that Medicare beneficiaries with $5,726.25 or less in annual prescription drug expenditures will also pay a significant percentage of their drug costs.

Example: Wendy and her husband Keith have annual prescription drug costs of $2,600 and $5,726.25 respectively. (Wendy's costs are about the average prescription drug costs for Medicare recipients.)

Wendy and Keith will each receive $1,676.25 under their Medicare prescription drug plans. This amount equals 75 percent of the first $2,235 in drug costs exceeding the deductible. In Wendy's case, she will have out-of-pocket costs equal to $1,283.75, or slightly more than 49 percent of her expenditures. This $1,283.75 figure is calculated as follows:

Premium ($30/month)	$ 360.00
Deductible	275.00
25% of first $2,235 above deductible	558.75
100% of expenses in excess of $2,510	900.00
	$1,283.75

In Keith's case, his expenses above $2,510 are $3,215.25, and his total out-of-pocket costs and premium are $4,410, or 77 percent of his drug expenditures.

The percentage of drug costs that a beneficiary pays drops as costs exceed $5,726.25 because Part D plans pay 95 percent of this excess amount. For example, a beneficiary with annual drug costs of $50,000 will pay about 12 percent of this amount, and a beneficiary with annual drug costs of $100,000 will be responsible for about 9 percent.

Medicare prescription drug plans can incorporate certain cost-saving features found in many other types of prescription drug plans. These include prior approval for certain drugs, quantity limits, and the use of step therapy.

Covered Drugs

Each Medicare prescription drug plan has a formulary, which is a list of approved drugs that the plan will cover. Formularies do not need to cover every prescription drug. By law, they must include at least two drugs in every therapeutic class. (There are 146 therapeutic classes.) Most plans cover more than the minimum required number of drugs. Medicare drug plans, however, are required to cover a majority of drugs in certain classes. These classes include antidepressant, antipsychotic, anticonvulsant, antiretroviral, anticancer, and immunosuppressant drugs.

Some drugs are excluded from Medicare coverage by law. These include nonprescription drugs, prescription vitamins and minerals, certain barbiturates and benzodiazepines, and drugs for anorexia, weight loss or weight gain, fertility, cosmetic purposes, hair growth, and relief of such symptoms of cold as cough and stuffy nose. Plans may provide enhanced benefits and cover some of these excluded drugs. However, charges for the excluded drugs will not count towards meeting out-of-pocket limits.

Two other important points need to be mentioned about covered drugs: formulary changes and the coverage of nonformulary drugs.

Formulary Changes

A prescription drug plan is allowed to make formulary changes during the year as long as the changes are approved by the Centers for Medicare & Medicaid Services. Such formulary changes must be posted on the plan's Web site at least 60 days prior to the change. In addition, members affected by a formulary change must also be notified at least 60 days before the change. However, persons already taking the drug can continue to have coverage for refills until the end of the calendar year.

Nonformulary Drugs

If a prescription drug is not on a plan's formulary, a beneficiary has the right to request that the plan cover a medically necessary drug. An "exception" to the formulary is allowed under either of two circumstances:

- The drug is currently being used and is removed from the plan's formulary for reasons other than safety.
- The beneficiary's doctor prescribes a nonformulary drug because the doctor believes a formulary drug will not work for the beneficiary.

If the plan turns down the exception, there is an appeals process that has several levels.

Plan Variations

Very few Medicare prescription drug plans are exactly like the standard benefit plan. In fact, fewer than 15 percent of persons with Medicare prescription drug coverage have such plans. There are several major ways in which most plans provide more comprehensive benefits, but there are significant variations in how they do this.

Formulary Drugs

Most, if not all, plans have more drugs on their formularies than required by law. In some cases, the additional drugs are mostly generics; in other cases, there are both generic and brand name drugs.

Reduced Deductibles

Although many drug plans have an annual calendar-year deductible of $275, the majority of drug plans have no initial deductible. A small number of plans have a deductible that is less than $275 (often $100).

Tiered Copayments

In lieu of paying 75 percent of the cost of each drug after meeting the deductible, most plans have a tiered copayment structure. This is acceptable as long as the average amount paid by the plan for the initial level of benefits is at least 75 percent.

The following examples show some of these variations.

Example 1: The plan has a three-tiered copayment structure. Tier I consists of generic drugs and has no copay.

Tier II is preferred brand name drugs and has a $15 per-prescription copay. The copay is $50 for other brand name drugs, which make up tier III.

Example 2: The plan has a four-tiered copayment structure. It is similar to the plan in example 1, except there is a fourth tier for certain unique and expensive specialty drugs. The copays for the first three tiers are $7, $30, and $60, respectively. The beneficiary must pay 25 percent of the cost of drugs in tier IV.

Benefits in the Coverage Gap

A small number of plans provide benefits in the coverage gap, when drug costs exceed $2,510 but are less than $5,726.25. Some plans cover generic drugs only; in other cases, both generic and brand name drugs are covered.

When there is coverage in this gap, the full cost of the drugs is used to calculate whether the $5,726.25 threshold has been met.

Where Prescriptions Can Be Filled

Prescription drug plans use a network of pharmacies to dispense drugs. Some plans operate on a national basis; others operate within defined regions. In some cases, the network may include many local pharmacies; in other cases, it may consist of a single large retail chain.

Beneficiaries are allowed to use out-of-network pharmacies only if they cannot reasonably be expected to use a network pharmacy and they do not regularly get their drugs from the out-of-network pharmacy.

All plans must include walk-in pharmacies. Most plans also fill prescriptions through mail-order pharmacies that can be accessed by mail, telephone, fax, or Internet. Unlike other types of prescription plans, Medicare plans do not allow prescriptions to be filled for longer periods of time if a mail-order pharmacy is used. For example, if a 90-day supply can be obtained by mail order, a 90-day supply must be available at local pharmacies. However, some plans have a financial incentive, such as lower copayments, to use mail order.

Cost

The federal government pays a significant subsidy out of general tax revenue to each Medicare prescription drug plan. On the average, this subsidy is about 75 percent of the cost for a plan with the standard benefit structure. There are, however, significant variations in the premiums that a beneficiary must pay. Nationally, the premiums average less than $30 per month, but some stand-alone plans cost less and others significantly more. Premiums for drug coverage under Medicare Advantage drug plans are generally somewhat lower, and a few plans even offer the benefit at no extra cost.

These variations are a function of several factors, including the drugs covered, deductibles, copays, the pharmacies used, and the plan's ability to negotiate with manufacturers of drugs. Some lower-cost plans are also attempting to buy market share.

Subsidies in the form of waiver of premiums and copayments are available to beneficiaries who have low incomes and limited assets.

Enrollment

The initial enrollment period for a person who becomes eligible for Medicare is the 7-month period that includes the month of eligibility and 3 months before and after that date. This is the same as the enrollment period for Part B of Medicare. If an individual enrolls during the first 3 months of this period, coverage begins on the first day of the month of Medicare eligibility. If the individual enrolls later, coverage begins the first day of the month after the plan receives the application.

creditable prescription drug coverage

If an individual fails to enroll in a Medicare prescription drug plan at the time of initial eligibility, there is a penalty unless the person had prior *creditable prescription drug coverage*. Creditable coverage includes prescription drug coverage under other plans that is at least as good as Medicare's. These other plans, such as an employer or union plan, must certify the actuarial equivalency of their plan benefits with Medicare. It is not necessary that these plans meet the Medicare prescription drug plan rules; they only must be at least as good. For example, an employer plan might have higher copays than permitted for Medicare plans when prescription costs exceed a specified amount, but this might be offset by no coverage gap. By law, health plans that provide prescription drug coverage must notify persons aged 65 or older whether their prescription drug coverage is creditable or not.

If an individual fails to enroll in a prescription drug plan and has not had creditable coverage, there is a penalty added to the premium. The penalty equals 1 percent of the average national Medicare prescription drug plan premium for each month of late enrollment. The percentage does not change after an individual enrolls, but the size of the penalty changes each year as the average premium changes.

An individual may change prescription drug plans, without evidence of insurability, during an annual election period that runs from November 15 until December 31 of each year. The new plan is effective on the following January l.

There are also special enrollment periods when certain events take place. These include

- moving out of the plan's service area
- losing creditable prescription drug coverage by retirement or any other reason that is not the beneficiary's fault
- returning to original Medicare from a Medicare Advantage plan
- entering or leaving a long-term care facility
- losing coverage because a Medicare prescription drug plan stops offering coverage, fails to provide timely benefits, or misled the beneficiary about benefits

Making Choices

It is obvious from the prior discussion that the Medicare prescription drug plan is very complex. Medicare beneficiaries need to make decisions on whether to obtain coverage, and if so, which plan to purchase. Some will need help in making their decisions. Information is available on Medicare's Web site (www.medicare.gov) and those of consumer groups, such as AARP (www.aarp.org), as well as from financial services professionals.

Many factors that should enter into these decisions have previously been addressed. In this final section on Medicare prescription drug plans, these factors are summarized and in some instances discussed in greater detail.

Necessity of Coverage

Medicare beneficiaries fall into three categories as to the necessity for prescription drug coverage: those with creditable coverage, those with less-than-creditable coverage, and those with no coverage.

Those with Creditable Coverage. Some Medicare beneficiaries are eligible for prescription drug coverage from an employer or union health plan. If this coverage is creditable, there is probably little reason to join a Medicare prescription drug plan. There may be some circumstances when the Medicare plan has features that make it more attractive than the current coverage. However, a decision to drop existing coverage must be made with caution because the individual may not be able to rejoin the plan at a later date. He or she may also be unable to drop the drug coverage without also dropping the entire medical expense coverage under the employer or union plan.

Example: Wilma is retired. She has prescription drug coverage from her previous employer. That employer notifies her that her current coverage on average is at least as good as Medicare prescription drug coverage. She reviews the information provided by her previous employer and decides to keep the coverage. Because her current coverage is at least as good as Medicare prescription drug coverage, if she later decides to get Medicare prescription drug coverage, she won't have to pay a penalty. If her employer later stops offering prescription drug coverage, she can join a Medicare drug plan within 63 days after her current coverage ends and avoid paying the penalty.

Those with Less-Than-Creditable Coverage. Some Medicare beneficiaries have employer or union drug coverage that is not creditable. In this case the individual has several choices:

- Keep the current plan and join a Medicare drug plan to obtain more complete protection. If an employee is subject to the Medicare secondary rules, the employer's plan pays its drug benefit first and Medicare is secondary.
- Drop the current plan and purchase a stand-alone plan along with original Medicare or join a Medicare Advantage plan that has prescription drug coverage. The same caveats previously mentioned for dropping coverage apply in this situation as well.
- Do nothing. Unfortunately, the penalty premium will be charged if a Medicare prescription drug plan is purchased later.

Those with No Coverage. Some persons without prescription drug coverage prior to enrollment in Medicare will easily realize the importance of prescription drug coverage—particularly if they are already incurring significant drug expenses. Others may question the need for coverage if they currently incur few or no prescription drug expenses. They should be aware that the use of medications increases with age and the failure to purchase coverage when initially eligible will result in increased premiums if purchased in the future. Some who advise Medicare beneficiaries suggest that they be encouraged to buy the least expensive plan available; they can always change without penalty to another plan that better meets their circumstances.

Cost

As previously mentioned, the premiums and cost sharing for Medicare prescription drug plans vary considerably. In comparing costs, however, keep in mind that a lower-cost plan may not be the best choice if it does not cover all the drugs an enrollee is taking, has higher copayments, or requires prescriptions to be filled at inconvenient locations.

Covered Drugs

Not all formularies are alike. Before purchasing a Medicare prescription drug plan, an individual needs to ascertain whether the drugs he or she is taking are included on the drug plan's formulary. Plans have Web sites that include this information. If the drugs are not available, perhaps a different plan is better. Alternatively, the individual might consult his or her physician to see if a formulary drug is an acceptable substitute.

Example: Ian takes a relatively expensive drug for his arthritis. He is considering purchasing a Medicare prescription drug plan that does not include this drug on its formulary. Ian's physician says he should not take the drugs that are on the plan's formulary because of possible side effects. The physician says he can request an exception but feels Ian should try to find a plan that includes the current drug on its formulary. Ian finds another plan, but it is slightly more expensive.

Convenience. Convenience is important to many seniors. For example, they need to be able to obtain prescription drugs easily and in the way they prefer.

Example: Claire, a widow, has been in frail health for the last few years. When she became eligible for Medicare, her sister who lives in another state suggested a prescription drug plan that she liked very much and felt provided excellent benefits at a reasonable cost. Unfortunately, the plan uses the pharmacies of a large discount chain, and the store nearest to Claire is 18 miles away. She is also reluctant to use mail order. Claire checks with her local pharmacy that is only a block's walk away and finds that it participates in two plans that cover the drugs she takes. She has a modest fixed income and selects the lower-cost plan that uses the local pharmacy.

CHAPTER REVIEW

Key Terms

original Medicare
Medicare supplement (medigap) insurance
Medicare SELECT policy
Medicare Advantage
Medicare prescription drug plans
coverage gap (doughnut hole)
creditable prescription drug coverage

Review Questions

Review questions are based on the learning objectives in this chapter. Thus, a [10-3] at the end of a question means that the question is based on learning objective 10-3. If there are multiple objectives, they are all listed.

1. With respect to original Medicare:
   a. Who is eligible? [10-1]
   b. How do they enroll? [10-1]
   c. What do they pay? [10-1]
2. What types of benefits are provided by original Medicare ? [10-1]
3. a. What are the gaps in original Medicare? [10-2]
   b. What types of coverages are available to fill these gaps? [10-2]
4. a. In addition to standardizing the policies, what other Medicare supplement features resulted from federal legislation? [10-3]
   b. What restrictions are applicable to Medicare supplement sales activities? [10-3]
5. a. What are the basic benefits applicable to the 10 original Medicare supplement plans? [10-3]
   b. What additional benefits might be available under plans B through J? [10-3]
6. Describe the Medicare supplement plans that have consumer-directed features. [10-3]
7. a. Who is eligible for a Medicare supplement policy? [10-3]
   b. What restrictions might apply to preexisting conditions? [10-3]
8. How does Medicare Advantage increase the options available to Medicare beneficiaries for obtaining medical expense coverage? [10-4]
9. a. When can a Medicare beneficiary enroll in or switch Medicare Advantage plans? [10-4]

b. What factors should be considered to determine whether enrollment is an appropriate option? [10-4]

10. Describe the prescription drug coverage available under Part D of Medicare with respect to each of the following?
    a. eligibility [10-5]
    b. types of plans [10-5]
    c. standard benefit structure [10-5]
    d. covered drugs [10-5]

11. What are the variations among Medicare prescription drug plans? [10-5]

11

Interim, Ancillary, and Other Supplemental Medical Expense Policies

Learning Objectives

An understanding of the material in this chapter should enable you to

11-1. Describe the nature of and need for interim medical expense policies.

11-2. Describe the features of ancillary benefit policies as contained in dental and vision benefit products.

11-3. Describe the characteristics of policies designed to supplement principal policies of medical expense insurance.

Chapter Outline

Many persons may want to purchase one or more of several specialized types of medical expense insurance. Some of these policies can be used to cover needs that are temporary because of a gap in permanent medical expense protection or that sometimes arise but are not addressed by principal medical expense insurance. Other types of policies are of a more permanent nature and provide protection that principal policies exclude or supplement principal policies. This specialized medical expense insurance can be classified as interim, ancillary, and supplemental.

INTERIM MEDICAL EXPENSE INSURANCE

interim medical expense insurance

While most policyowners purchase medical expense insurance without an explicitly predetermined period of coverage in mind, many do purchase coverage to meet a need for only a specifically identified period. This type of policy is called *interim medical expense insurance* and includes temporary and international travel policies. The less comprehensive nature of this protection, plus its temporary nature, keep the premiums relatively low. Interim policies may supplement existing coverage or serve as a principal insurance policy if they represent the insured's underlying or fundamental program of benefits.

These medical expense policies may be relevant to anyone who needs coverage for a limited period of time. If a person is between jobs or is near Medicare eligibility at age 65, a temporary policy may function as a bridge for that person and provide coverage for his or her spouse and dependents, if any.

Before traveling abroad, everyone with a principal policy of medical coverage should review its provisions carefully for exclusions or restrictions on payment for medical treatment in foreign countries. International travel insurance includes coverage and benefits that may be excluded or limited under Medicare or private medical expense insurance. As a result, anyone whose principal policy excludes or limits benefits when traveling abroad needs international travel medical expense insurance. Such coverage is essential for retired persons age 65 and over who travel abroad; in general, Medicare excludes benefits for medical treatment outside of the United States.

Finally, students who are frequently covered under their parents' benefit plan at work may turn to a separate policy of student insurance if their parents retire.

The following sections present interim medical expense insurance under the headings of temporary, international travel, and student policies.

Temporary Medical Policies

temporary medical policies

Temporary medical policies provide individuals and families with medical expense insurance for limited periods of time. They are generally marketed to those who lack coverage because they are

- losing employer-provided coverage but will not be eligible for Medicare for a year or two
- between jobs
- recent college graduates
- part-time and temporary employees
- newly divorced
- dependents who are no longer eligible under their parents' benefit plan
- employees during temporary interruptions of employment
- foreigners temporarily residing in the United States

Eligibility

Eligibility under temporary policies usually includes individuals under 65, their spouses, and dependent children through age 20 (age 24 if full-time students). Coverage can be for a family or self only. If self-only coverage is written for children, they must be between specified ages, such as 2 through 19.

Certain situations typically create ineligibility for temporary coverage. These include:

- the existence of any hospital, major medical, group medical, or other medical insurance currently in force
- pregnancy, or in family coverage, a family member who is pregnant
- denial of insurance due to health reasons or the presence of health conditions that would make a person ineligible for individually underwritten insurance
- coverage by Medicare or Medicaid, or attainment of age 65 during the term of coverage
- permanent residency in the United States for less than a specified number of years
- the need for coverage while traveling abroad

Coverages and Benefits

Temporary medical expense policies are almost always major medical insurance that provides coverage for the core services listed in chapter 8. Additional coverage may include prescription drugs, private-duty nursing, skilled-nursing facility care, home care, and ambulance services with identified limits.

Temporary policies offer a broad spectrum of benefit choices. Deductibles, which may apply to the policy term or on a per cause basis, are usually available in a range from $250 to $2,500. Once the deductible is satisfied, a coinsurance benefit (usually 80 percent, although it may be lower) applies to the next $5,000 or $10,000 of covered expenses. Thereafter, the policy often pays 100 percent of covered expenses up to the policy's maximum benefit. An aggregate policy maximum benefit may be $1 million to $2 million. Reasonable and customary limits apply to benefits for covered services. Lower out-of-pocket costs encourage the use of network participating providers and precertification of hospital admissions and surgeries.

Coverage Period

Most policies require the purchase of a minimum coverage period of 30 days. Some companies allow longer periods in daily or monthly increments up to the maximum coverage period of 6 or 12 months. Alternatives for premium payment include a single payment option if the exact number of days of desired coverage is known, or monthly billing allowing the insured to pay for protection as needed on an ongoing basis up to the maximum coverage period.

Because a temporary policy is designed to fill a specific need during a defined policy period and is not intended to be permanent, it is usually not renewable but may be rewritten for a subsequent period. The subsequent policy is usually not a continuation of coverage from the first policy. Therefore, the insured must reapply and satisfy eligibility requirements, including underwriting, that normally exclude conditions or symptoms that may have occurred during a previous policy period. Indeed, if a claim has been filed or the health of the individual has significantly changed since taking out the initial policy, the reapplication for a subsequent policy period is likely to be denied.

Insurer practices regarding the rewriting of temporary policies for additional periods vary widely. Some companies offer no additional coverage periods; others limit the periods to two or three; and still others rewrite additional periods indefinitely. In addition, some companies continue benefits for covered conditions that occurred during a previous coverage period.

Exclusions and Limitations

Exclusions and limitations are also typical of those listed previously for major medical policies. However, preexisting conditions are excluded from coverage, with a look-back period of 3 to 5 years from the policy's effective date. In addition, limits apply to the benefits for the following conditions or services, if covered:

- transplants
- AIDS
- mental or nervous disorders
- substance abuse
- childhood immunizations

Even when these policies do not include other managed care restrictions, they frequently require completion of a treatment authorization for selected services (usually elective surgery and hospitalization) to receive maximum benefits (that is, to avoid a coinsurance benefit reduction) or any benefits in some cases, such as for organ transplantation.

Extension of Coverage

Because of the policy's interim nature, the extension of coverage for treatment that is in progress upon the policy's expiration is an important issue. Temporary medical policies may include two provisions that extend coverage beyond this date. First, if a covered person becomes totally disabled and is being treated for the disabling condition during the benefit period, the policy extends benefits to the earliest of (1) 12 months following the termination date, (2) the end of total disability, or (3) the date on which treatment is no longer required. Other policies may simply specify that even if the insured is receiving benefits for services on the date the policy terminates, coverage does not continue beyond 90 days from the otherwise regular termination date. Second, a benefit of up to $1,000 may be provided for follow-up care for any injury or sickness that occurred during the policy period. To qualify, the insured must have met the policy deductible and the expense must be incurred within 60 days of policy expiration.

International Travel Medical Policies

international travel medical policies

International travel medical policies may also provide a principal program of benefits for international travelers. Not all medical expense programs—for example, Medicare—cover medical services received by Americans in foreign countries. Many principal medical expense policies limit coverage to emergency medical care subject to defined maximums, such as up to 30 days of treatment within the first 180 days of travel. In addition, international travelers from other countries with national health service programs are not likely to receive benefits for medical care services received outside their home countries. Thus, people traveling abroad for any reason may seek interim medical expense insurance.

Fortunately, medical insurance programs are available for people, regardless of age, who are traveling, working, or living away from their home countries or countries of residence. U.S. citizens and foreign nationals with international destinations, as well as foreign nationals visiting the United States, may purchase some form of this coverage for themselves, their spouses, and their dependent unmarried children within identified age brackets, such as over 14 days but under age 19. Child-only coverage is also available.

International travel policies feature medical expense benefits but also cover emergency medical evacuation and repatriation of mortal remains; they may include additional types of insurance and provide nonhealth-related benefits. Premiums are usually based on either the trip's duration or the coverage's duration, although in some cases, such as vacation travel, the premium may vary based on the value of the trip.

Medical Coverages and Benefits

Covered medical services are quite similar to those identified under the core services of a major medical policy and generally include

- hospital services
- physicians' services
- prescription medicines
- laboratory and X-ray services
- outpatient services
- local ambulance

Available maximum benefit amounts for these services range from \$10,000 to as much as \$2 million or more. Maximums may apply as an aggregate amount for the coverage period or to covered services for each distinct unrelated condition. Within these limits, the policy benefits are similar to major medical insurance. A single deductible during the period of coverage, such as \$100 to \$2,500, may be featured. After the deductible has been met, the policy's coinsurance benefit could be 80 percent of the next \$5,000 or \$10,000 of covered expenses. Thereafter, the policy may pay 100 percent of covered expenses up to the selected maximum benefit. Some policies pay 100 percent of covered expenses immediately after satisfying the deductible. Reasonable and customary charge limits may also be stipulated.

An international travel policy may also include a hospital indemnity benefit (such as \$100 per night), a supplemental accident benefit (such as \$300 per injury), and an emergency dental benefit (such as \$100 per tooth). Stand-alone dental policies for international travelers provide broader coverage for emergency dental care.

Available Coverage Periods

Available coverage periods vary widely as well, depending on the type of trip being taken. Policies are tailored to meet individual market needs of short-term or long-term travel. Minimums may be a few days, 2 weeks, or even 6 months for some policies. Additional periods may be added beyond the minimum in daily, weekly, or monthly increments, depending on the policy. Representative maximum coverage periods are 90 days, 180 days, and 12 months.

Coverage usually ceases when the insured returns home, but policies written for periods of 3 or more months frequently cover all trips taken during the specified coverage period. Many policies allow single or multiple renewals; thus a 12-month initial period may extend to 3 or even 5 years. Some policies are designed specifically for persons who spend extensive periods away from home, such as retired couples living full-time or for several months in a foreign country. These policies have the characteristics of permanent medical insurance; the policy requires an annual premium and is annually renewable, the coverage is continuous when renewed, and the lifetime benefits may be $5 million or more. Note, however, that retirees who qualify as permanent residents of a foreign country are also eligible for government or private health plans in that country.

Exclusions

Exclusions are similar to those listed under major medical policies, with preexisting-conditions exclusions having a look-back period that may range from 180 days to 3 years or even as long as 5 years, depending on the policy. In addition, treatment paid for or furnished under any other policy or health plan, whether private sector or government sponsored, is a common travel policy exclusion.

Because of the interim nature of the insurance, the dates of treatment received after the trip for an illness or injury that occurred during the trip may become an issue. A policy typically limits coverage to expenses incurred within 6 months of the occurrence of an illness or injury. Initial treatment of an injury must occur within 60 days of an accident, and sickness must first manifest itself during the period of coverage.

Other Medical Benefits

Separate benefit limits are usually set for other medically related coverages. For example, emergency medical evacuation covers transportation associated with medical emergencies or situations where relocation is necessary in order to receive appropriate medical care. Available benefits range from $10,000 to $100,000. In addition, if a physician decrees that a family member should accompany the insured during the medical evacuation, that family member's travel and lodging expenses are covered up to a set maximum (for example, $10,000). If the insured is traveling with a minor child when hospitalized, the additional expense associated with returning the child to his or her home country is also covered up to a set maximum, such as $2,500. Emergency dental treatment, usually as a result of an accident during a trip, may be covered up to $1,000. Repatriation of an insured's mortal remains to his or her home country may be limited to $20,000.

Additional Coverages

Travel policies frequently include accidental death and dismemberment coverage. The benefit amount is usually available at various optional levels that may range from $25,000 to $250,000 or more. The insured's spouse is usually covered at the same benefit amount, with dependent children covered at a lower level, such as 20 or 25 percent of the parents' amount. Policies written for periods of 3 or more months may also include an offer of term life insurance.

Optional riders may provide coverage for a range of hazardous activities that includes motorcycling, skydiving, and surfing; specified athletic activities; and continued benefits at a reduced level for a limited period during an incidental home country trip.

In addition, nonhealth-related coverage often provides benefits for baggage delay and baggage loss or damage. These may be set, for example, at $300 and $2,500, respectively. Travel policies may also provide a formal assistance program that includes the following:

- 24-hour medical care location
- provider payment guarantees
- medical case monitoring and arrangement of communication between patient, family, physicians, consulate, etc.
- medical transportation arrangements
- emergency message service for medical situations

When purchasing coverage through a travel agent, protection is usually available for the value of the travel arrangements themselves. For example, coverage in the event of trip cancellation and interruption may be provided in amounts to $10,000, with delayed arrival and missed connection benefits up to $1,000.

Student Medical Expense Policies

There is a market for student medical expense insurance. Many family policies exclude dependent children when they turn 19, get married, or when they are no longer full-time students. Thus, a part-time college student after age 19, a full-time student after an age specified in a family policy (such as age 24), and married students need a principal program of medical expense insurance. In addition, HMOs or other exclusive-provider benefit plans may be unable to offer network services to students in the vicinity of the college or university under their parents' family plan. Indeed, purchasing an individual student policy separate from family coverage may be more economical than continued coverage under the parent's plan.

Student medical insurance coverage is available both as an individually purchased product and through school sponsorship. In both cases, eligibility requirements usually stipulate that the student must be taking a specified class load, such as 9 or more credit hours, or be a full-time graduate student in attendance at an accredited college or university.

Independently Purchased Policies

A range of individual policies purchased independently of the academic institution are available from an insurance agent. If purchased apart from the institution's sponsorship, the student may maintain coverage in the event of a transfer to another school, a reduction to part-time status, or even when taking a semester off. Such programs are usually renewable to certain ages.

These plans also follow the core benefits of major medical plans. However, the total aggregate plan maximum may be as low as $50,000 or as high as $1 million. The coinsurance benefit is usually 80 percent for covered services, with available out-of-pocket limits of $5,000 to $10,000. Available overall plan deductibles may range from $250 to $2,500. In addition, limitations may be placed on the maximum benefit for each illness or injury, such as $25,000 or $100,000.

Covered Services and Exclusions

Covered services under these plans typically include

- semiprivate hospital room and board as well as intensive care
- physicians' office visits
- emergency care
- surgery
- inpatient and outpatient services
- X-ray and laboratory services
- medical equipment and supplies
- home health care
- ground ambulance and medical evacuation

Benefit exclusions, some of which have pointed application to students, typically include

- expenses for preexisting conditions incurred in the first 12 months after the effective date of the policy

- maternity benefits for normal pregnancy and childbirth
- weight-reduction programs and related surgery
- medications to stimulate growth
- sterilization and treatment for infertility
- genetic testing or counseling
- routine physical exams and immunizations
- removal of tonsils and adenoids
- mental illness
- substance abuse
- custodial care
- intercollegiate sports injuries
- prescription drugs
- free services
- cosmetic treatment or surgery
- medical services incurred outside the United States or Canada

Some of these policies cover students only; others allow coverage for spouse and dependents to be added. Premiums may be paid on an annual or semiannual basis.

Institution-Sponsored Plans

Insurers also work with academic institutions to sponsor a student medical plan. Often students may decline these sponsored plans only upon documentation of comparable coverage. These sponsored programs take on the nature of a voluntary association, which may be written on a group or individual product basis. The high participation levels allow these plans to be more comprehensive in many aspects than independently purchased plans, with such additional benefits as

- spouse and dependent coverage, including maternity, routine preventive examinations, well-baby care, child care, and required immunizations
- inpatient and outpatient mental health and substance abuse services
- prescription drugs
- preventive dental services
- annual eye exams

Sponsorship by the institution allows the plans to set up or participate in hospital and physician networks in the local area and removes many specific coverage limits on outpatient visits, inpatient days, and fee levels. Unallowed charges above reasonable and customary limits are also eliminated when using the network. In addition, these programs produce savings by integrating the student health center into the plan of benefits as a source of primary care and provider referral. It is not unusual to find these sponsored programs offered in conjunction with at least modest accidental death and dismemberment coverage at principal amounts as low as $1,000.

SELECTED ANCILLARY MEDICAL EXPENSE POLICIES

Dental and vision coverage are two forms of ancillary or limited benefit insurance that are available in the individual market. Persons familiar with dental and vision plans in a former employer group setting will find that individual policies are more likely to include a lower maximum benefit, lower internal benefit limits, higher out-of-pocket payments, and longer waiting periods. This should not be surprising because those who purchase these individual plans have a high likelihood of using them and insurers are trying to keep the premiums low.

The cost of these coverages, although much less than a principal policy, is still relatively expensive in relation to the benefits provided. From a strict insurance point of view, ancillary coverage appears difficult to justify; the yearly premiums may represent as much as a third to more than half of the annual maximum benefits insureds could receive. Nevertheless, especially in the case of dental insurance, ancillary benefit policies are attractive. Persons purchasing these forms of coverage are in effect largely prepaying, rather than insuring, their routine vision and dental services. These insureds are apparently pleased to do so knowing that they will almost certainly use the covered services and wish to have benefits available to help pay for them. However, the market remains quite narrow; fewer than 3 percent of persons with dental benefits have individual coverage and the statistics for individual vision coverage are even lower.

In an effort to make the ancillary coverage more attractive, insurers frequently include discount cards for the purchase of dental, vision, and other ancillary services as a value-added feature with their policies. Persons with coverage simply present the card when purchasing services from providers identified as honoring the card. Discounts, which reduce the retail or objectively determined price, usually range up to 30 percent but can be higher. The discount card supplements or extends the purchasing power of an insured ancillary benefit policy when services are obtained from providers participating in the discount program. For example, the insured benefit may apply to dental or vision services subject to the discount, thereby reducing the insured's out-of-pocket costs. Alternatively, an insured benefit may apply to specified services, such as a routine dental or vision exam, with noncovered services and materials available at a discounted price.

Some card program sponsors also market their discount card programs directly to consumers who may or may not have dental, vision, or any other type of medical expense insurance.

Dental Insurance

Dental insurance is fairly common, but it is usually provided through employer-sponsored programs. However, dental coverage is also purchased in the individual market. In some cases, dental coverage is offered as an optional benefit or rider to a comprehensive medical policy for an additional premium. In other cases, dental coverage is purchased as a stand-alone policy.

The subsequent discussion considers dental insurance under the headings of unique benefit features, benefit payment methods, and managed care plans.

Unique Benefit Features

Dental insurance usually contains features that are unique to the management of dental claims expenses. These features include service-level groupings, least expensive treatment alternatives, prior authorization, benefit maximums, frequency limitations, program phase-in, and other limitations and exclusions.

Service-Level Groupings. Dental insurance typically aggregates professional treatment categories into four service-level groups for plan design purposes:

- service level I—routine preventive and related diagnostic services, including cleanings, oral exams, X rays, and applications of topical fluoride
- service level II—basic services, including minor restorative procedures (fillings) as well as endodontic, periodontic, and oral surgery services
- service level III—major services, including major restorations (crowns, inlays, onlays, veneers) and prosthodontic procedures (dentures, bridges)
- service level IV—orthodontic services. Benefits for this level service, if provided in an individual policy, are limited to dependent children under age 19 (or older if a student).

A typical dental policy provides its most complete payment for level I services, somewhat less complete payment for level II services, and the least complete benefit for level III and level IV services (if covered). Benefits for these service levels give insureds financial incentives to seek routine services for prevention of future expenses and have a greater stake in decisions for more costly major services. The objective is to reduce spending on optional care and promote cost-effective dental practices.

Least Expensive Professionally Acceptable Treatment. Because dental problems can often be successfully treated in more than one way, insurers usually focus their benefits on the least expensive professionally acceptable treatment. For example, a policy pays for an amalgam filling that effectively repairs a tooth but not for a gold inlay or crown, which would also be effective but much more expensive. If the more expensive option is used, then the insured pays the difference between the amalgam filling and the gold inlay or crown. Thus the insured has a substantial incentive to obtain the least expensive, but acceptable, treatment.

Nevertheless, if the more expensive treatment is used, patient cost sharing encourages the insured to protect his or her investment by practicing good oral hygiene and taking advantage of routine diagnostic and preventive services, usually provided at little or no out-of-pocket cost.

Prior Authorization. An insurer frequently requests the insured's dentist to complete a preauthorization-of-benefits form for major services and orthodontia that describes the dental diagnosis, the proposed treatment, and the charges. This process is called prior authorization (also commonly referred to as predetermination, precertification, or pretreatment estimate) and consists of filing a claim form in advance of treatment when anticipated charges exceed a stated amount, such as $300. The insured or the dentist sends the completed form to the insurer's claim office. Frequently, X rays, photographs, and models for orthodontia are also submitted to substantiate the required treatment and to avoid delaying benefit payment pending a subsequent request.

Prior authorization promotes better quality dental care and reduces costs by identifying unnecessary expenses, treatments that cannot be expected to last, and charges that exceed policy allowances. Prior authorization also gives the insurer some control over the performance of procedures; before extensive and expensive work begins, both the dentist and the insured understand that benefits will be limited to the least costly alternative or perhaps even denied.

Benefit Maximums. Virtually all individual dental policies feature a calendar-year maximum benefit, usually in the range of $750 to $1,500, that applies in the aggregate to all dental expenses except orthodontia. Insureds over age 65 are likely to have an annual limitation on payments for certain services, such as major restorations, dentures, and bridges. Calendar-year maximums encourage insureds to seek less costly care, and they may help to spread out dental expenses over several years. Policies that provide coverage for orthodontia services have a separate lifetime maximum benefit, such as $750, as well as a per year maximum, such as $300.

Frequency Limitations. Dental policies include limitations on the frequency of covered services. Typical frequency limitations are as follows:

- bitewing X rays—one set every 12 consecutive months
- prophylaxis (cleaning)—one in any 6 consecutive months
- filling replacements—after 24 months from initial filling
- crown replacements—after 84 months from initial restoration
- bridges and denture replacements—after 84 months from initial delivery

Program Phase-in. Program phase-in, as table 11-1 displays, can occur in a number of ways, including the following:

- waiting periods
- incremental benefit levels
- incremental annual maximums

Waiting Periods. Dental policies frequently impose a waiting period before certain types of expenses are covered. For example, there may be no coverage for major dental services (level III) until the second policy year. Orthodontic benefits (level IV), if included, would be payable after the beginning of the third year.

Incremental Benefit Levels. Dental policies may also phase in the benefit level for covered services starting at a lower coinsurance benefit level; increasing percentages in each subsequent year encourage insureds to spread out claims. For example, the preventive and maintenance benefit may be initiated at 100 percent to encourage routine care, but benefits for major services (level III) could be 60 percent of expenses in the first year, increasing to 70 percent in the second, and finally to 80 percent thereafter.

Incremental Annual Maximums. An annual maximum can be introduced at a lower level and incremented annually, limiting the claims expense in the policies' early years while still encouraging diagnostic and preventive services.

Other Limitations and Exclusions. Dental policies exclude coverage for all cosmetic services. In addition, they frequently limit or exclude coverage for medical services, temporomandibular joint (TMJ) dysfunction, and orthodontia. Orthodontic benefits, if covered, are limited to persons under age 19.

Termination. Benefits for a dental service received after termination may still be covered as long as (1) the charge for the service was incurred prior to the termination date, and (2) treatment is completed within 60 or 90 days after termination.

Benefit Payment Methods

The two common benefit payment methods under individual dental insurance are dental major medical and scheduled maximum payments.

Dental Major Medical Benefits. Dental major medical is a common method of benefit payment and utilizes the same provisions discussed in chapter 8 under major medical insurance—namely, deductibles and coinsurance benefits. However, this benefit payment method uses an annual maximum benefit and has no overall out-of-pocket limit. Table 11-1 presents a benefit summary of this method based on an individual stand-alone dental product.

TABLE 11-1
Individual Dental Major Medical Benefit Summary (Stand-Alone Product)

	First Year	Second Year	Thereafter
Level I—preventive and diagnostic services (exams, X rays, cleanings)	75%	80%	85%
Level II—basic services (fillings, extractions, oral surgery)	50%[a]	60%	70%
Level III—major services (crowns, bridges, dentures, root canals, periodontal surgery)	Not covered	50%[b]	50%
Level IV—orthodontic services (straightening teeth)	Not covered	Not covered	50%[c]
Deductibles	$25 lifetime and $75 per calendar year per insured except for level I services, which have a $35 one-time deductible		
Maximums	$1,000 per calendar year for all Level I to Level III services per insured $400 per calendar year for Level IV services and $1,000 lifetime per insured		

a. 3-month waiting period
b. 18-month waiting period
c. 24-month waiting period

Note: All benefit percentages apply to allowable amounts based on reasonable and customary dental fees.

Individual stand-alone dental products tend to have lower benefits than dental coverage purchased in conjunction with or as a rider to a principal medical expense policy. Such products, because of their greater potential for adverse selection, use more stringent benefit design to control the cost of coverage. More generous benefit designs are evident in subsequent tables.

Dental deductibles usually are written on a calendar-year or lifetime basis, with the calendar-year approach being typical. Annual deductibles for an individual range from $50 to $100 per person. Dental deductibles in individual policies often differ by service level, although a lower or one-time deductible may apply to preventive services. Lifetime deductibles in such policies are usually low; they function somewhat like an initiation fee and are only paid once.

The coinsurance benefit level, as under major medical insurance, leaves the insured to pay a portion of the allowable charges. However, in most dental policies, the coinsurance benefit is uniquely structured to reduce spending on optional care while promoting cost-effective practices by varying the benefits for the different service levels.

- level I—Preventive and diagnostic expenses (for example, cleanings, examinations, and X rays) generally are reimbursed between 80 and 100 percent of allowable fees.
- level II—The reimbursement level for restorative, replacement, and surgical procedures generally is lower than for preventive and diagnostic procedures, typically 70 to 85 percent. In some cases, reimbursements for replacements and major surgery may be lower. Some policies categorize X rays as level II services.
- level III and level IV—Major replacements (crowns and prostheses) and orthodontics have the lowest reimbursement levels; in most instances, reimbursement is no more than 50 to 60 percent of the reasonable and customary fees for these procedures.

Scheduled Maximum Payment Benefits. Individual dental policies may use the scheduled maximum payment (SMP) method. Under this method, benefits are paid up to the amount specified in the dental fee schedule for an all-inclusive list of services. For example, the benefit may be $40 for a cleaning and $300 for root canal therapy. If a service is not on the list, it is generally covered, but only at the listed rate for a suitable substitute. The SMP method provides benefits on a first-dollar basis and usually contains no deductibles or specified coinsurance percentages, although there may be exceptions. In order to encourage diagnostic and preventive services, dental schedules are designed so that the fees for these services are more completely covered, while benefits for other dental services are paid at a lower level.

Table 11-2 presents a benefit summary using a scheduled maximum payment method.

TABLE 11-2
Individual Dental Scheduled Maximum Benefit Summary

Covered Services	Benefit	Waiting Period
Level I—preventive and diagnostic services	Fee schedule ($40 for a cleaning)	None
Level II—basic services	Fee schedule ($80 for a filling)	6 months
Level III—major services	Fee schedule ($250 for a crown)	18 months for crowns and dentures 12 months for all others
Level IV—orthodontic services	50% of reasonable and customary charges	18 months
Maximums	$750 per calendar year for level I and II services per insured $1,000 per calendar year for levels I, II, and III services per insured $750 lifetime maximum for level IV services per insured (benefit limited to insureds under age 19)	

Dental Managed Care Programs

Managed care has become common in individual dental insurance with the use of dental PPO products. They are similar in concept to PPO arrangements for medical benefits discussed earlier. Individual dental HMO products are also available, but are less common. Managed care arrangements are a more likely feature of dental coverage offered in conjunction with medical benefits than when dental coverage is offered as a stand-alone product. Insureds are rarely required to fill out claim forms or other paperwork when they receive services from dentists in managed care arrangements.

Dental PPOs. A dental PPO is an arrangement between an insurer and a network of dentists whereby the dentists agree to accept a negotiated payment (usually less than their customary fees) in anticipation of a higher volume of patients. Typically, the agreement requires the participating dentists to take part in utilization review and quality assurance programs.

However, these programs are usually not as extensive as those found in dental HMOs.

The higher volume of patients results from a benefit structure that gives the insured financial incentives to use dentists in the network. These incentives typically take the form of reduced cost sharing or greater benefits. Preferred-provider dental products frequently use the dental major medical benefit method. As with medical expense insurance, insureds are not required to use participating dentists, but they receive more liberal benefits if they do. Insureds who go outside the network are responsible for additional out-of-pocket expenses for charges that exceed either what a network dentist would have been reimbursed or a determined reasonable and customary amount.

Some PPO products create an even greater incentive to use the network by increasing the indicated deductible and/or patient payment participation levels as indicated in table 11-3, which compares benefits when using a typical dental preferred-provider network with those that would be provided outside the network.

TABLE 11-3
Dental PPO Benefit Summary

Covered Services	Network Benefits	Nonnetwork Benefits
Level I—preventive and diagnostic services	100% of negotiated charge[a]	100% of R&C[b]
Level II—basic services	85% of negotiated charge	75% of R&C
Level III—major services	50% of negotiated charge	50% of R&C
Level IV—orthodontic services	50% of negotiated charge	50% of R&C
Deductible[c]	$50 (individual) $100 (family)	$75 (individual) $100 (family)
Orthodontia Lifetime Maximum	$1,000	$1,000
Annual Maximum for Other Benefits	$1,000	$1,000

a. Negotiated charge—fee that the dentists participating in the network accept as payment in full
b. Reasonable and customary—charge based on prevailing fees charged by dentists in the area, although an insurer may determine an allowed amount on another basis, such as a negotiated payment rate
c. Not applicable to level I

Other PPO dental products may use a combination of benefit payment methods. For example, the benefit may pay 100 percent for preventive and diagnostic services received from a network dentist and have a scheduled maximum benefit if such services are received outside the dental PPO network. Services in all other categories may be paid at a scheduled maximum amount regardless of whether or not they are received from dentists participating in the network. However, the insured pays less out of pocket if services are received from participating dentists because the insurer has negotiated favorable rates with them.

Dental HMOs. A dental HMO (DHMO) is a prepaid health plan that provides dental care services to insureds in a defined geographic area. It accepts responsibility for delivery of services (not just the payment); pays participating dentists either a fixed periodic amount based on the number of insureds (capitation) or a negotiated charge per service; and is organized under state law as a dental HMO. Capitation payments are common in DHMOs and are usually made on a monthly basis for each individual or family regardless of the number or types of services rendered or the number of insureds seen. Thus the dentist or dental group is at financial risk for the insureds' utilization and has every incentive to encourage dental health and avoid unnecessary procedures.

Because DHMOs provide service benefits, in contrast to nonmanaged and PPO products, they typically have no deductibles and no maximum benefit level. Flat copayment amounts are associated with benefits for basic services (such as $20 for a filling), major restorative services (such as $300 for a crown), and orthodontic services (such as $2,500 for braces). However, some DHMOs use coinsurance benefits for the payment of major restorative and orthodontia services. Prior authorization is usually not used in DHMO programs. Typically, the member is limited to the dentists participating in the DHMO network unless the plan has a point-of-service option that allows the insured to seek treatment outside the DHMO at a reduced benefit level.

Vision Benefit Products

In the individual market, products that cover routine services to correct vision are available. Most principal medical insurance policies cover diagnosis and treatment of eye diseases and injuries. Procedures to improve vision in the absence of disease or trauma are explicitly excluded. Even the most comprehensive medical policies, when they cover routine eye care, limit services to examinations and glaucoma and vision acuity testing and do not cover corrective eyewear. Discounts for vision products and services are offered with medical policies, however. Under these arrangements, the insured is eligible for discounts for exams and eyewear, including frames, lenses, and contact lenses, at designated retail optical locations. Discounts may range from 15 percent to 50 percent depending on the service or product selected. Sometimes an initial eye exam may be provided at no charge.

Nevertheless, there are stand-alone insurance products that provide routine vision care benefits for individuals and families, as tables 11-6 and 11-7 exemplify. Individual vision benefit products are discussed under the headings of benefits, eligibility, and exclusions.

Benefits

Benefits may be offered in conjunction with other ancillary coverages, such as dental coverage, or with principal policies of medical expense insurance. As with other types of medical expense insurance, benefits for vision care plans may have a major medical, scheduled maximum payment, or managed care structure.

Table 11-4 illustrates a major medical structure with a calendar-year deductible and coinsurance benefits using reasonable and customary charges with a limited annual maximum. Similar to stand-alone dental products, there is no out-of-pocket limit, and a minimal one-time or lifetime deductible is used. The product design phases in the benefits and covered services over a 2-year period. The frequency limits for exams and eyewear are also identified.

TABLE 11-4
Individual Vision Benefit Coverage Summary: Major Medical Structure

	First 12 months	Second 12 months	Thereafter	Frequency Limits
Eye exam	75%	80%	85%	1 per year
Eyewear (lenses, frames, and contact lenses)	Not covered	50%	50%	1 pair every 2 years
Deductibles	$25 lifetime and $75 per calendar year per insured			
Maximum	$300 per calendar year per insured			

Table 11-5 illustrates both the scheduled maximum payment and managed care benefit structures to which phase-in and frequency limits would also apply.

Eligibility

Coverage may restricted to individuals who are under age 65 as well as eligible dependents, including a spouse and unmarried children from birth to age 19 (extended to age 24 or some other specified age if a full-time student).

TABLE 11-5
Individual Vision Benefit Coverage Summary: Scheduled Maximum Payment and Managed Care Structures

Benefit	Scheduled Maximum Payment	Managed Care Member Payment
Examinations	$75	$0 (plan pays in full)
Frames		
Basic	$65	$0 (plan pays in full)
Premium	$65	$50
Designer	$65	$80
Other	$65	80% of charges over $60
Lenses		
Single vision	$50	$0 (plan pays in full)
Bifocal	$75	$40
Trifocal	$90	$60
Progressive	$75	$100
Contact lenses		
Conventional	$115/$180†	Charges over $120 allowance
Disposable	$115/$180†	Charges over $120 allowance

* Insured pays the balance of charges.
† Higher amount for medically necessary contact lenses

Exclusions

The cost of a lens in excess of the cost of a standard lens is not covered, and the insured, therefore, would pay an extra charge. (A standard lens fits a frame with an eye size less than 56 millimeters in diameter.) Charges for replacement lenses are not covered unless there is a change in prescription.

The cost of a frame in excess of the cost of a standard frame is also not covered. A standard frame is defined by a specific retail value, such as $80 or less. The cost of replacement frames is not covered unless the existing frame is not compatible with the replacement lenses.

In addition to excluding any services or materials not listed as an eligible expense, the following expenses are not covered:

- any procedure, service, or supply that is covered under other medical expense insurance
- special procedures, such as orthoptics (treatment of eye movement disorders), vision training, and subnormal vision aids
- prescription and nonprescription sunglasses

- medical or surgical treatment of the eyes, including hospital expenses
- replacement of lost or broken lenses and/or frames

OTHER SUPPLEMENTAL MEDICAL EXPENSE POLICIES

Chapter 10 discussed policies that supplement original Medicare. In addition, there are other medical expense policies designed to supplement the benefits of principal policies. These other supplemental medical expense policies—hospital indemnity insurance, specified disease insurance, and critical illness insurance—share certain characteristics. The insured is assisted with the significant additional financial consequences of a serious episode of illness or injury by receiving direct cash payments, usually made in addition to any benefits received from other coverages. These payments may be used for

- out-of-pocket expenses of medical treatment left uncovered by even principal medical expense insurance
- associated nonmedical expenses, such as travel, lodging, meals, dependent care, and loss of income

Hospital indemnity insurance, specified disease insurance, and critical illness insurance are described below. However, they are no substitute for adequate medical expense and disability income insurance.

Hospital Confinement Indemnity Insurance

hospital confinement indemnity insurance

Hospital confinement indemnity insurance provides covered individuals with a fixed daily cash benefit during a hospitalization. A spouse or dependent child is usually eligible for coverage, although benefits may be reduced. Table 11-6 is an example of a schedule of benefits under a hospital confinement indemnity policy.

The policy provides daily benefits in the event of hospital confinement at a specified dollar amount (such as $250 per day) for a defined period (such as 180 days). These additional benefits are available as a standard feature or as a rider:

- a lump-sum payment on the first day of hospital confinement
- an intensive care benefit, such as $400 for a specified number of days, in addition to the standard daily payment

TABLE 11-6
Hospital Confinement Indemnity Insurance
Schedule of Benefits

Benefits	Covered Persons	
	Policyowner	Spouse/ Dependent
Inpatient Hospital		
Daily payment[a]	$ 250	$175
First day of confinement	$1,000	$500
Intensive care/coronary care[b]	$ 400	$200
Outpatient Sickness[c]		
Emergency room	$100	$100
Outpatient physician treatment	$ 50	$ 50
Emergency Accident [d]		
Emergency room	$300	$100
Physician services	$300	$100

a. Maximum benefit period per confinement is 180 days. Two or more confinements for the same or related causes in one or more hospitals and separated by less than 30 days are considered the same confinement.
b. Benefit is paid for a 30-day maximum in addition to the daily hospital benefit.
c. Indicated benefits are per sickness, with a family maximum of $500 per calendar year.
d. Benefits are provided per accident.

- surgical and anesthesia benefit for surgery performed by and anesthesia administered by a physician, with scheduled limits and a yearly maximum
- payment for emergency room and related physician services due to an illness or accident, with limitations on duration or expense per event or per year
- outpatient sickness benefit, with limits per treatment and per year
- daily payment for recovery after a qualified hospital stay
- an accidental death and dismemberment benefit

Exclusions are those typically listed in principal medical insurance policies, which are found in chapter 8. However, the preexisting-conditions exclusions period may be limited to a 12-month delay in benefits for any condition that occurred 12 months prior to the effective date of the policy. As discussed previously, benefits for fully disclosed conditions may also be limited or excluded.

Accident-only policies are a variation of hospital confinement indemnity policies and constitute another category of supplemental insurance. They provide cash payments in the event of injury or death resulting from a covered accident within a specified period but not for hospitalization resulting from illness.

Specified (Dread) Disease Insurance

specified (dread) disease insurance

Specified (dread) disease insurance provides benefits to insured individuals and covered family members upon the occurrence of medical events or diagnoses related to the treatment of a disease named in the policy. It does not cover accidents or injuries. Specified disease insurance for cancer only has been the most prevalent form of this insurance. Today, however, policies frequently cover cancer in addition to other listed diseases that might include many or all of the following:

- Addison's disease
- amyotrophic lateral sclerosis
- botulism
- Budd-Chiari syndrome
- cystic fibrosis
- diphtheria
- encephalitis
- histoplasmosis
- Legionnaires' disease
- lupus erythematosus
- malaria
- meningitis
- multiple sclerosis
- muscular dystrophy
- myasthenia gravis
- osteomyelitis
- poliomyelitis
- Q fever
- rabies
- Reye's syndrome
- rheumatic fever
- Rocky Mountain spotted fever
- sickle-cell anemia
- Tay-Sachs disease
- tetanus
- toxic shock syndrome
- trichinosis
- tuberculosis
- tularemia
- typhoid fever
- undulant fever
- whooping cough

Specified disease policy benefits vary widely. Benefit provisions may utilize a combination of three payment structures: per-day or per-service, expense-incurred, or a lump-sum payment. Benefits are contingent on a diagnosis of the specified disease, but payments will cover the first day of care or confinement even though the diagnosis is made at some later date. This retroactive application of benefits usually applies to relevant services received within 90 days prior to the diagnosis. Table 11-7 presents a summary of illustrative benefits.

Specified disease policies frequently offer a first-occurrence benefit that pays a one-time amount ranging from $1,000 to as high as 50,000 or more for each covered person who receives a diagnosis of internal cancer.

TABLE 11-7
Specified Disease Insurance
Example of Benefits

Service	Benefit
Hospital confinement	$300 daily for up to 90 days; $600 daily in coronary or intensive care unit up to 30 days
Surgery	Up to $7,500 per fee schedule
Anesthesia	Up to 25 percent of the surgical benefit
Physician's attendance	Actual charges up to $35 per day for in-hospital visits
Chemotherapy, radiation, immunotherapy, or radioactive isotopes therapy	50 percent of the first $50,000 of charges and 100 percent of the next $100,000, limited to $125,000 per calendar year
Experimental treatment	Up to $25,000 for experimental bone marrow transplant and $2,500 for donor-related expenses plus transportation
Transportation and lodging	Up to $50 per day for lodging, mileage, or coach airfare for travel for insured and companion (each)
Ambulance	Actual charges for an ambulance to the hospital and up to $5,000 for air ambulance
Artificial limbs and prostheses	Actual charges with lifetime maximum of $2,000 per insured person
Equipment	Up to $1,000 per calendar year for rental or purchase

Critical Illness Insurance

critical illness insurance

Critical illness insurance (sometimes referred to as serious illness insurance) is a relatively new form of supplemental medical insurance that provides a substantial one-time lump-sum cash benefit for a listed critical illness. Some of these conditions result from injury as well as disease and include specified major surgeries.

The applicant selects a maximum benefit amount, which can range from $10,000 to several hundred thousand dollars. The maximum benefit is payable only once—upon the first diagnosis of a listed condition or in combination with a specified surgical treatment or condition that is also covered. Each covered condition and surgical treatment is explicitly defined in the policy. Typically, the maximum benefit is payable for the following medical conditions or major surgery:

- Alzheimer's disease
- blindness
- deafness
- life-threatening cancer
- heart attack
- major organ transplant
- multiple sclerosis
- paralysis
- renal failure
- stroke

The policy may also provide a partial benefit, such as 25 percent of the maximum benefit, for each of the following:

- initial coronary angioplasty (surgical treatment)
- initial coronary artery bypass (surgical treatment)
- initial diagnosis of cancer in its original site (other than skin cancer)

Companies may offer other benefits. For example, a partial or maximum benefit may be paid when medical bills for any condition or combination of covered medical problems not specifically listed in the policy exceed $100,000 in a 12-month period.

Benefits are payable only once. If the insured receives a partial benefit, the maximum benefit is reduced by the amount paid and the premium is also reduced accordingly. The policyowner is notified of the new maximum amount and the new premium. Coverage terminates on the date the maximum benefit amount is paid under the policy's terms. Optional coverage may provide disability income and/or accidental death and dismemberment benefits.

CHAPTER REVIEW

Key Terms

interim medical expense insurance
temporary medical policies
international travel medical policies
hospital confinement indemnity insurance
accident-only policy
specified (dread) disease insurance
critical illness insurance

Review Questions

Review questions are based on the learning objectives in this chapter. Thus, a [11-3] at the end of a question means that the question is based on learning objective 11-3. If there are multiple objectives, they are all listed.

1. a. What types of policies may be considered interim medical expense insurance? [11-1]
   b. Why may they qualify as principal insurance programs? [11-1]
2. a. To whom are temporary medical expense insurance policies marketed? [11-1]
   b. What are the criteria for eligibility and ineligibility? [11-1]
3. Describe temporary medical expense insurance policies with respect to
   a. coverages and benefits [11-1]
   b. coverage periods and renewal [11-1]
   c. extension of coverage provisions [11-1]
4. a. To whom are international travel policies marketed? [11-1]
   b. What is the range of available coverage periods? [11-1]
   c. What other medical benefits and types of insurance coverage may be available with these policies? [11-1]
5. a. Why do students need their own medical expense policies? [11-1]
   b. What are the advantages and disadvantages of individually purchased policies compared to institution-sponsored plans? [11-1]
6. a. How may individual dental and vision service plans differ from employer-sponsored plans? [11-2]
   b. How may persons with discount cards for ancillary services use them in conjunction with their insured plans for these services? [11-2]
7. Describe each of the following dental benefit features:
   a. service-level groupings [11-2]
   b. least expensive professionally acceptable treatment [11-2]

c. prior authorization [11-2]
d. benefit maximums [11-2]
e. frequency limitations [11-2]
f. program phase-ins [11-2]
g. other limitations and exclusions [11-2]
h. benefits for services after termination [11-2]

8. What are the differences between a major medical and scheduled maximum payment benefit structure for dental insurance? [11-2]

9. What are the differences between a dental PPO plan and a dental HMO plan? [11-2]

10. Describe vision benefit products with respect to each of the following:
    a. benefits [11-2]
    b. eligibility [11-2]
    c. exclusions [11-2]

11. For what types of expenses can benefits from supplemental policies be used? [11-3]

12. a. In what ways are the benefits under a hospital confinement policy similar to those available under a specified disease policy? [11-3]
    b. In what ways do they differ? [11-3]

13. a. What types of illnesses and surgeries do critical illness policies often cover? [11-3]
    b. How might the benefits paid under such a policy differ? [11-3]
    c. Under what circumstances does the policy terminate? [11-3]

12

Introduction to Disability Income Insurance

Learning Objectives

An understanding of the material in this chapter should enable you to

12-1. Explain the need for disability income insurance.

12-2. Describe the market for disability income insurance.

12-3. Explain how underwriting requirements influence the market for disability income insurance.

12-4. Describe the characteristics of purchasers of disability income insurance.

12-5. Explain the meaning of income for purposes of disability income insurance.

12-6. Explain the relationship between earned income and issue limits for disability income insurance.

12-7. Describe the definitions of total disability.

12-8. Explain how disability income policies may offer benefits for less-than-total disability.

Chapter Outline

This is the first of four chapters on disability income insurance, the purpose of which is to replace the income of a person who is unable to work because of disability resulting from injury or sickness. This chapter examines the need for disability income insurance, the extent to which the American population has disability income protection, the meaning of *income,* and the various definitions of *disability*.

Chapter 13 looks at the ways to finance disability income, including personal resources, government programs, employer-provided coverage, and finally individually purchased disability income policies.

Chapter 14 examines the contract provisions that are found in disability income policies purchased by individuals. These provisions can vary and, in many instances, the policyowner is required to make choices. It also looks at how an individual can determine the appropriate type and amount of coverage to purchase.

Finally, chapter 15 explores the many business uses of disability income insurance, including business overhead expense insurance, disability buy-sell funding, and key person insurance.

Certain topics that have applicability to all types of health insurance are covered in earlier chapters. These include historical development, general contract provisions, underwriting, regulation, and taxation. However, certain aspects of these topics are unique to disability income insurance and are addressed in more detail in chapters 12 through 15.

THE NEED

Most people seem to be aware of the need to provide income to their families if they should die prematurely. However, they do not seem to have the same awareness of the need to provide such income if they are disabled. In both cases, income ceases. In the case of disability, however, family expenses—instead of decreasing because the family has one less member—may actually increase due to the cost of providing care for the disabled person.

The following facts highlight the need for disability income insurance:

- About one in three working Americans will suffer a disability of at least 90 days prior to age 65.[1] The figures in table 12-1 show this for workers at various ages.

TABLE 12-1
Probability of Becoming Disabled for at Least 90 Days

Age	Probability
25	37%
30	36
35	34
40	31
45	28
50	25
55	20

- The average duration of a disability that has lasted at least 90 days is 3.1 years.[2] This duration is slightly over 2 years for persons disabled at age 25 and becomes higher as age increases. At age 55, it is 4.6 years.
- Ten percent of persons disabled for 90 days or more will be disabled for 5 years or more.[3]
- At all ages, the possibility of suffering a disability of at least 90 days is significantly greater than the possibility of death. For example, it is 2.7 times as likely at age 27 and 3.5 times as likely at age 42.[4]
- Poor health, as well as the accompanying medical bills and lost income, contributes to about 50 percent of personal bankruptcies.[5] Although many people buy life insurance so that their families can afford mortgage payments in case they die, the odds of mortgage foreclosure due to disability are 16 times greater than the risk of foreclosure due to death.[6]
- Although many persons feel that work-related injuries, which will be covered by workers' compensation insurance, are the leading cause of disability, two-thirds of disabling injuries occur off the job.[7] In addition, most disabilities result from illnesses rather than injuries. The largest writer of disability income insurance recently reported that half of all long-term disability claims arose from five sources. These include cancer (12.1 percent), complications of pregnancy (11.7), joint/muscle/connective tissue diseases (10.1), back injuries (8.2), and cardiovascular disease (8).[8] The major reasons for short-term disability claims were normal pregnancy (20 percent), injuries other than back injuries (9), digestive/intestinal diseases (7), reproductive/ urinary system diseases (7), and pregnancy complications (7).[9]

- The potential for lost income because of disability is significant, as table 12-2 shows for various ages and monthly income levels.[10] The table assumes no change in earning levels, and the figures would be significantly higher, particularly for persons at younger ages, if assumptions were made about lost future increases in earnings over time.

TABLE 12-2
Potential Lost Income to Age 65

Age	Monthly Income			
	$2,000	$5,000	$7,000	$10,000
25	$960,000	$2,400,000	$3,360,000	$4,800,000
30	840,000	2,100,000	2,940,000	4,200,000
35	720,000	1,800,000	2,520,000	3,600,000
40	600,000	1,500,000	2,100,000	3,000,000
45	480,000	1,200,000	1,680,000	2,400,000
50	360,000	900,000	1,260,000	1,800,000
55	240,000	600,000	840,000	1,200,000

THE MARKET FOR DISABILITY INCOME INSURANCE

Despite the previous statistics, only about one-half of American workers have any form of private disability income insurance.[11] Most of this coverage is through employer plans, with the number of in-force individual policies totaling slightly over 5 million.[12] Several reasons are given for this significant gap in the financial plans of many Americans. These include the following:

- Many people underestimate the potential loss from disability.
- Many people assume that employer-provided coverage or Social Security will provide the disability income benefits they need. As discussed more fully later in this chapter and in chapter 13, such benefits are often limited in amount or duration. In addition, Social Security benefits may be difficult to collect because of the stringent definition of disability.
- Many people cannot afford every type of insurance that they need because of budget constraints. Automobile insurance, homeowners insurance, medical expense insurance, and life insurance have a higher priority for most Americans than does disability income insurance. In addition, many persons also put a higher priority on saving for specific needs, such as retirement and educating children.

- The insurance industry overall has not marketed the product as aggressively as other types of insurance. Historically, much of the disability income insurance that was sold was marketed by agents of life insurers. Many of these insurers have withdrawn from the disability income market, and the policies currently being sold are mostly from a small number of insurers. Even though these life insurance agents often still broker disability income insurance, the companies they represent are much more likely to encourage them to sell life insurance products, annuities, and mutual funds. Disability income insurance is also viewed as a complex product that is more difficult to sell than many other types of insurance and one that requires a high degree of due diligence. (This situation also has plagued the sale of long-term care insurance.) Despite all this, there are agents who specialize in disability income insurance and make a good living selling the product.

The market for disability income insurance can be looked at from three perspectives—the types of persons who have a need for the policies, the types of persons who meet the underwriting requirements to obtain them, and who actually purchases disability income insurance.

Who Has a Need?

Self-employed persons and many employees have a need for individual disability income insurance. Such policies are also needed in business situations and, depending on the circumstances, may be purchased by either individuals or the business entity.

Self-Employed Persons

Unless they purchase individual disability income insurance or can rely on personal financial resources, self-employed persons have little protection against the loss of income resulting from disability. Most of them have potential long-term disability benefits under Social Security, but the duration of disability must be expected to last at least one year, and many types of disabilities do not satisfy the stringent definition of disability required for such benefits.

Example: Four years ago, Simon, then aged 35, quit his job and became a self-employed graphic designer. At that time, Although he purchased medical expense coverage for himself and his family at that time, because of financial constraints he did not purchase any individual life insurance or disability income protection to replace his lost employer-provided benefits. Over time, his business and income continued to grow. Two years ago, he purchased a new home and decided to buy an individual life insurance policy. He also has been contributing to a tax-deferred retirement plan.

Last year, Simon fell from a ladder and broke his back. For the next 9 months, he was unable to work and suffered a total loss of income. Even though he is now back to work, many of his old clients have not returned and he still is physically unable to work full-time.

If Simon had purchased an individual disability income policy, he would have been able to receive benefits for much of this lost income. Because of his lack of coverage, he and his family have been barely able to make ends meet with his wife's income and they have exhausted almost all the family savings. The only way he has been able to keep his new home is because his parents have assumed a portion of the mortgage payments.

Employees

Many employees have a need for disability income insurance. In some cases, their employer provides no disability income benefits. In other cases, the benefits are limited in duration or amount.

Example 1: Angelina's employer provides a salary continuation plan under which her income will continue for up to 6 months if she is disabled. After that time, the employer provides no disability income benefits.

Angelina has a need for a long-term disability income policy.

Example 2: Brad makes $240,000 as an executive with a large corporation that has an excellent benefit package. If he is disabled, his income will continue in full for 6 months. After that time, he is covered by an employer-provided plan that pays 65 percent of his income up to a maximum $8,000 per month. Unfortunately, that is only $96,000 for him on an annual basis, or 40 percent of his income.

Brad can supplement his employer-provided coverage with the purchase of an individual disability income policy.

Example 3: Arnoldo is a nationally known professor at a major university. He has excellent employer-provided disability income benefits with respect to his salary. The university encourages professors to do outside consulting, and Arnoldo has a very lucrative practice. However, the university benefits do not consider this income when calculating disability income benefits.

Arnoldo should explore the purchase of an individual policy to replace his lost consulting income if he is disabled.

Business Uses

As discussed in much more detail in chapter 15, there are several reasons for using disability income insurance for business purposes. These policies account for a relatively small portion of the number of policies in force, but the policies often pay large benefits and have high premiums.

Meeting Underwriting Requirements

The market for disability income insurance is influenced by the underwriting standards of the insurers that sell the policies, as discussed in chapter 4. For some persons, these standards result in the denial of any coverage. For other persons, these standards affect the amount of coverage and policy provisions that are available. Because underwriting standards vary among insurers, a person who might not meet the underwriting standards of some insurers may be viewed as an acceptable business risk by other insurers. Underwriting decisions are also often a combination of several factors, and no one factor alone determines the final underwriting decision. However, there are some factors that by themselves may make an individual ineligible for coverage. These factors relate to age, income level, occupation, hours worked, and health. They are often explicitly spelled out in agent manuals to discourage agents from submitting such applications.

Anyone who is unable to obtain insurance coverage will need to rely on other financial resources to pay his or her living expenses if disabled.

Age

Insurers place age limits on persons to whom they will issue coverage. At the lower end, the ages may vary from 18 to 21. Persons younger than these ages often have low income levels. Policies issued to such persons also have very high lapse rates so that the insurer cannot recover initial acquisition expenses.

Insurers also have maximum ages above which they will not issue coverage, commonly ages 55 or 59. Persons above these ages may decide to "retire" if they are disabled and not have the motivation to return to work. Older persons may also seek coverage because they fear they are in the early stages of conditions that may lead to disability.

Income Level

Most insurers will not write coverage for persons who have income below a specified amount, usually in the range of $18,000 to $25,000. Such persons tend to have more claims than average, often because of job instability and/or lack of motivation to return to work after becoming disabled.

Insurers are also concerned about persons with significant unearned income and high net worth. Such persons will often have the resources needed to provide a large amount of income if they are disabled and may have little motivation to return to work. Rather than disqualifying a person for coverage, these characteristics are more likely to affect the amount of coverage the insurer will issue, as discussed in chapter 13.

Occupation

Every insurer has a list of occupations for which it will not issue coverage. Often these are hazardous occupations, but they may also be occupations that are associated with bad claims history.

Example: One insurer has a lengthy list of occupations that make a person ineligible for coverage. Some of these occupations include the following:

- actors
- airline flight attendants
- air traffic controllers
- armed services personnel
- asbestos workers
- bartenders

- billboard hangers
- chimney sweeps
- crop dusters
- dog catchers
- domestic servants
- fishermen
- forest rangers
- game wardens
- jockeys
- loggers
- masseurs and masseuses
- models
- professional athletes
- professional sky divers
- toll collectors
- zoologists

Part-Time Employees

Most insurers write coverage only for persons who are employed full-time. This is often defined as working at least 30 hours per week. Persons working fewer hours are less likely to have the motivation to return to work, particularly if they have a spouse who works full-time.

Health

Insurers are obviously very concerned about the health of applicants for disability income insurance. Most insurers have weight limitations that vary by height. Persons significantly below or significantly above specific parameters are ineligible for coverage.

Insurers also have underwriting guides that list specific medical conditions that make a person ineligible for coverage. In other cases, however, they might write coverage with an exclusion rider for certain specific conditions.

Example: One insurer has a list of medical conditions that generally make a person ineligible for coverage. A few of these include:

- cerebral thrombosis

- cancer, other than skin cancer, if less than 7 years have elapsed since successful treatment
- juvenile onset diabetes
- coronary artery disease
- chronic migraines
- multiple sclerosis
- Parkinson's disease
- benign tumors that are still present

Characteristics of Purchasers

An understanding of the market for disability income insurance is not complete without some data on who the purchasers are and the types of policies they purchase. Research organizations, such as LIMRA International Inc. (www.limra.com), conduct studies of DI insurance buyers to determine profiles of their demographic characteristics. LIMRA studies have compiled information on hundreds of thousands of DI insurance contracts from numerous insurance companies. In addition to demographic information, LIMRA collects attitudinal and financial product ownership information from DI insurance buyers and owners; participating companies represent a mix of large, mid-size, and small DI insurance writers, with in-force contracts sold in both retail and employer-sponsored markets. These reports investigate buyer demographic characteristics such as gender, age, occupational class, and type of policy purchased as they relate to the DI insurance marketplace. Consider the information in table 12-3, which was extracted from LIMRA's *The Disability Income Buyer Study: United States, A 2004 Report.*

MEANING OF INCOME

Although disability income insurance is designed to replace lost income, it is not always easy to determine precisely what income is from the standpoint of disability income insurance; the determination may vary somewhat from one insurer to another. An applicant's determination of income is extremely important in disability income insurance. If it is overstated, the amount of insurance issued may result in overinsurance. This often leads to an increased incidence of claims and a lack of motivation to return to work.

In addition, the amount of disability income insurance that an insurer will issue is limited to only a percentage of the lost income.

TABLE 12-3
Demographic Characteristics of Individual DI Insurance Buyers

Percentage of Policies Purchased	
Gender	**Percentage**
Male	68%
Female	32%
Age	**Percentage**
60 and over	2%
50–59	15%
40–49	32%
30–39	38%
less than 30	13%
Commissioners Individual Disability Table A (CIDA) Class Underwriting Class	
Class	**Percentage**
Class 1: the lowest premium class; includes professional, technical and managerial occupations that are generally office duties only	72%
Class 2: supervisory and other skilled clerical and skilled technical people	19%
Class 3: nonhazardous light manual workers	6%
Class 4: hazardous work with heavy manual labor or using heavy equipment	3%
Policy Type	
Policy	**Percentage**
Noncancelable	72%
Guaranteed renewable	28%

Source: The Disability Income Buyer Study: United States © 2004, LIMRA International, Inc.®

financial underwriting

As mentioned in chapter 4, the calculation and analysis of income, which this chapter and chapter 13 expand upon, is often referred to as *financial underwriting*. It is equally as important as medical underwriting.

Determining Income

In analyzing income, it is important to look at earned income, unearned income, expenses associated with disability, and the verification of income.

Earned income

earned income

The type of income that is properly insurable is *earned income*. For most individuals, this is the income generated from an individual's own efforts in a profession or trade. It includes wages, salary, bonuses, fees, commissions, and any other fees for services rendered. Some insurers will also include deferred compensation amounts and retirement plan contributions paid to or on behalf of an applicant. Insurers are also very concerned about the stability of income. For example, if an applicant received an unusually large bonus just before applying for coverage, the insurer would want to be certain that such a bonus would continue in the future. If not, they would be unwilling to consider the entire bonus in calculating earned income.

For a sole proprietor and a general partner in a partnership, earned income is often defined as the individual's share of the business's gross revenue minus his or her pro rata share of the normal business operating expenses. These expenses are tax deductible and include office operating expenses, employee salaries, and business travel expenses.

For an owner of a closely held corporation, earned income may include a share of the profits generated from his or her involvement in the business.

Unearned Income

unearned income

Unearned income is income that will not stop if disability strikes and is not insurable for purposes of disability income insurance. Examples include interest on savings or investments, dividends, rental income, pension payments, annuity income, trust payments, royalties, and any other income not derived from the individual's job activities.

Differentiating between earned and unearned income requires a determination of whether the individual is actively involved in the generation of the income. For example, a person may own rental property and receive income from it. If the owner actively manages the property, the net rental income may be considered earned income if disability would result in the loss of this income. However, if the owner takes no active part in the property's management, the rental income is most likely to be considered unearned investment income.

Expenses Associated with Disability

Disability results not only in lost income, but also in increased expenses arising from medical bills and the care of a disabled individual. Disability income insurance does not cover these extra expenses. For them, an individual needs medical expense insurance and long-term care insurance.

Verifying Income

Insurers need a basis for verifying an applicant's income. At a minimum, they will require that the individual's latest Form 1040 personal federal income tax return be submitted along with the application. In some cases, they may also want returns for prior years. Business owners will also be required to submit business tax returns.

Limits on Amounts of Coverage

Every disability income insurer has a maximum amount of coverage that it will write for an applicant based on the applicant's earned income. Table 12-4 shows these limits for one insurer by selected incomes. Such limits are often referred to as issue and participation limits. An *issue limit* is the maximum amount of coverage that an insurer is willing to write and includes the amount of any coverage an applicant already has in force with that insurer. A *participation limit* takes into account the amount of insurance in force from other insurers.

issue limit

participation limit

Example: Taylor has an annual earned income of $100,000. He currently has no disability income insurance and would like a monthly benefit of $6,000. However, the first insurer that he approached told him it had an issue limit of $4,400. A second insurer he contacted had an issue limit of $4,600. Therefore, he bought that policy. He then turned around and applied for an additional monthly benefit of $1,400 from the first insurer. This insurer informed Taylor that it also had a monthly participation limit of $4,400. Because he already had more than that amount of coverage from another insurer, the first insurer declined to issue a policy.

TABLE 12-4
Issue/Participation Limits for Individual Coverage

Annual Earned Income	Monthly Indemnity Individually Paid Coverage	Monthly Indemnity Employer-Paid Coverage
$20,000	$1,200	$1,400
30,000	1,650	2,100
40,000	2,150	2,850
50,000	2,600	3,550
60,000	3,100	4,350
70,000	3,550	5,100
80,000	4,000	5,400
90,000	4,200	5,700
100,000	4,400	5,950
110,000	4,600	6,200
120,000	5,000	6,500
130,000	5,300	6,900
140,000	5,600	7,300
150,000	6,000	7,700
160,000	6,300	8,100
170,000	6,700	8,500
180,000	7,000	8,900
190,000	7,350	9,300
200,000	7,700	9,700
210,000	8,000	10,000
220,000	8,250	10,000
230,000	8,500	10,000
240,000	8,705	10,000
250,000	9,000	10,000
260,000	9,200	10,000
270,000	9,400	10,000
280,000	9,600	10,000
290,000	9.800	10,000
300,000 and over	10,000	10,000

In most cases, the issue and participation limits are the same when an applicant has only individual coverage.

The limits in table 12-4, which are for individual policies, differ by whether the applicant or the applicant's employer pays the premium. In the latter case, the insurer will issue larger amounts of coverage because benefits from employer-financed coverage are subject to income taxation, whereas benefits are income tax free if the insured pays the premiums. Note that the amount of the monthly benefit decreases as a percentage of earned income as earned income increases. For example, with individually paid coverage, an insured with $20,000 of earned income would receive an annual disability income benefit of $1,200 x 12, or $14,400. This represents 72 percent of the insured's annual earned income. At $30,000 of earned income, the percentage decreases to 60. At earned incomes of $60,000, $100,000, $150,000, $200,000, and $300,000, the percentage is 60, 52.8, 48, 46.2, and 40, respectively. Such a percentage is referred to as a *replacement ratio.* These ratios are typical of those used by most insurers.

replacement ratio

The maximum amount of coverage that this insurer will issue is limited to a monthly indemnity of $10,000 per month. Some insurers will issue higher amounts, such as $15,000 and occasionally more. In addition, most insurers will have lower maximum limits for certain occupational classifications. For example, the limits in table 12-4 apply only to the top four of the insurer's occupational classifications. Other occupational classifications have maximum limits that vary from $2,500 to $7,000.

Note that limits such as those in the table are maximum amounts. Insurers also have minimum amounts of coverage that they will issue. These are often in the range of a monthly benefit of $300 to $$500. Insurers may also have special-issue limits for some young professionals without earnings records because they are just starting their careers. For example, one insurer will offer a monthly benefit of $4,500 to first-year physicians, $3,000 to medical residents, $2,500 to medical interns, and $3,000 to first-year attorneys, CPAs, engineers, and architects. Insurers reduce these limits by the amount of other group and individual coverage in force.

DEFINITIONS OF DISABILITY

Disability can mean different things to different people and is not defined the same way in every disability income policy. However, an insured will receive benefits only if he or she satisfies the precise definition that is contained in a disability income policy.

The remainder of this chapter discusses the various definitions of disability. After looking at definitions of total disability, the focus changes to looking at the definitions of less-than-total disability.

Total Disability

Early disability income contracts focused solely on the concept of total disability. The insured was either disabled totally or not at all. All contracts still cover total disability, but as explained later they may also provide benefits when a disability is not total. Definitions of total disability fall into two broad categories—any occupation and own occupation. However, there are variations in each of these categories.

Any Occupation

The narrowest and most strict definition of total disability is the inability to perform the duties of any occupation because of injury or sickness. Defining total disability in this way means that a person capable of doing anything at all for remuneration would not be considered disabled.

Example: Charlie is well educated and was a successful traveling salesman. He was severely injured after falling off a ladder and is now confined to a wheelchair. Despite extensive rehabilitation efforts, Charlie is only at the point that he can sell newspapers and magazines at a kiosk established by a local charitable organization. However, this would make him no longer disabled under the strictest any-occ definition.

As explained in chapter 13, Social Security incorporates this type of definition of disability. Fortunately, private disability income policies no longer use such a definition.

In an effort to match coverage more closely with an individual's needs, a more liberal any-occupation definition was developed. This definition is commonly referred to as an *any-occ definition of disability*. With this definition, total disability is defined as a condition that prevents a person from performing the duties of any occupation for which that person is reasonably suited by education, training, and experience.

any-occ definition of disability

Example: Let's return to Charlie from the previous example. Assume that his rehabilitation has been such that he can return to an office job in the marketing department of one of the firms whose products he formerly sold. Even though his salary is less than what he earned as a traveling salesman, Charlie will no longer be considered disabled because he is suited for the job by his education (a degree in marketing), training, and experience.

Own Occupation

own-occ definition of disability

Some insurers issue policies with an *own-occ definition of disability*. With such a definition, an insured is considered totally disabled if he or she is unable to perform the substantial and material duties of his or her regular occupation at the time of disability. Even if the person returns to work in another occupation, the insurer will still pay the full disability income benefits as long as the insured can no longer perform the duties of the former regular occupation.

Example: Fiona was a successful architect who was severely disabled by a neurological disorder. She is no longer able to draw the plans and blueprints required of her former occupation. However, she has been able to secure a job as lecturer at a local university. With an own-occupation definition of disability, she will also be able to collect her full disability income benefits.

The own-occ definition of disability as previously described was once more commonly available than it is currently. Today, insurers are more likely to use variations that are more restrictive.

modified own-occ definition of disability

One variation is to terminate benefits at any time that the insured returns to work in any gainful employment position for which he or she is suited by education, training or experience. However, partial or residual disability income benefits may become payable at this time. This variation is sometimes referred to as a *modified own-occ definition of disability*

dual (or split) definition of disability

Another variation is to use a *dual (or split) definition of disability*. An own-occ definition is used for a limited period of time that might range from 2 to 5 years. After that time, an any-occ definition is used.

What Do Insurers Use?

Many insurers will use several of the definitions of total disability previously described. In their most preferred occupational classes, they may be willing to issue a policy with an own-occupation of disability as long as certain underwriting criteria are met. For other occupational classes, they may use a version of dual definition of disability. For the least preferred occupational classes, they will use an any-occ definition.

Less-Than-Total Disability

As disability income contracts evolved and became more competitive, there were complaints that the total definition of disability did not take into account disabilities that were not totally disabling, but resulted in lost income because the insured was unable to perform some of the duties of his or her regular occupation. As a result, insurers developed several approaches to pay benefits when the insured is less than totally disabled. These approaches, which are usually in the form of a rider to a basic disability income policy for total disability, include

- partial disability benefits
- residual disability benefits

The availability of benefits for less-than-total disability is often an incentive for an insured to return to work.

Partial Disability Benefits

partial disability

The earliest form of coverage for less-than-total disability was benefits for *partial disability*. This is defined as the inability to do some of the specific duties relating to a job. Its purpose is to pay limited benefits to an insured who is attempting to return to work after a minimum specified period of total disability. Typically, the benefit is equal to 50 percent of the basic total disability benefit and is only paid for a limited period, such as 3, 6, or 12 months. The benefit is a fixed amount and has no relationship to the income earned upon return to employment. In fact, the insured may return to a job that pays the same wages as prior to disability.

Example: Rose is a consultant and used to travel frequently for her job. She was totally disabled for several months and received a monthly indemnity of $4,000 from her disability income policy. After recovering from the total disability, she was able to return to work, but unable to travel. Her former employer gave her a job that utilized her skills, but it paid less than her previous position. Rose is eligible for a partial disability if such a benefit is in her policy. Even if the new position had the same salary as her old position, she would also be eligible for the partial disability benefits because she could not fully perform her old job.

Residual Disability Benefits

residual disability

Partial disability benefits are not as common as they once were and have largely been replaced by residual disability benefits. A *residual disability* is defined as a disability that results in the insured's inability to perform some of the duties of his or her own occupation, resulting in a loss of income. It is typically coupled with an own-occ definition of total disability.

Residual benefits focus on the loss of income rather than on the physical limitations of the disability. The benefits can be paid if the insured returns to either full-time or part-time employment. Residual benefits continue until the end of the benefit period specified in the policy as long the insured continues to meet the definition of disability.

Example: Herb is an attorney who previously earned $240,000 per year, or $20,000 per month. For several months, he was totally disabled as a result of a serious heart attack. Eventually, he was able to return to work on a part-time basis, at an annual salary of $150,000, or $12,500 per month. Herb suffered a residual loss of income of $90,000 on an annual basis, or $7,500 on a monthly basis.

---

qualification period

The actual mechanics of understanding residual disability benefits are somewhat more complicated than this example indicates. First, there may be a *qualification period* before an individual is eligible for residual disability benefits. This is the period that the insured must be totally disabled before qualifying for such benefits. Common periods are 30, 60, and 90 days.

Second, the insurer starts the benefit calculation by comparing income before and after the disability to determine the percentage loss of income. This percentage is then multiplied by the benefit for total disability to determine the residual disability benefit.

Example: Let's return to the example of Herb. Assume that his monthly disability income benefit for total disability is $12,000. His $7,500 monthly loss of income is 37.5 percent of his pre-disability income of $20,000. Therefore, his residual disability benefit will be 37.5 percent of his $12,000 total disability benefit, or $4,500.

Third, residual benefits often cease (or are not paid initially) if the income loss is below a certain percentage (usually 20 percent) of pre-disability earnings. Conversely, policies are likely to continue paying the total disability income benefit if earnings fall significantly. This figure used for this calculation is usually 75 or 80 percent. In addition, there may be a minimum residual disability benefit, such as 50 percent of the total disability benefit, during the first few months that residual disability benefits are paid. This period is commonly 6 months, after which benefits are based on the actual reduction in income.

Example: Let's return again to Herb and assume that his insurer uses the percentages previously mentioned. Let's further assume that Herb returns to work and finds that he is able to work almost full time and his salary increases to $16,000 per month. The decrease in his income is now $4,000 per month, or 20 percent of his pre-disability income. Therefore, his insurer would stop his disability income benefits. On the other hand, assume he is only able to work one day per week at a monthly income of $4,000. This represents a drop in income of 80 percent, and the insurer would continue to pay the total disability income benefit of $12,000 per month.

Fourth, it is important to look at how pre-disability earnings are calculated. There are several possible variations. For example, an insurer may calculate an average monthly income based on the last 3 years of earnings. Another insurer might use only the prior 6 or 12 months, or the highest 12 months in the prior 3 years. For insureds whose incomes fluctuate, the calculation used can make a significant difference in the benefit received. Some insurers also index prior earnings for inflation, often based on the consumer price index. Without such indexing, the residual disability benefit will decrease as the insured receives future pay increases during disability.

Finally, there are variations in what types of work result in the receipt of residual benefits. Under some definitions of residual disability, loss of income is measured as the difference between pre-disability income and post-disability income from the same occupation. If the insured takes a job in another occupation, the full total disability benefits are still paid as long as the insured cannot perform all the duties of his or own occupation. This can sometimes result in an insured having a larger income than prior to disability.

loss-of-earnings policy

Several insurers now issue what is called *a loss-of-earnings policy*. With this approach, loss of income is measured as the difference between pre-disability income and post-disability income from *any* occupation. In this case, total disability benefits are not paid if the insured returns to work. However, the insured is then eligible for residual disability benefits.

CHAPTER REVIEW

Key Terms

- financial underwriting
- earned income
- unearned income
- issue limit
- participation limit
- replacement ratio
- any-occ definition of disability
- own-occ definition of disability
- dual (or split) definition of disability
- modified own-occ definition of disability
- partial disability
- residual disability
- qualification period
- loss-of-earnings policy

Review Questions

Review questions are based on the learning objectives in this chapter. Thus, a [12-3] at the end of a question means that the question is based on learning objective 12-3. If there are multiple objectives, they are all listed.

1. Why is there a need for disability income insurance? [12-1]
2. Why is there a gap in the financial plans of many Americans with respect to disability income insurance? [12-2]
3. Who has a need for disability income insurance? [12-2]
4. How do underwriting standards affect the availability of disability income insurance? [12-3]
5. What are the characteristics of purchasers of disability income insurance? [12-4]
6. a. How do insurers determine earned income for purposes of disability income insurance? [12-5]
   b. What is the relationship between earned income and the maximum issue limits of insurers? [12-6]
7. Why is it important to understand the definition of disability used in a disability income policy? [12-7]
8. Cheryl is a plastic surgeon. Why would she prefer a disability income policy with an own-occ definition of disability rather than one with an any-occ definition? [12-7]
9. Sam, an electrical engineer, was totally disabled as a result of being struck by lightning and severely burned. After several months of rehabilitation, he is

able to return to his old job on a part-time basis. Before his disability, Sam earned $10,000 per month and had a total disability benefit of $6,000 per month under a policy with an own-occ benefit. When he returns to work, he expects to earn $5,000 per month. If his policy provides residual disability benefits, how much will Sam collect from his policy? [12-8]

10. What are the ways in which total disability benefits might be calculated if a disabled person with residual disability benefits returns to work in a new occupation? [12-8]

NOTES

1. Society of Actuaries, Commissioner's Individual Disability Table A.
2. Ibid.
3. Ibid.
4. Web site of Disability Resource Insurance Center: www.di-resource-center/statistics.html.
5. Himmelstein, D. U. et al., "Illness and Injury as Contributors to Bankruptcy," *Health Affairs*, Feb 2, 2005.
6. National Safety Council, *Injury Facts*, 2004.
7. Ibid.
8. UNUM disability databases, 2006.
9. Ibid.
10. MetLife, *DI Reference Manual*, 3d ed.
11. Ibid.
12. LIMRA, *U.S. Individual Disability Income Survey*, first quarter, 2006.

13

Financing of Disability Income

Learning Objectives

An understanding of the material in this chapter should enable you to

13-1. Explain why it is important for individuals and insurers to understand the resources available to finance disability income benefits.

13-2. Describe the nature of Social Security disability income benefits.

13-3. Explain the extent to which workers' compensation laws provide disability income benefits.

13-4. Describe the nature of state temporary disability income benefits.

13-5. Identify the ways in which social insurance programs are coordinated with individual disability income insurance.

13-6. Describe the benefits available under employer-provided sick-leave plans.

13-7. Explain the characteristics of employer-provided group disability income plans.

13-8. Explain how employer-provided disability income benefits are coordinated with individual insurance.

13-9. Explain how insurers might take unearned income and net worth into consideration when determining disability income issue limits.

Chapter Outline

Disability income insurance was introduced in chapter 12. However, other sources are often available to individuals to finance the loss of income because of disability. An understanding of these sources is important from the perspective of both individuals and insurance companies that provide coverage. An individual needs to understand these sources of benefits in order to determine if there is still a need to purchase additional protection. If so, these sources need to be considered in calculating the proper amount of coverage to purchase. Insurers need to be aware of all sources of income available to an applicant to ensure that the amount of coverage issued, when combined with these other resources, does not result in overinsurance.

FIGURE 13-1
Listing of Compensation Systems

Federal Disability Compensation Systems

- Primary Social Security Disability Benefits
- Dependents' Social Security Disability Benefits
- Armed Services Disability Benefits
- Veterans Administration Disability Benefits
- Veterans Administration Pension Disability Benefits
- Civil Service Disability Benefits
- Federal Employees Compensation Act
- Black Lung Benefits Act of 1972
- Longshore and Harbor Workers' Compensation Act
- Railroad Retirement Act

Employer-, Union-, and Association-Sponsored Compensation Systems

- Employer/Union or Association Group Life Waiver of Premium
- Employer/Union or Association Hospital
- Indemnity
- Employer/Union or Association Accidental Death and Dismemberment
- Employer/Union or Association Travel Accident
- Employer/Union Group Long-Term Disability
- Employer/Union Group Short-Term Disability
- Employer/Union Group Life Total and Permanent Disability (TPD) Benefit
- Employer/Union Retirement Disability
- Employer Deferred-Compensation Plans
- Employer Profit-Sharing and Savings Plans
- Association Disability Income

State and Local Government Compensation Systems

- Workers' Compensation
- State Cash Sickness
- State Vocational Rehabilitation
- Supplemental Security Income
- Aid to Families with Dependent Children
- Food Stamps

Individually Purchased Insurance Industry Compensation Systems

- Disability Income
- Automobile No-Fault Disability
- Automobile (Other Than No-Fault) Disability
- Hospital Indemnity
- Disability Buy/Sell
- Travel Accident
- Accidental Death and Dismemberment
- General and Individual Liability
- Business Overhead Expense
- Mortgage Disability Income
- Creditor Disability Income
- Individual Insurance Waiver of Premium

Miscellaneous Sources of Income

- Underground Employment
- Recoveries through Litigation
- Unearned Income

Source: *Compensation Systems Available to Disabled Persons in the United States*, Health Insurance Association of America, 1979.

This chapter looks at the five most common "insurance" sources of disability income other than individual insurance and describes how they are coordinated with private insurance. These are

- Social Security
- workers' compensation benefits
- state temporary disability benefits
- employer-provided sick-leave plans
- employer-provided group disability income plans

The first three items are government social insurance programs and the last two items are what most people refer to as employee benefits.

In addition, an individual may have personal resources in the form of assets and income other than earned income to provide support during a disability. These resources are also discussed.

Before continuing, note that disability income can come from many other sources, some of which are not discussed in this chapter. A study conducted by the Health Insurance Association of America identified 42 possible sources of disability income. These are shown in figure 13-1.

SOCIAL SECURITY

Many people think of the Social Security program as providing only retirement benefits. However, it is also the largest disability income insurer in the United States. It provides potential benefits to over 95 percent of all Americans with earned income. The program annually provides $90 billion of benefits to almost 9 million American workers[1] and their families and is financed by a portion of the Social Security taxes paid by employees, employers, and the self-employed.

The following discussion looks at Social Security disability income program from the perspective of eligibility, determination of disability, benefit amounts, duration of benefits, rehabilitation, and taxation. The treatment is relatively brief and readers who desire more detail about all its often complex rules and procedures can find additional information on the Social Security Web site at www.ssa.gov.

Eligibility

To qualify for disability benefits, a worker must satisfy certain eligibility requirements in addition to satisfying the program's disability criteria. Benefits are only available to persons who are disabled prior to their *full retirement age*. This is the age at which nonreduced Social Security

full retirement age

retirement benefits are initially available. The full retirement age, once 65, has been increasing and most workers now have a full retirement age between 66 and 67, depending on their year of birth. Persons who continue to work past their full retirement age and then become disabled can apply for Social Security retirement benefits, which are comparable in amount to disability benefits.

disability insured

The person must be *disability insured.* Such a status requires a person to meet two criteria. He or she must be fully insured and must have a minimum amount of work experience under the Social Security program within a specified period.

Fully Insured

A person is fully insured under Social Security—and never loses this status—if he or she has 40 credits under the program. For 2008, a worker receives one credit for each $1,050 in annual earnings on which Social Security taxes are paid. However, a worker can earn no more than four credits in any calendar year. Consequently, a worker who pays Social Security taxes on as little as $4,200 ($1,050 x 4) at any time during the year will receive the maximum four credits. This $1,050 is subject to annual indexing, just like the wage base on which Social Security taxes are paid.

Obviously, most workers will have little trouble obtaining fully insured status as long as they have at least 10 years of coverage by Social Security. However, there is also a second alternative for a worker to obtain fully insured status as long as he or she has a minimum of six credits. Such a person is fully insured if he or she has at least as many credits as there are years elapsing *after* the year in which age 21 is attained and *before* the year in which he or she became disabled. The major beneficiaries of this alternative are younger persons who have been in the work force for fewer than 10 years.

Example: Max reached age 21 in 2000 and was disabled in 2008. He started working after college and had only 19 Social Security credits. However, all he needs to be fully insured is seven credits.

Recent Work Experience

The second criterion is a recent amount of work experience under the Social Security program. A worker aged 31 or older meets this requirement as long as he or she has earned 20 credits during the 40 calendar quarters ending with the quarter in which disability occurs. Workers aged 24 through

30 must have earned credits equal to at least one-half the number of calendar quarters from the time they turned 21 until the quarter in which disability begins. Workers under age 24 must have earned at least six credits during the prior 12 calendar quarters.

A special rule for blind persons exempts them from the recent-work rules, but they still must be fully insured.

Determination of Disability

The basic Social Security definition of disability is the inability to engage in any substantial gainful activity by reason of any medically determinable physical or mental impairment that can be expected to result in death or can be expected to last for a continuous period of not less than 12 months. There is a somewhat more liberal definition for persons who are at least age 55 and legally blind.

One very important point needs to be made about the term "substantial gainful activity." It does not mean that a person is so disabled that he or she can earn no income. However, the disability must be severe enough that a person can earn no more than a stated monthly amount, which is indexed annually. For 2008, this monthly amount is $940 ($1,570 for blind persons).

The Social Security Administration uses a five-step process to determine whether an applicant for benefits is disabled:

- Step 1—They look at whether the applicant is still working. If the applicant is earning more than the stated income mentioned above, Social Security denies the disability claim. Otherwise, they go to step 2.
- Step 2—They look at whether the impairment is severe. This means that the impairment must significantly limit the applicant's ability to do such basic work activities as walking, sitting, and remembering for at least one year. If not, Social Security denies the claim. If it is severe, they go to step 3.
- Step 3—They have a list of impairments that describes medical conditions that are considered so severe that the conditions automatically qualify an applicant for benefits by law. If the applicant's condition is on the list, Social Security approves the claim. If it is not on the list, they go to step 4.
- Step 4—They decide if the impairment prevents the applicant from being able to do the work he or she did before. If the applicant is able to do the work, Social Security denies the claim. If not, they go to step 5.
- Step 5—They look at whether the applicant can engage in other substantial gainful activity, based on the applicant's medical condition, age, education, past work experience, and skill. If they

determine that an applicant cannot do such work, the claim is approved. Otherwise, they deny the claim.

The Social Security Administration informs the applicant by letter of the final decision. If they approve a claim, the letter shows the amount of the benefit and when it starts. If they deny the claim, the letter explains why and tells the applicant the process for appealing the decision if he or she does not agree with it.

Benefits Amounts

primary insurance amount (PIA)

Social Security bases the amount of disability benefits (as well as retirement and survivor's benefits) on a worker's primary insurance amount. The *primary insurance amount (PIA)* is the monthly amount the worker will receive if he or she is disabled. It is also the amount on which any additional benefits for family members are based. The actual PIA calculation is complex and performed by the Social Security Administration when a beneficiary is eligible for benefits. It involves indexing past wages on which Social Security taxes were paid, eliminating some years with the lowest or no earnings, and averaging the indexed wages for the remaining years. The result is then put into a formula that is weighted in favor of low-income earners.

Worker Benefits

For 2008, the PIA (and benefit) for workers who have paid the maximum Social Security taxes can be as high as between $2,075 and $2,300 per month. The higher figure is for workers who are disabled at younger ages. However, the estimated average Social Security benefit for all disabled workers is about $1,000 per month. Workers earning $20,000 per year can expect their benefits to be approximately 50 percent of their pre-disability earning. This percentage gradually decreases for workers with higher pre-disability earnings, and a worker with pre-disability earnings of $100,000 can expect a benefit of about 25 percent of annual earnings.

Workers are also eligible for Medicare benefits after they have been receiving disability benefits for 2 years.

Family Benefits

Social Security disability benefits, like other Social Security benefits, are also payable to eligible dependents. These benefits are in addition to the amount payable to the worker. The most frequently paid benefit is to unmarried dependent children. This benefit is payable to each child as long as the child is under age 18, but continues until age 19 if the child is still enrolled full-time in secondary school. In addition, benefits are payable to any disabled dependent children, regardless of age, as long as their disability began before age 22 and still exists when the worker files for benefits.

A worker's spouse may also receive benefits under certain circumstances as long as the spouse is not entitled to a larger retirement or disability benefit based on his or her own earnings record. Benefits are payable to a spouse who is aged 62 or older. They are also payable to a spouse who is taking care of a worker's child as long as the child is under age 16 or disabled.

The benefits payable to each eligible dependent are 50 percent of the benefit payable to the disabled worker. In many cases, a spouse will not apply for benefits because he or she has current earnings that are high enough to eliminate his or her benefit because of the Social Security earnings test.

There is a maximum overall family benefit. Like the PIA, it is determined by a formula and is usually reached when two or three family members (including the disabled worker) are eligible for benefits. If total benefits would exceed the family maximum, the worker's benefit is not affected, but the benefits of other family members are reduced proportionately.

Example: Karen is receiving a monthly Social Security disability benefit of $1,200. Her husband, who earns $100,000 per year, did not apply for a spouse's benefit. However, they submitted a benefit claim for their two children. If there were no family maximum, each of the children would receive a monthly benefit of $600. However, there is a monthly family maximum of $1,900 in her situation. Her benefit will remain at $1,200, but the children will receive only $700 more, or $350 each.

If Karen had only one child, that child's monthly benefit would be $600, for a total monthly family benefit of $1,800.

Offset for Other Benefits

Social Security reduces the benefits of a disabled worker who also receives workers' compensation benefits or disability benefits from certain other federal, state, or local disability programs to the extent benefits payable (including family benefits) exceed 80 percent of the worker's average current earnings at the time of disability. This reduction does not apply to private disability income benefits received.

Cost-of-Living Increases

Social Security benefits are subject to annual cost-of-living adjustments, based on changes in consumer price index (CPI).

Duration of Benefits

When describing the duration of Social Security disability benefits, it is necessary to determine when benefits begin and when they end.

When Benefits Start

elimination period

As a general rule, benefits start with the sixth full month of disability. Benefits are not paid for the month in which a disability commences. This is then followed by a 5-month elimination period, which the Social Security Administration refers to as a waiting period. An *elimination period* is a period of time after an individual otherwise satisfies the criteria for benefits but before benefits begin. Elimination periods are also found in other social insurance programs as well as in private disability income insurance and long-term care insurance.

Example: It was determined by Social Security that Heather became disabled on January 15. She received no benefits for that month or for the months of February, March, April, May, or June. She received he first disability check, effective July 1.

The process for approving Social Security disability claims tends to be lengthy, with periods of 3 to 5 months not uncommon. Therefore, a beneficiary should file a claim as soon as possible in order for benefits to start on time. However, if a claim approval is not received until a later date, benefits are paid retroactive to the beginning of the sixth full month of disability.

There is an exception to the general rule if a new disability arises within 5 years after a previous disability ended. In that case, benefits begin with the first full month of the new disability.

When Benefits Cease

Benefits for a worker cease under three circumstances. The first is when a worker dies. At that time, any family benefits also cease, but the family members become eligible for Social Security survivor's benefits.

Benefits for the worker and family member also cease when a worker is no longer disabled. However, benefits continue through the month of recovery and the following 2 months. As explained later, benefits may also continue for a period if a worker is in a vocational rehabilitation program.

Finally, benefits cease when a worker attains the Social Security full retirement age. At that time, the benefits (including any family benefits) automatically convert to Social Security retirement benefits.

Even when a disabled worker is eligible to continue receiving benefits, the benefits of family members cease when they no longer meet the eligibility requirements. For example, a child might reach the maximum age for benefits.

In addition to benefits ceasing, there are also circumstances in which Social Security does not pay benefits. For example, benefits are suspended while a worker is imprisoned in the United States for conviction of a felony committed at any time. However, benefits for family members continue.

Rehabilitation

The Social Security program has provisions to encourage a disabled worker to return to work. These include the Ticket to Work program and incentives for trial work periods.

Ticket to Work Program

Ticket to Work program

The purpose of the *Ticket to Work program* is to encourage persons receiving disability benefits to obtain vocation rehabilitation, job training, job referrals, and other employment support services that will enable them to return to work. The program is voluntary and failure to use it will not jeopardize future disability benefits.

Essentially, the Social Security Administration issues a ticket to disabled workers so they can, at no charge, obtain the provided services. Each worker can take his or her ticket to a state vocational rehabilitation agency or an employment network, which is a private or government agency that works with the Social Security Administration to provide these services. This agency then develops a plan for the disabled worker. If the worker is satisfied, he or she signs the plan and begins working with the agency.

The Social Security Administration agrees to continue paying disability benefits until the worker completes the plan, even if the worker recovers sufficiently so that he or she no longer meets the criteria for benefits.

Trial Work Periods

The trial work period allows a disabled worker to test his or her ability to work. During this time, the worker receives full Social Security benefits, regardless of earnings, as long as he or she continues to have a disabling impairment. A trial work month is any month in which earnings are $670 or more (in 2008 and subject to annual indexing). The trial work period continues until a person has worked 9 months within a 60-month period.

After the trial work period ends, the worker still has 36 months during which disability benefits are payable if earnings are not substantial ($940 in 2008 or $1,570 if a person is blind). If earnings are substantial, the Social Security disability benefits cease, but there are provisions that allow the worker to continue receiving Medicare benefits as long as he or she otherwise continues to meet the definition of disability.

Tax Treatment

Any benefits received in the form of monthly income under Social Security are partially subject to federal income taxation for some Social Security recipients. To determine the amount of Social Security benefits subject to taxation, it is necessary to calculate modified adjusted gross income, which is the sum of following:

- the taxpayer's adjusted gross income (disregarding any foreign income and savings bond exclusions)
- the taxpayer's tax-exempt interest received or accrued during the year
- one-half of the Social Security benefits for the year

If the modified adjusted gross income is $25,000 or less for a single taxpayer ($32,000 or less for married taxpayers filing jointly), Social Security benefits are not taxable. If the modified adjusted gross income is between $25,001 and $34,000 ($32,001 to $44,000 for married taxpayers filing jointly), up to 50 percent of the Social Security benefit is includible in taxable income. If the modified adjusted gross income exceeds $34,000 ($44,000 for married taxpayers filing jointly), up to 85 percent of the Social Security benefit is includible in taxable income. The exact amount of the taxable Social Security benefit is determined by complex formulas that are beyond the scope of this discussion.

WORKERS' COMPENSATION BENEFITS

Prior to the passage of workers' compensation laws, it was difficult for employees to receive compensation for their work-related injuries or diseases. Group benefits were meager, and the Social Security program had not yet been enacted. The only recourse for employees was to sue their employer for damages. In addition to the time and expense of such actions (as well as the possibility of being fired), the probability of a worker winning such a suit was small because of the three common-law defenses available to employers. Under the contributory negligence doctrine, a worker could not collect if his or her negligence contributed in any way to the injury. Under the fellow-servant doctrine, the worker could not collect if the injury had resulted from the negligence of a fellow worker. And finally, under the assumption-of-risk doctrine, a worker could not recover if he or she had knowingly assumed the risks inherent in the trade.

workers' compensation law

To help solve the problem of uncompensated injuries, each state enacted a *workers' compensation law* to require employers to provide benefits to employees for losses resulting from work-related accidents or diseases. These laws are based on the principle of liability without fault. Essentially, an employer is absolutely liable for providing the benefits prescribed by the workers' compensation laws, regardless of whether the employer would be considered legally liable in the absence of these laws. However, benefits (with the possible exception of medical expense benefits) are subject to statutory maximums.

In addition to all states, the federal government has enacted several similar laws. The Federal Employees Compensation Act provides benefits for the employees of the federal government and the District of Columbia. The Federal Employer's Liability Act covers railroad employees and workers aboard ships, and the Longshore and Harbor Workers' Compensation Act covers stevedores, dock workers, and workers who repair ships.

Type of Law

Most workers' compensation laws are compulsory for all employers covered under the law. A few states have elective laws, but most employers elect coverage. If they do not, their employees are not entitled to workers' compensation benefits and must sue for damages resulting from occupational accidents or diseases. In such cases, the employer loses the right to the three common-law defenses previously described.

Financing of Benefits

Most states allow employers to comply with the workers' compensation law by purchasing coverage from insurance companies. Several of these states also have competitive state funds from which employers may obtain coverage, but these funds usually provide benefits for fewer employers than insurance companies provide. Five states have monopolistic state funds that are the only source for obtaining coverage under the law.

Almost all states, including some with monopolistic state funds, allow employers to self-insure their workers' compensation exposure. These employers must generally post a bond or other security and receive the approval of the agency administering the law. While the number of firms using self-insurance for workers' compensation is small, these firms account for approximately one-half the employees covered under such laws.

In virtually all cases, the employer bears the full cost of providing workers' compensation benefits.

Covered Occupations

Although estimates are that workers' compensation laws cover about 90 percent of the workers in the United States, the percentage varies among states from less than 70 percent to more than 95 percent. Many laws exclude certain agricultural, domestic, and casual employees. Some laws also exclude employers with a small number of employees. Furthermore, coverage for employees of state and local governments is not universal.

Eligibility

Before an employee can be eligible for benefits under a workers' compensation law, he or she must work in an occupation covered by that law and be disabled or killed by a covered injury or illness. The typical workers' compensation law covers accidental occupational injuries (including death) arising out of and in the course of employment. In all states, this includes injuries arising out of accidents, which the workers' compensation law generally defines as sudden and unexpected events at a definite time and place. Most workers' compensation laws exclude self-inflicted injuries and accidents resulting from an employee's intoxication or willful disregard of safety rules.

Every state has some coverage for illnesses resulting from occupational diseases. While the trend is toward full coverage for occupational diseases, some states cover only those diseases specifically listed in the law.

Benefits

Workers' compensation laws typically provide disability income benefits as well as rehabilitative services for disabled workers. In addition, they provide benefits for medical care as well as death benefits.

Disability Income

For an employee to collect disability income benefits under workers' compensation laws, his or her injuries must result in one of the following four categories of disability:

- temporary total. The employee cannot perform any of the duties of his or her regular job. However, full recovery is expected. Most workers' compensation claims involve this type of disability.
- permanent total. The employee will never be able to perform any of the duties of his or her regular job or any other job. Several states also list in their laws certain disabilities (such as loss of both eyes or both arms) that result in an employee automatically being considered permanently and totally disabled even though future employment might be possible.
- temporary partial. The employee can perform only some of the duties of his or her regular job but is neither totally nor permanently disabled. For example, an employee with a sprained back might work part-time.
- permanent partial. The employee has a permanent injury, such as the loss of an eye, but may be able to perform his or her regular job or may be retrained for another one.

Most workers' compensation laws have an elimination period for disability income benefits that varies from 2 to 7 days. However, benefits frequently are paid retroactively to the date of the injury if an employee is disabled for a specified time or is confined to a hospital.

Disability income benefits under workers' compensation laws are a function of an employee's average weekly wage over some period, commonly the 13 weeks immediately preceding the disability. For total disabilities, benefits are a percentage (usually 66 2/3 percent) of the employee's average weekly wage, subject to maximum and minimum amounts that vary substantially by state. Maximums in the range of $400 to $700 per week are common, and they are over $1,000 per week in a few states. Benefits for permanent total disabilities usually continue for life but have a limited duration (such as 10 years) in a few states.

Benefits for partial disabilities are calculated as a percentage of the difference between the employee's wages before and after the disability. In most states, the duration of these benefits is subject to a statutory maximum. Several states also provide lump-sum payments to employees whose permanent partial disabilities involve the loss (or loss of use) of an eye, an arm, or other body member. These benefits, which are determined by a schedule in the law, may be paid in lieu of, or in addition to, periodic disability income benefits.

Rehabilitation Benefits

All states have provisions in their workers' compensation laws for rehabilitative services for disabled workers. Benefits are included for medical rehabilitation as well as for vocational rehabilitation, including training, counseling, and job placement.

Other Benefits

Workers' compensation laws usually provide benefits for medical expenses in full, with no limitations on time or amount. They are not subject to an elimination period.

Most workers' compensation laws provide two types of death benefits: burial allowances and cash income payments to survivors.

Burial allowances are a flat amount in each state, and vary from $300 to $5,000 (benefits of $1,000 and $1,500 are common).

Cash income payments to survivors, like disability income benefits, are a function of the worker's average wage prior to the fatal injury. Benefits are usually paid only to a surviving spouse and to children under 18.

Tax Treatment

Workers' compensation benefits are received free of federal income taxes.

Extent of Coverage

Labor unions have been particularly critical of workers' compensation insurance because of its incomplete coverage of workers. State laws do not cover all workers because of elective laws, numerical exemptions, and exclusions or less-than-full coverage for certain groups. These groups include agricultural, domestic, and casual workers. Estimates indicate that nationally between 10 percent and 15 percent of workers are without coverage; this figure is as high as 30 percent in some states.

STATE TEMPORARY DISABILITY BENEFITS

temporary disability laws

At their inception, state unemployment insurance programs were usually designed to cover only unemployed persons who were both willing and able to work. Benefits were denied to anyone who was unable to work for any reason, including disability. Some states amended their unemployment insurance laws to cover the unemployed who subsequently became disabled. Five states—California, Hawaii, New Jersey, New York, and Rhode Island—and Puerto Rico went one step further by enacting *temporary disability laws* under which employees can collect disability income benefits regardless of whether their disability begins while they are employed or unemployed. While there are variations among the states, these laws—often referred to as nonoccupational disability laws because benefits are not provided for disabilities covered under workers' compensation laws—are generally patterned after the state unemployment insurance law and provide similar benefits.

In the six jurisdictions that have temporary disability laws, most employers must provide coverage for their employees. In most jurisdictions (except Rhode Island, which has a monopolistic state fund), coverage may be obtained from either a competitive state fund or private insurance companies. Private coverage must provide at least the benefits the law prescribes, but the coverage may be more comprehensive. As with workers' compensation insurance, self-insurance is generally permitted. Depending on the jurisdiction, an employer's program cost is borne entirely by employee contributions, entirely by employer contributions, or by contributions from both parties.

Eligibility

Before an employee is eligible for benefits under a temporary disability law, the employee must satisfy (1) an earnings or employment requirement, (2) the definition of disability, and (3) an elimination period.

Earnings or Employment Requirement

In order to qualify for benefits, every jurisdiction requires that an employee must have worked for a specified time and/or received a minimum amount of wages within some specific period prior to disability.

Definition of Disability

Most laws define disability as a worker's inability to perform his or her regular or customary work because of a nonoccupational injury or illness, including maternity. As with workers' compensation laws, certain types of disabilities are not covered. In most jurisdictions, these include disabilities caused by self-inflicted injuries or by illegal acts.

Elimination Period

The usual elimination period is 7 days. However, in some jurisdictions, the law waives the elimination period if the employee is hospitalized.

Benefits

Benefits are a percentage of the employee's average weekly wage for some period prior to disability. The benefits usually range from 50 percent to

66 2/3 percent, subject to maximum and minimum amounts. Most states have a maximum weekly benefit of $500 or less, but it is almost $1,000 in California. Benefits are generally paid for at least 26 weeks if the employee remains disabled that long. However, they can continue for up to one year in California.

Tax Treatment

Benefits are considered a form of unemployment compensation for federal tax purposes and subject to income taxation.

COORDINATION OF SOCIAL INSURANCE BENEFITS WITH INDIVIDUAL INSURANCE

When disability income policies were first issued, there was no reason for insurers to be concerned with social insurance benefits because social insurance programs did not exist. However, the passage of such programs and the magnitude of their benefits made it imperative that insurers consider these benefits in determining the amount of coverage they would issue. As explained in a later section of the chapter, group insurance benefits usually have direct offsets for such benefits, which is not the case with individual policies.

Initially, individual insurers took a piecemeal approach. For example, they might issue a base amount of coverage and then use riders to provide additional benefits when Social Security benefits or workers' compensation benefits were not available. Some insurers also issued policies that covered nonoccupational disabilities only.

social insurance offset rider

Today, the most common practice is to issue a basic amount of coverage in conjunction with a *social insurance offset rider*. Such riders vary among insurers, but they essentially provide additional benefits (often referred to as social insurance substitute benefits) when specified social insurance programs pay nothing or less than the benefit under the rider.

Example: Martin is self-employed and applied for an individual disability income policy. The insurer's guidelines indicated that it could issue a policy with a monthly benefit of up to $4,500. However, if Martin is disabled and able to collect Social Security benefits, the Social Security benefits will amount to $2,000 per month. Therefore, the insurer is willing to issue Martin a policy with a basic benefit of $2,500 per month. To this policy, the insurer will attach a social insurance offset rider with a monthly benefit of $2,000.

An insurer may evaluate each applicant individually to determine the appropriate amount of coverage under a social insurance offset rider. However, it is common for an insurer to have a basic benefit limit and then provide an additional amount of coverage under the social insurance rider. This latter benefit reflects the approximate Social Security benefit available to persons at their annual income levels. Table 13-1 shows one insurer's issue/participation limits for selected annual earned incomes if an individual pays for the coverage. The basic benefit, but not the benefit under the social insurance rider, is higher if an employer pays the premium. This is because the employer-paid benefits result in taxable income.

At a minimum, social insurance offset riders apply to Social Security and workers' compensation benefits payable to an insured. Many riders also apply to benefits paid under state temporary disability laws and any other government disability program. There are some insurers that offset Social Security benefits only. In such cases, the rider is usually referred to as a Social Security offset rider.

These riders may also differ with respect to how the offset is applied. The most common approach uses a dollar-for-dollar offset. This means that the insurer reduces the monthly benefit available under the social insurance rider by the amount of the social insurance benefit. This insurer typically freezes the offset amount so that benefits under the rider are not reduced if the social insurance benefit increases because of cost-of-living adjustments.

TABLE 13-1
Issue/Participation Limits

Annual Earned Income	Basic Monthly Benefit	Monthly Benefit under Social Insurance Rider	Total Monthly Benefit
$20,000	$500	$800	$1,300
30,000	700	1,100	1,800
40,000	1,000	1,300	2,300
50,000	1,300	1,600	2,900
60,000	1,500	1,800	3,300
70,000	1,800	1,900	3,700
80,000	2,100	2,000	4,100
100,000	2,800	2,000	4,800
120,000	3,350	2,000	5,350
140,000	3,850	2,000	5,850
160,000	4,600	2,000	6,600
180,000	5,300	2,000	7,300
200,000	5,700	2,000	7,700
300,000	7,500	2,000	9,500
400,000	9,000	2,000	11,000
500,000	10,200	2,000	12,200

Example: Let us return to Martin in the previous example. If he does not qualify for Social Security disability benefits, he will receive the full additional $2,000 monthly benefit payable under the rider. If he does qualify for Social Security disability benefits, he will receive nothing under the rider if the Social Security benefits are $2,000 or more. However, if the Social Security benefits are only $1,879, he will receive $121 dollars from the rider. If the Social Security benefit increases to $1,923 next year as the result of the annual cost-of-living increase, he will still receive $121 under the rider.

Insurers sometimes use one of two other approaches to determine the benefit under the offset rider. Under the first approach, the insurer pays no benefits if the insured receives social insurance benefits, regardless of the amount. Under the other approach, the insurer reduces the benefits payable under the rider by a percentage of any social insurance benefits received.

It is obviously in the insurer's interest to have an insured apply for social insurance benefits, and many insurers assist the insured in performing this task. It is also common for insurers to deny benefits if an insured fails to apply for any potential social insurance benefits.

One final point is worth mentioning: The rider may reduce benefits at any time. For example, an insured may collect full benefits under the rider but later be eligible for Social Security benefits because of a deteriorating condition. The insurer then reduces the benefits under the rider. Conversely, an insured may no longer meet the Social Security definition of disability. The insurer restores any reduction under the rider as long as the insured still meets the insurer's definition of disability.

EMPLOYER-PROVIDED SICK-LEAVE PLANS

sick-leave plan

Employers provide short-term disability benefits to employees through two approaches: sick-leave plans and short-term disability income insurance plans. *Sick-leave plans* (often called salary continuation plans) are usually uninsured and generally fully replace lost income for a limited period, starting on the first day of disability. In contrast, short-term disability income insurance plans (which are covered in the next section of this chapter) usually provide benefits that replace only a portion of an employee's lost income and often contain an elimination period before benefits start, particularly for sickness.

paid time off (PTO) program

In recent years, a few employers have combined their sick-leave plans with other types of payments for time not worked, such as vacations, holidays, and personal leave into a single *paid time off (PTO) program*. One rationale for such programs is that many employees view sick days as a right and will take the maximum number of days available, whether sick or not. With a PTO program, the employer gives an employee a specified bank of days off with full pay, and the employee can take this paid time off for any reason. The bank of days is usually slightly less than the total number of days under the prior programs, but within the range of the number of days that most employees took off. PTO programs have generally had the effect of lowering the number of days that employees call in sick, because employees can use these days for other purposes. This lowers an employer's benefit costs and minimizes other problems associated with unscheduled absences.

Eligibility

probationary period

Almost all sick-leave plans are limited to permanent full-time employees. Most plans also require an employee to satisfy a short *probationary period* (commonly 1 to 3 months), which is the period an employee must work before being eligible for benefits. Sick-leave plans may also be limited to certain employees, such as top management or nonunion employees.

Benefits

Most sick-leave plans are designed to initially provide benefits equal to 100 percent of an employee's regular pay. Most plans, however, provide a reduced level of benefits after an initial period of full pay.

Several approaches are used to determine the duration of benefits. The most traditional approach credits eligible employees with a certain amount of sick leave, such as 10 days each year. Most plans with this approach allow employees to accumulate unused sick leave up to a maximum amount, which rarely exceeds 6 months (sometimes specified as 180 days or 26 weeks).

Another approach bases the duration of benefits on an employee's length of service. For example, an employee with less than 3 months of service may get no sick days. After this limited period, the employee may get 5 days during the next year, with the number of days increasing to 30 with 10 years of service.

An alternative to this approach provides benefits for a uniform length of time (such as 26 weeks) to all employees, except possibly those with short periods of service. However, benefits are reduced to less than full pay after some period that is related to an employee's length of service. For example, an employee with 2 years of service might get 4 weeks of sick leave at full pay and 22 additional weeks at half pay. After each additional year of service, the number of weeks at full pay increases by 4, until all 26 weeks would be available at full pay after 6 years of service.

Most sick-leave plans are coordinated with social insurance programs. For example, if an employee is entitled to 100 percent of pay and receives 60 percent of pay as a workers' compensation benefit, the sick-leave plan pays the remaining 40 percent.

EMPLOYER-PROVIDED GROUP DISABILITY INCOME PLANS

Insured group disability income plans consist of two distinct products: short-term coverage and long-term coverage. In many respects, the contractual provisions of both short-term and long-term disability income contracts are the same or very similar. In other respects—notably, the eligibility requirements, the definition of disability, and the amount and duration of benefits—they differ significantly.

Eligibility

Many of the eligibility requirements in group disability income insurance plans are similar to those in other types of group insurance contracts. In addition to being in a covered classification, an employee must usually work full-time and be actively at work before coverage commences. Any requirements concerning probationary periods, insurability, and premium contributions must also be satisfied.

Disability income insurance plans frequently differ in both the classes of employees who are eligible for coverage and the length of the probationary period. Employers are more likely to provide short-term benefits to a wider range of employees, and it is not unusual for short-term plans to cover all full-time employees.

Long-term disability plans often limit benefits to salaried employees because claims experience has traditionally been less favorable for hourly paid employees. Some long-term plans also exclude employees below a certain salary level because this category of employees, like hourly paid employees, is considered to have a reasonable level of benefits under Social Security.

Long-term disability income plans tend to have longer probationary periods than short-term disability income plans. While the majority of short-term disability plans either have no probationary period or have a probationary period of 3 months or less, it is common for long-term disability plans to have probationary periods ranging from 3 months to 1 year. Whereas short-term plans require only that an employee be actively at work on the date he or she is otherwise eligible for coverage, long-term plans sometimes require that the employee be on the job for an extended period (such as 30 days) without illness or injury before coverage becomes effective.

Definition of Disability

Disability income insurance contracts pay benefits only if the employee meets the definition of disability as specified in the contract. Virtually all short-term disability income insurance contracts define disability as *the total inability of the employee to perform each and every duty of his or her regular occupation.* A small minority of contracts use a more restrictive definition, requiring that an employee be unable to engage in any occupation for compensation. Partial disabilities are usually not covered, but a few newer plans do provide benefits. In addition, the majority of short-term contracts limit coverage to nonoccupational disabilities because employees have workers' compensation benefits for occupational disabilities.

A few long-term disability income contracts use the same liberal definition of disability that is commonly used in short-term contracts, but the term *material duties* often replaces the term *each and every duty.* The majority of long-term disability contracts use a dual definition under which benefits are paid for some period of time (usually 24 or 36 months) as long as an employee is unable to perform his or her regular occupation. After that time, the contract provides benefits only if the employee is unable to engage in any occupation for which he or she is qualified by reason of training, education, or experience. The purpose of this combined definition is to require and encourage a disabled employee after a period of time to adjust his or her lifestyle and earn a livelihood in another occupation.

A more recent definition of disability in some long-term contracts contains both an occupation test and an earnings test. Under the occupation test, a person is totally disabled if he or she meets the definition of disability as described in the previous paragraph. However, if a person does not satisfy the occupation test, he or she is still considered disabled as long as the person satisfies an earnings test—that is, his or her income has dropped by a stated percentage, such as 20 percent, because of injury or sickness. This newer definition makes a group insurance contract similar to an individual disability income policy that provides residual benefits.

The definition of disability in long-term contracts may differ from that in short-term contracts in several other respects. Long-term contracts are somewhat more likely to provide benefits for partial disabilities. However, the amount and duration of such benefits may be limited when compared with those for total disabilities, and the receipt of benefits is usually contingent on a previous period of total disability. In addition, most long-term contracts provide coverage for both occupational and nonoccupational disabilities. Finally, short-term contracts usually have the same definition of disability for all classes of employees. Some long-term contracts use different definitions for different classes of employees—one definition for most employees and a more liberal definition for executives or salaried employees.

Exclusions

Under certain circumstances, disability income contracts do not pay benefits even if an employee satisfies the definition of disability. Common exclusions under both short-term and long-term disability income contracts specify that no benefits will be paid

- for any period during which the employee is not under the care of a physician
- for any disability caused by an intentionally self-inflicted injury
- unless the period of disability commenced while the employee was covered under the contract
- if (or to the extent that) benefits are payable under workers' compensation or similar laws

It was once common for contracts to exclude disabilities resulting from pregnancy. Such an exclusion is now illegal under federal law if an employer has 15 or more employees. Employers with fewer than 15 employees may still exclude pregnancy disabilities unless they are subject to state laws to the contrary.

Additional exclusions are often found in long-term contracts. These commonly deny benefits for disabilities resulting from

- war, whether declared or undeclared
- participation in an assault or felony. Some insurers have recently expanded this exclusion to include the commission of any crime.
- mental illness, alcoholism, or drug addiction. However, most contracts provide benefits for an employee who is confined in a hospital or institution that specializes in the care and treatment of such disorders; other contracts provide employees with benefits but limit their duration (such as for 24 months per disability).
- preexisting conditions

The purpose of the exclusion for preexisting conditions is to counter the adverse selection and potentially large claims that could occur if an employer established a group disability income plan or if an employee elected to participate in a plan because of some known condition that is likely to result in disability. Although variations exist, a common provision for preexisting conditions excludes coverage for any disability that commences during the first 12 months an employee is covered under the contract if the employee received treatment or medical advice for the disabling condition both (1) prior to the date the employee became eligible for coverage and (2) within 90 consecutive days prior to the commencement of the disability.

Benefits

Group disability income contracts contain benefit schedules that classify employees and specify the amount of disability income that the contract provides. They also include provisions pertaining to the length of time that benefits are paid and the coordination of benefits with other available sources of disability income.

Benefit Schedules

There are a variety of benefit schedules in group disability income contracts. Benefits may be available to all employees or limited to specific groups of employees. In addition, benefits may be expressed as either flat-dollar amounts, varying dollar amounts by classification, or a percentage of earnings.

Giving a disabled employee a level of income that is comparable to his or her regular earnings encourages absenteeism and diminishes the incentive to return to work. In general, employers design disability income plans to provide a level of benefits that replaces between 50 and 70 percent of an employee's gross income. Although this may appear to represent a substantial reduction of regular earnings, remember that a disabled employee does not have the usual expenses associated with working, such as transportation costs. In addition, disability income benefits financed with after-tax employee contributions are not subject to Social Security and Medicare taxes, and employer-financed benefits are subject to Social Security and Medicare taxes only during the last calendar month in which an employee worked and during the 6 months that follow.

Many short-term disability income plans and the majority of long-term plans base benefits on a single percentage of regular earnings (excluding bonuses and overtime). This percentage varies widely for short-term plans, and benefits as low as 50 percent or as high as 100 percent are not unusual. Many insurers are reluctant to underwrite plans that provide benefits higher than 70 percent of earnings. In some instances, short-term plans may use different percentages, such as 100 percent of earnings for 4 weeks and 70 percent of earnings for the remaining benefit period. The length of time for which an employee receives the higher level of benefits may also be a function of the length of the employee's service.

Long-term plans typically provide benefits that range from 50 to 70 percent of earnings; 60 and 66 2/3 are the most prevalent percentages. Some plans also use a sliding scale, such as 66 2/3 percent of the first $4,000 of monthly earnings and 40 percent of earnings in excess of $4,000.

Plans that determine benefits as a percentage of earnings also commonly place a maximum dollar amount on the benefit that they provide, regardless of earnings. For example, a long-term plan might be subject to a monthly maximum that varies from $1,000 for some small groups to $4,000 or $5,000 (and sometimes higher) for large groups. The purpose of the maximum is to prevent the absolute benefit from being so high that an employee, by adjusting his or her lifestyle, could live comfortably on the disability income benefit and thus have no financial incentive to return to work.

Period of Benefits

To determine the period for which benefits are paid, it is necessary to determine when benefits begin and how long they are paid. In both respects, there are differences between short-term and long-term plans.

Short-Term Plans. Short-term disability income contracts commonly contain an elimination period, which is the length of time for which an employee must be disabled before benefits begin. The typical short-term contract has no elimination period for disabilities resulting from accidents, but has an elimination period of 1 to 7 days for disabilities resulting from sicknesses. Some plans have a single elimination period that applies to disabilities from either accidents or sicknesses; a few plans have no elimination periods for either. Elimination periods are occasionally longer than 7 days, particularly when there is a sick-leave plan to provide benefits during the initial portion of a disability. In a few cases, plans pay benefits retroactively to the date of disability if the disability lasts for a predetermined period, but it is generally felt that retroactive benefits cause employees to prolong their return to work in order to receive benefits for the full period of their disability.

Once an employee begins to receive benefit payments under a short-term disability contract, the benefits continue until the end of the benefit period the contract specifies as long as the employee remains disabled for that long. Although short-term contracts may provide benefits up to 2 years (with long-term contracts providing benefits for periods over 2 years), benefits rarely continue for more than 1 year. In fact, the majority of short-term contracts stipulate that benefits last for either 13 or 26 weeks; the latter period is more prevalent.

Long-Term Plans. Long-term disability income plans have elimination periods of 3 to 6 months; 6 months is most common. The length of the elimination period often corresponds to the length of time benefits are paid under a firm's short-term disability income plan or salary continuation plan. Unlike short-term plans, the elimination periods for sicknesses and accidents are the same.

Long-term disability income benefits may be paid for a duration as short as 2 years or as long as the disabled employee's lifetime. At one time, it was common for long-term disability income benefits to stop at age 65, but an age 65 termination limit is no longer permissible under the Age Discrimination in Employment Act. Several different approaches that are acceptable under the act are now used for older employees. In a few cases, benefits are paid until age 70 for any disability that occurred before that age. For disabilities occurring at age 70 or later, benefits are paid for a reduced duration. A more common approach is to use a graded benefit period and give benefits to age 65 for employees who are disabled before a specified age. Employees disabled after the specified age receive benefits for a limited duration, as shown in table 13-2.

TABLE 13-2
Duration of Disability Income Benefits

Age at Commencement of Disability	Benefit Duration
59 and younger	To age 65
60–64	5 years
65–69	To age 70
70–74	1 year
75 and older	6 months

Integration with Social Insurance and Other Benefits

To minimize the possibility of an employee's receiving total benefits higher than his or her pre-disability earnings, disability income plans commonly stipulate that benefits are integrated with other sources of disability income. In general, most states' insurance laws or regulations allow a reduction in plan benefits because of any payments from social insurance programs and other group insurance or retirement plans the employer provides, but not because of benefits from individual disability income contracts unless the employer purchased them.

Benefits under short-term plans are generally integrated with (1) workers' compensation benefits, if the plan covers occupational disabilities, (2) temporary disability laws, if they are applicable, and (3) Social Security benefits, if the maximum benefit period is longer than 5 months.

Long-term disability income benefits are usually integrated with benefits provided under the following:

- Social Security
- workers' compensation laws
- temporary disability laws
- other insurance plans for which the employer makes a contribution or payroll deduction

- pension plans for which the employer has made a contribution or payroll deduction to the extent that the employee elects to receive retirement benefits because of disability
- earnings from employment, either with the employer or from other sources

It is possible for the integration with other benefits to totally eliminate a long-term disability benefit. To prevent this from happening, many plans provide (and some states require) payment of a minimum benefit, such as $50 or $100 per month. Most plans also contain a provision freezing the amount of any Social Security reduction at the initial level that was established when the claim began.

As a general rule, both the insured and the insurer profit if the insured is able to collect Social Security benefits for a disability; the insured has an increased overall benefit, and the insurer has a substantially lower claim to pay. Consequently, insurers are often willing to assist claimants by helping them file Social Security claims and appeal decisions when claims are denied.

Supplemental Benefits

It is becoming increasingly common to find group long-term disability income plans that provide employees with a base of employer-paid benefits and that allow each covered employee to purchase additional coverage at his or her own expense. For example, a plan may provide basic benefits of 50 percent of earnings and an option for an employee to increase this amount to 55, 66 2/3, or 70 percent of earnings. These *buy-up* (or supplemental) *plans* are becoming more popular because employers want to control the costs of benefits by shifting a greater burden of the cost to employees.

buy-up plan

Some plans are also designed as *carve-out* plans to provide benefits for certain employees, typically key executives. For example, an employer might design one plan to cover most of its employees, but it might cover top executives with another group plan that provides enhanced benefits in the form of a larger percentage of earnings and a more liberal definition of disability. Another variation of a carve-out plan would provide executives with a lower benefit percentage than other employees would receive, but it could include supplemental benefits in the form of individual disability income policies. In addition to more favorable policy provisions, a carve-out plan might offer better rate guarantees and an overall higher benefit than a group plan could offer. Furthermore, the portability of the individual policy might be attractive to executives but might not necessarily appeal to the employer.

carve-out (benefit plan)

Additional Benefits

Group long-term disability income contracts occasionally contain several types of additional benefits that the employer can elect to include. The most common are a cost-of-living adjustment (COLA), a pension supplement, and a survivors' benefit.

Some disability income plans have cost-of-living adjustments to prevent inflation from eroding the purchasing power of disability income benefits that an employee receives. Under the typical COLA formula, benefits increase annually during the period of disability, along with changes in the consumer price index.

Many firms make provisions in their pension plan for treating disabled employees as if they were still working and accruing pension benefits. Such provisions require that contributions on behalf of disabled employees be made to the pension plan, usually from the employer's current revenues. However, some disability income contracts stipulate that the contract will pay the contributions necessary to fund a disabled employee's accruing pension benefits.

Note also that some pension plans provide disability income benefits by allowing disabled employees to begin receiving retirement benefits when they are totally and permanently disabled. It is common, however, to limit these early retirement benefits to employees who have satisfied some minimum period of service or reached some minimum age. Recently, employee benefit consultants seem to feel that separate retirement and disability income plans are preferable.

Some long-term contracts provide a benefit to survivors in the form of continued payments after the disabled employee's death. In effect, the disability income payments are continued, possibly at a reduced amount, for periods ranging up to 24 months (3 to 6 months is more common). Payments are generally made only to eligible survivors, who typically are the spouse and unmarried children under age 21.

Other types of additional benefits are even less common. Examples include child-care payments for disabled employees who can work on a part-time basis, spousal disability benefits payable to the employee, and benefits to pay premiums for medical expense coverage.

Tax Treatment

The federal income tax treatment of employer-provided disability income benefits is described in chapter 6. In summary, benefits are included in an employee's income for tax purposes to the extent the benefits were purchased with employer funds. They are tax free to the extent an employee paid for them.

COORDINATION OF EMPLOYER-PROVIDED BENEFITS WITH INDIVIDUAL POLICIES

Just as with social insurance benefits, insurers that issue individual disability income contracts are concerned with overinsurance because of an insured's having disability income coverage under an employer-provided plan. If the insured's existing coverage is under a sick-leave plan or short-term disability income plan, the solution may be to require the insured to select an elimination period equal to the duration of these short-term benefits.

Insurers have separate issue/participation limits for those situations when an applicant wants to purchase individual disability income coverage in addition to his or her long-term disability income benefits from group insurance. As with the issue/participation limits discussed earlier in this chapter and in chapter 12 for situations involving only individual disability income policies, there are also two sets of limits for situations involving group disability income insurance coverage. Insurers use one set of limits if the applicant pays for the individual coverage and a second set if an employer pays for the individual coverage. Table 13-3 shows these limits at selected earned income levels for the same insurer used in table 13-1. It is important to note that the maximum monthly benefit allowed when there is a combination of individual and group disability income coverage is higher—often much higher—than if a person had only individual coverage.

TABLE 13-3
Maximum Issue/Participation Limits with Combination of Individual and Group Long-Term Disability Income Benefits

Annual Earned Income	Monthly Benefit If Employee Pays for Individual Coverage	Monthly Benefits If Employer Pays for Individual Coverage
$20,000	$500	$500
30,000	700	900
40,000	1,000	1,400
50,000	1,450	1,900
60,000	1,600	2,000
80,000	2,200	3,350
100,000	3,300	4,450
120,000	4,400	5,800
140,000	5,200	7,050
160,000	6,200	8,300
180,000	7,200	9,350
200,000	8,200	10,050
300,000	12,750	15,550
400,000	16,400	18,500
500,000	18,150	20,750

From these limits, insurers subtract all or a portion of the amount of other coverage—both individual and group. There is often a full-reduction if the employee pays for the coverage and benefits are not included in an employee's income for federal tax purposes. In most cases, however, the employer pays for the benefits and an employee will have taxable income when benefits are received. In this situation, the insurer often lowers the issue limit by a percent of the benefit from the employer-provided coverage. Such reductions are usually in the range of 80 percent, but possibly lower for persons in high income tax brackets.

Example: Alicia wants to purchase individual disability income coverage to supplement the monthly benefit of $4,000 that her employer's noncontributory group insurance plan provides. Because she has group insurance benefits, the insurer has a maximum issue limit of $6,200. The insurer lowers this amount by 80 percent of her group insurance benefit because it is taxable. Therefore, the insurer will issue an individual policy with a monthly benefit of $3,000 ($6,200 less 80 percent of $4,000). If Alicia is disabled, she will receive total benefits of $7,000—$3,000 from her individual policy and $4,000 from her group benefits.

It is important to point out that the existence of group insurance often eliminates the need for the issuer of an individual policy to make any adjustment for social insurance benefits because such benefits have already been integrated with the group benefits.

PERSONAL RESOURCES

Individuals often have personal resources that can be used to provide income if they are disabled. These include unearned income and net worth. Insurers are concerned with both, but there are significant variations in how they consider them when determining issue limits.

Unearned Income

As unearned income increases as a percentage of earned income, the frequency of disability claims increases and the motivation to return to work decreases after a disability commences. Most insurers reduce issue limits if unearned income exceeds a certain percentage of earned income or a specified dollar amount. For example, one insurer reduces its issue limit if an applicant's annual unearned income exceeds earned income by the lesser of 10 percent of earned income (before taxes) or $30,000. The reduction is equal to one-half the amount of earned income in excess of this threshold. Another insurer evaluates its issue limit if the applicant's unearned income exceeds 20 percent of after-tax income.

Net Worth

An individual can often liquidate net worth to generate unearned income. Some insurers have precise criteria concerning net worth. For example, one insurer will not issue a disability income policy to anyone with a net worth in excess of $5 million. Another insurer reduces its issue limit by one-half the amount that net worth exceeds $3 million. Other insurers, however, look at each case individually and are able to use discretion. For example, a person who is actively involved in his or business and has been responsible for its net worth may be properly motivated to return to work. On the other hand, an individual who has inherited significant net worth (and unearned income) may be a poor risk for disability income coverage.

CHAPTER REVIEW

Key Terms

full retirement age
disability insured
primary insurance amount (PIA)
elimination period
Ticket to Work program
workers' compensation law
temporary disability laws
social insurance offset rider
sick-leave plan
paid time off (PTO) program
probationary period
buy-up plan
carve-out (benefit plan)

Review Questions

Review questions are based on the learning objectives in this chapter. Thus, a [13-3] at the end of a question means that the question is based on learning objective 13-3. If there are multiple objectives, they are all listed.

1. Why is it important for individuals and insurers to understand the sources available to finance the loss of income from disability? [13-1]
2. How does the Social Security program determine eligibility for disability benefits? [13-2]

3. a. How are disability benefit amounts determined under Social Security? [13-2]
   b. What is the duration of the benefits? [13-2]
4. How does the Social Security program encourage the rehabilitation and return to work of disabled beneficiaries? [13-2]
5. To what extent are Social Security disability benefits subject to federal income taxation? [13-2]
6. a. What is the nature of workers' compensation programs? [13-3]
   b. To what extent do they provide disability income benefits? [13-3]
7. What is the nature of state temporary disability laws? [13-4]
8. How are social insurance benefits coordinated with individual disability income insurance? [13-5]
9. How might employer-provided sick-leave plans provide disability income benefits? [13-6]
10. a. How might the eligibility requirements under employer-provided disability income plans vary? [13-7]
    b. What is the usual definition of disability? [13-7]
11. What are the benefit provisions in employer-provided disability income plans with respect to each of the following?
    a. integration with social insurance and other benefits [13-7]
    b. supplemental and additional benefits [13-7]
    c. benefit schedules [13-7]
    d. period of benefits [13-7]
12. What are the ways in which employer-provided disability income benefits are coordinated with individual disability income policies? [13-8]
13. a. What personal resources might a person have to provide disability income? [13-9]
    b. How might insurers consider these resources when determining issue limits? [13-9]

NOTE

1. December 2006 statistics from the Social Security Administration Web site: www.ssa.gov.

14

Disability Income Policy Provisions and Riders

Learning Objectives

An understanding of the material in this chapter should enable you to

14-1. Identify the provisions in disability income policies that are common to all forms of health insurance.

14-2. Describe the provisions in disability income policies that pertain to the definition of disability.

14-3. Explain the provisions in disability income policies that apply to benefits.

14-4. Explain the provisions in disability income policies that apply to renewability and premiums.

14-5. Describe the optional riders that can be added to disability income policies to increase policy benefits.

14-6. Identify the miscellaneous types of riders that might be available for use with disability income policies.

14-7. Explain how an applicant can evaluate disability income policies and select the appropriate benefit provisions and riders.

Chapter Outline

Disability income insurance policies are among the most complex types of insurance contracts. Over time, the provisions in medical expense insurance have become somewhat uniform because of state laws and insurer practices. Provisions in long-term care insurance contracts have become more uniform because of the federal rules that pertain to long-term care insurance contracts that want to obtain "qualified" status in order for favorable tax treatment to apply to premium payments and benefits. More variations are found in disability income contracts. There tends to be less uniformity in the way policy provisions are organized as compared to other forms of health insurance. There are numerous variations in the names that insurers use to describe various types of policy provisions. In addition, the provisions may vary by underwriting class. The terminology used to describe optional riders, as well as their provisions, also vary.

The first part of the chapter looks at the provisions and riders found in disability income contracts. Because earlier chapters of this book discuss some of these provisions and riders, this chapter will not repeat that discussion but rather expand upon it when necessary. This discussion looks at disability income contracts from the perspective of the following:

- provisions common to all forms of health insurance
- provisions pertaining to the covered disabilities
- provisions pertaining to benefits
- provisions pertaining to renewability and premiums
- policy riders

As with other forms of health insurance, purchasers of disability income contracts must make certain decisions about the provisions in their contracts and the riders they will add. With proper planning, an applicant has considerable latitude in tailoring a policy to best meet his or her needs.

The final portion of this chapter looks at how an applicant for disability income insurance can evaluate and compare policies. Unfortunately, not everyone has the resources to fund fully all their financial planning needs. The chapter also addresses how a purchaser of disability income insurance may have to make decisions when the cost of coverage exceeds the applicant's available financial resources.

PROVISIONS COMMON TO ALL FORMS OF HEALTH INSURANCE

Earlier chapters addressed many of the provisions that are common to all forms of individual health insurance. Many of these provisions are a result of the Uniform Individual Accident and Sickness Policy Provision Law (UPPL) that is discussed in chapters 5 and 6. In some cases, these provisions are mandatory and must be in every disability income contract. These include provisions pertaining to the following:

- entire contract
- incontestability
- grace period
- reinstatement
- notice of claim
- claim forms
- proof of loss
- time of payment of claims
- physical examinations and autopsy
- legal action

The UPPL also has some optional provisions. Most disability income policies contain provisions that apply to misstatement of age and conformity with state statutes. Disability income policies seldom contain a provision dealing with the payment of claims when there is duplicate coverage because the underwriting process addresses this issue, as described in chapter 13. In addition, the application, which the insured signs, becomes part of the insurance contract. The insured is asked to list all current disability income insurance that he or she currently has and whether the new policy will replace any of that coverage. If the insured fails to list any existing coverage, this is a fraudulent statement that would give the insurer the right to rescind coverage. If the insured fails to follow through on canceling existing coverage, typically within 90 days of the new policy's effective date, the application often states that the insurer will rescind coverage or lower the issue limit to what would have been issued with the existing policy remaining in force. If not so stated, the insured is typically required to sign a policy amendment that has the same effect. An agent who is involved with a replacement situation also needs to be sure that he or she is in compliance with any state requirements in this regard.

One optional provision that is not commonly used but which is sometimes found in disability income policies deals with changes of occupation. If the insured has a claim after changing to a more hazardous occupation, the insurer will adjust the benefits. The payment will be what the premium would have purchased based on the premium rate for the more hazardous occupation. If the insured changes to a less hazardous occupation, the insurer lowers the premium and refunds any excess premium from the date of the occupation change. Newly issued policies rarely contain this provision, but it is found in some existing policies.

PROVISIONS PERTAINING TO COVERED DISABILITIES

There are numerous provisions in disability income policies that pertain to covered disabilities. These include definitions of disability as well as provisions for presumptive total disability and recurrent disabilities.

Definitions of Disability

Every disability income policy clearly spells out what the insurer means by the term *disability*. There is a definition of total disability. There are also definitions for partial disability, residual disability, and/or loss of earnings (if they are included in the contract). Chapter 12 covers all of these definitions in detail, including their variations.

injury

Because disability income is paid only if it arises from injury or sickness, each of these terms is also specifically defined in a policy. *Injury* is usually defined as an accidental bodily injury that occurs while the policy in force. However, a few policies use a much more restrictive definition and specify that the injury must also result from accidental means. For example, assume that an insured breaks a leg while skiing. Clearly, the insured is injured. However, the activity leading to the injury (skiing) was an intentional act, and a policy with the more restrictive definition might not consider it an injury within the policy definition. Note that some insurers use the term *accident* instead of the term *injury*, but the meaning is the same.

sickness

Sickness is usually defined as an illness or disease that is diagnosed and treated while a policy is in force. Unless specified otherwise, the definition includes both mental and physical illnesses. However, as mentioned under the section on exclusions and limitations, insurers may provide more limited benefits for mental illnesses.

Policies have a requirement that a person collecting benefits must be under the regular care of a physician during the period he or she is collecting benefits. However, many policies have a provision that the insurer will waive this requirement if the continued treatment or care is no longer beneficial or required. Most policies also state that a physician whose specialty is appropriate for treatment of the disabling injury or sickness must provide the care.

concurrent disability provision

Finally, it is common for disability income contracts to contain a *concurrent disability provision.* Such a provision states that if the insured is disabled as the result of more than one cause, the amount and duration of the benefits will not be greater than that for any one of the causes.

Presumptive Total Disability

presumptive total disability provision

In some cases, disability is of such a catastrophic nature that an insured is automatically considered to be totally disabled. Most policies contain a *presumptive total disability provision.* Under such a provision, an insured will receive benefits for a total disability if he or she has a total and complete loss of any of the following:

- the sight of both eyes
- the hearing of both ears
- the power of speech
- the entire use of two arms, two feet, or one arm and one foot

Benefits continue as long as the loss lasts until the end of the maximum policy benefit period, even if the insured returns to work. Benefits commence from the date of loss, and the insurer waives the elimination period. In addition, other requirements pertaining to total disability—such as being under the care of a physician—do not apply.

Recurrent Disability Provision

An insured may sometimes recover from a disability and no longer be eligible for disability income benefits. If the insured suffers a subsequent disability, it is important to determine whether this situation qualifies as a recurrent disability. If it does, the insurer treats it as a continuation of the prior disability. No new elimination period is required, and the benefits from the prior disability are applied to any maximum benefit period. If the new disability is not classified as recurrent, there is a new elimination period (unless it is waived, as described later) and a new maximum benefit period.

recurrent disability provision

The usual *recurrent disability provision* specifies that a new disability is considered recurrent if it arises from the same cause or causes and is not separated from the original disability by a recovery period of more than 6 or 12 months. Twelve months is the common duration for policies with lengthy benefit periods, such as for life or until age 65. Six months is common when policies have shorter benefit periods.

A subsequent disability is not considered recurrent if it arises from a different cause.

Example 1: Martha has a disability income contract that provides benefits until age 65. She received disability income benefits when she was disabled and receiving treatment for breast cancer. After her cancer was in remission, Martha returned to work and her disability income benefits ceased. Nine months later, Martha again was unable to work because her breast cancer had spread to other organs. As long as her policy has the usual 12-month period for separate disabilities, Martha is treated as having a recurrence of the original disability and benefits will commence immediately. If Martha has a period of remission (and no disability benefit payments) of more than 12 months, she will be considered to have a new disability.

Example 2: Hal returned to work 3 months ago after collecting disability income benefits because of a heart attack. He was recently disabled again when a distracted driver, who was text messaging, failed to observe a red light and hit Hal's car. This is a new disability.

PROVISIONS RELATING TO BENEFITS

Disability income policies contain numerous provisions that apply to benefits. The following discussion broadly categorizes these provisions in the following ways:

- benefit amounts
- when benefits commence
- duration of benefits
- effect of earned income on benefits
- additional types of benefits that are often a standard part of disability income policies
- exclusions and limitations
- suspension of coverage

Benefit Amounts

The full benefit amount is stated in the declarations section of a disability income policy. In many cases, an applicant selects the maximum amount of coverage that the insurer offers. However, the applicant can select a lower amount, usually in increments of $100, subject to the minimum amount of coverage for which the insurer will issue a policy. A lower limit decreases the premium accordingly. Before selecting a lower limit, however, an applicant needs to do (or have someone else do) a thorough analysis of what his or her financial situation would be like following a disability. Such an analysis typically involves cash flow projections and estimates of both necessary and discretionary uses of financial resources.

There are two primary reasons that an insured may select a lower limit than the amount of coverage an insurer is willing to write. The most common reason is cost. Not every applicant has the resources to pay for the maximum amount of coverage, particularly if a policy provides many of the often-desirable optional policy features. The example at the end of the chapter focuses on this issue. Many insurance and financial planners feel that the benefit amount is the most important policy feature, and any attempts to lower cost should first look at other alternatives, such as increasing the elimination period, lowering the maximum benefit period, and/or eliminating optional benefits.

An applicant may also feel (either rightly or wrongly) that the maximum limit available is more than is needed to sustain a desired lifestyle if a disability occurs.

Commencement of Benefits

Benefits from disability income contracts will not begin unless the insured satisfies a policy's definition of disability. In addition, the insured must satisfy the policy's elimination period.

Characteristics of the Elimination Period

The insured typically has the choice of several elimination periods. Durations of 30, 60, 90, 180, and 365 days are often available, with 90 days being the most commonly selected. Some insurers offer longer elimination periods, such as 730 days. The same elimination period almost always applies to disabilities from any cause. However, a few insurers offer a zero-day elimination period that applies only to disabilities arising from injuries.

The available elimination periods vary among insurers, and a different assortment of elimination periods may apply to different underwriting classes.

Some policies require that the elimination period be satisfied with consecutive days of disability. However, most policies allow the elimination period to be satisfied with nonconsecutive days of disability from the same cause during a specified period referred to as an *accumulation period.* This period is typically two or three times longer than the elimination period.

accumulation period

Some policies also waive future elimination periods if the insured becomes disabled within a period (often 5 years) after the end of a disability for which the insurer paid benefits.

Example: Joan has a disability income policy with an elimination period of 90 days and an accumulation period of 180 days. She was disabled and unable work for 30 days because of a back injury. After she had therapy, she returned to work to work for 15 days. Because of extreme pain, she was unable to work for another 20 days. After returning to work for an additional 10 days, Joan had major back surgery and has been unable to work for the last 6 months.

Prior to the surgery, Joan had satisfied 50 days of her elimination period. Therefore, her benefits commenced after she had been able to work for 40 additional days following her surgery.

Selecting the Elimination Period

When selecting an elimination period, an applicant needs to consider several factors. By far the most important is whether the applicant has the resources to pay living costs and other expenses until benefit payments commence. These resources may come from the insured's assets, income of other family members, or employer-provided benefits. It is important to point out that disability income benefits are paid in arrears. This means that the insurer makes the first benefit payment one month after the elimination period is satisfied. Thus, if an insured has a 90-day elimination period, he or she will receive the first benefit payment 4 months after the onset of disability.

Another important factor is cost. Because many disabilities are relatively short-term in nature, significant premium savings are available with longer elimination periods.

Example: Harold, aged 35, needs to determine the appropriate elimination period for his disability income policy, which will provide a $3,000 monthly benefit until age 65. His agent informs him that the premium will be the following for different elimination periods.

Elimination Period	Annual Premium
30 days	$2,602
60 days	$1,675
90 days	$1,241
180 days	$1,091
365 days	$1,009

Harold has an employer-provided salary continuation plan that will pay benefits for 60 days. He also has an emergency fund and can afford to support himself for another 30 days. Therefore, Harold decides that a 90-day elimination period is appropriate.

Benefit Duration

Just as with the length of the elimination period, an applicant usually has options with relation to the duration of benefits and must make a choice. The duration of benefits is referred to as the *benefit period* and is the maximum

benefit period

period that benefits are paid under the contract for a claim after the elimination period is satisfied. Unless a claim is recurrent, a new benefit period applies to each disability.

Types of Benefit Periods

Possible benefit periods include one year, 2 years, 3 years, 5 years, 10 years, to age 65 or age 67, or even the insured's lifetime. However, an insurer usually makes only a few of these options available to an applicant, and the possible choices commonly vary by underwriting class. For example, one insurer allows persons in its least favorable underwriting classes a choice of 2 years or 5 years. Persons in its most favorable underwriting classes also may elect benefits until age 65. Some insurers that previously offered benefits to age 65 have changed the benefit duration to age 67. This reflects the increase in the age that a person must attain to receive full Social Security retirement benefits. There are a few insurers that specialize in writing policies only for short durations, usually 5 years or less.

Many insurers do not offer lifetime benefits and, if they do, this option is available only to their most favorable underwriting classes. When a policy provides lifetime benefits, the insurer typically pays such benefits only if the disability commences before a specified age, such as 50, 55, or 60. Disabilities that commence after that age are often limited to benefit periods of 2 or 5 years or may terminate at a specified age, such as 65, 68, or 70. In other words, lifetime benefit payments are available only for disabilities that initially occur before a specified age and remain continuous and uninterrupted for the remainder of the insured's life.

A few insurers are willing to tailor the benefit period to almost anything the insured wishes to purchase, even though it is not one of their standard benefit periods. For example if a disability occurs, an employee might want to supplement employer-provided disability income benefits until children graduate from college in 12 years, or a business owner might want additional benefits until business loans are repaid in 7 years. If the insured is disabled, the insurer makes benefit payments only until the insured satisfies his or her specific financial obligation. At that time, the policy terminates. This type of coverage is sometimes referred to as *decreasing term disability income insurance* because the potential benefit period decreases each year that the insured is not disabled.

decreasing term disability income insurance

In most cases, the same benefit period applies to all disabilities, regardless of whether they arise from injury or sickness. However, some policies do make a distinction. These policies often provide lifetime benefits if a disability results from injury but limit benefits to age 65 or 67 if the disability stems from sickness. Although a few insurers allow an applicant to select different benefit periods for injury and sickness, the benefit period for sickness cannot exceed the benefit period for injury.

Termination of Benefits

As long as an insured remains disabled according to policy provisions, benefits are payable for the length of the benefit period. Insurers often require repeated verification that a disability still satisfies the qualifications for benefit eligibility. Benefits for total disability generally cease when an individual no longer satisfies the criteria for disability. However, as explained in chapter 12, an insured may have a policy that pays residual disability benefits if he or she returns to work at a reduced income.

Selecting the Benefit Period

The selection of the benefit period is another important decision facing an applicant for disability income insurance. In many cases, an applicant will select the maximum benefit period for which he or she is eligible. However, as the following example shows, the length of the benefit period has a significant effect on the premium for a policy.

Example: Let's return to Harold from the previous example and assume that Harold has selected a 90-day elimination period. When Harold asks his agent how the length of the benefit period will affect his annual premium, the agent provides Harold with the following information:

Benefit Period	Annual Premium
2 years	$514
5 years	$769
to age 65	$1,241
Lifetime	$1,715

Harold selects the benefit period to age 65. He feels that 2-year and 5-year benefit periods are too short, and that a lifetime benefit is too expensive.

Disabilities sometimes last for many years, and the selection of a short benefit period may prove to be woefully inadequate. However, as chapter 12 points out, many disabilities last only a few years, and only 10 percent of disabilities last more than 5 years after a 90-day elimination period. If an applicant can afford only a short elimination period, it will be adequate for many disabilities and is better than having no coverage at all.

Effect of Earned Income on Benefits

If a disability income policy provides benefits only for total disability, the policy pays benefits as long as the insured meets the definition of disability. However, as chapter 12 explains, some policies provide benefits for less-than total disability. When this is the case, the policy must define the term *earned income*. The policy must also specify whether and how it adjusts pre-disability earned income for changes in the cost of living when benefits are calculated. Chapter 12 discusses the definition of earned income, including possible variations.

When determining the amount of post-disability earned income that is considered in calculating benefits, insurers use amounts that the insured reported or will report for federal income tax purposes. However, they may allow the insured to elect either cash or accrual accounting. Under the cash method of accounting, earned income includes only that income actually received during the month for which a benefit is claimed. Under the accrual method of accounting, earned income includes income earned during the month for which benefit a is claimed, even though it might not be paid until a later period; any income received for work in prior claim periods is not considered.

Additional Benefits

Disability income contracts often contain some additional benefits as standard contract provisions. The following discussion looks at a few of these provisions, but readers should not view this as a complete discussion of every such provision that might be found or introduced in the future.

Perhaps the most common is a provision providing benefits for rehabilitation. Chapter 5 introduces this concept. The provision is often rather general and states that the insurer, at the insured's request, will consider joining in a program of rehabilitation. The insurer's role is determined by a written agreement with the insured, and the insurer pays benefits in accordance with this agreement. Even if a policy does not have a rehabilitation provision, the insurer may pay benefits for rehabilitation if it feels these benefits will lower the amount of a claim because the insured will return to work sooner.

A disability may occur if an individual donates an organ for transplant to another person. In the absence of a provision to the contrary, an insurer would not pay a disability income benefit because the disability did not arise from the insured's injury or sickness. However, the majority of policies now treat a disability resulting from such a circumstance as a sickness, without any special limitations. A few policies also treat disabilities from cosmetic surgery in the same way. Because of a policy's elimination period, it is very unlikely that such claims will occur unless the insured has complications from the surgery. Some policies that have such provisions require that the policy has been in force for a minimum of 6 or 12 months before the benefit becomes available.

transition benefit

Some policies contain what is often referred to as a *transition benefit.* With such a provision, benefits continue to survivors for a short period after an insured's death. The insured must have been receiving disability benefits at the time of death for a minimum period, often 24 months. The duration of the transition benefit is usually in the range of 3 to 6 months.

capital sum

Some policies pay what is usually called a *capital sum.* This is a lump sum payable if the insured suffers a serious injury, such as the loss of sight in one eye with no possibility of recovery or the severance of a hand or foot above the wrist or ankle. It is payable if the insured survives the loss for a certain period, such as 30 days. The lump-sum amount is typically either 6 or 12 times the policy's basic monthly disability benefit.

A few insurers build small annual benefit increases into their policies as a standard benefit. Other insurers provide this benefit as one type of rider for inflation protection. The section of this chapter on policy riders discusses such riders.

A small number of insurers have classes of disability income policies that allow the insured to convert the policy to a long-term care insurance policy. The conversion is allowed at certain ages, even if an insured is disabled, with no medical evidence of insurability required. The insurer builds the cost of the conversion privilege into the policy's basic premium. However, the premium for the new long-term care policy is based on the insured's attained age and benefits selected at the time of conversion. The insured usually has a more limited choice of benefit provisions than is available to most persons who are eligible for long-term care insurance in the regular marketplace.

Exclusions and Limitations

Although most disability income policies contain relatively few exclusions and limitations, there tends to be very little uniformity among policies regarding which exclusions and limitations are included.

Exclusions

Most, if not all policies exclude disabilities resulting from war. In addition, they have an exclusion relating to disabilities arising from any preexisting condition that was not disclosed or was misrepresented in the application. However, policies are not consistent in how they define a preexisting condition. For example, one insurer considers a condition preexisting if it resulted from an accident or sickness that occurred within 5 years before a policy's issue date. No benefits will ever be paid for such a condition. Another insurer is much more liberal and only excludes benefits for a disability that arises from a preexisting condition if the disability commences during the first 2 policy years. That insurer also uses much shorter time periods to determine whether a condition is preexisting. A 2-year period applies to any condition for which the insured received medical advice or treatment during that time. A one-year period applies to conditions for which an insured sought no advice or treatment, but for which a prudent person would usually seek advice or treatment.

Policies may also exclude benefits for disabilities in one or more of the following situations:

- occurring while the insured is a member of the armed services
- during the period an insured is incarcerated
- arising from intentional self-inflicted injury
- arising from attempted suicide
- arising from the use of drugs or alcohol
- sustained during the commission of a felony
- caused by, contributed to, or which results from the suspension, revocation, or surrender of the insured's professional license or certification.

Limitations

Policies may also contain limitations that either delay the start of benefit payments or restrict their duration.

Most policies apply a 90-day elimination period to disabilities arising from a normal pregnancy if the specified policy elimination period is of a shorter duration. If the disability arises from complications of pregnancy, the normal elimination period applies.

A few policies limit the duration of benefits if the insured resides in a country other than the United States or Canada. The period of benefits under such a limitation is normally 12 or 24 months.

Some policies limit the duration of benefits for disabilities resulting from mental or nervous disorders. Typically, the insurer pays a benefit for only 24 months unless the insured is continually confined in a mental hospital or institution. In that case, the regular benefit period applies.

Suspension of Coverage

A few disability income contracts have provisions that may result in the temporary suspension of coverage. However, such provisions are not particularly common.

One such provision suspends coverage if the insured goes on active duty in the armed services of any country or international authority. The suspension does not apply to reservists who go on active duty for 90 days or less for military training. The insured can reinstate coverage as of the date of discharge without evidence of insurability or earned income by applying in writing and commencing premium payments within 90 days of discharge. The premium is based on the age and class of risk when the policy was first issued. If the insured was disabled during military service (for which he or she should be receiving government disability income benefits), the insurer will only cover a disability arising from the same cause if the insured recovers from the initial disability for at least 6 months. When there is no policy provision for suspending coverage, there may be a provision that provides the same reinstatement right if the insurer voluntarily terminates coverage while in the armed services.

Another provision allows the insured to voluntarily suspend coverage if he or she is unemployed and receives government unemployment benefits for at least 2 months. The suspension can last for up to 6 months or until the insured returns to work, if earlier. At that time, the insured can place the policy back in force without evidence of insurability and at the prior premium rates.

RENEWABILITY AND PREMIUM PROVISIONS

Every disability insurance policy has a provision that relates to renewability. Other things being equal, the more liberal the renewability provision is, the higher the premium. Other factors also affect premiums.

Renewability Provisions

Virtually all disability income policies are guaranteed renewable for the benefit period that the insured selects. All the insured has to do to keep the policy in force is pay the required periodic premium. However, the insurer can change the premium on a class basis. This usually occurs because of adverse claims experience for a block of business.

Many policies are also noncancelable. This means that the premium, with certain exceptions, cannot change during the renewability period beyond what is specified in the policy declarations. These exceptions include additional premiums that result from increased benefit levels because of automatic benefit increases or the insured's exercising an option to purchase additional benefits.

Although noncancelable policies are common, insurers are more restrictive in who can purchase a policy with this provision than they were a few years ago. In many cases, insurers offer policy forms with the provision only to the most favorable occupation classifications.

Many policies are renewable until a specific age, often 65 or 67. After that period, the insurer may allow the policy to be renewed further on a conditionally renewable basis. Generally, the insurer allows the insured to renew the policy on an annual basis without evidence of insurability as long as the insured is gainfully employed for at least 30 hours per week. The right to renew ends on the first policy anniversary on which the insured is not so employed. Benefits are often provided only for total disability. The premium for each year of renewal is based on the insured's age and the insurer's rates in use at the time of renewal.

Other Premium Provisions

Numerous factors, discussed in this and other chapters, affect the premium for a disability income policy Although these factor are typically part of the rating process and not actual policy provisions, some of the factors are affected by choices made about specific policy provisions. Insurers typically consider all or most of the following:

- age
- health
- gender
- occupation
- geographic location
- benefit level
- elimination period
- benefit duration
- mode of premium payment
- smoking status
- optional benefits selected

Premiums are usually level during the duration of a disability income policy. However, some insurers have step-rate plans so that young professional employees can pay lower premiums for the early years of their careers. The premium is level, but lower than normal until the insured reaches a specified age, such as 35 or 40. At that time, the premium increases to a higher amount that remains level thereafter. Some insurers also offer annually renewable premiums as an alternative to level premiums. This premium structure is much like that found in an annually renewable term life insurance policy. For example, at age 35 an annually renewable premium may be about half the cost of a level premium. However, within about 15 years, the premiums will be comparable. After that point, the annual premium will exceed the level premium by increasing amounts.

Disability income policies typically contain a waiver-of-premium provision as a standard policy feature. For some policies, however, it is a rider for which the insurer charges an extra premium. In most cases, the insurer waives the premium if the insured is disabled for a period of 90 days or the policy elimination period, if shorter. Once the insured is eligible for the waiver, most insurers also refund any premiums paid during the period needed to qualify for the waiver.

There are variations in how long insurers will waive the premium. In most cases, the waiver lasts as long as premiums are payable and the insured is receiving benefits. However, some insurers terminate the waiver at age 65 or age 67 if a policy has lifetime benefits. Some insurers continue to waive the premium for a period (often 90 days) after the insurer returns to work.

As with the elimination period, the insurer may require that the period to qualify for the waiver of premium be satisfied with consecutive days of disability. Other insurers allow the use of nonconsecutive days.

OPTIONAL RIDERS

There are many types of optional riders available to purchasers of disability income polices. These are divided into three categories. The first category includes riders designed to offset social insurance benefits, and chapter 13 discusses these riders.

The second category consists of riders designed to increase policy benefits, either before after a claim occurs. The three types of such riders include the

automatic increase rider

- *automatic increase rider*. This rider automatically adjusts policy benefits each year, based on cost-of-living increases. The increase is in the benefit amount prior to the time a disability occurs.

future increase option rider

- *future increase option rider*. This rider gives the insured the option to increase policy benefits at periodic intervals without evidence of insurability. There is the potential to purchase significant amounts of coverage in excess of what an automatic increase rider provides. Again, the increase is in the benefit amount prior to the time a disability occurs.

cost-of-living adjustment rider

- *cost-of-living adjustment rider*. This rider adjusts claim payments during the period of disability for changes in the cost of living.

Most insurers offer the riders in these first two categories, and it is common for applicants to select them. In the third category, there are numerous other miscellaneous riders that some insurers also make available to applicants. However, they are elected by far fewer applicants than the previously mentioned riders.

As with the policy provisions described earlier, there are variations among insurers with respect to the provisions of these riders as well as their names. Often the terminology *benefit* or *option* is used rather than the term *rider.*

Automatic Increase Rider

Most individuals receive annual pay increases that are at least equal to cost-of-living changes. The purpose of the automatic increase rider is to increase the amount of insurance protection at approximately the same percentage. The typical rider provides that the basic amount of coverage under the policy will increase on each annual policy anniversary by a specified percentage. In some polices, this is a flat percentage. Four percent is often used because it approximates the historic long-term average annual increase in the cost of living. In most cases, the increase is based on the actual change in the consumer price index (CPI) during the prior year. The increase, however, is usually subject to a maximum annual percentage, such as 8 percent, and may also be subject to a minimum percentage, such as 3 or 4 percent. The increase is typically on a compound interest basis, but it may be on a simple interest basis.

Example: Jerry purchased a disability income policy with a monthly benefit of $4,000. The policy has an automatic increase rider that increases the benefit amount by the CPI, subject to a minimum annual increase of 4 percent and a maximum increase of 8 percent. Assuming the CPI over the next year is 3.5 percent, Jerry's policy benefit will increase by 4 percent to $4,160 on the policy's first annual anniversary. Further, assume that the CPI increase is 5 percent the following year. Jerry's benefit will increase by this percentage. If the increase is based on simple interest basis, the additional amount of protection will be 5 percent of the original $4,000 benefit, or $200. Therefore, Jerry will then have $4,360 of protection. If the increase is on a compound interest basis, the 5 percent is applied to the prior year's benefit of $4,160, and Jerry's protection will increase to $4,368.

Automatic benefit increases are exactly that—automatic—and no evidence of medical insurability is required. In addition, the insured does not have to justify any financial need for the additional coverage. The insured is sent a notice of the benefit increase and is billed an amount that reflects an increased premium for the additional coverage at attained-age rates. However, the insured does not have to accept the increase. He or she may notify the insurer and have the coverage and premium adjusted to the prior year's amounts.

The rider is usually effective for a limited period, most often 5 years. However, the rider often terminates if the insured fails to accept a certain number of automatic increases, such as two. At the termination of the rider, the insured can usually renew it as long as he or she is under a certain age, such as 60. Renewal does not require evidence of medical insurability. However, it is contingent upon the insured's demonstrating that the amount of coverage then in force does not exceed the insurer's underwriting limits.

If an insured is disabled, benefit payments are based on the amount of coverage in force at the commencement of disability. They remain level as long as the insured remains disabled unless the insured has some type of cost-of-living adjustment rider. However, policy benefits for future disabilities sometimes continue to increase.

Example: Let's return to the prior example of Jerry. Assume that Jerry is disabled 2 years after he purchased his policy and has a monthly benefit of $4,368. In the absence of a cost-of-living adjustment rider, Jerry's benefit would remain level at that amount during the claim period. When Jerry recovers 2 years later, his insurer treats him as having accepted the automatic benefit increase and having the additional premium paid by the waiver-of-premium provision. Therefore, if the benefit would have increased to $4,800—for example, if he had not been disabled—it will also increase to $4,800 on his recovery.

Because benefit increases are automatic and most insureds accept them, there is minimal adverse selection with this type of rider. As a result, its cost is relatively modest. For, example one insurer charges an additional annual premium of about $50 for a 45-year-old male who initially elects a monthly $5,000 benefit for disability income coverage.

Future Increase Option Rider

Few provisions or riders for disability income insurance have as many variations in what an insurer titles it as the future increase option rider. It sometimes goes by such names as an additional purchase benefit, a guarantee of insurability rider, or a guaranteed purchase option. However, no matter what its name, it has the same basic purpose—to allow the insured to apply for additional amounts of coverage in the future without providing medical evidence of insurability. This rider is of particular value to persons who expect to have significant income increases over their remaining working years.

The typical rider allows the insured to apply for additional amounts of insurance at specific intervals in the future. For example, the option dates are often on each policy anniversary that is nearest the insured's 25th, 30th, 45th, 40th, 45th, and 50th birthday. Some policies may also allow further option dates, such as at age 55 and age 60. In general, the insured can exercise the option within the period that begins either 30 or 60 days before an option date and ends 30 or 31 days after the option date. There may also be special option dates, such as the following:

- the insured's marriage
- the birth of the insured's child
- the completion of the insured's legal adoption of a child
- the termination of group coverage by the insured's employer
- the date an insured's annual earned income is 20 percent greater than the last time an insurer issued a policy on the insured

Most riders have a specified amount of coverage that an insured can request as a special option as well as an overall maximum amount of additional coverage available under the rider. The following example is typical of those issued by the majority of insurers.

Example: Shirley, aged 33, recently purchased a disability income policy that allows her to apply for additional coverage on the policy anniversary nearest her 35th birthday and each 5 years thereafter until she is 55. At each option date, she can apply for up to $1,000 of additional coverage. This means that over the life of her policy, she will be able to increase her disability income benefits by as much as \$5,000. Her policy specifies this is an absolute maximum and will not increase if she exercises any special options. In other words, the exercise of a special option will mean that she will be unable to exercise any future options after she has met the \$5,000 maximum limit. In addition, the failure to exercise any available option reduces the maximum by \$1,000.

Some insurers take a different approach, as the following example shows:

Example: Rod, Shirley's twin brother, purchased a disability income policy that specifies only a \$5,000 additional benefit under his future increase option rider. Until he is age 45, he can purchase any amount of coverage on any annual policy anniversary date until he reaches the aggregate \$5,000 limit. At age 45 and older, his maximum annual increase can be no more than one-third of the maximum benefit limit during any option period—assuming of course that he has not already obtained the maximum amount of additional coverage.

The previous discussion used the word *apply*. Although the insurer cannot use medical underwriting, the amount of additional coverage an insurer will actually issue is limited by the insurer's financial underwriting criteria that it applies to earned income, employment, and existing insurance. In other words, the insured is treated just like a new applicant in determining insurance limits.

Example: Jill applied to exercise an option to purchase \$1,000 of additional disability income coverage. After analyzing her financial situation and existing disability income coverage, the insurer decided that the requested amount exceeded its underwriting limit by \$400. Therefore, she was only able to obtain \$600 of additional coverage.

The additional coverage is almost always provided through a separate policy rather than as an increase in the benefit amount of the policy to which the future increase option rider is attached. The new policy is in the same underwriting class as the old policy, and the premium for the additional protection is at attained-age rates. The insured may or may not be able to select different options than were in the original policy, such as the length of the elimination period and the benefit duration.

If the insured is disabled when he or she could ordinarily exercise an option, the option usually can still be exercised. For purposes of the benefit amount that the insurer will issue, the insured is treated as still working and having an income based on a specified period prior to disability, such as 12 months. Any increased benefit, however, applies only to future disabilities and not current disability payments.

The cost of adding a future increase option rider to a policy is significant and may increase the premium for the basic coverage by 10 to 20 percent. This is because of adverse selection; persons in poor health are more likely to exercise options than persons in good health.

Cost-of-Living Adjustment Rider

After a person becomes disabled and starts collecting disability income benefits, there is no provision in a basic disability income policy to increase the benefit payments because of increases in the cost of living. Such increases will take place, however, if the insured has added a cost-of-living adjustment rider to the policy. Without these increases, there is likely to be a significant decrease in the purchasing power of the benefit payments, particularly for a lengthy disability. Historically, for example, the purchasing power or the dollar has decreased by about 50 percent over 20-year periods.

Benefit payment increases as a result of the rider generally go into effect after a claim has been paid for one year and are made on an annual basis thereafter. Like the automatic increase rider, the increase may be a flat annual percentage or based on changes in the CPI, subject to maximum and minimum percentage increases. In either case, increases may be calculated on a simple or compound interest basis. Some insurers have a benefit cap and provide no further increases after the original benefit has doubled or tripled. Most insurers that provide lifetime benefits cease increases at age 65.

Example: Kurt was totally disabled, and his disability lasted for 3½ years. His initial monthly benefit was $4,000. His policy contained a cost-of living adjustment rider that provided a 5 percent increase calculated on a compound interest basis. During the first year of his disability, he received $4,000 per month. During the second year, the benefit increased to $4,200 per month. The monthly benefit payments increased to $4,410 and $4,630, respectively, for the following 2 years.

There are variations in how insurers determine the disability income benefit a person has after he or she recovers from a disability for which the rider has increased benefit payments. In some cases, the benefit reverts to its original amount prior to the disability, or $4,000 in the previous example. (However, this amount may have increased because of provisions in an automatic increase rider or future increase option rider that the insured has.) In other cases, the benefit under the policy for future disabilities increases to the indexed amount paid under the rider at the time of recovery ($4,630 in the example) without the insured's having to pay any additional premiums. Finally, some insurers permit the insured to increase the policy benefit to the indexed amount by exercising a *buy-back provision.* With this provision, the insured can increase the policy benefit to the final indexed level by purchasing an additional amount of coverage ($630 in the example), based on attained-age rates at the time of return to work. Under any of these circumstances, the provisions of the rider come into effect again for subsequent disabilities.

buy-back provision

A cost-of-living adjustment rider is expensive and often increases the basic policy premium by 20 to 50 percent, depending on the amount of the potential increase, the insured's age, and other benefit options selected.

Miscellaneous Riders

There are numerous other riders that may be available to an applicant for disability income insurance. The following discussion describes some of these riders. Readers, however, should be aware that insurers currently might offer other riders or develop new riders in the future.

Return-of-Premium Riders

Some insurers are reluctant to purchase disability income policies because the feel they will get nothing in return if they pay significant premiums for many years and have no claims. As a result, insurers frequently offer a *return-of premium rider*, which "refunds" all or a portion of the premiums paid for a policy if the insured's claim experience is favorable. There are two basic approaches used with return-of-premium riders. With one approach, the policy builds a cash value, usually starting with the third

return-of-premium rider

policy year. At that time, the cash value is typically equal to about 5 percent of the aggregate premiums paid. This percentage increases over time. If the insured surrenders the policy, he or she receives the cash value that has built up at that point in time, minus the amount of any claims that the policy has paid. By age 65, the percentage is 100 and the policy expires. The insured then receives a refund of all the premiums he or she has paid, minus any claim payments he or she received over the policy's duration.

Example: Bertha has a disability income policy that has a return-of-premium rider. After 17 years, she has paid premiums that total $30,000. Currently, her policy has a cash value of 53 percent of this amount, or $15,900. If Bertha never had a claim, she could surrender the policy and receive this amount. However, assume Bertha received claim payments of $37,000 for a disability she suffered s few years ago. Because this exceeds the cash value, Bertha will receive nothing if she surrenders the policy.

The second approach refunds a portion of the premiums paid during specific intervals, again minus any claims paid. Depending on the insurer, the percentage may vary from 50 to 80 percent, and the intervals from 5 to 10 years. However, there is no need to surrender the policy, and the insurer makes an additional refund at the end of the next interval if the policy is still in force.

The number of insureds purchasing return-of-premium riders is relatively small, primarily because of their cost. They add anywhere from 25 to 100 percent to the cost of a policy's basic premium. Because they provide more generous refunds, riders that use the second approach are more expensive than riders that use the first approach.

Own-Occupation Riders

Standard disability income contracts are much less likely than in the past to use own-occupation definitions of disability. However, in selected cases, they may be willing to write such coverage. This is usually accomplished with the *own-occupation rider*, which modifies the definition of total disability in the policy to which the rider is attached.

own-occupation rider

Pension Supplement/Completion Riders

pension supplement/ completion rider

Many individuals allocate part of their income to funding retirement plans. Unfortunately, maximum issue limits often make it difficult for a disabled person to have enough resources to continue such funding. And disability benefit payments are more likely than in the past to cease at age 65 or 67. With a *pension supplement/completion rider*, an applicant can purchase an additional benefit amount that will be paid to a funding vehicle for retirement benefits. The funding vehicle is usually some type of trust established by the insurer that writes the disability income coverage. The insured often has discretion with regard to how the insurer invests his or her funds. At age 65 or 67, the funds are distributed to the insured.

Catastrophic Benefit Riders

catastrophic benefit rider

Several insurers offer what is commonly referred to as a *catastrophic benefit rider*. This rider provides additional benefits in certain situations when an insured is so severely disabled that he or she is likely to incur significant extra expenses because of a disability. Coupled with the basic disability income policy, this rider may enable an insured to have a benefit amount for catastrophic disability that is as high as 100 percent of predisability income.

Depending on the insurer, the events that trigger benefits vary, but they typically include one or more of the following:

- The insured is unable to perform two or more activities of daily living. This is like the benefit trigger in long-term care insurance contracts, which chapter 18 discusses.
- The insured has a severe cognitive impairment, such as Alzheimer's disease.
- The insured is a paraplegic or quadriplegic.
- The insured has a presumptive disability.

A few insurers have a somewhat more limited rider that provides additional benefits if an insured is confined to a nursing facility while receiving disability income benefits. Often referred to as a nursing-facility confinement rider, the rider typically increases the basic disability income benefit by a stated proportion. This rider was once more common than today, primarily because some insurers have replaced it with a broader catastrophic benefit rider.

A few insurers also still offer riders that provide additional benefits if an insured is hospitalized. One type of this rider waives the usual elimination period if the insured is hospitalized, but does not increase policy benefits. Another variation of this rider pays an additional monthly benefit, along with the regular monthly benefit, if an insured is hospitalized.

Mental and Nervous Disorder Riders

As mentioned earlier, some disability income policies limit the duration of disability benefits for mental or nervous disorders unless the insured is in a mental hospital or institution. Insurers who issue such polices may offer a rider that deletes the exclusion and treats such disabilities like any other disability.

Most insurers, however, do treat disabilities from all causes in the same way. Some of these insurers may offer a rider that allows the insured to elect a shorter benefit duration for disabilities resulting from mental and nervous disorders. This rider often results in a premium savings of about 10 percent.

Long-Term Care Purchase Option Riders

A very small number of insurers have a rider that permits the insured to purchase long-term care insurance at specified future dates without evidence of insurability. There is an additional premium for the rider, but it is modest because the rider is usually made available only to relatively young applicants. Its provisions are similar to those of the future increase option rider for disability income insurance. Like the conversion provision to long-term care coverage, there may be limits on the available policy provisions, and the premium is based on the insured's age at the time an option is exercised. Unlike the conversion provision, however, the insured is not exchanging the disability income policy for a long-term care policy. Rather, he or she is purchasing a long-term care insurance policy in addition to the disability income policy.

At least one insurer has a rider that gives a credit to the insured if he or she purchases a long-term care insurance policy from the same insurer. The credit is a reduction in the first-year premium for the long-term care insurance policy equal to 2 percent of the cumulative premiums paid for the disability income policy. The insured, however, must apply for and meet the normal underwriting criteria for the new policy.

CHECKLIST FOR EVALUATING AND COMPARING DISABILITY INCOME POLICIES

As the previous discussion in this and earlier chapters shows, there is no such thing as a standard disability income policy. The variations are numerous—not only among different insurers but even among contracts issued by the same insurer. Although this makes the evaluation of a policy or a comparison of proposed policies difficult, consumers must often make such evaluations. Probably the best way to do this is by using a checklist like the one below.

☐ What is the annual policy premium?

☐ What is the renewability provision?

☐ What is the definition of total disability?

☐ What is the amount and frequency of total disability benefits?

☐ What is the duration of total disability benefits?

☐ Is there a presumptive disability provision?

☐ Is there coverage for disabilities arising from organ donations?

☐ Are partial-disability benefits covered? If yes,

___ What is the definition of partial disability?
___ What period of total disability is required before benefits are payable?

☐ Are residual-disability benefits covered? If yes,

___ What is the benefit amount?
___ How long are benefits payable?
___ Is a period of total disability required?
___ How are prior earnings calculated?

☐ What are the policy exclusions and benefit limitations?

- ☐ Is there a provision or option for increasing benefit amounts prior to disability: If so, by how much?

- ☐ Is there a provision for cost-of-living increases when disability payments are being made? If so, what is the increase?

- ☐ Does the policy contain any modifications from standard issue? If so, what are they?

- ☐ What is the waiver-of-premium provision?

- ☐ Is there a return-of-premium option?

- ☐ What are the rehabilitation benefits?

- ☐ Does the policy contain riders? If so,

    ___ What do they provide?
    ___ What is the additional premium?

PUTTING IT ALL TOGETHER

Planning for disability should be part of anyone's overall financial plan. In addition to meeting regular living expenses, financial planning must consider many other factors in addition to providing income during periods of disability. Individuals must also make decisions about paying for medical expenses and long-term care, funding children's education, and providing income for retirement. Unfortunately, few Americans have the financial resources to do everything they might like to do, and they must establish priorities. On one hand, disability planning should not take place without regard to other financial needs. On the other hand, individuals should not become so overwhelmed with other financial goals that they ignore the need for disability income. Without it, individuals may not achieve these other goals if disability robs them of needed income.

The following example shows how an individual might approach disability planning. Of course, everyone is unique and another person might come up with a different solution.

Example: Ken, aged 45, is married with four children. His wife works part time as a freelance editor. His oldest daughter just started college, and his son is a high school sophomore. He also has twin daughters who just turned 6.

Ken recently left a secure job to work for a friend who has a small and growing company. Ken has a salary that is slightly less than he earned previously, but there is the potential for very large salary increases if the firm does well. His new employer provides a good medical expense plan for Ken and his family. There is also a 401(k) plan to which the company provides a modest contribution. In addition, Ken has stock options which will provide significant retirement income if the firm prospers. However, there is a minimal employer-provided disability income plan. The plan will provide benefits equal to 100 percent of his salary if he is disabled, but only for a maximum of 2 months. This contrasts with his prior coverage, which provided benefits until age 65.

Ken realizes he has an urgent need for an individual disability income policy. He approaches a friend who sells disability income insurance, and asks the agent for a proposal from a good company. They discuss all the possible options, but Ken does not tell the agent that he is only expecting to pay an annual premium of $3,000 or less.

The proposal delivered by the agent contains the following:

- monthly benefits of $6,000, which is the underwriting limit based on Ken's earned income.
- a 60-day waiting period to coordinate benefits with the employer-provided coverage
- a benefit period to age 65
- a rider for residual benefits
- an automatic increase rider
- a future increase option rider
- a cost-of-living rider

Ken is stunned when the agent tells him that the annual premium for this coverage is $9,210. The agent then tells Ken that the premium will decrease to $5,090 if the waiting period is 90 days. Ken thinks that this is a very good idea, because he has an emergency fund that will easily cover lost income for an additional 30 days. When Ken inquires about a longer waiting period, he finds that increasing it to 180 days will only lower the premium by another $300.

Ken is still concerned about the premium and decides to explore further the ways to reduce the premium. He rejects the idea of lowering the monthly benefit, because he feels that $6,000 is the minimum amount needed for his family to maintain a standard of living close to their current one. The agent then gives Ken the following premium breakdown:

- basic monthly benefit $3,477
- residual benefit rider 552
- automatic increase rider $56
- future increase option rider $453
- cost-of-living adjustment rider $552

Ken likes the concept of residual benefits and an automatic increase of benefits and decides to accept these riders, which lowers the premium to $4,085. He feels that he can afford this premium with a little belt tightening. The future increase option rider is of little interest to him, because he feels that the basic policy benefit with any automatic increase will at least enable his family to initially live adequately if he is disabled. In addition, there is the possibility that his employer will have a long-term disability income plan in the future.

Ken also likes the concept of a cost-of-living rider but rejects it, as the premium is already higher than he wants to pay. In making this decision, he considers the fact that children leaving home and additional income when his wife returns to full-time employment as soon as the twins are a little older will offset increased living costs.

CHAPTER REVIEW

Key Terms

injury
sickness
concurrent disability provision
presumptive total disability provision
recurrent disability provision
accumulation period
benefit period
decreasing term disability income insurance
transition benefit
capital sum
automatic increase rider
future increase option rider
cost-of-living adjustment rider
buy-back provision
return-of-premium rider
own-occupation rider
pension supplement/completion rider
catastrophic benefit rider

Review Questions

Review questions are based on the learning objectives in this chapter. Thus, a [14-3] at the end of a question means that the question is based on learning objective 14-3. If there are multiple objectives, they are all listed.

1. What types of provisions are common to disability insurance policies as well as other forms of health insurance policies? [14-1]
2. What types of provisions do disability income policies contain with respect to covered disabilities? [14-2]
3. Why might an applicant select a lower benefit amount than an insurer is willing to issue for disability income? [14-3]
4. a. What options are often available to an applicant with respect to the length of the elimination period in a disability income policy? [14-3]
   b. What factors should an applicant consider when selecting the elimination period? [14-3]
5. a. What options may be available to an applicant with respect to the length of the benefit period in a disability income policy? [14-3]
   b. What factors should an applicant consider when selecting the benefit period? [14-3]
6. In addition to the actual definition of earned income, what provisions are contained in a disability income policy with respect to earned income? [14-3]

7. What are some of the additional types of benefits that an insurer might incorporate into a disability income contract as a standard feature? [14-3]
8. What types of exclusions and limitations might be found in disability income policies? [14-3]
9. What are some of the circumstances under which coverage under a disability income policy might be suspended? [14-3]
10. Describe the types of renewability provisions that might apply to disability income policies. [14-4]
11. What factors typically influence the premiums for disability income policies? [14-4]
12. What variations are found in the waiver-of-premium provisions of disability income policies? [14-4]
13. What variations might automatic increase riders contain? [14-5]
14. How might future increase options differ? [14-5]
15. a. What variations exist in cost-of-living adjustment riders? [14-5]
    b. How might the amount of a disability income benefit be determined after an insured has recovered from a disability for which the rider increased benefit payments? [14-5]
16. What are some of the ways that miscellaneous types of riders might broaden the coverage available to purchasers of disability income policies? [14-6]
17. What factors need to be considered when evaluating or comparing disability income policies or proposals? [14-7]

15

Business Uses of Disability Income Insurance*

Learning Objectives

An understanding of the material in this chapter should enable you to

15-1. Identify the disability needs facing business owners and professionals.

15-2. Explain the purpose of and describe the provisions of business overhead expense insurance.

15-3. Explain the purpose of buy-sell agreements, and describe their provisions.

15-4. Describe the provisions of disability buyout insurance.

15-5. Explain the purpose of and describe the provisions of key-person disability insurance.

Chapter Outline

* Portions of this chapter are based on material written by Ted Kurlowicz, James F. Ivers III, and John J. McFadden for *Planning for Business Owners and Professionals*, 11th edition (Bryn Mawr, PA: The American College Press, 2007).

As mentioned in other chapters, businesses often provide disability income protection to their owners or key executives. The business may cover them under sick-pay plans or group insurance arrangements that protect all or, at least, a much larger group of employees. However, some businesses have separate disability income plans for different groups. One plan may apply to rank-and-file employees, and another plan to owners and executives. The latter plan, for example, may have a more liberal definition of disability and/or a longer benefit period. Other businesses—particularly smaller, closely held organizations—may have a long-term disability income plan that applies only to a smaller group of owners and executives.

Businesses may fund disability income plans for owners and executives with group insurance, but individual policies are often used. In many cases, the business pays the premium, and benefits are taxable. In other cases, the owner or executive pays the premium or is treated as having paid the premium. This results in tax-free benefits. Chapter 6 describes the tax treatment of disability income premiums and benefits.

The purpose of this chapter is not to explore further the need for disability income insurance to protect the income of owners and executives. Rather, it is to look at other business needs for disability income insurance that often confront the business owner or professionals—particularly those with sole proprietorships, closely held businesses, or professional practices. The frequency of long-term disability is a problem that the closely held business owner or professional cannot afford to ignore. Recent statistics reveal that a firm established by two 35-year-old co-owners faces a 75 percent probability that at least one owner will sustain a long-term disability prior to age 65. If the firm was formed by six or more co-owners, it is almost a certainty that there will be at least one long-term disability before the owners reach age 65. Because many disabilities lasting at least 3 months may continue for more than 5 years, even one such occurrence could have a devastating effect on a closely held business.

The disability of a business owner or professional presents unique and complex problems. Fortunately, there is a variety of special disability products available to cover specific business-related losses due to disability.

For the sole proprietor or professional, disability threatens not only his or her earned income but also the continued existence of the business. The owners of a closely held business may also be placed in a difficult situation if one or more of them should become disabled. The typical closely held business owner or professional receives all (or a substantial portion) of his or her income from the closely held business or professional practice. Furthermore, the ownership interest in the closely held business or practice is likely to be the owner's most substantial asset.

In addition to providing disability income for themselves, there are three other risks that business owners or professionals must protect against the possibility of disability:

- business overhead expenses—Certain business expenses continue during a business owner's or professional's disability. These must be paid to allow the business or practice to remain viable during the disabled owner or principal's recovery and return to work. This need can best be answered by a disability contract specifically designed to cover business overhead expenses.
- buy-sell funding—Although business overhead expense disability coverage is designed to provide reimbursement for business expenses during relatively short disabilities, a business owner's permanent or long-term disability requires a different solution. A specially designed disability contract will help fund the buyout of the disabled owner's share of the business.
- key-person protection—Finally, in some instances the closely held business may be especially dependent upon the special skills of a key employee. The disability of this key person may substantially impair the business's finances, especially for the short term. Again, there are specially designed disability products to fund this need.

This chapter discusses these three business disability needs. It is important to understand, however, that the basic disability income product that has been the focus of earlier chapters is specifically designed to replace the insured's lost income and is *not* designed to meet the business needs of overhead expenses, buy-sell funding, or key-person disability. These three needs do not involve protecting the disabled owner's income, but rather are situations that address the financial problems the business experiences when an individual is disabled. Consequently, specifically designed contracts to meet these unique business needs are the best and most efficient means to satisfy the risks. Attempting to solve these business needs with the basic disability income contract usually creates unnecessary complexity. For example, the specially designed business overhead, buy-sell, and key-person contracts each have elimination periods, benefit periods, and contract language to meet these specific needs. In addition, underwriting rules and limits specifically recognize each situation's unique needs. The basic disability income contract is not designed to dovetail with the specific business needs of overhead expense, buy-sell, and key-person coverages.

BUSINESS OVERHEAD EXPENSE INSURANCE

business overhead expense (BOE) policy

The oldest and most commonly sold form of business disability insurance is the *business overhead expense (BOE) policy*. The purpose of this contract is to provide reimbursement for certain specified expenses so that a business or professional practice may remain viable during the recovery and return to work of the disabled owner or principal. These benefit payments are usually for the relatively short term and assume that the business owner will return to work.

This risk is particularly important for the professional operating a solo practice or partnership. The professional practitioner can lose clients, goodwill, valuable employees, and indeed the business as a whole if office expenses cannot be paid during a period of disability. The professional's career could be destroyed even with a short-term disability.

Eligibility Requirements

The basic need for BOE insurance depends on whether or not the business entity will be able to generate the income to cover expenses during the owner's absence because of disability. Underwriting requirements help identify the professional or business owner whose disability would create a significant loss of revenue and thus a loss of monies to pay expenses. The law firm with five or fewer principals, for example, would clearly have a change in revenue if one of those principals was disabled for even 2 or 3 months. The owner of a small business who is also key to the success of the business would similarly have difficulty paying certain fixed expenses if disabled, especially if he or she does not have other employees to carry on the same work with the same skills. On the other hand, a large group practice of 30 physicians in the same specialty will not usually suffer much overall loss of revenue if one of those individuals is disabled for a period of time. Criteria to determine eligibility may involve the nature of the business, occupation class, and the number of principals, as well as the number of employees doing the same or similar work as the owner or directly involved with the generation of revenue.

Covered Expenses

Most BOE contracts cover fixed monthly expenses that are ordinary and necessary for the operation of the business or profession and would continue in the event of disability. These expenses may include but are not limited to rent, utilities, equipment rental, employee salaries, certain interest expenses, office supplies, and property taxes. If expenses are shared with other principals, the amount of coverage per individual is limited to the individual's share of expenses. Expenses that are not covered usually include those directly associated with the generation of income and therefore would not occur during disability. Examples of these expenses are the purchase of new equipment, salary payments to the insured or his or her replacement, and expenses not causing cash reimbursements, such as depreciation or premium payments waived because of disability.

Certain types of businesses may present particular challenges in the area of overhead expenses if the owner's disability does not significantly affect the income of the business, especially on a short-term basis. Even though the owner/manager is important to the BOE coverage of the business, employees of the firm may continue to generate some income while he or she is disabled. In these situations, the amount of BOE coverage should be reduced in proportion to the risk being considered.

Definition of Disability

Total disability is usually defined as the insured's inability to perform his or her own occupation in the business or professional practice. Most insurers also have a presumptive disability clause in their policies. It is also common for them to include or offer benefits for partial and/or residual disabilities.

Benefits

The purpose of the BOE contract is to provide benefits until the disabled principal or owner recovers or, in the event of a longer-term disability, until a decision can be made regarding the future of the business with a permanently disabled principal or owner. Elimination periods are generally short (30 to 90 days); benefit periods range from 12 to 24 months, but can be as short as 6 months or as long as 36 months. Monthly benefit limits range from $2,000 to $20,000 or $30,000 per month, depending on the particular circumstances and the insurer. Some BOE products offer a limited survivor benefit in the event of death, such as one or two times the monthly benefit limit.

Benefit payments are based on reimbursement of actual expenses, and claim examiners require verification that the expenses have been incurred. Although the benefit limit is expressed as a uniform monthly amount, many actual expenses vary from month to month. BOE policies contain provisions to address this issue, but provisions differ among insurers. Most insurers allow unused benefits in a given month to be applied to benefit payments for months during which expenses exceed the monthly benefit limit. Some insurers make a single payment at the end of benefit period or when a disability ceases, if earlier. Other insurers apply the unused benefits to expenses on a monthly basis. Some insurers also extend the benefit period if there are any unused benefits. The following examples show some of these variations, which are important for an insured to understand when evaluating BOE policies.

Example 1: Clint has a BOE policy that has a monthly benefit limit of $6,000, after a 30-day elimination period. He was disabled for 4 months following a skiing accident. During this time, his business overhead expenses were as follows:

Month	Expenses
1	$4,900
2	$4,800
3	$8,000 (property taxes were due)
4	$5,100

His policy paid nothing the first month because of the elimination period. It paid his actual expenses of $4,800 the second month; the remaining $1,200 was credited to a carryover account. Clint collected the $6,000 maximum monthly benefit the third month. For the fourth month, he collected $5,100, and $900 was added to the carryover account. This brought its balance to $2,100.

Clint returned to work in the fifth month. At that time, the insurer totaled his expenses for the 3 months when benefits were payable. This amount ($17,900) exceeded the benefits he collected ($15,900) by $2,000. Therefore, the insurer paid him that amount from the carryover balance.

Example 2: This is the same as example 1, except Clint's policy did not wait until the end of his disability to apply the carryover balance. For the second month, he received the same $4,800. However, for the third month, he received $7,200. This consisted of the $6,000 monthly benefit limit plus $1,200 from the carryover account. The account was now running a deficit of $800. His total expenses for the 2 months had been $12,800, but he had collected only $12,000 from his BOE policy.

For the fourth month, Clint received $5,900. This consisted of his $5,100 in expenses for the month and the $800 deficit. In the final analysis, Clint received the same total benefit amount as in example 1, but its timing was different.

Example 3: Monique has a BOE policy with a 12-month benefit period. The policy has a $5,000 monthly benefit limit. She was disabled because of a stroke. It is questionable if she will return to work, but she continues to keep her office open in hopes that she will. During the benefit period, she was paid her actual overhead expenses of $48,000. Because her potential benefit was $60,000, her insurer will continue to pay benefits beyond 12 months until she receives an additional $12,000.

Other Contract Provisions and Riders

Some provisions in BOE policies are like those in regular disability income policies (discussed in chapter 14). The exclusions are similar, and there is usually a waiver-of-premium provision. Future-increase-option riders and return-of-premium riders are typically available.

Other contract provisions and riders are unique to the business overhead expense contract or differ from those found in regular disability income contracts. There are typically no policy provisions or riders to increase benefit payments for cost-of-living changes because the benefit period is short, but a small number of insurers do provide them.

Although there is a trend away from noncancelable policies in traditional disability income policies, this more favorable renewability provision is more likely to be available with BOE policies.

Another unique feature of BOE policies is that some have a conversion privilege. This provision allows the insured to convert to a regular disability income policy if he or she is no longer responsible for overhead expenses. The insured usually must exercise the conversion before a certain age, and the eligibility for the new policy does not require evidence of physical insurability. The new policy's issue limits are typically those of the BOE policy up to a maximum limit, subject to the issue and participation limits in effect by the insurer on the date of conversion. The length of the benefit period is relatively short and is usually the longer of the benefit period of the BOE policy or the minimum period for which the insurer will issue a regular policy. The premium for the new policy is based on attained-age rates or issue-age rates, depending on the insurer.

substitute salary expense rider

As mentioned earlier, the BOE policy does not cover the expenses of hiring a replacement for the disabled insured. The rationale for this is that the cost of hiring the replacement will result in income to pay the salary. However, in some cases, it may take a period of time for this to occur. The optional *substitute salary expense rider* addresses this issue. The rider pays a specified portion of the replacement's salary for a limited duration.

Tax Treatment

The federal income tax treatment of BOE insurance differs from taxation of individual disability income insurance. The business may deduct the premiums for BOE insurance as a business expense, which is similar to property and liability coverages. Unlike individually owned disability income insurance benefits, the benefits from BOE insurance are taxable income to the business. This is not usually a problem, however, because the income is offset by the deductibility of overhead expenses that the policy benefits are used to pay.

DISABILITY BUYOUT INSURANCE

The purpose of disability buyout coverage is the same as that of life buyout insurance (that is, to fund the purchase/sale of the insured's ownership interest in a business or professional practice by his or her partners, co-shareholders, or the business entity). The triggering event is the disability, as opposed to the death, of one of the principals. Unfortunately, continuation of the business usually receives less attention in relation to the owner's disability than it does in relation to the owner's death, but the need is just as important.

When a disabled owner begins to feel the financial strain resulting from the loss of earned income from the business, an obvious solution is to sell the business interest. This solution will offer satisfactory results for all the parties involved if it is planned for in advance. In the absence of a prearranged binding agreement, the disabled owner is likely to be dissatisfied with the sale proceeds. It may be difficult to dispose of a closely held business interest to an outsider, particularly if the disabled owner holds a minority interest in the business. Similarly, if the disabled owner has unique and special skills that affect the value of the business, it may be difficult to find a buyer who is willing to pay an amount that is acceptable to the disabled owner.

If the disabled owner and the healthy co-owners can reach an agreement, the disabled owner's interest can be transferred to the remaining owners, preventing any unwanted outsiders from entering the business. However, the disabled owner will be in a precarious bargaining position, particularly if he or she has a minority interest. The healthy owners can terminate income payments to the disabled owner at their whim. Under these circumstances, the disabled owner is likely to be compelled to accept a purchase price far below the fair value of the interest.

In some circumstances—for example, a partnership in which any general partner can force liquidation or any corporation in which the disabled shareholder holds a majority interest—the disabled owner may be in a position to force the liquidation of the business. However, a forced liquidation is unlikely to satisfy any of the parties because it results in business assets being disposed of quickly and generally at below fair market value. The business also may lose goodwill, and the healthy owners will temporarily lose their livelihoods.

Disability Buy-Sell Agreements

An obvious solution to the problems created by a business owner's long-term disability is to draft a comprehensive buy-sell (purchase-and-sale) agreement between the business and its owners prior to the occurrence of any triggering events. It is at this time that all parties to the agreement are in their strongest bargaining or negotiating position. Because the continuation problems created by an owner's death are similar to those created by an owner's disability, it is common to incorporate a provision in the life insurance buy-sell agreement to consider the latter contingency.

buy-sell agreement

The purpose of a *buy-sell agreement* is to provide an orderly transfer of ownership in the event of death, retirement, voluntary or involuntary termination, or disability. By stipulating the disposition of an owner's interest in the business before a triggering event occurs, the agreement allows for continued ownership and uninterrupted operation of the business. It also protects the remaining owners from undesired new owners, and it protects an owner's value in the business. Buy-sell agreements are complex and need to be carefully drafted. This is usually done by an attorney, and, in fact, insurers often require this before they will issue an insurance policy to fund the agreement.

disability buyout insurance

Disability buyout insurance, as with life insurance, is simply a funding vehicle to the underlying buy-sell agreement. It safeguards the parties from certain financial losses that may occur if an owner who was actively and productively involved in the business becomes disabled. The types of losses that may occur are the drain on business assets in order to support the disabled owner, the disabled owner's lack of productivity that may cause the value of the business to decline, and the reduction of future profitability for the remaining active owners.

Buy-sell agreements that become operative at the disability of a closely held business owner are structured in the same basic form as life insurance agreements. The business entity or the co-owners can be the intended

cross-purchase agreement

entity buy-sell agreement

purchasers of the business interest. In a partnership, a *cross-purchase agreement* is an agreement among partners for each partner to purchase the partnership interest (or a portion of it if there are more than two partners) that a disabled partner holds when the agreement becomes operative. Each partner must purchase a disability buyout policy on each of the other partners. In an *entity buy-sell agreement*, the partnership is a party to the agreement and is the designated purchaser of a disabled partner's interest. Only one policy on each partner is necessary. This minimizes the number of policies needed. As a result, this is the usual form of buy-sell agreement if there are more than two partners involved.

Example: Eric, Susan, Alex, and Robert are partners in an accounting firm. They have decided to explore a buy-sell agreement in case one of them is disabled. When they look into a cross-purchase agreement, they soon realize that Eric will need to purchase three disability buyout policies—one on each of the other three parties. Susan, Alex, and Robert will need to do the same. Therefore, it will take 12 policies to fund the agreement.

However, if they enter into an entity buy-sell agreement, the partnership will only need to purchase one policy on each partner for a total of four policies.

For businesses structured as corporations, disability buy-sell agreements are designed as either cross-purchase or stock-redemption plans. Again, in the cross-purchase agreement, each shareholder agrees to purchase a designated portion of a disabled co-shareholder's stock when a disability triggers the agreement. Each co-shareholder entering the cross-purchase agreement is similarly bound to sell his or her stock when the specific nature of the disability meets the provisions described below. The *stock-redemption agreement* (the name for an entity buy-sell agreement when a corporation is involved) binds the corporation to redeem a disabled shareholder's stock. Each shareholder entering the agreement must agree to have his or her stock redeemed when he or she becomes disabled, according to the terms of the agreement.

stock-redemption agreement

The disability buy-sell agreement can be designed in a mandatory fashion as described above, or the owners can be given an option to buy a disabled owner's stock. An optional agreement offers flexibility to the parties by delaying the actual decision to purchase the disabled owner's interest until the circumstances are known. However, the basic purpose of a disability buy-sell agreement dictates the use of a mandatory agreement. Such an agreement ensures that a disabled owner will have a guaranteed market for his or her business interest and will receive fair proceeds that can be used by the owner and his or her family during the period of disability. At the same time, the healthy owners can enjoy the assurances that a binding agreement provides—that is, they will not have to deal indefinitely with a potentially disabled and disgruntled co-owner who might sell to outsiders or force the liquidation of the business.

Provisions of a Disability Buy-Sell Agreement

Typically, disability buy-sell agreement provisions will be incorporated in one agreement providing for all the contingencies the owners stipulate to trigger a buy-sell agreement—death, disability, retirement, and so on. The inclusion of disability as a triggering event creates the need for the following provisions:

trigger date

- elimination period—The elimination period in a disability buy-sell agreement is the amount of time that must elapse following the onset of the owner's disability before the purchase must occur. The date the buyout becomes operative is also referred to as the *trigger date.* The elimination period in the agreement must be consistent with the elimination period in the disability buyout policy.
- definition of disability—This provision specifies the degree of disability that an owner must face before a purchase becomes mandatory. Here again, the definition of disability should be the same as in the disability policy, and the determination of disability is typically left to the insurer.
- recovery of the disabled owner—The possibility exists that a disabled owner will recover sufficiently to provide the usual services to the business. This recovery could occur either during or after the elimination period. If recovery occurs during the elimination period, it is commonly provided that a new elimination period will have to be satisfied if the disabled owner returns to work for a reasonable length of time. If recovery occurs after the elimination period, the buyout will already have been triggered, and it is normal for the buyout to be completed.
- funding—A disability buy-sell agreement offers more certainty if it is funded in advance, and specially designed disability buyout insurance is the most efficient vehicle to use. If the agreement is to be insured, this provision will stipulate all the specifics related to the insurance funding, including the purchaser, the premium payer, and the beneficiary of each policy.

- disposition of policies held by the seller after a buyout has become effective—If a disability buy-sell agreement is funded with insurance, there will be one or perhaps several policies covering each owner. Each owner may also be covered by life insurance as a means to fund the buy-sell agreement's death provisions. This provision will specify the method of disposition of any unnecessary insurance policies after a buyout occurs following either the death or the disability of an owner.
- premature death during the period of disability buyout—Disability buy-sell agreements are often carried out through installment obligations. In such a situation, the disabled owner may die before all the installment payments are made. It is usually recommended that the life insurance covering each owner under the life insurance buy-sell agreement be continued until the disability installment payments are completed. This provision might stipulate that the disabled owner's death will accelerate the installment obligation and the balance will be due in one lump sum. The purchasers can then use the proceeds of the life insurance policies to complete the buyout.

Triggering the Buyout

The selection of the operative event for the disability buy-sell agreement gives some discretion to the parties that is not available in the buy-sell agreement at death. That is, death is relatively easy to define and offers no chance of recovery, whereas disability occurs in varying degrees and may be either temporary or permanent in duration or either total or partial in severity. The effect of an owner's disability on a closely held business will vary depending on the owner's status and the type of business. For example, a business that does not depend on the personal services of the owners may be able to operate with a disabled owner for an indefinite period of time. A professional who provides counseling services to clients may be able to perform substantially all of his or her normal duties after sustaining a disability that causes substantial physical impairment. The drafter of the buy-sell agreement's disability provisions must take the specific circumstances of each closely held business and its owners into consideration when designing the provision of the agreement specifying the event that will trigger the buyout.

Definition of Disability

The definition of disability in an insured agreement should never be more liberal than the definition used in the disability buyout policy. Otherwise, the parties could become bound to a mandatory buyout at a time when no benefits are forthcoming from the funding insurance contract. For this reason, legal and financial services professionals typically recommend that the insured disability buy-sell agreement contain the identical definition of total disability used in the disability buyout policy. This places the burden on the insurer to determine when the benefits will be paid and thus when the buyout will occur. The use of the insurer's definition removes the potential for a dispute among the parties to the agreement. Furthermore, it ensures that benefits will be forthcoming when the agreement becomes effective.

Insurers currently offer policies with varying definitions of disability to suit the needs of specific business and professional clients. (The specific types of disability definitions are discussed elsewhere in this book.) Many disability buyout policies, however, have a hybrid definition of disability that is specifically applicable to the closely held business buy-sell situation. Under this definition, benefits will be provided if the insured is unable to perform the duties of his or her regular occupation and any other occupation *within the business organization* for which the insured is reasonably suited in consideration of education, training, and experience. Under these circumstances, the buyout will be completed and the benefits will be paid when the disabled owner or professional is unable to contribute productively to his or her specific business or professional practice.

The following example, which focuses on the definition of disability, shows why it is so important for a disability buyout policy to be consistent with a disability buy-sell agreement and the intentions of the buyers and sellers.

Example: Ted and John are partners in a law firm that specializes in criminal defense litigation. The partners form a binding insured cross-purchase disability buy-sell agreement triggered by a disability that satisfies the insurer's definition of total disability. Unfortunately, Ted, John, and their advisors were not careful in selecting the disability buyout policies and secured protection that provides benefits only when the insured satisfies the "any-occupation-for-which-the-insured-is-reasonably-suited" requirement.

When the high-pressure nature of the work overcomes Ted and extreme hypertension results, several doctors advise him that he will no longer be able to handle the stress of being a trial lawyer. However, the physicians see no reason why Ted cannot engage in basic legal research or perhaps teach at a law school. The insurer views these other tasks as occupations for which Ted is reasonably suited by his education and training, and it will provide no benefits under the policy. Because the buy-sell agreement was not triggered since the insurer's definition of disability was not satisfied, John is not required to purchase Ted's interest. A conflict will probably arise since Ted will want continued income payments while John will soon be dissatisfied with carrying the caseload of both partners. This problem could have been avoided if the partners had secured a policy with a more favorable definition of disability.

The Disability Buyout Policy

Unlike business overhead expense policies, disability buyout policies are not noncancelable or guaranteed renewable in the strict sense. The insurer often conditions renewability of the contract on

- the insured's being actively at work in the business
- the insured's owning not more than 90 percent or less than 10 percent of the business
- a written buy-sell agreement in place

Because the purpose of the policy is to fund a one-time event (that is, the disposition of the insured's interest in a specific business), the policy benefit is paid only once. As previously mentioned, it is important that the provisions of the *agreement* and the *policy* be consistent. Like business overhead expense policies, disability buyout policies reimburse the policyowner for actual expenses. Because the policyowner is not the insured, the reimbursement requirement protects both insured and insurer from a situation in which the policy proceeds are used for something other than purchasing the insured's ownership interest. A unique provision of many buy-sell contracts is that the insured is presumed to remain disabled once the buy-sell benefit becomes payable. This provision ensures that benefits will be available to fund the purchase even if the insured recovers from the disability before all benefits are paid.

The typical elimination period under a disability buyout policy is 12 or 24 months. Some insurers offer optional elimination periods with higher benefit amounts for longer elimination periods. The length of the elimination period must take into consideration the specific business's needs; however, with each successive month that an owner is disabled, there will be increasing pressure on the healthy owners. Consequently, a one- to 2-year time frame is usually the selected elimination period.

Insurers will issue disability buyout policies with benefit limits up to a specified percentage of the purchase price for the disabled owner's interest.

The percentage participation limits may vary from 80 to 100 percent, but virtually every insurer reduces its participation after the insured business owner reaches age 59. Aggregate limitations also exist for this type of policy, which may also be somewhat restrictive. The regular policy limitations range from $500,000 to $2 million depending on the insurer, and they are affected by the combination of the elimination period and benefit period selected. Again, the coverage available will vary with the type of occupation class for the business, the type of business, and any unique situations in the specific business. Policies with higher limits may also be negotiated with specialty underwriters.

Many disability buyout policies have a conversion provision. If the owner leaves the business before a certain age (such as 60), he or she is able to convert the policy to a regular disability income policy without evidence of medical insurability as long as he or she is still working. The maximum monthly benefit and benefit duration available under the conversion policy are spelled out in the disability buyout policy, but they are subject to the insurer's issue limits at the time of conversion. The premium for the new policy is usually at original age rates, but some insurers use attained-age rates.

A few insurers allow the insured under a disability buyout policy to be changed if the original insured ceases to be one of the business owners. However, such a change typically requires both new medical and financial underwriting.

Form of Buyout Payments

The purchase price for a disabled owner's interest will be in the form of either a lump sum or an installment obligation. Lump-sum purchases are impractical to fund in disability buy-sell agreements unless there is a specific insurance contract providing the funding. It is simply not realistic that a business entity could accumulate enough cash in anticipation of a possible buyout.

Several insurance companies offer disability buyout policies that provide a lump-sum benefit when the elimination period has been satisfied. Other buyout policies provide for periodic payments over a 2-, 3-, or 5-year period once the buyout is triggered. However, the maximum benefit available under such contracts is usually limited to a specific percentage of the value of the insured's ownership interest. Therefore, even if a disability buyout contract is purchased, there may be a gap between the amount of proceeds and the required lump-sum purchase price.

The traditional and most common method of payout is the periodic payout. Usually, the insurer will provide higher total benefits on a periodic-payout basis than on a lump-sum basis. The longer the period of payout, the higher the benefits are likely to be.

Financial Underwriting of the Disability Buyout Policy

Insurers carefully underwrite the disability buyout risk. As previously mentioned, insurers may provide protection for only a specified percentage of the actual purchase price. It is usually required that the purchase price be fixed in the agreement, including a provision for annual review. Insurers will demand financial data from the closely held business to determine that the purchase price is not excessive. Insurers apply some type of formula evaluation method to the data to arrive at the estimate of the fair market value.

Careful medical and financial underwriting are necessary in the disability buyout underwriting process to avoid situations in which an older owner may be encouraged to "retire" on the disability contract to effect the buyout.

The sales and underwriting processes for disability buyout situations are lengthy and more complex than those for the regular disability income sale. The coordination between the buyout agreement and the policy itself and the underwriting of multiple owners add to this complexity.

Claims

The administration of a disability buyout claim is significantly different from other types of disability insurance claims. Besides determining if the insured meets the definition of disability, the claim examiner must also determine if an actual buyout has or will occur with the business entity named in the application. Thus the examiner must obtain not only medical documentation but also documentation of the buy-sell transaction.

The long elimination periods that are part of buyout policies encourage late-notice claim problems. Examiners should anticipate these problems by using the documentation of disability required under regular disability or business overhead expense policies to address a potential disability buyout claim. When it becomes clear that a claim is probable, the examiner should obtain the buy-sell agreement and begin to become familiar with the potential buy-sell transaction. The examiner will also request up-to-date financial information to determine the current financial condition of the business. This preparation will enable the examiner to make timely requests for stock transfer certificates, promissory notes, or other documents that might be unique to the disability buyout claim.

Tax Treatment

The federal tax rules applicable to lifetime sale, liquidation, or redemption of an owner's business interest are applicable to the disability buy-sell situation. Table 15-1 summarizes these tax specifics. Note that most limited liability companies are treated as partnerships for tax purposes.

TABLE 15-1
Federal Tax Treatment of an Insured Disability Buy-Sell Agreement

	Partnership	Corporation
Cross-purchase Agreement	Premiums paid by partners are nondeductible. Disability benefits are received tax free by partners. Sale proceeds received by disabled partner are • ordinary income to the seller to the extent they represent unrealized receivables, appreciated inventory, and depreciation recapture • capital gain to the extent they are received for the partnership interest including goodwill (no basis step-up available)	Premiums paid by share-holders are nondeductible. Disability benefits are received tax free by shareholders. Sale proceeds received by the disabled shareholder are capital gain to the seller (no basis step-up available)
Entity (Stock-redemption) Agreement	Premiums paid by partnership are nondeductible. Disability benefits are received tax free by the partnership. Liquidation payments received by the disabled partner are • ordinary income to the extent they represent unrealized receivables, appreciated inventory, and depreciation recapture • capital gain to the extent they are received for the partnership interest (including goodwill if specified in the agreement (no step-up)	Premiums paid by the corporation are nondeductible. Disability benefits are received tax free by the corporation. Redemption amounts received by the disabled shareholder are • ordinary income if redemption fails to qualify for sale-or-exchange treatment under IRS Code Sec. 302 • capital gain if redemption qualifies for sale-or-exchange treatment under IRS Code Sec. 302

KEY-PERSON DISABILITY INSURANCE

key-person disability income insurance

The final disability business need is *key-person disability income insurance*. Its purpose is to indemnify a business for the extra costs resulting from a key employee's disability. It can be used to provide indemnity for lost sales, lost profits, lost contracts and orders, and lost goodwill. It can also be used to hire and train a replacement.

There is no quarrel with the basic assumption that, particularly in a small business, there are key employees who are critical to the business's continuing financial success. However, the unique stability and motivation characteristics of the disability contract pose certain challenges. How much does the loss of the key person affect the firm's income during that person's disability? How long does this effect last during the key person's disability? How unique is the skill of this particular employee? Are there other employees who perform the same or similar functions? How can the insurer be certain that the key employee today will also be a key employee at the time of a claim? How does the insurer avoid the employer's temptation to fund early retirement for the older employee who was once a key person? Because of these unique variable factors, the underwriting of key person disability income insurance is very strict and limits the sales and marketing potential of the product. As a result, there are fewer sales of this product than either BOE insurance or disability buyout insurance. This is also the primary reason that few disability insurers write the coverage.

Policy Provisions

Key-person disability income policies are owned by the business, and the business receives the policy benefits. The insured is usually someone in the sales, marketing, product development, or financial departments of the business. Persons with significant ownership interest in the business and their relatives are generally not eligible for coverage.

Most polices have short elimination periods, such as 30, 60, or 90 days. Benefit periods rarely exceed 3 years, and 6 to 18 months is the more common range. Policies are typically noncancelable and can be renewed until the insured is 65, as long as he or she continues to work full-time (or at least 30 hours per week) for the business and does not have a significant ownership interest in the business.

An own-occ definition of disability is typically used. Benefits are provided if the insured is totally disabled. Some policies also provide benefits for partial disability. However, benefits for residual disability are not available.

Benefit limits are subject to strict underwriting and rarely exceed twice the key-person's salary. The policy usually pays benefits on a monthly basis for the benefit period as long as the insured remains disabled. A few insurers provide lump-sum payouts, but they typically underwrite more strictly and require a longer elimination period.

replacement benefit

Some insurers offer a *replacement benefit*, which the policyowner can elect in lieu of other benefits. This benefit covers the costs associated with hiring a replacement for the disabled worker as well as the new employee's salary for a short period. This benefit is typically available only after the key employee has been disabled for a minimum time, such as 6 months. Unlike the regular policy benefit, the policyowner is indemnified only for actual expenses, which must be substantiated.

As with the business overhead policy, there may be a conversion provision for the insured and the ability to change the insured.

Tax Treatment

The premiums paid by the business are not deductible for federal income tax purposes, and the business receives the benefits tax free.

CHAPTER REVIEW

Key Terms

business overhead expense (BOE) policy
substitute salary expense rider
buy-sell agreement
disability buyout insurance
cross-purchase agreement
entity buy-sell agreement
stock-redemption agreement
trigger date
key-person disability income insurance
replacement benefit

Review Questions

Review questions are based on the learning objectives in this chapter. Thus, a [15-3] at the end of a question means that the question is based on learning objective 15-3. If there are multiple objectives, they are all listed.

1. In addition to providing disability income for themselves, what are the other disability risks facing business owners and professionals? [15-1]
2. What criteria are often involved in determining eligibility for business overhead expense (BOE) insurance? [15-2]
3. What are the provisions in BOE insurance with respect to each of the following?
   a. covered expenses [15-2]
   b. definition of disability [15-2]
   c. benefits [15-2]
4. a. How are BOE policies similar to regular disability income policies? [15-2]

   b. What provisions do they have that are unique? [15.2]
5. What is the tax treatment of BOE premiums and benefits? [15.2]

6. What are the reasons for needing a disability buy-sell agreement? [15-3]
7. What are the basic forms that a disability buy-sell agreement may take for each of the following?
   a. a partnership [15-3]
   b. a corporation [15-3]
8. What types of provisions should be included in a disability buy-sell agreement? [15-3]
9. Why should the definition of disability usually be the same in a disability buy-sell agreement and the disability buyout policy to fund the agreement? [15-3]
10. What provisions are found in disability buyout policies with respect to each of the following?
    a. renewability [15-4]
    b. payment of policy benefits [15-4]
    c. length of the elimination period [15-4]
    d. policy limits [15-4]
    e. conversion [15-4]
    f. change of insured [15-4]
    g. form of buyout payments [15-4]
11. What issues complicate the financial underwriting process for disability buyout insurance? [15-4]
12. What unique situations accompany the claims process for disability buyout policies? [15-4]
13. What are the tax considerations with respect to disability buyout situations? [15-4]
14. What unique problems face the underwriter of key-person disability income insurance? [15-5]
15. What are the policy provisions found in key-person disability income policies? [15-5]
16. What is the tax treatment of premiums for and benefits from key-person disability income policies? [15-5]

16

Introduction to Long-Term Care Insurance

Learning Objectives

An understanding of the material in this chapter should enable you to

16-1. Describe the various component services that constitute long-term care.

16-2. Identify the persons who make up the categories of caregivers, and explain their roles in providing care.

16-3. Describe the various care settings in which long-term care is provided.

16-4. Explain why there is a growing need for long-term care.

16-5. Summarize the circumstances that make it increasingly difficult for families to provide long-term care.

16.6 Describe the magnitude of the cost of long-term care.

16.7 Briefly identify the sources of payments for long-term care.

Chapter Outline

Long-term care often describes the help a person receives for an extended period of time due to physical or mental limitations. Although long-term care fitting this description has existed since the beginning of the human family, heightened concern about meeting its financial need is more recent. Over the last few decades, demographic, economic, and social factors have combined with advances in medical treatment and technology to raise awareness of that concern among most Americans.

As individuals and as a society, we are getting older. Americans are living longer, and as a result, the elderly population is increasing. Yet at the very time we are more likely to need someone to take care of us (and our parents), we are less likely to look to our families to meet that need fully or even to a great extent. Whether at home or in a nursing home, professionals and institutions provide a rapidly increasing portion of long-term care—care that is costly and must be paid for. Nevertheless, Americans often pay little attention to how they will deal with long-term care financing.

This chapter and the four remaining chapters of this book are about long-term care and the ways to meet the financial need associated with it. Whether the reader is a financial services professional or a consumer, the underlying goal of these chapters remains the same: a better understanding of long-term care, the options to provide and pay for it, and the importance of planning to meet its financial need. The financial burden associated with an extended, sometimes indefinite, period of long-term care argues persuasively that a person's financial plan is not complete or even adequate unless the resources required to alleviate this burden are identified. These resources may include personal resources, government programs, and traditional health insurance. The limitations of these options, however, make a strong case that, for many people, a properly designed financial plan, especially relating to a secure retirement, should include long-term-care insurance.

This chapter sets the stage for the subsequent chapters on long-term care by (1) defining it through component services, (2) describing caregivers and care settings, (3) explaining its growing need and cost, and (4) providing a brief summary of available financial resources to pay for it. Each of these resources is covered in much greater depth in later chapters.

Chapter 17 identifies the personal resources and programs that might be available to meet the financial need of long-term care. These resources and programs, although they may have limitations, often can be integrated with long-term care insurance, however.

Chapter 18 introduces long-term care insurance as an important resource to meet the financial needs of long-term care. It reviews the development and evolution of policy features and the effect that government legislation and regulation has had on them. Government is more than just a regulator of long-term care coverage, however; it often acts as an advocate for long-term care insurance. Chapter 19 presents insurance policy characteristics common in the market today.

Chapter 20, the final chapter, discusses the key role of consumers in the continued development of this new insurance product and the purchase patterns of available policies that indicate how consumers value specific benefit features. The chapter also addresses several of the decisions that consumers face in selecting the most appropriate policy. In addition, the chapter includes checklists or guidelines that aid consumer evaluation and comparison of long-term care policies and the companies that offer them. The chapter concludes with a review of group and hybrid policies that can also provide long-term care coverage.

LONG-TERM CARE SERVICES

long-term care

Long-term care is defined by its component services—a broad range of medical, custodial, social, and other care services that assist people who have an impaired ability to live independently for an extended period. This period can range from a few weeks to the remainder of a person's life. As explained in more detail later in this chapter, people often need more than one type of long-term care service at a given point in time. Needs may also change over time. Long-term care excludes *acute care* services in which a patient receives medical care for a period of time for a severe episode of illness (such as pneumonia), accident or other trauma, or recovery from surgery. Hospitals usually provide acute care.

acute care

Long-term care is provided in a wide variety of settings, including the home, community, and alternate living arrangements and institutions, such as nursing homes, assisted-living facilities, and Alzheimer's facilities. The benefits available to meet long-term care needs from both government and private sources depend on the type of long-term care needed as well as its setting.

The types of long-term care services—medical care, custodial care, social care, and other support services—require some further explanation. The subsequent sections explain in greater detail the role that caregivers and care settings have in providing those services.

Medical Care

skilled care

Medical care services for long-term care recipients are professional services prescribed by and under the supervision of a physician. These services are usually classified as *skilled care* (often referred to as skilled-nursing care) and are available 24 hours a day or on a daily basis. Skilled care when provided less frequently than daily, perhaps 2 to 4 days per week, is sometimes called intermediate care. The most common setting for skilled care is in a nursing home that is classified as a skilled-nursing facility. Intermediate care may also be provided in a nursing home, an intermediate-care unit of a nursing home, or at home.

Skilled and licensed health professionals, such as nurses, licensed practical nurses, and therapists, provide both forms of care. Procedures and treatments include injections, administration of medications, changing of dressings, and observation and monitoring of a patient's condition, including his or her temperature, pulse, respiration, and blood pressure. Specific forms of therapy are physical, speech, respiratory, infusion, and occupational.

The services of a medical social worker may also be required to deal with the social, emotional, and other problems associated with an illness or disability. Although both skilled and intermediate care usually anticipate rehabilitation or recovery from an accident or illness, the duration of care is often unspecified.

Example: Charlene was recently discharged from a hospital and is recovering from a serious automobile accident. Her lack of mobility requires extensive physical therapy and other medical services. Although her period of long-term care is uncertain, she is expected to make a complete recovery and return to a fully independent life. Charlene's long-term care consists primarily of medical care, which is covered by her medical expense insurance.

Custodial Care

custodial care

Custodial care, often called personal care, assists a person who has a limited ability to conduct his or her routine daily activities because of deficiencies in physical and/or cognitive functions. Someone can usually provide custodial care without professional medical skills or training. Family members often give custodial care at home, and it is the most common type of care in nursing homes, where unlicensed professionals (such as nurse's aides) often provide it.

Physical Functions

activities of daily living (ADLs)

Physical functions are basic and necessary tasks of everyday life and are often called the *activities of daily living (ADLs)*. They include

- bathing
- dressing
- grooming/personal hygiene
- using the toilet
- maintaining continence
- eating
- walking/ambulating
- mobility inside the home
- transferring in and out of a bed, chair, or wheelchair

Example: David, a patient with crippling arthritis, needs care in the form of assistance with ADLs. His period of long-term care has no foreseeable conclusion because he shows little progress toward recovery or self-sufficiency. David's long-term care need is primarily for custodial care.

Cognitive Functions

cognitive functions

Cognitive functions pertain to the mental processes of comprehension, judgment, memory, and reasoning. Recognizable symptoms and standardized tests identify and measure deficiencies in cognitive functions. Deficiencies in intellectual capacity are reflected in the necessary activities of life that require a greater degree of skill, judgment, and independence than ADLs. These activities include *instrumental activities of daily living (IADLs)*, such as the following:

instrumental activities of daily living (IADLs)

- shopping for personal items
- managing money
- using the telephone
- preparing meals
- managing medication
- doing housework

In addition to assistance with performing the above activities, individuals with diminished cognitive abilities often need substantial supervision to maintain their safety. Without this supervision, these persons may, for example, become lost, neglect to turn off stoves and other appliances, or fail to maintain proper hygiene. In the earliest stages of cognitive impairment, there may be the need only for some simple reminders. Cognitive impairments usually become worse over time, however, and continuous supervision may eventually be needed.

Social Care

social care

Social care consists of those services that help maintain an individual's personal interactions and identity as a member of a community. Obviously, a family—the basic social unit—maintains a primary responsibility to assist its cognitively impaired or physically disabled members to avoid the loneliness and isolation that can often accompany long-term care. If the care recipient resides in a nursing home or other institutional setting, the place of residence has a major responsibility to create and maintain a sense of community. Volunteer organizations established by churches, charities, and the government may have formal programs of visitation to long-term care recipients, as well as daily telephone communication.

Other Support Services

Other support services encompass any nonpersonal, nonmedical service that enhances the care recipient's security and well-being. These services include providing durable medical equipment and such services as home modification and home management. The following are examples of modifications that adapt the home environment to the care recipient's needs:

- ramps to allow wheelchairs and walkers to bypass stairs where possible
- medical response systems
- medication monitoring/dispensing systems
- stairway elevator seats

- bathroom balance bars
- enlarged shower stalls
- widened doorways
- improved lighting
- easier access to and operation of switches and controls
- nonslip flooring
- phones with amplification capability and larger, more legible dial pad buttons

Home management services maintain and repair a home as the care recipient becomes less able to perform such tasks.

CAREGIVERS

care continuum

Long-term care is provided by caregivers and delivered in specific settings. Among the caregivers and the settings, there is a progression of care from less intensive to more intensive as the care delivered moves from family members to professionals and from the home setting to supportive-living arrangements. This progression is often called a *care continuum.* A care recipient's level of independence and the care options that satisfy his or her needs and match a family caregiver's availability and capacity determine the care recipient's place in the care continuum. Thus, although the home is usually the best care setting in which to maintain independence, it may not be the option selected. A supportive-living arrangement may better correspond with a family's caregiving limits and more completely satisfy the care recipient's need for social interaction.

Formal and informal caregivers are the two main types of caregivers. In addition, respite caregivers, care coordinators, and even daily money managers provide long-term care services.

Informal Caregivers

informal caregiver

An *informal caregiver* is an individual who voluntarily cares for a long-term care recipient without pay and without formal education and training in long-term care. Informal caregivers include immediate family members such as spouses, children, brothers, and sisters, as well as others related to the care recipient by blood or marriage, such as aunts, uncles, cousins, and in-laws. Friends, neighbors, and volunteers from churches, charities, and community groups may also be informal caregivers. The informal caregiver with overall responsibility for a person's long-term care (usually a family member) is called a *primary caregiver*. All other informal caregivers are *secondary caregivers*.

primary caregiver
secondary caregiver

Formal Caregivers

formal caregiver

A *formal caregiver* in a long-term care setting is an individual who provides care as a profession or occupation and earns a living by rendering services to long-term care recipients. Formal caregivers include physicians, nurse caregivers, other licensed medical personnel, and nonlicensed personnel. Families may retain formal caregivers on an individual professional basis. However, formal caregiver services other than those furnished by physicians and other doctors are often obtained through home care agencies that assist informal caregivers in the home care setting.

Physicians

Physicians are formal long-term caregivers because they usually authorize and direct the medical care and other necessary services provided to long-term care recipients. Physicians may treat long-term care recipients directly for acute illness, such as pneumonia, or medically manage a chronic condition, such as Parkinson's disease. A *geriatric physician* specializes in the treatment of the aged. Chapter 19 explains physician certification of an insured as eligible for long-term care insurance benefits.

geriatric physician

Nurse Caregivers

nurse caregiver

A *nurse caregiver* is a registered nurse or a licensed practical or vocational nurse who is responsible for the medical treatment of actual or potential health problems with the goal of rehabilitating a care recipient or stabilizing his or her medical condition. A registered nurse supervises the conduct of nursing services that may include custodial services in conjunction with medical care. Thus, nurse caregivers also direct the services provided by nonlicensed personnel, such as nursing assistants (aides). Nursing assistants in the home care setting are often called home health aides. Nurse caregivers are principal providers of skilled and intermediate care (discussed earlier).

Other Licensed Medical Personnel

Other licensed medical personnel are those with special health care skills obtained through training and experience, such as therapists, speech-language pathologists, social workers, and dietitians. These professionals often work together, sometimes in teams, to care for their patients and advise nurse caregivers and physicians on important aspects of patient care.

therapist

Therapists. A *therapist* is a trained medical specialist who commonly performs one or more of the following services:

- physical therapy—treatment of physical impairments through the use of special exercise, application of heat or cold, and other physical modalities
- respiratory therapy—treatment that maintains or improves the breathing function through the administration of medications and oxygen and/or the use of ventilator equipment
- infusion therapy—introduction of fluids, electrolytes, or drugs directly into a vein, tissue, or organ
- occupational therapy—functional enhancement of persons who have physical, social, and emotional deficits arising from physical injury, illness, emotional disturbance, congenital or developmental disability, or aging

speech-language pathologist

Speech-Language Pathologists. A *speech-language pathologist* is a professional with advanced training and education in human communications, its development, and its disorders. Individuals with these skills measure and evaluate language abilities, auditory processes, and speech production and treat those with speech and language disorders. Speech-language pathologists often work with stroke victims.

social worker

Social Workers. A *social worker* is an individual with advanced education in dealing with social, emotional, and living environment problems associated with physical or cognitive impairments.

dietitian

***Dietitians*.** A *dietitian* is a professional trained in the application of the principles of nutrition to the planning, preparation, and serving of foods to promote health and treat disease. For example, proper nutrition can be used to control high blood pressure and diabetes—two conditions that increase with age and affect many seniors. Monitoring weight gains and losses and planning special diets for people on tube feedings are also a dietitian's responsibility.

Nonlicensed Personnel

nonlicensed personnel

Nonlicensed personnel are employed to assist long-term care recipients with nonmedical tasks that usually relate to activities of daily living (ADLs), such as bathing and feeding, and instrumental activities of daily living (IADLs), such as cleaning, laundry, meal preparation, shopping, paying bills, and completing other chores. In the home setting, these nonlicensed personnel are called homemakers, companions, and chore workers. Although these caregivers are usually unlicensed, some states require that certain categories of personnel be certified. Personnel at this level may receive training in geriatric care, including helping persons with cognitive impairments.

Respite Caregivers

respite caregiver

respite care

A *respite caregiver* is an alternate caregiver who provides long-term care services to relieve a primary caregiver from the physical and emotional stress of rendering care over a long period of time and/or to allow the primary caregiver to have some period of personal time. This service is called *respite care*. Respite care may occur in a number of settings and can be provided by informal and formal caregivers. Respite care can be relatively brief. For example, a neighbor who relieves a caregiver for an hour a day several days a week provides respite care by giving the primary caregiver the opportunity to take a break or pursue personal interests. Respite care can also have an extended duration. Usually, the longer the period of respite care, the more likely it is to be provided by formal caregivers. For example, a care recipient living at home could receive services from a home care agency or be placed in an assisted-living facility or a nursing home for a week or two when the caregiving family takes a vacation.

Care Coordinators

A care coordinator, also known as a care manager, geriatric care manager, or care planner, assesses an elderly patient who exhibits some degree of physical or cognitive impairment to determine care needs and to develop a care plan to meet those needs. The plan also identifies and assesses the care resources available from the family (including financial resources) and resources available in the community. The plan effectively places the care recipient in the care continuum by recommending the proper care setting and the appropriate caregivers (or combinations of caregivers) in a manner that respects the care recipient's independence and needs and the informal caregivers' availability and capacity. A social worker typically functions as the care coordinator and develops the care plan. The charge for this service is usually on a fee-for-service basis and costs about $100 per hour.

A family caregiver or physician may request a care coordinator's services, or the care coordinator may be part of the certification process to determine eligibility for benefits under a long-term care insurance policy (discussed in chapter 19). The primary family caregiver or the coordinator can manage the plan by monitoring the quality and effectiveness of care and making changes as the care recipient's and caregiver's needs change.

Daily Money Managers

daily money manager (DMM)

A *daily money manager (DMM)* assists clients who, for any reason, may have difficulty conducting their routine personal financial affairs. Services that DMMs provide relate to budgeting, paying routine bills, and keeping track of financial matters. In addition, DMMs may balance checkbooks, make bank deposits, organize tax records and other paperwork, and confer with creditors. Many persons retain these professionals because they may simply have little time for or interest in managing their routine daily money matters. However, DMMs in effect serve as long-term caregivers when they assist a person with physical and/or cognitive disabilities, usually precipitated by aging, that inhibit the ability to manage one's own finances. These disabilities include limited vision, arthritis or other conditions that hamper writing ability, and cognitive impairments that reduce the ability to complete tasks. The goal is to help persons with such limitations continue living independently. An adult child of an older person may seek the assistance of a DMM if the child does not have the time or ability to manage a parent's financial affairs.

Most DMMs charge for their services on an hourly basis. Some local government agencies, church groups, and other not-for-profit organizations provide referrals to DMMs and may offer reduced fees or free services for low-income clients.

CARE SETTINGS

care setting

A *care setting* is an environment in which health care services may be given to care recipients. Long-term care settings also occur along a care continuum that begins with home care provided by informal caregivers. They advance to supportive-living arrangements outside the home with the use of formal caregivers. As the care recipient's needs become more intensive and complex, informal caregivers often need support to maintain the home as the care setting. Although supportive-living arrangements outside the home may indicate that the care continuum requirements exceed the home environment's capabilities, these care settings are often an alternative to the home environment when they involve independent living and assisted-living facilities. As supportive-living settings progress from independent living through assisted living and to nursing home care or Alzheimer's facility care, they also represent a care continuum. Because the nursing home or Alzheimer's facility setting provides the most intensive and complex form of long-term care using formal caregivers, these facilities often constitute an end point on the care continuum. Hospice care, which can be offered in many settings, and hospital care also mark the end of the care continuum for some long-term care recipients.

The key to the appropriate placement of a care recipient within the continuum of care is to select the setting and level of services that best meet the care recipient's needs. At the same time, the care recipient should maintain a maximum degree of independence and as normal a living situation as disability or declining health permits. In other words, the assistance should meet, but not exceed, the care recipient's needs and should allow as independent a life as possible. Because there are alternative settings that might be suitable, individuals and their families should discuss the settings for future care in advance of its need.

aging in place

Aging in place is a term that is frequently used to summarize this approach to placement in the care continuum; care recipients avoid nursing home care by receiving care where they live, usually at home and in the community, through a combination of formal and informal caregiver services.

Home Health Care

home health care

Home health care, as the name implies, takes place where the care recipient resides and encompasses virtually any home environment other than a nursing home. Home may be the familiar family residence of many years or a new residence acquired by spouses for their retirement. The proximity of family members and reduced home maintenance and repair burdens are often the reasons seniors relocate, especially as they become less independent or after the death of a spouse. The care recipient's home may also be in a family member's residence, an independent living facility, or assisted-living facility.

The spectrum of long-term-care services available in the home setting is quite broad, encompassing medical and custodial services that use both informal and formal caregivers. These services are provided to the extent and in the combination necessary to meet the recipient's changing needs and the family caregivers' availability and capacity. Nationwide, a landmark report documented that there were 22.4 million families providing physical and emotional assistance to older loved ones or friends during the year surveyed.[1] For more than half of these care recipients, these caregivers represent their only source of long-term care.[2] More than 10 million Americans over age 65 live alone, and many have no one to turn to if they need help.[3]

Most care recipients and their families view the home as the ideal care setting, at least at the beginning of the care continuum when care needs are more easily managed. With familiar surroundings, possessions accumulated over a lifetime, and proximity to established neighbors and friends, the care recipient can flourish and function at a high level of independence despite a disability or chronic condition. To the extent recovery is possible after an illness or injury, it is often quicker when care is delivered in a preferred setting, such as at home. In the home setting, family members, to the extent they are available and have the capacity to do so, may provide the needed custodial services by assisting with activities of daily living, instrumental activities of daily living, and home maintenance. Assistance may be hands-on or in the form of supervision to make sure these tasks are properly and safely completed.

Many elderly with some disabilities live by themselves and need only minor assistance at the beginning and end of the day. Although the ideal location is the care recipient's own residence, the care recipient may move into a family member's home to make it easier for the family caregiver to provide assistance.

Example: Jane's mother, Dorothy, recently widowed at age 78, remains in reasonably good health, but she is becoming increasingly frail and suffers from macular degeneration that restricts her vision. Jane visits her mother two or more times a week to pay bills and to handle financial matters that are now beyond Dorothy's current abilities. When she visits, Jane brings her mother groceries and other necessary purchases. Jane also closely monitors her mother's routine daily activities, such as dressing and bathing, to make sure that she is completing them without major difficulty. Jane's husband cuts the grass, shovels snow, and keeps Dorothy's house in repair.

Jane, as the primary caregiver, and her husband are able to take care of Dorothy's current needs quite well as her informal caregivers in Dorothy's home where, despite some limitations, she maintains significant independence. They are giving Dorothy long-term care at a relatively low level in the care continuum by assisting with the IADLs and the ADLs, frequently on a stand-by basis, and performing home maintenance.

As care needs change with increased dependency, a family caregiver may have to seek additional assistance to maintain the care recipient at home. This assistance can include a range of support through home health care agencies, adult day care centers, and community services. The services that these groups provide allow a family member to maintain a relative in the home care setting when the relative's increasing needs exceed the informal caregiver's availability and/or capacity. In the absence of these services, the family caregiver would have little choice than to turn to supportive-living arrangements.

Home Health Care Agencies

home health care agency

A *home health care agency* is a private company that specializes in care to the elderly and disabled. Many of these agencies employ a range of formal caregivers that frequently includes those previously listed under the headings of nurse caregivers, other licensed medical personnel, and nonlicensed personnel. These agencies can provide medical and custodial services. Specifically, they may provide intermediate nursing services; help the care recipient with bathing, dressing, and meals; and offer socialization and housekeeping. Some agencies, however, provide little medical care and specialize in home health aides (nursing assistants) and other nonlicensed personnel (such as homemakers, companions, and chore workers) who may maintain and repair a home. These agencies are more appropriately referred to as home care agencies.

Example: To continue the previous example, Dorothy falls and breaks her hip. After release from the hospital and a less-than-30-day stay in a nursing home, she returns home to complete her recovery. A home health care agency now provides medical services in the form of nursing care services and physical therapy three times a week. A home health aide visits every weekday to help Dorothy with dressing, bathing, and transferring in and out of bed and chairs.

Jane has just received a letter from Medicare informing her that Dorothy's recovery is now complete to the extent that she no longer requires nursing care. The services of the home health aide who assisted Dorothy with her ADLs are also no longer covered because Medicare does not pay for custodial care in the absence of a need for intermediate nursing care.

Because Dorothy is left with limited agility after her surgery and is becoming more frail, Jane and Dorothy agree to retain the home health care agency's services for a few hours every weekday to assist with dressing, bathing, and personal hygiene while Jane and her husband are at work. On the weekend and sometimes during weekday evenings, Jane and her husband continue to care for Dorothy as they did before her accident. However, her needs now include hands-on assistance with ADLs that the home health aide provides during the week.

Dorothy has returned to a lower level of care than when she required nursing care during her recovery from surgery. Nevertheless, although Dorothy remains at home, her increased dependency and the continuing services of a formal custodial caregiver have clearly advanced her along the care continuum beyond the point at which Jane and her husband began to care for her.

Home health care agencies are usually state licensed, but regulation varies widely among states and by the type of services provided. However, only about one-half of licensed home health care agencies meet the standards to receive the federal certification required for payment of services under the Medicare and Medicaid programs. The National Home Care Council, the Joint Commission on Accreditation of Healthcare Organizations, and the Community Health Accreditation Program are three prominent standard-setting organizations that accredit home health care agencies. State licensure, federal certification, and accreditation are important indicators of the home health care agency's staff qualifications and, therefore, of the quality of its services.

Adult Day Care Centers

adult day care center

The *adult day care center* is a relatively new care setting that provides social, medical, and rehabilitative services to people with physical and mental limitations. These centers are designed for the elderly who may be severely impaired but live at home and whose family caregiver may be unavailable to stay at home during the day because he or she is working. In addition, care in this setting allows the caregiver a break and an opportunity for personal activities. It also provides the elderly person with social interaction. Without the services these centers provide, many people could not remain at home.

Adult day care centers are usually open 5 days a week from 6 to 12 hours per day and typically offer a full range of long-term care services. Custodial care is provided. Indeed, most of those receiving care at adult day care centers are frail and need help with the activities of daily living. Many have cognitive impairments, including the early stages of Alzheimer's disease. The centers also provide meals under the direction of a dietitian and meet social needs through recreational and educational activities. Many programs offer transportation between home and the center. Medical services include nursing care, as well as physical, speech, and occupational therapy. Not all centers provide medical services, however. Daily charges range from around $50 to over $100 if medical services are provided. These centers are frequently sponsored by community service agencies.

Insurance industry representatives often use the terms "adult day center" and "adult day services" to describe this form of long-term care, thereby avoiding the words "day care," which seniors may find offensive.

Community Services

Community services include community-sponsored programs and services funded by the Administration on Aging.

Community-Sponsored Programs. Almost every community, through volunteers, community groups, charities, churches, and the government, provides various arrays of services that support family caregivers and enhance a care recipient's ability to remain at home. Indeed, the development of adult day care centers discussed above demonstrates the important role community services can play in long-term care. Many communities offer organized classes ranging from art to exercise. Other social services include group sightseeing, scheduled transportation to local shopping facilities, and regularly scheduled movies. These services keep seniors not only physically active, but also mentally engaged. The significant variations in specific services that communities sponsor are beyond the scope of this text. However, a review of the categories of services funded by the Administration on Aging identifies the services that are common across communities.

Services Funded by the Administration on Aging. The federal Older Americans Act established the Administration on Aging (AOA), which supports local area agencies on aging (AAAs) through funds provided to each state. Nationwide, over 650 area agencies on aging receive funding from their respective states. The AAAs contract with public and private groups to offer services, or they may provide services directly to support in-home and community services for individuals aged 60 or older. There are several categories of these services[4]:

- in-home services—meals-on-wheels, housekeeping, chore services, telephone reassurance, friendly visiting, energy assistance and weatherization, emergency response systems, home health services, personal care services, and respite care
- information and access services—information and referral/ assistance, health insurance counseling, client assessment, care management (coordination), transportation, caregiver support, and retirement planning and education
- community-based services—employment services, senior centers, congregate meals, adult day care services, and volunteer opportunities
- housing services—senior housing and alternative community-based living facilities
- elder rights—legal assistance, elder abuse prevention programs, and ombudsmen services for complaint resolution

Each community determines its own priorities for the services it offers within these categories and the extent to which they are offered. Consequently, services may differ markedly among adjacent communities. Eligibility requirements may relate both to income levels and care priorities, such as the homebound elderly with no family caregiver. Community services, even those with federal funding, do not constitute an entitlement program like Medicare or Medicaid. Budgets are limited; often, there are waiting lists for those who are otherwise eligible. In an effort to expand the reach of their services, agencies are accepting payments that vary and extending income eligibility requirements above their traditional thresholds.

Families are encouraged to contact local agencies to determine the specific services offered in their communities, as well as eligibility and payment requirements. AAAs are listed in telephone directories, usually under city or county government headings. With funding provided by the AOA, the state and area agencies on aging have established an Eldercare Locator administered in cooperation with the National Association of State Units on Aging. The Eldercare Locator helps elderly adults and their caregivers to find local services for seniors through a toll-free service at 800-677-1116; some locator features are available through the Internet at www.eldercare.gov. Many churches also have volunteers who are valuable resources for finding local caregivers.

Supportive-Living Arrangements

With advancing age, many seniors—although they continue to be in generally good health or have only minor limitations—become less willing to maintain a traditional home, especially if they live alone. They may need some degree of assistance from time to time or at least want the security of knowing that it is available. In addition, they may feel isolated living at home and miss the companionship of others, often after the death of a spouse. At the same time, they wish to remain as independent as possible for as long as possible before entering a nursing home. Supportive-living arrangements for these individuals are available in settings across a care continuum that ranges from independent housing to an assisted-living facility and eventually to a nursing home. Which setting individuals or couples may enter is directly related to their level of independence. Because these living arrangements are often available through unrelated facilities on a stand-alone basis, they are described separately. However, in many other cases, a combined facility may offer two or more types of supportive-living arrangements. This discussion excludes adult retirement communities that are typically designed for younger retirees in good health who must provide entirely for their own medical and long-term care needs.

Independent Housing

independent housing

Independent housing is a collective term for the array of supportive living arrangements for seniors in a domestic or homelike environment. Residents are free to come and go as they please and do not require facility-based care (described in the following sections). The support these arrangements afford may range from companionship when desired to special meal and recreation programs. Local transportation to shopping and community events may also be available. Limited assistance with daily activities, if offered under these arrangements, is provided on a scheduled basis, not on demand.

Examples of independent housing are shared residences, senior apartments, home sharing, and accessory apartments. In a shared residence, a number of seniors live in the same house as a family, usually with each resident having the privacy of a separate bedroom. A senior apartment is a unit in a "seniors only" complex that provides a sense of community and security. Shared housing is an arrangement in which a person, known as the host and usually elderly, agrees to share space in his or her own home with one or more elderly guests. The housemates can provide companionship and assistance to each other and the host may receive additional income from the guest(s). An accessory apartment is a separate living unit that is constructed, often for a family member, in a single-family home. Such a unit is called an elder cottage if it is built as a separate structure on the property of the single-family home.

Frequently, community, religious, and other charitable and not-for-profit organizations facilitate and/or operate independent housing programs. Although many of these living arrangements are licensed, the regulations governing their operations vary widely, as does the quality of the housing and services provided. Zoning requirements also regulate the construction of accessory apartments and elder cottages.

Assisted-Living Facilities

assisted-living facility

An *assisted-living facility* provides supportive-living arrangements for older residents who, despite some degree of impairment, remain independent to a significant degree but require continuing supervision and the availability of assistance on an unscheduled basis. There may be separate sections of assisted-living facilities devoted to caring for individuals with such cognitive impairments as Alzheimer's disease.

Residents may have single rooms or their own apartments with kitchens, or they may live in separate units. Services usually include meals, laundry, housekeeping, personal services (such as a hairdresser or a barber), and transportation outside the facility. Services also include assistance with one or more activities of daily living, and medication monitoring is routine. A nurse may be called for an assisted-living resident who needs limited amounts of nursing care. If constant nursing and/or custodial care is required, the resident may no longer qualify as a candidate for assisted living. Facilities, however, may use an aging-in-place approach in the assisted-living-care setting and avoid relocation of a resident to a nursing home or to another unit by allowing a higher than normal level of care in certain situations, such as when hospice care is needed.

Assisted-living facilities may serve as many as several hundred residents, but most are smaller. Although costs also vary widely, average annual costs are approximately $34,000[5], or about half the cost of a nursing home. Board-and-care homes and adult foster care are much smaller in scale than assisted-living facilities, yet provide similar supportive services.

Example: To continue the previous example further, Dorothy's deteriorating condition impairs her independence to the point where the home care agency visits that assist her with bathing and dressing are insufficient to meet her changing needs. Dorothy can no longer be left home alone.

After performing an assessment, the care coordinator Jane hired agrees that Dorothy needs a higher level of care that includes continual supervision and hands-on assistance with bathing, dressing, and transferring in and out of bed and chairs. The coordinator recommends either an assisted-living facility or an adult day care center in the community if Jane is able to take care of Dorothy's needs after work and on weekends. Both options require Dorothy to give up her home of many years. Because Dorothy prefers the independence of a home-like setting, she decides to move to Jane's home, rather than an assisted-living facility, to allow her daughter to care for her on a daily basis. Jane is willing to meet the additional care needs, and having her mother live with her makes it possible. Dorothy applies and is accepted at the adult day care center. Jane and her husband adjust their work schedules to accommodate the center's hours. They are pleased that Dorothy receives care and supervision throughout the day, makes new friends, and is more active than she was previously.

This arrangement continues successfully for quite some time until Dorothy's needs at home increase to the point that they are more than Jane and her husband can handle. Somewhat reluctantly, Dorothy moves to an assisted-living facility where she receives supervision and the availability of support services on a continuing basis.

Dorothy continues to advance along the care continuum. Initially, a higher level of care at the adult day care center met her increased needs; the home remained the care setting, and informal caregivers provided more care. With the move to the assisted-living facility, both the setting and the dominant involvement of formal caregivers indicate that Dorothy is now at an even higher level on the care continuum.

Nursing Homes

nursing home

A *nursing home* is a state-licensed facility that provides skilled, intermediate, and custodial care services; the care recipient's condition determines the combination and extent of services provided. Nursing homes typically have separate sections or units for each level of service. Nursing homes are classified as approved skilled-nursing facilities when they meet the accreditation criteria required for reimbursement of services provided to Medicare and/or Medicaid patients. Not all nursing homes that offer skilled-nursing care services seek Medicare or Medicaid approval.

Hospitals usually discharge patients to nursing homes to complete their recovery from an acute illness or injury. Indeed, approximately two-thirds of people discharged from nursing homes were admitted from a hospital and stayed for 3 or fewer months.[6] Those who stay longer are often chronic long-term care recipients who enter a nursing home when they need more care than a home care setting or assisted-living setting can provide. These care recipients need around-the-clock care at least for custodial care and possibly nursing care. Other factors that affect the decision to enter a nursing home are

- the absence of a willing or available family caregiver
- limitations on an available family caregiver's capacity to provide home care even with the support of community and professional home care services
- the determination that the cost of home care needed to meet the recipient's needs makes the nursing home a more economical option

Nursing homes frequently represent the highest level of care and an end point on the long-term care continuum. They provide the most intensive long-term care services because of their setting and the array of formal caregivers available on a 24-hour basis.

Alzheimer's Facilities

Individuals with Alzheimer's disease and other serious forms of dementia often need specialized or unique forms of care that are not given to all patients in most nursing homes. This care requires a high level of staffing to provide the social interaction, close monitoring, and significant personal assistance that these generally mobile patients need throughout the day. As a result, the *Alzheimer's facility* has been developed to furnish care to Alzheimer's patients and other persons with similar needs. These may be stand-alone facilities, but most Alzheimer's facilities are separate units of nursing homes or assisted-living facilities that are devoted to this type of care.

Alzheimer's facility

An Alzheimer's facility has a staff that is specially trained to deal with persons who have dementia. Such facilities are physically designed to alleviate the stress of disoriented patients. For example, the facilities may have few doors and a traffic flow to minimize dead-end corridors. There are numerous activities for patients and high levels of security—other than medication and restraints—to keep patients from harming themselves or wandering away.

Combined Facilities

A combined facility offers two or more supportive-living arrangements that offer the same housing and services described previously under separate facility settings. Some combined facilities provide independent and assisted living, while others provide assisted living and nursing home care. In both of these situations, the combined facility usually gives no assurance or guarantee to the resident regarding access to or the cost of the next level of care, should it be required. By contrast, a *continuing care retirement community (CCRC)*, also known as a life-care facility, offers the full continuum of supportive-living arrangements and is obligated to provide access to housing and defined long-term care services at each level of care for the life of the resident.

continuing care retirement community (CCRC)

Typically, CCRC residents must be capable of fully independent living upon entry, but they are assured of assisted living and nursing home levels of care as their future needs change. In some facilities, the residents may receive occasional home care services when they reside in their independent living accommodations. When a resident needs continuing supervision, he or she is usually required to move to the assisted-living unit of the CCRC. If, however, care needs escalate to the point where skilled care or custodial care is required on a continuing basis, the resident then moves to the CCRC's nursing home facility. Return to assisted living or independent living remains a possibility if the resident's/patient's condition improves. A resident spouse capable of independent living remains in the independent accommodations where the couple initially resided. Religious and other not-for-profit organizations sponsor CCRCs. Large corporations also develop them.

The financial arrangements under which the CCRC obligates itself to house and care for residents for life (discussed in chapter 17) vary widely because they constitute a use of personal assets to meet long-term care needs.

Hospice Care

hospice care

Hospice care is a system of treatment designed to relieve the discomfort of a terminally ill individual and to maintain quality of life to the extent possible throughout the phases of dying. When hospice care is available, the cost of treating terminally ill patients is usually much less than the cost of traditional hospitalization. It is not designed to produce a cure. Hospice care, only recently considered a long-term care component, has a number of unique patient care features.

First, as the definition suggests, the care emphasizes comfort and palliative treatments to manage pain rather than the performance of heroic medical treatment and surgical procedures.

Second, in addition to the array of formal caregivers described previously, the hospice care team includes psychologists, spiritual advisors, and bereavement counselors. Counseling for the patient and family members from these professionals is a standard component of hospice care.

Third, hospice care can be provided in multiple settings, depending on the care recipient's needs and circumstances. The home is the typical setting because of familiar surroundings and the likely presence of family members who are often caregivers. Individuals without family caregivers may enter a freestanding hospice facility, which provides a home-like setting, professional staff, and continuous access by family members. Nursing homes and hospitals may also serve as hospice care settings.

Finally, because hospice care is provided at the very end of an individual's continuum of care, its duration is usually measured in weeks or months, not years.

THE GROWING NEED FOR LONG-TERM CARE

The need for long-term care is most often associated with the elderly, but it has no age barrier. Many younger persons are unable to care for themselves because of handicaps resulting from birth defects, mental conditions, illnesses, or accidents. For example, victims of accidents with severe head trauma and such illnesses as a stroke or multiple sclerosis may be any age. Indeed, more than a third of individuals who receive help with everyday activities are working-age adults.[7] Most of this care is provided at home or through community services, and approximately 10 percent of nursing home patients are younger than 65.[8]

Nevertheless, the growing need for long-term care is related to age and increasing longevity.

Age

The greatest single predictor of the need for long-term care is advancing age and the gradual, inevitable decline in physical and mental abilities that usually accompanies it. The effect of age on the need for long-term care is obvious enough, but a few often-quoted statistics easily confirm this reality:

- Age-related disabling conditions, although not initially life threatening but causing a deterioration of health (for example, arthritis, senile dementia, and Alzheimer's disease), affect 20 percent of those over age 65. This figure jumps to about one in two for those older than 85.[9]
- Those who attain age 85 are nearly four times as likely to need long-term care as those who have attained age 65 (50 percent versus 14 percent).[10]

Not surprisingly, the older we become, the more vulnerable we are to the conditions that require long-term care. A healthy and long life brings many rewards but increases the chances of dependence on someone else. Simply put: Getting older is dangerous to your independent living!

Hidden in the average numbers above is an important gender difference with respect to the need for long-term care. Women generally live longer than men do. They usually outlive their husbands. They are more likely to live alone, and they are more likely to need institutional care. Indeed, women are twice as likely as men to use nursing home care after age 65.[11]

Increasing Longevity

As sobering as the previous statistics may be for anyone of advancing years, they become even more compelling with the realization that they are not static. Thanks to continuing giant strides over the last century in living conditions, nutrition, public hygiene and sanitation, maternity and infant care, inoculations, and other medical advances to treat infectious and acute illnesses, we are living longer. In 1900, life expectancy at birth was 47 years. By 1960, life expectancy had increased to 70 years; in 2002, life expectancy at birth was 79.9 years for women and 74.5 years for men. Perhaps more significantly, people who survive to age 65 can expect to live an average of 18.2 more years.[12]

Thus, there are more people entering the age categories discussed previously in which dependency on others is more prevalent. The baby-boom generation[13] that will reach age 65 between 2011 and 2029 will swell these numbers significantly. A few statistics using the population projections in figure 16-1 make the case:

- In 2000, there were approximately 35 million people aged 65 and over, constituting 12.5 percent of the country's population of 282 million; by 2030, after the last of the baby-boom generation reaches age 65, there will be slightly over 70 million seniors, constituting about 20 percent of the population (363.6 million).
- Individuals aged 85 and older are the fastest-growing segment of the senior population. This segment is expected to increase from 4.3 million, or 1.6 percent of the population, in 2000 to almost 9.6 million by 2030, when it will represent over 2.8 percent of the population.
- By 2050, when the full effect of the baby-boom retirees is felt, the age-85-and-over category will be almost 21 million and constitute almost 5 percent of the population (419.8 million).

FIGURE 16-1
Projected Growth in U.S. Elderly Population (in Millions)

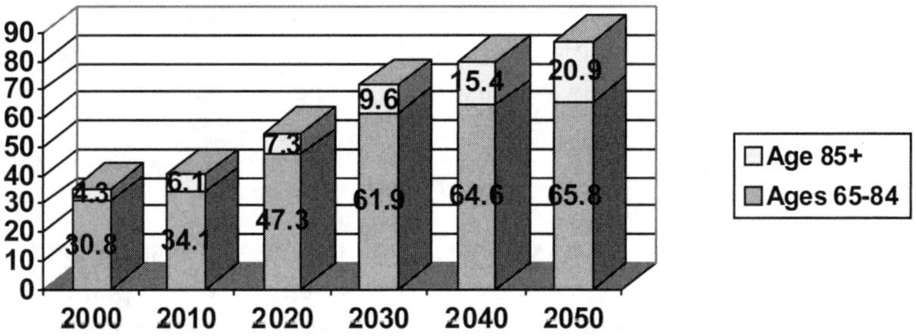

Source: U.S. Interim Projections by Age, Sex, Race, and Hispanic Origin, U.S. Census Bureau, Washington DC, March 2004, Table 2a.

In other words, individuals are not only aging; they are getting even older and growing in number. A society of aging individuals presents new challenges. The increasing need for long-term care is a significant one. In the past, many persons needed long-term care because they suffered from such acute conditions as heart disease and stroke—ailments with formerly high mortality rates. But the age-adjusted death rate for heart disease and stroke has declined by one-third since 1981.[14] In the future, a larger portion of the elderly will be incapacitated by chronic conditions, such as Alzheimer's disease, arthritis, and osteoporosis—conditions that are more likely to require continuing assistance with day-to-day needs. Despite any declines in their rates of disabilities, the disabled elderly will increase in total with the rise in the number of the elderly population, especially those at more advanced ages. As a result, the aggregate need across the entire population will demand a growing share of national resources to pay for health facilities and professionals.

LIMITS ON THE ABILITY OF FAMILIES TO PROVIDE THE COMPLETE RANGE OF CARE

Family members (often at considerable personal sacrifice) provide a great deal of long-term care for their older relatives. More than 20 million families, almost one-fourth of all American households, provide informal and unpaid care for an older relative or friend who is ill or disabled. Cumulatively, such care represents approximately 70 percent of the long-term care rendered in the home. This care would cost over $200 billion per year if furnished by paid caregivers and would constitute the main source of seniors' long-term care financing.[15] Moreover, these caregivers spend additional billions of dollars of their own money in the process of providing that care; total out-of-pocket payments for long-term care made by care recipients and their families exceed $44 billion per year.[16]

Studies show that the principal caregivers are daughters (26.6 percent), spouses (23.4 percent), other female relatives (17.5 percent) and sons (14.7 percent). Almost 20 percent of caregivers for the elderly live with the person for whom they are caring. Cumulatively, women, including nonrelatives, make up over 63 percent of informal caregivers. The average age of family caregivers for someone aged 50 and older is estimated to be 46; almost half of these caregivers are over age 65.[17]

Because most families prefer to care for their older relatives at home, informal caregivers will continue as a principal source of long-term care. However, it is becoming more difficult for families to provide that care at the very time that the need for long-term care is increasing. Limits arise from demographic, economic, and social factors that can be categorized under the headings of availability and capacity.

Availability

Compared to previous generations, family members today are simply less available to meet the needs of their elderly parents because of a higher percentage of women in the paid workforce, lower birth rates, and geographic dispersion of families.

Higher Percentage of Women in the Paid Workforce

Women have been and continue to be the major providers of long-term care. However, their availability has become restricted because of their increased participation in the paid workforce. Due to economic necessity, the desire for a higher standard of living, and/or the pursuit of their own careers, a majority of women have joined their male counterparts in the workplace. Regardless of the motivation, the hours they spend at work are unavailable for caregiving and often exclude assistance to a parent who needs continuous care, thereby precipitating the need for professional care at home or in a nursing home. Still, many women (and also men) with jobs provide care to elderly parents. Indeed, over a third of family caregivers are employed, with over three-quarters of them employed full-time.[18]

Lower Birth Rates

Unlike the baby-boom generation, today's average family is smaller, and there are fewer larger families. Because of the cost of living, standard-of-living concerns, and marriages later in life, families are having fewer children. In addition, there are more childless families, and more people are remaining single. As a result, today's aging parents have fewer children to look to for their care than in previous generations.

Geographic Dispersion of Families

Family members are dispersed geographically to a greater extent than in previous generations. Sons and daughters and brothers and sisters often leave the area in which they grew up when they marry or simply to take advantage of employment and career opportunities. To the extent they are dispersed geographically, family members are unavailable to care for elderly parents or other relatives.

Capacity

The capacity of family members to provide long-term care may be limited by an individual's capabilities, a family's situation, and the condition of the family member being cared for. These capacity limitations frequently arise from multiple priorities, increased longevity, divorce, and the need to use medical technology.

Multiple Priorities

sandwich generation

Even when family members are available to care for an aging parent or relative, they often face multiple priorities that restrict their ability to provide care. The caregiver may still be taking care of dependent children, or he or she may have a spouse who also needs care. Such people who provide care to children or spouses as well as older relatives are referred to as the *sandwich generation*. Financial priorities may also conflict if the family caregiver must pay a portion of a parent's long-term care expenses while meeting his or her own financial obligations for retirement and education of children.

Increased Longevity

Longevity makes it difficult to predict the availability of family support. An extended life span leaves a greater proportion of older people who require support from a younger but aging generation. Thus, family members are increasingly at an advanced age when they find themselves responsible for their spouse or their 80- or 90-year-old parents. At this period in their lives, their own declining capabilities could make them unable to provide the extent of care required by the age and condition of their loved one. A retiree's limited financial and other resources could easily be insufficient to support both the caregiver and a disabled spouse or parent, especially if medical care or other expensive services are needed.

High Divorce Rates

Divorce has the effect of restricting the capacity to provide informal care in several ways. Not surprisingly, a person is more likely to care for the parents of a spouse than for the parents of an ex-spouse. Aged divorced persons, especially fathers, are less likely to receive care from their adult children. Stepparents are only half as likely to receive care from their stepchildren as parents of natural children are. Single-parent families, often created by divorce, have lower incomes on average than two-parent families and are often below the poverty level. They are, therefore, less able to assume the burdens of or contribute to the care of a parent or other relative.

The Need to Use Medical Technology

The level of assistance a family gives an elderly relative at the initial stages of a chronic condition may be nothing more than occasional visits to check on or observe routine activities and offer help when needed. Inevitably, the initial level of assistance almost always escalates to continuous care with the caregiver assuming a major responsibility for meeting a broad range of needs. At some point thereafter, available medical technology to improve nutrition, provide therapy, and prevent infection may be necessary, even if the care setting is maintained in the caregiver's or recipient's home. Such technology continues to evolve and increase in cost. While the family member may continue to provide custodial care, the use of the medical technology may require professional assistance 1 or more days a week.

THE COST OF LONG-TERM CARE

The Congressional Budget Office (CBO) estimated the year 2004 national expenditures for care for the elderly in institutional settings at over $92 billion, with home health care exceeding $42 billion.[19] These expenditures, about 11 percent of national health care expenditures, are increasing faster than inflation because of the growing demand for nursing home beds and the shortage of skilled medical personnel. By 2020, these annual amounts are expected to rise to approximately $139 billion for nursing home care and $69 billion for home care.[20]

The out-of-pocket payments for long-term care by individuals who must use personal resources can be astronomical. Currently, average annual nursing home costs for a semiprivate room are approximately $69,000 and can be much higher.[21] While over half of current residents have been in their nursing homes for at least one year, the average length of stay since admission is 2.4 years.[22] Two visits a day by a home health aid to help with bathing and dressing and household chores can cost more than $2,500 a month. By 2030, the annual cost of nursing home care is expected to approximate $207,000 with comparable increases in home care charges.[23]

SOURCES OF PAYMENT FOR LONG-TERM CARE

Table 16-1 shows projections for the long-term care expenditures of the elderly in 2010 and 2020 by payer category.

Although the statistics in table 16-1 illustrate total overall payments by source, any individual might rely solely on government programs, solely on personal resources, or on a combination of the two. Other chapters cover these alternative sources in detail. However, they are briefly presented here to summarize their limits and provide the basis for introducing long-term care insurance covered in depth in chapters 18 through 20.

Government Programs

Medicare, Medicaid, and veterans' benefits are frequently cited government sources of payment for long-term care services.

TABLE 16-1
Projections of National Long-Term Care Expenditures for the Elderly (in Billions of Inflation-Adjusted Dollars)

Services Provided in Institutional Settings			
	2000	2010	2020
Medicare	$12.3	$ 16.0	$ 19.5
Medicaid	36.2	52.0	57.7
Private long-term care insurance	*	11.2	25.9
Out of pocket	34.3	29.3	35.6
Other	*	*	*
	$85.8	$108.5	$138.7
Services Provided in the Home			
	2000	2010	2020
Medicare	$17.1	$23.8	$31.0
Medicaid	7.1	14.9	17.1
Private long-term care insurance	*	5.5	10.2
Out of pocket	8.5	6.3	7.3
Other	*	*	*
	$37.2	$52.2	$68.6

* Less than $5 billion.

Source: Congressional Budget Office.

Medicare

Medicare is a medical expense insurance program for people aged 65 or older, people under age 65 with disabilities, and people with end-stage renal disease (permanent kidney failure requiring dialysis or a transplant). Medicare provides coverage for acute hospital, surgical, and physician's care but pays only limited benefits for long-term care expenses. These benefits do not extend to custodial care unless this care is needed along with medical or rehabilitative treatment (post-acute-skilled care) in nursing facilities or at home. Unfortunately, Medicare's limited coverage of post-acute services in a skilled-nursing facility and payment of certain home health care services often gives the mistaken impression that Medicare provides payment for custodial long-term care services required by the elderly with chronic conditions.

Medicaid

Medicaid (discussed in detail in chapter 17) is a federal/state-funded entitlement program that provides medical assistance for individuals and families with low incomes and resources. Medicaid is also the largest source of payment for long-term care services. To qualify for benefits, one must essentially be impoverished. In fact, many people do spend down their assets to meet the means test their state of residence requires. Others transfer ownership of their resources to qualify. However, there are a number of significant shortcomings to considering Medicaid eligibility as an appropriate source for financing a personal program of long-term care.

Veterans Administration Benefits

The Department of Veterans Affairs (VA) may provide limited nursing home benefits (discussed in chapter 17) for veterans in one of its own facilities or in private nursing homes. Service-connected disabilities and illnesses or low income are eligibility requirements for admission to VA nursing homes. This care is always further conditioned on available space. Use of private nursing homes is possible upon discharge from a VA facility, but it is normally not provided in excess of 6 months unless service-related care is required. Direct admission to a private nursing home is almost always limited to care for a service-related condition.

Personal Resources

Personal resources (covered in chapter 17) include income, savings, and assets that constitute one's personal or family wealth. The single question most relevant to personal resources is their sufficiency in total to pay long-term care expenses often incurred at unanticipated times and for extended or indefinite periods at the levels mentioned previously. Statistics indicate that 50 to 75 percent of all couples are impoverished within 1 year after one of them enters a nursing home, and only 15 percent of Americans can afford to pay for more than a 3-year nursing home stay at today's rates.[24] Even if personal wealth is sufficient to meet expenses for a specific episode of long-term care, the adequacy of the remaining resources to maintain a spouse's or a family's desired standard of living and an estate to pass to heirs must also be considered.

An often overlooked—but very real—personal resource in discussions of long-term care is the support of family members. This support can be in the form of caregiving or monetary contributions.

Benefits from traditional forms of life and health insurance may also be used under some circumstances to meet long-term care needs. However, these benefits are limited in both the amount and the situations in which they are available.

Long-Term Care Insurance

Finally, there is long-term care insurance, which is covered in detail in subsequent chapters. It is a form of health insurance that usually provides coverage for personal or custodial care, intermediate care, and skilled care in various settings. These settings may include nursing homes and at-home care, as well as adult day care and assisted-living facilities. Benefits often vary by setting and the kind of care received. These benefits may be in the form of either reimbursement of expenses incurred (usually up to a maximum) or payment of a defined amount.

CHAPTER REVIEW

Key Terms

long-term care
acute care
skilled care
custodial care
activities of daily living (ADLs)
cognitive functions
instrumental activities of daily living (IADLs)
social care
care continuum
informal caregiver
primary caregiver
secondary caregiver
formal caregiver
geriatric physician
nurse caregiver
therapist
speech-language pathologist
social worker
dietitian
nonlicensed personnel
respite caregiver
respite care
daily money manager (DMM)
care setting
aging in place
home health care
home health care agency
adult day care center
independent housing
assisted-living facility
nursing home
Alzheimer's facility
continuing care retirement community (CCRC)
hospice care
sandwich generation

Review Questions

Review questions are based on the learning objectives in this chapter. Thus, a [16-3] at the end of a question means that the question is based on learning objective 16-3. If there are multiple objectives, they are all listed.

1. What factors have raised awareness about long-term care? [16-1]
2. How do providers of custodial care differ from providers of skilled care? [16-1]
3. What types of assistance do individuals with diminished cognitive abilities often need? [16-1]
4. What other types of support services might be provided to an individual who needs long-term care? [16-1]
5. What factors determine a long-term care recipient's place on the care continuum? [16-2]
6. What are the roles of each of the following in providing long-term care?
   a. physicians [16-2]
   b. nurses [16-2]
7. What are the types of therapy that might be provided to an individual who needs long-term care? [16-2]
8. How does a care coordinator get involved in the process of assessing long-term care and monitoring its delivery? [16-2]
9. a. Describe how care settings change along the care continuum. [16-3]
   b. How should a care setting be selected? [16-3]
10. a. In what types of settings might home health care be provided? [16-3]
    b. Why is the home often viewed as an ideal setting for long-term care? [16-3]
    c. What types of assistance may be available to a family member who provides home health care? [16-3]
11. What types of services might be provided by each of the following?
    a. home health care agencies [16-3]
    b. adult day care centers [16-3]
12. Describe the types of community services that might be available to a person who needs long-term care. [16-3]
13. Why may an individual need or desire supportive-living arrangements? [16-3]
14. What factors may affect the decision that a nursing home is the appropriate long-term care setting? [16-3]

15. a. What care settings are used to provide hospice care? [16-3]
    b. Why is the home the typical setting? [16-3]
    c. What are the other unique features of hospice care? [16-3]
16. Why is the need for long-term care not limited to the elderly? [16-4]
17. What are the primary factors that have resulted in a growing need for long-term care? [16-4]
18. a. To what extent do family members provide long-term care? [16-5]
    b. Why is it becoming increasingly difficult for family members to provide this care? [16-5]
19. a. What is the cost of long-term care? [16-6]
    b. Identify the resources that may be available to meet long-term care needs. [16-7]

NOTES

1. *National Family Caregiver Survey,* National Alliance for Caregivers and AARP, Washington, DC, 1997.
2. *A Decade of Informal Caregiving,* Center on an Aging Society, Georgetown University, February 2005, p. 4.
3. *A Profile of Older Americans: 2003,* The Administration on Aging, available at www.aoa.gov/prof/statistics/profile/2003/6.asp, accessed on April 25, 2007.
4. *Area Agencies on Aging: A Link to Services of Older Adults and their Caregivers*, National Association of Area Agencies on Aging, from its Web site at www.n4a.org/aboutaaas.cfm, accessed on April 25, 2007.
5. *Assisted-Living—Long-Term Care Facility Survey,* Prudential Insurance Company of America, 2006.
6. *The National Nursing Home Survey: 1999 Summary*, Centers for Disease Control and Prevention (CDC)/National Center for Health Statistics (NCHS), June 2002.
7. *Who Needs Long-Term Care?,* Georgetown University Long-Term Care Financing Project Fact Sheet, May 2003.
8. Centers for Disease Control and Prevention (CDC)/National Center for Health Statistics (NCHS), *1999 National Nursing Home Survey*, Table 3.
9. Congressional Budget Office, *Financing Long-Term Care for the Elderly,* April 2004, Section 3, p. 1.
10. *Who Needs Long-Term Care?,* Georgetown University Long-Term Care Financing Project Fact Sheet, May 2003.
11. Centers for Disease Control and Prevention (CDC)/National Center for Health Statistics (NCHS), *1999 National Nursing Home Survey*, Table 3.
12. *National Vital Statistics Reports,* vol. 53, no. 6, November 10, 2004, Table II.
13. During the World War II years from 1941 to 1945 and to some extent during the depression years that preceded them, many Americans put their plans for having families on hold. At the conclusion of WW II, the birth rate increased significantly. This period of increased birth rates beginning in 1946 and generally accepted as ending in 1964 is known as the "baby boom." Currently, this population cohort is between the ages of 43 and 61 and will reach the traditional retirement age of 65 in 2011 to 2029. At that time, the combination of the elderly's

increasing life spans and the surge of baby-boom retirees will cause those aged 65 and over to constitute 20 percent of the total population (compared to the current level of 13 percent).

14. *Older Americans 2004: Key Indicators of Well-Being,* Federal Interagency Forum on Aging-Related Statistics, from its Web site at www.agingstats.gov/chartbook2004.
15. *Long-Term Care: Aging Baby Boom Generation Will Increase Demand and Burden on Federal and State Budgets,* statement of David M. Walker, Comptroller General of the United States before The Special Committee on Aging, U.S. Senate, March 21, 2002, pp. 11–12.
16. *The Economic Value of Informal Caregiving*, Arno, P.C. Levine, and M. Memmot, 1999, Health Affairs 18(2), pp. 182–188.
17. Family Caregiver Alliance: Selected Caregiver Statistics, accessed at www.caregivers.org, January 14, 2005.
18. *A Decade of Informal Caregiving,* Center on an Aging Society, Georgetown University, February 2005, p. 4.
19. Congressional Budget Office, *Financing Long-Term Care for the Elderly,* April 2004, Section 3, p. 1.
20. *Projection of Expenditures for Long-Term Care Services for the Elderly,* The Congressional Budget Office, March 1999, pp. 3 and 4.
21. *The MetLife Market Survey of Nursing Home & Assisted Living Costs,* October 2007, The MetLife Mature Market Institute, p. 4.
22. Ibid., p. 6..
23. *Long-Term Care Insurance: Protection for the Future,* American Council of Life Insurance, from its Web site at www.acli.org, accessed on April 25, 2007.
24. *The John Hancock/National Council on Aging 1997 Long-Term Care Survey,* prepared by Matthew Greenwald and Associates, Washington, DC, Report of Findings, p. 15.

17

Integrating Other Resources with Long-Term Care Insurance

Learning Objectives

An understanding of the material in this chapter should enable you to

17-1. Evaluate income as a resource for meeting long-term care needs.

17-2. Evaluate medical expense insurance as a resource for meeting long-term care needs.

17-3. Explain how noninsurance service plans help finance long-term care expenses.

17-4. Describe the role of family support in meeting long-term care needs.

17-5 Evaluate the use of assets to meet long-term care needs.

17-6. Explain various methods of reconfiguring assets that can help finance long-term care expenses.

17-7. Describe how Medicaid and veterans' benefits meet long-term care needs.

Chapter Outline

Many individuals have personal resources—other than long-term care insurance—that they can use to help finance long-term care if the need arises. In most cases, personal resources will be integrated with long-term care insurance. These resources may take numerous forms. Many individuals may have current or retirement income. Private medical expense insurance may provide limited benefits. A newer product—noninsurance service plans—may also be of help. An often overlooked but frequently used resource is the services and financial support of family members and friends. Finally, most Americans have assets in the form of savings and investments.

This chapter looks at these resources, including their limitations for meeting long-term care needs. It also discusses the ways in which assets can be reconfigured to better finance long-term care expenses while meeting an individual's other financial objectives. This reconfiguration may take many forms; these forms are as diverse as entering a continuing care retirement community, the purchase of annuities, the use of accelerated benefits or viatical settlements, the establishment of charitable remainder trusts, and home equity conversions.

Two important points need to be made concerning the use of personal resources for long-term care. First, as has happened to many individuals in recent years, personal resources may diminish significantly in value. Potential economic changes need to be considered when planning for future contingencies.

Second the personal resources discussed in this chapter are often adequate to finance long-term care needs only for limited periods and/or up to limited amounts. In many cases, personal resources will be inadequate to fully finance long-term care expenses, and an individual may need to rely on government programs to meet long-term care needs.

As a result, this chapter concludes with an examination of two government programs that cover long-term care—Medicaid and veterans' benefits. Of course, another alternative to depleting personal resources is the purchase of long-term care insurance. Chapters 18 through 20 of this book are devoted to the use and characteristics of long-term care insurance.

INCOME

The majority of individuals who need long-term care will have some sources of personal income available to them. However, the amount of the income and the degree to which it can be used to finance long-term care expenses vary significantly. The following discussion examines these sources of personal income, the extent to which this income might be available to finance long-term care needs, and the factors that might cause the adequacy of the income to change.

Sources

In analyzing sources of income, it is appropriate to look at the income of a household unit in which each member of the household is committed to supporting any other member of the household. In most cases, this household unit is a husband and wife, but it might also consist, for example, of a mother and daughter or two or more siblings.

Possible sources of income include the following:

- income of a spouse or other household member
- Social Security retirement benefits
- private pension benefits
- Social Security disability income benefits
- private disability income benefits
- investment income
- annuity income
- trust fund income

Availability for Long-Term Care Needs

Even though an individual who needs long-term care may have financial resources in the form of periodic income, much or all of this income may be necessary for other purposes. As the following examples illustrate, the amount of the income and the specific circumstances determine the income's availability to finance long-term care.

Example 1: June and Rich, both aged 55, have annual incomes of $40,000 and $60,000, respectively. Both have employer-provided disability income insurance that, along with Social Security benefits, will replace 60 percent of their incomes until age 65 if they became disabled and need long-term care. They have a daughter who is still in high school, and they recently purchased a new home that has a higher monthly loan payment than their older home did. They estimate that a family income of $80,000 is necessary to maintain their current lifestyle and to pay for their daughter's education. If Rich needs long-term care, June's income and Rich's disability benefit of $36,000 will provide no resources to pay long-term care costs. If June needs long-term care, Rich's income and June's disability benefits of $24,000 will provide only $4,000 per year toward long-term care expenses.

Example 2: April and Glenn, aged 64 and 67, respectively, live very comfortably on his annual retirement income of $100,000 per year. Their home is paid for, and they have annual investment income of $40,000. April and Glenn want to remain in their home as long as possible if either or both need long-term care. They estimate that they could continue to live well, excluding any long-term care expenses, on an annual income of $75,000. Therefore, they have $65,000 of annual income that could be used to finance long-term care.

Example 3: Macy, a 68-year old widow, has retirement income of $20,000. After paying $800 per month for her subsidized apartment, Macy has no additional income that could be devoted to long-term care expenses provided at home. However, if she went into a nursing home, most of her income could be devoted to its cost.

Example 4: Kirk, aged 78, has annual retirement and investment income of $45,000. His home is paid for, and his personal expenses do not exceed $30,000. He uses the remaining $15,000 of his income to help finance the care of a developmentally disabled granddaughter. Kirk feels he has no income resources that could be used to finance his own home health care because he has no intention of ceasing payments for his granddaughter's care. However, most of the $30,000 on which he lives could be devoted to facility care.

Example 5: Bruce, a 58-year-old bachelor, has an annual income of $150,000 and no financial debts or personal obligations. He expects to have an income of $90,000 if he retires at age 65 or is disabled prior to that time. He feels that $60,000 of this income could be devoted to home health care or $75,000 to facility care.

Future Adequacy of Income

Individuals who plan to rely on income to finance all or a portion of any future long-term care must be aware that all sources of income do not continue indefinitely. For example, a spouse's income may cease because of the spouse's retirement or his or her own need for long-term care. Private disability income benefits often cease at age 65. Social Security disability income benefits are replaced with comparable retirement benefits. This may not be the case, however, in the private market with individual or employer-provided disability income benefits. Income from an annuity or liquidation of an investment may also have a finite duration.

Consideration must also be given to the effects of inflation and other economic conditions. As the following example illustrates, what appears to be adequate income today may not keep up with the inflationary increases in the general cost of living or in long-term care costs.

Example: When Lou and Fran retired several years ago, they felt they would be able to devote at least $20,000 of their annual retirement incomes to home health care expenses. Since that time, their mostly fixed retirement income has failed to keep up with inflation, and they have had to lower this figure to $15,000. At the same time, home health care costs have increased at a much faster rate of inflation, thus further diminishing the percentage of these costs that their retirement incomes can finance.

Similarly, changes in other economic conditions can also wreak havoc with plans to finance long-term care needs.

Example 1: Mark and Helen, both aged 58, retired 4 years ago when their 401(k) plans were worth $3 million. They felt that these plans would generate sufficient income to meet their living needs as well as finance any necessary long-term care expenses. However, the plans were invested in employer stock and have diminished greatly in value. Now Mark and Helen must reenter the workforce just to finance current living expenses.

Example 2: Cal and Rhoda have always been conservative investors. By the time they retired 13 years ago at age 62, they had substantial income from certificates of deposit. As these certificates are maturing, however, the interest rates for new certificates are significantly lower. Cal and Rhoda had expected that they would be able to finance a sizable portion of any long-term care costs with their investment income. Now they will have to liquidate other assets that they had intended to leave to their children.

MEDICAL EXPENSE INSURANCE

Individuals may have limited coverage for certain long-term care expenses from private medical expense insurance, through either individually purchased policies or employer-provided coverage. The situation is slightly different, depending on whether or not the individual is covered under Medicare.

Individuals Covered by Medicare

About two-thirds of individuals covered by Medicare have additional medical expense insurance to reimburse them for some health care expenses that Medicare does not cover. This coverage may be in the form of an individually purchased Medicare supplement policy or a continuation of coverage under a former employer's plan. However, in no case is this coverage a substitute for long-term care insurance or other resources to meet long-term care needs.

Medicare Supplement Insurance

Medicare supplement insurance (covered in chapter 10) is primarily designed to fill the deductible, coinsurance, and copayment gaps in Medicare's benefits for covered services that would otherwise result in out-of-pocket expenses for beneficiaries. However, in a few situations, additional benefits are provided.

Some of the standard Medicare supplement policies in the marketplace provide benefits for services that could be described as long-term care. Most policies provide reimbursement for the copayment required during days 21 through 100 for care in a skilled-nursing facility. Some of the Medicare supplement policies also provide benefits of up to $1,600 per year of at-home assistance with activities of daily living for persons who are recovering from illness, injury, or surgery at home or at any other location other than a hospital or skilled-nursing facility.

Continued Employer-Provided Coverage

Somewhat over one-quarter of currently retired employees have some type of employer-provided coverage to supplement Medicare.

Some employers furnish coverage to supplement Medicare in a manner similar to what is provided by one of the standard Medicare supplement policies. Other employers use a Medicare carve-out under which the employer's medical expense plan reduces benefits to the extent that a retired employee has coverage under Medicare. The long-term care benefits under a Medicare carve-out are similar to those discussed below for individuals not covered by Medicare.

Individuals Not Covered by Medicare

Individuals not covered by Medicare usually have medical expense coverage through employer-provided plans or individually purchased policies. Some persons may also have a critical illness policy or specified disease insurance. As with the other types of medical expense coverage already discussed, there is limited coverage for long-term care expenses.

Medical Expense Coverage

Group and individual medical expense insurance primarily covers acute medical care for illness or injury. However, coverage often includes some benefits for services that may be received over an extended period of time in a variety of long-term care settings, such as a home, nursing home, or hospice. Coverage in these settings, as under Medicare, is limited to medical services rendered by licensed medical practitioners (such as physicians, nurses, and therapists) and to the cost of medical supplies and equipment (such as hospital beds and wheelchairs). Benefits are also subject to limitations. For example, nursing home benefits may be limited to 60 days for each episode of care, home health care may be limited to 100 visits per year, and hospice care may be capped at $5,000.

Medical expense policies also frequently contain a specific exclusion for custodial care, the most common form of care required by the elderly and others with chronic physical and cognitive impairments. The custodial care exclusion is defined broadly to eliminate coverage for the following:

- assistance with activities of daily living
- services that do not seek to cure or are provided during periods when the patient's medical condition is not changing
- services that do not require continued administration by trained medical personnel

Coverage of domiciliary care, which would include homemaker and chore services, as well as respite care is also typically excluded.

It should also be noted that insurers will sometimes pay for long-term care expenses that are not otherwise covered as long as this care is a less expensive alternative to covered services under a policy (such as hospitalization).

Critical Illness Policies

Critical illness insurance (covered in chapter 11) provides a one-time lump-sum cash benefit if the insured is afflicted with a covered critical condition, and the insured can use these funds for whatever purpose he or she sees fit. This use might include family support, payment of nonreimbursed medical expenses, or payment for long-term care services. The specified conditions for which benefits are paid may result from injury, disease, or major surgery. The lump-sum benefits from such policies, assuming they are significant (such as $100,000), could help pay long-term care expenses for a limited period of time. However, the types of covered conditions are often restricted to no more than 10. Moreover, benefits in force after age 65 (if the policy is renewable after that age) are typically reduced by as much as 50 percent.

Specified Disease Insurance

Although benefits under specified disease insurance (also covered in chapter 11) can be significant, they have limited applicability to long-term care because of the covered condition restrictions, the need for acute care rather than chronic care, and/or the limited nature of the benefits themselves.

Coverage under specified disease policies frequently extends limited benefits to care in certain long-term care settings, if related to a covered disease. Skilled-nursing facility care and home care may be covered, but benefits are usually less than $100 a day. In the case of skilled-nursing facility care, benefits are often paid only for a duration of care equal to that of a prior hospital stay for which policy benefits are paid. Benefits for home care also have a maximum duration, such as 2 weeks. However, expenses for hospice care in a hospital, hospice center, or a home may be paid up to $100 per day with a lifetime maximum of 180 days.

Substantial benefits under these policies are related to acute care, not to care for chronic illnesses and disabilities. For example, subject to policy limitations, benefits of up to $125,000 per calendar year may be available for the expenses of chemotherapy, $25,000 per year for bone marrow transplant expenses, or $600 a day for up to 30 days of hospital intensive care. These benefits are paid in addition to benefits provided by other insurance. If a primary program of medical benefits covers the expenses of these services, then the insured may use the specified disease policy's benefits for other purposes, including payment of long-term care services for a limited period.

Specified disease policies also frequently offer a first-occurrence benefit that pays a one-time lump-sum amount for each covered person who receives a diagnosis of internal cancer. This amount may range from $1,000 to $50,000 or more and could also help pay long-term care expenses to some extent.

NONINSURANCE SERVICE PLANS

noninsurance service plan

The *noninsurance service plan*, also known as a buying service or a buying club program, for the purchase of health care services is becoming increasingly common. This type of plan is also called a discount program, because its prominent feature is the assurance of a discount on the purchase of specified professional services and products from a designated list or network of providers and suppliers. For example, discounts may apply to services received from physicians, dentists, vision care providers, hearing specialists, dentists, optometrists, and to prescriptions and over-the-counter medications. These plans may also offer health assessments, access to health information, and assistance in locating health care services, often at no additional charge other than the membership fee. Depending on the services offered, the membership fee may be nominal, or it may be as much as several hundred dollars per year, sometimes with an initial application charge. Just as with discount stores that have membership fees, the savings will depend on the amount of services, the product purchased, and the size of the discount.

Organizations that offer noninsurance programs are adapting them more specifically to the market for long-term care services. They list home health care agencies, assisted-living facilities, and nursing homes as network participants. Discounts may range up to 10 percent at assisted-living facilities and up to 20 percent for home health care services and nursing homes.

These plans are often marketed to employees through their employer or directly to individuals. Insurers, through agreements with plan sponsors, may also offer them as an alternative when applicants for long-term care insurance are unable to qualify for coverage. The Federal Long Term Care Insurance Program discussed in chapter 18 offers such an alternative as a noninsurance service package.

Noninsurance service plans may also extend the benefits of an existing long-term care insurance policy. If services are obtained at a discount, the daily, weekly, or monthly benefit payment will cover a greater portion of expenses and reduce the insured's out-of-pocket payments. Similarly, a policy with a pool of funds as a benefit maximum (unless the maximum is unlimited) can purchase more care if the charges for services are discounted than if they are not.

Some insurers are considering the use of discounts to encourage insureds to receive services covered under their long-term care policies from preferred providers. Few, if any, companies have marketed such a product, however, because location, reputation, and services offered—not price—typically dominate an insured's selection of long-term care providers.

FAMILY SUPPORT

For many individuals, long-term care needs are met with the support of family members, or even friends. In some cases, family members may act as caregivers themselves; in other cases, they may give financial support to provide the care. Families may offer this support because the relative who needs care has no other resources. They may also furnish the care because they feel it is their obligation.

One of the most important steps that any family can take to provide for any relative's future long-term care is to discuss this contingency in advance. In this way, all family members have an understanding of the situation's potential magnitude and the role that each person may have to play in the future.

Family Members as Caregivers

As mentioned in chapter 16, family members provide about 70 percent of home health care, often at great personal sacrifice to themselves. However, demographic, social, and economic factors are making it increasingly difficult for family members to provide this care. As the following examples illustrate, the availability of family members as caregivers and the acceptance of such care can vary.

Example 1: Paul and Shirley have modest financial resources to pay for long-term care. They are both in their late 70s and beginning to show signs of failing health. Their four children all live nearby and are devoted to their parents. The children and their spouses have agreed that they will do everything possible to see that Paul and Shirley are cared for as long as possible in their home of 50 years. One daughter and one daughter-in-law who do not work outside the home are willing to provide some home care services during the day. Other family members are willing to help out at night and on weekends.

Example 2: Claire, aged 85, receives home health care services from Medicare, but these services are now insufficient to meet the level of care required to remain in her apartment. She has one daughter who would like to be of assistance, but the daughter lives 2,000 miles away. Her other daughter, who lives nearby, is unwilling to take on caregiver responsibilities and suggests that her mother apply for Medicaid to provide care in a nursing home.

Example 3: Albert, aged 75, is a lifelong bachelor and has no close living relatives other than an 84-year-old widowed sister. She is in frail health and would be unable to act as a caregiver. In fact, Albert helps care for her, and without his assistance, she will need to enter a nursing home. Most of his friends are older than he and could be of no assistance in caring for him at home.

Example 4: Hortense, aged 87, is barely able to care for herself at home. Although her children are willing to provide some care, Hortense has made up her mind that she will not be a burden to them and refuses their assistance.

Financial Support

Family members may also have the means to provide financial resources to relatives who are in need of long-term care. The support may be in the form of paying for long-term care expenses or long-term care insurance premiums.

Example 1: Carolyn, age 68, is concerned about her ability to finance any future long-term care needs. Even though she could afford to pay the premiums for a long-term care insurance policy, she has certain health impairments that make her uninsurable. However, both of her children are financially secure and can pay any long-term care expenses that she is unable to afford. In fact, her son has even established a trust that should be able to finance any portion of future nursing home costs that Carolyn is unable to pay.

Example 2: George and Marlene, both in their late 60s, would like to buy long-term care insurance but are unable to afford payment of the entire premium. Their three children are unable to provide any care because of geographic location and their own family responsibilities. In addition, they cannot afford to finance the cost of prolonged care for their parents. Among the children, however, they are able to provide the additional $3,000 that their parents need each year to purchase long-term care insurance policies.

Continued Availability of Family Support

Just as financial resources can diminish over time, so can the availability of family resources, as the following examples illustrate.

Example 1: Carmela, aged 94, has continued to live in her own apartment, despite many frailties of old age. This has been possible because of the assistance of her two children. However, her son recently died and her daughter now has the task of caring for a husband who suffered a stroke. The daughter cannot care for both her mother and her own husband.

Example 2: Ryan's father, aged 95, is in a nursing home, and his mother, aged 92, is in an assisted-living facility. Although his parents accumulated substantial resources for their retirement, these assets are now largely depleted, and Ryan is paying a large portion of their expenses. Ryan, who is 68, worked past his normal retirement age to help finance their needs. A recent heart attack forced him to retire, and he no longer has the financial resources to be of much assistance to his parents after his own needs are met.

ASSETS

Many individuals have some—even significant—assets that can be used to finance long-term care. However, when determining the possible use of assets for this purpose, an individual or couple must answer three basic questions: Are the assets available for this purpose? Are the assets adequate? Is this the way that the individual or couple wants to use the assets?

Availability of Assets

In determining the availability of assets to finance long-term care expenses, it is necessary to ascertain the extent that the assets are needed for other purposes. As the examples below indicate, availability can vary significantly among persons who have similar amounts of assets.

Example 1: Joe and Beth, aged 67 and 65, respectively, recently sold their dry cleaning business and now have $1 million of assets, exclusive of their home and personal possessions. Their only retirement income is from Social Security, and they will need to invest most of their assets to provide them with the additional income necessary to have the comfortable lifestyle for which they have planned. Only limited assets will be available if one of them needs to enter a nursing home.

Example 2: Grant and Lindsay are also aged 67 and 65, respectively, and have $1 million of assets, exclusive of their home and personal possessions. They recently retired but have sizable pensions from their former employers. They have no need to use their assets to provide a retirement income and could use all their assets to finance long-term care expenses if the need arises.

In addition, assets may be unavailable because they cannot be easily liquidated.

Example: Jacques, aged 65, had a successful career as a businessman. Last year, he sold two-thirds of his business to his two sons and is living off the income from this sale. He still retains ownership of the remaining one-third of the business, and this asset constitutes most of his $900,000 investment portfolio. It is highly unlikely that anyone other than his sons would purchase this minority business interest. In addition, his sons went heavily into debt to buy their shares of the business and are not in a position to take on more debt at this time. Therefore, the business asset could not easily be turned into cash to pay long-term care expenses.

Adequacy of Assets

Although some seniors have sufficient assets to entirely finance their long-term care needs, most seniors do not. They have not saved enough. In some cases, this lack of savings may be a result of individuals living beyond their means. In many cases, however, there is simply insufficient income left for savings and investments beyond the expenses of raising and educating a family. And, as mentioned earlier, accumulated assets are often needed to generate income for normal living expenses during retirement. However, the assets that have been accumulated—unless they are needed for other purposes—can be used to finance at least a portion of future long-term care expenses.

As is discussed in more detail in chapter 20, an individual must estimate the future expenses that will be incurred if long-term care is necessary. These expenses will vary as a result of many factors, such as age, type of long-term care desired, and inflation projections. Once the potential expenses are determined, the individual must determine the resources that are available to finance these expenses. As previously discussed, these resources may come from many sources, such as income or family support. Moreover, an individual must determine the extent to which accumulated assets can be used to generate additional income to pay another portion of these expenses. Depending on an individual's preferences, this additional income may come from the earnings generated by these assets and/or a liquidation of principal. This process of comparing needs with resources will indicate whether an individual has unfilled needs that can be met through other means—such as the purchase of long-term care insurance.

Example 1: Bryan is a 67-year-old bachelor who has a retirement income of $65,000 a year and $900,000 in accumulated assets. If he were to need nursing home care today, his income would finance the cost of that care in his community. However, Bryan is aware that nursing home costs are rising, and he feels he might need an income of $150,000 or more to finance such care in the future if he lives into his 90s like some of his relatives have. Considering that his assets will continue to grow, even if invested conservatively, Bryan's income and assets will be able to finance any future long-term care costs for many years. He could get by without long-term care insurance.

Example 2: Jose and Maria, both aged 65, are able to live on their Social Security and pension income of $40,000. In addition, they have $250,000 in accumulated assets other than their home and personal possessions. Their financial advisor has indicated that these assets could generate about $20,000 in income if either of them needed long-term care. However, the cost of such care where they live is about $45,000 per person per year. They could not fully finance long-term care expenses for a lengthy period of time, particularly if both need care. They are candidates for long-term care insurance to make up this shortfall in their personal resources.

Just as with income, economic conditions may affect the value of assets and the income it can generate.

Example: When Irv and Rebecca retired 17 years ago, they felt they had sufficient assets to meet their future financial needs. Now that they are approaching 80, however, they realize that their conservatively invested assets have grown more slowly that the cost of long-term care. Furthermore, current economic conditions no longer make it possible to safely generate the investment income from these assets that they once had expected.

Desired Use of Assets

Some individuals have no qualms about using their accumulated assets to finance their future expenses, including long-term care. However, there are probably a larger number of individuals who would prefer to put their assets—or at least a portion of them—to different uses. As the following examples show, these uses might range from bequests to meeting special needs.

In each of these cases, the individuals could help finance their potential long-term care needs with long-term care insurance.

Example 1: Jack and Pauline worked very hard to accumulate almost $700,000 by the time they retired. They do not want these assets lost to long-term care expenses. Rather, they wish to leave the assets to their four children.

Example 2: Beryl could probably finance any future long-term care expenses as a result of a $1 million settlement from a lawsuit. Because she has no close relatives, Beryl would like to leave most of her assets to the church that has been her "family" for the last 40 years.

Example 3: Cal and Betty have nearly $1 million in assets. They have a profoundly learning disabled son whom they have cared for at home for more than 40 years. Although he would be eligible for assistance in a state-funded facility if they could no longer provide care, they want him to receive care in a better facility. In addition, they do not want themselves or their son to rely on public assistance. Their desire is to use their assets for their son's care.

Example 4: Rudy has $300,000 in assets that could be devoted to his long-term care needs. His preference, however, is to use these assets to help pay for the college education of his nine grandchildren.

RECONFIGURATION OF ASSETS

An individual's assets are not always in the optimal form to generate the funds necessary to finance long-term care expenses. However, there are many ways that assets might be reconfigured to better provide these funds. In some cases, this reconfiguration might take place at the time long-term care is needed. In other cases, the reconfiguration might occur in anticipation of such a need in the future, possibly in a way that also allows the individual to meet other financial objectives at the same time.

This section of the chapter looks at certain techniques that are sometimes used to reconfigure assets. These include

- entering continuing care retirement communities
- purchasing annuities
- accelerating life insurance benefits
- selling life insurance policies through viatical settlements
- converting home equity into income

These techniques might be used as an alternative to long-term care insurance, as a way to supplement long-term care insurance, or because an individual has no long-term care insurance as a result of inadequate planning or uninsurability. Note that each of these techniques has tax and financial planning ramifications and should be discussed with financial advisors and family members.

Continuing Care Retirement Communities

As mentioned in chapter 16, one type of supportive-living arrangement is the continuing care retirement community (CCRC). In the simplest sense, a CCRC offers all the types of living arrangements that an older individual or couple needs. The individual or couple occupies an independent living unit, but access is guaranteed to the assisted-living facility or nursing home portion of the facility if the need arises. There are, however, many variations of the CCRC, and the services and amenities vary among them.

CCRCs have increased in popularity in recent years, and estimates are that between 500,000 and 750,000 older Americans now reside in these facilities. The financial commitment to enter some CCRCs that are sponsored by religious and fraternal organizations may be within the means of even lower-income individuals, but most CCRCs require a significant monetary outlay. Depending on the type of living unit selected, the amenities, and the services provided, entrance fees typically fall in the range of $100,000 to $300,000 (and sometimes significantly more). Monthly fees per resident can range from $1,000 to more than $3,000.

The CCRC Contract

Upon entering a CCRC, a resident agrees to a contract that spells out the accommodations and services provided, the entrance fee, and the monthly fee, which is usually subject to annual increases. The contract also specifies the portion of the entrance fee that will be refunded if the resident leaves the facility for any reason—including death. Some CCRC contracts specify that a portion of the entrance fee will be forfeited for each month of occupancy. Other CCRC contracts specify that a portion, or all, of the entrance fee will be refunded. Other things being equal, the larger the portion of the entrance fee that will be refunded, the larger the monthly fee and/or the higher the entrance fee. The following are two examples of the arrangements found.

Example 1: Anne paid a fee of $100,000 to enter a CCRC. The fee is forfeited at the rate of 2 percent for each month of occupancy. If Anne decides to leave after 20 months of occupancy, she will receive a refund of $60,000. Her heirs will receive the same amount if she dies after 20 months. Once Anne has lived in the facility for 50 months, there is no refund.

Example 2: Clyde and Irma are about to enter a CCRC and are considering the possible financial arrangements. The entrance fee is $250,000. They can elect to receive a 50 percent refund if they leave at any time for any reason. With this option, their per person monthly fee will be $2,000. If they elect an 80 percent refund, the monthly fee will be $2,600. And if they elect a 100 percent refund, the monthly fee will be $3,000. The refund is also paid to their heirs if Clyde and Irma die while residing in the facility.

The prior discussion is based on the typical form of CCRC. A few CCRCs operate on a rental basis and have no entrance fee. Some CCRCs are structured so residents can purchase their units as if the units were part of a condominium or cooperative. They can also sell their units to new residents who meet the facility's entrance criteria.

Just as refund provisions affect the cost of CCRC contracts, so does the extent to which coverage is included for nursing home care. A CCRC contract takes one of three approaches with respect to the provision of nursing home care. One approach, usually referred to as an extensive contract, stipulates that all levels of care will be provided at essentially the same monthly fee. The second type of contract, referred to as a modified contract, guarantees access to all levels of care, but the duration of covered nursing home care is limited. After that period has ended, the resident must pay for the cost of nursing home care, although often at a discounted rate. The third type of contract, referred to as a fee-for-service contract, also guarantees access to all levels of care, but the resident must pay the cost of all required nursing home care.

Some Considerations

The decision to use a CCRC to meet the potential need for long-term care should take many factors into consideration. These factors include age at entrance, the CCRC's location, future costs, and the facility's financial stability.

Age at Entrance. CCRCs typically have a minimum entrance age of 65 for an individual or at least one spouse in the case of a couple. Most residents, however, enter in their mid-70s. At the time of entrance, applicants are underwritten to determine whether they meet the physical requirements of being able to reside in an independent living unit for a period of time. Applicants who are currently receiving long-term care or who have conditions that make it likely that care will be needed very soon are denied entrance. As a result of this underwriting, an applicant may find that he or she has waited too long to use a CCRC. Therefore, anyone considering a CCRC for the future should have contingency plans if this alternative becomes unavailable. These plans might include the purchase of long-term care insurance.

Location. Individuals need to think seriously about the location of a CCRC. It is not unusual for individuals who retire to move to locations far away from their families and then return home when their health begins to fail. Similarly, older seniors who have not moved to a new location may want to relocate to an area where they have relatives. Even though their intention is not for their families to provide long-term care, they are looking for the emotional support and occasional assistance that close family members can offer. If they leave a CCRC, this relocation can result in a significant financial loss as well as a loss of their guaranteed access to future care.

Future Costs. As previously mentioned, monthly costs in CCRCs are typically subject to annual cost increases. Unfortunately, residents' monthly incomes are often largely fixed. Most CCRCs take this into account when they underwrite new applicants and require that applicants have enough income (or assets to generate income) to pay their future monthly fees and to furnish the other items of needed personal support. For example, a CCRC might require that an applicant have an income equal to 200 percent of the initial monthly fee.

If a CCRC uses a modified or fee-for-service contract, a resident may also be faced with higher monthly costs in the future because of the need for nursing home care. As a result, some CCRCs require that residents carry long-term care insurance to meet these potential costs.

Even when a CCRC carefully analyzes an applicant's financial situation, there will always be some residents who suffer financial reversals and are unable to make their monthly payments. Many CCRCs set aside funds to provide limited assistance to these persons. Circumstances may still arise, however, where some residents can no longer afford to remain in a CCRC.

Financial Stability. CCRCs, like any other type of enterprise, can have financial difficulties. Some have had to raise fees significantly; others have even declared bankruptcy. In many cases, the difficulties have arisen as the residents have aged and the demand for nursing home care has increased. Therefore, a CCRC's financial stability—both present and future—is of utmost importance.

For several reasons, CCRCs today tend to be in a significantly better financial situation than in the past. Actuarial estimates of future long-term care utilization are much more accurate. Close to 40 states also have legislation and regulations that apply to CCRCs, including standards for reserves to meet future costs. The nursing home and assisted-living portion of the facilities are subject to state and federal health care regulations. Finally, most CCRCs are accredited by the Continuing Care Accrediting Commission (CCAC) program of the Commission on Accreditation of Rehabilitation Facilities (CARF). This program, known as CARF-CCAC, publishes a list of the facilities it accredits as having met its standards for financial resources and disclosure and other characteristics of a CCRC. These characteristics include governance and administration as well as resident life, health, and wellness.

Use of Annuities

annuity

An *annuity* is a series of periodic payments that begins at a specific date and continues throughout a fixed period or for the duration of a designated life or lives. Although a detailed analysis of annuities is beyond the scope of this book, a few words can be said about their variations. Any annuity can be characterized in the following ways:

- An annuity may be purchased with periodic premiums (an installment annuity) or with a lump-sum premium (a single-premium annuity).
- Benefits may commence in the distant future (a deferred annuity) or shortly after funding (an immediate annuity).
- Payments can be received for a specified period of time (an annuity certain) or for the duration of one life (a single life annuity). Payments may also be received for as long as the first of two or more persons lives (a joint life annuity) or until the last of two persons dies (a joint-and-last-survivor annuity).
- Payments may cease at the death of the last annuitant (a pure annuity), or some of the purchase price may be returned to a beneficiary (a refund annuity).
- Payments may be a fixed number of dollars (a fixed annuity), or they may vary with investment earnings of the annuity company (a variable annuity).

charitable gift annuity

private annuity

Life insurers issue most annuities, but some organizations specialize in annuities only. In addition, there are charitable gift annuities and private annuities. A *charitable gift annuity* involves the transfer of money or other assets to a charitable or nonprofit foundation. The foundation then provides a contractually established income for the life of the donor. In most cases, this income is generally determined in part using an actuarial assumption that on average 50 percent of the value of the donated assets is returned to the annuitant. A *private annuity* is a transaction between two parties, but the person or organization that assumes the obligation for the annuity payments is not in the business of selling annuities.

Many individuals are concerned about the future financial well-being of themselves and their families. This has led to an increasing interest in financial planning for their retirement years and the creation of an estate for their heirs. No financial plan, however, is complete without considering long-term care needs, and the use of annuities often plays many roles in this planning. Although annuities, along with many other types of investment vehicles, are often used in the general process of wealth accumulation, this book does not contain a discussion of this aspect of financial planning. However, annuities can play a role in guaranteeing a lifetime income to meet long-term care expenses or pay long-term care insurance premiums. Annuities may also be used to fulfill long-term care needs of individuals and couples when long-term care insurance is not an available alternative and to meet long-term care needs of heirs. As with any financial product, there are many considerations that must be addressed when using annuities—including the annuity company's ability to meet its future obligations.

Guaranteeing a Stream of Income

For many individuals and couples, the ability to meet future long-term care needs depends on a steady stream of income that will last until death. As the following examples show, there are many ways that annuities might be used to generate this income.

Example 1: Bill and Cathy are both in their early 60s. When they retire, they expect that their pension and Social Security income will be adequate to meet their basic living needs. In addition, they bought long-term care insurance policies 5 years ago. When they purchased the policies, they were concerned about their ability to pay the premiums after retirement. As a result, they used part of a small inheritance from Bill's mother to purchase single-premium deferred annuities for each of them. The annuities will provide an annual lifetime income, starting at age 65, equal to the premium payments for the long-term care insurance policy.

Example 2: Hans recently retired at age 62 and had a significant amount of money in his employer's employee stock ownership plan (ESOP). He has no heirs to whom he wishes to leave anything, and his sole financial goal is to satisfy his own needs, including long-term care. However, he is concerned about the possibility of his former employer's stock decreasing in value. By using the proceeds of his ESOP, he was able to purchase an annuity that pays him $170,000 per year for the rest of his life.

Example 3: At ages 75 and 77, respectively, Henry and Gay have decided to move to a continuing care retirement community. One of their financial goals has been to leave a substantial amount of money to their church at their deaths. Now that their long-term care needs are met, they feel they can do this immediately. Through the use of a charitable gift annuity, they can give the church $1 million, while receiving a lifetime income of $71,000 per year from the annuity. This income will be more than adequate to pay their monthly resident's fees.

Example 4: Nick and Gloria, aged 71 and 69, respectively, recently retired from the construction company that they founded 40 years ago. Almost all their assets were tied up in this business, and Nick and Gloria want to convert it into retirement income that can be used for their support, including long-term care. They entered into a private annuity with their daughter and son-in-law, whereby the daughter and son-in-law obtain the business and agree to pay Nick and Gloria $100,000 per year as long as both are alive. At the death of either Nick or Gloria, the survivor will get $60,000 per year for the remainder of his or her life.

Meeting Specific Long-Term Care Needs

Annuities can also be used to plan for specific long-term care needs, often when an individual is unable to qualify for long-term care insurance. In fact, some types of annuities are designed for this purpose.

One example is an annuity that contains a long-term care rider. With such a rider, the periodic payment increases when the annuitant is determined to need long-term care. For the most part, this involves satisfying the same criteria that trigger benefits under a long-term care insurance policy. These criteria are discussed in chapter 19. However, the additional monthly benefit is available only after the contract has been in force for a period of time, often 6 or 7 years. In addition, the benefit is usually paid for a limited number of months.

Eligibility for a long-term care rider is underwritten much less stringently than long-term care insurance. Coverage can often be obtained if an individual is in the early stages of a condition that may require long-term care in the distant future.

Example: Grace recently retired at age 63 and is interested in turning some of her assets into a lifetime income stream to supplement her retirement income. She was recently diagnosed with the very early stages of

Parkinson's disease. Her physician has told her that her health will slowly decline, but it should be several years before she needs any type of long-term care. Although Grace cannot qualify for long-term care insurance, she is able to purchase a single-premium annuity that will guarantee her $2,000 of monthly income. The annuity has a rider that after 6 years increases this amount to $4,000 per month for a 36-month period if Grace satisfies the criteria for needing long-term care. Grace feels that the annuity payments and her other resources will be sufficient to meet her future needs, whether or not they involve long-term care.

---

impaired risk annuity

Unlike life insurance underwriters, who are concerned with applicants dying too soon, underwriters of annuities are concerned with applicants living too long. In determining the annuity payments for a given outlay, there is an assumption about an insured's life expectancy. Individuals who need long-term care have life expectancies, on the average, that are of shorter duration. This factor is taken into consideration if an applicant purchases an *impaired risk annuity*. With such annuities, an applicant's health is considered in the underwriting process, and the annuity payments are increased (or the premium lowered) in relation to the shorter life expectancy. This type of annuity is frequently used as part of structured settlements that arise out of legal liability judgments.

Considerations When Using Annuities

As the previous examples have shown, annuities may be valuable in planning for long-term care needs. The use of annuities in financial planning is complex, however, and the ramifications of their use are not always considered or fully understood by consumers or even some financial advisors who recommend and sell these products. Proper financial and tax advice is essential.

Annuities often have significant tax advantages, such as the tax-deferred growth of funds during the accumulation period. However, several of the previous examples involve the conversion of other assets into annuities. Some of these transactions may trigger capital gains when the older assets are disposed of in the conversion process. Other transactions may actually have a beneficial tax impact. For example, the sale of an asset to buy an annuity may result in a capital loss that can be used to offset capital gains that would otherwise be taxed. The purchase of a charitable gift annuity may result in significant tax benefits in the form of charitable deductions.

The income and estate tax treatment of any death benefits must also be considered. A deferred annuity has a death benefit payable to the annuitant's beneficiary if the annuitant dies during its accumulation period. A refund annuity may also have a residual value that is paid to a beneficiary if an annuitant dies after benefits commence. Without proper planning, there may be some unpleasant surprises when the taxation of these death benefits becomes apparent to heirs.

Annuities often make fixed benefit payments over time. To the extent a fixed annuity is used to finance future needs, the available resources will not grow as inflation drives future costs higher. If a variable annuity is used, future increases in annuity payments are uncertain because of the volatility in the securities markets. Some insurers sell annuities that are designed so that benefits increase from year to year, such as 4 percent per year on a compound basis. For the same dollar outlay, such an annuity will have lower initial benefit payments than a fixed annuity, but payments will increase over time and eventually be higher.

Annuities, like insurance, involve the law of averages. Although there are average life expectancies that are used to calculate premiums, some people live much longer than others. For those who outlive their life expectancies by many years, a life annuity was a great "investment" from a financial standpoint. However, when large amounts of money are used to purchase an annuity, little if any of these funds may go to heirs if the annuitant dies soon after the purchase. On one hand, the use of annuities to meet long-term care needs may free heirs from having to provide or finance care for a relative. On the other hand, it may also result in a smaller inheritance than other alternatives when the relative dies.

An annuity may be difficult to access to meet long-term care needs. In the case of a deferred annuity, there may be a substantial penalty for an early withdrawal of funds. Some annuities, however, do allow penalty-free withdrawals under certain circumstances, such as the need for long-term care.

The final consideration mentioned here is probably the most important—the security of the benefit payments. Private annuities are generally not secured, and defaults do occur. In the previous example about Nick and Gloria, what happens if the business fails because their daughter and son-in-law are not as good at business as Nick and Gloria were? Where will the funds then come from to support Nick and Gloria?

Even insurers that sell annuities have occasionally had financial difficulties and been forced into liquidation. Although annuitants usually receive something, it is typically in the form of reduced annuity payments or a lump-sum settlement that is inadequate to purchase a comparable annuity. It is important for a consumer to evaluate the company from which an annuity is purchased, not only in terms of the annuity's cost, but also in terms of the company's financial strength and reputation. The considerations with respect to annuity companies are essentially the same as those for long-term care insurers and are discussed in chapter 20.

Use of Life Insurance

An insured can reconfigure the asset value of a life insurance policy in a number of ways to yield funds that may be used to pay for long-term care. Life insurance policy provisions usually allow for policy loans, withdrawals, or policy surrenders. However, these alternatives often yield minimal funds because they are limited to the policy's cash value, which is likely to be inadequate to pay the cost of long-term care for a significant period.

Accelerated benefits and viatical settlements, on the other hand, can yield significantly greater proceeds because they are based on a percentage (or in some cases all) of a policy's death benefit. Consequently, accelerated benefits and viatical settlements are the more likely alternatives to which some persons with life insurance policies may turn when seeking funds to pay for long-term care. Nevertheless, the use of these transactions is no substitute for long-term care insurance. Although no one should buy a life insurance policy just to obtain its proceeds to meet long-term care expenses, those who have policies should be aware of the resources that can be made available. This use of a life insurance policy may be appropriate for someone who cannot afford long-term care insurance or does not qualify for it due to poor health. However, such a financial transaction also has its limitations.

First, these benefits are often available only if the insured is terminally ill and has a limited life expectancy. Many individuals who need long-term care services do not fit these criteria.

Second, the proceeds of a life insurance policy received through accelerated benefits or viatical settlements, even if substantial, may give the insured a false sense of security that long-term care needs are being met. In fact, the proceeds are very likely to be inadequate to cover prolonged periods of long-term care. For example, if an insured received $100,000, that amount would cover skilled care in a nursing home for no more than 2 years. Not surprisingly, the use of accelerated benefits or viatical settlements occurs most frequently when death is a near-term prospect rather than in chronic illness situations.

Third, the receipt of a life insurance policy's death benefit while the insured is still living diminishes or eliminates the resources available after the insured's death to meet the needs for which life insurance was purchased in the first place. If the policy was bought to pay estate taxes, retire a mortgage balance, and provide income for surviving family members, there may little or no money available to handle these financial needs. However, many of the purposes for which life insurance is initially purchased can diminish over time. Dependent children become independent adults, and major debts, such as a home mortgage, are significantly reduced or paid off.

A characteristic that accelerated benefits and viatical settlements have in common is the tax-preferred status that may apply to the proceeds received by the insured under certain circumstances. The proceeds received by a terminally ill patient are tax free if a licensed health care professional certifies that the individual is expected to die within 24 months after the date of certification, even if death occurs later. The payment may also be tax free to those with chronic, but not terminal, illnesses if the proceeds are used to pay for long-term care services not covered by long-term care insurance. HIPAA's requirements for the determination of a chronically ill patient and tax-qualified long-term care benefits are also applicable and discussed in chapter 18.

Accelerated benefits and viatical settlements are both vehicles to obtain proceeds from the death benefits of a life insurance policy while the insured is still living, and both may have tax-preferred treatment of an insured's receipt of those proceeds. However, they are vastly different transactions. One involves receiving some policy proceeds in advance; the other involves the sale of the policy.

Accelerated Benefits

accelerated-benefits provision

Many insurers now include an *accelerated-benefits provision* in newly written life insurance policies as a standard feature and/or allow a policyowner to collect accelerated benefits from policies that do not contain an explicit provision. Under such a provision, an insured is entitled to receive a portion of his or her death benefit while still living if one or more of the following events, known as triggers, occur:

- diagnosis of a terminal illness or physical condition for which death is likely to occur within a specified number of months, usually 12 months or less
- occurrence of one of a number of specified medical conditions, such as dread diseases or catastrophic illnesses, that would result in a drastically limited life span with extensive or extraordinary medical treatment
- the need for extended long-term care in a nursing facility, at home, or in the community due to an inability to perform daily activities
- permanent confinement to a nursing home

The categories of triggering events and their specific definitions vary among insurers and are subject to state regulation. Most insurers, however, restrict the accelerated benefits trigger to a single event, which is most frequently terminal illness.

The amount of the accelerated benefits available is a percentage of the basic life insurance coverage and may range from 25 to 100 percent. In addition, many insurers limit the maximum benefit to a specified dollar amount. This amount varies widely among insurers and can be as low as $25,000 or as high as $500,000 or more. The proceeds can be distributed as monthly payments, which in turn reduce the cash value and death benefit of the policy each month. Any amount not accelerated is paid to the beneficiary upon the insured's death.

Other than the tax-qualified requirements discussed previously for those with chronic rather than life-terminating conditions, there are no limitations on how the accelerated benefit can be used. It may be used to pay medical expenses and nursing home care not covered by other insurance; it can even be used to prepay funeral expenses.

Example 1: Jay, a 72-year-old widower, has insufficient income to pay the full cost of his home health care. He has two life insurance polices, each with a $50,000 death benefit and a cash value of $20,000. The policies were purchased several years ago, and neither has an accelerated-benefits provision. Jay can borrow the cash value or surrender the policies to receive $40,000. However, he would like to receive a larger amount. When he inquires about the possibility of obtaining an accelerated benefit, both insurers indicate that they offer such benefits but only if the insured is certified as having a life expectancy of 1 year or less. Because Jay does not meet this criterion, he then explores the possibility of a viatical settlement. Although some viatical companies are willing to buy his policies, he finds that they will offer only about $10,000 more for each policy than he can obtain through a policy loan or surrender.

Example 2: Kay, aged 80, has incurred significant long-term care expenses, and her assets are nearly depleted. She has a $100,000 life insurance policy with a $30,000 cash value. Because she has been certified as having a life expectancy of less than 1 year, she can elect an accelerated benefit of 92 percent of the policy benefit ($92,000) rather than surrendering the policy for its cash value.

Viatical Settlements

viatical settlement

A *viatical settlement* is another arrangement that gives the insured a cash advance against all or a portion of the death benefit of a life insurance policy while the insured is still alive. Under the arrangement, the policyowner (who may be the insured or someone else, such as a spouse) typically sells the policy to obtain financial resources to pay for expenses at the end of the insured's life. These expenses may include payment of long-term care costs.

Typically, a viatical company purchases the policy at a percentage of the death benefit that ranges from 50 percent to 80 percent if the usual regulatory guidelines for the remaining life expectancy of terminally ill individuals are used. The viatical company becomes the owner and beneficiary of the policy and assumes responsibility to pay the premium required to maintain the policy in force.

Other factors also affect the amount of the proceeds. If a waiver-of-premium provision is in effect when a policy is sold, the viatical company incurs less expense and is in a position to provide the insured with a higher settlement percentage. The financial strength of the insurance company that issued the policy and that of the viatical company itself affects the amount of the settlement that the viatical company is willing and able to offer the insured.

When the insured dies, the viatical company or investor to whom the policy has been sold, not the original policyowner, collects the death benefit. Usually, although not always, the viatical company or investor makes a profit. The viatical settlement paid to the insured plus administrative expenses and premium payments, if any, are expected to be less than the death benefit received when the insured dies.

Viatical settlements have been a source of controversy. Although accelerated benefits are subject to state regulations, many viatical settlements have taken place in an unregulated environment. This has often led to the policyowner's receiving proceeds that are significantly less than justified by the insured's life expectancy and a reasonable profit for the viatical company or investor.

Some states now regulate the minimum proceeds that the policyowner receives in a viatical settlement and the types of persons who can be owners of a viatical company or solicit such transactions. However, regulations do not exist in every state. As a result, many financial advisors suggest that a viatical settlement should be considered only if the amount of the proceeds exceeds that of an accelerated benefit or if the insured does not qualify for an accelerated benefit.

Reverse Mortgages

For many seniors, their home represents their greatest single source of financial wealth. They have spent many years paying off a mortgage loan, while experiencing significant appreciation in home values. As a result, they have accumulated many thousands of dollars in home equity—a significant personal resource. There is a spectrum of financial transactions that allow homeowners to reconfigure this resource to provide cash and/or income to meet the expenses of retirement and old age, including long-term care.

Traditionally, homeowners—either as individuals or as couples—have accessed their equity through a home equity loan or the sale of their home. Both transactions have drawbacks. A home equity loan creates a new repayment obligation that may cut into scarce spendable dollars and increase the risk of foreclosure. Selling one's home to meet expenses represents a major life disruption, and a new place to live must be found.

Homeowners may retain occupancy after the sale of their home through a sale-leaseback arrangement. Depending on the lease terms, they may also free themselves from such ownership responsibilities as maintenance and the payment of taxes and insurance. However, the homeowners are giving up ownership of their home and are subject to the lease terms that are unlikely to anticipate their changing needs.

Homeowners may also take advantage of the increased cost of housing by renting a part of their home to generate additional income or to obtain such services as home upkeep and personal care in exchange for rent. Although attractive in concept, rental arrangements also have drawbacks. They are temporary, unadaptable to changing circumstances, and frequently undependable. Moreover, rental income is often modest.

A relatively new financial transaction, known as a reverse mortgage, avoids the drawbacks of these alternatives. As explained later, however, this technique has some other limitations. A reverse mortgage is unsuited to a borrower who has little equity in a home, regardless of the home's value.

reverse mortgage

A *reverse mortgage* may be defined as a nonrecourse, first mortgage loan against a home's value that advances cash to the borrower, who remains the homeowner. It requires no installment repayments, although such payments may be made to restore, in whole or in part, the amount of available cash. Proceeds from the sale of the home are used to repay the loan when the borrower no longer maintains the home as a principal residence.

The loan is a nonrecourse loan because the home is the only asset available to satisfy the repayment obligation, even if the amount of the loan exceeds the home's value—a situation possible under circumstances that are explained later. All other assets, including investments, savings, and personal property, are unencumbered by this transaction and can continue to be used at the homeowner's discretion or left to heirs without regard to the mortgage loan liability.

A reverse mortgage is also a first mortgage loan because it has the priority right of repayment over any other loan against the home. Thus, the balance of any existing regular mortgage loan must be repaid as a condition for obtaining a reverse mortgage or repaid from its proceeds.

Loan Proceeds and Payout Options

Under a reverse mortgage, the amount of the cash payout to the borrower, known as the loan proceeds, depends on four factors:

- the borrower's age
- the home's value
- the borrower's equity in the home
- the expected level of interest rates

Generally, when interest rates are low, borrowers who are older and own more expensive homes with no mortgage receive higher loan proceeds than other borrowers. The borrower's age, which usually must be at least 62, is particularly significant because it affects the interest expense portion of the loan's total cost. Because they are expected to live fewer years and, therefore, incur less total interest expense until the loan is repaid, older borrowers are able to receive a greater portion of their home's value as loan proceeds. Often lenders allow up to three co-owners to become borrowers under a reverse mortgage, in which case the age of the youngest borrower determines the amount of the proceeds. Interest rates are usually adjustable annually.

Under a reverse mortgage, borrowers can elect one or a combination of the following three basic options to receive the payout of the proceeds from their home equity:

- The lump-sum option allows a borrower to receive the entire amount of the loan proceeds at one time.
- The credit-line option allows the borrower to draw the loan proceeds entirely, partially, or not at all, as future events unfold and needs arise.
- The monthly payment option provides the loan proceeds as a steady source of funds in a prescribed amount, somewhat like an annuity. Payments may be for a specific term or the borrower's tenure in the home. Under a tenure plan, monthly checks continue as long as the borrower maintains the home as a principal residence, even if the payments continue longer than expected and eventually exceed the home's value.

Lenders offer variations on these three basic options based on the borrower's financial circumstances and needs. The credit-line and monthly payment options may be offered in a constant amount or at amounts that increase with the home's value. Borrowers may choose to take part of the proceeds as a lump sum and part as monthly payments.

The payout option selected affects the total interest cost of the reverse mortgage, which in turn determines the amount of the proceeds the borrower receives; the greater the cumulative interest expense is, the smaller the portion of a home's value that is available as proceeds to the borrower. Thus, all other things being equal, the proceeds accepted as a lump sum, which incur immediate interest charges on the full amount, are likely to be less than cumulative proceeds received through monthly payments over the course of the borrower's tenure in the home.

The total cost of a reverse mortgage to the borrower can be difficult to calculate, especially under a monthly payment option. Federal law requires that lenders disclose the estimated total annual loan cost (TALC) of every reverse mortgage. The TALC is most useful for comparing one type of reverse mortgage to another because it combines the loan amount, interest, closing costs, points, and the monthly loan service fee into a single rate. Lenders are required to illustrate the TALC rate for their loans at the end of 2 years following closing, at the end of the borrower's life expectancy, and at a period that is 40 percent beyond life expectancy.

Example 1: Marcia, an 83-year-old widow, has been able to live on her monthly Social Security benefits. She has no other income and her only asset, other than $5,000 in a bank account, is her home. Marcia realizes that she will need to rely on Medicaid if she ever has to go to a nursing home. She would like to remain in her home as long as possible, but her physical condition is making this more difficult. Marcia has found that she is eligible for a reverse mortgage that will pay her $500 per month. By taking the reverse mortgage, she will be able to afford assistance that will help her postpone the time when nursing home care will be needed.

Example 2: Mark and Julie, both in their 70s, have sufficient retirement income to pay their normal living expenses. They have become aware of the cost of long-term care and realize that they have insufficient resources to pay for these costs if they both should need care. The cost of long-term care insurance policies, for which they are eligible, is beyond their financial means. However, they are eligible for a reverse mortgage on their home. The lump-sum proceeds will be enough to purchase paid-up long-term care insurance policies that, when used to supplement their other resources, should meet any future long-term care expenses.

Repayment

The obligation to repay the reverse mortgage loan typically occurs when the borrower or the last surviving borrower sells the home, moves, or dies. If the borrower does not live in the home as a principal residence for 12 consecutive months, even when due to illness, the loan becomes payable. The borrower, who remains the homeowner, can also trigger the reverse mortgage repayment obligation through a failure to pay property taxes, pay homeowners insurance premiums, or make necessary repairs. Generally, lenders have the option to use loan funds, if available, to pay these required expenses and add the amount to the balance owed.

Other borrower actions that could make a reverse mortgage immediately repayable are:

- bankruptcy
- abandonment of the home
- renting the home, even in part
- adding a new owner to the home's title
- changing the home's zoning classification

As a general rule, the amount of repayment is equal to the total amount of the loan advance paid out plus accrued interest and any fees that have been rolled into the loan, not to exceed the home's value. A borrower who moves but wishes to retain ownership may repay the loan from other resources. If the home is sold, any proceeds remaining after satisfying the loan obligation belong to the borrower or, in the instance of death, to the borrower's heirs. (Note, however, that the loan amount and accumulated interest may exceed the home's value if the borrower continues to live in the house for a long enough period.) Heirs may wish to maintain the home in the family and pay off the reverse mortgage obligation with a traditional mortgage loan or by using life insurance proceeds, for example.

Sources

Reverse mortgages are available through lending institutions as well as state and local governments. Loans from state and local governments are often provided in lump-sum amounts for limited purposes, such as home improvement or the payment of property taxes. Under the term of these loans, borrowers typically must also qualify under income limitation requirements. Although lending institutions in the private sector make reverse mortgages broadly available, they most frequently do so in accordance with the requirements of the programs offered by the U.S. Department of Housing and Urban Development (HUD) and the Federal National Mortgage Association (Fannie Mae). The Federal Housing Administration (FHA) is part of HUD.

Both HUD and Fannie Mae provide reverse mortgages through approved lending institutions that may include banks, mortgage companies, credit unions, and savings and loan institutions as well as state and local housing authorities. HUD's reverse mortgage, known as a Home Equity Conversion Mortgage (HECM), is a federally insured private loan. HECM loan amounts, although they may be lower than other reverse mortgage alternatives, contain a growth feature that allows amounts under the line of credit payout option to increase as the home's value increases. In other respects, however, HUD and Fannie Mae reverse mortgage are similar; there are no limitations on the use of loan advances and no borrower income limits or qualifications. In addition, both programs offer the three loan advance payout options discussed previously. Both HUD and Fannie Mae place a limit on the loan amount. The basis of the HUD limit is the cost of housing in each geographical area; Fannie Mae uses the average home price in the United States as the basis for its maximum loan. Fannie Mae also sponsors a special program that allows seniors to use their reverse mortgage loans to make the transition from a larger home to a smaller one without a mortgage payment while drawing a monthly income.

Information on HUD-approved and Fannie Mae–backed reverse mortgages is available on their respective Web sites at www.hud.gov and www.fanniemae.com. AARP also provides information on reverse mortgages at www.aarp.org, under the link "Money and Work."

Payment for Long-Term Care

The loan advances from a reverse mortgage can be significant and may be used for long-term care. They are often sufficient to pay the long-term care insurance premiums for those who are insured or insurable. In the absence of long-term care insurance, the loan amounts may be enough to entirely pay for the cost of care for an extended period or for the purchase of an annuity to generate income, which together with other personal resources may be available for long-term care.

Like all personal resources, reverse mortgages have limitations when used to pay long-term care expenses. The loan advances may be less than expected and insufficient to cover the high cost of long-term care. For example, even at low interest rates, the proceeds a borrower aged 65 receives from a reverse mortgage on a $300,000 home may be no more than 55 percent under a credit-line option and less than $1,000 under a monthly payment option for the borrower's tenure. Moreover, estimates of long-term care expenses that served as the basis for determining an adequate amount and appropriate payment option today may be outstripped by inflation and/or the need for more extensive care in the future.

Also, the circumstances under which the reverse mortgage must be repaid are often unpredictable or inopportune. For example, a person may obtain a reverse mortgage to pay for long-term care at home, only to subsequently require nursing home care. Also, a person living in the home and using the reverse mortgage payments for a spouse's nursing home care may die unexpectedly or suffer a debilitating illness that also requires care outside the home. In both cases, repayment of the reverse mortgage is required. Any loan advances taken as monthly payments or a line of credit would cease at the very time they are most needed.

GOVERNMENT PROGRAMS TO MEET LONG-TERM CARE NEEDS

As stated as the beginning of this chapter, personal resources may be inadequate to fully finance long-term care expenses. Persons who have exhausted their resources to pay for long-term care and have no benefits available to them under a long-term care policy may be eligible for benefits under certain government programs to meet long-term care needs. Significant among these programs are Medicaid and veterans' benefits.

Medicaid

As stated in chapter 7, Medicaid is the largest source of medical care for eligible individuals and families with low income and assets. Medicaid is also the nation's largest single payer of long-term care services; it accounts for 40 percent of all long-term care services delivered and almost half of all nursing home expenditures. [1]

The discussion begins by considering how persons of means may relate to the Medicaid program and then proceeds to review long-term care services provided, qualifying for Medicaid, transfers of wealth, and estate recovery. It then addresses Medicaid's shortcomings

The discussion concludes by enumerating the drawbacks of Medicaid planning and suggesting a better alternative for many persons—long-term care insurance.

Medicaid rules were significantly affected by the Deficit Reduction Act of 2005 (DRA). In general, DRA strengthens safeguards to restrict the ability of persons of means from qualifying for Medicaid. In fact, the new restrictions are so substantive, especially due to the increased look-back period for asset transfers at less than fair market value and the new penalty period start date, that states must establish specific criteria for hardship waivers and notify Medicaid applicants about them. Indeed, nursing homes are now eligible for limited payments while their patients' hardship waiver applications are pending.

Medicaid and Persons of Means

Most persons of means usually do not anticipate a need for Medicaid. Medicaid is a public assistance or "safety net" program that these persons normally do not need. Nevertheless, unanticipated circumstances may cause persons of means to need such a safety net to pay for medical and long-term care services. For example, a calamitous personal financial loss can wipe out substantial resources accumulated over a lifetime. Similarly, the protracted cost of treatment and care as well as a loss of income arising from an illness, accident, or disability can have the same outcome for persons who are usually considered well off.

Many other persons who may be financially independent but have modest personal incomes and assets may be more likely to need a safety net. These persons may rely largely on a combination of Social Security income and Medicare, which they supplement with their own resources. They, too, may need the Medicaid program if faced with major adverse events.

Still other persons of means who need long-term care shelter much of their assets, spend down remaining resources to pay for the care, and then qualify for Medicaid. Adopting this strategy is a personal decision. Some persons will make every attempt to avoid public assistance and will apply for Medicaid only as a payer of last resort. Other persons have no qualms about accepting Medicaid and view it as their right.

Long-Term Care Services Provided

States provide long-term care services under Medicaid either as a result of a federal mandate or at the state's option.

The *mandated services* include nursing facility care and certain home care services. Nursing facility care includes medical, nursing, and custodial care. Mandated home care services include nursing services, home health aide services, medical supplies, and medical equipment and appliances that are suitable for use in the home. In conjunction with the mandated home care benefits, states may also provide audiology services and such therapeutic services as physical therapy, occupational therapy, and speech pathology.

Approximately 30 states provide optional *personal care services* to assist persons with physical and cognitive impairments to remain in their homes and communities. Personal care services encompass assistance with activities of daily living and instrumental activities of daily living.

States also have the option to provide *home and community-based services* to keep beneficiaries from being institutionalized. States that provide these services often target them to individuals over age 65 with nondevelopmental disabilities. Home and community-based services include homemaker/home health aide services, adult day health services, habilitation services, and respite care. Habilitation services are defined as services designed to assist individuals in acquiring, retaining, and improving the self-help, socialization, and adaptive skills necessary to reside successfully in home and community-based settings. Some of these services overlap with other existing optional service categories, such as personal care services. All states offer at least some services in the home and community-based category.

Qualifying for Medicaid

As chapter 7 also states, persons who qualify for Medicaid must be in an eligible category and meet financial need requirements. They must also demonstrate a need for long-term care.

Eligible Category. Because most persons needing long-term care are age 65 or older, they are, by virtue of their age, in a Medicaid-eligible category. Persons under age 65, however, must be disabled in order to be categorically eligible for Medicaid.

Over 7 million lower-income seniors and persons with disabilities constitute a group known as dual eligibles because they qualify for Medicaid and are eligible for Medicare as well. Indeed, the majority of Medicaid expenditures for dual eligibles are for long-term care services; nearly one-quarter of dual eligibles are in nursing homes. Medicare pays first for services that both programs cover, and Medicaid pays the difference up to the state's coverage and payment limit. Medicaid as the payer of last resort makes sure that its recipients become dual eligibles with Medicare whenever possible.

community spouse

Financial Need. Every state uses income and asset-limitation tests to determine a Medicaid applicant's inability to pay for care. All states are required to protect the income and assets of a Medicaid recipient's spouse, known as a *community spouse*. These provisions help ensure that a community spouse is able to live with at least some degree of independence.

Income. Income is all the money an individual receives from any source, such as Social Security benefits, pension, trusts, annuities, investments, or any payments received on a one-time or continuing basis. For the elderly and persons with disabilities who need long-term care services, these limits are tied to the Supplemental Security Income (SSI) program administered by the Social Security Administration. In 2008 that limit is $637 per month, although states often do set higher limits.

Thirty-three states allow a medically needy category, in which the income test is more liberal. In these states, income must be less than an individual's medical and/or long-term care expenses. If this is the case and the applicant becomes income eligible, Medicaid simply makes up the difference between the individual's income that must be devoted to care for him or her and what Medicaid would pay in the absence of this income.

In addition, because of the high cost of nursing home care specifically, almost 40 states allow persons needing nursing home care to qualify with personal incomes up to three times the SSI benefit level ($1,911 per month in 2008). This approach is known as the special income rule or income cap test. Many states use this approach in conjunction with the medically needy category to set an upper limit on the income a person may have and still qualify for nursing home care under Medicaid. If income is above that level, Medicaid eligibility is denied even if the individual has no assets and cannot afford to pay for long-term care. Persons who qualify under this test must, nevertheless, contribute what income they have to offset the cost of their care.

In every state, the community spouse's income is not considered available to the applicant, and the two individuals are not considered a couple for income eligibility purposes. The state uses the income eligibility standard for one person rather than two, and the Medicaid income test applicable in the state is used.

In addition, there is a separate process for the treatment of income after Medicaid eligibility is determined that also affects a community spouse's income. The posteligibility process ascertains how much the Medicaid recipient must contribute toward the cost of care and also determines how much of the recipient's income is protected for use by the community spouse. The protected amount is known as the community spouse income allowance and in 2008 can range from $1,712 to $2,610 per month. The process applies to any financial eligibility criteria for Medicaid that a state may use for nursing facility residents. States may, but are not required to, use this process when one member of a couple receives Medicaid home and community based services.

Under the posteligibility process, if the community spouse has his or her own income, the amount of that income reduces the community spouse's monthly income allowance. Similarly, any income of family members, such as dependent children, reduces the family monthly income allowance. Once the above items are deducted from the Medicaid recipient's income, any remaining income is contributed toward the cost of care.

Example 1: Shortly after Chuck and Ann's 50th wedding anniversary, Chuck's growing dementia and physical frailties cause him to enter a nursing home. Their household income is based on Social Security payments of $1,500 per month to Chuck and $1,200 per month to Ann. In addition, Chuck has monthly income of $1,000 from a trust fund. Chuck applies for Medicaid and meets his state's medically needy income test: His total income of $2,500 per month is less than the $3,300 per month that Medicaid pays for nursing home care in his state.

The community spouse income allowance in Chuck's state is $2,610 per month. However, Ann will receive only $1,410 of this allowance from Chuck's income because she has $1,200 of her own income. This leaves $1,090 of Chuck's $2,500 income that must be applied to the cost of Chuck's care, minus personal and medical expenses.

Example 2: Margaret and Arthur are just beginning retirement when tragedy strikes. A cycling accident leaves Margaret paralyzed and with severe cognitive impairment. After discharge from the hospital, she needs nursing home care on a long-term basis and applies for Medicaid. Her only income now is $1,500 per month from Social Security. She meets her state's income cap test of $1,869 per month because only her income is considered. When she becomes eligible for Medicaid, Arthur receives no community spouse allowance because his Social Security benefits and pension income exceed the state-approved amount.

Assets. Medicaid applicants in every state must also pass an asset-limitation test, which may be set at as low as the SSI resource standard of $2,000 for an individual and $3,000 for a couple. This test is applied, however, at the conclusion of a somewhat complicated calculation to determine exempt and countable assets as well as determination of protected resource amount for a community spouse.

The state Medicaid agency makes this determination by first classifying assets as either exempt or countable. Medicaid recipients, including those residing in nursing homes, may retain the following exempt assets without affecting Medicaid eligibility:

- the cash surrender value of life insurance policies with an aggregate face value of $1,500 or less
- personal property (such as clothing and jewelry) up to reasonable limits
- prepaid burial insurance
- a burial space
- an automobile, within certain limits
- a home and its furnishings. A home is exempt, provided it is the Medicaid recipient's principal place of residence and the recipient's home equity is within the threshold amount mentioned below. The home remains exempt after the recipient enters a nursing home, as long as a community spouse or a minor, blind, or disabled child continues to live there. Technically, a home could become a countable asset that would have to be spent for care if the recipient has no family in these categories. However, as a matter of practice, nursing home residents may continue to claim a home as their principal residence by making a declaration of their "intent to return," regardless of their actual likelihood of eventual discharge from the nursing home back to the community. Nevertheless, any person with home equity above $500,000 (up to $750,000 at a state's option) who has no spouse or a minor, blind, or disabled child is ineligible for Medicaid.

Virtually any asset that is not exempt is considered countable. Examples include

- cash and checking and savings accounts
- investments of all kinds, such as stocks, bonds, money market funds, certificates of deposit, and Treasury obligations

- retirement accounts, such as pensions, individual retirement accounts, and annuities
- second homes and vehicles

Countable assets include the purchase price of an exclusive right to live in a home limited to one's lifetime (known as a life estate) with the remaining interest going to another party. This requirement is inapplicable, however, if the purchaser resides at the property for 1 year or the transferee is a family member. Entrance fees paid upon admission to a continuing care retirement community or life-care facility also may be considered countable assets. Loans of any type (including promissory notes and mortgages) are included as countable assets unless the repayment terms are actuarially sound, provide for equal payment, and prohibit the cancellation of the balance upon the lender's death. New rules explicitly include as countable certain previously excludible annuities and require the state to be named as the remainder beneficiary.

The countable assets of the applicant and the community spouse, regardless of ownership, are combined. If the applicant is in or is entering a nursing home, the total marital assets are calculated, not on the date of the Medicaid application, but as of the date the applicant enters the nursing home. To determine whether an applicant with a community spouse meets the state's resource standard for Medicaid, the following procedure is used. From the couple's combined countable resources, a protected resource amount (PRA) for the community spouse is subtracted. The PRA is the greatest of

- the spousal share, which is equal to one-half of the couple's combined resources but subject to a maximum of $104,400 in 2008. (This amount is adjusted annually.)
- the spousal resource standard amount adopted by the state at any amount between $20,880 and $104,400 in 2008 and adjusted annually
- an amount of resources transferred to the community spouse for support as directed by a court order
- an amount of resources designated by a state hearing officer as necessary to generate income for the community spouse up to the minimum maintenance needs standard

After the PRA is calculated and subtracted from the couple's combined countable resources, the remainder is considered available to the applicant as countable resources. If the amount of countable resources exceeds the state's resource standard amount, the individual is ineligible for Medicaid and must spend down those resources to the standard amount to qualify under the test. If the amount of countable resources is below the state's resource standard, the individual meets the test. Once a person qualifies for Medicaid, any resources belonging to the community spouse are no longer considered available to the spouse on Medicaid.

In the case of both the income and resource protections, the law allows for exceptions to the general formulas in individual cases through both administrative and judicial procedures.

Need for Care. Often overlooked in the discussion of Medicaid qualification are the need-for-care criteria. These criteria, also called the level-of-care criteria, determine whether an individual is considered an appropriate recipient of long-term care and whether that individual should receive care in a nursing home, at home, or in the community. Need-for-care criteria vary by state and the type of service provided. States may also impose controls on utilization of services.

Transfers of Wealth

Federal Medicaid law attempts to discourage individuals from transferring savings and other countable resources to adult children, siblings, or others in order to satisfy the Medicaid resource test and qualify for nursing facility coverage. It does so by imposing, for a specified period of time, an exclusion of nursing facility coverage upon those individuals who engage in such transfers.

Asset Transfers. Under the transfer-of-assets provisions, states must withhold or delay payment for various long-term care services for individuals who dispose of assets for less than fair market value. The term "assets" in this case includes both assets and income. These provisions apply when assets are transferred by individuals who are in long-term care facilities or receiving home and community-based services. They also apply to transfers by their spouses or someone else acting on their behalf. Now states can "look back" to find transfers of assets for 60 months prior to the date the individual is institutionalized or, if later, the date he or she applies for Medicaid. The look-back period for asset transfers taking place prior to the enactment of the Deficit Reduction Act (DRA) on February 8, 2006, is only 36 months, however. For certain trusts, this look-back period continues to be 60 months, as explained later.

If a transfer of assets for less than fair market value is found, the state must withhold payment for nursing facility care (and certain other long-term care services) for a period of time referred to as the penalty period. The length of the penalty period is determined by dividing the value of the transferred asset by the average monthly private-pay rate for nursing facility care in the state. There is no limit to the length of the penalty period. If there is more than one transfer, all penalty periods are added and expire consecutively (not concurrently).

Under current rules, the penalty period begins on the date that an applicant would have been Medicaid eligible except for the penalty amounts. Prior to DRA, the penalty period began with the date the asset transfer at less than market value occurred.

Once one spouse qualifies for Medicaid, the community spouse is able to transfer his or her own assets without having the transfer affect the other spouse's Medicaid eligibility.

Example: Roberta recently gave each of her six grandchildren a gift of $10,000.

Assume the following:

- Two years later, she suffers a severe stroke and requires ongoing nursing home care.
- After 2 years in a nursing home, she is unable to pay for her care and applies for Medicaid.

Under these circumstances, the state delays her Medicaid eligibility by imposing a 10-month penalty. The period is calculated by dividing the $60,000 in total gifts to her grandchildren by the state-determined $6,000 monthly private-pay rate for nursing home care. The penalty period begins as of the date her lack of resources would have made her eligible for Medicaid except for the penalty. Roberta now applies for a hardship waiver of the penalty based on health or life-threatening circumstances. Meanwhile, Medicaid will pay her nursing home care for up to 30 days while her hardship waiver application is pending.

A transfer of a home to a close family member, however, may be made without penalty. The permitted transferees are

- a spouse
- a minor, blind, or disabled child

- one or more siblings who already have partial ownership of the home and who have lived there for at least a year before the transferor needed nursing home care
- a caregiver child, who for a period of at least 2 years provided hands-on care that delayed the need for nursing home care

Treatment of Trusts. When an individual, his or her spouse, or anyone acting on the individual's behalf establishes a trust using at least some of the individual's funds, that trust may be considered available to the individual for purposes of determining Medicaid eligibility.

As a general rule, payments actually made to or for the benefit of the individual are treated as income to the individual. Amounts that could be paid to or for the benefit of the individual, even if not paid, are also treated as available resources. Amounts that could be paid to or for the benefit of the individual but are paid to someone else are treated as asset transfers.

If a trust is revocable by the Medicaid applicant, the principal of the trust is always considered a countable asset for purposes of Medicaid eligibility. If a trust is irrevocable, any amount of the principal that could be removed by the trustee on a discretionary basis for the individual's care is also treated as a countable asset. In the situation in which the Medicaid applicant cannot receive invasions of principal for any reason, monies put into an irrevocable trust are treated as asset transfers and subject to a 60-month look-back period.

There are a few exceptions to the trust rules previously described. For example, a trust is not counted as an asset available to an individual if the state determines that counting the trust would present an undue hardship. In addition, three specific types of trusts are not counted as being available to the individual:

- trusts established by a parent, grandparent, guardian, or court for the benefit of an individual who is disabled and under the age of 65, using the individual's own funds
- trusts established by a disabled individual, parent, grandparent, guardian, or court for the disabled individual, using the individual's own funds, where the trusts are made up of pooled funds and managed by a nonprofit organization for the sole benefit of each individual included in the trusts
- trusts composed only of pension, Social Security, and other income of the individual in states that make individuals eligible for institutional care under the special income rule or income cap test

In these three situations, the trust must provide that the state receive any funds remaining in the trust when the individual dies, up to the amount of Medicaid benefits paid on the individual's behalf.

Estate Recovery

States must try to recover the cost of Medicaid benefits from the estates of certain nursing home residents and older persons who received home and community-based services. This law, referred to as *estate recovery*, applies to individuals who were aged 55 or older when they received Medicaid. At a minimum, states are required to file claims in probate court against the estates of certain deceased Medicaid beneficiaries.

estate recovery

Under probate laws, an estate is usually defined as all real estate and personal property that pass from a deceased person to an heir through a will or by rules of intestate succession. Property that passes directly to joint owners or to beneficiaries under a trust is normally not considered part of the probate estate. However, federal legislation gives states the option to expand the definition of estate to include these types of interests and any other property that the individual has any title to or interest in at the time of death.

There are limits on a state's right to recover Medicaid benefits. Recovery cannot be made in the following circumstances:

- before the death of a surviving spouse. During a surviving spouse's lifetime, the state Medicaid agency cannot require repayment of the cost of Medicaid benefits provided to the deceased spouse. After the surviving spouse dies, however, the state may file a claim for repayment. Heirs receive their inheritance only after Medicaid's claim is paid.
- if the individual has a surviving child who is under age 21 or who is blind or permanently disabled
- against one's home on which the state placed a lien unless additional protections for siblings and adult children are satisfied

Shortcomings of Medicaid

Medicaid has several related shortcomings from the recipient's perspective.

First, a Medicaid recipient is on public assistance and loses significant authority to direct his or her own care. The state, as the payer for care, largely determines when, where, and how care is provided.

A second and related drawback is the diminished availability of provider services. The Medicaid recipient may not use any available provider, but must select one approved by Medicaid. As the largest payer for nursing home services, Medicaid negotiates rates that are substantially below those paid by private patients and Medicare. Payment and budgetary tensions between long-term care providers and Medicaid agencies are chronic; providers believe they are paid far too little as state agencies face ever-growing expenses and tighter budget constraints. This situation, which limits providers' availability to serve Medicaid patients, is evident in several ways.

Nursing homes become highly selective in their admissions as they attempt to attract and maintain patients that are profitable, or at least more profitable than Medicaid patients. Some of these nursing homes, if they become greatly dissatisfied with Medicaid payments, may cancel their Medicaid contract or reduce the beds available to Medicaid patients to the minimum that Medicaid requires, preferring instead to admit higher-paying private-pay or Medicare patients. Other nursing homes as a general policy admit private-pay or private-pay and Medicare patients only. These homes take the position that Medicaid patients require an unfair subsidy of the true cost of care by their private patients and would compromise the high level of service they provide. State agencies, on the other hand, may decertify the number of available beds or decline to approve new beds to control utilization and maintain their budgets. The net result for the Medicaid recipient is a limited choice of nursing homes and a possible wait for placement. An available provider may be at a location inconvenient to the recipient or recipient's family. This problem becomes more acute as nursing home occupancy rises.

The policies of Medicaid-approved nursing homes with regard to patient transfer or discharge must be identical for all individuals, regardless of source of payment. It is illegal to evict a Medicaid recipient or a person who becomes Medicaid eligible from a nursing home that accepts Medicaid residents. Nevertheless, if a Medicaid nursing home patient enters a hospital because of illness or injury, Medicaid will pay the nursing home to hold the bed for only a week or two. After that time, the bed may be given to another patient, and the recovering Medicaid patient once again may have to look for a facility.

Despite Medicaid's standards, a third drawback is frequently a lower level of service compared to that received by private patients. The likelihood of lower service levels is usually directly related to the proportion of Medicaid patients in a nursing home. Nursing homes with large Medicaid patient populations have difficulty maintaining profitability. A lower level of service may affect the quality of patient care if programs and staff are reduced to cut costs. Reduced service levels are reflected in the amenities, which are far fewer than those provided to and paid for by private-pay patients. Medicaid patients may have spartan accommodations and sometimes share a four-bed room. Common areas can be austere. The patient or the patient's family must often supply TV, telephone, and other personal services and items for the Medicaid recipient's convenience, comfort, or enjoyment.

Medicaid Planning

Medicaid planning

Medicaid planning is the process of rearranging a person's financial resources to make that person eligible for Medicaid while sheltering his or her financial resources for use by a spouse, children, or others. Unlike someone who exhausts financial resources as a private-pay patient and turns to Medicaid to pay for care as a last resort, a person who uses Medicaid planning turns to Medicaid as the first resort. Medicaid planning is usually associated with qualification for Medicaid benefits for nursing home care. However, a person may plan to divest himself or herself of resources to obtain Medicaid coverage for a significant medical event, such as an organ transplant, which is often accompanied by continuing and expensive follow-up care.

Despite the restrictions on asset transfers and the use of trusts and estate recovery, strategies to qualify for Medicaid while shielding financial resources remain available. A discussion of the specifics of these extensive and quite complicated arrangements is beyond the scope of this book. Medicaid planning usually requires legal and tax advice. Congress tried to safeguard Medicaid as a program for the poor by imposing criminal penalties on those who use Medicaid planning or advise someone to make such arrangements. However, subsequent legislative amendments or injunctions against enforcement have nullified these enactments.

Even if Medicaid planning is successful in achieving eligibility while shielding assets, there are major drawbacks. These include the following:

- The individual is placed on public assistance and becomes subject to the shortcomings of the Medicaid program discussed previously.
- If done in advance of the need for long-term care, Medicaid planning may turn out to be a bad choice for a person who never requires long-term care.
- The federal and state Medicaid requirements in effect at the time long-term care may be required could eliminate the effectiveness of the prior planning strategies used to shelter resources.
- The sale or transfer of assets or the creation of a trust to satisfy Medicaid planning may disrupt normal estate planning and could create losses or additional tax liabilities.
- The loss of legal control of one's financial resources creates dependence on the decisions of others for routine needs and when unanticipated circumstances arise.
- The individual may at some future date no longer need long-term care and find that there are insufficient assets to provide support outside a nursing home.

These serious drawbacks to Medicaid planning are more than sufficient to encourage anyone with even modest financial resources to at least consider other alternatives for financing his or her long-term care needs. One alternative is the use of available resources to purchase long-term care insurance tailored to meet an individual's financial objectives. A number of states, recognizing the value of an individual's financial independence and the need to avoid Medicaid, have programs that actively encourage the purchase of long-term care insurance. These programs, known as partnerships, generally allow those who purchase approved policies to maintain assets equal to the amount of long-term care benefits purchased should they exhaust their insurance benefits and have to turn to Medicaid as a last resort. Chapter 18 explains partnership programs.

Veterans' Benefits

Another potential government source of long-term care for eligible individuals is the health care program of the Department of Veterans Affairs (administered by the Veterans Health Administration), often referred to as the VA. As stated in chapter 7, the VA determines benefits and the eligibility for benefits on the basis of Congressional appropriations to the department. Chapter 7 also briefly describes criteria for benefit eligibility.

Long-term care benefits may be available to certain veterans in addition to the basic medical benefits. Benefits include nursing home care, domiciliary care, adult day care, and outpatient geriatric evaluation. The VA also supports state programs for elderly veterans.

Nursing Home Care

The VA will provide nursing home care to veterans who need skilled-nursing care and related medical services because of a service-related disability and to veterans with a service-connected disability rated at 70 percent or more who need the care for any reason. Other veterans may also receive care to the extent that resources are available. The VA provides nursing home care to over 31,000 veterans on a daily basis—8,500 in its own facilities and over 23,000 in community and state nursing homes at VA expense.[2] Care in the latter facilities is designed to allow a veteran to make the transition from a hospital to the community.

Domiciliary Care

The VA also provides care on a daily basis to over 9,500 veterans in its own domiciliary facilities or similar state-owned facilities.[3] These facilities are designed to provide rehabilitative and long-term care for veterans who need minimal medical care but not the level of skilled-nursing care provided by VA nursing homes.

Adult Day Health Care

There are a few VA programs that provide adult day health care programs for veterans. These programs are therapeutically oriented and offer maintenance and rehabilitative services to veterans in a congregate, outpatient setting.

Geriatric Evaluation and Management

The majority of VA centers have programs to provide care and services to the frail elderly. This care can be given to persons who are already in VA facilities or on an outpatient basis to prevent unnecessary institutionalization.

Support of State Programs

Several states have veterans' homes to provide long-term care for frail elderly veterans. The VA supports these homes through construction grants, as well as per diem payments for certain veterans.

CHAPTER REVIEW

Key Terms

noninsurance service plan
annuity
charitable gift annuity
private annuity
impaired risk annuity
accelerated-benefits provision
viatical settlement
reverse mortgage
community spouse
estate recovery
Medicaid planning

Review Questions

Review questions are based on the learning objectives in this chapter. Thus, a [17-3] at the end of a question means that the question is based on learning objective 17-3. If there are multiple objectives, they are all listed.

1. What are the possible sources of income that might be available to meet long-term care needs? [17-1]

2. a. Why might income not be available to meet long-term care needs? [17-1]
   b. Why might there be concerns about the future adequacy of the income? [17-1]
3. What is the extent of long-term care benefits that might be available from private medical expense coverage for individuals who are covered by Medicare? [17-1]
4. To what extent might each of the following provide financing for long-term care benefits for individuals not yet covered by Medicare?
   a. medical expense insurance [17-2]
   b. critical illness policies [17-2]
   c. specified disease insurance [17-2]
5. How might noninsurance service plans be of value in financing long-term care expenses? [17-3]
6. a. How can family members provide financial support to meet long-term care needs? [17-4]
   b. What types of situations might make this support decrease? [17-4]
7. Why might the assets of an individual or a couple not be available to meet long-term care needs? [17-5]
8. Under what circumstances might a reconfiguration of assets be used to finance long-term care expenses? [17-6]
9. a. What is the nature of a typical contract for a continuing care retirement community (CCRC)? [17-6]
   b. How might such contracts vary? [17-6]
   c. What approaches might a contract take with respect to the provision of nursing home care? [17-6]
10. What types of considerations should be addressed before entering into a contract for a CCRC? [17-6]
11. What issues must be addressed when considering the use of annuities to meet long-term care needs? [17-6]
12. a. When might the use of a life insurance policy be appropriate for financing long-term care needs? [17-6]
    b. What are the possible limitations of using a life insurance policy to finance long-term care expenses? [17-6]
13. a. What types of benefit triggers are usually used with accelerated-benefit provisions in life insurance policies? [17-6]

b. What variations are found in the amount of benefits that can be accelerated? [17-6]

14. a. What factors affect the amount of benefits available under viatical settlements? [17-6]
    b. Why are such settlements a source of controversy? [17-6]

15. a. What payment options are available under reverse mortgages? [17-6]
    b. What factors affect the loan amounts available under these payment options? [17-6]

16. a. What triggers an obligation to repay a reverse mortgage? [17-6]
    b. What is the amount of repayment under a reverse mortgage? [17-6]

17. What are the sources for reverse mortgages? [17-6]

18. What are the limitations of using reverse mortgages to pay long-term care expenses? [17-6]

19. What types of long-term care services does Medicaid provide? [17-7]

20. a. Describe the income and asset tests to qualify for Medicaid. [17-7]
    b. What provisions are made for spouses of Medicaid recipients? [17-7]

21. When Alicia, aged 74, became ill 4 years ago, her widowed daughter moved into Alicia's home to provide the care needed to delay her mother's move to a nursing home. During this period, Alicia deeded the home to her daughter and also gave her daughter her remaining assets of $60,000. Now that Alicia must enter a nursing home, what effect will these transfers have on her eligibility for Medicaid? The cost of the nursing home will be $4,000 per month, and the average private-pay rate in her state is $5,000 per month. [17-7]

22. What are the Medicaid rules that apply to the establishment of a trust that is funded with at least some of an individual's assets? [17-7]

23. What are the limitations to a state's right to recover Medicaid benefits from a beneficiary's estate? [17-7]

24. What are Medicaid's shortcomings? [17-7]

25. What are the potential disadvantages of shielding assets from Medicaid? [17-7]

26. Briefly describe the types of VA benefits that might be available for long-term care. [17-7]

NOTES

1. *Medicaid's Long-Term Care Beneficiaries: An Analysis of Spending Patterns*, Kaiser Commission on Medicaid and the Uninsured, Kaiser Family Foundation, Washington, DC, November 2006, p. 1.
2. Fact Sheet: VA Long-Term Care, January 2005, from the Department of Veteran's Affairs Web site, www.va.gov.
3. Ibid.

18

Development of Long-Term Care Insurance

Learning Objectives

An understanding of the material in this chapter should enable you to

18-1. Describe the NAIC model legislation that affects the policy provisions of long-term care insurance policies.

18-2. Describe the NAIC model legislation that affects the marketing of long-term care insurance.

18-3. Explain HIPAA's requirements for favorable tax-treatment of long-term care insurance policies.

18-4. Identify the ways that government acts as counselor regarding long-term care insurance.

18-5. Describe the implications of the Federal Long Term Care Insurance Program for long-term care insurance.

18-6. Explain the importance of partnership programs for long-term care and describe their features.

Chapter Outline

As stated in chapter 1, the evolution of long-term care insurance products has been dramatic with respect to the magnitude of the changes and the speed with which these changes have occurred. The development of this relatively new form of health insurance protection accelerated in large part due to the effect of the NAIC model legislation and HIPAA on the provisions of today's long-term care policies. This chapter examines the features and significance of these two forms of government regulation. When it comes to long-term insurance, however, government is more than just a regulator; it is an advocate. The chapter also reviews how government as a counselor, sponsor, and partner encourages the development of private-sector coverage of long-term care expenses.

NAIC MODEL LEGISLATION

Because of its widespread adoption by the states, it is appropriate to discuss the NAIC model legislation regarding long-term care. The legislation consists of a model act that is designed to be incorporated into a state's insurance law and a model regulation that is designed to be adopted for use in implementing the law. This discussion is based on the latest version of the model legislation, which, as mentioned earlier, seems to be amended almost annually. Even though most states have adopted the NAIC legislation, some states may not have adopted the latest version. However, the importance of the model legislation should not be overlooked. Because most insurers write coverage in more than one state, it is likely that the latest provisions have been adopted by one or more states where an insurer's coverage is sold. Also, because most insurance companies sell essentially the same long-term care product everywhere they do business, the NAIC guidelines are often, in effect, being adhered to in states that have not adopted the legislation.

Before proceeding with a summary of the major provisions of the NAIC model legislation, it is important to make two points. First, although the model legislation establishes guidelines, insurance companies still have significant latitude in many aspects of product design. Second, many older policies that were written prior to the adoption of the model legislation or under one of its earlier versions are still in existence.

The model legislation states that *long-term care insurance* is any insurance policy or rider that is advertised, marketed, offered, or designed to provide coverage for not less than 12 consecutive months for each covered person in a setting other than an acute care unit of a hospital for one or more of the following: necessary or medically necessary diagnostic, preventive, therapeutic, rehabilitative, maintenance, or personal care services. This definition is broad enough to include policies or riders that provide coverage for long-term care in a single setting, such as the home, or a variety of alternative settings that range from the home to a skilled-nursing facility. The 12-month period has been the source of considerable controversy because, in effect, it allows policies to provide benefits for periods as short as 1 year. Many critics of long-term care insurance argue that coverage should not be allowed unless benefits are provided for at least 2 or 3 years. Statistics would seem to support their views. Approximately 55 percent of all persons currently in nursing homes have been there in excess of one year. This figure drops to about 30 percent for stays of 3 years or longer. On the average, the length of stay for persons currently in nursing homes has been about 2.5 years.[1] However, about 14 percent of stays exceed 5 years, and stays for such conditions as severe arthritis and Alzheimer's disease sometimes exceed 10 years.

The model act specifically states that the term "long-term care insurance" also includes group and individual annuities and life insurance policies or riders that directly provide or that supplement long-term care insurance. Long-term care insurance *does not* include an insurance policy that is offered primarily to provide any of the following:

- Medicare supplement coverage
- basic hospital expense coverage
- basic medical-surgical expense coverage
- hospital confinement indemnity coverage
- major medical expense coverage
- disability income or related asset-protection coverage
- accident-only coverage
- specified disease or specified accident coverage
- limited benefit coverage

In addition, long-term care insurance *does not* include life insurance policies (1) that accelerate the death benefit specifically for one or more of the qualifying events of terminal illness, a medical condition that requires extraordinary medical intervention, or permanent institutional confinement *and* (2) that provide the option of a lump-sum payment for the previous benefits if neither the benefits nor the eligibility for benefits is conditional upon the receipt of long-term care.

The act specifies, however, that any product advertised, marketed, or offered as long-term care insurance is subject to the act's provisions even if it is included in the previous list of policies or riders otherwise excluded from the definition of long-term care insurance.

The model legislation focuses on two major areas—policy provisions and marketing.

Policy Provisions

Many of the criteria for policy provisions pertain to definitions, renewal provisions, limitations and exclusions, prior levels of care, incontestability, inflation protection, and nonforfeiture benefits.

Definitions

Many words or terms cannot be used in a long-term care insurance policy unless they are specifically defined in the policy and are in conformity with the model legislation. Examples include activities of daily living (ADLs), adult day care, cognitive impairment, home health care services, mental or nervous disorder, personal care, and skilled-nursing care. These terms as defined are consistent with their use in other sections of this book.

Renewal Provisions

No policy can contain renewal provisions other than guaranteed renewable or noncancelable. With either type of provision, the insurance company cannot make any unilateral changes in any coverage provision or refuse to renew the coverage.

Under a guaranteed renewable provision, coverage is also continued by the timely payment of set premiums, but the insurance company is allowed to revise premiums on a class basis.

Under a noncancelable provision (very rarely used with long-term care insurance), premiums are established in advance and the insured has the right to continue the coverage in force by the timely payment of premiums. The term *level premium* can be used only with a noncancelable policy.

Exclusions and Limitations

Exclusions and limitations by type of illness, treatment, medical condition, or accident are prohibited, except in the following cases:

- preexisting conditions. The definition of preexisting conditions, however, can be no more restrictive than to exclude a condition for which treatment was recommended or received within 6 months prior to the effective date of coverage. In addition, coverage can be excluded for a confinement for this condition only if it begins within 6 months of the effective date of coverage.

- mental or nervous disorders (but this does not permit the exclusion of Alzheimer's disease)
- alcoholism and drug addiction
- illness, treatment, or medical condition arising out of war, participation in a felony, service in the armed forces, suicide, and aviation if a person is a non-fare-paying passenger
- treatment provided in a government facility, unless required by law
- services for which benefits are available under Medicare or other governmental programs, with the exception of Medicaid
- services for which benefits are available under any workers' compensation, employer's liability, or occupational disease law
- services available under any motor vehicle law
- services provided by a member of the covered person's immediate family
- services for which no charge is normally made in the absence of insurance
- expenses for services or items available or paid under another long-term care insurance or health policy

In addition, the model legislation permits exclusions and limitations for services provided outside the United States and for legitimate variations in benefit levels to reflect differences in provider rates.

Prior Levels of Care

No policy can provide coverage for skilled-nursing care only or provide significantly more coverage for skilled care in a facility than for lower levels of care, such as custodial care.

Eligibility for benefits cannot be based on a prior hospitalization requirement, and eligibility for benefits provided in an institutional care setting cannot be based on the prior receipt of a higher level of institutional care.

A policy that conditions eligibility for noninstitutional benefits on a prior receipt of institutional care cannot require a prior institutional stay of more than 30 days.

Incontestability

A policy must contain a provision that makes the policy incontestable after 2 years on the grounds of misrepresentation alone. The policy, however, can still be contested after 2 years on the basis that the applicant knowingly and intentionally misrepresented relevant facts pertaining to the insured's health.

If the policy has been in force for less than 6 months, an insurer can rescind the policy or deny an otherwise valid claim upon a showing of a misrepresentation that was material to the insurer's acceptance of coverage. If the policy has been in force for at least 6 months but less than 2 years, the insurer can rescind the policy or deny an otherwise valid claim upon showing that the misrepresentation was both material to the insurer's acceptance of coverage and pertains to the condition for which benefits are sought.

The insurer cannot recover any benefits paid under a policy prior to the time the policy is rescinded.

Inflation Protection

Insurance companies must offer the applicant the right to purchase coverage that allows for an increase in the amount of benefits based on reasonable anticipated increases in the cost of services covered by the policy. The applicant must specifically reject this inflation protection if he or she does not want it. This provision does not apply to life insurance policies that provide accelerated benefits for long-term care. Chapter 19 discusses in detail the various types of inflation protection that long-term care policies may provide.

Nonforfeiture Benefits

Insurance companies must offer the applicant the right to purchase a nonforfeiture benefit. If the applicant declines the nonforfeiture benefit, the insurer must provide a contingent nonforfeiture benefit that is available for a specified period of time following a substantial increase in premium rates. This provision, like the inflation-protection requirement, does not apply to life insurance policies that provide accelerated benefits for long-term care. Chapter 19 also explains the types of nonforfeiture provisions that long-term care policies may contain.

Marketing

Some of the provisions of the model legislation that pertain to marketing include outline of coverage, shopper's guide, 30-day free look, standards for appropriateness of coverage, limitations on post-claims underwriting, third-party notification of pending policy lapse, and policy replacement.

Outline of Coverage

An outline of coverage must be delivered to a prospective applicant at the time of the initial solicitation. Among the information it must contain is

- a description of the principal benefits and coverage provided in the policy
- a statement of the policy's principal exclusions, reductions, and limitations

- a statement of the terms under which the policy may be continued in force or discontinued
- a statement that the outline of coverage is a summary only, not a contract of insurance, and that the policy contains governing contractual provisions
- a description of the terms under which the policy or certificate may be returned and premium refunded
- a brief description of the relationship of the cost of care and benefits
- a statement whether the policy is intended to be federally tax qualified

Shopper's Guide

A shopper's guide must be delivered to all prospective applicants. The guide must either be in the format developed by the NAIC or one developed by the state insurance commissioner. In the case of agent solicitations, the guide must be presented prior to the presentation of an application or enrollment form. Shopper's guides are discussed in more detail in chapter 20. A few states also require that information on Medicare supplement policies be provided to applicants aged 65 or older.

30-Day Free Look

The policy must allow applicants to have a 30-day free look after the policy's delivery. During that time, an applicant may have the premium refunded if, after examining the policy, he or she is not satisfied for any reason. The policy is then void from its inception. A notice of this provision must be prominently displayed on or attached to the policy's first page.

Standards for Appropriateness of Coverage

Any entity that markets long-term care insurance, other than life insurance policies that accelerate benefits for long-term care, must develop and use suitability standards to determine whether the purchase or replacement of coverage is appropriate for the applicant's needs, and agents must be trained in the use of these standards. Chapter 20 discusses appropriateness of coverage and suitability in detail.

Limitations on Post-Claims Underwriting

post-claims underwriting

An issue that has been of concern to regulators, consumers, and insurance professionals is *post-claims underwriting.* This practice occurs when an insurer does little underwriting at the time of the initial application for coverage. Then, after a claim is filed, the insurer obtains medical information that could have been obtained earlier and may rescind the policy or deny the claim based on this new information.

To control post-claims underwriting, applications for insurance must be clear and unambiguous so that an applicant's health condition can be properly ascertained. Except for policies that are guaranteed issue, the application must also contain a conspicuous statement near the place for the applicant's signature that states the following: "If your answers to this application are incorrect or untrue, the company has the right to deny benefits or rescind your policy."

If an application contains a question about whether an applicant has had medication prescribed by a physician, the application must also ask the applicant to list the medications that have been prescribed. If the policy is issued and the insurer knew or should have known at the time of application that the medications listed in the application were related to a condition for which coverage would normally be denied, it cannot rescind the policy for that condition.

The insurer is also required to obtain additional information on applicants aged 80 or older. This includes at least one of the following: a report of a physical examination, an assessment of functional capacity, an attending physician's statement, or copies of medical records.

Finally, a copy of the completed application must be delivered to the insured no later than the time of the delivery of the policy unless it was retained by the insured at time of application.

Third-Party Notification of Pending Policy Lapse

No policy can be issued until the applicant has been given the option of electing a third party to be notified of any pending policy lapse because of nonpayment of premium. The purpose of this provision is to eliminate the problem of policy lapse because a senile or otherwise mentally impaired person or a person with a loss of functional capacity fails to pay the premium.

Policy Replacement

If one long-term care insurance policy replaces another, the new insurer must waive any time periods pertaining to preexisting conditions and probationary periods for comparable benefits to the extent that the original policy had such provisions.

The model regulation also requires applications to contain questions as to whether the applicant has other long-term care insurance in force and whether a long-term care insurance policy is intended to replace any other medical expense policy or long-term care insurance policy in force. These questions include the following:

- Do you have another long-term care insurance policy?
- Did you have another long-term care insurance policy in force during the last 12 months? If so, with which insurer? If that policy lapsed, when did the lapse take place?
- Do you intend to replace any medical or other health insurance coverage with this policy?
- Are you covered by Medicaid?

Agents must also list any other health insurance policies they have sold to the applicant that are still in force as well as any policies sold to the applicant in the past 5 years that are not in force.

If it is determined that a sale will involve a policy replacement, an insurer or its agent must furnish an applicant with a notice regarding the replacement of long-term care coverage and its potential disadvantages. The applicant retains a copy of the notice; the insurer retains another copy, signed by the applicant. In addition, the insurer replacing coverage must notify the existing insurer of the proposed replacement within 5 days of the earlier of the date of application or the date the policy is issued.

EFFECT OF HEALTH INSURANCE PORTABILITY AND ACCOUNTABILITY ACT (HIPAA)

The enactment of HIPAA in 1996 made the tax treatment of long-term care insurance more favorable. Chapter 6 discussed specifically the income tax-treatment of long-term care policies. Because favorable tax treatment is given only if long-term care insurance policies meet prescribed standards, the nature of most long-term care insurance coverage has changed. In many cases, the imposition of federal standards resulted in broader coverage for consumers. However, Congress seemed to have been concerned with the revenue loss associated with this tax legislation. As a result, policies that were modified to comply with the federal standards sometimes actually provide more limited access to benefits than had been previously required in several states. Moreover, the amount of long-term care insurance premiums that can be deducted for income tax purposes is subject to limitations.

It should be emphasized that the long-term care changes in the act are primarily changes in the federal income tax code. States still have the authority to regulate long-term care insurance contracts. They have no obligation to bring state rules and regulations into conformity with these tax changes. However, all states allow tax-qualified contracts so that consumers can obtain the favorable federal tax benefits.

Requirements for Favorable Tax Treatment

To understand whether a long-term care insurance policy will receive favorable tax treatment under HIPAA, it is necessary to understand the meaning of several terms. These include qualified long-term care insurance contract, qualified long-term care services, and chronically ill individual.

Qualified Long-Term Care Insurance Contract

qualified long-term care insurance contract

The act provides favorable tax treatment to a *qualified long-term care insurance contract.* This is defined as any insurance contract that meets all the following requirements:

- The only insurance protection provided under the contract is for qualified long-term care services. The act does allow a contract to satisfy this requirement, however, if payments are made on a per diem or other periodic basis (such as $150 per day) without regard to the expenses incurred during the period to which the payments relate.
- The contract cannot pay for expenses that are reimbursable under Medicare or would be reimbursable except for the application of a deductible or coinsurance amount. However, this requirement does not apply to expenses that are reimbursable if (1) Medicare is a secondary payer of benefits, or (2) benefits are paid on a per diem or other periodic basis without regard to the expenses incurred during the period to which the benefits relate.
- The contract must be guaranteed renewable.
- The contract does not provide for a cash surrender value or other money that can be (1) borrowed or (2) paid, assigned, or pledged as collateral for a loan.
- All refunds of premiums and all policyowner dividends must be applied as future reductions in premiums or to increase future benefits. A refund in the event of the insured's death or a complete surrender or cancellation of the contract cannot exceed the aggregate premiums paid under the contract.
- The policy must comply with various consumer protection provisions. For the most part, these are the same provisions in NAIC model legislation and already adopted by most states.

Under the act's provisions, a qualified long-term care insurance contract also includes the portion of a life insurance contract that provides long-term care insurance coverage by a rider or as part of the contract as long as the above criteria are satisfied.

Furthermore, the act allows any contract issued before January 1, 1997, that met the long-term care requirements in the state where the policy was issued to be considered a qualified long-term care insurance contract even though the contract does not meet the above requirements. If such a "grandfathered policy" undergoes a material change, however, the policy must then conform to the HIPAA requirements to retain this status. An example of a material change is the addition of a new covered service for which an increased premium is charged.

Although the term "qualified long-term care insurance contract" is used in HIPAA and the Internal Revenue Code, different terminology is often used for the sake of brevity. Thus, it is common to see these contracts referred to just as qualified contracts (or policies), TQ contracts (or policies), or tax-qualified contracts (or policies). The latter terminology is used in this book. Similarly, contracts (or policies) that are not tax qualified are referred to as non-tax-qualified or NTQ.

To further complicate the issue of terminology, the terminology for qualified contract is sometimes preceded by the word *federally* to clarify that HIPAA provides favorable tax treatment with respect to federal tax laws, not state tax laws. It is left to the reader to determine the tax treatment of long-term care insurance in his or her own state. It should be noted, however, that most states do not tax long-term care insurance benefits, and about half the states that levy income taxes provide some type of tax deduction or tax credit for the purchase of long-term care insurance.

Qualified Long-Term Care Services

qualified long-term care services

The act defines *qualified long-term care services* as necessary diagnostic, preventive, therapeutic, curing, treating, and rehabilitative services, as well as maintenance or personal care services required by a chronically ill individual and provided by a plan of care prescribed by a licensed health care practitioner.

Chronically Ill Individual

chronically ill individual

A *chronically ill individual* is one who has been certified by a licensed health care practitioner as meeting one of the following requirements:

- The person is expected to be unable to perform, without substantial assistance from another person, at least two activities of daily living (ADLs) for a period of at least 90 days due to a loss of functional capacity. The act allows six ADLs: eating, bathing, dressing, using the toilet, maintaining continence, and transferring into or out of a bed, chair, or wheelchair. A tax-qualified long-term care insurance policy must contain at least five of the six. (The Secretary of the Treasury in consultation with the Secretary of Health and Human Services is permitted to prescribe regulations so that a person who has a level of disability similar to the level of disability of a person who cannot perform two ADLs would also be considered chronically ill. However, no action has ever been taken in this regard.)

- Substantial supervision is required to protect the individual from threats to health and safety because of severe cognitive impairment.

For purposes of certifying an individual as chronically ill, a licensed health care practitioner is a physician, registered nurse, licensed social worker, or other person who meets any requirements prescribed by the Secretary of the Treasury. Recertification of an individual as chronically ill must occur at least every 12 months.

GOVERNMENT AS ADVOCATE

Government typically assumes the role of an insurance regulator; a role that we have seen also extends to long-term care insurance. More recently, however, government has taken on a role that arguably can be described as an advocate of long-term care insurance. That role is evident as counselor, sponsor of the Federal Long-Term Care Insurance Program, and partner through Medicaid programs.

Government as Counselor

The emerging role of government as counselor with regard to long-term care insurance is evident in the State Health Insurance Assistance Program and in the Long-Term Care Consumer Awareness Campaign.

State Health Insurance Assistance Program

State Health Insurance Assistance Program (SHIP)

Each state has a *State Health Insurance Assistance Program (SHIP)* that receives money from the federal government to give free local health insurance counseling to people with Medicare. Generally, SHIP counselors assist Medicare beneficiaries with their questions about benefits, claim denials and appeals, complaints about care or treatment, and selecting an appropriate Medicare plan. Significantly, among its other specific responsibilities, SHIPs offer guidance about the purchase of long-term care insurance. Medicare's Web site at www.medicare.gov identifies and provides contact information for each state's SHIP by following the home page search tools under helpful phone numbers and Web sites. The home page also provides links to information on long-term care services and options to pay for them, including long-term care insurance.

Long-Term Care Consumer Awareness Campaign

Long-Term Care Consumer Awareness Campaign

The *Long-Term Care Consumer Awareness Campaign* is a multistage project started in January 2005 as a cooperative effort between several participating states and agencies of the federal government to increase awareness among the public of the need to plan for long-term care.

The ultimate goal of the campaign, called "own your future," is to measure the effect that increased awareness of long-term care needs among retirees and near-retirees will have on their increased planning and use of private-sector options, including long-term care insurance, to pay for long-term care. The campaign's fundamental premise is that the burden of public financing of long-term care services under Medicaid will decline with the increased use of private-sector payment options.

The project's immediate activities are state based direct mail campaigns supported by each participating state's governor, and targeted to households with members between the ages of 45 to 70. Campaign materials include a Long-Term Care Planning Kit and state specific information and resources.

The results from a 2006 study of the responses generated by five initially participating states are encouraging.[2] On average, nearly 8 percent of the targeted population in these states requested the planning kit. While interest in planning is evident across all the socio-demographic groups within the target population, the typical responder across the five states is as follows:

- age 58 and married
- a household income of $60,000–$75,000
- a homeowner with a median home value of $130,000
- some college education

Significantly, these respondents are individuals of more moderate income and assets who are potentially vulnerable to spend down to Medicaid if they do not learn about and adopt such planning options.

Another key finding from this study asserts that public sector sponsorship is critical to achieving good response rates on any campaign that promotes private responsibility for long-term care planning; it ensures consumer confidence in the objectivity of the information provided. Moreover, the study authors concluded that the campaign helped to renew collaboration between the public and private sectors with the unified objective of raising awareness and education on long-term care planning issues.

Fifteen states are currently participating in the campaign, which is now coordinated through the National Clearing House on Long-Term Care

Information. Further information on the campaign and a copy of the Long-Term Care Planning Kit is available at www.longtermcare.gov.

The Federal Long Term Care Insurance Program

A major development in long-term care insurance was the group plan that the federal government established for its employees in 2001. Although the federal government is by far the largest employer to offer long-term care insurance, it is not the only government employer to do so; more than 30 states currently offer or are in the process of offering long-term care insurance to their employees and/or retirees.[3] Complete information on The Federal Long Term Care Insurance Program (FLTCIP), including eligibility, covered services, and benefits as well as a premium calculator, is available at www.opm.gov/insure/ltc.

Many in the insurance industry viewed the creation of the FLTCIP as a positive development that could serve to promote long-term care insurance.

First, the passage of the Long-Term Care Security Act addresses many long-standing sources of consumer reluctance to purchase long-term care insurance. In effect, the federal government is telling the members of its own federal family that the likelihood of needing long-term care is real, and they should consider a program to pay for it because current government and private medical insurance programs are insufficient. Enactment of the new law also implies that a government-sponsored and paid-for social insurance program to provide long-term care for all Americans is unlikely in the foreseeable future.

Second, the federal government, as the nation's largest employer, becomes a model for other employers and encourages them to establish employer-sponsored long-term care insurance programs. The significant education program during the open-enrollment period (referred to as the open season), with thousands of educational meetings, satellite broadcasts, and videos, also serves to raise the awareness of employees outside the federal program of their need for long-term care coverage and the possibility that their employers could offer it.

Finally, the action further validates the professional standing of insurance companies and their agents in their work to provide long-term care insurance to their clients.

Partnership Programs For Long-Term Care

The partnership programs for long-term care are alliances between certain state governments and insurance companies to encourage the sale of approved long-term care policies. The goals of these programs are to protect people from being impoverished by long-term care expenses and to avoid their immediate dependence on Medicaid. These programs also provide further evidence of government's advocacy of long-term care insurance. Indeed, the states that currently have partnership programs make a concerted effort to inform and counsel their residents about the value of purchasing long-term care insurance.

Partnership programs are summarized with respect to their impetus, program development, state requirements, program types, and limitations. The removal of a federal legislative impediment to widespread expansion beyond the original partnership states is also discussed.

Impetus

Many middle-class people in nursing homes qualify for Medicaid by spending virtually all of their assets on long-term care or by transferring the assets to put themselves in a state of poverty. The result has been a staggering financial burden on Medicaid that endangers its mission to care for the poor in many states. The cycle of spending down to Medicaid dependence can be broken if more middle-class Americans—especially those of more modest means who are likely to spend down to qualify for Medicaid—could be broadly encouraged to purchase long-term care insurance.

The potential savings to the Medicaid program are obvious. If the policy's benefits prove sufficient to meet the cost of care, a person with long-term care insurance may not have to rely on Medicaid at all. Moreover, a comprehensive policy provides resources to care for someone at a much lower cost at home. If the person was on Medicaid, higher nursing home costs might be incurred.

In return for the potential cost savings generated by reducing Medicaid dependence, states are willing to offer an incentive for the purchase of long-term care insurance. Policymakers agreed that an effective incentive from the state is to allow people who purchase long-term care insurance to qualify for Medicaid while maintaining a higher-than-usual personal asset level. As a result, purchasers of long-term care insurance with significant assets could still qualify for Medicaid without having to spend down all their assets to meet the state's otherwise required level.

Program Development

In 1987, the Robert Wood Johnson Foundation funded a study by the state of Connecticut. The study concluded that collaboration between insurers and the state could help reduce the burden on the Medicaid program through the use of private long-term care insurance. The foundation subsequently awarded program development grants to four states: California, Connecticut, Indiana, and New York. The resulting and continuing programs in these four states, known as the partnership programs,[4] became operational in the early 1990s. The Department of Health and Human Services granted the required approval or waivers that permitted these states to change the Medicaid asset spend-down requirements. Purchasers of long-term care insurance policies under these programs could then maintain some or all of their assets and still qualify for Medicaid without having to spend down their assets to levels typically required for Medicaid eligibility.

State Requirements

Insurers participating in the partnership programs are required to meet the state's requirements for qualified policies and reporting.

Requirements for Qualified Policies. Insurance companies that participate in partnership programs must develop special products to qualify for approval in each state. The plans, which may be individual or employer sponsored, must meet HIPAA standards for tax-qualified policies. The state's approval further boosts consumer confidence in purchasing the plan. Policy requirements of most partnership programs, which were considered innovative a decade ago when they were first introduced, include the following:

- availability of both facility-only and comprehensive policies
- minimum and maximum benefit amounts and durations
- inflation protection
- single lifetime elimination period
- a care coordinator or consultant, often from a state-approved or state-required agency, to assist in planning for care and obtaining appropriate services
- protection against policy lapse due to nonpayment of premium through waiver of premium and notification of a specially identified third party in the event of the insured's failure to pay the premium
- state role in the claims process to ensure prompt payment and review of denials
- agent training in partnership policies

Some states require insurers to offer upgraded partnership products when new products are issued in the nonpartnership market. At least one state (California) requires any new policy enhancements also to be offered to current partnership policyowners.

An important objective of partnership programs is to encourage individuals of modest means to purchase coverage. To keep the cost of partnership policies affordable, the state programs may allow shorter benefit durations than otherwise allowed by state regulations. For example, California and Indiana allow the sales of policies with benefit durations of 1 year, and Connecticut allows sales of policies with a 2-year benefit duration. Purchase of policies with shorter duration periods has ranged from 30 percent to more than 50 percent of partnership policies sold in some years.

Reporting Requirements. Partnership states require insurers to report activity on program-approved policies regularly. The reporting requirements encompass the following:

- new insureds, both individual and employer sponsored
- insureds who have changed or dropped coverage
- claimants, including those assessed for benefit eligibility and those meeting elimination periods
- applicants denied coverage

The partnership states have developed a single uniform data set and streamlined their requirements to ease reporting by insurers that participate in more than one state. In addition, the states themselves can more easily track partnership program progress.

Program Types

Two basic partnership models were developed—the total-assets model and the dollar-for-dollar model.[5] Both models have minimum requirements on the amount of coverage that a consumer is required to purchase. As with all Medicaid recipients, insureds who become eligible for Medicaid must contribute their income toward the cost of care.

Total-Assets Model. The total-assets model initially adopted by New York requires that participants select a minimum daily benefit amount for 3 years of nursing home care and 6 years of home health care, or a combination of the two. When total minimum benefits are exhausted (even if policy benefits are greater), the insured's income, which must be dedicated to paying for care, determines Medicaid eligibility, regardless of assets. However, New York's minimum coverage requirements, which are high compared to other partnership states, tend to discourage enrollment of middle- and lower-income persons. As a result, the state has added several versions of the dollar-for-dollar model as new consumer options.

Dollar-for-Dollar Model. The dollar-for-dollar model also allows consumers to protect their assets through the purchase of a partnership policy that has a state-approved level of coverage and benefits. When policy benefits are utilized, an amount of assets equal to the benefits that were paid for long-term care services is disregarded in determining financial eligibility for Medicaid. In general, the minimum policy must cover at least 1 year in a nursing home at a minimum daily benefit amount. Three states—California, Connecticut, and Indiana—initially adopted this model.

Indiana later changed to a hybrid arrangement that allows a total-assets model for coverage amounts above an annually increasing threshold level ($228,045 for 2008) with a dollar-for-dollar model for coverage levels below the threshold amount. Policies purchased prior to March 1998 are grandfathered into total asset protection if their original maximum policy amount was at least $140,000.

Limitations

A person with a partnership policy has all the advantages of long-term care insurance discussed throughout this book. The limitations of the program occur if those with approved policies qualify for Medicaid under the partnership program. Although assets are protected as enrollees turn to Medicaid to pay for their care, they must keep in mind the Medicaid shortcomings discussed in chapter 17.

In addition, as mentioned previously, although assets are protected, income is not. Program beneficiaries must therefore spend essentially all their income, allowing certain limited amounts for the support of a spouse who continues to live at home. This standard Medicaid requirement effectively eliminates participation in partnership plans by high-income persons.

Although insureds under this program may receive their insurance benefits in any state, their assets are protected only in the state where they purchased their partnership-program-eligible policy. This is currently a major drawback as many people relocate at or during retirement for leisure living or to be near family. However, with the approval of the Department of Health and Human Services, Connecticut and Indiana have established reciprocity of program benefits between them, whereby residents with partnership policies in one state who relocate to the other are eligible for asset protection in the determination of Medicaid eligibility. If many states implement partnership programs, reciprocity among them would be a significant advantage, creating a further incentive to purchase coverage under the program.

Program Experience

More than 15 insurance companies participate in partnership programs in one or more of the original four partnership states.[6] Since the inception of the programs through 2005, a study reported that combined sales of partnership-approved policies in these states exceeded 211,000. Although the number of policies increased significantly since the programs began, a decline in sales in recent years is regarded as reflecting general market trends.

Approximately 172,000 policies were in force at the end of the study period. At that time, 1,209 active policyowners were currently receiving long-term care insurance benefits, with over 899 having died while receiving benefits. An additional 251 insureds had exhausted their benefits, with only 119 of this number accessing Medicaid. State officials believe that the remaining 132 persons are not accessing Medicaid because they are spending down income or unprotected assets, their health has improved, or their families are providing informal care.

In some ways, the available data may be encouraging regarding success of partnership programs to reduce Medicaid spending. For example, the number of persons with partnership policies who died while accessing their benefits is more than three times the number of those who exhausted their benefits. Available data, however, remain insufficient to confirm the effectiveness of partnership programs in relieving the long-term care cost burden on Medicaid. Current studies do not answer such key questions as whether the policies are purchased by people who otherwise would not buy insurance, whether the partnership policies are a substitute for other long-term care insurance policies, or if participants would have used Medicaid regardless of their long-term care insurance. The answers to these questions require continued evaluation.

Moreover, to be successful, partnership programs must encourage enrollment of persons at middle and lower-middle income levels because they are generally less likely to purchase long-term care insurance and more likely to become Medicaid eligible by spending down their assets. Thus far, available data from the partnership states indicate that the program encourages many upper-middle income persons to obtain long-term care insurance—but they are already the most common buyers of this type of insurance.

Removal of a Federal Legislative Impediment

The Deficit Reduction Act of 2005 (DRA) removed a long-standing impediment to the expansion of partnership programs beyond those implemented in the initial four states.

The Omnibus Budget Reconciliation Act of 1993 (OBRA) effectively eliminated an important feature of state partnership programs approved by the Department of Health and Human Services after May 14, 1993. Any partnership program approved after that date was no longer able to exempt amounts from Medicaid's estate recovery requirements for individuals who applied to Medicaid after exhausting their private long-term care insurance benefits. Even though a new partnership program could continue to allow a participant to retain greater asset amounts upon application for Medicaid, the state was required to recover Medicaid's long-term care expenditures from the participant's estate, including the previously protected assets. Thus, the asset-protection component of any new partnership program would be in effect only while the participant was alive. This requirement effectively removed the asset-protection incentive essential to consumer interest in any long-term care insurance policy that a new state partnership program might offer.[7]

DRA restored the ability of states to obtain a Medicaid plan amendment that allows exemption from the estate recovery requirement for qualified partnership programs. However, these partnership programs may exempt only the amounts of the insurance benefits made to or on behalf of an individual under a long-term care policy that meets the requirements specified in the law. These standards are consistent with the practices of the four active programs and conform to NAIC and HIPAA provisions.

As a result, new state programs may qualify for partnership program status. However, while the act grandfathers programs approved prior to OBRA, new qualified partnership programs must use only the previously described dollar-for-dollar model (not the total-assets model) to determine the amount of assets exempt from estate recovery.

DRA also promotes the expansion of state partnership programs through new initiatives:

- a national clearinghouse of information to educate consumers on long-term care
- standards for uniform reciprocal recognition of long-term care policies offered through states with qualified partnership programs
- an annual report to Congress by the Secretary of Health and Human Services on qualified partnership programs

Anticipating a change in the federal law, over 20 states have already enacted legislation or approved regulations that allow the establishment of new partnership programs. However, at the time this book is being written, no new programs are in operation.

CHAPTER REVIEW

Key Terms

post-claims underwriting
qualified long-term care insurance contract
qualified long-term care services
chronically ill individual
State Health Insurance Assistance Program (SHIP)
Long-Term Care Consumer Awareness Campaign

Review Questions

Review questions are based on the learning objectives in this chapter. Thus, a [18-3] at the end of a question means that the question is based on learning objective 18-3. If there are multiple objectives, they are all listed.

1. How does the NAIC model legislation affect long-term care insurance policies? [18-1]
2. What types of limitations and exclusions does the NAIC model legislation allow in long-term care insurance policies? [18-1]
3. How does the NAIC model legislation affect an applicant with respect to inflation protection and nonforfeiture benefits? [18-1]
4. What types of information are contained in the outline of coverage that must be given to an applicant for long-term care insurance? [18-2]
5. What provisions are contained in the NAIC model legislation with respect to each of the following?
   a. shopper's guide [18-2]
   b. free-look period [18-2]
   c. standards for appropriateness of coverage [18-2]
6. How does the NAIC model legislation control post-claims underwriting? [18-2]
7. What is the purpose of a third-party notification of pending policy lapse? [18-2]
8. What regulations apply to the replacement of long-term care insurance policies? [18-2]
9. What is the general nature of the HIPAA provisions that apply to long-term care insurance? [18-3]
10. a. How does HIPAA affect long-term care policies issued before January 1, 1997? [18-3]
    b. What effect does HIPAA have on state tax laws for long-term care insurance? [18-3]
11. a. What are the six activities of daily living (ADLs) that may be contained in a federally tax-qualified long-term care insurance policy? [18-3]
    b. How many of these ADLs must be contained in such a policy? [18-3]
12. What two programs suggest that the federal and state governments are working cooperatively as counselors to the public on the need for protection against the expenses of long-term care? [18-4]

13. What are the implications of FLTCIP for the growth of long-term care insurance? [18-5]

14. a. What is the nature of partnership programs for long-term care? [18-6]
    b. What is the impetus for such programs? [18-6]

15. What is the nature of long-term care insurance policies sold under partnership programs? [18-6]

16. Describe each of the following types of partnership programs for long-term care:
    a. total-assets model [18-6]
    b. dollar-for-dollar model [18-6]

NOTES

1. *The National Nursing Home Survey, 1999 Summary*, Centers for Disease Control and Prevention (CDC)/National Center for Health Statistics (NCHS), June 2002.
2. *Pilot Long-Term Care Awareness Campaign: Phase I Final Report, Executive Summary*, U.S. Department of Health and Human Services, February 24, 2006, pages 2–4.
3. The Minnesota Department of Employee Relations conducted a *Survey of States that Offer Long-Term Care Insurance to Employees and/or Retirees*. The survey, updated in August 2003, identified 31 states that offer such long-term care insurance programs. The California program, self-insured through a trust established by the California Public Employees Retirement System (CalPERs), is by far the largest of these programs with over 170,000 enrollees. With the exception of the program in Alaska, which like that in California is self funded, all other state programs are insured.
4. Detailed information on the specific partnership programs is available from each state's Web site as follows: California (www.dhs.ca.gov/cpltc), Connecticut (www.CTpartnership.org), Indiana (www.IN.gov/fssa/iltcp), and New York (www.nyspltc.org).
5. Program descriptions are taken from the Center for Health Policy, Research, and Ethics, George Mason University, from its Web site at www.gmu.edu/department/chpre/index.html.
6. The discussion on program experience is based on *Overview of Long-Term Care Partnership Program*, a letter to Committee on Finance, United States Senate, from John E. Dicken, Director, Health Care, United Sates Government Accountability Office, September 9, 2005 and *The Long-Term Care Partnership Program: Issues and Options,* George Washington University School of Public Health and Health Services, December 2004.
7. At the time of OBRA's enactment, states other the original four states with active programs had shown interest in partnership programs.

   Because its plan amendment was approved before the OBRA legislative deadline, the Iowa partnership program can offer asset protection with an exemption from estate recovery under Medicaid. Massachusetts is also not subject to the estate recovery conditions of the legislation, but its partnership program provides no up-front protection of assets upon application for Medicaid. Illinois and Washington also undertook partnership program initiatives, but both programs are subject to the estate recovery requirement. All these programs experienced little or no insurer interest.

   With DRA's enactment, the above-mentioned states as well as other states enacting new enabling legislation may pursue active implementation and/or establishment of partnership programs for long-term care insurance.

19

Characteristics of Individual Long-Term Care Insurance

Learning Objectives

An understanding of the material in this chapter should enable you to

19-1. Explain who may be an insured under a long-term care insurance policy.

19-2. Describe the circumstances under which an insured may be eligible for benefits.

19-3. Identify the types of care that might be covered by a long-term care insurance policy.

19-4. Describe the benefit variations by type of care among long-term care insurance policies.

19-5. Describe benefit payment amounts associated with long-term care insurance policies.

19-6. Describe the period of benefits provisions that may be found in long-term care insurance policies.

19-7. Describe policy provisions with respect to restoration of benefits, inflation protection, and exclusions.

19-8. Describe the provisions in long-term care insurance policies with respect to nonforfeiture options, premiums, and renewability.

Chapter Outline

For many types of insurance, policy provisions are relatively standardized. For long-term care insurance, the opposite is true. Significant variations (and therefore differences in cost) exist from one insurance company to another. An applicant also has numerous options with respect to policy provisions.

The policy provisions covered in this chapter include the definition of the insured, eligibility for benefits, types of care covered, benefit variations, benefit amounts, period of benefits, restoration of benefits, inflation protection, exclusions, nonforfeiture options, premiums, renewability, and claims. The provisions and practices described represent the norm in that most policies fit within the ranges that are described. However, the norm covers a wide spectrum. This, coupled with the large number of options available to an applicant, makes the evaluation and comparison of long-term care insurance policies more difficult than the evaluation and comparison of most other forms of insurance.

DEFINITION OF INSURED

Most long-term care insurance policies provide coverage for only one person and define the insured as the person named in the policy. However, some insurance companies issue joint policies on more than one individual. These joint policies usually involve a husband and wife but occasionally can include other family members as well. Most insurers will even issue joint policies to domestic partners who live together. In these cases, the insured will be defined as any of the persons listed in the policy.

The purchase of long-term care insurance is often a joint purchase by a married couple, and insurers encourage this action with premium discounts and favorable policy provisions. As a result, some insurers have a single application that both spouses can use. More often than not, however, an insurer's practice will be to issue each spouse a separate policy.

ELIGIBILITY FOR BENEFITS

benefit trigger

All tax-qualified long-term care insurance contracts use the same two criteria, each known as a *benefit trigger,* to determine whether an insured is chronically ill and eligible for benefits. The insured is required to meet only one of the two. The first criterion is that the insured is expected to be unable, without substantial assistance from another person, to perform at least two of either five or six of the ADLs that are acceptable under HIPAA for a period of at least 90 days due to loss of functional capacity. Most insurers use a benefit trigger of the inability to perform two or more of all six ADLs.

hands-on assistance

standby assistance

The definition of substantial assistance can vary among policies. Policies that have the most restrictive definition require actual *hands-on assistance.* This means that the insured must need actual physical assistance from another person to perform the ADLs. Other policies require only that the insured need *standby assistance*, which means that the insured requires the presence of another person within arm's length who can intervene to prevent physical injury. Standby assistance can also be defined to include cueing to accomplish an ADL. Cueing includes verbal prompting, gestures, and other demonstrations. In some policies, either hands-on assistance or standby assistance constitutes substantial assistance.

Although insurers are also allowed to use less restrictive definitions than those below, the six ADLs and their definitions under the NAIC model regulation are the following:

- bathing—washing oneself by sponge bath, or washing oneself in either a tub or shower (including the task of getting into or out of the tub or shower)
- continence—the ability to maintain control of bowel and bladder function; or, when unable to maintain control of bowel or bladder function, the ability to perform associated personal hygiene (including caring for a catheter or a colostomy bag)
- dressing—putting on and taking off all items of clothing and any necessary braces, fasteners, or artificial limbs
- eating—feeding oneself by getting food into the body from a receptacle (such as a plate, cup, or table) or by a feeding tube or intravenously
- toileting—getting to and from the toilet, getting on and off the toilet, and performing associated personal hygiene
- transferring—moving into or out of a bed, chair, or wheelchair

substantial supervision

The second criterion is that substantial supervision is required to protect an individual from threats to health and safety due to severe cognitive impairment. *Substantial supervision* is the continuous presence of a person directing and watching over another and may also be defined to include cueing. Most policies use the definition of cognitive impairment in the NAIC model regulation, which is a deficiency in a person's (1) short- or long-term memory, (2) orientation as to person, place, and time, (3) deductive or abstract reasoning, or (4) judgment as it relates to safety awareness.

Tax-qualified policies require that someone certify whether the insured is chronically ill. Some insurers use the broadest definition allowed by HIPAA and state only that certification must be by a licensed health care practitioner. As defined in chapter 18, this definition includes physicians, registered nurses, and licensed social workers. However, regulations allow insurers to use a subset of this definition. As a result, some insurers have more restrictive requirements. For example, they may require that the certification be from a physician or from a licensed health care practitioner employed by an organization with whom the insurer contracts.

medical necessity

Non-tax-qualified long-term care insurance contracts, on the other hand, may have more liberal eligibility requirements. Many of these contracts use the same benefit triggers that are in tax-qualified contracts except that there is no time period that applies to the inability to perform ADLs. A small number of non-tax-qualified contracts require only the inability to perform one ADL and/or use more than the six ADLs allowed by HIPAA. Finally, many non-tax-qualified contracts make benefits available if a third criterion—*medical necessity*—is satisfied. This generally means that a physician has certified that long-term care is needed, even if neither of the other criteria is satisfied.

TYPES OF CARE COVERED

There are many types of care for which benefits may be provided under a long-term care insurance policy. These can be broadly categorized as nursing home care, assisted-living care, hospice care, Alzheimer's facilities, home health care, respite care, caregiver training, care coordination, and alternative sources of care. A long-term care insurance policy may provide benefits for one, several, or all of these types of care. Most of these care settings have already been discussed in a general sense in chapter 16. The following discussion focuses on the specific provisions of long-term care insurance policies that apply when each of these types of care is covered.

Nursing Home Care

Nursing home care is a term that encompasses skilled-nursing care and custodial care in a licensed facility.

bed reservation benefit

Policies that provide nursing home care often also provide a *bed reservation benefit*, which continues payments to a long-term care facility for a limited time (often 21 or 30 days per calendar year) if a patient temporarily leaves because of hospitalization or any other reason. Without a continuation of payments, the bed may be assigned to someone else and unavailable upon the patient's release from the hospital. Policies that cover care in assisted-living and/or hospice facilities (discussed in the following sections) often include a bed reservation benefit for those settings as well.

The definition of a nursing home (sometimes referred to as a nursing care facility) is very specific in long-term care insurance policies and varies somewhat among insurers. It usually includes the following requirements:

- The facility must be licensed or legally authorized.
- A doctor must be available to furnish care in case of an emergency.
- Nursing services must be provided 24 hours a day under the supervision of a full-time nurse.
- The facility must maintain records for all patients.
- The facility must have appropriate procedures to handle medications.

The definition is broad enough to include facilities that provide nursing care only as well as distinct units of other facilities (such as hospitals) that meet the definition. However, the definition excludes several types of facilities, such as places designed primarily for rest, the aged, drug addicts, alcoholics, the mentally retarded, treatment of the mentally ill, or education.

Assisted-Living Facility Care

Assisted-living facility care is provided in facilities that care for the frail elderly who are no longer able to care for themselves but do not need as high a level of care as is provided in a nursing home.

As with nursing homes, long-term care insurance policies have very specific definitions of assisted-living facilities. Again, definitions vary, but the following requirements are commonly included:

- The facility must be licensed, if required by the state in which it operates.
- The facility must serve a minimum number of residents, such as 5 or 10.
- The facility must serve meals and accommodate special dietary needs.
- Trained personnel must be on duty and ready to respond at all times to provide care.
- There must be formal arrangements for the services of a physician or nurse to provide medical care in case of an emergency.
- There must be appropriate procedures for handling medications.

Hospice Care

Hospices for the treatment of terminally ill persons are a recent development in the area of medical care. A hospice may be a separate facility, but this type of care can also be provided on an outpatient basis in the dying person's home. Most comprehensive long-term care insurance policies that provide benefits for hospice care make no distinction in the setting. However, some policies provide benefits only for care in a facility because Medicare provides home care benefits for those persons eligible for Medicare.

Alzheimer's Facilities

The states require long-term care insurance policies to cover Alzheimer's disease and related forms of degenerative diseases and dementia under the same terms as they cover other conditions that qualify an individual as chronically ill. Therefore, coverage is provided if an individual receives services in a nursing home, in an assisted-living facility, or at home—as long as the specific type of care is covered in the policy. Most policies, however, have some specific reference to Alzheimer's facilities. In some cases, they are included as part of the definition for assisted-living facilities. In other cases, they are referred to separately but defined as a facility that must meet the policy's definition of either a nursing home or an assisted-living facility.

Home Health Care

homemaker companion

Home health care includes part-time skilled-nursing care, therapy, and part-time services from home health aides. It also often includes help from a *homemaker companion* who is an employee of a state-licensed home health care agency. The companion may assist with such tasks as cooking, shopping, cleaning, bill paying, or other household chores.

Adult Day Care Centers

Comprehensive policies of long-term care insurance that cover home care services typically cover care in an adult day care center as well. An adult day care center, defined in a previous chapter, is designed for impaired elderly persons who reside at home, but who are able to benefit from the specialized services this type of facility can provide during the day outside of the home. Policies define the requirements that such a center must meet before benefits for adult day care services are paid, however.

Some policies may define an adult day care center loosely as a day-program of social and health-related services for a specified number of frail, impaired elderly, or other disabled adults who can benefit from care in this setting. Other policies go further by specifying required staffing levels and qualifications, on-duty personnel minimums, a written record of services provided to each care recipient, and a provision for emergency medical care. Facilities that provide predominantly recreational or social activities are typically excluded from coverage.

Respite Care

Respite care, also defined in a previous chapter, provides temporary relief to a primary caregiver from his or her responsibilities for a chronically ill person being cared for at home. The scope of coverage under a policy usually determines the services for which a respite care benefit may be paid. For example, a facility-only policy may pay for respite care in a nursing home, assisted-living facility, or hospice facility for a person who would otherwise be eligible for benefits in a facility, but is normally cared for at home. If the policy also covers home care, the services of a formal (and sometimes informal) caregiver at home or at an adult day care center may be paid. Limits, such as 30 times the amount of the daily benefit per calendar year, apply to respite care benefits.

Benefits for respite care and caregiver training, explained in the following paragraph, usually reduce a policy's overall benefits. In some ways, however, both of these types of benefits are independent of other policy benefits. Thus, for example, an insured person may receive benefits for respite care and/or caregiver training before becoming eligible to file a claim for facility and/or home care services.

Caregiver Training

caregiver training

Caregiver training is the instruction of an informal caregiver to provide needed assistance so that a chronically ill person can remain at home. Usually, family members, friends, and anyone who would normally live with an insured are eligible for such training as a benefit under a policy that covers this service. All policies that cover this service will limit the benefit; a lifetime benefit equal to 7 times the amount of the daily benefit is one example of such a limit.

Care Coordination

Many policies (either as a standard provision or an optional benefit) provide the services of a care coordinator who works with an insured, his or her family, and licensed health care practitioners to assess a person's condition, evaluate care options, and develop an individualized plan of care that provides the most appropriate services. The care coordinator may also periodically reevaluate ongoing plans of care and act as the insured's advocate. Some long-term care policies mandate that the insured use the services of the care coordinator in order to receive benefits.

In many cases, the care coordinator is recommended by the insurance company but is not its employee or an employee of a care provider. If the recommended care coordinator is voluntarily used, additional benefits might be available to the insured, such as waiving elimination periods, increasing benefit levels, and not decreasing maximum policy benefits because of the cost of the care coordinator. When care coordination is provided, there may or may not be coverage if the insured or his or her family selects a care coordinator not recommended by the insurer.

Alternative Plans of Care

Many policies provide benefits for alternative plans of care, even though the types of care might not be covered in the policy. For example, a policy covering nursing home care only might provide benefits for care in an assisted-living facility if these benefits are an appropriate and cost-effective alternative to care in a nursing home. A policy provision permitting alternative plans of care also allows for adaptation to new forms of care. As a general rule, the alternative plan must be acceptable to the insurance company, the insured, and the insured's physician.

Other Benefits

Most long-term care policies contain at least some other benefits. These benefits usually focus on enabling a person to continue living at home. They may be included as a part of the home health care benefit but more often are separate benefits with their own limits of coverage. They include

- the purchase or rental of needed medical equipment and emergency alert systems
- modifications to the home, such as a ramp for a wheelchair or bathroom modifications
- payment of a transitional benefit to assist in meeting immediate needs resulting from the onset of loss of functional capacity

BENEFIT VARIATIONS

It is probably only a slight exaggeration to say that there are almost as many variations among long-term care policies as there are insurance companies writing the product. Much of this variation is related to the types of care for which benefits are provided. These benefit variations fall into three broad categories: facility-only policies, home health care policies, and comprehensive policies. Some insurance companies write only one type of policies; other insurance companies may write all three.

Facility-Only Policies

nursing home policy

facility-only policy

Many early long-term care policies were designed to provide benefits only if the insured was in a nursing home. This type of policy was frequently referred to as a *nursing home policy*. Such policies still exist, but they frequently also provide benefits for care in other settings, such as assisted-living facilities and hospices. The term *facility-only policy* is often used to describe this broader type of policy, and the term, in its most generic sense, also includes nursing home policies.

Home Health Care Policies

home health care policy

Home health care policies were originally developed to be used either as an alternative to nursing home policies or to complement such policies if more comprehensive coverage was desired. A *home health care policy* is designed to provide benefits for care outside an institutional setting. Some home health care policies also provide benefits for care in assisted-living facilities, and this is one area in which they often overlap with facility-only policies.

Although some insurers still write stand-alone home health care policies, many other insurers have exited this market and now write the coverage as part of a broader comprehensive policy.

Comprehensive Policies

comprehensive long-term care policy

Most long-term care policies written today can be described as comprehensive policies. A *comprehensive long-term care policy*, sometimes referred to as an integrated policy, combines benefits for facility care and home health care into a single contract. However, variations exist within this type of policy with respect to what is covered as part of the standard policy and what is an optional benefit that the applicant may select. For example, some policies cover almost all care settings as part of their standard benefits; other policies provide facility-only coverage as a standard benefit with home health care covered as an option for an additional premium.

Some Examples

The following examples of actual long-term policies in the marketplace illustrate some of the wide variations in benefits.

Example 1: This policy is advertised as a nursing home policy. The policy provides coverage for

- nursing home care
- hospice-facility care
- a bed reservation benefit
- an alternative plan of care

Example 2: The policy is advertised as a long-term care insurance policy providing facility benefits only. The policy provides coverage for

- nursing home care
- assisted-living facility care
- hospice-facility care
- a bed reservation benefit
- an alternative plan of care

Example 3: The policy is advertised as a home health care policy and provides coverage for

- home health care
- adult day care
- a care coordinator

- caregiver training
- a homemaker companion
- respite care

Example 4: The policy is advertised as a home health care policy and provides benefits for

- home health care
- adult day care
- a care coordinator
- an alternative plan of care
- caregiver training
- respite care

Example 5: The policy is a comprehensive policy with standard benefits for facility care and optional benefits for home and community-based care. The standard benefits are for

- nursing home care
- assisted-living care
- hospice care
- a bed reservation benefit
- a care coordinator
- an alternative plan of care

Optional coverage includes a rider that provides benefits for

- home health care
- adult day care
- caregiver training
- a homemaker companion

Example 6: The policy is a comprehensive policy that provides benefits for

- nursing home care
- assisted-living facility care
- hospice care
- a bed reservation benefit
- home health care
- adult day care
- respite care
- an alternative plan of care
- caregiver training

- transitional care
- informal care
- a home health care coordinator

BENEFIT AMOUNTS

When purchasing long-term care insurance, the applicant selects the level of benefit he or she desires up to the maximum level the insurance company will provide. Benefits are often sold in increments of $10 per day up to frequently found limits of $200 or $250 or, in a few cases, as much as $400 or $500 per day. The benefit level selected is known as the daily benefit amount (DBA). Most insurance companies will not offer a DBA below $40 or $50. Some policies base benefits on a monthly (rather than daily) amount that can vary from $1,000 to $9,000 or more.

The same DBA is often provided for all levels of institutional care. Most comprehensive policies that provide home health care benefits once limited the daily benefit for home care services to one-half the DBA for institutional stays. However, many insurers now allow applicants to select home health care limits up to 100 percent of the DBA for institutional care; a few insurers even offer limits as high as 125 percent or 150 percent. If a policy provides home health care benefits only, the daily amount of that benefit is what the applicant selected.

Generally, the DBA for institutional care also determines the level of the other benefits that a long-term care policy may provide, as the following examples show:

- bed reservation—DBA for 21 days per calendar year
- respite care—60 percent of the DBA for up to 21 days per calendar year
- caregiver training—payment of up to 3 times the DBA per claim period
- informal care—25 percent of the DBA for up to 50 days per calendar year
- transitional care—one-time payment equal to 3 times the DBA

Policies pay benefits in one of two basic ways: reimbursement or per diem.

Reimbursement Policies

The majority of newer policies pay benefits on a reimbursement basis. These contracts reimburse the insured for actual expenses up to the specified policy limit. For example, a policy with a daily benefit amount of $200 will pay only $150 if that was the insured's actual charge for care. Tax-qualified policies that provide benefits on a reimbursement basis must be coordinated with Medicare except when Medicare is the secondary payer of benefits.

Home health care services may not be needed every day of the week, and the cost of the services can vary on the days that they are received. Some insurers pay benefits on a weekly or monthly basis at the time of claim. Even though the insured must select a daily benefit amount, claims are paid as if the benefit is seven times this amount when a weekly basis is used.

Example: Francesca's long-term care insurance policy has a daily benefit of $100 for home health care services. On each day of the week, she receives care from a home health aide at a cost of $50 per day. On Mondays, Wednesdays, and Fridays, a nurse and a physical therapist also visit her. Their combined charges total an additional $90 on each of these days. Thus, Francesca's total home health care costs for the week are $620.

If Francesca's policy pays benefits on a daily basis, she will receive her benefit maximum of $100 for Mondays, Wednesdays, and Fridays, and $50 for each of the remaining days of the week. Her total weekly reimbursement is therefore $500.

However, if Francesca's policy pays a weekly benefit, she has an aggregate benefit amount of $700 that can be used anytime during the week. As a result, her entire expenses of $620 for the week will be reimbursed.

As the example illustrates, the payment of benefits on a weekly or monthly basis increases claim costs. Some insurers that pay claims in this manner do so automatically and build the extra claim costs into their basic rate structure. Other insurers may make this payment method a policy option for which the insured pays a higher premium.

Per Diem Policies

Some policies provide benefits on a per diem basis once care is actually being received. This means that benefits are paid regardless of the actual cost of care. In this case, a policy with a daily benefit of $200 will pay $200 even if actual long-term care charges for the day are only $150. Per diem contracts are seldom coordinated with any benefits that are payable under Medicare. If home health care benefits are provided, most per diem policies pay benefits regardless of the service provider. In such cases, benefits are paid even if care is provided by a family member at no charge. Some policies, however, define the type of service provider from whom care must be received.

Example: Lynn, aged 70, recently entered a nursing home following a lengthy hospitalization. The cost of her care is $200 per day. Because she will need skilled-nursing care for a few months, Medicare will pay the cost of the first 20 days of care in full and provide an additional 80 days of benefits with a daily copayment. Lynn also has a tax-qualified long-term care insurance policy that will provide benefits of $150 per day after a 30-day elimination period.

If Lynn's policy provides benefits on a reimbursement basis, no benefits will be payable as long as Lynn is collecting any benefits from Medicare. When Medicare payments cease after 100 days, Lynn requires only custodial care for a few more weeks. Beginning on the 101st day, she will collect $150 per day because her policy counts the days she was receiving Medicare benefits toward the elimination period.

If Lynn's policy provides benefits on a per diem basis and if the policy is not integrated with Medicare, Lynn will collect a daily benefit of $150 beginning on the 31st day regardless of any Medicare reimbursement.

Note that per diem policies are sometimes referred to as indemnity policies even though the usual insurance meaning of indemnity implies payment of benefits for actual expenses up to policy limits. In this sense, reimbursement policies, not per diem policies, are actually policies of indemnity.

disability-based policy

A few insurers offer a variation of the per diem policy that pays benefits as long as the insured satisfies the policy's benefit triggers, even if no long-term care is being received. Such a policy is referred to as a *disability-based policy.*

PERIOD OF BENEFITS

To determine the period of benefits under a long-term care insurance policy, it is necessary to look at the elimination period and the maximum duration of benefits.

Elimination Period

The applicant is required to select an elimination period, which some long-term care insurers call a waiting period or a deductible period. Most insurers allow an applicant to select from three to five optional elimination periods. For example, one insurer allows the choice of 20, 60, 100, or 180 days. Choices are typically as low as 0 days or as high as 365 days. Some states limit the length of the elimination period to a maximum duration of 180 days, for example, although a few states allow longer durations, such as 2 years.

In a comprehensive policy, there is normally a single elimination period that can be met by any combination of days during which the insured is in a long-term care facility or receiving home health care services. The days of care that satisfy the elimination period need not be consecutive or associated with the same episode of care; all days of care accumulate until the elimination period is satisfied. However, some insurers require separate selections for facility benefits and home health care benefits. The two elimination periods may be for the same length of time, and days used for one elimination period may or may not offset days used for the other.

Some policies require the insured to meet the elimination period for each separate stay in a long-term care facility or each period of home health care. Under either approach, policies may or may not allow days that were applied to a prior elimination period, which was not satisfied, to be carried over to satisfy a new elimination period. Newer policies, however, typically do not require that more than one elimination period be satisfied during the insured's lifetime. The following are examples of varying provisions among policies with a single elimination period.

Example 1: The policy requires the satisfaction of only one elimination period during the insured's lifetime but does not require that days used to satisfy the elimination period be consecutive. Assume Gary has a 90-day elimination period, is certified as chronically ill, and received services covered under his tax-qualified policy. Because he spent only 35 days in a nursing home before being discharged, he is ineligible for benefits because the elimination period was not satisfied. However, when he later enters a nursing home for an indefinite stay, there will be a period of only 55 days before he is eligible for benefit payments. If he leaves the nursing home after 55 days, there will be no additional elimination period for a subsequent stay in a long-term care facility or for home health care.

Example 2: The policy requires the satisfaction of only one elimination period during the insured's lifetime, but it must be satisfied during the same time period for which the insured is certified as needing long-term care. Using the same facts as in example 1, Gary will not satisfy the elimination period during the first nursing home stay. Benefit payments will begin after Gary has been in the nursing home for 90 days during the second nursing home stay. If he is later discharged, there will be no additional elimination period for subsequent long-term care services.

Example 3: The policy requires the satisfaction of a new elimination period for each period of long-term care if there is a gap of more than 6 months between periods of care. Using the same facts as in the previous example, Gary would satisfy the elimination period after he had been in the nursing home for 90 days during the second stay. If he were later discharged, a new elimination period would need to be satisfied for any subsequent long-term care services if the subsequent services begin more than 6 months after the discharge.

As mentioned in chapter 10, Medicare may provide benefits for up to 100 days in a skilled-nursing facility. In addition, long-term care policies are permitted by the NAIC model legislation to exclude benefits for services that are provided under Medicare, and tax-qualified policies written on a reimbursement basis must generally have such an exclusion. Nevertheless, the vast majority of these policies allow an insured's Medicare-covered days in a skilled-nursing facility to be counted toward the elimination period.

However, the long-term care insurance policies of a few insurers—frequently their older policies—do not permit these days to be counted.

There are several ways that home health care services can be counted toward the elimination period. Some policies count only those days when actual services are received for which charges are made and that will be covered after the elimination period is satisfied. If an insured receives services 3 days during the week, this counts as 3 days. If the insured's policy has a 60-day elimination period, benefit payments will not begin until the insured had been receiving services for 20 weeks (or 140 days). Some policies count each week as 7 days toward the satisfaction of the elimination period if services were received on any number of days in the week, even 1 day. In this case, the insured will start receiving benefit payments after 60 days have elapsed from the first service.

Another variation is for the insurer to start counting days toward satisfaction of the elimination period as soon as long-term care is certified as being necessary, even if services are received from someone who does not make a charge. Therefore, family members or friends could provide the services until the elimination period is satisfied, and the insurer will then start paying benefits for the services of a paid caregiver.

One final comment about the elimination period concerns its relationship to the requirement that tax-qualified policies cannot pay benefits for the inability to perform ADLs unless this inability is expected to last at least 90 days. Actually, despite what some people think, there is no relationship! If an insured is certified as being unable to perform the requisite number of ADLs for at least 90 days, benefit payments will start after the satisfaction of the elimination period, be it 0, 20, 60, or any other specified number of days. If the insured makes a recovery after the elimination period is satisfied but before the end of the 90-day period, the insured is fully entitled to any benefits received because the period was *expected* to be at least 90 days.

In some cases, an insured will not be eligible for benefits because a medical practitioner does not believe and will not certify that the insured will need care for as long as 90 days. If, in fact, the period of necessary care continues for 90 days or longer, the situation can be reevaluated and benefits paid retroactively from the end of the elimination period.

Maximum Duration of Benefits

The applicant is also given a choice as to the maximum period for which benefits are paid. This benefit period begins from the time benefit payments start after satisfaction of the elimination period. In addition, the benefit period does not necessarily apply to each separate period for which long-term care services are received. Rather, it applies to the aggregate time benefits are paid under the policy. When the maximum benefits are paid, the policy will terminate. However, if benefits are only partially exhausted during a course of long-term care, they may be restored under certain circumstances, as explained later. Also, as explained later, the length of the benefit period may actually differ from the period chosen if a policy uses a pool-of-money concept. Some benefits—such as those for respite care, caregiver training, informal care, and transitional care—may not count toward the maximum benefit, however.

Most insurers require the applicant to select the benefit period, and they make several options available. For example, one insurer offers durations of 2, 3, and 5 years as well as lifetime benefits. Some comprehensive policies have separate benefit periods for stays in a long-term care facility and home health care. For example, if each of these periods is 3 years, an insured could potentially collect benefit payments for up to 6 years—3 years while receiving benefits at home and an additional 3 years after entering a long-term care facility.

There are actually two ways that the benefit period is applied in the payment of benefits. Under one approach, benefit payments are made for exactly the benefit period chosen. If the applicant selects a benefit period of 4 years and collects benefits for 4 years, the benefit payments cease. The other approach, most commonly but not exclusively used with reimbursement policies, uses a *pool of money*. Under this concept, there is an amount of money that can be used to make benefit payments as long as the pool of money lasts. Until recently, the applicant did not select the amount in the pool of money; it was determined by multiplying the daily benefit by the benefit period selected. For example, if the daily benefit is $200 and the benefit period is 1,460 days (or 4 years), then the pool of money is $292,000 ($200 x 1,460). Most policies still use this approach, but some insurers allow the insured to select a pool of money as a lifetime maximum benefit. Several important points about this pool of money should be mentioned:

pool of money

- Daily benefit payments from the pool of money cannot exceed the daily policy benefits.
- Under comprehensive policies, the pool of money is typically determined by using the daily benefit amount for institutional care.
- Adjustments are made to the pool of money during periods of benefit payments to reflect any inflation protection that applies to the policy benefits. This increase may apply to the original pool amount or any balance remaining in the pool after a claim commences.

Example: Renee has a comprehensive long-term care insurance policy that provides benefits on a reimbursement basis for a benefit period of 4 years. Her daily benefit is $200 for care in a long-term care facility and $100 per day for home health care. The policy makes benefit payments using the pool-of-money concept. Assume that Renee is chronically ill and receives home health care for 2 years at a cost of $80 per day for 5 days each week after she satisfies her elimination period. At that time, her condition deteriorates and she enters a nursing home that has a daily cost of $230.

Under a pool-of-money concept, the amount available for Renee's benefit payments is $292,000, as previously calculated. During the 2 years (104 weeks) that Renee receives home health care, the policy will make benefit payments equal to the full cost of her care because it is less than $100 per day. This totals $41,600 ($80 x 104 x 5). Therefore, the pool of money is reduced by this amount to $250,400 by the time she enters the nursing home. The policy will then pay a daily benefit but only up to the policy limit of $200 per day. (The extra $30 per day is her responsibility.) Consequently, Renee can receive benefits for an additional 1,252 days ($250,400 ÷ $200). The net effect is that Renee will actually receive benefit payments over a period that is equal to almost 5 1/2 years. This period would be somewhat longer if an inflation increase had been assumed for the pool of money.

Some insurance companies have developed special benefit duration alternatives that meet the concerns of prospective insureds who may be worried about exceeding a specific benefit period, but are unwilling to incur the expense of buying a policy with a lifetime benefit maximum.

shared benefit

A few insurers use the concept of a *shared benefit* when a husband and wife are insured under the same policy or with the same insurer. Under this concept, each spouse can access the other spouse's benefits. For example, if each spouse has a 4-year benefit period and one spouse has exhausted his or her benefits, benefit payments can continue by drawing on any unused benefits under the other spouse's policy. In effect, one spouse could have a benefit period of up to 8 years as long as the other spouse receives no benefit payments. If the insurer uses a pool-of-money concept, a single pool that combines the benefits of both spouses is created, and either or both spouses can receive benefit payments from the pool. There are also other variations on this theme. An insurer might allow the transfer of any unused benefits to a surviving spouse's policy. Or an insurer might allow the spouses to purchase an extra benefit, equal to each spouse's separate benefit. If either or both spouses exhaust their individual benefits, this third benefit amount or pool can be accessed. There is at least one insurer that offers a shared benefit when any related family members are insured under its policy.

Another alternative is to offer an additional pool of money at the end of the benefit period. Thus, for example, an insured might have a pool of a specified amount of money available as an additional benefit, should the payments under a selected 5-year benefit period be exhausted.

RESTORATION OF BENEFITS

Some policies written with less than a lifetime benefit period provide for a restoration of full benefits if the insured previously received less-than-full policy benefits and has not required long-term care covered by the policy for a certain time period, often 180 days. In some cases, this provision is a standard part of the policy; in other cases, it is offered as a rider for an additional premium. If a policy does not have such a provision, the benefits available for a subsequent claim are reduced by the benefits previously paid.

INFLATION PROTECTION

Most states require that a long-term care policy offer some type of automatic inflation protection. The applicant is given the choice to select this option, decline the option, or possibly select an alternative option. The cost of an automatic-increase option is usually built into the initial premium, and no additional premium is levied at the time of an annual increase.

As a result of the NAIC model act and HIPAA, the standard provision in almost all policies is a 5 percent benefit increase compounded annually. The increase may be over the life of the policy, until a certain age, or until the policy benefit has reached a specified amount (such as twice the original policy benefit). Under such a provision, the amount of a policy's benefits increases by 5 percent each year over the amount of benefits available in the prior year. New benefit amounts are often rounded to the nearest dollar. A small number of insurers offer compound benefit increases that use other percentages (such as 6 percent), and at least one insurer has an option tied to actual price inflation as determined by the CPI.

A common alternative that many insurers make available is based on simple interest, with each annual automatic increase being 5 percent of the original benefit amount. Other options that are occasionally found are increases (either simple or compound) based on different fixed percentage amounts, such as 3, 4, or 6 percent. Note that each state can determine which alternative options that an insurer may offer.

The effect of an automatic increase in daily benefits can be dramatic, as table 19-1 indicates. However, such a provision is also accompanied by a significant premium increase.

TABLE 19-1
Effect of Automatic Increase on $100 Per Day Benefit

End of Policy Year	No Increase	5% Simple Interest	5% Compound Interest
5	$100	$125	$128
10	100	150	163
15	100	175	208
20	100	200	265
25	100	225	339
30	100	250	432

future purchase option

If an automatic-increase option is not selected, some policies have a *future purchase option* (called a guaranteed purchase option by some insurers), which allows the policyowner to increase benefits without evidence of insurability on a pay-as-you-go basis at specified intervals, such as every 1, 2, or 3 years. Each benefit increase is accompanied by a premium increase based generally on attained-age rates for the additional coverage. Over time, with regular benefit increases, the total annual premium will increase significantly. In order to moderate the increase, some policies base the premium for the future purchase option on the insured's age when the policy was purchased initially. Such a policy would have a higher initial premium, however.

The amount of the periodic benefit increase under a pay-as-you-go option may be a fixed dollar amount, such as a daily benefit increase of $20 every third year, or based on a specified percentage or an index, such as the CPI. Some insurers have an aggregate limit on the total amount of benefit increases or an age beyond which they are no longer available. Failure to exercise a periodic increase or a series of increases over a specified period typically terminates the right to purchase additional benefits in the future or to obtain them without evidence of insurability.

Inflation increases also affect the lifetime maximum benefit or pool of money under a long-term care insurance policy. In most cases, the inflation increase applies only to the amount of unused benefits.

It is important to note that increases in benefits can be inadequate to offset actual inflation in the annual cost of long-term care, which for certain periods has been more than 5 percent.

EXCLUSIONS

With some exceptions, most long-term care insurance policies contain the exclusions permitted by the NAIC model legislation. These exclusions are enumerated in chapter 18.

Some of the other areas where an insurer's exclusions might differ from the NAIC model legislation include the following:

- Most policies no longer have exclusions for nervous or mental disorders and treat them like any other condition with regard to the need for nursing home or home care. Typically, however, no coverage is provided if care is received in an institution licensed primarily for the care of patients with mental illness.
- Most policies do not exclude benefits for expenses or services covered under another policy. Rather, the issue of other insurance is a factor taken into consideration during the underwriting process.
- Policies written on a per diem basis seldom have an exclusion for services or expenses provided under Medicare. Policies written on a reimbursement basis do contain such an exclusion. For tax-qualified policies, the exclusion also applies to amounts Medicare does not pay because of its deductible and coinsurance provisions. For non-tax-qualified policies, the exclusion is usually only for actual duplicate coverage.
- Although many policies do not cover services or treatment received outside the United States, some insurers provide benefits while the insured is in Canada. A few insurers also provide benefits for services or treatment received in any foreign country, but benefit levels might be reduced or the coverage period might be limited to a year or an even shorter period, such as 30 to 60 days.
- Some policies have a preexisting-conditions provision that specifies that benefits are not paid within the first 6 months for a condition for which treatment was recommended or received within 6 months of policy purchase. Most policies, however, have no such provision or state that the provision does not apply to preexisting conditions listed on the policy application. There is little need for such a provision because insurers are required in most states to underwrite at the time coverage is written and are not allowed to use post-claims underwriting. If the policy is underwritten properly at the time of application, claims within the usual preexisting-conditions period are unlikely to occur. Elimination periods for benefits often serve a similar purpose.
- Policies in a few states limit the use of a war exclusion.
- Many policies no longer contain an aviation exclusion.

NONFORFEITURE OPTIONS

nonforfeiture benefit

Most companies give an applicant for long-term care insurance the right to elect a nonforfeiture benefit. Indeed, offering such a benefit is required by some states, the NAIC model legislation, and the requirements for a federally tax-qualified policy. With a *nonforfeiture benefit*, the policyowner will receive some value for a policy if the policy lapses because the required premium is not paid in the future.

The most common type of nonforfeiture option, and the one almost always available in tax-qualified policies, is a shortened benefit period. With this option, coverage is continued as a paid-up policy, but the length of the benefit period (or the amount of the benefit if stated as a lifetime maximum) is reduced. Under the typical provision, the reduced coverage is available only if the lapse is on or after the policy's third anniversary. The amount of the benefit is equal to the greater of the total premiums paid for the policy prior to lapse or 30 times the policy's daily nursing home benefit.

return-of-premium rider

Some policies offer a *return-of-premium rider*, under which a portion of the premium is returned, usually if a policyowner dies after a specified number of years. For example, one insurer's policy pays nothing if the insured dies before the policy has been in force for 5 full years. Fifteen percent of the total premiums paid are returned if the policy was in force for 6 years, 30 percent for 7 years, 45 percent for 8 years, 60 percent for 9 years, and 80 percent for 10 or more years. Other insurers may refund as much as 100 percent of the premiums paid. There are also some policies that refund all premiums paid if the insured dies before age 65; after age 65, the percentage of the premiums refunded gradually decreases to 0 over a period of time, such as 10 years. Depending on the insurer, any benefits paid while coverage was in force may or may not be deducted from the refund.

contingent nonforfeiture benefit

The NAIC model legislation and an increasing number of states that require an insurer to offer a nonforfeiture benefit also stipulate that a policy must contain a *contingent nonforfeiture benefit* (also called a contingent benefit upon lapse) if the policyowner does not purchase the nonforfeiture benefit. Some insurers also include this provision in their contracts even when it is not required. The provision gives the policyowner the right to elect certain options each time the insurer increases the premium rate to a level that results in a cumulative increase of the annual premium equal to or exceeding a specified percentage of the premium at the time of policy issue. The percentage is a sliding scale determined by the issue age. For example, the percentage is 130 if the policy was issued when the insured was 45 to 49 and 110 at issue ages 50 to 54. The figure continues to drop to 70 percent for an issue age of 60, 40 percent for an issue age of 70, and 20 percent for an issue age of 80. The options are a reduction in benefits to a level sustainable by the current premium or the conversion of the policy to a paid-up status with a shorter benefit period. The policyowner must be notified of the rate increase and of these options prior to the increase, usually either 30 or 45 days. However, the policyowner is not required to select either of these options and can continue to pay the higher premium and maintain the current policy benefits.

PREMIUMS

In discussing the premiums payable for a long-term care insurance policy, it is necessary to look at the premium-payment period, the mode of payment, and provisions for waiver of premium and a grace period. In addition, the provisions for reinstating a lapsed policy must be addressed.

Premium-Payment Period

The majority of long-term care insurance policies have premiums that are payable for life and determined by the insured's age at the time of issue. For example, a policy may have an annual cost of $800 at the time of purchase. Assuming the policy is guaranteed renewable, this premium will not change unless it is raised on a class basis. A few insurers, however, promise not to raise premiums for a specified period after a policy has been written, such as 3, 5, or 10 years. In the past, guaranteed renewable policies were often advertised as being "level premium." This is misleading because premiums may be (and in some cases have been) increased by class. As a result, the current NAIC model act prohibits the use of this term unless a policy is noncancelable, which means that rates cannot increase.

In recent years, insurers have increasingly begun to offer accelerated (or limited) premium-payment periods. These shorter periods, which result in higher annual premiums, are popular with many applicants who want to have their policies paid for prior to retirement. They are also popular in executive incentive packages if the employer pays all the premiums for an executive's long-term care insurance. Some of the options include the following:

- a single-premium option, which is a one-time payment
- a higher first-year premium and a reduced premium thereafter
- a paid-up-at-65 option under which the policyowner pays an annual premium until he or she reaches age 65
- a higher premium until age 65 and a reduced premium thereafter
- a shortened payment period, such as 5, 10, or 20 years

Once these premiums are paid, the policy is paid up and no subsequent premiums are required to keep it in force.

With premiums paid on an accelerated basis, the policyowner has a lot to lose if the policy terminates in a short period of time because of either death or cancellation. As a result, some states require that an accelerated payment period of a short length, such as 10 years or less, be accompanied by some type of return-of-premium rider or nonforfeiture benefit.

Regardless of the length of the premium-payment period, the policyowner is normally given the option of paying the annual premium in semi-annual, quarterly, or monthly installments.

Waiver of Premium

Most long-term care insurance policies contain a waiver-of-premium provision, under which the policyowner does not have to pay premiums after the insured has begun to receive benefit payments or has received them for a period of time. While the premiums are being waived, the policy remains fully in force.

Unlike the similar provisions in life insurance and many other types of health insurance, there are a variety of conditions that might apply to the waiver-of-premium provision for long-term care insurance:

- Some policies begin waiving premiums at the time the elimination period has been satisfied. Other policies do not waive premiums until the insured has been collecting benefits under the policy for a period of time, such as 30, 60, or most commonly 90 days. Most, but not all, policies require that this period consist of consecutive days. A third possibility is that premiums will be waived after a specified period during which the insured has been receiving long-term care, regardless of the length of the elimination period. In this case, it might be possible for the premium waiver to begin before the elimination period is satisfied.
- Many comprehensive policies waive premiums if the insured is receiving benefit payments either in an institution or at home. Waiver of premium when care is received at home may have specific restrictions, however. For example, one insurer waives premiums after the insured has been confined in a long-term care facility for 90 days. Premiums are also waived after 90 days of benefits for home health care but only if the care had been received for at least 5 days per week. Further restrictions often apply to waiver of premium when covered services are received outside the United States.
- The waiver of premiums usually ceases when the insured is no longer receiving daily benefits under the policy. However, some policies waive the premiums for the life of the insured, even if the

insured recovers from the condition that resulted in the need for long-term care.

- Some policies waive the premiums for both spouses if either spouse is receiving benefits as long as each spouse is insured with the same company. A few policies contain a provision, often called a survivorship benefit, that waives the premium for a surviving spouse after the other spouse dies as long as the company insured both spouses and the policy had been in force for a certain period of time, such as 10 years.

Grace Period and Third-Party Notification

Most policies have a 31-day grace period. To prevent the inadvertent lapse of a policy, particularly by an elderly person, the NAIC model legislation for long-term care insurance policies requires that the applicant be given the option of designating a third party to receive notification of the cancellation of a long-term care insurance policy for nonpayment of premium. This designee is sometimes referred to as an alternate premium payer. The provision requires the insurer, after the premium is overdue by at least 30 days, to notify both the policyowner and the designee that (1) the premium is overdue and (2) the policy will lapse at the beginning of the 36th day after the notice is mailed unless the premium is paid prior to that time. (Note: Technically, the insured is given 30 additional days to pay the overdue premium after the notification is received. However, the mailing period for the receipt of the notification is deemed to be 5 days.)

Some insurers allow an applicant to name two or three alternate designees.

Reinstatement

Another provision to protect the insured is a requirement that an insurer reinstate a lapsed policy within a specified period following the lapse if the insurer receives proof that the insured was cognitively impaired or had a loss of functional capacity at the time the premium was due. The NAIC requires that this period be at least 5 months, but some insurers use a somewhat longer period. The reinstatement is retroactive to the date of lapse and made without the insured's having to show any evidence of insurability. However, any overdue premiums must be paid.

If a policy lapses for any other reason, reinstatement is at the insurer's option, as explained in chapter 6.

RENEWABILITY

Long-term care policies currently being sold are almost always guaranteed renewable, which means that an individual's coverage cannot be canceled except for nonpayment of premiums. Although premiums cannot be raised on the basis of a particular applicant's claim, they can (and sometimes are) raised by class.

Insurers are allowed to issue policies that are noncancelable, but very few policies of this nature are written because of the uncertain nature of future claim costs.

CHAPTER REVIEW

Key Terms

benefit trigger
hands-on assistance
standby assistance
substantial supervision
medical necessity
bed reservation benefit
homemaker companion
caregiver training
nursing home policy
facility-only policy
home health care policy
comprehensive long-term care policy
disability-based policy
pool of money
shared benefit
future purchase option
nonforfeiture benefit
return-of-premium rider
contingent nonforfeiture benefit

Review Questions

Review questions are based on the learning objectives in this chapter. Thus, a [19-3] at the end of a question means that the question is based on learning objective 19-3. If there are multiple objectives, they are all listed.

1. How might the definition of insured vary under a long-term care insurance policy? [19-1]
2. a. Describe the two benefit triggers used in tax-qualified long-term care insurance contracts. [19-2]
   b. How might the benefit triggers differ in non-tax-qualified contracts? [19-2]

3. What requirements must a facility have in order to satisfy the usual definition of a nursing home found in a long-term care insurance policy? [19-3]

4. What types of benefits might be included in coverage for home health care? [19-3]

5. How might coverage for care coordination vary between long-term care insurance contracts? [19-3]

6. Under what circumstances might a long-term care insurance policy provide coverage for alternative plans of care? [19-3]

7. How might long-term care benefits vary by type of care? [19-4]

8. Samantha has a long-term care policy that provides a daily facility benefit of $250. Her actual charges, however, are only $215. How much will she collect from her insurer if the policy is the following?
   a. a per diem contract [19-5]
   b. a reimbursement contract [19-5]

9. Describe the policy variations that might be found with respect to elimination periods. [19-6]

10. What, if any, relationship exists between a tax-qualified contract's elimination period and the requirement that an insured must be expected to be unable to perform ADLs for at least 90 days? [19-6]

11. Conrad's long-term care policy provides a daily benefit of $250 for institutional care and $200 for home health care. The benefit period is 3 years.
    a. What is the amount of money available to Conrad if his "typical" policy uses a pool-of-money concept? [19-6]
    b. What amount of money will be paid by the policy if Conrad incurs daily home health care expenses at $250 for 2 years prior to his death? [19-6]

12. What type of provision might be found in a long-term care insurance policy to restore full benefits after an individual has recovered from a prior period of long-term care? [19-7]

13. a. What alternatives for automatic benefit increases might be available under a long-term care insurance policy? [19-7]
    b. What is the advantage of selecting an increase that uses compound interest? [19-7]

14. How might exclusions in long-term care contracts differ from those contained in the NAIC model legislation? [19-7]

15. a. What types of accelerated premium-payment options might be found in long-term care insurance policies? [19-8]
    b. Why might they be used? [19-8]

16. What variations might be found in waiver-of-premium provisions that are used in long-term care insurance contracts? [19-8]

17. a. What provisions are contained in long-term care insurance policies to prevent their inadvertent lapse? [19-8]
    b. What reinstatement provision is found in such policies? [19-8]

20

Consumers and Long-Term Care Insurance

Learning Objectives

An understanding of the material in this chapter should enable you to

20-1. Describe the perceptions that form consumer attitudes toward long-term care insurance.

20-2. Identify the characteristics of individuals who purchase long-term care insurance policies and describe their purchase patterns.

20-3. Describe the factors that consumers should consider to determine if a long-term care policy is appropriate for them and when it should be purchased.

20-4. Describe the factors that consumers should consider when choosing the type, extent of coverage, and benefit provisions of a long-term care policy.

20-5. Describe the factors that consumers should consider when comparing policies, switching policies, paying premiums, and evaluating insurers.

20-6. Describe how group plans sponsored by employers and hybrid policies may provide long-term care insurance and the factors consumers should consider if they use these alternatives.

Chapter Outline

Like many types of insurance, long-term care insurance is a consumer product. Consumers include the public at large, those who decline coverage (referred to later as nonbuyers), and those who purchase or are in the process of purchasing long-term care insurance. Just as with homeowners insurance, automobile insurance, and other health insurance products, consumers must perceive long-term care insurance as offering needed financial protection. In addition, the product must be affordable and understandable so that consumers can make intelligent choices among policies and policy options and be satisfied with their purchase.

Making long-term care insurance appealing to consumers is especially important because of the product's market challenge. Persons who are more able to pay the premiums and obtain coverage because they are working and younger perceive less need to protect themselves from the consequences of a financial risk they often believe is distant. Persons who feel a greater need for the insurance are frequently less able to pay premiums and obtain coverage because they are often retired, older, and more likely to have chronic medical conditions.

In the final analysis, the product's success requires that, over time, long-term care insurance play a meaningful role in meeting the financial need of long-term care for many (if not most) Americans, especially those who are elderly. In the meantime, progress toward that goal can be measured by the growth in the number of policies issued and increases in covered services and benefit levels. On one hand, consumers need the availability of an easily understood process to select policies and policy features. On the other hand, consumers must be able to tailor the product to their specific needs, resources, and preferences. Unfortunately, these two objectives are often in conflict.

This chapter discusses consumers and long-term care insurance as they relate to consumer attitudes, the purchasers and purchase patterns of available policies, and the decision-making process in the selection of coverage, benefits, and other policy features. In some cases, the consumer's decision-making process extends to the use of group insurance, usually at work, and various kinds of hybrid policies as sources of long-term care coverage. The chapter concludes with a review of these alternatives.

CONSUMER ATTITUDES

Long-term care insurance is a relatively new product developed to meet a real and growing risk that is gradually surfacing in the public's consciousness. Consumer attitudes toward long-term care insurance grow out of their perceptions of the potential need for long-term care and the means to pay for it as much as from their perceptions of the long-term care insurance products themselves. Surveys show that many consumers continue to be significantly uninformed.

Considerable consumer education is required to increase public awareness of the likely need for long-term care, correct broadly held misconceptions on how to pay for it, and provide an understanding of the value of long-term care insurance. This education, essential to informed decision making, is ongoing; progress has been made in many areas. Indeed, as the following discussion points out, consumers are much more informed today than previously.

Perceptions of the Need for Long-Term Care

Unless individuals believe they are likely to need long-term care sometime in their lives and to be personally responsible for the high cost associated with it, they will not seek an insurance plan to protect themselves. Many Americans are not looking for a solution to a problem they do not perceive. Previous studies indicate that most people give the need for long-term care very little or no thought, and only 12 percent claim to give it a great deal of thought. Interestingly, over two-thirds are unconcerned or only somewhat concerned about affording long-term care in the future.[1] However, there are signs of growing awareness.

A recent survey reports an increased perception of the need for long-term care among nonbuyers, defined as those who chose not to buy long-term care insurance after a solicitation and presentation of policy details. In the past decade, the percentage of such nonbuyers who believed they had a greater than 50 percent chance of needing nursing home care in their lifetimes more than doubled, increasing from 27 percent to 53 percent. Comparable statistics for home health care went from 31 percent to 59 percent.[2]

Perceptions of Available Means of Payment

Consumers also have significant misconceptions about the financial aspects of long-term care, including its cost, sources of payment, and available insurance coverage.

Cost of Care and Sources of Payment

Americans, including many who profess at least some familiarity with long-term care services, often do not know what these services cost. Fewer than one in 10 Americans over age 45 who responded to an AARP survey can estimate the national average cost of nursing home care within 20 percent; over 60 percent were too low.[3] Not surprisingly, consumers also have a limited understanding of how long-term care costs are paid.

Until recently, many people believed that Medicare covers nursing home stays for 3 months or more for age-related or other chronic conditions. In fact, Medicare does not cover extended nursing home stays for such conditions. More than 4 in 10 erroneously believe Medicare covers assisted living residence care.[4] In addition, nonbuyers of long-term care insurance are roughly twice as likely as buyers to agree with the statement that ". . . the government will pay for the cost of long-term care if services are ever needed."[5]

However, some misconceptions are giving way to reality. The percentage of nonbuyers who cite their belief that Medicare and Medicaid will pay for long-term care services as an important or very important reason for not buying coverage has declined from almost 60 percent to 20 percent over the last several years. Indeed, over 90 percent of nonbuyers and more than three-quarters of other surveyed individuals who generally have less experience with long-term care policies agree with the following statement: "Whatever health reforms come about in the next few years, it is more likely that individuals will have to rely on themselves to plan and pay for long-term care."[6]

Perceived Insurance Coverage

Many Americans believe they have long-term care coverage, when in reality they probably do not. Almost 30 percent of Americans over age 45 report having some type of long-term care insurance. Many of these persons are mistaken because research reveals that fewer than 10 percent of retirement-age persons (age 55 and over) have private long-term care coverage.[7]

Other studies[8] show additional misconceptions by persons over age 45 about coverage for long-term care services:

- more than 4 in 10 are unaware that Medicare provides only limited coverage for skilled-nursing facility care
- 46 percent of those who currently have health (medical) insurance believe that it would cover most of the cost of long-term care
- 30 percent are unaware that while Medicaid does provide long-term care coverage, it is only available to those who have depleted nearly all of their financial resources

To a great extent, then, many persons thinking they have long-term care insurance may have an unfounded sense of protection against the costs of long-term care. Many persons believe, often mistakenly, that they are already covered or have some other means to pay for long-term care, or simply do not know how long-term care services will be paid. One analysis suggests that this may explain in large part why the decision not to purchase long-term care insurance seems rational.[9]

Perceptions of Long-Term Care Insurance Policies

Industry reports document that there is a growing awareness of long-term care insurance policies. In 1995, less than 40 percent of those surveyed from the general population were aware of insurers that offered long-term care policies. More recently, that recognition level was 66 percent. Significantly, 44 percent of the group surveyed also report being approached to buy long-term care insurance and 38 percent had considered buying coverage; much higher percentages than the 28 percent and 21 percent recorded respectively in these same categories 10 years earlier.[10]

Although awareness and even interest in long-term care and long-term care insurance is increasing, in most cases it is insufficient to motivate consumers to purchase the product. The reluctance to purchase long-term care insurance, even among those who are aware of it, has many reasons. Undoubtedly, many of these reasons are based on a lack of understanding about long-term care and the sources to pay for it. There are also other reasons that can generally be grouped as psychological/emotional considerations and practical considerations.

Psychological/Emotional Considerations

More than one industry report points out that many Americans are simply ignoring the long-term care issue, even when they are realistic about the likelihood of needing long-term care and being affected by its financial ramifications.[11] Researchers attempt explanations. Some believe that reluctance to purchase coverage continues to be a matter of awareness and that long-term care insurance is simply an undiscovered necessity for some people. Other researchers believe that many older adults are in denial. Indeed, some study participants expressly admit they are ignoring the issue.[12] Just the consideration of their dependency and the loss of dignity associated with long-term care may repel those who are healthy and physically active from thinking realistically about the protection being offered. More important, they do not see that coverage for these services makes any real difference to them in the quality of care they can expect to receive.

Another group of researchers observe that, in spite of more recent restrictions, Medicaid's rules remain generous and flexible, and typical middle-class elderly persons who need long-term nursing home care can qualify for public benefits even without elaborate Medicaid planning. Because Medicaid provides a safety net, it is argued that many individuals can effectively ignore the financial risk of long-term care. Thus, these researchers conclude that trying to overcome consumer reluctance to purchase long-term care insurance by emphasizing asset protection is misplaced. In the current Medicaid environment, only an emphasis on access to quality care that long-term care insurance provides can be effective.[13]

Practical Considerations

There are important practical considerations that make people reluctant to purchase long-term care insurance. Although cost is the biggest obstacle, there are other challenges, such as those related to confusion and credibility.

Cost. Cost in terms of premiums remains the greatest practical obstacle to the purchase of long-term care insurance.[14] In many cases, consumers unfamiliar with actual long-term care insurance premiums overestimate the premiums by as much as 5 to 10 times because they assume the cost of care is the cost of coverage. Consumers in this category become more interested in coverage when informed of actual premiums.[15]

In addition, over 80 percent of nonbuyers, who by definition are presented with detailed policy information, consistently report that cost remains the most significant barrier to purchase. No more than 25 percent of nonbuyers would pay the premium for policies selling to their age group. Thus, typical nonbuyers are assumed to believe that the policy value is less than its cost, or they are not convinced of or do not understand the value of the policy relative to its cost.[16]

Confusion. Industry reports consistently identify what can only be labeled as confusion about evaluating policies and the many options and features that accompany them. In addition to the complexity of long-term care insurance, financial planning experts' mixed messages about its value and the timing of its purchase have heightened consumer confusion. There is reason to be optimistic, however, because this situation, while by no means satisfactory, is improving significantly. In 1990, 87 percent of nonbuyers indicated an important or very important reason in their decision not to buy long-term care insurance was confusion that prevented them from determining which policy was appropriate. More recently, this figure has dropped by more than half to 40 percent.[17]

Credibility. The lack of trust consumers have in the integrity of insurers and their representatives relates to the issue of confusion. Here, too, there is reason to be optimistic because confidence is growing in the integrity of insurance companies that provide long-term care insurance. In 1990, over 70 percent of nonbuyers did not believe that companies would pay benefits as stated in the policy; this figure is now 42 percent.[18]

PURCHASERS AND PURCHASE PATTERNS OF AVAILABLE POLICIES

As chapter 1 discusses, 4.5 million persons have individual policies of long-term care insurance in force, a slight increase over the prior year.[19] An additional 1.9 million persons had group coverage under employer-sponsored plans for the same period, a 5 percent increase over the prior year.[20] While the individual market provides approximately 70 percent of long-term care coverage, that percentage is expected to decrease as the employer-sponsored market continues to grow more rapidly. Based on a trend from statistics reported previously, approximately 200,000 persons may have group coverage sponsored by associations.[21]

Although the amount of coverage in force has been increasing slightly, the sales of new policies has been trending downward. However, some insurers have been enjoying increasing sales.

The characteristics of purchasers and their purchase patterns reflected in the policy design features that individual buyers select generally reveal important insights into the consumer/purchaser attitudes toward long-term care insurance.

Purchasers

The average person who purchases individual long-term care insurance is getting younger—around age 60 today compared to 68 in 1990. Perhaps more significantly, the proportion of buyers under age 65 has grown from one quarter to two-thirds of all individual long-term care insurance buyers. Purchasers of coverage in the employer-sponsored market are on average in their 40s.[22]

Persons with long-term care insurance coverage share many characteristics. They are typically more affluent and more highly educated than the general population. They are also more likely to be married, and in the vast majority of cases, each spouse has coverage. About 57 percent of the population with long-term care insurance are women.[23]

In contrast to the general population (discussed earlier), people with long-term care coverage are significantly more realistic with respect to the need for long-term care and their personal responsibility to pay for it. Virtually all insureds agree that it is important to plan now for the possibility of needing long-term care services sometime in the future. As might be expected, they do not look to the government and other types of health insurance as major payment sources for long-term care services. Buyers generally have the same objectives in deciding to acquire long-term care coverage. Over 90 percent of buyers cited one of the following four reasons as the most important in their decision to purchase long-term care insurance:

- protecting assets/leaving an estate
- avoiding dependence
- guaranteeing the affordability of needed services
- protecting living standards

Among these, protecting assets/leaving an estate is the single most important reason for the purchase. Easing the long-term care burden on one's family and choice of long-term care providers are also important considerations.[24]

Purchase Patterns of Individual Policies

A multiyear study shows that the purchase patterns of buyers of individual long-term care insurance policies vary by income and age. Changes in purchase patterns have occurred over time and are likely to continue. Table 20-1 presents the policy design choices and premiums paid by individual long-term care insurance buyers by income levels.

Not surprisingly, as the table shows, persons at higher income levels are more likely to buy policies with more comprehensive coverage, longer benefit duration, higher benefit levels, and greater inflation protection. Elimination periods, which are fairly close across all income levels, are an exception to this rule. Perhaps these periods do not decline appreciably as income increases because higher-income insureds can more easily afford to pay for the initial periods of long-term care out-of-pocket.

Table 20-2 profiles by age the same policy choices and premium levels in table 20-1. Older buyers tend to purchase less coverage, lower benefits, and fewer optional features. Age and income factors are interrelated, and both are often present in many decisions. For example, older individuals pay a much higher premium than their younger counterparts, usually at a time in their lives when they are retired and their incomes are lower. Thus, those who lack home care coverage tend to be older insureds. Older buyers also tend to select shorter benefit durations and/or lower daily benefit amounts and are less likely to buy the automatic inflation-protection feature. This may be a rational choice for these buyers, who expect to access benefits sooner than younger insureds and anticipate that inflation will be less of a problem.

Table 20-3 shows how purchase patterns change over time. Overall, coverage, benefits, and the purchase of optional features have increased during the periods shown—in some cases significantly. For example, in a recent 5-year period, the average nursing home and home care benefits have increased by around 30 percent—outpacing the general rate of inflation. The proportion of policies that cover both institutional care and home care have has grown from 37 percent in 1990 to 90 percent today. Particularly noteworthy is the increase in the election of an automatic inflation protection (automatic benefit increase) option, which jumped from 41 percent in 2000 to 76 percent.

Despite this growth, premiums reflected a relatively small increase, averaging only 11 percent over the period from 1995 to 2000. More recently, however, premiums are increasing more rapidly. New insureds paid on average an annual individual policy premium of $1,918, a 14 percent increase over 2000, a relatively large increase considering that that the average age of the purchaser decreased by 6 years. However, the reduction in premium due to the younger average age of new policyowners is offset by the increased selection of automatic inflation protection, higher daily benefits, and more comprehensive coverage. Thus, analysts conclude that recent premium increases are commensurate with the value of the policies that are being purchased.[25]

CONSUMER DECISIONS

Consumers are faced with many decisions when purchasing long-term care insurance. Helping them make these decisions intelligently requires that insurance agents and other financial advisors have the knowledge to guide consumers through the maze of questions that must be answered. These questions include the following:

TABLE 20-1
Key Policy Design Parameters Chosen by Individual Long-Term Care Insurance Buyers, by Level of Income

Policy Features	Level of Income			
	Less than $25,000	$25,000–$49,999	$50,000–$74,999	$75,000 and Over
Benefit Duration				
Average	3.6 years	5.1 years	5.3 years	5.6 years
1–2 years	35%	8%	9%	8%
3–4 years	35	52	47	38
5–6 years	24	16	15	23
7–8 years	—	6	7	7
Lifetime	6	18	22	24
Nursing Home Benefit Amount				
Average	$116	$121	$131	$147
Up to $80	14%	16%	9%	7%
$81–$100	38	28	23	15
$101–$120	14	11	14	8
$121–$150	22	37	35	38
$151 and Over	12	9	19	32
Home Care Benefit Amount				
Average	$105	$116	$126	$142
Up to $80	18%	23%	14%	10%
$81–$100	43	26	24	15
$101–$120	19	13	14	9
$121–$150	15	29	32	37
$151 and Over	5	10	18	29
Percentage with Inflation Protection	44%	67%	71%	86%
Average Elimination Period	73 days	79 days	85 days	79 days
Percentage with Home Care	94%	89%	96%	97%
Average Annual Premium	$1,807	$2,079	$2,011	$1,844
Monthly Premiums				
Up to $50	11%	3%	3%	8%
$51–$75	15	7	13	13
$76–$100	13	15	12	12
$101–$125	11	18	17	13
$126–$150	15	10	12	14
$151–$200	11	18	17	21
$201 and Over	23	29	26	20

Source: America's Health Insurance Plans.[26]

TABLE 20-2
Key Policy Design Parameters Chosen by Individual Long-Term Care Insurance Buyers, by Age

Policy Features	Age Category				
	Less than 55	55–64	65–69	70–74	75 and Over
Benefit Duration					
Average	5.9 years	5.6 years	4.4 years	3.8 years	3.0 years
1–2 years	8%	6%	16%	21%	33%
3–4 years	32	41	50	55	57
5–6 years	24	24	20	16	8
7–8 years	7	5	4	—	1
Lifetime	29	24	10	8	1
Nursing Home Benefit Amount					
Average	$151	$142	$132	$119	$112
Up to $80	6%	6%	10%	16%	29%
$81–$100	16	22	25	33	28
$101–$120	8	11	12	13	11
$121–$150	37	35	33	26	21
$151 and Over	33	26	20	12	11
Home Care Benefit Amount					
Average	$146	$136	$127	$113	$106
Up to $80	8%	10%	14%	23%	30%
$81–$100	16	21	25	32	33
$101–$120	11	12	13	15	10
$121–$150	35	34	30	20	20
$151 and Over	30	23	18	10	7
Percentage Choosing Inflation Protection	87%	85%	62%	39%	19%
Average Elimination Period	78 days	83 days	80 days	88 days	82 days
Percentage with Home Care	98%	97%	94%	92%	91%
Average Annual Premium	$1,740	$1,877	$2,003	$2,341	$2,604
Monthly Premiums					
Up to $50	10%	5%	4%	4%	3%
$51–$75	12	10	11	8	8
$76–$100	16	14	14	11	10
$101–$125	15	17	14	10	15
$126–$150	14	15	11	10	9
$151–$200	15	17	17	18	16
$201 and Over	18	22	29	39	39

Source: America's Health Insurance Plans.[27]

TABLE 20-3
Individual Long-Term Care Insurance Policy Designs Selling by Purchase Year

Attributes of Policies	Percentage of 2005 Sales	Percentage of 2000 Sales	Percentage of 1995 Sales	Percentage of 1990 Sales
Types of Policies Sold				
Nursing Home Only	3%	14%	33%	63%
Comprehensive Policies	90	77	61	37
Home Care Only	7	9	6	—
Nursing Home Duration				
1–2 years	11%	17%	24%	23%
3 years	22	23	20	12
4 years	17	14	18	15
5 years	16	11	6	12
6 years	6	5	2	5
7–8 years	5	—	—	—
Lifetime Benefits	23	30	30	33
Average Duration	5.4 years	5.5 years	5.1 years	5.6 years
Nursing Home Daily Benefit				
Up to $30	–	1%	1%	2%
$31–$59	2%	5	12	25
$60–$89	6	17	40	51
$90–$119	25	43	38	18
$120 and Over	67	34	9	4
Average Daily Benefit	$142	$109	$85	$72
Home Health Care Duration				
1 year	4%	5%	20%	N/A
2 years	10	14	31	
3 years	22	22	21	
4 years	17	13	5	
5 years	16	10	10	
6 years	6	7	1	
7–8 years	4		—	
Lifetime Benefits	22	30	12	
Average Duration	5.2 years	5.4 years	3.4 years	
Home Health Care Daily Benefit				
Up to $30	—	1%	3%	25%
$31–$59	3	8	26	60
$60–$89	9	17	33	13
$90–$119	26	41	31	2
$120 and Over	62	33	8	—
Average Daily Benefit	$135	$106	$78	$36

Table 20-3 continues on the next page.

Elimination Period				
0 days	1%	23%	28%	25%
15–20 days	6	3	17	41
30–60 days	20	16	16	12
90–100 days	67	55	39	22
More than 100 days	6	3	—	—
Percentage Choosing Inflation Protection	76%	41%	33%	40%
Simple	23	17	14	
Compound	49	22	15	N/A
Indexed to Consumer Price Index	4	2	4	
Total Annual Premium				
Up to $500	4%	5%	10%	19%
$500–$999	18	24	29	40
$1,000–$1,499	25	26	23	21
$1,500–$1,999	20	18	15	11
$2,000–$2,499	12	9	9	5
Greater than $2,500	22	18	14	4
Average Annual Premium	$1,918	$1,677	$1,505	$1,071
Source: America's Health Insurance Plans.[28]				

- Is coverage appropriate?
- When should coverage be purchased?
- Is it better to purchase a tax-qualified policy or a non-tax-qualified policy?
- Is it better to purchase a per diem policy or a reimbursement policy?
- What types of coverage should be purchased?
- What is the appropriate amount of coverage?
- What is the best way to plan for future inflation?
- Is a nonforfeiture option needed?
- How should policies be compared?
- What are the considerations for switching policies?
- How should premiums be paid?
- How can insurers be evaluated?

Long-term care insurance is relatively expensive, and for many consumers the amount of premium they will pay is an important factor. As the following discussion addresses each of the above questions, it takes cost considerations into account when appropriate. The following sections of this chapter summarize and expand upon these cost considerations.

In the final analysis, however, many of these questions do not have precise answers. The answers lie with the consumer's personal preferences.

Appropriateness of Coverage

The first major decision in purchasing long-term care insurance is to determine whether such coverage is appropriate to meet an individual's needs. From the standpoint of the insurer, the agent, and the financial advisor, this process is often referred to as suitability.

The NAIC Long-Term Care Insurance Model Regulation addresses the issue of suitability. The regulation requires any insurer marketing long-term care insurance to develop and use suitability standards and to train its agents to use the standards. These standards must take the following into account:

- the applicant's ability to pay for the proposed coverage and other financial information appropriate to its purchase
- the applicant's goals or needs with respect to long-term care insurance and the advantages and disadvantages of insurance to meet these goals and needs
- the values, benefits, and costs of any of the applicant's existing insurance compared to the values, benefits, and costs of the recommended purchase or replacement

personal worksheet

The insurer or agent, if one is involved, must make a reasonable effort to obtain the preceding information. This includes the presentation to the applicant of a long-term care insurance *personal worksheet.* The information on the worksheet and the questions asked vary among insurers, based on their practices and state insurance regulations. Insurers in some states are allowed to use a brief worksheet that the applicant signs to acknowledge that he or she has considered the following information:

- the current and future obligations for keeping the policy in force
- the current costs of nursing home care, home health care, and community-based services in the area where the applicant lives
- the average use of services covered by the policy. For example, these include the average length of stay in a nursing home and the average number of home health care visits in a week.

Other states require the use of a much more comprehensive worksheet that is in line with what the model regulation recommends. Such worksheets contain information about the premium for the coverage being considered, the insurer's right to increase premiums, and the insurer's history of rate increases. Worksheets also ask the applicant to answer the following questions:

- How will you pay each year's premium—from income, from savings and investments, or with family help?

- Have you considered whether you can afford to keep the policy if the premium goes up by 20 percent?
- What is your annual income?
- How do you expect your income to change over the next 10 years—increase, decrease, or not change?
- Will you buy inflation protection? If not, have you considered how you will pay the difference between future costs and your daily benefit amount?
- What elimination period are you considering, and how do you plan to pay for your care during this period?
- Other than your home, what is the approximate value of your assets?
- How do you expect your assets to change over the next 10 years?

The applicant must sign a statement that the insurer or agent has reviewed the worksheet with him or her. In addition, the applicant must indicate that the answers to the questions describe the applicant's financial situation or that he or she chooses not to provide the information.

The insurer then compares the applicant's financial information with its suitability standards. For example, the insurer may have adopted standards that premiums should not exceed more than 7 percent of an applicant's income and that the applicant should have an annual income of at least $35,000 and assets (excluding a home and automobile) of at least $75,000. In addition, the applicant should be able to absorb an increase in future premiums of up to 30 percent.

If an applicant does not meet an insurer's suitability standards or does not choose to provide financial information, the insurer may decline the application or send the applicant a letter stating that the insurer has suspended the final review of the application. If the applicant believes the policy is what he or she wants, however, the applicant, within the next 60 days, can check the appropriate box on the letter and return it to the insurer. The insurer will then continue to review the application and issue a policy if the applicant meets its underwriting standards. Although many persons who fail to meet the insurer's suitability standards could rely on Medicaid, there are still drawbacks to Medicaid, as explained in chapter 17.

It is important to point out that many individuals who are unable to afford long-term care insurance may have family members who are willing to pay part or all of the cost. After all, it is these same family members who may otherwise be called upon to provide long-term care services if and when these services are needed.

Suitability standards focus on determining minimum standards for the appropriateness of long-term care insurance. There are individuals, however, for whom coverage might not be appropriate—for example, individuals who have purchased alternative types of coverage, such as residence in a continuing care retirement community. There are other individuals whose wealth makes it possible to self-fund their long-term care expenses. Nevertheless, as mentioned in chapter 17, these individuals may still have valid reasons for purchasing long-term care insurance. Finally, there are the very elderly for whom a short life expectancy and the very high cost of coverage make the purchase of long-term insurance financially questionable, assuming they are even eligible for coverage.

Time to Purchase Coverage

It can be argued that an individual is never too young to buy a long-term care insurance policy. Even a young person can need long-term care services as the result of an accident or illness. In addition, the younger an applicant is, the less likely that he or she will fail to meet the insurer's underwriting standards.

Most purchasers of individual long-term care policies postpone buying coverage until they approach or are past retirement age. In some ways, this is understandable. At earlier ages, these persons still have the expenses of supporting a family and are more concerned with purchasing life insurance and disability income insurance to replace lost income should they die or become disabled.

Postponing the purchase of long-term care insurance, in addition to increasing an individual's likelihood of being uninsurable, also confronts him or her with increasing premium costs. For example, one insurer sells a tax-qualified, facility-only policy that has a $100 daily benefit, a 5-year benefit period, a 90-day elimination period, and a 5 percent compound inflation rider. The annual premium is $510 at age 50, $690 at age 55, $980 at age 60, $1,330 at age 65, and $2,000 at age 70. Moreover, as the following example shows, the situation is actually much more dramatic when the benefit amount needs to be adjusted for inflation.

Example: Betsy, aged 50, purchased a tax-qualified comprehensive long-term care insurance policy that has an unlimited lifetime benefit of $100 per day. The policy also has a 90-day elimination period and a 5 percent compound inflation rider. Her annual premium is $1,100.

Betsy's friend Rosemary, also aged 50, decides to wait until she turns 60 to purchase her policy even though she knows that the insurer's annual premium for an identical policy with a $100 daily benefit will be $1,900 for an insured aged 60. However, what Rosemary fails to realize is that in 10 years, Betsy's daily benefit will have increased to $163 because of the inflation rider. Therefore, a policy identical to Betsy's at that time will require Rosemary to pay a premium of $3,097 for a daily benefit of $163 at the rates for a 60-year-old. In addition, during that 10-year period, it is also possible that the insurer will make matters even worse for Rosemary by raising its premium rates.

The lower premiums at younger ages also make it financially easier for many applicants to elect broader benefits. There is also an increased likelihood that both automatic inflation protection and nonforfeiture benefits are purchased.

Tax-Qualified versus Non-Tax-Qualified Policies

Since the passage of HIPAA, there has been disagreement over whether consumers should purchase tax-qualified or non-tax-qualified policies. However, most insurers now offer only tax-qualified policies, and these policies account for about 98 percent of long-term care insurance policies sold in a recent year.[29] The two types of policies differ with respect to tax treatment and benefit triggers.

Tax Treatment

The primary reason for the predominance of tax-qualified policies seems to be their more favorable income tax treatment. As pointed out in chapter 6, a policyowner who itemizes deductions may be able to deduct a portion of the premium cost if medical expenses exceed 7.5 percent of his or her adjusted gross income. In addition, benefits are received tax free, with the possible exceptions of benefits from per diem contracts that exceed $270 per day (in 2008).

As chapter 6 states, premiums for non-tax-qualified policies are not deductible and there is uncertainty over the tax status of benefits received from non-tax-qualified policies. With this uncertainty, many consumers naturally shy away from non-tax-qualified policies. Many agents are also reluctant to sell these policies because of the potential legal liability of selling a policy whose benefits are subject to such ambiguity. However, some advocates of non-tax-qualified policies note that an agent might be just as liable for not letting a client know about the existence of such policies.

Benefit Triggers

HIPAA requires specific benefit triggers for tax-qualified policies. Most non-tax-qualified policies have somewhat less restrictive benefit triggers that make it easier to qualify for benefits. As a result, insurers that offer both types of policies tend to have premiums that are 5 to 10 percent higher for non-tax-qualified policies.

Although the two types of policies may differ with regard to the number and types of ADLs that an insured must be unable to perform, the majority of non-tax-qualified policies use the same criteria as in tax-qualified policies. The major differences are in the time period for which an insured must be expected to be unable to perform ADLs and the use of a medical necessity trigger.

90-Day ADL Period. As mentioned in chapter 18, for purposes of a tax-qualified policy, a chronically ill person must be expected to be unable to perform at least two activities of daily living for at least 90 days. Non-tax-qualified policies do not have this 90-day requirement.

Example: Ian has a comprehensive long-term care insurance policy with a 20-day elimination period. He recently broke both his arms as a result of a freak accident. His physician certified that he would need help with several activities of daily living but only for the next 50 to 75 days.

If Ian has a tax-qualified policy, he will not be eligible for benefits because his disability is not expected to last for at least 90 days. However, if he has a non-tax-qualified policy, he can start receiving benefits after 20 days.

Although advocates of non-tax-qualified policies often emphasize this distinction, there are those who point out that it is of little or no significance to most insureds. First, as shown in table 20-3, the majority of insureds are subject to elimination periods of 90 days or longer. For them, claim payments will begin at the same time under either type of policy. Second, as explained in earlier chapters, coverage for certain long-term care services of short duration is provided under Medicare and private medical expense insurance. (However, the coverage might not pay for the type or duration of care needed.) Finally, many insureds have the resources to pay for long-term care services for relatively short periods of time.

Medical Necessity. Perhaps a more significant distinction is that many non-tax-qualified policies use medical necessity as a benefit trigger. Such a benefit trigger is not allowed in a tax-qualified policy. From a consumer standpoint, there are individuals, particularly the frail elderly, who do not meet the benefit triggers of tax-qualified policies but who still require long-term care services.

Per Diem versus Reimbursement Policies

A consumer must decide whether to purchase a policy that pays benefits on a per diem basis or a reimbursement basis. Note, however, that most policies pay benefits on a reimbursement basis, and many insurers do not offer per diem policies.

In general, a per diem (or indemnity) policy will be 10 to 15 percent more expensive, particularly if the daily benefit is high and there is the possibility of its exceeding the actual costs that would be paid under a reimbursement policy. One advantage of a per diem policy is that, if the insured receives a benefit in excess of the cost of long-term care services, he or she can use this additional money to pay extra costs associated with such services. These costs might include payments to informal caregivers, payments for prescription drugs, or family support because of lost wages. The latter, however, is better provided under some type of disability income insurance. The insured could also save the money to pay for future long-term care services that might exceed the daily benefit.

Another advantage of a per diem policy is that the claims process tends to be somewhat simpler and faster. With a reimbursement policy, the insured must submit actual invoices to the insurer in addition to verification that he or she qualifies for benefits. With a per diem policy, it is only necessary to show that eligibility for benefits has been satisfied.

In addition to a per diem policy's higher premium, benefits are subject to federal income taxation if they exceed more than $270 per day (in 2008) and are used for anything other than the payment of qualified long-term care services.

Type of Coverage

More than 15 years ago, most buyers of long-term care insurance policies purchased coverage only for care in facilities like nursing homes. As shown in table 20-3, there has been a significant change in recent years, with a large majority of buyers now selecting comprehensive policies. The public has become more aware of the need for long-term care services in the home environment and wants protection for this need even though it may increase the cost of a facility-only policy by 60 to 70 percent.

There are situations in which a facility-only policy may still be appropriate, however. It is a viable alternative if cost is a consideration, particularly if there are family members or others who will provide necessary services in the home. It may also be an appropriate choice if an insured has some resources that could be used to pay for home health care services before nursing home care becomes necessary.

There are also situations in which a stand-alone home health care policy may be a logical option. For example, an individual with limited resources may wish to remain at home for as long as possible. Once the person needs nursing home care, he or she may have no qualms about relying on Medicaid. Residents of continuing care retirement communities sometimes purchase stand-alone policies so they can obtain care in their independent-living units rather than having to move to the facility's assisted-living portion.

Amount of Coverage

The decision about the amount of long-term care coverage to purchase actually involves a series of decisions about the size of the daily benefit, the elimination period, and the benefit duration. Such factors as an applicant's age, income, assets, and tolerance toward financial risk also influence the decision. There are no precise answers. Each situation is unique, and the final amount of insurance selected in many cases is a balance between what the applicant feels is appropriate and what he or she can afford.

At one extreme, an individual could purchase a policy with a daily benefit equal to the cost of long-term care services (and appropriate increases for inflation), a 0-day elimination period, and lifetime benefits. However, such a policy would be unaffordable to many applicants and is also unnecessary. Virtually all applicants have some resources that can be used to finance at least a portion of their long-term care needs. As explained in chapter 17, these resources may also include accumulated assets and financial support from family members.

Daily Benefit

The first step in selecting the proper daily benefit is to find out the cost of care in the geographic region where care might be received. It should be noted that this might be a different region from where an applicant currently lives. For example, an applicant may feel that the city where a child lives might be a more appropriate location for long-term care if it is needed.

The average daily cost for nursing home care varies significantly from one geographic region to another. For example, one recent study of nursing home costs shows that the average cost is $213 for a private room and $189 for a semiprivate room.[30] However, there are significant cost differences among regions, with the average daily cost of a private room averaging $123 in Shreveport to $510 in Alaska. Even within regions, the variations from the average cost are sometimes greater than 50 percent. Although an applicant might prefer to be in the most expensive nursing home in town, he or she might be able only to afford insurance that will pay for care in a less expensive facility. Although published averages are helpful, they are no substitute for relying on an agent who is familiar with local nursing home costs. It may also be helpful to actually visit nursing homes to determine if they are acceptable and to obtain their rates. Nursing home rates can also be obtained from the local area agencies on aging, which were established by the Older Americans Act.

Other statistics in the same study show that the hourly cost of home health care provided by a home health aide working for a licensed home care agency was $19. Again, there are significant variations from one region to another and within regions. Even with these figures in hand, an estimate must be made about the need and frequency of home health care services. For example, if around-the-clock care is needed, the cost of home health care can exceed the cost of nursing home care. Most insurers, agents, and financial planners recommend that the daily home health care benefit be equal to somewhere between 75 and 100 percent of the daily nursing home benefit. As shown in table 20-3, individual policies are near the 100 percent figure ($135 versus $142). Note, however, that reducing the percentage of home health care benefits to 80 percent of nursing home benefits will usually lower the premium about 10 percent. A decrease from 100 percent to 50 percent often results in a premium saving of 25 to 30 percent.

The next step to determine the appropriate daily benefit is to subtract the daily costs that the applicant has determined can be made from other resources.

It should be pointed out that the cost of long-term care insurance is essentially proportional to the daily benefit chosen. All other things being equal, a policy with a daily benefit of $200 will cost twice as much as a policy with a daily benefit of $100.

Elimination Period

Recent applicants for individual long-term care insurance policies select elimination periods that average 80 days. [31] Averages are deceiving, however, because many applicants elect an elimination period of either 90 days or 30 days or less. If all other factors are equal, an increase in the elimination period from 20–30 days to 90–100 days will usually result in a premium saving of between 10 and 20 percent. It is necessary to balance this saving in premium against the potential cost that an insured must assume if he or she needs long-term care. For example, with a 90-day elimination period, the insured would have to pay $18,000 out of pocket before benefits commence if nursing home costs are $200 per day. This figure may increase substantially by the time an insured needs long-term care several years in the future, whereas the insured's available resources remain stable or decrease during retirement years. Although the premium saving for the longer elimination period is significant, so is the potential out-of-pocket cost.

Benefit Duration

As indicated in chapter 16, the average stay in a nursing home is approximately 2.5 years. Although different statistics are often cited, it appears that somewhere between 10 and 20 percent of nursing home stays exceed 5 years. As table 20-3 indicates, for the years reported many insureds selected a benefit duration of 5 years or more, but a large percentage select less. If these persons have long-term care needs that exhaust their benefits, they will need to liquidate their assets, rely on financial support from relatives, and possibly apply for Medicaid.

Ideally, a policy would have an unlimited benefit period, but the realities of cost often dictate otherwise. Many long-term care experts feel that, at a minimum, a person should have a benefit period somewhere in the neighborhood of 4 to 6 years. However, even that might be unaffordable to some insureds. As a general rule, the cost to increase a benefit period from 2 to 4 years is approximately 50 percent. Going from a 2-year benefit to a lifetime benefit requires a premium increase in the range of 70 to 80 percent.

Inflation Protection

The amount of long-term care insurance coverage may be perfectly appropriate at the time a policy is purchased. However, the initial amount of coverage may be inadequate in the future because of the effect of inflation on long-term care costs.

Example: Five years ago when she retired at age 65, Sylvia purchased a long-term care insurance policy with a $100 per day nursing home benefit. The policy included no increase in benefits for inflation. At that time, the benefit amount was equal to the average cost of nursing home care in her community. However, nursing home costs there have risen at a rate of 6 percent over the last 5 years, and the average nursing home cost is now $133 per day. If this inflation rate continues, daily nursing home costs will increase to $179 in another 5 years and to $240 in 10 years. Sylvia's assets are currently insufficient to cover this increase in nursing home costs if she has a nursing home stay of more than a few months.

Sylvia's twin sister, Salvia, bought a similar long-term care insurance policy at the same time. However, Salvia purchased a policy with a 5 percent compound inflation rider even though the extra premium meant that she would have to manage her retirement expenses more carefully than her sister would. After 5 years, Salvia's daily benefit has risen to $128. (See table 19-1 in chapter 19.) It will continue to rise to $163 in another 5 years and to $208 in 10 years. Although Salvia's benefit has failed somewhat to keep up with the actual increase in costs, she is in a better position than her sister to make up the shortfall out of her assets because the difference is much smaller.

This example illustrates two very important points. First, protection against the effects of inflation may be a determining factor in whether an individual's long-term care protection adequately meets future needs. Second, the inflation protection in many policies may not keep benefit limits in line with the real inflation in long-term care costs.

There may be some policyowners who feel that they have other resources to offset the effects of inflation. Although this may be true in some circumstances, many policyowners may change their minds when the true magnitude of inflation's effects is explained to them.

There are two ways to plan for inflation in long-term care costs. One is to purchase some type of automatic benefit increase; the other is to periodically purchase additional benefits. The characteristics of these types of inflation increases are described in chapter 19.

Automatic Benefit Increases

The election of an automatic benefit increase results in a significantly higher premium, and the magnitude of this increase varies widely among insurers. However, the increased premium remains level over the life of the contract unless an insurer increases rates by class. The cost of adding automatic inflation protection varies by insurer because of such factors as age and the particular type of plan selected. The authors of this book randomly picked three different comprehensive long-term care insurance policies from three different insurers and found that premiums increased by the factors in table 20-4 if 5 percent compound inflation protection was included. For example, a factor of 2.0 indicates that a policy with the inflation protection would be twice as expensive as a policy without it.

TABLE 20-4
Increase for 5 Percent Compound Inflation

Age	Insurer 1	Insurer 2	Insurer 3
40	3.3	2.5	2.0
55	2.4	2.0	1.9
65	2.0	1.5	1.8
75	1.6	1.4	1.6

Insurer 2 was the only insurer in table 20-4 that also offered a 5 percent simple inflation option. The factors for this option are 1.9, 1.6, 1.4, and 1.3, respectively. Unfortunately, benefits will eventually fall significantly behind those of a policy with 5 percent compound inflation protection, as shown in table 19-1 in chapter 19. However, a simple inflation option does result in a lower premium and may provide adequate future protection if an insured has (or expects to accumulate) other resources that can be also be used to finance future cost increases if long-term care is needed or if the insured has a very short life expectancy.

Future Purchase Options

Many insurers allow insureds to increase benefits periodically on a pay-as-you-go basis without evidence of insurability. This means that the initial premium will be much lower than that of a policy with an automatic benefit increase. However, there are some drawbacks to purchasing additional benefits in the future.

Each election of a subsequent benefit increase raises the premium as the price for the increased benefit is determined by the insured's attained age. Eventually, the premium will surpass that of a policy written with an automatic benefit increase, and these increases will grow steadily larger. At some point, the cost of these increases may become unaffordable to some insureds. Furthermore, insurers may place an aggregate limit on the amount of benefit increases or have an age limit beyond which benefit increases cannot be purchased. Finally, the failure to purchase a specified number of either consecutive or cumulative scheduled benefit increases typically terminates the right to exercise future benefit increases without evidence of insurability.

The use of a future (or guaranteed) purchase option appears to have declined dramatically in the individual marketplace in recent years. This conclusion is inferred by the increase in those choosing the automatic inflation protection which grew from 41 percent of sales in 2000 to 76 percent of sales more recently. Persons declining the automatic inflation protection most frequently have a future purchase option provided to them, however. This shift is largely due to the declining age of applicants. Many of these persons, who are in or near retirement, are unwilling to face large premium increases later, at a time when they expect less income to be available to afford them. If they currently can afford to purchase inflation protection, they prefer the more predictable future premiums of a policy with an automatic inflation increase.

Nonforfeiture Benefits

In addition to deciding what, if any, type of inflation protection to include in a long-term care insurance policy, an applicant must decide whether to elect some type of nonforfeiture benefit. Few purchasers of individual policies elect such an option. There are several reasons for this. One reason is cost. For example, including a shortened benefit period option will typically increase premiums by 20 to 40 percent, depending on the insurer and the insured's age at which the policy is purchased. A refund-of-premium rider to a non-tax-qualified policy may increase premiums by 50 percent or more if 100 percent of the premiums are refunded. Applicants who are on tight budgets are probably better off if they use their limited resources to purchase an adequate benefit amount and include inflation protection.

Another reason most purchasers do not elect a nonforfeiture option seems to be that most applicants purchase long-term care insurance to meet future needs and do not plan to let a policy terminate later in life—a time when they are much more likely to need coverage. Therefore, they see little value in a nonforfeiture benefit, particularly when they realize the extra premium required. Moreover, they are not used to receiving any type of benefit when most other types of insurance terminate.

Finally, some financial planners question whether a nonforfeiture option makes good financial sense. They argue that if the policyowner can afford such an additional premium, he or she would be better off in the long run to invest the additional premium. In this way, additional funds will be available in the future whether a policy terminates or not.

It should also be noted that purchasers of group coverage are much more likely to have a nonforfeiture benefit. These purchasers tend to be considerably younger than purchasers in the individual marketplace and, therefore, have significantly lower premiums. This, coupled with the fact that these buyers are typically working (because most group coverage is provided under employer-sponsored benefit plans), makes the cost of a nonforfeiture benefit more affordable.

Policy Comparisons

Consumers and financial services professionals are often faced with the daunting task of comparing long-term care insurance policies. Although most consumers are not interested in comparing every available policy, they are often presented with proposals from more than one agent or with more than one proposal from a single agent. If the agents or insurers have done a proper evaluation of their client's needs, the policies will have many similarities, but there will also be differences. Thus, a systematic approach to compare the policies is needed. Note, however, that an agent's presentation of too many policies to a client can be overwhelming and may actually discourage the client from purchasing coverage. As a result, many agents are trained to ask probing questions at the onset of the sales process so that a limited number of policies can be presented, based on such factors as affordability and client needs.

Several insurance companies, consumer groups, and financial publications have prepared what are referred to as checklists or worksheets for this purpose. Perhaps the best known of these is the worksheet in the NAIC's *A Shopper's Guide to Long-Term Care Insurance.* This worksheet is reproduced in figure 20-1.

FIGURE 20-1
How to Compare Long-Term Care Insurance Policies

Fill in the information below so that you can compare long-term care insurance policies. Most of the information you need is in the outline of coverage provided in the policies you are comparing. Even so, you will need to calculate some information and talk to the agent or a company representative to get the rest.

Insurance Company Information	**Policy 1**	**Policy 2**
1. Name of the insurance company's agent		
2. Is the company licensed in your state?	yes/no	yes/no
3. Insurance rating service and rating		
What levels of care are covered by this policy?		
4. Does the policy provide benefits for these levels of care?		
• Skilled nursing care?	yes/no	yes/no
• Personal/custodial care?	yes/no	yes/no
(In many states, both levels of care are required.)		
5. Does the policy pay for any nursing home stay, no matter what level of care you receive?	yes/no	yes/no
• If not, what levels aren't covered?		
Where can you receive care covered under the policy?		
6. Does the policy pay for care in any licensed facility?	yes/no	yes/no
• If not, what doesn't it pay for?		
7. Does the policy provide home care benefits for:		
• Skilled nursing care?	yes/no	yes/no
• Personal care given by home health aides?	yes/no	yes/no
• Homemaker services?	yes/no	yes/no
• Other ____________________?	yes/no	yes/no

8. Does the policy pay for care received in:		
• Adult day care centers?	yes/no	yes/no
• Assisted living facilities?	yes/no	yes/no
• Other settings? (List)		
How long are benefits paid and what amounts are covered? (You may be considering a policy that pays benefits on a different basis, so you may have to do some calculations to determine comparable amounts.)		
9. How much will the policy pay per day for:		
• Nursing home care?	$	$
• Assisted living facility care?	$	$
• Home care?	$	$
10. Are there limits on the number of days or visits per year for which benefits will be paid? If yes, what are the limits for:	yes/no	yes/no
• Nursing home care?	days	days
• Assisted living facility care?		
• Home care? (days or visits?)		
11. What is the length of the benefit period that you are considering?	years	years
12. Are there limits on the amounts the policy will pay during your lifetime? If yes, what are the limits for:	yes/no	yes/no
• Nursing home care?	$	$
• Assisted living facility care?	$	$
• Home care? (days or visits?)	$	$
• Total lifetime limit	$	$
How does the policy decide when you are eligible for benefits?		
13. Which of the "benefit triggers" does the policy use to decide your eligibility for benefits? (It may have more than one.)		
• Unable to do activities of daily living (ADLs)	yes/no	yes/no
• Cognitive impairment (Older policies may discriminate against Alzheimer's; newer ones don't.)	yes/no	yes/no
• Doctor certification of medical necessity	yes/no	yes/no
• Prior hospital stay	yes/no	yes/no
• Bathing is one of the ADLs	yes/no	yes/no
When do benefits start?		
14. How long is the waiting period before benefits begin for:		
• Nursing home care?	days	days
• Assisted living facility care?	days	days
• Home health care?	days	days
• Waiting period—service days or calendar days	service days	calendar days
15. Are the waiting periods for home care cumulative or consecutive?		
16. How long will it be before you are covered for a preexisting condition? (Usually 6 months)	months	months

17. How long will the company look back in your medical history to determine a preexisting condition? (Usually 6 months)	months	months
Does the policy have inflation protection?		
18. Are the benefits adjusted for inflation?	yes/no	yes/no
19. Are you allowed to buy more coverage? If yes,	yes/no	yes/no
• When can you buy more coverage?		
• How much can you buy?	$	$
• When can you no longer buy more coverage?		
20. Do the benefits increase automatically? If yes,	yes/no	yes/no
• What is the rate of increase?	%	%
• Is it a simple or compound increase?		
• When do automatic increases stop?		
21. If you buy inflation coverage, what daily benefit would you receive for:		
Nursing home care:		
• 5 years from now?	$	$
• 10 years from now?	$	$
Assisted living facility care:		
• 5 years from now?	$	$
• 10 years from now?	$	$
Home health care:		
• 5 years from now?	$	$
• 10 years from now?	$	$
22. If you buy inflation coverage, what will your premium be?:		
• 5 years from now?	$	$
• 10 years from now?	$	$
• 15 years from now?	$	$
What other benefits are covered under the policy?		
23. Is there a waiver of premium benefit? If yes:	yes/no	yes/no
• How long do you have to be in a nursing home before it begins?		
• Does the waiver apply when you receive home care?	yes/no	yes/no
24. Does the policy have a nonforfeiture benefit?	yes/no	yes/no
If yes, what kind?		
25. Does the policy have a return of premium benefit?	yes/no	yes/no
26. Does the policy have a death benefit?	yes/no	yes/no
If yes, are there any restrictions before the benefit is paid?	yes/no	yes/no
27. Will the policy cover one person or two?	one/two	one/two
Tax-qualified status		
28. Is the policy tax-qualified?	yes/no	yes/no
What does the policy cost?		
29. What is the premium excluding all riders?		
• Monthly	$	$
• Yearly	$	$

30. What is the premium if home care is covered?		
• Monthly	$	$
• Yearly	$	$
31. What is the premium if assisted living is covered?		
• Monthly	$	$
• Yearly	$	$
32. What is the premium if you include an inflation rider?		
• Monthly	$	$
• Yearly	$	$
33. What is the premium if you include a nonforfeiture benefit?		
• Monthly	$	$
• Yearly	$	$
34. Is there any discount if you and your spouse both buy policies?	yes/no	yes/no
• If yes, what is the amount of the discount?	$	$
• Do you lose the discount when one spouse dies?	yes/no	yes/no
35. What is the total annual premium including all riders and discounts?		
• Total monthly premium	$	$
• Total annual premium	$	$
36. When looking at the results of questions 29 through 35, how much do you think you are willing to pay in premiums?	$	$

Source: *A Shopper's Guide to Long-Term Care Insurance*, Worksheet 2: How to Compare Long-Term Care Insurance Policies,

Switching Policies

Policyowners are sometimes faced with the situation in which they would like a "better" long-term care insurance policy—possibly because their existing policy has less-than-adequate benefits or more restrictive policy provisions than are currently available in the marketplace. Should they terminate the old policy and switch to a new policy? Such a change must be made with a careful and thorough determination that the new policy is better than the old policy and that the insured will qualify for the new policy. The difference in premiums must also be considered because the new policy will be written at attained-age rates that may be higher than those used for the old policy. In addition, an old policy should never be terminated before a new policy is actually issued. An insured must also be aware of any preexisting-conditions provision in the new policy, whereby benefits otherwise payable under the old policy would be denied. Finally, the insured must take into account any difference in the tax status of the old and new policies.

There are many reasons for considering a new policy. For example, an insured may wish to increase the daily benefit, add inflation protection, or add home health care. It is always prudent to determine if the existing insurer will raise its benefits at a lower cost than the additional premium for a new policy. Such increases in benefits require evidence of insurability, and the additional premium is usually based on attained-age rates. The rates that apply to the original benefits, however, will remain at the old issue-age level.

As mentioned in chapter 18, insurers have continued to enhance their newer policies, and the ability of and cost to existing insureds to obtain these benefits varies among insurers. However, it is always worth the effort to explore the possibility of upgrading an older policy before replacing it with a newer policy. In some cases, replacing an older policy may be justified; in other cases, it may not.

A final alternative to switching policies is to purchase an additional policy. For example, an insured with an acceptable facility-only policy may have decided that he or she would like benefits for home health care. The insurer, however, may be unwilling or unable to add this coverage for reasons that include jeopardizing a grandfathered policy's tax status or state laws that no longer allow issuing the home health care rider formerly used with the policy. Rather than purchasing a new comprehensive policy, the insured may find that it is less expensive to buy a separate home health care policy. An additional policy may also be a viable alternative if an insured is unable to increase daily benefit amounts under an existing policy.

Premium Payments

One of the final steps in the purchase of long-term care insurance is the determination of how to pay the premium. As mentioned in chapter 19, there are several options. These include: pay it over the applicant's lifetime, pay it periodically over an accelerated period, or pay it in a single lump sum. The most appropriate method is the one that best fits the applicant's financial circumstances and attitude toward uncertainty. A large majority of insureds have elected to pay premiums over their lifetimes.

Lifetime Payments

Over 95 percent of applicants elect to pay their premiums over their lifetime in annual, semiannual, quarterly, or monthly installments.[32] The periodic payment is level and predetermined, but it might increase if the insurer raises premiums on a class basis. The insurer bills the insured unless an election is made at some point to have payments made automatically from a bank account—an approach that is often required if payments are made monthly.

Accelerated Payments

As mentioned in chapter 19, some insurers allow applicants to make premium payments over limited periods of time, such as 10 years or until age 65. After that time, no more premium payments are required to keep coverage in force. In addition, an insured will not be subject to any rate increases that an insurer might impose for policies that are still in the premium-payment period. Such options are increasingly popular with younger purchasers of long-term care insurance who want a paid-up policy by the time they retire, possibly with a lower income than they had during their working years. Other purchasers like the peace of mind that having a paid-up policy will give them. Less than 5 percent of applicants select to pay premiums in this way.[33]

The major drawback to accelerated payments is cost. For example, one insurer offers 55-year-old applicants a policy that will be paid up at age 65 if they make periodic premium payments for 10 years that are 2.1 times the annual premium payments for a policy with a lifetime payment period. This factor is 2.3 at age 45 and 1.9 at age 65. Needless to say, many applicants are unable to afford such increased premiums. Moreover, accelerated payments are likely to cause otherwise tax-deductible premiums to exceed the annual deduction limits identified in chapter 18. The loss of a tax advantage for premium amounts above these limits effectively serves to increase a person's premium costs even further.

As a result, some financial planners feel that the applicant would be better off by investing this additional premium and would need only modest return to generate enough income to make premiums payments for life.

One final point is worthy of mention. Premiums during an accelerated-payment period, like those paid over an insured's lifetime, can be made in annual or shorter periodic intervals.

Single Payments

Some insurers allow an applicant to purchase a paid-up policy with one single payment at the time of purchase. If an applicant has liquid resources that are not earning a sufficient return, this will enable him or her to avoid future premiums and rate increases. Less than one percent of applicants use this premium payment method.[34]

Again, a major obstacle to this option is cost. For example, the insurer mentioned previously charges a premium at age 55 that is 16.8 times as much as a premium paid over the insured's lifetime. The policyowner also loses potential future income tax deductions if the policy is tax qualified.

Furthermore, the insured's estate will be reduced if the insured dies in the near future unless the policyowner purchased some type of nonforfeiture or return-of-premium option. As mentioned earlier, such an option would have resulted in a significant further increase in the premium.

Evaluating Insurers

Chapter 2 discusses the criteria a consumer should use when selecting an insurance company from which to purchase a health insurance policy. This process, which focuses on financial strength, reputation, and cost, applies equally to the selection of an insurer from which to purchase a long-term care policy. Nevertheless, a review of premium rate variations among insurers for similar policies can be an important element in selecting a policy and in evaluating the insurer.

One recent survey compared 38 policy forms from 23 insurance companies with respect to cost under varying assumptions.[35] Table 20-5 shows the premium variations for policy forms from 10 of these companies at selected ages for one particular set of policy assumptions. The comparison is based on the insurer's best preferred rates for a single-life comprehensive policy with the following characteristics:

- $100 daily benefit for both facility care and home health care
- lifetime benefit
- 90-day elimination period
- 5 percent annual compound inflation increase

TABLE 20-5
Premium Comparisons among Insurers

	Age 40	Age 50	Age 60	Age 70
Insurer 1	$1,231	$1,955	$3,052	$5,113
Insurer 2	1,347	1,547	2,150	4,450
Insurer 3	1,487	1,516	2,167	3,863
Insurer 4	1,512	1,879	2,643	5,359
Insurer 5	1,594	1,820	2,565	5,142
Insurer 6	1,615	1,924	2,669	5,125
Insurer 7	1,678	1,942	2,661	4,387
Insurer 8	1,734	2,006	2,860	5.077
Insurer 9	1,848	1,968	2,784	5,688
Insurer 10	2,151	2,506	3,473	6,031

As this table shows, there are substantial premium variations among insurers, and the array of companies from lowest to highest premium is not the same at different ages. Moreover, all the companies in the survey offer a discount when both spouses purchase coverage. Compared to the single insured rate, the cost of the additional spouse's coverage is discounted from 12 to as much as 38 percent, with 30 percent being most common. In addition, the same pattern of price variation by insurer may differ significantly for other policy assumptions.

However as chapter 2 also cautions, when evaluating insurers, cost comparisons must be used with care. Policies, although comparable, are rarely identical with respect to all the provisions that affect their cost. Significantly, an insurer's financial strength, policyowner service, and stable premiums over time are more important considerations that an initially low premium.

A Decision-Making Example

The effect of cost on consumer decisions has been woven throughout much of this chapter. However, the discussion has focused on the way in which one factor, such as the length of the elimination period or the inclusion of inflation protection, affects the final premium. As this final example illustrates, an insured must often make several decisions before the final selection of a long-term care insurance policy.

Example:

Fred, aged 65, has decided that he needs long-term care insurance. Five years ago, he and his wife sold their small jewelry store and were able to retire comfortably. Their plans of a leisurely life during retirement years were soon shattered when Fred's wife had a serious stroke. For 3 years, Fred was able to care for her at home with the assistance of professional caregivers. After she was totally paralyzed 2 years ago by a second stroke, Fred found it necessary to put her in the nursing home where she recently died.

Having spent almost $250,000 to provide his wife with the best care possible, Fred is fully aware of the effect that long-term care can have on a family's assets. He wants to make sure that any long-term care expenses he might incur will not further deplete the $500,000 in remaining assets that he and his wife spent a lifetime accumulating and intended to leave to their children and grandchildren.

Fred has contacted a well-respected insurance agent whom he has known for several years and asked her to help him find a long-term care insurance policy that meets his objectives. Fred has indicated that he would like a policy that provides these benefits:

- a daily facility benefit of $150. A top-quality nursing home in Fred's town will cost about $250 per day, but Fred feels he can afford to pay $100 from his Social Security and retirement income.
- a home health care benefit of $150 per day
- a lifetime benefit period
- a 20-day elimination period
- 5 percent annual compound inflation protection

Fred's agent calculates that such a policy will have an annual premium of $5,060. Fred feels that this is somewhat more than he can pay without withdrawing funds from his assets and asks her what can be done to reduce the premium to about $4,000 per year. She comes up with the following alternatives:

- If Fred lowers the daily benefit to $130 per day, the premium will drop to $4,380. A further decrease to $120 per day will result in a premium of $4,050. Fred decides to consider this option.
- If Fred decreases the home health care benefit to 50 percent of the facility benefit, the premium will drop to $4,130. Fred realizes how costly home health care can be and doesn't like this option.
- If Fred elects a 5-year benefit period, the premium will drop to $4,135. For a 4-year benefit period, the premium will be $3,800. Fred is aware of some patients in his wife's nursing home who had been there for as long as 10 years and doesn't like this option either.
- If Fred increases the elimination period to 90 days, the premium will drop to $4,150. The premium for a 180-day elimination period will further decrease the premium to $3,750. Fred is willing to think about a 90-day

elimination period, but he feels that 180 days is too long.

- If Fred changes the inflation protection from compound interest to simple interest, the premium will drop to $4,260. Fred hopes to live for many more years and realizes the effect that inflation will have on long-term care costs. This option doesn't appeal to him.

Fred decides to take a day or two to think about his options. He calculates that the longer elimination period will increase his out-of-pocket costs by $10,500 (70 days times $150) over what they would otherwise be if he needs long-term care. He also calculates that the lower benefit amount of $120 will increase his annual out-of-pocket costs by $10,950 (365 days times $30). Fred realizes that these additional out-of-pocket costs will come from his accumulated assets. He also understands that he could afford the benefits he originally desired if he were willing to reduce his assets by about $1,000 per year to pay the $5,060 premium.

Fred finally decides that the policy with the $5,060 premium is the most appropriate choice. Its benefits will make it more likely that his family will provide the level of care he wants if he is unable to make decisions for himself.

USING GROUP AND HYBRID POLICIES

As mentioned previously, the consumer's decision-making process may extend to the use of group insurance, usually at work, and various kinds of hybrid policies as sources of long-term care insurance.

Group Coverage

Many persons can obtain long-term care coverage at work if their employers sponsor such a program. As stated previously, about 1.9 million persons or 30 percent of those with long-term care coverage obtain it in this way. In addition, approximately 200,000 persons purchase coverage through group plans offered by associations and affinity organizations that make coverage available as a member benefit. Examples of these types of organizations include the U.S. Chamber of Commerce, AARP, banks, service clubs, and alumni associations. Although the plans sponsored by employers and associations are typically referred to as group insurance coverage, in some cases, they might be mass-marketed plans of individual coverage.

The following discussion of group long-term care insurance focuses primarily on the plans sponsored by employers because they are by far the most common situation in which group coverage is obtained.

A recent industry study found that as many as one out of four shoppers for long-term care coverage said the fact that their employers offered such a plan prompted them to consider its purchase.[36] Almost 4 out of 10 of these shoppers did purchase coverage at work, while 2 out of 10 went on to purchase their coverage elsewhere, usually in the individual market. All of these shoppers are consumers who found themselves in a position where they must weigh the advantages of employer-sponsored group coverage against the purchase of an individual policy of long-term care insurance. To a great extent, group coverage is similar to the coverage under policies sold in the individual marketplace. Group products currently available are tax qualified and as such meet all the requirements imposed by HIPAA. These products are also subject to the provisions of the NAIC model act and regulation. There are good reasons, then, why a majority of these surveyed shoppers chose group coverage. The following discussion presents group product features under the headings of eligibility, premiums, benefits, underwriting, and portability. Nevertheless, a third of the shoppers surveyed who could have chosen employer-sponsored group coverage found an individual policy more appealing. Thus, the discussion also points out why an individual policy of long-term care insurance can be a better choice.

Eligibility

As long as an employee falls within an eligible classification, group coverage is available for the employee and/or spouse as long as the insurer's underwriting criteria are satisfied. Many plans also extend eligibility to retirees and other family members, such as adult children, parents, parents-in-law, grandparents, grandparents-in-law, or siblings.

Plans vary as to when an eligible person may apply for coverage. When a group plan is first installed, eligible persons must usually elect coverage within a defined enrollment period. To minimize adverse selection, eligible persons who initially declined coverage are often unable to enroll until the next open enrollment period, which might be on an annual basis or as infrequently as every 2 or 3 years. In addition, an employee who delays enrollment will usually be subject to a more stringent level of underwriting.

Premium Cost

The majority of group programs are voluntary benefit plans with the employee (and other covered persons) paying the full cost of coverage. Unlike medical expense premiums, which employees pay at a composite or average premium rate for the entire group, long-term care premiums are charged at the age rate applicable to each participant. In the unusual situation where an employer pays a portion of the cost of coverage, the employee would have a strong incentive to purchase coverage at work. Such a contribution usually applies only to an employee's coverage, however.

Depending on the plan, premiums may be payable for the employee's life or over the employee's working years. Payroll deduction is also commonly used to collect the employee's cost for coverage. Payroll deduction is popular with employees and encourages participation in group long-term care plans. In some cases, however, employees are billed directly in the same manner as if they had purchased coverage in the individual marketplace.

When payroll deduction is used, an employee can usually elect to have the deduction include the cost of a spouse's coverage. The cost of coverage for other eligible family members is usually paid on a direct-bill basis, even if the employee pays the premium. Retirees may be billed directly or allowed to have the premium deducted from pension payments they receive from the employer.

The cost of employer-provided coverage tends to be 5 to 15 percent less expensive than coverage purchased in the individual marketplace because of administrative and marketing cost savings.

Just because the cost of coverage in the group marketplace may be less in general than the cost of individually purchased coverage, it should not be assumed that group coverage is always the best purchase for a consumer. As table 20-4 displays, there are significant price variations among insurers. If a high-cost insurer provides the group coverage, a person may be able to find less expensive coverage in the individual marketplace. In addition, the person may be able to design a benefit package to better fit his or her specific needs by purchasing coverage elsewhere.

Benefits

Some employer-sponsored plans offer as wide an array of benefit choices as in the individual marketplace. However, most plans simplify the decision process by limiting the available options from which an employee must select. This simplification may be to allow choice among several specific benefit options or choice among selected predesigned benefit packages.

Regardless of the approach, the available options usually are more limited than in the individual market because they are determined by negotiation between the employer and the insurer. For example, an employer's plan may automatically include inflation protection or may not have an option for a 0-day elimination period.

At the same time, the packages offered may require the inclusion of costly benefits or benefits that a prospective insured may not wish to pay for such as caregiver training, payment of informal caregivers, or respite services. Individual policies allow greater flexibility in tailoring a benefit package to personal choices.

Underwriting

There are levels of underwriting frequently applicable to employer-sponsored group plans, including long-term care insurance, that are more liberal than the underwriting requirements of individual policies. These levels include:

- guaranteed issue—coverage is issued to all who apply for it
- modified guaranteed issue—coverage is issued after satisfactory responses to a limited number of medical and activity questions
- simplified issue—coverage is issued after satisfactory responses to additional , but still limited number of medical and activity questions

Less restrictive underwriting is possible because adverse selection tends to be less of a problem with employees; they tend to be healthier as a result of their being actively at work. Moreover, the employee group as a whole must meet criteria to minimize adverse selection, especially for guaranteed issue and modified guaranteed issue underwriting. These criteria, which are also common to group underwriting for other types of insurance, often establish requirements for group size, type of employee to be covered, plan participation levels, and industry and company stability. Guaranteed issue, which is often limited to eligible employees, is also often accompanied by a higher premium than other levels of underwriting. Simplified-issue underwriting might be used for all applicants, or it might be used for all applicants other than employees when the employees are subject to less stringent underwriting.

In some cases, a group plan will use the same full underwriting as in the individual marketplace (sometimes referred to as long-form underwriting), which is discussed in chapter 4. This type of underwriting is likely to be used when the group is very small or otherwise fails to satisfy the insurer's group criteria, as well as for eligible enrollees other than employees.

Nevertheless, group underwriting, unlike individual underwriting, generally provides no discount rate classification for enrollment of both spouses or partners and has no mechanism for a preferred risk rate. Thus, in some cases, the categories available in underwriting individual policies can produce more attractive rates than a group policy.

Portability

continuation of coverage

If an insured leaves the employer where the coverage was provided initially, he or she can elect to maintain coverage. Under a group policy, the NAIC model regulation requires that the insurer provide the insured with a basis for continuation or a conversion provision. Under a *continuation of coverage*, the insured retains coverage under the group contract but pays premiums directly to the insurer. This same arrangement would occur if the insured's coverage is in the form of an individual policy paid through payroll deductions. Under a conversion provision, the insured is issued an individual policy that must be identical or substantially equivalent to the group coverage. The premium for the converted policy is based on the rates for the individual policy at the insured's attained age when the original group coverage was obtained.

Hybrid Policy Alternatives

hybrid product

As the sales of long-term care insurance grew in the 1990s, several insurers began to introduce insurance contracts that combined long-term care insurance and either life insurance or annuities into a single policy. Such a policy, which is called a *hybrid product* in this book, is also referred to by several other names, including a linked policy, blended policy, combination policy, and package policy. Hybrid policies are discussed under the headings of attractions, experience, life insurance hybrids, annuity hybrids, and guaranteed purchase options.

Attractions

Hybrid policies have potential attractions. First, hybrid policies address the concern of potential buyers who consider a stand-alone long-term care policy to be a significant expense for services they may need to no great extent or not at all. Such persons may view a hybrid more favorably because it allows the purchase of a single product with two types of protection, one of which may have an investment or savings component. As result, they or their heirs would receive value through the payment of life insurance or annuity benefits of a hybrid policy even if long-term care was never needed.

There is also some evidence that a hybrid policy may offer some savings compared with the separate purchase of a long-term care policy. A recent study finds a premium savings of around 5 percent in hybrids of annuities and long-term care insurance.[37] The study also suggests that other hybrid products may provide savings in administration, processing, and commissions. Conversely, however, this means that the hybrid purchase simply makes a single premium payment for two forms of coverage which if purchased separately at the same benefit level would represent a combined premium that is roughly the same.

Second, because of the broad acceptance of life insurance, annuities, and disability income insurance, consumers may be more likely to consider these products in hybrid form more favorably as vehicles to address the growing concern about how to pay for long-term care. Moreover, because these forms of financial protection are typically purchased at younger ages during working years, including a long-term care component under a hybrid arrangement could be achieved with a lower premium and more favorable underwriting than if coverage were purchased separately later.

Third, the Pension Protection Act of 2006 makes the tax laws more favorable to hybrids of long-term care insurance and life insurance and annuities, but not disability income insurance. Transfers of money from a life insurance policy or an annuity for the purchase or funding of long-term care coverage are now allowed tax free. Previously, transfers for such a purpose would have resulted in a tax liability on at least some of the funds withdrawn.

However, the new law, in an effort to limit lost revenues from the more favorable tax treatment, decreases the financial incentive for insurers to offer hybrids by increasing corporate taxes on the premiums of such products when they do. As a result, the net effect on promoting hybrid policies is unclear as the liberalization and additional tax may simply offset each other.

Experience

The sales growth for these policies has been quite modest, and most companies' marketing efforts seem to be less intense than was once the case. This slow growth is due to several factors. First, many hybrid products were designed to take advantage of the high interest rates and the continually increasing stock market values. Instability in interest rates and the stock market make these products less attractive. Second, hybrid products combine complex long-term care policies with complex types of life insurance and annuities. The resulting products were often difficult for agents to understand and to explain to clients and their financial advisors. Third, many financial advisors view long-term care insurance as meeting a different need than life insurance, disability income insurance, or annuities, and feel that separate products should be used for each need.

Despite these impediments to the growth of hybrid products, there are circumstances where their use is appropriate. However, not all the tax ramifications are clear—particularly with regard to withdrawals from single-premium products—and competent tax advice is recommended before their purchase.

Life Insurance Hybrids

Life insurance hybrid products can take the form of most types of cash value policies. However, most policies that have been sold are universal life insurance, including variable universal life insurance. Although premiums can be paid in any mode, most sales involve the payment of a single premium.

Purchasers of this type of policy tend to be persons of moderate-to-high net worth who transfer assets from traditionally low-yielding investments, such as money market accounts and certificates of deposit. As alluded to previously, they also tend to be persons who feel that their heirs should receive something (that is, a death benefit) from their long-term care coverage to the extent that they do not use the benefits. In addition, they prefer to keep control of their own financial options, they like the tax-favored nature of life insurance, and they want to avoid ongoing premium payments.

The long-term care coverage under hybrid life insurance policies is designed to be tax qualified and is subject to most of the same HIPAA and state regulations that apply to stand-alone long-term care insurance policies. These products, however, are considered life insurance policies or riders that accelerate long-term care benefits and, as such, are sometimes treated differently under state regulations. For example, the insurer does not have to offer a nonforfeiture option because the cash value tends to serve this function.

The coverage under hybrid policies is comparable to that under comprehensive policies sold on a stand-alone basis. Depending on the insurer, the benefit may be paid on a per diem or reimbursement basis. The insured has some of the choices available to purchasers of stand-alone policies. However, there also tend to be several differences:

- The amount of the long-term care benefit is a function of the amount of life insurance protection purchased. Conversely, the benefit amount selected dictates the amount of the life insurance that must be purchased.
- Benefit periods are often limited to 2, 3, or 4 years. However, some insurers make lifetime benefits available.
- There is typically no choice of elimination period. The usual period in these policies is 90 days.
- There is usually no option for automatic inflation increases. Rather, the insured can elect each year to increase both the death benefit and long-term care benefit by 5 percent of the amount of the prior year's coverage. The additional coverage is at the insured's attained age at the time of the election and must be paid with an additional lump sum if the original policy was purchased with a single premium. Failure to exercise an annual option results in the forfeiture of the right to elect additional coverage in the future.
- There is no nonforfeiture option.

A form of simplified issue underwriting is sometimes used for younger issue ages and small amounts of coverage. However, full individual underwriting is used for most coverage. Rates vary by the same classification categories as discussed in chapter 4 for health insurance policies such as age, gender, underwriting class, and possibly use of tobacco.

Example: The contract is a universal life policy, and the insurer requires a minimum single premium of at least $10,000. The policy also includes a long-term care insurance benefit that in the aggregate is double the life insurance death benefit. The long-term care coverage provides benefits on a reimbursement basis from a pool of money, and the benefits can be used for all types of long-term care. Benefits can be increased by 5 percent each year by the payment of an additional lump-sum premium.

Helen wishes to purchase this policy at age 60 and have 4 years of benefits at $200 per day. She wants total long-term care benefits of $292,000 (1,460 days times $200). If Helen fits into the insurer's best underwriting classification, her lump-sum premium is $52,000. For this premium, she also receives a $146,000 death benefit.

If Helen decides to purchase the policy and dies without needing the long-term care benefit, her beneficiary will receive the $146,000 death benefit. If she receives up to $146,000 in long-term care benefits before her death, her beneficiary will still receive a $146,000 death benefit.

If Helen's long-term care benefits are greater than $146,000, the excess will be deducted from the death benefit. For example, assume she receives $200,000 in long-term care benefits. Then the death benefit will be reduced by $54,000 ($200,000 minus $146,000) to $92,000. This policy, like the policies of many other insurers, has a minimum death benefit equal to 10 percent of the life insurance benefit. Therefore, her beneficiary will always receive at least $14,600.

Note that the previous benefit amounts would have been different if Helen had purchased any additional benefits, received any policy loans, or made any withdrawals.

Annuity Hybrids

As mentioned in chapter 17, annuities may be used to finance long-term care expenses with impaired-risk underwriting or through contract provisions that increase payments when annuitants need long-term care. These are not hybrid products, however, because the contracts themselves do not provide any type of long-term care insurance.

Only a small number of insurers sell hybrid annuity contracts. As with the hybrid life insurance contracts, these annuities are usually purchased with a large single premium by persons who have moderately high income and net worth and want to transfer assets from some other source.

There are probably almost as many variations of these hybrid annuities as there are insurers offering them. The following are two examples of such contracts.

Example 1: With one insurer's annuity, the annuitant funds a deferred annuity with a single premium equal to the deferred annuity's face amount. This premium also buys an additional amount of long-term care protection equal to twice the annuity premium. As with any long-term care protection, there is a specified level of benefits. The annuity fund grows tax deferred at a fixed rate of interest, and the annuitant has all the usual annuity options. If the annuitant has long-term care expenses, the first benefit payments are considered a liquidation of the annuity. After the annuity is liquidated, the remaining long-term care benefits come from the long-term care portion of the contract. If the annuitant dies before receiving any long-term care benefits from the contract, a death benefit equal to the original deposit is paid to a beneficiary.

Example 2: With another insurer's annuity, the annuitant purchases a deferred variable annuity. The initial deposit is split between two accounts—one for the annuity and the other to fund the desired long-term care benefit. The insured has the choice of several options for each account, and the final annuity amount and long-term care benefits depend on investment results. This insurer's product provides two totally separate benefits. If the annuitant withdraws annuity benefits, there is no effect on the long-term care benefits. Similarly, if the annuitant uses long-term care benefits, the annuity account remains unaffected. There is a guaranteed death benefit under the contract so that the insured's beneficiary always receives an amount at least equal to the annuitant's initial investment.

Options to Purchase Long-Term Care Insurance

A very small number of insurers have recently introduced riders that can be added to life insurance or disability income policies to guarantee the insured's right to purchase long-term care insurance in the future without evidence of insurability. However, the riders, for which there is a premium charge, are underwritten at the time of issue and are available only to applicants who meet the insurer's standards at that time. These riders, which are referred to by various names, are likely to be introduced by other insurers if they find acceptance in the marketplace.

The rider of one life insurer allows the insured to purchase a long-term care insurance policy at any 5-year age interval starting at age 25 (or older if the policy was purchased at a later age) and continuing until age 60. However, the option cannot be exercised unless it has been in force for at least 2 years. The option can be exercised only once, and when it is exercised the insured can purchase any individual policy that is then being sold by the insurer. The only restriction on benefits is that there is a maximum daily benefit available. This limit varies from $110 to $220, depending on the geographic region in which the insured resides. Other than a somewhat higher premium to include this option, exercising it has no effect on the policy to which it is attached; the insured can continue that policy in force.

A few insurers offer a rider to a disability income policy that allows the insured to convert it for a long-term care insurance policy without undergoing additional underwriting. Chapter 14 discusses this type of rider.

CHAPTER REVIEW

Key Terms

personal worksheet
continuation of coverage
hybrid product

Review Questions

Review questions are based on the learning objectives in this chapter. Thus, a [20-3] at the end of a question means that the question is based on learning objective 20-3. If there are multiple objectives, they are all listed.

1. Describe consumer perceptions with respect to each of the following:
   a. need for long-term care [20-1]
   b. cost of care and sources of payment [20-1]
   c. extent of current insurance coverage [20-1]

2. Describe the reasons consumers are often reluctant to purchase long-term care insurance coverage. [20-1]

3. a. What are the characteristics of persons who buy individual long-term care insurance? [20-2]
   b. What are the purchase patterns of persons who buy this coverage? [20-2]

4. a. What does the NAIC model regulation require that suitability standards take into consideration? [20-3]
   b. How can an agent make a reasonable effort to obtain the information necessary to meet suitability standards? [20-3]
   c. What are the insurer's obligations if the suitability standards are not met? [20-3]

5. What are the consequences of waiting too long to buy long-term care insurance? [20-3]

6. a. Why do agents and consumers often shy away from non-tax-qualified policies? [20-4]
   b. What advantages might such policies have? [20-4]

7. What are the pros and cons of purchasing a per diem long-term care insurance policy rather than a reimbursement policy? [20-4]

8. a. Why might a facility-only policy be appropriate? [20-4]
   b. Why might a stand-alone home health care policy be appropriate? [20-4]

9. How can an individual determine the appropriate daily benefit for a long-term care insurance policy? [20-4]

10. What considerations must be addressed in determining the length of an elimination period? [20-4]

11. a. For what reason might the amount of long-term care coverage initially purchased be inadequate in the future? [20-4]
    b. Under what circumstances might a simple inflation option be an appropriate alternative to a compound inflation option? [20-4]
    c. What are the drawbacks to a future purchase option? [20-4]

12. Why do few consumers elect nonforfeiture options when purchasing long-term care insurance? [20-4]

13. What types of questions are asked on checklists or worksheets to compare long-term care insurance policies? [20-5]

14. a. Why might a policyowner consider switching long-term care insurance policies? [20-5]
    b. What are the alternatives to switching policies? [20-5]

15. a. What drawbacks are associated with accelerated premium payments for long-term care insurance? [20-5]
    b. What is an additional drawback of purchasing a paid-up policy with a single payment? [20-5]

16. What characteristics might shoppers for long-term care coverage find in each of the following areas of their employer-sponsored group long-term care plan?
    a. eligibility [20-6]
    b. premiums [20-6]
    c. benefits [20-6]
    d. underwriting [20-6]
    e. portability [20-6]

17. Why would shoppers for long-term care coverage find an individual policy preferable to a plan offered by their employer? [20-6]

18. a. What are the attractions of hybrid long-term care insurance products? [20-6]
    b. Why has the growth of such hybrid products been relatively modest? [20-6]

19. What types of persons tend to purchase hybrid policies that combine universal life insurance with long-term care insurance? [20-6]

20. What is the nature of the long-term care insurance that is contained in universal life insurance hybrid policies? [20-6]

21. a. What types of persons usually purchase hybrid annuity products? [20-6]
    b. Why is it difficult to characterize these products? [20-6]

22. What is the purpose of an option to purchase long-term care insurance that is sometimes added to a life insurance or disability income policy? [20-6]

NOTES

1. *Long-Term Care Insurance: An Undiscovered Necessity*, American Council of Life Insurance, 1999, and Roper Organization Survey of 1990 Americans, 1998, figures 12, 13, and 15.
2. *Who Buys Long-Term Care Insurance? A 15-Year Study of Buyers and Nonbuyers, 1990–2005,* prepared for America's Health Insurance Plans by LifePlans, Inc., April 2007, pp. 23 and 24.
3. *The Costs of Long-Term Care: Perceptions Versus Reality in 2006*, AARP, Washington, DC, December 2006, Fact Sheet and Report, p. 25.
4. Ibid., Report, pp. 77–100.

5. *Who Buys Long-Term Care Insurance? A 15-Year Study of Buyers and Nonbuyers, 1990–2005,* p. 21.
6. Ibid., pp. 45 and 46, 51.
7. *The Costs of Long-Term Care: Perceptions Versus Reality in 2006*, pp. 8 and 9.
8. Roper ASW Study, sponsored by the American Society on Aging and funded by State Farm Life Insurance Company, May 2003.
9. *Who Buys Long-Term Care Insurance? A 15-Year Study of Buyers and Nonbuyers, 1990–2005,* p. 25
10. Ibid., p. 53.
11. *Long-Term Care Insurance: Consumer Perceptions*, a report by LIMRA International, Inc., Windsor, Connecticut, and the Health Insurance Association of America, Washington, DC, 2002, p. 3, and *Long-Term Care Insurance: An Undiscovered Necessity*, figure 13.
12. *Long-Term Care Insurance: Consumer Perceptions*, pp. 3, 4.
13. *The Myth of Unaffordability: How Most Americans Should, Could, and Would Buy Private Long-Term Care Insurance*, Center for Long-Term Care Financing, Seattle, WA, September 1, 1999, pp. iv, 11, 35.
14. *Who Buys Long-Term Care Insurance? A 15-Year Study of Buyers and Nonbuyers, 1990–2005,* p. 44.
15. *Long-Term Care Insurance: Consumer Perceptions,* p. 3.
16. *Who Buys Long-Term Care Insurance? A 15-Year Study of Buyers and Nonbuyers, 1990–2005,* pp. 45, 50.
17. Ibid., p. 45.
18. Ibid., p. 45.
19. *Individual Long-Term Care Insurance, Annual Review 2006,* LIMRA International, Inc., 2007, p. 2
20. *Group Long-Term Care Insurance, Annual Review 2006* , LIMRA International, Inc., 2007, p. 2.
21. *U.S. Group Long-Term Care Insurance, Executive Summary, Annual 2004,* LIMRA International, Inc., 2005, pp. 2–4.
22. *Who Buys Long-Term Care Insurance? A 15-Year Study of Buyers and Nonbuyers, 1990–2005,* p. 9, and *Who Buys Long-Term Care Insurance in the Workplace? A Study of Employer Long-Term Care Insurance Plans,* prepared for the Health Insurance Association of America by LifePlans, Inc., October 2001, p. 14.
23. *Who Buys Long-Term Care Insurance? A 15-Year Study of Buyers and Nonbuyers, 1990–2005,* pp. 9–10.
24. Ibid., pp. 33–35.
25. Ibid., pp. 28–29.
26. Ibid., p. 30.
27. Ibid., p. 31.
28. Ibid., p. 27.
29. *Individual Long-Term Care Insurance, Annual Review 2006,* p. 2.
30. *MetLife Market Survey of Nursing Home & Assisted Living Costs,* October 2007, MetLife Mature Market Institute, pp. 4, 12–14.
31. *Who Buys Long-Term Care Insurance? A 15-Year Study of Buyers and Nonbuyers, 1990–2005,* p. 28.
32. *Individual Long-Term Care Insurance, Annual Review 2006,* p. 2.
33. Ibid.
34. Ibid.
35. "Ninth Annual Long-Term Care Insurance Survey," *Broker World,* July 2007.
36. *U.S. Buyers and Nonbuyers of Long-Term Care Insurance*, LIMRA International, Inc., 2007, p. 15.
37. *A Look at Hybrid Insurance Products with Long-Term Care Insurance*, by Marc P. Freiman, Ph.D,, AARP, 2007, p. 10.

Glossary

accelerated-benefits provision • a life insurance policy feature that allows the policyowner to receive a portion of the death benefit while the insured is still living if one or more specified events occur. *Compare* viatical settlement.

accidental death and dismemberment (AD&D) insurance • a policy or a rider to a policy that designates a dollar benefit (the *principal amount*) that is payable at the insured's accidental death. Payment of all or part of the principal amount is also made in the event of the accidental loss of a hand, foot, and/or eye, or at a degree of complete and irreversible paralysis of the limbs.

accident-only policy • a variation of a hospital confinement policy that provides cash payments in the event of injury or death resulting from a covered accident within a specified period. *See* hospital confinement indemnity insurance

accumulation period • the period of time specified in a disability income policy during which the insured is allowed to satisfy the elimination period

activities of daily living (ADLs) • physical functions that are the basic and necessary tasks of everyday life and usually include eating, bathing, dressing, transferring from bed to chair, using the toilet, and maintaining continence. *Compare* instrumental activities of daily living (IADLs).

acute care • medical care received for a relatively brief time for a severe episode of illness, an accident or other trauma, or recovery from surgery. Acute care is usually given in a hospital.

additional purchase benefit • *See* future increase option rider.

Administration on Aging (AOA) • an agency within the U.S. Department of Health and Human Services created by the Older Americans Act (OAA) that funds assistance and services for older persons and their caregivers

adult day care center • a care setting that provides social, medical, and rehabilitative services during the day to persons with physical and mental limitations who normally reside in their own homes and whose family caregiver is unable to stay at home during the day. *Also known as* adult day centers.

adverse selection • the tendency for those who know that they are highly vulnerable to loss to be more likely to purchase insurance to cover that loss

agent (insurance) • a legal representative of an insurance company with authority to act on behalf of the insurer

agent's statement • a declaration in an insurance application signed by the agent attesting that the agent personally interviewed the applicant, determined the appropriateness of the coverage, witnessed the applicant's signature, and reported all available information and observations relative to the applicant's insurability

aggregate maximum • the overall amount of benefits payable under a policy for all covered services on behalf of each insured as long as the policy is in force. *Also known as* lifetime maximum

aging in place • a term frequently used to summarize the approach to placement in the care continuum under which the care setting and the level of services provided best meet the care recipient's needs while maintaining a maximum degree of independence and as normal a living situation as possible

aleatory contract • a contract in which the values exchanged are not necessarily equal

alien insurer • an insurance company formed in a country other than the United States that writes business in the United States. *Compare* foreign insurer.

allowable charges • in medical expense insurance, the basis on which benefit payments are made for covered services. Insurers determine allowable charges using a provider's reasonable and customary fees or fees negotiated with providers participating in the insurer's network.

alternate premium payer • a designee authorized by the policyowner under a provision for third-party notification of policy lapse

Alzheimer's disease • a progressive mental deterioration or dementia accompanied by confusion, memory failure, isolation, restlessness, inability to recognize familiar objects and persons, speech disturbances, hallucinations, and the inability to carry out purposeful activity

Alzheimer's facility • a facility with a high level of staffing and other capabilities to provide the social interaction, close monitoring, and significant personal assistance individuals with Alzheimer's disease need. An Alzheimer's facility may be a stand-alone facility but most frequently is a separate unit of a nursing home or assisted-living facility devoted to this type of care.

amendment • *See* rider.

ancillary medical expense insurance • a policy that provides coverage and benefits for health care services that historically were considered incidental to medical care. Examples include dental, vision, hearing, and prescription drug services.

annuitant • a person who receives the periodic payment from an annuity • for purposes of federal benefit programs, retired federal government and postal employees—more specifically, the retirees who qualify to receive a pension in the form of a retirement annuity

annuity • a financial contract that typically provides a series of periodic payments beginning at a specific date and continuing throughout a fixed period or for the duration of a designated life or lives

annuity certain • an annuity in which payments are received for a specified period of time

any-occ definition of disability • a definition of total disability defined as a condition that prevents a person from performing the duties of an occupation for which that person is reasonably suited by education, training, and experience

area agencies on aging (AAAs) • public or private nonprofit agencies, designated by a state under the Older Americans Act (OAA) to address the needs and concerns of all older people in local communities

Archer MSA (medical savings account) • a tax-referred personal savings account established with a qualified high-deductible health plan that conforms to the provisions of the Health Insurance Portability and Accountability Act (HIPAA)

assisted-living facility • a supportive-living arrangement for elderly residents who, despite some degree of impairment, remain independent to a significant degree but require continuing supervision and the availability of assistance on an unscheduled basis. *Compare* independent housing.

association plan • an insurance benefit program established through an affiliation of independent members with a professional, industry, or other noninsurance relationship or as a construct by insurers (known as a discretionary or trust plan) to provide coverage to individuals who are unaffiliated other than for the purpose of obtaining insurance

at-entry rate • *See* issue-age rate.

attained-age rate • a premium rate for a policy or policy change that is based on the insured's age at the time the policy is written or the change is made. *Compare* issue-age rate.

attending physician's statement (APS) • as used in this text, may be the actual medical records from an insurance applicant's primary care physician, other physicians (for example, specialists), and/or hospitals that have treated the applicant for conditions bearing on underwriting. Alternatively, an APS may be a written explanation or statement from these health care providers regarding the history or significance of a specific condition.

attitudinal hazard • carelessness or indifference as to whether a loss occurs or the size of the loss if it does occur

authorization to release information • a statement or series of statements signed by an applicant for insurance that approves the release of the applicant's financial and/or and medical information to the insurer by individuals and organizations

automatic-increase rider • a long-term care or disability income policy rider that adjusts policy benefits each year, based on cost-of-living increases, by a stated percentage applied annually to either the initially selected benefit (simple) or the amount of benefits available in the prior year (compound)

bargaining contract • a contract in which both parties contribute to the terms and conditions. *Compare* contract of adhesion.

bathing • washing oneself by sponge bath, or washing oneself in either a tub or shower (including the task of getting into or out of the tub or shower)

bed reservation benefit • a long-term care insurance policy benefit that continues payments to a long-term care facility for a limited time (such as 20 days) if a patient temporarily leaves because of hospitalization or any other reason

beneficiary • the designated recipient of benefits from an insurance policy

benefit period • under a disability or long-term care insurance policy, the period after satisfaction of the elimination period for which benefits are paid

benefit trigger • under long-term care insurance policies, a criterion that determines whether an insured is chronically ill and eligible for benefits

bilateral contract• a contract in which both parties have a legal obligation to perform. *Compare* unilateral contract.

binding receipt • a type of receipt that provides interim coverage between the prepayment date and the date the insurer notifies the applicant of the underwriting decision. Under a binding receipt, the insurer reserves the right to reject the application, but does agree to provide coverage until underwriting is completed.

blended policy • *See* hybrid product.

brand-name drug • a drug manufactured and marketed under a trademark by a specific pharmaceutical company

broker • a marketing intermediary between the insurer and policyowner who represents the policyowner

business overhead expense (BOE) insurance • a disability policy designed to reimburse a business for expenses that continue when an owner or principal is disabled

buy-back provision • a provision in a cost-of-living adjustment rider that allows the insured to increase policy benefits following a disability to the amount that was being paid when the disability ceased

buy-sell agreement • a legal agreement between business owners that describes the circumstances under which the buyout of a disabled owner's share will occur because of death, retirement, termination, or disability

buy-up plan • a supplemental plan under which an employer provides a certain level of benefits and an employee can elect additional coverage at his or her own expense

calendar year maximum • an annual limit on total benefit payments imposed by some policies in addition to the aggregate (lifetime) maximum. *See also* aggregate maximum.

cancelable • a contract in which the insurance company reserves the right to terminate coverage at any time (and perhaps for any reason) during the term of coverage by notifying the insured. *Compare* noncancelable; guaranteed renewable; conditionally renewable; nonrenewable.

capital sum • a lump sum payable under some disability income contracts if the insured suffers serious medical condition, such as the loss of sight in one eye or the severance of a hand or foot, and survives the loss for a certain period, such as 30 days

capitated payment • payment to a health care provider or health plan using a flat per member per month amount without regard to the number or types of services rendered during the period

capitation • a payment mechanism in which payment to a health care provider is made per subscriber per month without regard to services rendered

care continuum • a progression of care from less intensive to more intensive as the care delivered moves from family members to professionals and from the home setting to supportive-living arrangements based on the care recipient's needs and the availability and capacity of family and other caregivers

care coordinator • a health care professional, often a social worker, who assesses an elderly patient with some degree of physical or cognitive impairment to determine the care needs and to develop a care plan to meet those needs. *Also known as* a care manager *or* care planner.

care manager • *See* care coordinator.

care planner • *See* care coordinator.

care setting • an environment in which long-term care services may be rendered to care recipients. Home health care and supportive-living arrangements are categories of care settings.

caregiver training • training of a family member or friend to provide care so that a person can remain at home

carve-out benefit • a certain class of services that is separated from a medical/surgical benefit plan and supplied under an alternative arrangement, usually involving a network of specialized providers, to achieve more effective care and/or efficiency. *See also* specialty benefit organization.

carve-out plan • an employee benefit plan under which certain employees (often executives) are provided benefits that are more generous than those provided to other employees

case management • a program of coordinated health care services for disproportionately high-cost patients with the goal of improving continuity, quality, and outcomes and lowering expenses through cost-effective resource utilization. *Also known as* large or catastrophic case management.

catastrophic benefit rider • a disability income policy rider that provides an additional benefit if the insured is so disabled that he or she is likely to incur significant extra expense because of disability

catastrophic high-deductible policies • medical expense policies that operate as umbrella major medical coverage to provide benefits after an extraordinary amount of medical expenses has been incurred, such as $20,000, or an underlying principal plan reaches its maximum. *Also known* as umbrella or excess major medical policies.

Centers for Medicare & Medicaid Services (CMS) • part of the U.S. Department of Health and Human Services that is responsible for the administration of the Medicare and Medicaid programs

centers of excellence • health care facilities that provide highly specialized care, such as transplants, and are designated as the providers of choice for such care under a contract with a health benefit plan

charitable gift annuity • an annuity that involves the transfer of money or other assets to a charitable or nonprofit foundation, which in turn provides an income for the life of the donor

chronic condition • a disease or disorder that develops slowly and persists for a long period of time, often the remainder of a person's life, although the condition is generally not immediately life threatening

chronically ill individual • a definition used in long-term care policies for someone who meets the criterion for benefit eligibility due either to a loss of functional capacity or a need for substantial supervision to protect the individual from threats to health and safety because of severe cognitive impairment

classification categories • the categories into which insurance applicants are assigned that determine the premiums they are charged and their acceptability for coverage

CMS • *See* Centers for Medicare & Medicaid Services (CMS).

COBRA • federal legislation that requires group health plans to allow employees working for companies with 20 or more employees to extend their current health insurance coverages at group rates for up to 36 months following a qualifying event that results in the loss of coverage for a qualified beneficiary

cognitive function • activities that pertain to the mental processes of comprehension, judgment, memory, and reasoning

coinsurance • the percentage of covered expenses under a major medical plan that will be paid once the deductible is satisfied. *Also known as* percentage of allowable charges; *compare* percentage participation.

combination policy • *See* hybrid product.

commingling of funds • an agent combining his or her premium funds with those of clients. Prohibited under the Unfair Trade Practices Act, some states prevent commingling by requiring a separate bank account for the agent's premium funds.

community rating • the practice of using the same rate structure for all enrollees in a medical expense plan, regardless of both their past or potential claim experience and whether coverage is written on an individual or a group basis

community spouse • the non-Medicaid dependent spouse of a person who applies for or is a recipient of Medicaid benefits

community-based services • a category of services provided by community groups under contract with area agencies on aging (AAAs) that includes employment services, senior centers, congregate meals, adult day care services, and volunteer opportunities

community-sponsored programs • various services provided by local volunteers, community groups, charities, churches, and government agencies that support family caregivers and enhance a care recipient's ability to remain at home

competent parties • an element of a binding agreement requiring individuals to be legally and mentally capable of entering into a contract and insurers to be organizationally and legally capable of entering into a contract

comprehensive long-term care policy • a long-term care insurance policy that combines benefits for facility care and home health care services into a single contract. *Also known as* an integrated policy. *Compare* facility-only policy; home health care policy.

concealment • a failure by one party to a contract to affirmatively disclose to the other all of the important facts that are the exclusive knowledge of the first party

concurrent disability provision • a provision in a disability income policy that specifies that if the insured is disabled as the result of more than one cause, the amount and duration of the benefits will be no greater than for any one of the causes

condition • a clause in an insurance contract in which one party's obligation to perform is subject to the other party's performance of specific acts

condition precedent • a condition in an insurance contract that must be fulfilled by the policyowner before the insurer can be held liable for a loss

condition subsequent • a condition in an insurance contract that must be fulfilled by the policyowner after the insurer has become liable in order to avoid the insurer's release from liability

conditional contract • an agreement in which one party's failure to perform relieves the other party of his or her obligation

conditional receipt • a receipt given for any payment with an insurance application. It may be an *approval type* or *insurability type*. With an approval-type receipt, coverage begins only upon approval of the risk by the company's underwriting department. With an insurability-type receipt, coverage becomes effective either on the date of prepayment or the date on which the last underwriting requirement is fulfilled.

conditionally renewable • a provision in some policies that allows the insurer to refuse to renew the policy for specifically listed conditions. *Compare* guaranteed renewable; noncancelable; nonrenewable; cancelable.

conformity-to-statute provision • a stipulation in a policy that any provision in conflict with any statute of the state where the policyowner lived when the policy was issued is amended to conform to that state statute

consideration • one of the requirements for a valid contract in which the parties to an agreement exchange a right or something of value, as in the case of an insured paying a premium in exchange for the insurer's assumption of an obligation to provide coverage

consumer-directed health care • a concept that attempts to control costs by making consumers of health care take a more active role in the purchase of such care; also a term that describes the use of high-deductible medical expense policies accompanied by tax-favored savings accounts. *Also known as* consumer-driven health care or consumer choice.

contestable period • usually a 2-year period after a policy is issued during which the insurer, in the event of a material misrepresentation on an application, has the right to deny claims and rescind the contract (with a return of premium) or deny the claim and offer to reform the contract

continence • the ability to maintain control of bowel and bladder functions or, when unable to do so, the ability to perform associated personal hygiene (including caring for a catheter or a colostomy bag)

contingent benefit upon lapse • *See* contingent nonforfeiture benefit.

contingent nonforfeiture benefit • a provision in some long-term care insurance policies whereby, if cumulative annual premiums increase beyond a specified level, the insured may elect to have reduced benefits sustainable by the current premium or a paid-up policy with a shorter benefit period

continuation of coverage • continued coverage under a group contract by an insured who is no longer a member of the group with the insured paying the premiums directly to the insurer. *Compare* conversion provision.

continuing care retirement community (CCRC) • a facility that offers the full continuum of supportive-living arrangements and is obligated to provide access to housing and defined long-term care services at each level of care for the life of the resident. *Also known as* a life-care facility.

contract • a binding or legally enforceable agreement between two or more parties for the provision of goods or services through an exchange of value

contract of adhesion • a contract that is prepared in all its details by one party, rather than having its terms bargained over between parties to the contract. In the event of ambiguity in insurance contract terms, courts are likely to rule in favor of the insured and against the insurer (the party that drew up the contract). *Compare* bargaining contract.

conversion provision • a provision in a group insurance plan that gives an employee whose coverage ceases the right to convert to an individual policy without providing evidence of insurability and without any limitation due to preexisting conditions

coordination-of-benefits provision • a provision in most group medical insurance plans that establishes priorities for paying benefits without duplication when an individual is covered under more than one plan

copayment • a fixed-dollar amount that the insured must pay for a covered service. *Also known as* copay; *compare* percentage participation.

cost-of-living adjustment rider • a disability income policy rider that adjusts claim payments during the period of disability for changes in the cost of living

cost shifting • the practice of unilaterally increasing the charges for the health care services of certain patients to recover the charity care costs and bad debts that are unrecognized in the rates paid by other paying patient

coverage gap (doughnut hole) • under Medicare prescription drug plans, the range in which the beneficiary must pay the full cost of prescription drugs

creditable prescription drug coverage • prescription drug coverage under other plans that is deemed to be equivalent to or better than the standard benefit plan for Medicare prescription drug coverage

creditable qualifying coverage • prior coverage under a group medical expense plan

critical illness insurance • supplemental medical expense insurance that provides a one-time lump-sum cash benefit if the insured is afflicted with a covered injury, disease, or major surgery. *Also known as* serious illness insurance.

cross-purchase agreement • a buy-sell agreement under which each business owner agrees to purchase a designated portion of a disabled co-owner's business interest when disability (or other event) triggers the agreement.

cueing • a form of assistance that involves verbal prompting, gestures, and other demonstrations to assist someone to accomplish an activity of daily living

custodial care • assistance given to a person who has a limited ability to conduct his or her routine daily activities because of deficiencies in physical and/or cognitive functions. *Also known as* personal care.

daily benefit amount (DBA) • the dollar amount selected by the insured as the benefit level for each day of covered services under a long-term care insurance policy that is paid either on a per diem or reimbursement basis depending on the terms of the policy. *Compare* weekly benefit.

daily money manager (DMM) • a person that assists clients who, for any reason, may have difficulty conducting their routine personal financial affairs

DBA • *See* daily benefit amount.

declaration • a factual statement in an insurance contract that identifies the specific person, property, or activity being insured and the parties to the insurance transaction

declination of issue • the decision to refuse coverage

decreasing term disability income insurance • a disability income policy that pays benefits only until a specified date

deductible • the initial amount of covered medical expenses that an individual must incur before he or she receives benefits under a medical expense plan

deductible period • *See* elimination period.

deferred annuity • an annuity with which benefits commence at a future date

definitions • explanations of the meaning of key terms in an insurance policy to clarify the coverage

dementia • a progressive mental disorder characterized by confusion, disorientation, and loss of intellectual capacity, memory control, and judgment

dental benefit plan service-level groupings • four groupings of professional treatment categories for dental services: level I—preventive and diagnostic services; level II—basic services, including fillings, as well as endodontic, periodontic, and oral surgery services; level III—major services, including major restorations (crowns, inlays, onlays, veneers) and prosthodontic procedures (dentures, bridges); level IV—orthodontic services

dental HMO • a prepaid managed care plan that provides dental care services to insureds in a defined geographic area

dental PPO • a managed care arrangement between a plan and a panel of dental providers whereby the providers agree to accept a negotiated payment (usually less than their customary fees) in anticipation of a higher volume of patients

dependent • a category of insured under a medical expense policy that usually includes a policyowner's husband or wife and unmarried children under a specified age (such as 19 or older if a full-time student), including adopted children

DHMO • *See* dental HMO.

dietitian • a professional trained in the application of the principles of nutrition to the planning and preparation of foods to promote health and treat disease

direct response • a method of marketing insurance without the intermediary of an agent or broker

disability-based policy • a long-term care insurance policy with a per diem basis of payment that provides benefits even if no care is being received as long as the insured satisfies the policy's benefit trigger

disability buyout insurance • a funding vehicle for financing the transfer of a business interest in accordance with a buy-sell agreement

disability income insurance • a form of health insurance that provides periodic payment when the insured is unable to work as a result of illness or injury

disability insured • the status a person must have under Social Security to receive disability income benefits. It requires that the person be fully insured and have a minimum amount of work experience under the Social Security program within a specified period.

disability management program • a comprehensive set of procedures and functions implemented by disability income insurers to rehabilitate an insured person who is receiving disability income benefits

discount program • *See* noninsurance service plan.

discretionary plan • *See* association plan.

discretionary trust • *See* association plan.

disease management • a continuous program of care conducted across a broad range of settings affecting the course of chronic illnesses (such as emphysema, asthma, diabetes, and heart disease) that incorporates the use of care guidelines by physicians and self-care education of patients

dollar-for-dollar model • a type of partnership program for long-term care in which the purchase of an amount of coverage through an approved policy allows an equal amount of the insured's assets to be disregarded (protected) in determining financial eligibility for Medicaid if the insurance benefits become exhausted

domiciliary care • rehabilitative and long-term care that involves a minimal level of medical care that excludes skilled-nursing care but often includes homemaker and chore services, as well as respite care

doughnut hole • See coverage gap.

dread disease insurance • *See* specified (dread) disease insurance.

dressing • putting on and taking off all items of clothing and any necessary braces, fasteners, or artificial limbs

dual definition of disability • a definition of total disability under which an own-occ definition is used for a limited period and then is replaced by an any-occ definition. *Also known as* split definition of disability.

dual eligibles • persons who are eligible for Medicare and any level of Medicaid assistance

E-SIGN • *See* Electronic Signatures in Global and National Commerce Act (E-SIGN).

earned income • income that an individual receives from working in his or her profession or trade. It excludes investment, rental, and retirement income.

eating • feeding oneself by getting food into the body from a receptacle (such as a plate, cup, or table), by a feeding tube, or intravenously

elder rights • a category of services for older individuals that includes legal assistance, elder abuse prevention programs, and ombudsmen services for complaint resolution

eldercare locator • a nationwide toll-free telephone service to help older adults and their caregivers find local services. Part of this service is available on the Internet.

electronic agent • a computer program instituted by its principals to do business in electronic form

electronic commerce • the conduct of business, including contracts and other transactions that relate to them, using computers and telephone or television cable lines. The Internet is the most common vehicle for these kinds of transactions, in which digitized information is communicated from one person or entity to another and stored without the use of paper.

electronic signature • an electronic sound, symbol, or process attached to or associated with a record and executed or adopted by a person with the intent to sign the record

Electronic Signatures in Global and National Commerce Act (E-SIGN) • federal legislation providing that a signature, contract, or other record may not be denied legal effect, validity, or enforceability solely because it is in electronic form and that a contract may not be denied legal effect, validity, or enforceability solely because an electronic signature or electronic record was used in its formation

elimination period • the period of time that must elapse after a person satisfies the criteria for benefits and the beginning of benefit payments. Elimination periods are commonly used in disability income insurance and long-term care insurance. *Also known as* a waiting period.

employee-pay-all benefits • *See* voluntary benefits.

end-stage renal disease • permanent kidney failure requiring dialysis or transplant

endorsement • *See* rider.

entire contract provision • a required provision of the UPPL stating that only those items actually included in a policy, including any riders or attachments, are part of the contract of insurance

entity buy-sell agreement • a buy-sell agreement under which a partnership purchases the ownership interest of a partner when disability (or other event) triggers the agreement

estate recovery • a state's program to recoup from the estates of certain Medicaid beneficiaries the cost of the Medicaid benefits they received

exclusion rider • a provision in an insurance contract stating that the insurer will not pay for a medical expense resulting from a particular medical problem (such as a back disorder) or an unusually hazardous occupation or avocation (such as automobile racing). *Also known as* a waiver.

exclusions • items that the insurer does not intend to cover

exclusive agency system • an insurance marketing system that uses exclusive agents

exclusive agent • an agent who represents only one insurer (or group of affiliated insurers); the insurer has ownership rights over the business written by the agent

execution clause • a clause in an insurance policy which signifies that the insurer has entered into the contract and will be bound by its terms

expense-incurred benefits • benefits that provide payments for specific amounts in relation to actually incurred medical expenses

experience rating • the practice by which the actual claim experience of a particular group is a factor in determining the premium the group policyowner is charged

extension of coverage • if an insured person is confined in a hospital or skilled-nursing facility because of covered injuries or sickness on the date insurance ends, coverage for that person is extended, but not past the date that the continuous confinement ends

extra premium • an additional premium paid by the insured to garner full protection. Extra premiums are used in cases where medical conditions are too difficult to define to be covered adequately by an exclusion rider (such as nervous disorders) or where the stated condition has too many complications that would have to be excluded (such as obesity, hypertension, or diabetes).

facility-of-payment provision • a policy provision that allows benefit payments to be made to a legal representative, frequently referred to as a guardian, if an insured person is physically, mentally, or otherwise incapable of giving a valid release (assignment) of any payment received

facility-only policy • a policy that provides benefits for care in a nursing home and other settings, such as an assisted-living facility and hospice. *Compare* comprehensive policy; home health care policy; nursing home policy.

Federal Long Term Care Insurance Program (FLTCIP) • a program authorized under federal legislation to provide long-term care insurance to federal and postal employees and annuitants, members and retired members of the uniformed services, and qualified relatives

financial underwriting • that portion of the underwriting process that determines an applicant's financial qualifications for insurance

first mortgage • a claim on real property, usually as security for a loan, that has a priority right of satisfaction over any other mortgage loan that may exist on the same property

fixed annuity • an annuity for which payments are a fixed number of dollars

flexible spending account (FSA) • a cafeteria plan account, usually funded by before-tax salary reductions by employees. Monies can be withdrawn from the account to pay unreimbursed medical expenses.

FLTCIP • *See* Federal Long Term Care Insurance Program.

foreign insurer • an insurance company doing business in a state other than the state in which it is incorporated; *also known as* a nondomestic insurer. *Compare* alien insurer.

formal caregiver • an individual who provides care as a profession or occupation and earns a living by rendering services to long-term care recipients. Formal caregivers include physicians, nurse caregivers, other licensed medical personnel, and nonlicensed personnel. *Compare* informal caregiver.

formulary • a plan's or pharmacy benefit manager's list of drug products that are preferred for dispensing to covered persons when appropriate; the list contains both generic and brand-name drugs

fraud • an active intent to deceive or intentionally mislead another person. In order to constitute fraud, intent must be shown, and the information concealed or misrepresented must be relied upon by and injure the other party. *See also* concealment; misrepresentation.

freedom of choice law • a type of managed care mandate that requires health plans to pay benefits to an enrollee when covered health care services are received from any qualified provider, even if the provider has not signed a contract with the managed care plan. *Also known as* managed care mandate, any willing provider law, and specialty care access law.

free-look period • a period of time, that may be as short at 10 days or as long as 30 days, after a policyowner receives a policy, during which the policyowner may return the policy for a full refund of any premium paid and the policy is void from its inception

FSA • *See* flexible spending account (FSA).

full individual underwriting • the most stringent form of underwriting. It requires the most extensive information of the applicant regarding medical history and current medical condition. *Also known as* long-form underwriting. *Compare* guaranteed-issue underwriting; modified guaranteed-issue underwriting; simplified-issue underwriting.

full retirement age • the age at which nonreduced Social Security retirement benefits are available. Social Security disability benefits are available only if a person is disabled before this age. At the full retirement age, any disability benefits being received are replaced with retirement benefit.

future increase option rider • a disability income or long-term care policy rider that gives the insured the option to increase policy benefits at periodic intervals without evidence of insurability

general agency system • a term used to describe an insurance marketing system whereby a general agent is granted a franchise by an insurer to build an agency force for marketing the insurer's products in a given geographic area

general agent • in the legal sense, an agent who has the authority to bind insurance for a client

generic drug • a drug product that is chemically equivalent to a brand-name drug whose patent has expired

geriatric care manager • *See* care coordinator.

geriatric physician • a physician who specializes in the treatment of the aged

grace period • a policy provision that gives an insured a specific number of days beyond the due date to pay each premium. States usually require a 31-day grace period for most policies.

group health plan • as used under COBRA, group health plans include medical expense, dental, vision care, and prescription drug plans, regardless of whether benefits are self-funded or provided through insurance companies, Blue Cross and Blue Shield plans, or HMOs

group insurance plan • a method of providing insurance coverage to members of a group, usually employees under an employer-sponsored plan, that is characterized by a master contract, group underwriting, and possibly experience rating

group underwriting • underwriting that evaluates the insurability of applicant employer groups that are organized for job, profession, or industry reasons. *Compare* individual underwriting.

guaranteed insurability rider • *See* future increase option rider.

guaranteed issue • requirements stating that carriers offering coverage in the individual market may not refuse coverage or enrollment to an eligible individual and must limit any preexisting-conditions exclusions with respect to such coverage.

guaranteed-issue underwriting • the most liberal form of group underwriting in which coverage is provided for all employees who apply for it. However, the insured group must satisfy certain insurer criteria to minimize adverse selection. *Compare* full individual underwriting; modified guaranteed-issue underwriting; simplified-issue underwriting.

guaranteed purchase option • *See* future increase option rider; long-term care purchase option rider.

guaranteed renewable • a provision in an insurance contract which gives the insured the right to renew coverage at each policy anniversary date, usually up to a stated age. Also, the insurer is not allowed to cancel coverage during the period of protection. However, the insurer does retain the right to raise coverage rates for broad classes of insureds. *Compare* noncancelable; nonrenewable; conditionally renewable; cancelable.

guaranty fund • a state fund to pay claims of insolvent insurers, usually funded by assessments of other insurers licensed in the state

hands-on assistance • actual physical assistance received from another person to perform activities of daily living

HDHP • *See* high-deductible health plan (HDHP).

health insurance • insurance policies that cover injury or sickness and encompass medical expense, disability income, and long-term care insurance

Health Insurance Portability and Accountability Act (HIPAA) • *See* HIPAA.

health maintenance organization (HMO) • an organized system of health care that provides a comprehensive array of medical services on a prepaid basis to voluntarily enrolled services within a specific geographic region. They finance health care as well as deliver medical services.

Health Maintenance Organization Act • a federal act passed in 1973 that introduced the concept of the federally qualified HMO. *See also* health maintenance organization (HMO).

health reimbursement arrangement (HRA) • a type of personal savings account from which unreimbursed medical expenses can be paid. An HRA can be established only by an employer for its employees.

health savings account (HSA) • a type of tax-preferred savings account or fund that a person with a qualified high-deductible health plan may establish to pay for certain medical expenses

high-deductible health plan (HDHP) • a medical expense plan that uses insurance policies with high-deductibles, usually no less than $1,000 and often as much as $5,000 or more. They are commonly used with consumer-directed medical expense plans. *See also* high-deductible major medical insurance.

high-deductible major medical insurance • a major medical policy with a deductible of $1,000 or more. These are specified deductibles that are required when these policies are used as part of certain consumer-directed health plans, such as those using health savings accounts. *See also* high-deductible health plan (HDHP).

high-risk pool • a mechanism, operated as a not-for-profit association, to broadly share the risk of above-standard financial losses for the benefit payments of comprehensive medical insurance offered to individuals whose preexisting health conditions denied them standard coverage in the private market

HIPAA • federal legislation for the primary purpose of making medical insurance more available, particularly when an employed person changes jobs or becomes unemployed. The legislation contains other provisions related to health care data standards and privacy, as well the requirements for the tax-preferred status of long-term care insurance policies that are described as contracts.

HMO • *See* health maintenance organization (HMO).

home and community-based services • under the Medicaid program, a special category of services that states may provide to keep beneficiaries from being institutionalized. Unlike other Medicaid services, these additional services may be targeted to specific populations and to certain geographic areas.

home care agency • company that provides little medical care but specializes in home health aides (nursing assistants) and nonlicensed personnel, such as homemakers, companions, and chore workers, who may maintain and repair a home. *Compare* home health care agency.

home health care • a setting that encompasses virtually any home environment outside of a nursing home in which the care recipient resides and receives care

home health care agency • company that specializes in medical and/or custodial care of the elderly and disabled in the home environment. Many of these agencies employ a range of formal caregivers that frequently include nurse caregivers, other licensed medical personnel, and nonlicensed personnel. *Compare* home care agency.

home health care policy • a long-term care insurance policy designed to provide benefits only for care outside an institutional setting, although some policies may provide benefits for care in assisted-living facilities. *Compare* comprehensive long-term care policy; facility-only policy.

homemaker companion • an employee of a state-licensed home health care agency who may assist with such tasks as cooking, shopping, cleaning, bill paying, or other household chores

hospice care • a system of treatment designed to relieve the discomfort of a terminally ill individual and to maintain the quality of life to the extent possible throughout the phases of dying

hospital • frequently defined in policies providing hospitalization benefits as "an institution licensed, accredited, or certified by the state which (1) is accredited by the Joint Commission on Accreditation of Healthcare Organizations; (2) provides 24-hour nursing service by registered nurses; (3) mainly provides diagnostic and therapeutic care under the supervision of physicians on an inpatient basis; and (4) maintains permanent surgical facilities or has an arrangement with another surgical facility supervised by a staff of one or more physicians"

hospital confinement indemnity insurance • a type of supplemental medical policy featuring cash benefits in the event of hospitalization and/or surgery resulting from illness or injury

HRA • *See* health reimbursement arrangement.

HSA • *See* health savings account (HSA).

hybrid product • an insurance contract that combines long-term care insurance and either life insurance or annuities into a single policy. *Also known as* a linked policy, blended policy, combination policy, or package policy.

immediate annuity • an annuity for which benefits commence one payment interval from the date of purchase

impaired risk annuity • an annuity for which an applicant's health is considered in the underwriting process and the annuity payments are increased (or the premium lowered) in relation to the shorter life expectancy

incontestable clause • a required provision of the UPPL that limits an insurer's right to rescind a policy to 2 years (3 years in some states) with respect to any misstatement made by the insured on the application. *Compare* time limit on certain defenses.

indemnity • a concept which means that the insured is entitled to payment only to the extent of financial loss or legal liability—in other words, the insured should remain in the same financial position that existed prior to a loss and should not profit from the loss

indemnity basis • in medical expense insurance, a policy benefit provision that reimburses a claimant for the incurred expense of medical services and requires documentation of each expense. *Compare* service basis. • in long-term care insurance, a designation often applied to a policy with a per diem basis of payment even though the usual insurance meaning of indemnity implies payment of benefits for actual expenses up to policy limits. *Also known as* a per diem policy.

independent housing • a wide range of supportive-living arrangements that include senior apartments, home sharing, and accessory apartments in which residents do not require constant supervision and are free to go and come as they please. Nonmedical support services that can be scheduled, such as meals, housekeeping, and laundry, are usually available. Assistance with some routine daily activities, such as bathing, dressing, and grooming, may be purchased as separate services.

independent living • *See* independent housing.

individual market • the market for health insurance coverage offered to individuals other than in connection with a group plan

individual medical expense insurance • a personally purchased contract of insurance that provides benefits in the event of an insured's illness or injury. Medical expense, disability income, and long-term care constitute the three forms of individual health insurance.

individual underwriting • underwriting that evaluates the insurability of each applicant separately. *Compare* group underwriting.

informal care • voluntary assistance, usually in the form of personal or custodial care, provided to a long-term care recipient by a person without pay and without formal education and training in long-term care

informal caregiver • a person who provides informal care. Informal caregivers include immediate family members, other relatives, friends, neighbors, and volunteers. *Compare* formal caregiver.

infusion therapy • the introduction of fluids, electrolytes, or drugs directly into a vein, tissue, or organ to improve a patient's condition

in-home services • a category of services provided by community groups that includes meals-on-wheels, homemakers, chore services, telephone reassurance, friendly visiting, energy assistance and weatherization, emergency response systems, home health services, personal care services, and respite care

injury • defined as "accidental bodily injury independent of disease, bodily infirmity, or other cause sustained while this policy is in force." Under some policies, it must also result from accidental means.

inspection report • the results of an investigation of an insurance applicant conducted by an independent agency that specializes in such investigations

installment annuity • an annuity purchased with periodic premiums

institutional advertisement • an advertisement having as its sole purpose the promotion of the reader's, viewer's, or listener's interest in the concept of insurance or the promotion of the insurer as a seller of an insurance product

instrumental activities of daily living (IADLs) • necessary and routine activities of life that require a greater degree of skill, judgment, and independence than activities of daily living (ADLs) and include shopping for personal items, managing money, using the telephone, preparing meals, managing medication, and doing housework. *Compare* activities of daily living (ADLs).

insurable income • that part of an individual's gross income that is insurable for disability income purposes

insurable interest • a right or relationship with regard to the subject matter of the insurance contract such that the policyowner would suffer financial loss from damage, loss, or destruction to the subject matter

insurance commissioner • the head of the state insurance department, an authorized administrative office that both issues and enforces rules and regulations

Insurance Information and Privacy Protection Model Act • NAIC legislation that includes restrictions designed to minimize intrusiveness, a mechanism to enable applicants to find out what information has been collected about them, prescribed procedures for granting individuals access to information, safeguards to limit disclosure, and notification of adverse underwriting decisions

insuring and consideration clause • the insurer's promise to pay benefits. The clause identifies the insurer, expresses the promise to pay, and states in general terms the scope and limits of coverage.

integrated policy • *See* comprehensive long-term care policy.

interim medical expense insurance • coverage that is purchased only for a specific period of time. Interim medical expense insurance includes temporary, international travel, and student policies.

intermediate care medical care services that may be provided or available perhaps 2 to 4 days per week. Intermediate care may be provided in a nursing home, an intermediate-care unit of a nursing home, or at home. *Also known as* intermediate-nursing care.

intermediate-nursing care • *See* intermediate care.

internal limit • *See* separate service maximum.

international travel medical policy • an interim medical expense insurance policy for persons who are traveling abroad

Internet • a global arrangement of computer networks that permits users to access and exchange information with any other computer that has access to the system

invitation to contract • an advertisement for insurance that does not qualify as an institutional advertisement, an invitation to inquire, or a lead-generating device and is assumed to directly solicit the purchase of insurance. *See also* institutional advertisement; invitation to inquire; lead-generating device.

invitation to inquire • an advertisement having as its objective the creation of a desire to inquire further about insurance that is limited to a brief description of the loss for which benefits are payable but may contain the dollar amount of benefits and the period of time during which they are payable. *See also* institutional advertisement; invitation to contract; lead-generating device.

issue-age rates • a premium rate for a policy or a policy change that is based on the insured's age at the time a policy was issued rather than at the time the change is made. *Compare* attained-age rate.

issue limits • a schedule that lists the maximum amount of coverage a disability income insurer will write at various income levels and occupation classes

joint-and-last-survivor annuity • an annuity from which payments are received until the last of two persons dies

joint life annuity • an annuity for which payments are received for as long as the first of two or more persons lives

key-person disability insurance • a policy specifically designed to provide benefits to a business for the loss of a key employee from disability

law of large numbers • a mathematical principle stating that, as the number of independent trials or events is increased, the actual results from those trials or events will come closer and closer to the results that one would expect to occur based on the underlying probability. *Also known as* the law of averages.

lead-generating device • any communication directed to the public that, regardless of form, content, or stated purpose, is intended to result in the compilation or qualification of a list containing names and other personal information of those to be to be solicited for the purchase of insurance. *See also* institutional advertisement; invitation to contract; invitation to inquire.

legal actions • a policy provision that requires an insured to wait at least 60 days after submitting proof of loss before starting legal action against the insurer. It also prohibits the insured from bringing legal action more than 3 years after proof of loss is required.

legal purpose • the stated object of a legally binding contract

licensed health care practitioner • for purposes of certifying a person as chronically ill under the HIPAA requirements for tax-qualified long-term care insurance contracts, a physician, registered nurse, licensed social worker, or other person who meets any requirements prescribed by the Secretary of the Treasury

Life and Health Insurance Policy Language Simplification Model Act • NAIC legislation that establishes readability requirements for insurance policies. The intent of the act is to simplify policy language so that an average consumer may easily comprehend it.

life-care facility • *See* continuing care retirement community (CCRC).

lifetime maximum • *See* aggregate maximum.

limitations • restrictions on the extent of coverage or benefits

limited agent • an agent who does not have the authority to bind the insurance company to provide coverage for an applicant

linked policy • *See* hybrid product.

list billing • a statement of a total premium amount submitted by an insurer to an employer that identifies employees who have individually purchased insurance offered at the workplace and serves as the basis for payroll deduction. *See also* voluntary benefits.

long-form underwriting • *See* full individual underwriting.

long-term care • the broad range of medical, custodial, social, and other care services that assist people who have an impaired ability to live independently for an extended period

Long-Term Care Consumer Awareness Campaign • a pilot project established as a cooperative effort between a number of participating states and agencies of the federal government to increase the awareness of the need for long-term care and to measure the impact on planning and the use of private-sector options, including long-term care insurance, to pay for such care

long-term care insurance • any insurance policy or rider that is advertised, marketed, offered, or designed to provide coverage for not less than 12 consecutive months for each covered person in a setting other than an acute care unit of a hospital for one or more of the following: necessary or medically necessary diagnostic, preventive, therapeutic, rehabilitative, maintenance, or personal care services

long-term care purchase option rider • a rider to a policy, such as a disability income or life insurance contract, that allows the insured to purchase long-term care insurance at specified future dates without evidence of insurability

loss-of-earnings policy • a disability income policy under which loss of income is measured as the difference between pre-disability income and post-disability income from any occupation

loss ratio • claims divided by premiums

lump-sum benefit • in a specified disease or critical illness policy, a benefit that pays a one-time amount for each covered person who receives a diagnosis of a covered disease or condition or undergoes a covered medical event

major medical insurance • a medical insurance policy designed to provide substantial coverage for most types of medical expenses arising from hospital, other facility, and physicians' services, as well as diagnostic tests and therapies, regardless of setting. Its benefit structure commonly uses deductibles, coinsurance payments, out-of-pocket limits, and aggregate and separate service maximums.

managed care • a health plan or insurance policy that tries to manage cost, quality, and access to health care; frequently used as a generic term applicable to HMOs, PPOs, and major medical policies with managed care features

managed care mandate • a law that mandates benefits specific to managed care plans and also dictates how managed care plans may conduct business, such as contracts that establish provider networks and the processes for referring patients to them. Major categories of these mandates are any willing provider laws, freedom of choice laws, and specialty care access laws.

managed care organization (MCO) • an entity that offers managed care plans

mandated benefits • state laws, usually applicable to medical expense insurance, that require policies to cover certain populations, providers, alternative care settings, specific conditions, diagnostic tests and exams, treatments, and services and products. *Compare* mandated option laws.

mandated option laws • legislation, usually state statutes, that requires insurers to offer mandated benefits in an insurance plan for purchase by consumers at their discretion. If consumers decline the mandated benefits, policies may be sold without them. *Compare* mandated benefits.

mandated services • under the Medicaid program, the category of services that states must offer to all who are eligible for Medicaid. Specifically required services are nursing facility care and certain home care services

mass-marketed individual insurance • a type of insurance product sold as individual polices of insurance through a sponsoring group, such as an employer or association

McCarran-Ferguson Act • a federal law that exempts insurance from certain federal regulations to the extent that individual states actually regulate insurance. It also stipulates that most other federal laws are not applicable to insurance unless they are specifically related to the business of insurance.

MCO • *See* managed care organization (MCO).

Medicaid • a federal/state public assistance or welfare program that provides health care benefits based on need. Each state has its own rules that must meet federal guidelines. In return, the federal government finances the major portion of each state's program.

Medicaid planning • the process of rearranging a person's financial resources to make that person eligible for Medicaid while sheltering the financial resources for use by a spouse, children, or others

medical-event benefit • in a specified disease policy, a benefit paid if an insured has inpatient care, surgical procedures, nonsurgical treatments (such as radiation and/or chemotherapy), or skilled-nursing care

medical expense insurance • a health insurance contract that pays for or provides access to medical care services required by illness or injury, usually of an acute nature. Coverage may include benefits in long-term care settings.

Medical Information Bureau • *See* MIB.

medical necessity • a benefit trigger in a non-tax-qualified long-term care insurance policy under which a physician certifies that long-term care is needed, even if no other criteria are satisfied

medical provider statement • a written report from a hospital or a physician that has provided medical services to the applicant. The underwriter asks for this statement if the application discloses any serious or questionable medical history.

medical services • the spectrum of health care provided by institutions, such as hospitals and other acute and nonacute facilities, and health care professionals, such as doctors and other licensed practitioners. Includes diagnostic and therapeutic services whose goal is to restore or maintain health.

medically needy • under the Medicaid program, a category of eligibility that states may establish for persons who have too much income to otherwise qualify for benefits but who are determined to be unable to afford needed medical care

Medicare • a federal social insurance program of medical expense benefits for most persons aged 65 or older, although certain younger persons are also eligible for benefits

Medicare Advantage • the program administered by the Centers for Medicare & Medicaid Services that allows Medicare beneficiaries to enroll in certain HMOs, PPOs, and other approved options as alternatives to receiving their benefits under the original Medicare program. *Also known as* Medicare Part C and originally called Medicare+Choice.

Medicare carve-out • a medical expense plan that reduces benefits to the extent that they are provided under Medicare

Medicare cost plan • an alternative to traditional Medicare in addition to Medicare Advantage. Under this alternative, the plan is paid on the basis of reasonable cost and the beneficiary may obtain covered services outside the plan's network.

Medicare Part A • the part of Medicare that covers hospitalization, confinement in certified skilled-nursing facilities, home health care, and hospice care under certain circumstances. *Also known as* hospital insurance.

Medicare Part B • the part of Medicare that covers most physicians' services as well as medical items and services not covered under Part A. Part B premiums are deducted from participants' Social Security or railroad retirement benefits.

Medicare Part C • *See* Medicare Advantage.

Medicare Part D • the part of Medicare that makes prescription drug coverage available to Medicare enrollees. Coverage is voluntary, and beneficiaries must pay a monthly premium. *See* Medicare prescription drug plans.

Medicare Prescription Drug, Improvement, and Modernization Act of 2003 (MMA) • federal legislation affecting Medicare and other health care areas. Among its major provisions are Medicare drug coverage in voluntary prescription drug plans (Part D of Medicare). It also strengthens and expands alternatives to traditional Medicare through Medicare Advantage and authorizes tax-preferred health savings accounts (HSAs).

Medicare prescription drug plans • private prescription drug plans in which Medicare participants can voluntarily enroll. The plans must meet certain standards established by Medicare, and beneficiaries must pay a monthly premium.

Medicare Savings Program • assistance under state Medicaid programs that provides payment of Medicare premiums and cost sharing (but not any other Medicaid benefits) to certain low-resource and low-income Medicare beneficiaries

Medicare secondary rules • regulations that specify when Medicare will be secondary to an employer's medical expense plan for active employees over age 65 and disabled employees

Medicare SELECT policy • a type of standard Medicare supplement insurance policy in which the beneficiary must use the insurance plan's designated hospitals and doctors for nonemergency services to be eligible for full supplemental insurance benefits

Medicare supplement (medigap) insurance • individual medical expense insurance designed to fill the deductible, coinsurance, and copayment gaps in Medicare's benefits for covered services that would otherwise result in out-of-pocket expenses for beneficiaries

Medicare+Choice •. *See* Medicare Advantage.

medigap • *See* Medicare supplement (medigap) insurance.

medsup insurance • *See* Medicare supplement (medigap) insurance.

MIB • a not-for-profit association of insurance companies that exchanges information among its members relevant to underwriting life, health, disability income, and long-term care insurance. Known formally as MIB Group Inc.

misappropriation • the unlawful keeping of funds belonging to another

misrepresentation • a false statement made by an applicant to an insurer at the time of or prior to the formation of a contract. *See also* concealment; fraud.

misstatement of age • an optional policy provision stating that, if the insured's age has been misstated, all benefits payable under the policy shall be at a level that the premium paid would have purchased at the correct age. In some cases, this provision may allow payment of the additional premium at the correct age if the insured understated the age but remains eligible for coverage. If the covered person is ineligible for coverage at the correct age, then the misapplied coverage is rescinded and any applicable premium is refunded.

modal premium • the premium amount at the interval allowed by the insurer and elected by the applicant, such as annually, semiannually, quarterly, or monthly

mode of premium payment • the frequency of premium payment selected by the applicant from the several options that an insurer may offer, such as annually, semiannually, quarterly, or monthly

modified guaranteed-issue underwriting • a form of group underwriting in which some medical questions are asked on the application to determine whether the applicant has recently received care, requires assistance, or has certain medical conditions. Although the insurer accepts most applicants, the answers to these questions may result in the declination of some applicants. *Compare* full underwriting; guaranteed-issue underwriting; simplified-issue underwriting.

modified issue • the decision to provide insurance with certain modifications to standard coverage, such as an exclusion rider, an extra premium, a change in benefits, or some combination of these options

modified own-occ definition of disability • a variation of the own-occ definition of disability under which total disability benefits cease when a person returns to any gainful employment for which he or she is suited by education, training, or experience. However, partial or residual disability benefits may be available at that time.

moral hazard • the perverse human tendency that increases the frequency and severity of a loss because insurance is in force

morbidity • the incidence of sickness and disability

MSA • *See* Archer MSA (medical savings account)

mutual holding company • a subsidiary of a mutual insurance company controlled by policyowners that in effect own the subsidiary as a stock insurance company. May be used as a device to generate investor capital for specific business areas while maintaining the advantages of the parent organization as a mutual insurance company.

mutual insurance company • a not-for-profit insurance company owned by its policyowners, who elect its board of directors

NAIC • *See* National Association of Insurance Commissioners (NAIC).

National Association of Insurance Commissioners (NAIC) • a voluntary association of all state insurance commissioners. The organization's specific objectives are the development of uniform regulatory policy and the coordination of regulations of multistate insurers.

National Association of State Units on Aging • a national nonprofit membership organization of 57 state and territorial government agencies on aging founded to respond to the needs of a diverse aging population

noncancelable • a renewal provision in an insurance contract whereby the insurance company cannot make any unilateral changes in any coverage provision or refuse to renew the coverage. The insured has the right to continue the coverage in force by the timely payment of premium rates that are established in advance and cannot be changed. *Compare* guaranteed renewable; nonrenewable; conditionally renewable; cancelable.

nondomestic insurer • an insurance company doing business in a state other than the state in which it is incorporated. *Also known as* a foreign insurer. *Compare* alien insurer.

nonforfeiture benefit • a provision in an insurance policy whereby the policyowner will receive some value for a policy that lapses because the premium is not paid in the future

noninsurance service plan • a program for the purchase of specified professional services and products at a discounted price from a designated list or network of health care providers and suppliers. *Also known as* a discount program.

nonlicensed personnel • individuals employed to provide long-term care recipients with personal care services of a nonmedical nature. In the home setting, these nonlicensed personnel are called home health aides, homemakers, companions, and chore workers.

nonrecourse loan • a loan arrangement in which the lender bases recovery of the amount loaned only on the asset that secures the loan with no encumbrance of the borrower's other assets or resources. In the case of a reverse mortgage, the asset is the borrower's home.

nonrenewable • a policy provision that gives the insurer the unlimited right to refuse to renew a policy at the end of any period for which premiums have been paid. *Compare* guaranteed renewable, noncancelable, conditionally renewable, cancelable.

non-tax-qualified • a type of long-term care insurance contract that fails to meet certain standards of the Health Insurance Portability and Accountability Act for favorable tax treatment. *Compare* tax-qualified.

notice of claim • a claims provision of the UPPL mandating that written notice be given to the insurer within 20 days of loss or as soon as is reasonably possible

number of insureds • a classification structure of persons covered under a medical expense policy that determines its premium; typical premium structures are (1) single male or single female, (2) applicant and spouse, (3) applicant and 1 child, 2 children, or 3+ children, and (4) family with 1 child, 2 children, or 3+ children. Coverage is often available for children only with premium classes for 1 child, 2 children, or 3+ children, usually with separate rates set by a child's age.

nurse caregiver • a registered nurse or a licensed practical or vocational nurse who is responsible for the medical treatment of actual or potential health problems with the goal of rehabilitating a care recipient or stabilizing his or her medical condition

nursing-facility confinement rider • a disability income rider that provides additional benefits if a disabled injured is confined to a nursing home

nursing home • a state-licensed facility that provides skilled, intermediate, and custodial care services; the care recipient's condition determines the combination and extent of services provided

nursing home policy • a type of long-term care insurance policy that is designed to provide benefits only if the insured is in a nursing home. *Compare* facility-only policy.

occupational therapy • treatment to enhance the capabilities of persons who have physical, social, and emotional deficits arising from injury, illness, emotional disturbance, congenital or developmental disability, or aging

offer and acceptance • one of the requirements for a valid contract in which an offer made by one party is accepted by the other party

Older Americans Act (OAA) • legislation that created the Administration on Aging (AOA) and authorized grants to states for community planning and service programs in the field of aging. The act also provides grants to area agencies on aging (AAAs) to meet local needs and provide support programs for the elderly, especially those who are in greatest economic and social need.

original Medicare • the term used to describe the traditional Medicare Parts A and B

other categorically needy • under Medicaid, a category or class of individuals and families who receive Medicaid benefits despite income levels that disqualify them as mandatorily eligible

out-of-pocket limit • the maximum sum of all payments by an insured for the amounts remaining after the coinsurance benefits for the allowable expenses of covered services in a yearly benefit period. *Also known as* stop loss.

own-occ definition of disability • a definition of disability in a disability income contract that guarantees payment of benefits if an individual is unable to perform the duties of his or her occupation, even if the individual is able to work at other occupations

own-occupation rider • a disability income policy rider to modify the definition of total disability to own-occupation if the basic policy provides a less favorable definition of disability

PACE • *See* programs of all-inclusive care for the elderly.

package policy • *See* hybrid product.

paid time off (PTO) program • an employer-provided program that combines sick-leave plans with other types of payments for time not worked, such as vacations and personal leave

palliative care • therapy designed to reduce pain or discomfort but not to produce a cure

paramedical examination • a medical examination of an applicant by trained personnel other than a physician

partial disability • the inability to do some of the duties relating to a job

Part A • *See* Medicare Part A.

Part B • *See* Medicare Part B.

Part C • *See* Medicare Advantage.

Part D • *See* Medicare Part D.

participation limit • the maximum amount of coverage a disability income insurer will issue when other sources of disability income are taken into consideration

partnership programs for long-term care • alliances between certain state governments and insurance companies to encourage the sale of approved long-term care policies. The goal of these alliances is to protect individuals from impoverishment by long-term care expenses that would result in their immediate dependence on Medicaid.

password • a sequence of characters intended to be used for authorized entry to a secure computer system or document

pay-as-you-go option • *See* future increase option rider.

PBM • *See* pharmacy benefit manager.

pension supplement/completion rider • a disability income policy rider that provides an additional benefit that will be paid to a funding vehicle for retirement benefits

per-cause deductible • a deductible amount that must be satisfied for each separate accident or illness before medical benefits are paid

percentage of allowable charges • *See* coinsurance.

percentage participation • the percentage of covered medical expenses that remains unpaid after the coinsurance benefit payment of a medical expense policy and that must be paid by the insured. *Compare* copayment; coinsurance.

per-day or per-service benefits • benefits that require specific services to be rendered in order to receive a cash benefit that may have little or no relation to specific charges

per diem basis • a method of paying benefits under long-term care policies in which the insured receives a specified daily or weekly benefit amount regardless of the actual cost of care. *Compare* reimbursement basis.

period of benefits • *See* benefit period.

persistency • the length of time an insurance contract remains in force

personal care • *See* custodial care.

personal care services • in general, services that assist with activities of daily living and instrumental activities of daily living • under Medicaid, the optional services that states may provide to assist persons with physical and cognitive impairments so they may remain in their homes and communities

personal identification number (PIN) • a numerical and/or character series used in electronic transactions that is unique to and identifies the individual making the transactions. *See also* electronic signature.

personal worksheet • a form containing questions to help assure that an insurance applicant has considered certain relevant information before buying insurance

pharmacy benefit manager (PBM) • the administrator of a drug benefit

physical therapy • treatment of physical impairments through the use of special exercise, application of heat or cold, and other physical treatment modalities

physician • a licensed health professional who has earned a degree of Doctor of Medicine or Doctor of Osteopathy at an approved medical school and completed National Board Examinations

physician examination • a medical examination of an applicant conducted by a physician. A physician examination is used if a paramedical exam yields uncertain or unfavorable results. Insurers may also require a physician examination because of the amount of coverage applied for, the applicant's age, or the need for more specific details of medical history.

PIN • *See* personal identification number (PIN).

point-of-service (POS) option • a hybrid arrangement that combines aspects of a traditional medical expense plan with HMO coverage. At the time of medical treatment, a participant can elect whether to receive treatment for specified services within the plan's network or outside of the network. However, full benefits are paid only for services received within the network. *Also known as* point-of-service (POS) plan.

policy • a written insurance contract

policy form • a standardized contract that an insurer offers to its policyowners. In many states, it must be filed with the insurance department.

policyowner • an insurance applicant becomes a policyowner when the contract of insurance is formed

pool of money • lifetime maximum benefit under a long-term care insurance policy calculated by multiplying the daily benefit by the benefit period to create a total amount of funds from which benefit payments may continue as long as the funds lasts. If the benefit period is unlimited, the pool of money ends with the life of the insured.

portability • under HIPAA, portability means that preexisting-conditions limitations for medical insurance are defined and, once satisfied, may not serve to deny, limit, or delay the issuance of a qualified person's group or individual medical coverage or the renewal of that coverage as required by the act

post-claims underwriting • an insurer practice of rescinding a policy or denying a claim based on medical information obtained at the time a claim is filed that could have been obtained and included in the underwriting process at the time the insured completed the application for insurance. State regulations attempt to minimize this practice.

PPO • *See* preferred-provider organization (PPO).

precertification • *See* prior authorization.

predetermination • *See* prior authorization.

preexisting condition • any condition, including illness or injury, not fully disclosed on a health insurance application that occurred within a specific time period prior to the policy's effective date, and either (1) for which symptoms existed that would cause a prudent person to seek diagnostic care or treatment, or (2) for which medical advice, treatment, or service was recommended by or received from a physician

preferred drug list • *See* formulary.

preferred-provider organization (PPO) • a managed health plan that is less restrictive than an HMO in that it allows patients to receive benefits for services rendered by any provider with increased benefits or lower out-of-pocket costs if a network provider is used. There is usually no specialist or service referral requirement, and utilization controls are less stringent. *See also* preferred-provider organization (PPO) arrangement.

preferred-provider organization (PPO) arrangement • the feature of a health benefit plan that makes available to insureds an identified network of participating providers or selected providers to obtain cost-effective medical services. The providers may or may not bear a financial risk for the utilization and cost of health services that is reflected in the payments they receive under the plan.

premium • the price charged for a period of coverage provided by an insurance policy. In health insurance, a specified amount of money paid for coverage by an insured that the insurer draws on to pay benefits for the covered expenses of insureds that incur them

prepayment • money paid by the applicant when the application for insurance is completed

presumptive total disability provision • a disability income policy provision that considers an insured to be totally disabled if he or she has a certain specified condition, such as the loss of sight in both eyes or the entire use of both feet

pretreatment estimate • *See* prior authorization.

primary insurance amount (PIA) • the monthly amount a worker will receive under Social Security if disabled. It is also the amount on which additional benefits for family members are based.

primary caregiver • the informal caregiver, usually a family member, with overall responsibility for a person's long-term care

principal amount • in the case of accidental death and dismemberment (AD&D) insurance, the designated dollar benefit to be paid by the insurer at the insured's accidental death. All or part of the principal amount is also paid in the event of the accidental loss of a hand, foot, and/or eye, or at the occurrence of complete and irreversible paralysis of the limbs.

principal medical expense insurance • a plan that provides substantial benefits for the major portion of the expenses for needed health care services and generally constitutes the policyowner's or beneficiary's fundamental program of medical expense protection. *See also* major medical insurance; managed care; interim medical expense insurance.

prior authorization • the process under an insurance plan for the review of a proposed course of treatment. For example, under a dental benefit program, the insured's dentist is asked to complete and submit a written request for preauthorization of benefits for major services and orthodontia that describes the diagnosis, the proposed treatment, and the cost. *Also known as* predetermination, precertification, and pretreatment estimate.

private annuity • an annuity arrangement in which the person or organization that assumes the obligation for the annuity payments is not in the business of selling annuities

private fee-for-service plans • a traditional insurance (such as major medical) benefit plan offered as an alternative to original Medicare that determines prospectively the payment rate of providers accepting the plan without placing them at financial risk for the utilization of services. Providers are allowed to bill beyond what the plan pays (up to a limit), and the beneficiary is responsible for paying whatever the plan does not cover and any additional premium the plan requires.

probate • the judicial process for the proof and registration of a deceased person's will and administration of a deceased person's estate

probationary period • a period of time an employee must work before becoming eligible for benefits

programs of all-inclusive care for the elderly (PACE) • optional benefit programs provided jointly by Medicare and Medicaid that focus entirely on older people who are frail enough to meet their state's Medicaid standards for nursing home care

proof of loss • a claims provision of the UPPL stating that proof of loss must be submitted within 90 days after the termination of the period for which the insurer is liable (for periodic benefits, such as disability insurance) or within 90 days after the date of such loss or as soon as is reasonably possibly but not later than one year from the end of the 90-day period except in the absence of legal capacity

protected health information (PHI) • individually identifiable health (medical) information

provider-sponsored organization (PSO) • a managed care plan established by doctors and/or hospitals that have formed their own program for the delivery and payment of health care services and deliver a substantial portion of services through their own or affiliated provider systems

pure annuity • an annuity in which payments cease at the death of the last annuitant

qualification period • in medical expense policies, a stipulated interval from the first diagnosis of a covered medical condition to the date when benefits become payable, which may vary by diagnosis as in the case of critical illness insurance. It is similar to an elimination period. In disability income policies, the number of days of total disability that is required before residual disability payments are made.

qualified beneficiary • as defined under COBRA, any employee, or the spouse or dependent child of that employee, who on the day before a qualifying event was covered under the employee's group health plan

qualified long-term care insurance contract • any long-term care insurance contract that meets the requirements of the Health Insurance Portability and Accountability Act (HIPAA) for favorable tax treatment. *Also known as* a tax-qualified policy.

qualified long-term care services • services that must be covered for a long-term care insurance policy to be a tax-qualified insurance contract under the Health Insurance Portability and Accountability Act (HIPAA)

qualifying event • as defined under COBRA, an event (such as termination of employment, reduction in hours worked, or death) that triggers the eligibility of a qualified insured to elect continuing coverage

reasonable and customary (R&C) fees • the smallest of the actual charge, the fee most often charged by the provider for the same service or supply, or the fee most often charged in the same area by providers with similar training and experience for comparable service or supplies

rebating • the return of any part of the premium (except as dividends) to the policyowner by the insurer or agent as a price-cutting sales inducement. Rebating is prohibited under the Unfair Trade Practices Act.

receipt • official acknowledgment of payment made with an application for insurance. Insurers may issue a conditional receipt, a binding receipt, or a temporary insurance agreement (TIA).

recision • revocation of a policy by the insurer

recurrent disability provision • a provision in a disability income contract that specifies that a new disability is considered recurrent if it arises from the same cause or causes as a prior disability, and there has not been a recovery period of more than a specified time such as 6 or 12 months. If a disability is recurrent, there is no new elimination period, and benefits from the prior disability are applied to any maximum benefit period.

refund annuity • an annuity for which some of the purchase price may be returned to a beneficiary

regulation • defined broadly to include legislation and administrative regulations as well as decisions of the courts that affect the business of insurance

rehabilitative benefits • benefits under disability income policies or programs to cover the costs of rehabilitating a disabled person. Benefits may be paid for medical rehabilitation as well as for vocational rehabilitation, such as training, counseling, and job placement.

rehabilitative services • care and treatment intended to restore an individual to normal functions after a disabling disease, injury, or incapacitation

reimbursement basis • the dominant method of paying benefits under newer long-term care policies that reimburse the insured for actual expenses incurred up to the specified daily or weekly benefit amount. *Compare* per diem basis.

reinstatement provision • a provision in an insurance contract that sets forth procedures for allowing an insured to request a policy to be restored to full effectiveness should a premium not be paid by the end of the grace period

renewal underwriting • although most medical expense policies are guaranteed renewable and not subject to renewal underwriting, renewal underwriting is used if an applicant is reclassified because of changes in age or place of residence, if an insured requests a reevaluation of previous underwriting decisions, or to reinstate a lapsed policy

replacement • the canceling of one policy and replacing it with another policy. States have rules that must be followed by insurers and agents who are aware that a replacement is taking place.

replacement benefit • a benefit under a key-person disability policy designed to provide funds for the hiring of a replacement of the disabled employee

replacement ratio • the ratio of disability benefits to income

representation • a statement made by an applicant to an insurer at the time of or prior to the formation of a contract

requalification questions • a series of questions at the beginning of an insurance application intended to immediately ascertain the ineligibility of an applicant for insurance and relieve the applicant from the need to complete the application and the agent from the need to submit it

residual disability • a disability that results in the inability of an insured to perform some of the duties of his or her own occupation, resulting in a loss of income

respiratory therapy • treatment that maintains or improves the breathing function through the administration of medications and oxygen and/or the use of ventilator equipment

respite care • a form of long-term care provided by informal or formal caregivers to relieve a primary caregiver from the physical and emotional stress of caring for a family member over a long period of time and/or to allow the primary caregiver to have some personal time. Respite care can be relatively brief or extended in duration.

respite caregiver • an alternate caregiver who relieves a primary caregiver to allow the primary caregiver to have some time off

restoration of benefits • a provision or rider in some long-term care policies written with less than a lifetime benefit period that provides for a reinstatement of full benefits if the insured previously received less than full policy benefits and has not required long-term care covered by the policy for a certain time period

return-of-premium rider • a rider under a disability income policy which "refunds" all or a portion of premiums paid if the insured's claims experience is favorable • a long-term care policy rider under which a portion of the premium is returned to the policyowner or beneficiary, usually if an insured dies after a specified number of years

reverse mortgage • a nonrecourse first mortgage loan against a home's value that advances cash to the borrower who remains the homeowner. It requires no installment repayments, and proceeds from the sale of the home are used to repay the loan when the borrower no longer maintains the home as a principal residence.

rider • a provision, also called an endorsement, in an insurance policy that can clarify, restrict, or expand coverage

right of examination • *See* free-look period.

risk • the possibility of undesired and unintended loss

salary continuation plan • a term applied to many types of employer-provided disability income plans

sandwich generation • persons who at the same time are caring for their own children as well as aging parents or relatives

SCHIP • *See* State Children's Health Insurance Program (SCHIP).

secondary caregiver • an informal caregiver other than the primary caregiver

self-funding • a method by which an employer finances the cost of an employee benefit plan by paying benefits from current revenue, administers (either directly or through an administrator) all aspects of the plan, and bears the risk that benefit payments will exceed those expected

separate service maximum • benefit limit applicable to specific services, such as organ transplants, substance abuse and dependency, mental illness, home health care, infertility treatment, and skilled-nursing home care. *Also known as* internal limit

serious illness insurance • *See* critical illness insurance.

service basis • in medical expense insurance, a policy provision that provides benefits as medical services received from providers under contractual agreements and generally requires no filing of claim forms by the insured

shared benefit • a long-term care insurance policy provision that allows a husband and wife insured under the same policy or with the same insurer to access each other's unused benefits

SHIP • *See* State Health Insurance Assistance Program (SHIP).

shopper's guide to long-term care insurance • a publication produced by government agencies, consumer groups, or insurers and other financial institutions to help consumers understand long-term care insurance and to assist them in the decision to buy a policy. The National Association of Insurance Commissioners (NAIC) publishes the best known of these guides.

sick leave plan • a short-term disability income plan of an employer. Benefits are generally uninsured and replace lost income for a limited period, starting on the first day of disability. *Also called a* salary continuation plan.

sickness • an illness or disease that is diagnosed while a health insurance policy is in force. Unless specified otherwise, it usually includes both mental and physical illness.

simplified-issue underwriting • a form of group underwriting in which the insurer tends to ask more medically related questions than are used with modified guaranteed-issue underwriting. Only if the answers to these questions are unsatisfactory does the insurer request further medical information—such as an attending physician's statement—or further medical assessments. *Also known as* short-form underwriting. *Compare* full individual underwriting; guaranteed-issue underwriting; modified guaranteed-issue underwriting.

single life annuity • an annuity in which payments are received for the duration of one life

single-premium annuity • an annuity purchased with a lump-sum premium

skilled care • medical care services that may be provided or available 24 hours a day or on a daily basis. The most common setting for skilled care is in a nursing home that is classified as a skilled-nursing facility. *Also known as* skilled-nursing care.

skilled-nursing care • *See* skilled care.

skilled-nursing facility • an institution, usually a nursing home, or part of an institution that meets the accreditation criteria required for reimbursement of skilled-nursing care provided to Medicare and Medicaid patients. *See also* skilled care.

social care • services that help maintain an individual's personal interactions and identity as a member of a community

social insurance offset rider • a rider to a disability income policy that will pay an additional benefit if a disabled person is not eligible for disability income benefits under a specified social insurance program or the program pays less than the benefits provided by the rider

social insurance program • government-run or government-regulated insurance program designed primarily to solve major social problems that affect a large portion of society. Distinguishing characteristics are emphasis on social adequacy, compulsory employment-related coverage, partial or total employer financing, benefits prescribed by law, and benefits as a matter of right.

Social Security • a federal social insurance program that provides disability income benefits as well as retirement income and benefits to survivors

Social Security offset rider • a rider to a disability income policy that will pay additional benefits when a disabled person is not eligible for disability income benefits under the Social Security program

social worker • an individual with advanced education in dealing with social, emotional, and environmental problems associated with physical or cognitive impairments

special enrollment period (for Medicare Part B) • a 7-month period after employer-provided coverage ends during which a person may enroll in Part B coverage without a late enrollment penalty

specialty benefit organization • an entity that provides services in one or more of the following areas: behavioral health care, chronic condition and disease management, rehabilitation after catastrophic injury, and transplant surgeries

specified (dread) disease insurance • supplemental medical insurance that provides per day, per service, expense-incurred, and/or lump-sum benefit payments upon the occurrence of medical events or diagnoses related to the treatment of a disease named in the policy

speech-language pathologist • a professional with advanced training and education in human communications, its development, and its disorders. Individuals with these skills measure and evaluate language abilities, auditory processes, and speech production and treat those with speech and language disorders.

split definition of disability • *See* dual definition of disability.

spousal discount • a reduction in otherwise applicable premium rates based on anticipated lower average claim expenses of those who live together in committed relationships and take care of each other before needing long-term care services

SSI • *See* Supplemental Security Income (SSI).

stability • permanence in personal, family, employment, and community relationships

stand-alone plan • a Medicare prescription drug plan that is available to persons enrolled in original Medicare or in a Medicare Advantage plan without prescription drug programs

standby assistance • the presence of another person within arm's length who can intervene to prevent physical injury or help with the completion of a task

standard issue • the usual insurer underwriting decision, which is approval of an insurance application as applied for

State Children's Health Insurance Program (SCHIP) • a federal program that gives grants to states to provide health insurance coverage to uninsured children who are 18 years old or under and are ineligible for Medicaid

State Health Insurance Assistance Program (SHIP) • a state program that receives money from the federal government to give free health insurance counseling and assistance to people with Medicare

state high-risk health insurance plan • a high-risk pool established through a not-for-profit association under state legislation that offers comprehensive medical insurance benefits to individuals whose preexisting health conditions deny them standard coverage

step therapy • the practice in prescription drug plans under which approval of higher-cost medications is contingent upon an individual first trying lower-cost, often well-established drugs to see if they are effective

stock insurance company • a profit-seeking insurance company owned by its stockholders

stock-redemption agreement • a buy-sell agreement under which a corporation agrees to purchase the ownership interest of a shareholder when the shareholder's disability (or other event) triggers the agreement

stock subsidiary • *See* mutual holding company.

stop loss • *See* out-of-pocket limit.

student medical expense policy • interim medical expense insurance for students attending institutions of higher education

substantial supervision • the continuous presence of a person directing and watching over another; may also be defined to include cueing

substitute salary expense rider • a rider to a business overhead expense policy that provides benefits for the expenses of hiring a replacement for the disabled insured

suitability • the process of finding insurance solutions that are appropriate for the needs and wants of consumers

supplemental accident insurance • a medical insurance policy that provides a specified dollar benefit (such as $500 or $1,000) for medical expenses incurred as a result of an accident. When offered in conjunction with a principal policy of medical expense insurance, supplemental accident insurance policies pay benefits without regard to otherwise applicable deductible, copayment, or other self-pay amounts, with covered expenses continuing to apply to the annual deductible.

supplemental medical expense insurance • a policy intended to augment and possibly extend insurance protection to expenses uncovered under a principal policy or other program of comprehensive coverage. *See also* hospital confinement indemnity insurance; specified (dread) disease insurance; critical illness insurance; Medicare supplement (medigap) insurance.

Supplemental Security Income (SSI) • benefit payments available under the Social Security Program to certain persons with limited incomes and financial resources. This group includes persons aged 65 or older as well as the blind or disabled.

survivorship benefit • a policy provision that waives the premium for a surviving spouse after the other spouse dies. It is used in situations in which a company insures both spouses and the coverage is in force for some period of time, such as 10 years.

TALC • *See* total annual loan cost (TALC).

tax-qualified • the type of long-term care insurance contracts that meet certain standards of the Health Insurance Portability and Accountability Act (HIPAA) for favorable tax treatment. *Compare* non-tax-qualified.

temporary disability laws • laws in a few states that require employers to provide short-term disability income benefits to employees

temporary insurance agreement (TIA) • a type of receipt for the prepayment of premium submitted with a completed insurance application that provides immediate interim coverage while the application is pending, yet affords some protection to the insurer

temporary medical policies • interim medical expense insurance for persons who lack coverage for various reasons, such as a temporary interruption of employment

temporomandibular joint dysfunction • *See* TMJ dysfunction.

therapist • a trained medical specialist who commonly performs physical, respiratory, infusion, or occupational therapy

third-party notification of policy lapse • a policy provision whereby the policyowner designates another person to receive notification of the imminent cancellation of a policy for nonpayment of premium

three-tier copayment or deductible structure • a managed health care plan benefit feature that requires members to pay one of three out-of-pocket amounts for services, such as hospital services, or products such as prescription drugs, depending on their cost to the health plan. *See also* copayment; deductible.

TIA • *See* temporary insurance agreement (TIA).

Ticket to Work program • a Social Security program designed to encourage a disabled beneficiary to return to work. The disabled worker is given a "ticket" that can be taken to specified vocational rehabilitation organizations that develop plans for disabled workers.

time limit on certain defenses • a required provision of the UPPL that restricts an insurer's right to rescind or void a policy because of nonfraudulent misstatement to 2 years (3 years in most states). However, if the misstatements were fraudulent, the time limit does not apply. *Compare* incontestable clause.

TMJ dysfunction • in dental treatment, any procedure that affects the way the teeth meet and changes the relationship of the temporomandibular joint is considered treatment of TMJ dysfunction. Because TMJ dysfunction is difficult to diagnose and there is little professional consensus on its appropriate treatment, TMJ dysfunction claims can be costly and subject to abuse.

toileting • getting to and from the toilet, getting on and off the toilet, and performing associated personal hygiene

total annual loan cost (TALC) • a calculation of the cost of a reverse mortgage that combines the loan amount, interest, closing costs, points, and monthly loan service fee into a single rate. Under federal law, lenders are required to illustrate the TALC rate for their loans at the end of 2 years following closing, at the end of the borrower's life expectancy, and at a period 40 percent beyond life expectancy.

total-assets model • a type of partnership program for long-term care in which consumers may purchase an approved long-term care insurance policy at a specified benefit level. It results in none of the insured's assets being considered in determining financial eligibility for Medicaid if the insurance benefits become exhausted.

total disability • a disability resulting from injury or sickness that prevents an individual from working. The precise definition is spelled out in the policy. *See* own-occ definition of disability; modified own-occ definition of disability; dual definition of disability.

transferring • moving into or out of a bed, chair, or wheelchair

transitional care benefit • payment under a long-term care policy to assist a person in meeting immediate needs resulting from the onset of loss of functional capacity

transition benefit • a benefit from a disability income policy that continues payments to survivors for a short period after a disabled insured dies

trial work period • a period of time a disabled worker can return to work and still receive Social Security disability income benefits as long as he or she still has a disabling impairment

trigger date • the date a buyout becomes operative under a buy-sell agreement

TROOP • stands for true-out-of-pocket costs, sometimes used to describe the out-of-pocket costs that an individual must incur before a Medicare prescription drug plan will pay 95 percent of covered drug costs

twisting • a form of misrepresentation in which the agent induces the policyowner to cancel disadvantageously the contract of another insurer in order to take out a new contract. Twisting is prohibited under the Unfair Trade Practices Act.

UETA • *See* Uniform Electronic Transactions Act (UETA).

unauthorized entity • an insurance company (or other organization, either real or fictitious) that has not gained approval to place insurance business from a department of insurance in the jurisdiction where it or an agent wants to sell insurance

underwriting • the insurer's classification and selection of insurance applications

underwriting manual • reference manual that gives the underwriter guidance and suggestions as to how to underwrite various physical and medical impairments

unearned income • income not derived from an individual's job activities, such as rental, investment, and pension income

unfair discrimination • under the Unfair Trade Practices Act, the insurer's ability to decline coverage and to underwrite and rate individuals applying for or seeking to renew health insurance is limited. Specific regulations also address gender, marital status, blindness, physical or mental impairment, and AIDS.

Uniform Electronic Transactions Act (UETA) • comprehensive model legislation developed by the National Conference of Commissioners on Uniform State Laws to provide uniform state rules for the governance of transactions in electronic commerce

Uniform Individual Accident and Sickness Policy Provision Law (UPPL) • a model law that establishes the rights and duties of both the policyowner and the insurance company, as well as claims procedures and other conditions

unilateral contract • a contract in which only one of the parties makes a legally enforceable promise. *Compare* bilateral contract.

upon-diagnosis benefit • in a specified disease policy, a benefit paid in a single lump sum upon the initial diagnosis of the covered disease, often with an incremental payment for each month the policy has been in force. *See also* medical-event benefit.

UPPL • *See* Uniform Individual Accident and Sickness Policy Provision Law (UPPL).

valued policies • insurance policies that pay a precise dollar amount per day, per week, or per month without a direct relation to an expense incurred or a loss sustained. In certain circumstances, persons may receive policy benefits that exceed the loss incurred.

variable annuity • an annuity with which payments vary with investment earnings of the annuity company

veterans' benefits • a program of the U.S. Department of Veterans Affairs, often referred to as the VA, that provides a broad spectrum of assistance and services to military veterans, such as health care services that include some types of long-term care

viatical settlement • an arrangement that provides the insured with a cash advance against all or a portion of the death benefit of a life insurance policy while the insured is still alive. Under the arrangement, the policyowner typically sells the policy to obtain financial resources to pay for expenses at the end of the insured's life. *Compare* accelerated-benefits provision.

void contract • an agreement that is entirely without legal effect and therefore unenforceable by either party. In essence, a void contract never was a contract.

voidable contract • an agreement that can be affirmed or rejected at the option of one of the parties but is binding on the other party. For example, if a policyowner has failed to comply with a condition of the contract, the insurer may elect to fulfill its part of the agreement or may choose to rescind the contract.

voluntary benefits • group or individual insurance products, usually made available by an employer, that an employee may purchase by paying 100 percent of the premium. *Also known as* employee-pay-all benefits, list billing arrangements, and worksite benefits.

waiting period • a term sometimes used to describe an elimination period or a probationary period, even though these two concepts differ. *See* elimination period; probationary period

waiver of premium • a policy provision under which the premium is waived when the insured is seriously disabled or incapacitated. The provision varies by form of health insurance.

weekly benefit • a benefit amount, usually applicable to home care benefits, that is determined by multiplying the insured's selected daily benefit amount by 7. Some insurers calculate the weekly benefit at the time of claim when several occasions of service occur on various days during a week. Other insurers offer a weekly benefit as an option, usually at a higher premium.

wellness • the state of being in good health

Women's Health and Cancer Rights Act • mandates that any policy providing medical and surgical benefits for mastectomy must also provide coverage for reconstruction of the breast on which the mastectomy was performed, surgery and reconstruction of the other breast to achieve a symmetrical appearance, prosthesis, and physical complications of all stages of mastectomy, including lymphedemas

workers' compensation • insurance that provides coverage for earnings lost due to occupational injuries and also pays for medical treatment for such injuries

workers' compensation law • state and federal laws that require employees to provide benefits when a covered employee is injured or dies from an on-the-job accident or sickness. Benefits include medical expenses, disability income, survivor benefits, and funeral benefits.

worksite benefits • *See* voluntary benefits.

Index